D1597263

The American Revolution in the Southern Colonies

To those courageous men who fought and died
under American and British flags
in the American Revolution in the Southern colonies

and

to my American and Southern family —
Harriet, Hollie and David.

The American Revolution in the Southern Colonies

by

David Lee Russell

McFarland & Company, Inc., Publishers
Jefferson, North Carolina, and London

Maps in this work are drawn from several sources, including:

Atlas of American History: Reprinted with the permission of Macmillan Library Reference USA, a division of Ahsoug, Inc., from *Atlas of American History*, edited by Kenneth T. Jackson. Copyright © 1943, 1971, 1978 by Charles Scribner's Sons.

Battles of the American Revolution: From Henry B. Carrington, *Battles of the American Revolution 1775–1781* (New York: A.S. Barnes, 1877).

A History of the Campaigns of 1780 and 1781: From Lieutenant-Colonel Tarleton T. Cadell, *A History of the Campaigns of 1780 and 1781 in the Southern Provinces of North America* (London: In the Strand, 1787).

Other maps were provided by the courtesy of the Hargrett Rare Book and Manuscript Library of the University of Georgia Libraries, and the Library of Congress.

Library of Congress Cataloguing-in-Publication Data
Russell, David Lee, 1947–
The American Revolution in the Southern colonies
/ by David Lee Russell.
p.   cm.
Includes bibliographical references and index.
ISBN 0-7864-0783-2 (illustrated case binding : 50# alkaline paper) ∞
1. Southern States — History — Revolution, 1775–1783 — Campaigns.
2. United States — History — Revolution, 1775–1783 — Campaigns.   I. Title.
E230.5.S7 R87   2000
973.3'3 — dc21   00-56869

British Library cataloguing data are available

*Front cover: Francis Marion (top), Battle of Cowpens (bottom).
Back cover: Siege of Charleston. All images ©2000 Art Today*

Manufactured in the United States of America

*McFarland & Company, Inc., Publishers
Box 611, Jefferson, North Carolina 28640
www.mcfarlandpub.com*

TABLE OF CONTENTS

ACKNOWLEDGMENTS

The research material for this book was almost exclusively obtained from the vast published works of the Wisconsin Historical Society on the campus of the University of Wisconsin in Madison. On the numerous occasions climbing the narrow steel stairs to the relevant floors of this aged library, it was as if I was returning to an earlier time. Like any Southern researcher I was impressed with the extensive collection of references covering Southern history in the colonial and revolutionary era. I look back with a special pleasure on those cold and sometimes sunny Saturday afternoons, roaming the stacks for published gems before departing with my borrowed research treasures across the central campus mall at State Street.

"The object is too important, the spirit of the British nation too high, the resources with which God hath blessed her too numerous, to give up so many colonies which she has planted with great industry, nursed with great tenderness, encouraged with many commercial advantages, and protected and defended at much expense of blood and treasure."

The King's Speech on Opening the Session of Parliament,
October 26, 1775, London

PREFACE

As we pass into the third millennium A.D., the English-speaking peoples of North America approach the 400th anniversary of their first colonization of this incredible land. For all those years the highest and most noble achievement for the American people was the gaining of their independence though the American Revolution. The historical account as presented in the following 20 chapters reveals in detail the most significant events as they occurred in the Southern colonies of British North America. It reveals an engaging period from 1763 to 1783 when the people of this loose collection of relatively autonomous colonial governments moved from the relative tranquillity after the French and Indian War to an ever increasing escalation towards conflict. Compelled to reject economic and political subjugation at the hands of the British, these new patriotic Americans came to be engaged in an involuntary struggle with their British forefathers to band together in a common spirit to form a United States of America.

Perhaps no nation since the birth of Christ has had such a grand and definitive beginning as the United States. As one researches the minute details of these profound events as I have attempted, the improbability of the ultimate success of the American Revolution comes to ultimate clarity. First encouraged by the intellectual and economically advantaged elite to seek with principle to rebel, these same leaders took up, with some trepidation, the difficult task of organizing a war effort against a worthy foe. The American cause saw few battles won outright against the British as the war plodded along in relative futility. But with a determined patriot leadership from a few skilled military leaders in the field, and the favorable circumstance of the latter events of the war in the Carolinas, the Chesapeake Capes and at Yorktown, the American cause came to fruition. These men dared to lead their common citizens to stare into the eyes of death in battle for the sake of independence.

My driving focus in the book was to present as comprehensive an account of the events as could be realized from available published material, while seeking not to violate the practical necessity of maintaining the reader's sense of flow. As measured by the overwhelming emphasis placed on events in the Middle and Northern colonies in the collective body of published accounts of the American Revolution, the full and published account of the Southern experience is not widely available in circulation today. This book favors coverage of the strategically critical occurrences in the South. I have chosen to spell place names as they appeared at that time. As the war progressed to the stalemate around New York, only in the South would the British finally come to terms with the reality of defeat at the hands of a local army, ill-equipped, yet favored with support from a stalwart French ally.

By modern standards the Revolution was fought in near slow motion. The action moved by land on slow horseback or at sea by graceful, yet deliberate, sailing vessel. But while the pace was often burdened, it was still a war of suffering and death. To see one's fellow comrade meet a horrible death by musketball, saber, or even a cannonball was but one outcome from a fierce battle on a field of red. Most of those who met their last day in battle died a lingering and often unbearable death. Patriots who did not expire on the battlefield still endured the personal miseries of unfilled stomachs, improper clothing, inclement weather, and extreme physical exhaustion. To marshal forces against an imposing, well-trained and thoroughly

1

equipped European army with such obstacles was a Herculean task in the mid–eighteenth century for the American patriot leadership. Despite this tremendous challenge — which many of these leaders did not meet — the American cause for independence at last prevailed, in no small part through the significant actions of the men who fought in the Southern colonies.

1

ORIGINS
OF THE
SOUTHERN COLONIES

The Citizens of America, placed in the most enviable conditions, as the sole Lords and Proprietors of a vast Tract of Continent, comprehending all the various soils and climates of the World, and abounding with all the necessaries and conveniences of life, are now by the late satisfactory pacification, acknowledged to be possessed of absolute freedom and Independency; They are ... peculiarly designated by Providence for the display of human greatness and felicity; Here, they are not only surrounded with every thing which can contribute to the completion of private and domestic enjoyment, but Heaven has crowned all its other blessings, by giving a fairer opportunity for political happiness, than any other Nation has ever been favored with.[1]

Such were the words of George Washington in his farewell address in September of 1796, concluding his national career and second term as president of the United States of America. Indeed, the achievement of this grand and new democratic Republic, along with "all the necessaries and conveniences of life," was certainly unmatched in modern civilization.

It was a time of challenge, of profound opportunity and of momentous events. In the period of the mid–eighteenth century in the southernmost British colonies of North America were some 700,000 citizens of the crown living on the coastal Atlantic in Maryland, Virginia, North Carolina, South Carolina and Georgia. These people, like their fellow subjects in the Middle and New England colonies, were about to engage in a long struggle to

create a new democratic nation of a type not seen in the history of the world. From these lands of the South came the statesmen, and later the soldiers, who, through their vision, courage and sacrifice, would create this new nation. Without the contributions of these Southern patriots, the American Revolution would not have been won and there would be no United States of America.

The grand hopes of the colonial experience in the Southern colonies began on March 25, 1584, when Queen Elizabeth granted a patent to Sir Walter Raleigh for lands not already taken by any "Christian Prince." Attempts at establishing a colony in North America began to take shape in earnest in June of 1585 when two ships with 107 passengers, including 17 women, landed to establish a settlement at Roanoke Island, in present day North Carolina. Sir Walter Raleigh's trip had taken him up the entire eastern Atlantic coast where he searched for promising settlement locations. He visited the Savannah River area and even surveyed the bluffs where the town of Savannah, Georgia, would later be built.[2] This group, under the authority of Sir Walter Raleigh, took formal possession of the country on July 13, 1587, and, in honor of Queen Elizabeth, named it "Virginia." While the settlers were valiant in their efforts to colonize, the colony ultimately disappeared for unknown reasons.

On April 10, 1606, James I of Britain divided Virginia into two colonies. The Southern lands (between 34 and 38 degrees north latitude), called South Virginia, were granted to the London Company for settlement. The Northern lands (between 38 and 41 degrees north latitude) were granted to the Plymouth Company.[3] Thus were established the two key legacy settlements that would begin the American colonial experience.

The origins of the American Revolution in the South may well have begun in London in December of 1606, when a little over 100 Englishmen, under the leadership of Captain Christopher Newport, loaded aboard three small ships, the *Susan Constant, Godspeed* and *Discovery*, and set sail to Virginia.[4] After four months at sea, these brave adventurers entered the Chesapeake Bay at Cape Henry on April 26, 1607, explored the area through May and then anchored 60 miles from the capes on the waters of the James River on June 22.[5] There they founded the first permanent English settlement in the South, Jamestown, in honor of their monarch, James Stuart, King of Scotland, in the fifth year of his reign.

Although this Southern settlement lost 66 of the 104 colonists who landed in its first year, it was clear that Englishmen and others, primarily from Europe, would immigrate in increasing numbers to this new land. Unknown to any at that time, the seeds of the Revolution were essentially planted by the ultimate success of those courageous, and soon to be independent, colonial adventurers, who survived the Atlantic crossing and endured the hardships of life in these eastern environs of North America.

Life in the first permanent English settlement in America and in the first Southern settlement, Jamestown, involved extreme hardships and privation. In December of 1608 Captain John Smith described the situation of the colonists as "the one halfe sicke, the other little better ... our dyet is of a little meale and water, and not sufficient of that." The settlement was only able to survive until the following July, when a supply ship would arrive with wine and biscuits, and due to help from the local Indians and the acquisition of oysters and some fish from the nearby waters. The next winter in Jamestown was to bring more famine and pestilence along with an Indian massacre. The struggling band of some 500 colonists included "not past sixty men, women and children, most miserable and poore creatures, and those were preserved for the most part by roots, herbes, acornes, walnuts, berries and now and then a little fish."[6]

Conditions continued to be so bad that when Sir Thomas Gates and Sir George Somers arrived in June of 1610 with another 150 settlers to join the local "wretches," the decision was made to abandon Jamestown. In the act of sailing out of the James River the colonists met Lord Delaware, who had come as the new governor for the settlement with three ships filled with provisions. From this point forward conditions seemed to improve somewhat for this Southern colonial settlement. The period often

known as the "starving time" was mostly over for the young settlement. The efforts to move from a "communal" group to separate households instigated by Governor and "High Marshal" Sir Thomas Dale in 1611 positively impacted the life in Jamestown. Each family was to have a house of four rooms or more, provisions for 12 months with 12 acres of land, along with planting tools, a cow, a few goats, poultry and swine. From these first beginnings of self-sufficiency on 12 acres evolved the proud "plantations" of the South including hundreds of acres or more.[7]

Back in Britain there was discontent over the slow progress of developing Virginia. So in 1612 a new group in the company, who believed that more economic and political freedom would result in increased profits for the London Company stockholders, took control and gained a new charter, abandoning the trading post concept. Now the planters in Virginia and the British stockholders were equals. On July 30, 1619, representatives of some 11 plantations and boroughs of Virginia met with the governor and his council in a Jamestown church. This was the first representative assembly held in America, and on that day this new body passed or considered laws on such topics as extravagant dress, education of Indians, the price of tobacco used as legal tender for paying taxes, and founding a college. Virginia had now moved from plantation to full status as a colony.

Through cultivation of the land, the sponsorship of the immigration of women to form family structures, an eventual peace with the local Indian tribes and a proper organization of a colonial assembly government, Jamestown survived and the colony of Virginia was created. In 1624, after disputes with the crown, some mismanagement of the colony and objectionable political activities by certain leaders, the London Company turned the colony and Jamestown over to the British Crown by act of the British court, which voided the patent. The colony now had a population of 1132 souls, with males outnumbering females by three to one. The London Company had spent £200,000 and was now bankrupt. As the new colony moved into a new era, it would become even more prosperous and secure.[8]

After Virginia had passed through the first 26 critical years, another Southern colony was about to be formed. On the 13th of June in 1633, during the reign of King Charles I, Cecilius Calvert, who was the first Lord Baltimore and a Roman Catholic, was granted a large tract of land 140 by 130 miles on the Chesapeake Bay. In order to escape the laws focused against Catholics in England, he wished to provide a place for many of his followers to settle in his granted lands.[9] After the departure of these 200 colonists from England aboard the *Ark* and *Dove* in November 1633, Lord Baltimore wrote a friend that he had finally succeeded in sending a "hopeful colony" into

The Southeast in 1694. (Library of Congress.)

Maryland with his two brothers, some 20 gentlemen of "very good fashion" and 300 laboring men. Though Lord Baltimore's letter made no mention of it, an account of the voyage by one who sailed with it revealed that women were also among the new settlers bound for Maryland. In March of 1634 the voyagers reached St. Mary's on the St. George River. They named the new colony "Maryland," in honor of Queen Henrietta Maria.[10]

Experience gained at Jamestown served to provide practical benefit to the new Maryland settlers. The settlers first selected a location for their town on a high bluff, not on marshy, bug-infested lowland as at Jamestown. They also made peace with the surrounding Indian tribes and were prudent to purchase land from them to minimize conflict. As the first "conditions of plantation" spelled out, Lord Baltimore granted to each male settler 100 acres, another 100 acres for his wife, 50 for each child, 100 for

each manservant and 60 for each female servant. The settlers hastened to plant crops. As in the Virginia example, the English tradition of male dominated, family based society was likewise promulgated in Maryland.

The settlement at St. Mary's prospered quickly with the support of the Indian population. By trade of English goods like cloth, hoes, axes and knives, the settlers were provided wigwams, as well as cornfields already cleared. They built simple dwellings, a guardhouse, storehouse and gardens. They also purchased cattle, hogs, poultry and fruit trees from Virginia. In addition, local Indians helped them to fish and hunt deer and turkey. As a result of their disciplined approach and focused work at building a strong colony, the Maryland colonists had no "starving time." In fact, they were so successful in farming that they were able to export a shipload of corn to England at the end of the first growing season. They made more progress in six months than the Jamestown settlers had made in their first six years.[11]

From the beginning, Lord Baltimore's dream was to create a near feudal state made up of large estates with their owners gaining significant control over their "subjects," as lords of the manor. Lord Baltimore granted a number of these manors, but the tenants were unwilling to be subjugated since land was cheap and available in surrounding areas. Marylanders took to the Virginia model and the plantation system as freemen. The feudal dream never came to pass, but the new colony did well. The only conflict associated with Maryland during its formative years came as a result of discontent among Virginia Puritans. They were granted land in Ann Arundell County, Maryland, in 1645 due to Lord Baltimore's religious tolerance, which he extended to Roman Catholics and Protestants. These immigrated Puritans soon began to oppose the system of land ownership in Maryland. When the civil war broke out in England and the king was executed, the Parliamentary Party of Puritans gained power as the new British monarchs, William and Mary, took power and declared Maryland to be disloyal. While Lord Baltimore retained his property rights, he lost his political rights until they were restored to the fourth Lord Baltimore in 1715.[12] Aside from these political events, Maryland was a most successful colony from the very beginning.

As the Virginia and Maryland colonies grew, the overflow population was seeking cheaper and better lands and gradually moved southward down the rivers of southeast Virginia into the sounds of the Carolinas. Favorable reports from these settlers about the new region brought more settlers into the Albemarle area of what is now North Carolina. News of this area soon reached the British elite. When King Charles II ascended to the throne in 1660 after much work and support from numerous friends, he granted eight of his most ardent supporters a tract of land each in America that they could rule as the "true and absolute Lords and Proprietors." Since Charles II owed them a great debt for their support, on March 24, 1663, he granted a charter for lands from 31 degrees to 36 degrees north latitude, stretching from sea to sea, to the Earl of Clarendon and seven others, the lands presently known as the Carolinas and Georgia.[13]

In August of 1669 these Lords Proprietor sent, under the command of Joseph West with Governor and Colonel William Sayle, a group of settlers aboard the 200-ton frigate *Carolina*, the *Port Royal* and the *Albemarle* to found a colony at Port Royal in the lower part of the province. After an adventuresome voyage, during which the ships *Port Royal* and *Albemarle* were lost, the colonists first made a brief visit to Port Royal, which they deemed too close to the Spanish. Then they moved north aboard the *Carolina* up the coast into a natural harbor and came ashore to make their first settlement at Albemarle Point on the west bank of the Ashley River in April 1670. They called it "Carolina." This was the third successful Southern colony. Some two years later they moved down the neck of the land between the Ashley and Cooper rivers to form Charles Town.[14]

The settlers had sailed from England with 15 tons of beer, 30 gallons of brandy, 59 bushels of flour, 100 beds and pillows, 12 suits of armor, 1200 hoes, 100,000 four penny nails, 765 fishing hooks, 240 pounds of glass beads, 288 scissors, garden seeds and medical equipment. The 93 new colonists included 29 "masters" (men of property) and free persons, 63 indentured white servants and one black slave. These first Carolina immigrants came to begin a new life, avoid debts and spouses and gain land. The proprietors granted each settler over 16 years of age 150 acres, plus 100 acres for every able-bodied manservant he brought with him. The settlement, christened Albemarle Point, was named in honor of the Duke of Albemarle, who was one of the proprietors.

The colonists first cleared the land to "extend their defensive perimeter," and built dwellings made of branches and mud, and later of clapboards. The colonists were well aware of how close they were to the Spanish at St. Augustine in Florida, only 200 miles away to the south. The local Indians were another threat. It was necessary for them to build defensive entrenchments and a military system to maintain constant watches. Under the proposed founding document, the Fundamental Constitutions of Carolina, a governor was elected along with a council and an assembly of representatives in the model of the British House of Commons. The outstanding defensive organization paid off the following August, when a combined Spanish and Indian attack was called off as the attackers were too intimidated by the defenses and a sudden summer squall. But the colony was to continue to live under the fear of a Spanish attack for another three generations.

Since the new colonists were able to obtain food from the other established colonies in the South, they did not die of starvation. However, at times the diets were not always adequate, which caused diseases like dysentery and malaria. During the warmer months the salt marshes were home to "pestiferous gnats, called Moschetoes." Some in the group turned to heavy drinking of rum to gain some degree of comfort in their new environment. Leaders complained of the low moral standards of the colonists, where people "prophanely violate" the Sabbath and commit other "grand abuses." The settlement took on the atmosphere of a rowdy port from the outset. Soon the Grand Council was to censure those who sold "strong drink" without a license and contributed to "drunkenness, idleness, and quarreling."

The first winter at Albemarle Point was a cold one,

as everyone was shocked to discover that for a time water froze to a thickness of one inch there. But the settlement survived the first year and continued to grow, and by 1672 it had a population of 268 men, 69 women and 59 children. Soon it was recognized that the better location for the settlement, from a defensive standpoint, was at the confluence of the Ashley and Cooper rivers at what was known as "Oyster Point." In February of 1671 the Grand Council selected the spot and in April John Culpeper was directed to "admeasure and lay out" the site of the town "in a square as much Navigable Rivers will permit." In July of 1671 the first Carolina Parliament met in Charles Town. By the late 1670s there were some 20 houses at Oyster Point and some 20 more under construction. Thus, in December 1679, the proprietors announced that "Oyster Point is ... a more convenient place to build a towne on than that ... pitched on by the first settlers," and that "the people's Inclinations tend thither." Therefore, "Oyster Point is the place wee doe appoint for the port towne ... which you are to call Charles Towne." Those who were granted lots in the new town were required to construct houses within two years. The streets were directed to be laid out in "broad and ... straight lines." By 1681 the Council had granted 33 lots. The previous May, Maurice Mathews estimated that there were "in all, men, women, and children, about 1000" citizens of Charles Town. In 1682 Thomas Newe wrote that he calculated that the town had "about a hundred houses ... of wood."[15]

The proprietary government in Carolina had so many problems over the years with the settlers that the British Parliament eventually stepped in to take the province under their care. While South Carolina had become a royal colony in 1719, North Carolina continued under the authority of the proprietors for ten more years. An agreement in 1729 gave seven of the eight proprietors £2,500 ($225,000) each from the crown for the property and jurisdiction, plus £5,000 ($450,000) to make up for lost land taxes, called quitrents, due them. The territory previously belonging to the proprietors of Carolina was divided into North and South Carolina and continued to be ruled as separate royal governments until American independence.[16]

An additional condition of the agreement of 1729 was that the eighth share of the land be granted to the descendant of Sir George Carteret, later titled Lord Granville. Lord Granville retained ownership of one-eighth of the land in the original grant of 1663, which was eventually known as the Granville District, defined as an area 60 miles wide in the northern half of North Carolina. This area contained two-thirds of the population and the largest percentage of the wealth. By agreement, Lord Granville was not allowed to have any voice in the government of the colony. This arrangement turned out to be a serious barrier to the development of North Carolina because of corrupt officers, squatters settling on the land and frustrated landowners. This condition continued until the beginning of the Revolution when the district was confiscated by the new state of North Carolina. After the Revolution, the Granville heirs tried to regain their property, but their suit was rejected in the United States District Court in Raleigh.[17]

Georgia, a much less populated region and generally considered to be a frontier colony, was the last colony to be established in North America. General James Oglethorpe, a member of the British Parliament, formed Georgia as the result of a visionary plan to create a buffer colony, between South Carolina and Spanish Florida, settled by the poorest class of London debtors. The plan called for proprietors to act as trustees to supervise the colony, which would be turned back over to the crown after 21 years. On June 9, 1732, King George II issued letters legally forming the colony. In honor of the king, the colony was named "Georgia."[18]

On January 13, 1733, the ship *Anne* arrived at Charles Town, where Carolina Governor Johnson received Oglethorpe, his party and his council. Being overwhelmingly supportive of the mission, the governor entered a successful motion in the Carolina General Assembly to provide Oglethorpe's party with 104 breeding cattle, 25 hogs and 20 barrels of rice. The governor also ordered a unit of his rangers to accompany the expedition to Georgia in scout boats to provide armed guards for Oglethorpe and company.

Oglethorpe and 130 men, women and children landed at Yamacraw, at the mouth of the Savannah River, in the spring of 1733 to begin the colony. Oglethorpe had with him Sir Walter Raleigh's written journal, which revealed area details of Raleigh's expedition in 1585.[19] Exploration found an elevated area on the banks of this navigable river. Oglethorpe immediately laid out the town of Savannah and soon began to encourage immigration. After only six years the colony had grown to population of 5000. Each settler was given 50 acres of land, which could not be sold, mortgaged or divided by the owner.

Parliament had forbidden importation of slaves to Georgia, but did allow indentured servants. But by 1749, under the pressure of settlers who envied the wealth of the plantation owners in South Carolina just across the river, Parliament repealed the act excluding slaves. From this point on, Georgia and her economy would evolve in step with that of its northern neighbor colony. By 1756 Georgia was exporting over a million pounds of rice and 2.5 tons of indigo per year. In 1751 the trustees turned over the administration of the colony to the crown as a royal colony. On the eve of the Revolution, Georgia was the most loyal of the Southern colonies due to the relative recentness of the colony.[20]

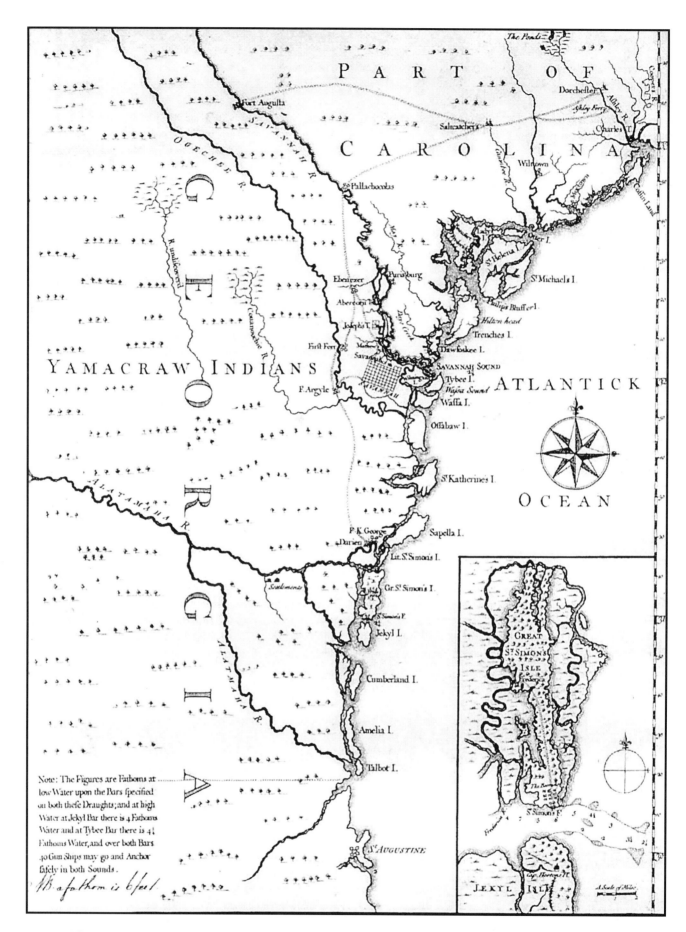

The Georgia coast in 1741. (Hargrett Rare Book and Manuscript Library, University of Georgia Libraries.)

From the very beginning the physical characteristics of the land and climate were to set the foundation for the Southern existence. These characteristics were common among all the five Southern colonies. Along the Atlantic coastal areas is the low, marshy, pine-forested, sandy soil region of the Tidewater. The Tidewater, from lower North Carolina southward, is a semi-tropical "paradise" of azaleas, flowering magnolias, palmetto plants, Spanish moss and live oaks. This region extends some 100 to 150 miles inland along the fertile river valleys. To the west of the Tidewater region is the Piedmont Plateau area where the rich clay soil and climate made for diversified crops. In 1767 an Englishman wrote about the Piedmont, remarking that it was more fruitful and healthy than the Tidewater, and once "peopled and secured," it would become a significant part of the "British dominions."[21]

Beyond the Piedmont, the Appalachian Mountains run from Canada to Georgia. This chain of mountains formed a natural barrier for the Southern colonists. In North Carolina, the Blue Ridge Mountains peak in 49 locations to over 6,000 feet above sea level. These pine-covered mountains, with the series of valleys like the Shenandoah and Tennessee, were the richest in the South. In 1755 James Glen, an early governor of South Carolina, wrote on an expedition to the Cherokee Nation of the upper Carolina a description calling the area the most delightful, as well as the most fertile, in the world, with large and extensive plains and savannas, swarming with deer and buffalo. John Logan wrote, "Up to the breaking out of the Revolutionary war, the woodlands in the upper portion of South Carolina were carpeted with grass, and the wild pea vine grew, it is said, as high as a horse's back, while flowers of every description were seen growing all around."[22]

The climate of the South has always prompted passionate comments from its visitors, even in colonial times. A German-born Hessian officer, who was obviously used to the cool European climate, wrote the following about the Tidewater area of South Carolina in 1779:

> Notwithstanding the fact that historians have endeavored to paint in beautiful colors the excellence of this climate for the fancy of the readers, no one is likely to put much faith in their delineations. On the contrary, nearly everyone who has put his foot in the province or has talked to an unprejudiced inhabitant is of an altogether different opinion. As is well known, the entire coast from Cape Hatteras southward is flat, marshy land, for the greater part still uncultivated and suited for the growing of rice only, a habitat of snakes and crocodiles, strewn with bodies of stagnant water and covered with impenetrable woods. Can this be a healthy climate?... The flat shore land, which extends into the sea (the reason hurricanes from NE. are so dangerous), increases the dampness of the soil. The endless forests, which cover the entire country, deprive the soil of the beneficial rays of the life-giving sun and fill the whole atmosphere with unhealthy miasmas.... All this considered, what remains then of the pure, beautiful climate of the promised land of the historian? There is probably no land which is subject to so many and such sudden changes of weather as this province. No two months, days, or hours are alike. Even in winter, in November and December, the sudden changes are common: from cold to almost unbearable heat, from rain to drought, from hurricane to pleasant air.... Summing up all this, we shall have had by the end of the year one pleasant day for every fifteen bad ones and not a single healthy day, suitable to the needs of the human body.[23]

Southern society was initially established around the geographic characteristics of the Tidewater. Land ownership was the primary force of social and economic class stratification. Over time there emerged the great planter class of aristocrats who possessed large tracts of fertile land, and the yeoman farmer class who owned small tracts of less productive land. With the combination of favorable climate and fertile land came the Southern drive towards an agricultural economy. It was this predominance of focus on the land and its crops that would indeed set the course of the South for over 300 years, from the time of the Jamestown landing.

As the American Revolution approached, the colonists had lived for over 150 years under British rule. As the descendants of those who founded permanent settlements like Jamestown, these hardy people moved out to homestead throughout the Atlantic Tidewater region. By the standards of life as measured by the conditions for the average citizen in the mother country or in continental Europe in this period, the American colonies were an outstanding place to live. Most emigrants left overcrowded, dirty villages or towns in the Old World to reach this land of unlimited possibility and prosperity across the Atlantic.[24]

From the days of Jamestown, when the colonists lived in the Atlantic coastal Tidewater areas, there was a gradual migration up the primary river valleys toward the interior Piedmont regions in all the Southern colonies. By 1763 there was still little settlement beyond the Appalachian Mountains. Some colonists tried but were forced back across the mountains because of hostile Indian tribes. A few colonists inhabited the Shenandoah Valley of Virginia, but the western portion of the Piedmont Carolinas and Georgia was virgin land.[25]

In initial settlements, the Southern colonial whites were primarily of British stock. Over time non–British Europeans began to come to the Southern colonies. They were mostly Protestant, belonging to the hardworking middle and lower-middle classes. In Virginia and Maryland the first settlers were English by birth. After the French and Indian War many Germans emigrated from the Rhine Valley after continual political and religious repression from their French rulers. They spread out into the Pennsylvania backcountry, Maryland, Virginia and even into Georgia. By the 1770s there were around 200,000 German colonists in America.[26]

Another large group of settlers was the Lowland Scottish Protestants who came from the province of Ulster in Northern Ireland. They came primarily to Virginia, but some later migrated into North Carolina and by 1776 there were some 150,000 Scots-Irish.[27] North Carolina was generally less English than the older Chesapeake colonies of Maryland and Virginia. This colony was settled as an overflow from Virginia. It was somewhat isolated from the Atlantic, and lacked the number of Tidewater rivers as found in Virginia. As early as 1653 a group of some 100 English had settled in the Albemarle Sound area. Most new arrivals to North Carolina were servants that had been released from their indentured status.[28] The first North Carolina inland settlements were between the Pee Dee and Dan rivers and they were English. Germans came from the low coastal areas and from the North. The Scots-Irish moved south from Virginia and gave North Carolina a significantly larger Scottish element.

In South Carolina and Georgia, the population in 1763 was of mixed origins, but was dominated by the English. The first settlers to Charles Town were English from the West Indies, specifically from Barbados, and from the mother country. Scottish Highlanders and French Huguenots also settled in the Charles Town region. In the 1730s South Carolina townships were formed in an arc 100 miles from Charles Town, and the provincial government offered immigrants bounty lands if they agreed to settle them. Designed as a ring of settlements to help protect the valuable rice-growing plantation areas, these townships were intended to increase European Protestant immigration.[29] Over time, Germans, Swiss and some Jews of Spanish, Portuguese and Dutch origin immigrated there. In most cases, this array of nationalities would quickly assimilate into the very English culture.[30]

South Carolina was known as the land of slaves and of large plantations growing rice and indigo. The plantation style of agriculture permeated from the experience of the settlers who came from the islands where plantations were the usual. These plantations were run more like those in Jamaica than Jamestown. Thus, the character of South Carolina was to be shaped from this unique heritage and mixture of cultures.

These Southern colonists came to the New World because of the conditions in their homelands. They were not generally problem peoples. They shared common desires to seek economic prosperity, as well as gain freedom from the Old World constraints of government and religion. They wanted to be free from the past. This mixture of European nationalities in the Atlantic colonies was indeed a unique phenomenon. It is interesting to note that of the 56 signers of the Declaration of Independence, 18 were of non–English extraction and eight were themselves immigrants.

In addition to dealing with the geographic conditions of the New World, the early colonists had to confront the Native American. The story of this ensuing tragedy was probably unavoidable from the very start, as the clash of cultures during the colonial times would ultimately leave the Indian peoples forced westward for survival. A noted expert in American culture once noted that these two civilizations were different in that one was "dynamic and searching," while the other was "static and unprogressive." Indians had no beasts of burden, lacked wheeled vehicles, used bows and arrows and tomahawks to hunt, lived in wigwams of poles, bark and hides, and had no system of written language to preserve their knowledge from generation to generation.[31]

The first report by a European of an encounter with Native Americans occurred in July 1524 when a Florentine navigator working for France, Giovanni da Verrazano, made a brief visit at the mouth of the Cape Fear River in North Carolina. He described the people as quite friendly, with russet color skin, thick black hair, wearing animal skins and "garlands of byrdes feathers." The first encounter by English with natives happened when an expedition of Philip Amadas and Arthur Barlowe, sent by Walter Raleigh, arrived off the Outer Banks of North Carolina in July of 1584. These Hatteras Island natives (Algonquian) were of "colour yellowish, and their haire blacke for the most." While all the experiences of the initial European explorers and settlers in the South with local Native Americans were essentially cordial, eventually conflict prevailed.[32]

Native Americans were quite a resourceful people who adapted well to the wilderness life. They had canoes for water travel, used skilled hunting and trapping methods, and grew corn, potatoes, squash, peanuts, beans and tobacco.[33] They lived primarily off game from the vast forests of the South. Though one can certainly find a place in their heart for these descendants of the first Americans; they were not in a position to deal with these European colonists. They would be killed either from battle with the "foreign" settlers or from the white man's diseases. By 1775 there were no more than 50,000 Native Americans within the Thirteen Colonies.[34]

Conflict between the colonists and the Native Americans was primarily over the land. The whites desired to acquire land for homesteads, based on their legacy of private property. Even when attempts were made to obtain the Indian land from negotiated treaties, the colonies usually overstepped their rights and took land they did not own. There was continual concern over the treatment of Southern Native Americans on the part of the British. In March of 1763, Lord Egremont, who was the secretary of state for the British Southern Department, wrote a letter to Royal Governor Dobbs of North Carolina indicating that he was concerned that the removal of the French and Spanish from the scene would alarm the Southern Native Americans.[35]

Subsequently, King George III directed the governors of the Southern colonies to meet with his superintendent of Indian affairs of the Southern District for a conference with the primary Southern Indian nations — the Creeks, Choctaws, Cherokees, Chickasaws and the Catawbas. The superintendent and Charles Town resident, Colonel John Stuart, was a prosperous owner of a 1500 acre plantation worked by 200 slaves.[36] The king issued a proclamation dated October 7, 1763, requiring that "all land and territories lying to the westward and northward of the sources of the rivers which fall into the sea from the west and northwest" should be reserved for the Native Americans. The congress, attended by some 700 Native Americans, met with Governor Dobbs and Colonel Stuart at Augusta, Georgia, during November 5 through 10, 1763. All parties agreed to the Treaty of Perpetual Peace and Alliance with these five Indian nations that intended to separate the Native Americans from the colonists.[37]

As the French departed the lower Mississippi River Valley at the end of the French and Indian War and the rather weak Spanish gained authority, the Southern Indians were now entirely dependent upon the British traders and officials for goods. The white man eventually played on these desires for goods that they had been used to having (rum, guns, powder, clothing, etc.), and persuaded these tribes to attack each other. The growing push westward for more land would leave these Indian people overwhelmed by the colonists. As the year 1763 came to a close, the white Southerners could look forward to fewer problems with Indian and foreign peoples.[38]

An event occurred in 1619 that would profoundly impact the Southern colonies to the present day. In that year the first 20 black slaves were brought to Jamestown, Virginia, in a Dutch ship. These blacks had been kidnapped from their homes in Africa by traders and sold to a Dutch ship captain. After arriving in the colony, he sold the blacks to the Virginia settlers. These first blacks were treated like indentured servants, and eventually were freed. But soon the idea developed that the blacks should be kept as slaves to work the fields. Thus began a dark period of 245 years of legal slavery in the South.

In the early days, the Dutch, Spanish and Portuguese slave traders found a better market for their human goods in the Spanish colonies to the South, so the slave population grew slowly in Virginia. Another significant factor that held the slave population down at this time was that slaves cost two to three times more than indentured servants did. Thus, the numbers grew slowly, and by 1649 there were only 300 black slaves in Virginia. In 1662, the Royal African Company was chartered under the protection of the crown to supply the American colonies with slaves.

The numbers of slaves began to grow, especially after 1680. The beginning of the shift from use of white indentured servants to black slaves occurred for a variety of economic, political and social reasons. Economic conditions had improved in England after 1675, and those willing to sign indentured contracts began to decrease. With the expansion of the size of tobacco fields on large plantations, and with a shift in attitude towards obtaining non-temporary labor, the black slave was considered the best alternative.

Black slavery was not a new phenomenon during the colonial period. It was indeed an established institution in the Caribbean and other areas in the Western Hemisphere. In fact, the trade of Africans to the American colonies represented only six percent of the total of such trade. The profit margins of those who transported slaves were a mere 8 percent to 12 percent as a rule. Plantations in the Caribbean had begun to shift to black slaves by 1640, when most of the arable land was occupied and opportunities for white immigrants diminished. The sad reality of slavery in the colonial period was that the major beneficiaries were the consumers of tobacco and sugar. These products were luxuries in Europe, but over the years the prices had fallen, which made the decision to shift to black slaves more expedient.[39]

Once the idea took hold for black slavery in the South, it progressed rapidly. In the six years beginning in 1683, the population of blacks in Virginia grew from around 3000 to 5000. The pace of slave importation increased to some 1800 per annum by 1705, and by the time of the Revolution, the colonies of Virginia and Maryland had a total black population of 206,000.[40] This growth in slave trade was profound even from a purely economic standpoint, for the average value of a slave in Virginia in the 1770s was £30 ($2700). While they were expensive, in South Carolina an entire ship of slave cargo was usually auctioned off in a single day, with each planter acquiring from two to 12 slaves.[41] The typical slaveholder, who used half of the output of a slave and sold the other half, could raise his standard of living by 15 to 20 percent.[42] The motivation to obtain the black slave was indeed recognized and exploited.

Slaveholding statistics differed between the planters in the upper South in the Chesapeake region, and those in the lower South centered at Charles Town. The average number of slaves owned by the Chesapeake planters was eight to ten, and only a few held more than 100. In the Charles Town Lowcountry region, covering southeastern North Carolina, South Carolina and northeastern Georgia, planters typically owned some 25 to 30 slaves, and a group of 79 planters held 100 or more slaves at their plantations.[43] Thus, it is not surprising that black slaves made up two-thirds of the population of South Carolina in 1775.[44] In the North, only New York, Newport and Providence had slave populations of over 10 percent, but in Charles Town, the majority of the city's population was slave.[45]

Conditions on the plantations were harsher to blacks in South Carolina than in the upper South primarily because the owners did not live year round on their plantations. These great planters of South Carolina spent much of their year in quarters in Charles Town, and left control to hired overseers. The reputation of some of these overseers was one of cruelty toward blacks. Because of the vast number of black slaves in South Carolina during the colonial era, the laws that evolved were also harsher. In the tobacco colonies the slave code was based on English law, which gave at least limited rights to slaves. But in South Carolina the slave code was based on Spanish law, where the owners maintained "absolute" power over their slave property.[46]

The treatment of the African blacks transported to the North American colonies and the West Indies was barbaric and inhuman. After the blacks were "collected," they were often marched naked and strapped together, single file, to the ships. Slave ships arriving in Charles Town between 1731 and 1769 held from 50 to 170 blacks.[47] They were confined aboard a ship for the long voyages in foul quarters, so small that they were too low to allow them to stand upright. The usual height of this "Middle Passage," as it was known, was from three feet three to three feet ten inches. Some slave ships had blacks on platforms between decks "stacked" like cordwood. There were many opportunities to die aboard these slave ships, including by suffocation, disease, and dehydration.[48] Toilet facilities were often open tubs, and the floors of these ships were covered with blood and mucus. Alexander Falconbridge, a surgeon aboard a slave ship, wrote, "It is not in the power of the human imagination to picture to itself a situation more dreadful or disgusting."[49] In the seventeenth century, one quarter of all slaves who boarded ships died en route. By the eighteenth century conditions had improved somewhat to a mortality rate of 10 percent.[50]

While the moral view of slavery as an evil was present in the colonial era before the Revolution, it was not considered of overwhelming social, economic or political significance at the time. Since the land in New England was not as favorable for crops as in the South and the growing seasons were shorter, the northern colonists did not pursue slavery with as much zeal as did the South. While the North never depended on slavery to any significant degree, primarily because of economic circumstances, they did condone slavery. Many men of significant standing in the North were slaveholders. Even the well-respected Ben Franklin bought and sold slaves in Philadelphia.[51] In the South, slavery was considered an economic reality. The dependence on slavery in the South was so great that even the most revered framer of the Declaration of Independence, Thomas Jefferson, who wrote the phase "that all men are created equal," owned nearly 200 slaves when he wrote the famous document. He would not release all his slaves until the death of his wife, when the economic impact was past. George Washington of Virginia died owning 277 slaves.[52]

Another curious group of human servants to the white colonist also came to North America before black slaves assumed their services over time. These colonists were indentured servants who came to the colonies under contract for a period of four to seven years to serve their masters. In return for transportation across the Atlantic, and for food, clothing and shelter, these people agreed to be indentured servants under a legal contract for a stated period. These contracts were of differing prices depending on the skills, age, sex, length of contract and, of course, the local demand for their talents. Thousands of willing white immigrants came to the Southern colonies in this way to seek a better life and often to eventually acquire land. Between 1630 and 1680 some two-thirds of all immigrants to Virginia were indentured.

Most indentured servant males served farmers to work the fields, while females handled the household chores. After their period of indenture, these people would usually receive some funds to help them get started in their new life in the colonies as free people. Even though they were servants for their indentured period, their general living conditions were not any worse, in most cases better, than they had known in their homeland. After 1680 black slaves replaced indentured slaves as the primary source of bonded labor in the Southern colonies. According to estimates, this unique method of supplying labor to the colonies brought some 350,000 indentured servants to North America during the colonial period. By 1774, the indentured servant population had decreased to around two percent.

The seeds of what was to later define the South as a sectional unit of America were present in society before the Revolution. In almost every face of life before the Revolution, there existed a differing set of realities between those who lived in the Southern colonies and their Northern counterparts. The South was focused on agriculture as the source of most wealth, held thousands of black slaves, had a common social order, and toiled on similar geography under the same hot, sun-drenched skies. Though there were already differences between the South and the other regions of America, the later sectional clashes were to develop during, and especially after, the American Revolution. In these pre–Revolutionary days, the focus was between colony and colony. An English visitor to the colonies during 1759 and 1760 wrote, "fire and water are not more heterogeneous than the different colonies in North America. Nothing can exceed the jealousy and emulation, which they possess in regard to each other."[53] But circumstances changed, and the new fixation was more especially centered between the colonies and the British.

As the Southern colonies approached the Revolution, there was a sense of confidence throughout the populace. While most documented history is focused upon the aristocrats of their day, the true foundation of what was great about the American and the Southern colonies was the "substance" of the common man and woman. The Southern colonists had created a successful environment that most peoples of the eighteenth century would envy. To describe the average Southern man of 1763 was to reveal a God-fearing, independent man with a basic, yet practical, education, a landowner, a small, hardworking farmer, a proud citizen, the father of a large household and a person actively engaged in the business of creating the greatness of America and the South. The colonists had taken all that was good about their European heritage and built a new foundation for an essentially improved and unique American society. Nowhere on earth were there so many possibilities. It was truly a time of promise for the Southern colonist. Like all Americans who spoke a common language, the colonist had a proud European — mostly British — heritage and believed in the opportunity and essential independence that had flourished for over 150 years in this New World.

On the third of November 1762 at Fountainbleau outside Paris, the preliminaries of the peace treaty ending the French and Indian War had concluded. The treaty, which would be formally signed on the following 10th of February in 1763, had just been initialed between the ministers of England and France to end this Seven Years' War. The words of the treaty required France to surrender to Great Britain all the lands in North America east of the Mississippi River, as well as the so-called "Neutral Islands" of the West Indies. The British gained political control of Bengal in India, and Spain gave up lands of East and West Florida. The war had sadly cost a million lives and devastated parts of Europe, while touching areas in all the four corners of the globe. But the faces of the English treaty ministers showed the gleam of victory. It was a time of incredible pride for England and its nearly three million subjects.[54]

In North America, the British Union Jack would now fly from Hudson Bay to the Florida Keys, providing to all the visible political success that had been gained through military means. An estimated 6,000 colonists had died along with their fellow British soldiers to gain this peace.[55] With the French, Spanish and Native Americans calmed, they felt a sense of security never experienced in the previous century and a half.

The political accomplishments of Great Britain at this time were equally matched by her colonial economic achievements. While the native-born American colonists by 1763 could not be expected to deal with the realities of their economic heritage, the true legacy in purpose for establishing colonial settlements from the very beginning was to build wealth for the mother country. Mercantilism, the dominant economic theme of the day in Great Britain, as it was in the other European states, had the stated aim of gaining national self-sufficiency and a favorable balance of international trade, while excluding trade with other states outside the "empire."[56] The commercial experiment of the Atlantic colonies, started in Jamestown in 1607, had served ultimately to enrich the English even though it did not meet the economic expectations of the founding investors. By 1763, Britain exported goods to the American colonies valued at some £3,730,900.[57] By 1772, the Southern colonies alone imported annually 16 percent (£1.6 million) of the exports of the mother country.[58]

In this hour of economic and political glory for the British king, the leaders of his government and the English people, who could imagine that in just over a decade the prosperous 13 American colonies would declare their independence and resort to armed conflict with their European "parents." At this point in history in 1763, Great Britain had reached the peak of her glory and prestige, and should have looked forward to decades of prosperity, along with her subjects in the American colonies. Unfortunately, the British would witness the decline and fall of their brightest economic hope in the empire. In just over a single decade the English government would destroy a colonial relationship built over 15 decades of economic growth and reasonable political cooperation.

The end of the French and Indian War was viewed in the Southern colonies in a different and more narrow perspective than it was in England. For the Southern colonies, a key objective of the war was securing the Ohio Valley and stabilizing their own Native American territories. The Southern colonists were proud of their financial and military contributions to the war. But the relationship between the British and the colonists was changing. The British never felt that the financial contributions to the war were adequate, and they downplayed the role of the Southern military men who supported the war. During the war the regular British troops felt that even the most junior British officer was higher in standing than a colonial officer, regardless of rank. In Virginia the British continued to protest the use of paper currency that had been issued to fund the war. The royal governor seemed to only cast bad press to the actions of the House of Burgesses. In Virginia, and throughout the South, there was a growing resentment of British criticism. It seemed that the British would always consider the Atlantic colonial peoples and their accomplishments as inferior in some way.[59]

Even before 1763, there was documented evidence that the idea of eventual independence of the Atlantic colonies was a possibility. A Swedish botanist, Peter Kalm, who visited New York in 1748, made such a prediction in the following:

I have been told by Englishmen, and not only by such as were born in America, but even by such as came from Europe, that the English colonies in North America, in the space of thirty or fifty years, would be able to form a state by themselves, entirely independent of Old England.

In 1761 in London, a pamphlet titled *Remarks on the Letter Address'd to Two Great Men*, and believed to be written by William Burke, a relative of the famous Edmund Burke, also presented such a case:

And as they increase daily in People and in Industry, the Necessity of a Connection with England, with which they have no natural Intercourse by a Reciprocation of Wants, will continually diminish. But as they recede from the Sea, all these Causes will operate more strongly; they will have nothing to expect, they must live wholly on their own Labour, and in process of Time will know little, enquire little, and care little about the Mother Country.[60]

The Maryland of 1763, in the upper South, looked much like the other Southern colonies, and it nearly mirrored its neighboring and larger colony, Virginia, in most respects. The Province of Maryland, the proprietary of Frederick, Lord Baltimore, was economically typical of the South, except that the white population outnumbered black slaves by a ratio of two to one, and there were few large plantations.[61] Of all the Southern colonies, Maryland had the smallest population by 1763, numbering 115,000. It was a small colony as many had emigrated to other lands, including beyond the Allegheny Mountains.

From the initial period of settlement up to 1763, Maryland and Virginia had shared similar economic and political legacies. Lord Baltimore had even been a stockholder in the founding Virginia Company. Both colonies had tobacco and slaves, and shared the fruits of the Chesapeake Bay environment. The earliest conflicts were with Virginia over Lord Baltimore's charter and the upper Chesapeake territory. Evidence of the economic closeness of the two colonies, though, is typified by the fact that customs data was combined on export trade reports to the British House of Lords.[62]

Maryland's early history revealed a period of prosperity and relative calm as the settlers built the colony and the government continued to defend its rights in England. The province not only enjoyed a favorable climate, but it also maintained a peaceful relationship, for the most part, with the Native Americans.[63]

The way of life in Maryland was considerably affected by the Chesapeake Bay and the bulk of the population resided in the lower region of the bay. Along the Chesapeake Bay the colonists settled in almost equal proportions on the Eastern and Western Shores. This was an area dominated by the growing of tobacco, which led to the growth in the slave population to cultivate it. The planters in this region had prospered, but in the 50 years before the American Revolution the cycles of chronic fluctuation in tobacco prices served to create economic depression and a certain degree of frustration in trade with Britain's merchants. Since the soil in Maryland best suited the growing of an "oronoko" type of tobacco, which was not favored in England and did not command the higher prices, the Maryland crops had to pass through English ports to be re-exported to other European countries due to trade regulations. With a growing population of planters, cyclic price variations, the process of soil exhaustion, trade regulations and even a war, it was not surprising that the tobacco planters of the lower Chesapeake experienced serious pressures on their financial well being. Even with these problems, the estimated annual production of tobacco hogsheads in Maryland by 1763 was 28,000, worth some £140,000 ($12.6 million).[64]

The other two evolving regions of Maryland included the upper bay, with the northern counties, and to the west, toward the frontier region, centered by Frederick County. In the upper bay the crop that dominated was wheat, which served to create the "grain culture." Iron ore production was also developed in this region centered on Baltimore, the largest town in Maryland. The growth of Baltimore was rather measured until a major road to western Maryland opened in the 1740s, when trade in the harbor flourished. Frederick County, which was exposed to the frontier of the French and Indian War, was a "rich and fruitful" area of the colony. Primarily Germans, who fostered grain agriculture over tobacco planting, populated it. The town of Frederick grew from 1763 until the Revolution to become larger than Annapolis, and second only to Baltimore in population.[65]

The Maryland Charter of 1632, which defined political and to some extent the economic parameters of the province, was quite liberal and unusual for its time. Lord Baltimore and his heirs enjoyed the most control over their domain of any other colony of Great Britain. He

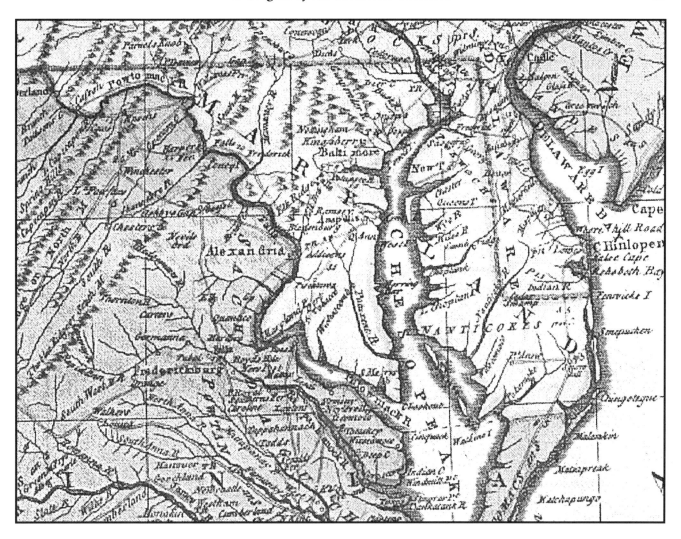

Maryland in 1771. (Library of Congress.)

could enact laws and regulations as needed "Providing the Laws were Consonant to Reason," and "Not repugnant or contrary but agreeable to the Laws, Statues, Customs and Rights of this our Kingdom of England." The charter also covered the requirement for a representative body to provide advice to the lord and his representatives. The colonists were to be considered peer citizens of England, with the same privileges, franchises and liberties of the English. The colonists were required to pay the same type of taxes and fees as would any Englishman, but the charter spoke that "Beyond that WE WILL that the Inhabitants of the aforesaid Province of the said land called Maryland shall not be burdened." In addition, the king pledged not to impose in the future any "Customs, or other Taxation Quotas or Contributions whatsoever in or upon the residents of the province for their goods, land or tenements, merchandise or within the ports or harbors of the province, laden or unladen."[66]

An assembly of delegates, as foreseen in the charter, first met in 1635. The principal requirement to be a member of this House of Delegates was to own 50 acres freehold or have an estate worth 40 pounds sterling. Four delegates were chosen from each county, and two from the town of Annapolis, where through special provision of the law, "all" homeowners were allowed to vote. The requirement of owning 50 acres was not a restrictive element since this was far below the average land holding of the typical farmer.[67] Over time an upper house was formed with a governor and his "Privy Council of State," who represented the interests of the Lord Proprietor.[68]

Maryland's political culture, like that of Virginia, was characterized as aristocratic and democratically idealistic by contemporary definition. As was true in the other Southern colonies, the assembly was dominated by the elite of the great planters, lawyers and wealthy merchants, with those of the less prosperous and "meaner sort" left with little direct voice. The political architecture was based on the principles of English constitutionalism and focused on the "Whig" view of the world. They rejected pure democracy as "all governments the worst" and desired that the colonial government must remain "steady, firm and respectable." While the great planters controlled the political realm in Maryland, even though the bulk of the population was farmers, they never exceeded five percent of the families in Maryland during the colonial period.[69] In Maryland the popular party of conservatives led the assembly toward Revolution and independence, but not with any idea of leaning towards a popular government of "commoners."

During the colonial era in Maryland there was little evidence of any east-west conflict as seen in several of the lower Southern colonies, even though there were rather significant differences. In the backcountry of the western counties were non–English populations like the Germans of Frederick County. In addition, they had differing religious backgrounds, with Anglican in the Chesapeake and Presbyterian, Baptist, and Lutheran out west. Economic variances existed also. In western Maryland few landholders owned slaves, while in the east slaves were common.[70]

Even though Maryland played no significant role in the French and Indian War, they did assist the British in funding the effort in several documented ways. On July 25, 1754, the Maryland Assembly passed an act to pay Governor Horatio Sharpe £6000 ($540,000) for services toward the defense of the colony of Virginia, then actually under attack by the French and Indians. These funds were financed by duties on peddlers, coaches, chairs, chaises, chariots, Madeira wine and a poll tax for indentured servants and black slaves. To help with the war effort the Maryland Assembly later voted an additional £40,000 ($3,600,000), paid for with duties on "Batchelors" over age 25, and on various writs and legal papers.[71]

As the people of Maryland reached 1763, they had little to complain about regarding the mother country or the provincial government. The people were not heavily burdened in support of their provincial government. Based on a report to Deputy Governor Sharpe to the Earl of Shelburne, released on May 14, 1767, the total financial demand on the people was less than £5500 annually, which equaled no more than one shilling per capita per year. No war debt existed and there was little other debt.[72]

The colony of Virginia in 1763 represented in excess of one-third of the entire Southern population, distributed in 54 counties. Between 1740 and 1770 the Virginia population would grow from approximately 180,000 to some 450,000.[73] Like Maryland, white colonists outnumbered blacks by two to one. Though the vast majority of the population was small farmers with perhaps a few slaves, there were a number of rather large plantations throughout the old colony. The lordly families owned the plantations of Virginia with dependents numbering in the hundreds. They most nearly resembled the landed

gentry of England, except that they had slaves to work their estates. In all of North America, this Virginia aristocracy exhibited the highest lifestyle, flair and luxury.[74]

Virginia was growing not only in population, but also economically, grounded on its primary crop of tobacco. Virginia had reaped the bounty in wealth almost exclusively because of the demand for tobacco in Europe. This expansion began at a serious pace around the 1620s when prices skyrocketed and had stabilized by the first quarter of the eighteenth century. Between 1740 and 1770 tobacco exports jumped from £165,000 to £476,000.[75] In 1763 the tobacco exports hit 50,000 hogsheads worth some £500,000 ($45 million).[76] Over the years the usual practice in Virginia called for merchants in England to provide credit to the debt-worthy planters if they agreed to pay their debts in the form of their annual tobacco crop. When the low tobacco prices and soil exhaustion started to create a serious indebtedness problem, these planters became a significant and somewhat embittered force in the political environment of the colony.

Another controversial issue at the time involved those frontier families who were settling on the west beyond the line defined in the Proclamation of 1763. The British forts that were located along the line, like Fort Pitt, were under orders to keep these settlers off the "Indian" lands. Eventually the issue was resolved in a series of treaties — Fort Stanwix, Hard Labor and Lochaber — with the tribes of the greatest Six Nations, which sold much of the valuable land to the settlers.[77]

As in other Southern colonies, some degree of sectional conflict existed between the older eastern counties and the newer western frontier counties in Virginia. Generally though, in Virginia the western counties were not all that unhappy. While the western districts were underrepresented, they did have some voice in the House of Burgesses in Williamsburg. Delegates were increased as the colonists populated the western areas. Actually, the Tidewater aristocracy encouraged the development of the west with their land speculation efforts. Apparently the western Virginia populace was not of a mind to challenge the economic and political power of the eastern planters.

By the mid–eighteenth century many Virginians became politically and economically discontent with the status quo. They were the product of a mature and prosperous existence nurtured in English heritage, yet profoundly "American" in attitude. An English visitor to Virginia in 1759, Andrew Burnaby, described evidence of this new attitude in reporting that Virginians were "haughty and jealous of their liberties, impatient of restraint, and can scarcely bear the thought of being controlled by any superior power." Also, he wrote, "Many of them consider the colonies as independent states, not connected with Great Britain, otherwise than by natural affection."[78] In the fall of 1766 Francis Fauquier, the royal governor of Virginia, wrote to the British Board of Trade that "the Blood of the people is soured by their private Distresses" and that "party feuds will run high" with the General Assembly. When attempts were made to calm the members of the House of Burgesses, they replied with an address on November 13, 1766, that revealed a strong distrust and thinly veiled threat to the British that the colonies and mother country might have their relationship "imperiled" should the Parliament violate their historic colonial rights.

On the topic of taxation in 1763, Virginia had no real issue. In fact, the tax burden on Virginians was lighter than it was for the typical Englishman. Virginians paid the salaries of the provincial officials with taxes on tobacco in the form of an export tax at the rate of two shillings per hogshead. Also, they paid a little over a shilling per ton on vessels trading in the colony, and six pence. for each person who arrived in Virginia by ship. By the spring of 1767 a surplus existed in Virginia of £1578, seven shillings and four pence. Other financial needs, such as funding the General Assembly, in supporting the College of William and Mary, and even compensating owners for slaves that were executed for capital offenses, were met with taxes of four pence per gallon on imported rum and wine, and some five percent of the value of a slave imported for sale into the colony. Service fees were charged for certain specific actions of officials, such as signing land patents, innkeeper licenses, marriage licenses, ship passes and the use of the great seal to authenticate papers.

While the tax burden was not heavy, there were occasional scandals in the colony surrounding fiscal action. During the period between 1757 and 1763 Virginia had issued over £412,962 in "treasury notes" which were repaid with tax revenue levied during these years. Rather than actually destroying these notes upon settlement, the treasurer of Virginia and the speaker of the House of Burgesses, John Robinson, simply reissued the notes as loans totaling some £100,000 ($9 million) to his friends, while accepting their personal papers as security for these debts. When Robinson died in the spring of 1766, the requirement to levy additional taxes on the colonists was mandated to correct the treasury deficit.

North Carolina in 1763, like Virginia, was seeing incredible growth and also some distressing disorder and incompetent government. The royal governor, William Tryon, had reported in 1767 to the Board of Trade that the colony was settling faster than any in North America, with migration coming from the North and settling in the Piedmont and backcountry of western North Carolina. The population was somewhere around 200,000 and it had doubled in the 20 years before 1754, when the population was only 77,000, and then doubled again during the next decade.[79]

Although North Carolina was gaining population and had been the location of the first attempt at English colonization at Roanoke Island, it had not become a major commercial region, even with the production of naval stores, which were so valued in Britain. The colony had no prevalent plantation aristocracy, few black slaves, and no large towns, which was in stark contrast to its Southern neighbor, South Carolina. The colony had little in common with its northern neighbor, Virginia, either, since North Carolinians were interested in local problems, Native American concerns, east-west sectional clashes, disagreements with their governor and others. North Carolina was also greatly affected by its geographic, and therefore economic, isolation. Coupled with these and other internal issues, a more "localized" view of the world emerged there at a time when those in other American colonies were developing a true "American" perspective.[80]

The character of the North Carolina populace was influenced by several factors beyond that of their backcountry status. Some settlers had left Virginia to avoid everything from a degree of religious intolerance, to debts, illegal activities and the aristocratic nature of the great landowners. They had developed little respect for the upper class, government and even religion. The laws that emerged in North Carolina held the settlers exempt of debt liabilities from another colony for five years, and exempt from taxation for the first year of residence. Thus began the continuing social conflict between the elite population of Virginia and the "commoners" of North Carolina. Many Virginians shared their contempt for North Carolinians, including Colonel William Byrd who, while negotiating the boundary between North Carolina and Virginia, showed his disgust for the shiftless population of the Carolina backcountry.[81]

The inhabitants of the interior of North Carolina were described by Robert Jones, the attorney general of the province, as bold and intrepid in the art of war as well as hospitable to strangers, and as dirty, impertinent and vain. In that region Presbyterianism was the predominant religion among those known as the Scots-Irish. In the backcountry were the rugged individualist farmers and ranchers. The Tidewater populations of North Carolina were the planter aristocracy affiliated with the Church of England.[82] As more settlers migrated to North Carolina, like the Germans and Swiss who founded New Bern, the Scots-Irish who moved to the western areas, and later the Scottish Highlanders, the character of the population changed to form a more stable culture. North Carolina became a place of little class division, in stark comparison to that of Virginia.

Sectionalism had, interestingly, been a dominant theme in North Carolina during the colonial period. The

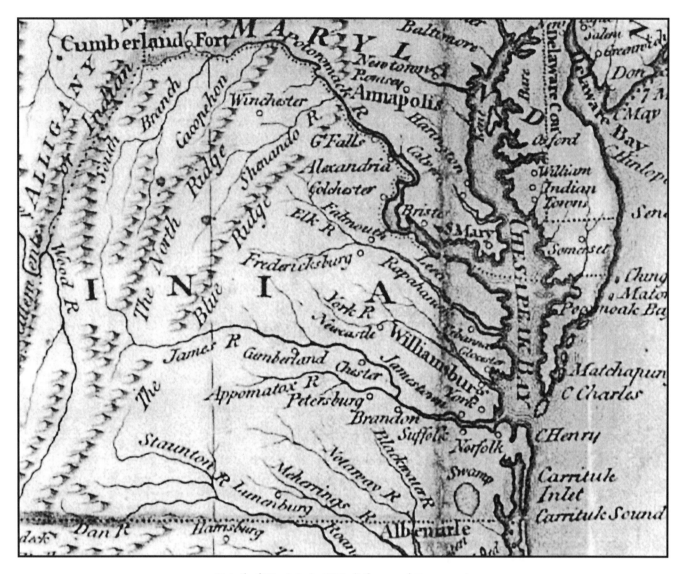

Detail of Virginia in 1783. (Library of Congress.)

first sectional problems occurred between the settlers in the Albemarle Sound region and those who moved down the Cape Fear River. Since Albemarle colonists dealt economically with the coastal Virginia area, while the Cape Fear colonists had their own access to the outside world, conflict often occurred. Conflict was fostered and led to inequities, like that of allowing the Albemarle counties to have five delegates to the Assembly when the Cape Fear and Neuse counties were allowed only two each. Into the 1740s the conflict included even the location of the capital. Cape Fear colonists wanted Wilmington as their provincial capital, but the peoples of the Albemarle counties refused to meet there, in favor of their choice, New Bern. Regardless, the capital was really the place where the royal governor lived. This capital issue was not resolved until Governor Tryon moved into Tryon Palace in New Bern in 1770.

The second, and for a few even deadly, sectional dispute in North Carolina centered around the conflict between the eastern and western populations. By the mid–eighteenth century the eastern counties were a mature society, as compared to western counties where life was still rather basic and frontier. One of the first well-publicized disputes began over the funding of the elegant "Governor's Palace" erected for Governor Tryon in New Bern, which was begun in 1766 and opened Christmas of 1770. This brick and marble building, which was among the most impressive facilities in North America, cost the citizens of the colony £15,000 ($1.35 million). It was to be paid for from a levy on imported wine, rum and liquor, and a poll tax. The western colonists were incensed by the lavishness of the building and the fact that very few of those citizens would ever see what they were being taxed for. A resident of Mecklenburg County in 1768 remarked that "not one in twenty in the four most populous counties will ever see this famous house when built, as their

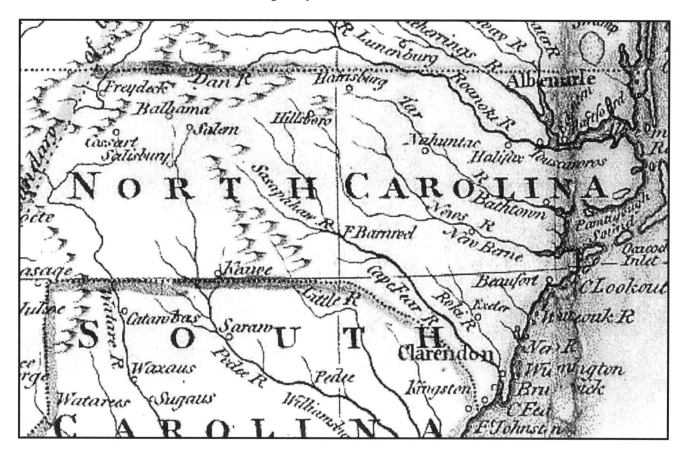

North Carolina in 1783. (Library of Congress.)

connections and trade do, and ever will, more naturally center in South Carolina." Thus, in his opinion, Charles Town was a better choice for a capital than New Bern from a practical "western" perspective. On August 2, 1768, in Orange County the residents told the sheriff that "We are determined not to pay the Tax for the next three years, for the Ediface or Governor's House." The trade of the Piedmont peoples was with South Carolina or with Virginia, but certainly not with the Tidewater North Carolinians.

This sectional conflict grew into what was known as the Regulator Movement, a term for the attempts of western people to take control of their affairs. The movement was caused by a number of valid grievances endured by these frontier colonists. Politically, there was a severe imbalance in the representation of the western peoples. In 1770 only 15 of the 81 members of the North Carolina Assembly were from the western counties, while the western counties contained one-third of the population. Also, there was significant fraud and corruption at the hands of the local officials. This corruption took numerous forms, including misappropriation of collected taxes, fraudulent handling of foreclosure activities, and excessive penalty fees. The most renowned and hated of individuals by the North Carolina Regulators was Edmund

Fanning, a New York native who moved to Hillsborough in 1760 for land speculation. He symbolically represented what would later be called the "carpetbagger" phenomenon in the South. Fanning, who was educated at Yale and Harvard, held a number of provincial and local offices — Assembly member, registrar of deeds, judge of superior court and militia colonel — and was primarily known for his cruelty, distaste for the common people and his arrogance.

As this western grievance festered, the Regulators began to take things into their own hands. The first documented conflict occurred in the Granville District in 1759 when the chief agent was seized by Regulators on his own plantation, but was later released. A riot broke out in Mecklenburg County in 1765 over attempts to survey lands owned by George Selwyn. This event was known as the "War of Sugar Creek." In June of 1765 George Sims, a schoolmaster and laborer, was arrested and brought to trial for a small debt he could not pay. He ultimately lost his horse, cattle, furniture and land over this £5 debt, but did deliver publicly his "Address to the People of Granville County" regarding his accusations of wrongdoing by lawyers, court clerks and the sheriff. He appealed to the Assembly but was ignored.

The formal organization of the Regulator Movement

took place in 1768, and was led by Herman Husband, Rednap Howell and James Hunter. The group declared their intention to pay no taxes, pay no fees greater than required by law, attend Regulator meetings regularly, help fund the movement and abide by the majority. The Regulators began to be more militant over time and started to become violent. In September 1770, a mob of 150 Regulators broke into the Superior Court building in Hillsborough, controlled by Judge Richard Henderson. With sticks in hand, they drove the judge out of the court and set up a mock court. They took an attorney out to the street and dragged him through the town. Reports indicated that Edmund Fanning was forcefully taken from his home, whipped, had his library burned, his furniture broken and his home destroyed. After various actions of civil disobedience by the Regulators, Governor Tryon began to take action against the North Carolina Regulators.[83]

The culmination of the governor's attempts to put down the Regulator Movement occurred in the spring of 1771 along the Alamance River. Governor Tryon gathered a militia force of 1452 men, primarily from eastern North Carolina, and marched to within six miles of a large force of about 2000 Regulators on May 14 at Great Alamance Creek, located just west of Hillsborough in Alamance County. Attempts to negotiate with the Regulators, to lay down their arms and submit to the taxes, went without success. The Regulators had never desired to engage in open fighting with Tryon and his militia. Eventually, a man named Thompson went to see Tryon at his encampment to negotiate, and was taken as a prisoner. When Thompson attempted to leave the encampment, Governor Tryon grabbed a gun and shot the man dead. The Regulators then fired on the flag of truce that the governor had sent out, as the parties approached each other. Tryon gave the word to "fire," but his men hesitated until the governor cried out, "Fire on them or on me." At this point his militia fired their weapons and men fell on both sides. Twenty-seven militia died as well as nine Regulators. There were many wounded.

The cruel treatment by Governor Tryon of the prisoners was a low moment in the events of the colony. The evening before the battle, the governor ordered the hanging of Regulator James Few without a trial and after this act proceeded to destroy what little property Few had to leave to his parents. The next sad event involved a Captain Messer who had been condemned to death by hanging the following day. On that day Captain Messer's wife came forward with her oldest son at her side, and appealed in tears to Tryon for leniency for her husband. The young boy of ten then told Tryon "Sir, hang me, and let my father live!" Tryon exclaimed, "Who told you to say that?" The boy replied, "Nobody," and then he continued, "If you hang my father, my mother will die, and the children will perish!" The Governor said, "Well," and being moved by the words of this child, said, "Your father shall not be hung today." On June 19, Captain Messer and five others were paraded through the streets of Hillsborough in chains and hanged just outside town.[84] This was the "apex" and close of Tryon's career in North Carolina. A few days after the victory at Alamance, he gave his farewell address to his militia and left for New Bern for preparations to move to New York as its new governor. This was the last significant event of the Regulators in North Carolina.

Because of the poor fiscal procedures and, in many cases, unlawful activities of many public officials, the public finances were in disarray by 1767. The Assembly had issued credit, paper money and debentures over the years that were to be covered by a poll tax and duties on liquor. The modest appropriations had been for officials' salaries, supporting a captain and ten men at Fort Johnson on the Cherokee boundary line, to fund small gifts to the Native Americans and payment of a bounty on hemp and flax. The total necessary annual expenses were only £1829 ($164,610). Even at the eve of the Revolution, the per capita tax of around a shilling was all that North Carolinians had to pay. Thus, there was no case for excessive taxation in North Carolina.[85]

South Carolina in 1763 was not a pioneering region like its northern neighbor, North Carolina, but it did have a wealthy aristocracy of great planters and successful merchants who led a mature society. What was unique about South Carolina was its relative political harmony interacting with a social fabric of significant contrasts. The white colonists showed a face of happy contentment in all areas of life, but with two-thirds of the population of 100,000 being black slaves, it is no surprise that they felt some sense of insecurity with the possibility of slave insurrections.[86] In some areas of the Tidewater Lowcountry the incredible ratio of blacks to whites reached seven to one.[87]

On the backs of their slaves the South Carolina planters prospered economically, with indigo and rice trade dominating. The aristocracy of the colony followed closely the English landed gentry in lifestyle and views, and like most Southern society, South Carolina based its political foundation on land ownership, with what one called a "country ideology." The entire colonial experience in South Carolina had been grounded on the idea of self-government and independence of religious, political and unquestionable economic freedom. Without the inhuman element to sour the moral reality, certainly the colony of South Carolina best exemplified the ideal of colonial success as originally envisioned by the British earlier in the seventeenth century.

South Carolina in 1783. (Library of Congress.)

The issue of taxation after 1763 to any great extent did not hurt South Carolinians. In spite of the rather large appropriations for the war, the taxes were not a burden. Taxes were delayed until 1769 and were collected through 1777.[88] The colony's economy had escaped the depression that followed the French and Indian War, and the rise of imports kept pace with the increasing exports. But, between 1760 and 1768 the local debt doubled, and by 1776 South Carolinians owed British merchants £347,000 ($31,230,000). The trade was flowing though and by 1760 the export of indigo reached £.5 million and rice over £43 million. The exports of South Carolina were some 15 percent of the total exports from the Thirteen Colonies. In addition, the imports into South Carolina by 1765 were 17 percent of all the imports of the American colonies.[89] The South Carolina economy was the best in the British Atlantic, and it made many a wealthy planter and merchant in the colony.

While most of the population lived in the Upcountry, the Tidewater life centered on the city of Charles Town. This seaport capital city of 10,000 was the economic, political and social focus of the entire Carolinas. With the highest per capita income for whites of any of the Thirteen Colonies flowing through the economy of Charles Town, the city and its peoples prospered. From the city's and colony's planter and merchant elite was formed a class of conservative-minded politicians who would lead the colony toward the Revolution with cautious, yet determined, steps. The government was made up of the governor and his council, various officials of the crown, and the Commons House of Assembly.[90] As these leaders responded to the coming British Parliamentary acts, they would continue to show a devoted commitment to maintaining the successful environment of economic, social and political stability, while coming to terms with the reality of British injustice, which was tipping the balance of forces toward loss of freedom. A symbol of that struggle was revealed by Henry Laurens, one of the leading merchants of the colony, who wept at the thought of independence from Britain, but subsequently joined his fellow patriots in the just cause and became the president of the Continental Congress.[91]

Several other towns provided support to the South Carolina planters. North of Charles Town was the small port of Georgetown located near the mouths of the Black, Pee Dee and Waccamaw rivers. The town became a depot for rice and indigo crops and provided a method to receive imported goods directly. South of Charles Town on the island of Port Royal was the town of Beaufort, which served the plantations of lower South Carolina.[92]

Sectionalism was a part of the colonial history of South Carolina, much like it was for its northern neighbor. The basis of the conflict was centered in the differences between the Lowcountry and Upcountry regions. In the Lowcountry were the aristocracy with their plantations, their capital, their Charles Town, slaves, rice and indigo crops, Anglican religion, wealth, and a heritage of English peoples intermingled with Scots, French and others. The Upcountry was populated with small farmers and cattlemen of moderate means and few slaves, from Scotch-Irish and German families with some English, French and Scots around. These people were poorly educated and lacked the social station of the Tidewater Lowcountry populace.

Out of these differing societies within the colony grew conflict. The Upcountry's key grievances were that they were under-represented in the Assembly and that they suffered because of few convenient courts and inadequate law enforcement. Rather than create new parish units, the South Carolina Assembly simply extended the western boundaries inland. It was difficult for the Upcountry peoples to determine which parish they were in, or even get to the polling place, which was usually at some distance from their home. The second grievance had resulted from the centralization of almost all legal services at Charles Town on the coast. There was no sheriff or circuit court outside the city to serve the Upcountry populace, and only a weak justice of the peace organization. It was extremely difficult to make the tough journey east to Charles Town to handle legal affairs. Another problem developed as a result of the lack of law enforcement, when various criminal types settled in the Upcountry to avoid the law. Reports told of much sinful activity in the Upcountry including public drunkenness, profanity, rape, murder, naked men and women bathing together, horse thievery, religious orgies, fornication, robbery and other varieties of wickedness.

Like the sectional conflict in North Carolina, these grievances between the Tidewater and Upcountry peoples led to the growth of the Regulator Movement in South Carolina. In the spring of 1767, the Upcountry people formed an association and then attacked some outlaw groups directly. The group demanded changes and planned a march in Charles Town for the fall. The governor, Lord Charles Montagu, then issued a proclamation that ordered the Regulators to disperse and asked the Assembly to set up some laws to restrain their growth. On November 7, 1767, Benjamin Hart, John Scott, Moses Kirkland and Thomas Woodward presented a written list of grievances, called the "Remonstrance," from some 4000 Upcountry colonists with details of the wrongs inflicted upon them. Montagu and the Assembly did attempt to correct the wrongs by sending out the militia and setting up a revised court system. Unfortunately the courts were not active until 1773 when the judges finally took their seats. With little real change for the Upcountry folks, the Regulators went back to their unlawful justice. To put down the movement, Montagu in February 1769 directed Joseph Coffell to leave with troops from Charles Town and seize some 25 Regulators. On the Saluda River his force met up with an armed group of Regulators, but no battle occurred. Eventually, the movement calmed down as the Revolution arrived.[93]

In 1763, Georgia had only been a colony for 31 years after its founding in 1732 as a trusteeship "for persons of lessor means and good character." Contrary to the mythology that developed over the years, Georgia was not founded by debtors. Those who came to its lands were principally "worthy" poor, indentured servants and others from Europe and the Carolinas. Having been founded to act as a buffer against the Spanish, the colony promoted the fur trade and various experiments in silk production. The dream of General James Oglethorpe evolved into a colony with much of the same legacy as the other Southern colonies. By 1763, Georgia took on the appearance of a frontier settlement, which approximated that of its Upcountry neighbors in South Carolina in most ways. During its brief history at that point, Georgia had developed a political and social elite, prospered economically, experienced Assembly government, grew in population, became more religiously diverse, and increasingly demographically heterogeneous.[94] Interestingly, Georgia suffered no east-west sectional conflict, primarily because it had no "west" to speak of.[95]

The population of Georgia had grown to 4000 inhabitants, but under the trusteeship had dwindled to some 500 by 1742 due to the original regulations that prohibited rum and slavery and limited landholding rights. By 1760 the population reached 6000 whites and around 3500 slaves. By 1766 the numbers were 9900 whites and 7800 slaves. The economy also grew during this period. Exports of rice in 1760 were 3400 barrels, and grew by

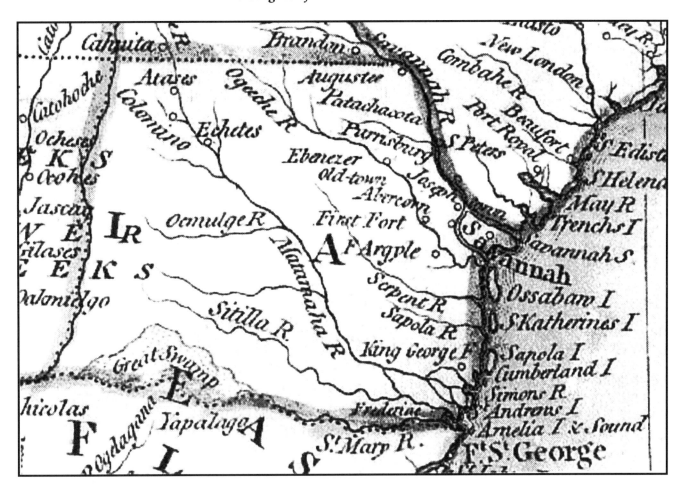

Detail of Georgia in 1783. (Library of Congress.)

1765 to 10,000 barrels. In 1761 it took 42 vessels to carry these goods from Savannah, but by 1765 it would take some 153 vessels. The planters grew indigo, corn, peas, cattle, pigs, horses and mules, as well as produced pine tree pitch, tar, turpentine, shingles, barrels and lumber. Imports from Britain, the West Indies, Africa and the Northern colonies had reached £137,000 ($12,330,000) by 1766, with over 500,000 acres of land having been distributed by 1767 to settlers. A planter aristocracy began to emerge like that of South Carolina.

While Georgia was seeing a good pace of economic growth by 1763, it still received annual grants from the British Parliament. These grants never dropped below £3000 ($27,000) during the remainder of the colonial period. In 1767 the grant was £4000. Even though the Parliament provided a grant of £4000 in 1767, the Georgia Assembly only granted £1843 to handle the government. Some funds were received from duties on Savannah shipping (to keep the lighthouse in repair), a deerskin duty, and a duty on goods imported from the Northern colonies to build the forts at Augusta and Frederica. While the British provided substantial aid to the new colony, the local Assembly showed its independence on numerous occasions. In 1767, an example of such an act involved the rejection of funding of the British garrison for Captain Phillips for support, as had been requested by Governor Wright in accordance with the Mutiny Act.[96]

As one considers the condition of Georgia in 1763, it goes without saying that those in the Assembly would proceed towards the Revolution with extreme caution. While the leaders of the young colony were to show their patriot drive over time, they were well aware of their "dependent state" and isolation from the other colonies on the southernmost fringe of the British Atlantic frontier. The people of Georgia would continue to be the most loyal British subjects in the Thirteen Colonies until the absolute brink of the Revolution. It was predictable that no official representatives from Georgia would attend the first or second Continental Congress.

Reflecting on the status of the five Southern colonies in 1763 is to see significant economic strength, a deep legacy of Assembly representative government, low taxes, a well-entrenched aristocracy, some sectional conflict, relative personal security from Native Americans and non–British foreigners, little public debt, and a wholly "American" people with a deep passion for personal independence.

2

REVOLUTIONARY SPIRIT AND THE FIRST CRISIS

Though the patriot leader John Adams insisted that the "Revolution was in the hearts and minds of men … with the first plantation in America," the momentous events that would ultimately lead to the American Revolution began after the conclusion of the French and Indian War with the Treaties of Paris in 1763. It was in that year that the British government began to take actions that served to change the method of administering the American colonies.[1] These actions would prove to be fatal to the historic economic and political relationship these colonies had established with their mother country. Perhaps the greatest tragedy was that through all these events, the British leadership never understood what had happened in America or how the colonists had changed. Even considering historic perspective, it is difficult to imagine the degree of arrogance present among the British political elite to continually make so many incremental errors. Indeed, 1763 was the "beginning of the end."

Early in the economic development of colonial America, the British had taken steps to maintain a level of control over the trade of the young Thirteen Colonies. Beginning in 1651 the Parliament passed the first in a series of "Navigation" Acts, which contained various restrictive elements, all designed to focus trade control through the British Empire. The specific objectives as outlined were to prevent vessels from foreign nations from doing business with ports of the empire without British approval, to force goods produced on the continent of Europe heading for the British colonies to pass through England, to require that the goods exported from the British colonies only be shipped through England or an authorized port, and to ensure that certain bounties for goods of special value to the British be provided.

These Navigation Acts thus filled the prescription for managing colonial trade, both in terms of exports of raw materials and agriculture to Britain, and with import restrictions for goods coming to the colonies. The goal was to have the colonies become fully dependent on the mother country by taking the colonial materials at lower prices and selling higher-valued manufactured goods to the colonial populace. In this way Britain could maintain a positive balance of trade with their colonial empire, with little outside interference.

While the impact of the Navigation Acts was felt in all the British Atlantic colonies, there is significant evidence that the Southern colonies suffered approximately 90 percent of the gross burden of this legislation. Southern income may have been penalized as much as 2.5 percent annually. Though the Southern planters shouldered the major burden, they did not complain about the Navigation Acts and it was not cited in public dialog as a key grievance during the period leading up to the Revolution. Southern planters did not complain, as did their Northern neighbors, because they had higher incomes than the Northern farmers and merchants.[2]

Even though the period between 1660 and 1764 saw Parliament enact nearly 30 acts associated with regulating commerce, not one single revenue act was passed. All the actions of the Navigation Acts were intended purely to manage the British view of colonial commerce, not to provide Britain with a source of revenue. For better or worse, under this policy of British mercantilism the commerce of the Atlantic colonies flourished as the British reveled in the glory of their economic wisdom and success. The export trade to the North American colonies in 1763 had reached a significant level. Britain was winning on the commercial front with the colonies of North America, and so were the colonials.

In April of 1763, George Grenville became the chancellor of the exchequer of Britain and began to made his mark on colonial policy. As a formal, stuffy and opinionated man of much financial renown, he intended to save the empire from the financial ruin created by the debts accumulated from the Seven Years' War, and at the hands of his predecessor, William Pitt. He was truly driven to stop the flow of red ink, to balance the budget and put the treasury on stable footing.[3] The centerpiece of his plan to clean up the fiscal condition was to tax the American colonies. The idea of taxing the colonies was not new. The first attempt actually began in 1739 when financier Robert Walpole, the Earl of Oxford, urged the Parliament to pass a revenue tax, without success.[4] But taxing the colonies was becoming a more popular idea.

As Grenville surveyed the British financial landscape, he was horrified at what he saw. The British national debt was £140 million ($12.6 billion), and the annual interest amounted to some £5 million ($450 million). By contrast, the total debt of the American colonies was believed to be only £2.6 million ($234 million). To complicate matters, the estimated public debt per British subject was £18 ($1,620), while the estimated debt for an American colonial subject was only eight shillings ($36).[5] The British taxpayer was already burdened with high taxes of various types. They had seen the Parliament add taxes on stamps, on the number of windows they had, even on the beer and cider they drank. The cider tax was eventually repealed in 1765 after violent resistance, but the beer tax continued to be the most unpopular tax to hit the average working man in Britain.[6]

English landowners justly complained of their plight at being taxed heavier than the merchants. Land taxes had risen from 10 percent of assessed value to 20 percent during the war. The continuing defense of the North American colonial frontier with some 7500 to 10,000 troops cost the British £135,000 ($31.5 million) annually, and represented nearly 12 percent of Parliament's annual operating budget.[7] The differences in the condition of the taxing situation between the British and the American colonist was expressed by Lord North in 1775 when he declared that Englishmen paid, on an average, 25 shillings ($112.50) annually in taxes, while the Americans paid only sixpence ($2.25).

Another serious problem for the British in 1763 was the condition of colonial customs. Non-adherence to the British customs regulations and outright smuggling was rampant. In order to collect £2000 it cost the British government some £8000. The customs posts were based in England and their agents in the colonies were poorly paid and easy prey to payoffs if they would look the other way. British officials had estimated that they lost £700,000 ($63 million) in merchandise annually, which represented a serious loss to British merchants. Grenville said that the colonies were worse than trade violators, they were really "Colonies of the Countries with which they trade" more than they were British colonies.[8] In Virginia and in Maryland tobacco was being smuggled out of the country by New Englanders, which actually deprived the College of William and Mary in Williamsburg, Virginia, of its proceeds from tobacco duties. In the eyes of Grenville, something had to be done.

Another significant factor in the minds of Grenville and his fellow Parliamentary supporters as they considered the idea of taxing the North American colonies was the prosperous colonial image that had been created. It was an image not far from the truth, at least in describing the wealthy aristocratic upper class. English travelers had come home with incredible stories of grand wealth and opulence in the New World. Southern colonial travelers had observed that "You may really go from house to house living upon Delicatesses, and drinking Claret you would not despise at the first tavern in London." Virginia planters were seen racing down the roads in their horse-drawn coaches with "Negro outriders."[9]

The genteel class had horse races, jockey clubs, theaters, great balls and even foxhunts. The colonial upper class was almost overdressed, and even the royal governor of South Carolina remarked that they should refrain from such extravagance and exhibit "Diligence, Industry, and Frugality." The observed dress of the colonial officers during the war with their silver, gold and jewels, as well as the elaborate colonial entertainment in lavish brick mansions, served to impress the British generals.[10] Philip Fithian, a young gentleman teacher from Princeton, New Jersey, noted that the Virginia belles were done up in the latest London fashions.[11] It was said that the new London fashions reached the Thirteen Colonies even before they reached the provincial towns in England. Certainly the colonial upper class, which had longed to live the life and have the style of the English county gentlemen, now saw their dreams come true.

The prosperity seen in the British colonies was not always confined to the wealthy. In Williamsburg, Virginia, as the House of Burgesses was in session, the town was buzzing with crowds of subjects "hurrying back and forwards from the Capitol to the taverns, and at night Carousing and Drinking in one Chamber and box and Dice in another, which Continues till morning Commonly." It came to later be a source of embarrassment for the American patriots as they pleaded a state of poverty in justification for not having to pay taxes. The British Parliament was not convinced.[12] Without question, many in the Thirteen Colonies including a healthy number of Southern gentlemen were not struggling in 1763.

Since the average Englishman, along with the English squire class, felt the colonies had become enriched at the expense of the British after the war, it was not difficult to see that Grenville would receive the necessary support. Many British citizens felt that the American colonists were, and would always be, "subservient" to the British in their "colonial" condition. As William Pitt put it, "Even the chimney sweepers on the streets talked boastly of their subjects in America."[13] This was an underlying problem that laid the foundation for viewing the colonial peoples unfairly in the following decade.

In March of 1764, the Parliament formally determined that it had the constitutional authority to tax any part of their empire. The time was right to take steps to raise funds to reduce the tax burden on the British peoples and reduce the national debt from the war. Since the estimated tax load on the American colonies was only £70,000 ($6.3 million) annually, it was logical in their minds that the British colonists in North America should accept a higher burden.

On April 5, 1764, the British Parliament passed the Sugar Act, also known as the Revenue Act of 1764. The preamble of this act states, "Whereas it is just and necessary, that a revenue be raised in America, for defraying the expenses of defending, protecting, and securing the same, We the commons, &c. towards raising the same, give and grant unto your majesty, after the 29th of September, 1764, upon clayed sugar, indigo, and coffee of foreign produce, [and on many other articles] the sum of..."[14]

The Sugar Act was a measure intended to essentially discourage trade between the Northern colonies and foreign colonies in the West Indies. The duty of three pence was not so much the key issue as was the actions defined to enforce the duties. It was said that the New England merchants felt this act was more alarming than even the darkest hour of the French and Indian War.[15] Grenville intended to "fix" the customs problems that had been defined as a major issue for England. Custom officials were ordered to begin to take their posts in the colonies and not via "agents" as in the past. The Royal Navy was also ordered to actively enforce the Acts of Trade and to reinstate the power of the Admiralty Courts to pass judgment on customs violations. Judges in Admiralty Courts were allowed to seize property in any of the colonies from an American merchant without redress, and could keep five percent of all collected fines. "Writs of assistance" could be issued which authorized the officers of the king to search for contraband.[16] Grenville also increased the paperwork required to be completed by colonial merchants in order to conduct trade business.[17]

Actually, the Sugar Act had been simply an extension of the Molasses Act of 1733, which had placed a duty of sixpence per gallon on molasses, nine pence for rum and five shillings per hundredweight of sugar for these commodities not produced in the British West Indies. The idea had been to improve the competitiveness of the plantations of the British "sugar islands." Due to the lack of effective enforcement and outright evasion of the Molasses Act, there was little real impact for the colonists.[18] In the South, the Sugar Act had limited effect, as the New England merchants bore the burden. The language of the Sugar Act was similar to that of other trade regulations and it was generally viewed as another moderate inconvenience, which had served to stifle lucrative trade with the West Indies.[19]

Reaction to the Sugar Act in the South was moderate. In August of 1764 the South Carolina Commons House took the first action of the Southern Assemblies to protest the act by having its Committee of Correspondence order its London agent to oppose the passing of any tax on the colony. During an October 1764 session in the North Carolina Assembly, the members expressed their feelings on the matter to the royal governor, Arthur Dobbs, at having "our Commerce Circumscribed ... and Burthened with new Taxes and Impositions laid on us without our Privity and Consent, against what we esteem our Inherent right and Exclusive privilege of Imposing our own Taxes..." Even with such words, the Assembly did not instruct its London agent to actively protest the Sugar Act.

In Virginia, the House of Burgesses, through its Committee of Correspondence, made up of the leading members Peyton Randolph, Richard Henry Lee, Landon Carter, George Wythe, Edmund Pendleton, Benjamin Harrison, Archibald Cary, John Fleming and Richard Bland, took upon the effort of drafting responses to the king and each of the houses of Parliament asserting the rights of the colony. Virginia's London agent, Edward Montagu, was told to protest the act and to indicate that freedom from taxation was a British right. His orders were to have the protests published if the House of Commons did not officially receive it in order that there would be no question in England just how Virginia stood on the issue.[20]

While the Sugar Act was not favorably received in the colonies, it was nothing to compare with the fevered outrage that occurred with the passage of what was to become the infamous Stamp Act. Grenville had listened to a number of proposals and ideas regarding how to best tax the Thirteen Colonies, as well as opinions on whether the colonies could pay more taxes. He met at 10 Downing Street in London with Lord North and the lords of the treasury to debate and consider the appropriate action. After some review, the feeling was that a revenue stamp on specific papers was a proper move and it would be difficult to evade such a taxing process.

Thus, in early spring of 1765 Grenville presented his formal plan to Parliament to lay a $1 million stamp tax on the American colonies. The Stamp Act passed in the House of Commons by an overwhelming margin of 294 votes to 42. The House of Lords passed it promptly and the king approved the act on March 22. Of interest was the fact that Lord Cornwallis, who was later to play a significant role in the American Revolution in the South, along with four others in the House of Lords, voted against the Stamp Act. The effective date of the Stamp Act was planned for November 1, 1765.

Even though the Stamp Act had passed by overwhelming numbers, there was some opposition of note in Britain. The most reputed opposition came from Colonel Isaac Barre, who had a unique perspective since he had once served in Colonial America. On February 27, 1765, during discussions in the House of Commons on the advantages for the colonies from the conquest of Canada, Colonel Barre reacted to comments from Charles Townshend. Townshend said, "And now will these American children, planted by our care, nourished up to strength and opulence by our indulgence, and protected by our arms, grudge to contribute their mite to relieve us from the heavy burden under which we lie."

Colonel Barre returned with perhaps the most articulate of possible comments, "They planted by your care! No; your oppressions planted them in America. They fled from your tyranny to the uncultivated, unhospitable country…. Yet, actuated by principles of true English liberty, they met all hardships with pleasure, compared with those they suffered in their own country from the hands of those who should have been their friends.

"They nourished up by your indulgence! They grew up by your neglect of them. As soon as you began to care about them, that care was exercised in sending persons to rule them in one department and another … men whose behavior on many occasions has caused the blood of those Sons of Liberty to recoil within them. They protected by your arms! They have nobly taken up arms in your defense; have exerted a valor amidst their constant and laborious industry, for the defense of a country whose frontier was drenched in blood, while its interior parts yielded all its little savings to your emolument. And believe me — remember I told you so — the same spirit of freedom which actuated that people at first will accompany them still. This people, I believe, are as truly loyal as any Subjects the King has…"[21] The term "Sons of Lib-

erty" would become a rallying phrase in the years to come for the patriots of the Thirteen Colonies.

Reaction to the Stamp Act in the colonies, and in the South, was the most profound political event since the Jamestown landing. Disregarding the fact that the Thirteen Colonies had been at least indirectly taxed for a century through the Navigation and Trade laws, the idea that the Parliament would tax with no approval from the colonial assemblies seemed intolerable. The use of stamps to tax citizens was not a new innovation, as the English had been taxed in this way since 1694. While the British had their fiscal justification for taxing the American colonies for support during the French and Indian War, as well as to cover the current expense outlays, the colonists saw it differently. In fact, the American view was that the colonies had collectively spent $16 million in their defense and they had received only $5 million from the British in repayment.

To the dismay of the crown's officials, the Stamp Act sparked action from even the wealthy upper class "Persons of Consequence" in the colonies, who rather than discouraging mob demonstrations, actually encouraged and helped organize such movements. Throughout the colonies, groups of patriots organized themselves into "clubs" and called themselves the Sons of Liberty, a term coined by Colonel Barre in his infamous speech. In all the colonies the public newspapers and pamphlets expressed the common outrage toward the Stamp Act. Even though the average Englishmen wanted tax relief dearly, it was also true that the majority of them believed that taxation without representation was a clear violation of the historical and constitutional rights within the empire.[22]

In the North news of the Stamp Act approval became known on May 26, 1765, in Boston. The citizens gathered to protest. Samuel Adams wrote of the act, "If taxes are laid upon us in any shape without our having a legal representative where they are laid, are we not reduced from the character of Free Subject to the miserable state of tributary Slaves? We claim British rights not by charter only! We are born to them." Later, when Adams was drafting a petition to the king, his daughter, Hannah, remarked, "Only think of it, that paper will soon be touched by the royal hand!" Adams responded with, "My dear, it will more likely be spurned by the royal foot."[23]

The most notable acts of protest against the Stamp Act were directed toward the "stamp masters" who had been appointed by George Grenville to collect the taxes. These men became the most hated men in the American colonies in 1765. This was the case in the South as well.

The first and most significant act of defiance to the Stamp Act occurred in Virginia. News of the passage of the Stamp Act arrived in Williamsburg while the House of Burgesses was in session. It was the young lawyer of age 29 and new member of the House, Patrick Henry, who watched the older members discuss the act with obvious leanings toward taking no action in opposition. Henry was not impressed with these proceedings. He retired to Raleigh Tavern and, by himself, without any advice or assistance, devised five resolves and three conclusions in response to the Stamp Act, which he recorded on a blank page of an old college law book. On May 29, 1765, Patrick Henry was to become the first voice of liberty in America as he presented his *Resolves* before the House of Burgesses.[24]

Henry said with passion, "All the Liberties, Privileges, Franchises and Immunities that at any Time have been held, enjoyed, and possessed by the People of Great Britain" and that among these privileges was an exclusive right of taxation. He continued that any attempt to vest that power in any body other than the Virginia Assembly "has a Manifest Tendency to Destroy American Freedom." In the course of his speech he delivered the fiery words, "Caesar had his Brutus, Charles the First his Cromwell, and George the Third..." At this point Speaker Robinson interrupted, crying out, "Treason, treason!" Henry paused and then calmly concluded, "may profit by their example. If this be treason, make the most of it." Standing by the door watching the events was the young Thomas Jefferson, a student at the College of William and Mary.[25]

Recorded accounts of the debates on Henry's *Resolves* that followed in the House indicate they were "most bloodly," in the words of Thomas Jefferson. The king's attorney general, Peyton Randolph, Richard Bland, Edmund Pendleton, George Wythe and all the old members of the body were opposed to the *Resolves*. Henry was ably supported by the powerful burgess of Fairfax County, George Johnston. The proceedings were heated as many threats were exchanged. After the voting, Speaker Robinson reluctantly revealed the measure approving four of the five resolves had carried by one vote, becoming officially the *Virginia Resolves*. The legislation was signed by the clerk of the House and forwarded to England by Governor Fauquier. As Peyton Randolph left the chamber, he passed the student Jefferson in the lobby and was heard to exclaim, "By God, I would have given 500 guineas for a single vote!"[26]

The spirited words of Henry's *Resolves* spread throughout the colonies, and were erroneously accepted as the actual ones (*Virginia Resolves*) adopted by the House of Burgesses. His words, published widely, served to inspire the colonial patriots everywhere to resist enforcement of the Stamp Act.[27] Patrick Henry had captured the essence of the American opposition in words of defiance never expressed prior to this time to the British government. His words, delivered in a fury, had come so unexpected to the House of Burgesses that all present were affected in one way or another. The new American spirit had been unearthed before their eyes. Patrick Henry of Virginia would spend the next ten years essentially "fighting the British." How fitting it was that the patriot words of American defiance would come from a son of Virginia, a product of this Southern colony and its Jamestown fathers.

From one of the wealthiest families in Virginia came the new Virginia stamp master, Colonel George Mercer. He returned from a trip to London to find that he had been burned in effigy, and even his own father wrote articles expressing his displeasure with the Stamp Act. He had been burned in effigy in early September in Dumfries, Virginia, and later on the 24th of that month in Williamsburg.[28] On October 30, 1765, a crowd gathered in front of the coffeehouse on the Duke of Gloucester Street in Williamsburg. The governor, accompanied by other officials including the speaker, approached the coffeehouse to greet the new stamp master, only to see him being mobbed by the crowd. The crowd of some of the best citizens in Williamsburg loudly threatened the governor's party and Colonel Mercer. The speaker attempted to ward off any items that might be thrown the governor's way using his large body as armor. To calm the crowd, Mercer agreed to make a swift decision to a resignation proposal. Even though the governor refused to let him resign, Mercer resigned the next day.[29] Mercer became a hero immediately. The crowd raised Mercer on their shoulders and carried him through the town to the music of French horns, bells tolling and bright illumination throughout the night. In spite of his new "status," Colonel Mercer left Williamsburg on the next ship to England.[30]

The first evidence in American history of a declaration of the "unconstitutional" nature of a legislative action occurred in a Northampton court in Virginia over the Stamp Act. Another protest came from Burgess member Richard Henry Lee, a 32-year-old resident of Chantilly, Virginia, in Westmoreland County and the third of six sons of the well-known family of Thomas Lee and Hannah Ludwell Lee. He wrote to a British correspondent, saying, "Many late determinations of the great, on your side of the water seem to prove a resolution, to oppress North America with the iron hand of power, unrestrained by a sentiment, drawn from reason, the liberty of mankind, or the genius of their own government. 'Tis said the House of Commons readily resolved, that it had a right to tax the subject here, without the consent of his representative...." He continued with, "Poverty and oppression, among those whose minds are filled with ideas of British liberty, may introduce a virtuous industry, with a train of generous and manly sentiments, which, when in future they become supported by numbers, may produce a fatal resentment of parental care being converted into tyrannical usurpation."[31] His words were indeed to ring true.

Governor Tryon, British governor of North Carolina, wrote in a letter referring to events of the Stamp Act: "It is with concern that I acquaint you that the obstruction to the Stamp Act passed by the last Parliament, has been as general in this province as in any Colony on the continent." In the first North Carolina Assembly, after Tryon became governor, the news of Parliament's passage of the Stamp Act arrived. In order to get a feeling for the potential problems with this act, Tryon interviewed the speaker of the North Carolina Assembly, John Ashe. Ashe replied that the act "would be resisted to blood and death." Tryon immediately issued a proclamation indicating that next Assembly meeting would be at New Bern, North Carolina, on November 30. This served to prevent the North Carolina Assembly from having an opportunity to send delegates to the infamous "Stamp Act Congress" of October 25, 1765. Resolutions were passed in public meetings held during the summer of 1765 supporting resistance of the Stamp Act.[32]

In North Carolina a significant demonstration against the Stamp Act took place in Wilmington on Saturday, October 19, 1765, at 7 P.M. Some 500 people assembled at the courthouse to burn in effigy the Earl of Bute, whom they had mistakenly blamed for the Stamp Act. The crowd proceeded to every home in the town, routed the men out and escorted them to a bonfire. The evening was concluded with a celebration of toasts to "Liberty, Property, and No Stamp Duty."[33]

The first armed resistance in the Thirteen Colonies against the Stamp Act also occurred in Wilmington. The sequence of events began on the 16th day of November, 1765, when Colonel and Speaker of the Assembly John Ashe and his followers gathered at Governor Tryon's house in Wilmington to demand to see William Houston, the new stamp master. Tryon refused and the mob threatened to burn the home. Tryon asked Ashe to discuss the issue with Houston inside his home, which he did. Houston realized the danger he was in, and agreed to accompany Ashe to the courthouse. Upon arriving, Houston took an oath and signed his resignation as stamp master to the mayor of Wilmington, Moses John De Rosset, and his aldermen, to the glad cheers of the crowd.[34]

In an attempt to influence support of the Stamp Act, Governor Tryon held a dinner for 50 of the leading citizens of Brunswick, New Hanover and Bladen counties at his home on November 18. He indicated that it was his intention to lobby London to exempt at least some of the legislation until the Stamp Act could be repealed fully, if only the people would support the Stamp Act for a short period. He pointed out the financial advantages for the colony to gain the trade that was being lost in the surrounding colonies. He even agreed to pay for the stamps required for the official documents coming from his office out of his own funds. But the men of the Cape Fear region declined the offer and the governor brought all business to a halt as a result.[35]

Ten days after the little Tryon dinner, the 12–gun British sloop of war *Diligence* arrived from Virginia with the stamp paper at Fort Johnston (now Southport, North Carolina), at the mouth of the Cape Fear River. Captain Constantine Phipps of the *Diligence* was surprised as he arrived at the Port of Brunswick, North Carolina, to deliver his paper to the collector of the port. He fired a salutation shot, giving white smoke, toward Fort Johnston, which received an answering salutation volley. Captain Phipps proceeded the eight miles up the Cape Fear to Brunswick. As the *Diligence* released the chains and attached anchor resting opposite the customs house of Brunswick, the captain noticed the unusual activity in the town. An armed body of men led by Colonel Hugh Waddell and Colonel John Ashe lined the streets and the shoreline. These two leaders informed Captain Phipps that the militia would fire on anyone attempting to land the stamp paper. The captain indicated that he would comply with their demands. Then the militia, after leaving an armed guard at Brunswick, took one of the boats off the *Diligence* and carted it to Wilmington, where upon arrival, there was a triumphal procession through the streets.[36] Tryon chose not to land the stamps and instructed Phipps to keep them on board. Phipps remained off the coast for more than two months.

Another armed event occurred as the Cape Fear patriots continued to resist the Stamp Act. Aboard the H.M.S. *Viper*, as it came up the Cape Fear, was Captain Jacob Lobb, who had decided to take a proactive stance in the enforcement of the Stamp Act. Using British authority, he seized three merchant ships that had entered the Cape Fear without stamped clearance papers. The king's attorney, William Dry, confirmed the seizures to be legal in every way and recommended to the collector of Brunswick that the ships be condemned. On February 12, 1766, an article appeared in the *North Carolina Gazette* under the name "Philanthropes" that presented a way to immediately open the closed ports. The article suggested arresting the offending officers rather than holding the vessels. The paper exclaimed, "Wilmingtonians, Brunswickers, and New Hanoverians, 'tis Liberty calls you, dear Liberty."

In Wilmington events were continuing to escalate. Crowds counted at over 1000, with many armed with weapons, gathered on February 18, 1766, to pledge their "faith and honor" to prevent the Stamp Act from succeeding. After choosing leaders — John Ashe (speaker of the lower house of the Assembly), Moses John De Rosset (Wilmington mayor), Cornelius Harnett, Hugh Waddell, Thomas Lloyd, and Alexander Lillington — the Wilmingtonians proceeded to the Port of Brunswick on the following day to join others in their threats of violence to British naval and civil officers if the three merchant vessels were not released. In response Governor Tryon asked captains Lobb and Phipps to defend Fort Johnston and the stamp paper against the mob.

While Captain Lobb indicated to Tryon that he would release all but one of the ships, he yielded to the demands of the citizens on February 20 by releasing the three ships after conferring with the patriot leaders. Within just a few hours every customs officer solemnly promised to make no further attempt to execute the Stamp Act. The following day the armed citizens marched triumphantly off to their homes with joy. Governor Tryon was frustrated by his own helplessness and failure to influence Lobb to resist the demands. Captain Phipps turned over the stamps in his possession to Captain Lobb, who placed them in Fort Johnston where nothing happened with them. The Stamp Act in North Carolina was now only a failed British initiative.[37]

Other public demonstrations against the Stamp Act also occurred in towns in North Carolina including Edenton, New Bern and Cross Creek. A pamphlet titled *The Justice and Policy of Taxing the American Colonies in Great Britain, Considered*, which was published in 1765 by Judge Maurice Moore, a native of the Lower Cape Fear, denounced the Stamp Act and rejected the right of Parliament to impose it on the colonies. He also rejected the prevalent English idea of "virtual representation" insofar as the colonies were concerned. He noted that direct representation of the colonies in Parliament was impractical and they could not "with the least degree of justice be taxed by the British Parliament."[38]

Without question, the actions of the hundreds of North Carolinians during the Stamp Act controversy were evidence of the patriotic spirit in that colony. In no other colony were the protests more orderly, prepared, effective and projected with armed intent. Through the brave actions of the local leaders and their followers, the Stamp Act died a swift death in North Carolina.

The Stamp Act became real in Maryland when the *Maryland Gazette* published news that an Annapolis merchant, Zachariah Hood, was returning from a business trip in London as the new stamp distributor for Maryland. The August 22, 1765, edition of the *Maryland Gazette* carried a letter from a "Gentleman in London," which revealed that it had been heard that Hood had said that if his country must be stamped, it might as well be done by a native. On the 26th a "considerable number of people, assertors of British American privileges," formed in Annapolis, led by 24-year-old Samuel Chase. Chase was a recently elected member of the Maryland House of Delegates, a lawyer, and a future Supreme Court justice. The crowd made an effigy of Hood, with mock stamp paper in his hand, and placed it on a cart that was displayed through the streets of the city.[39]

When Zachariah Hood arrived, he noted the mob demands and attitude, but refused to yield to their threats. As a result, his warehouse was pulled down, he was burned in effigy and he had numerous death threats against him. Out of fear he quickly fled from Maryland by horse to New York. He rode so hard to escape the mobs in Maryland that his horse died under him. He fled to Flushing, Long Island, where the New York Sons of Liberty found him and forced him to resign on November 28, after threatening to return him to the Maryland Sons of Liberty.[40] Later he returned to Maryland to find that he would not be able to continue to do business there. He then moved to the West Indies where he eventually became destitute. In 1771 he petitioned the crown for relief.

While the mob was riled up after the destruction of Hood's warehouse, a small tender from his majesty's sloop *Hornet* arrived at Annapolis. As the ship anchored, a number of men boarded it and asked the captain, Mewbray, whether the ship contained stamp paper as a cargo. While he had no stamps, the question angered him and he would not answer it. He then proceeded to eject the unwelcome citizens from his vessel. In fact, he had come up the bay trying to catch a smuggler. That night, while he was dining at a local establishment in Annapolis with his party, as local eyes glared, a man entered the room with a paper attached to his hat showing the words "No Stamp Act." Captain Mewbray was immediately upset and told the man to leave the place. He even posted sailors as "guards" to ensure the man did not return. Later on, one of Mewbray's drunk dinner guests came to a heated argument with John Hammond, who was a popular member of the lower house from Anne Arundel County. The words changed to blows as a fight ensued. Someone had alerted those on the street that Hammond was being murdered. As a result, a crowd gathered, with some of the members armed, as they forced Mewbray and his guests to flee and eventually to swim for their lives. While all is not entirely clear, it was reported that Captain Mewbray was wounded during the events of the evening. This turned out to be the last significant event in Annapolis during the Stamp Act period. While some of the "gentlemen" of the city disapproved of the Mewbray riot, including Maryland Governor Sharpe, the citizens of Maryland were to gain continued cohesion over the Stamp Act in the coming months.[41]

Governor Mercer of Virginia wrote a letter to Maryland Governor Sharpe informing him that he had received some stamps for use of Maryland, but that he was unable to forward them for he found it impossible to procure transportation.[42] Sharpe then informed General Gage that he could not prevent citizens from burning the stamps in shipment from Virginia "unless Your Excellency can order a Detachment of the King's Troops hither to guard it, & to assist in suppressing any Insurrection which might happen." Gage then sent Sharpe authorization that day to bring in 100 Royal Highlanders from Pittsburgh. Gage had suggested that it might be more appropriate to leave the stamps aboard a British man-of-war. After receiving the authorization from Gage and a consignment of stamps appeared in Chesapeake Bay, Sharpe accepted Gage's suggestion, and that of the lower house of the Maryland Assembly, to keep the stamps in the care of the British naval officers off the coast.[43] Governor Sharpe had been reluctant to hand over the stamps to the local militia because it was made up of numerous patriots. Sharpe gave the order to the arriving shipmaster to keep the stamps aboard and out in deep water.[44]

The county judges of Frederick County, Maryland, found a unique way to resist the Stamp Act, by declaring that since they had not received official notice of the act, they would continue to conduct business as usual. The Frederick Sons of Liberty were so happy, they honored the judges with a ball and many patriotic toasts. The Frederick patriots also held a mock funeral for the Stamp Act, with an effigy of Hood as a mourner. During that same month "freemen" gathered on the eastern shore in Talbot County and resolved to risk their lives and fortunes to preserve their rights against the Stamp Act. They proceeded to erect a 20-foot gallows in front of the courthouse, and hung an effigy of the stamp distributor as a reminder to all.[45]

The most provocative pamphlet published in support of the colonial position on fiscal matters taken by the British Parliament during the Stamp Act period was authored by a brilliant lawyer, Daniel Dulany of Maryland. In Dulany's *Considerations on the Propriety of Imposing Taxes in the British Colonies,* he indicated that the solution to Great Britain's financial problem did not come from taxing the colonies, but it was from "the Reduction of exorbitant Salaries, the Abatement of extravagant, and the Abolition of illegal Peruisites, the Extinction of useless Places, or the disbanding of undeserving or ill deserving Pensioners." Another patriot of Maryland, Charles Carroll of Carrollton, likewise challenged to know "what security remains for our property" if "a set of men at some great a distance, so little acquainted with our circumstances, and not immediately affected with the taxes laid upon us," were conceded the right to tax the colonies.[46]

Until the events of the Stamp Act, South Carolina had no real argument with the status quo in relations with the British government or the mercantile economic process. There was no talk of suffering at the hands of the Navigation Acts over the years, and in fact anyone who strolled the streets of Charles Town in 1763 would have felt that it was indeed a "most promising area" within the Thirteen Colonies. While there was some rising debt about this time, it was not of significance. The prosperous planters and merchants enjoyed purchasing all manner of goods from British merchants. The wealthy were ordering numerous luxury items from the profits of successful businesses. With a growing economy and opportunity everywhere, it was a great time to live in this Southern city.[47]

In the early stages of the Stamp Act controversy, the South Carolina Commons House took relatively moderate actions in expressing the rejection of the principles of the Stamp Act. The Commons was controlled by a small number of influential families, like the Pinckneys, Rutledges, Manigaults, Middletons and Lowndeses, who desired to maintain the status quo, while directing their London agent, Charles Garth, with instructions to deliver their anti–Stamp Act arguments to the Parliament in their name. Garth was instructed as early as August of 1764 "to oppose the passing of the Bill for Laying a Stamp Duty or any other Tax, on the Colony, and to give him such other Directions for the Benefit of the Inhabitants thereof." The Correspondence Committee, staffed by a distinguished group including Rawlins Lowndes, speaker of the House, Thomas Bee, Christopher Gadsden, Thomas Lynch, Isaac Mazyck, Charles Pinckney and John Rutledge, wrote the Garth document presenting the case, saying it was "that inherent right of every British subject, not to be taxed but by his own consent or that of his representative." To the average citizen, using stamps would be a major inconvenience. The stamps were required for college diplomas, wills, and even cards and dice.[48] But after the Stamp Act was instituted, the attitudes of moderation essentially vanished.[49]

Issues associated with the rights of the South Carolina Assembly to control the affairs of the colony in all areas had been under scrutiny for a time. The royal governor, Thomas Boone, had challenged the legislators the year before the Stamp Act on their rights to determine the validity of the election of Assembly members. Boone was then replaced through the encouragement of the Assembly with a well-respected Carolinian, William Bull, Jr., in a temporary role as lieutenant governor of the colony. With this change, the Assembly was favorably encouraged that it would continue to control the political direction of the colony in all areas including the right to tax.

The leader of the opposition to the Stamp Act and

the chief "enemy" of the former governor, Thomas Boone, was Christopher Gadsden. He was an ambitious and wealthy merchant of 41 years, with investments in a wharf and warehouses in Charles Town, who had an extremist reputation among the powered elite. He had served the Assembly since 1757. He was also the captain of the Charles Town militia, which gave him close ties to the working classes of the city. He had the opportunity to influence them with the potential threats to their well being as the result of British Parliamentary moves like the Stamp Act. Henry Laurens had privately criticized Gadsden for his actions in 1764 and described him as a "rash headlong Gentleman who has been too long a ringleader of people engaged in popular quarrels."

During the summer of 1765, Gadsden had led the Assembly in opposition of the Stamp Act and called upon his peers to support sending government representatives to the upcoming meeting in New York in October to protest the Stamp Act. As a result of Gadsden's influence, the South Carolina Assembly took the first action of any colony to elect delegates to what was to be known as the "Stamp Act Congress." The body elected the two radicals—the wealthy rice planter Thomas Lynch and Christopher Gadsden—and the moderate young Charles Town lawyer, John Rutledge, to the Congress. They sailed from Charles Town on September 4, 1765, for New York.

While Gadsden was gathering support against the Stamp Act in the Assembly in the summer of 1765, Charlestonians were beginning to raise their glasses to the news coming from the Northern colonies of mob actions. On October 18 stamps arrived in Charles Town aboard the ship *Planters Adventure.* Saturday, the next day, the British officials' concerns over the potential for mob actions was realized as a 40-foot gallows was erected at the intersection of Broad and Church streets with the engraved message, "Liberty and No Stamp Act." An effigy of the stamp distributor was also hanging from the gallows. That night the structure was loaded on a wagon and paraded down Broad Street before a crowd of some 2000. While the British officials watched in horror, the mob sacked the home of one of the stamp distributors, George Saxby, then headed off to burn the effigy and bury the coffin labeled "American Liberty." Afterwards, a number of the participants spent the rest of the evening in the local taverns drinking and toasting "damnation to the Stamp Act." Violence continued for the next eight days.

As the events unfolded, Lieutenant Governor William Bull directed that the stamps from the *Planters Adventure* be moved to Fort Johnson on James Island under armed guard. Henry Laurens was outraged by the actions of the mob, which had been led by the local "Sons of Liberty." Laurens said "Patriotism ... committed unbounded acts of Licentiousness & at length Burglary &

Robbery." Rumors began to surface that Laurens might be concealing stamps and on October 23 an armed group "heated with liquor" went to Laurens' home on Ansonborough Street to demand to search the home. Since Laurens was concerned for the safety of his pregnant wife, he allowed the group to inspect his house. Of the event, Laurens wrote, "Riot is in Fashion."[50]

Beginning on October 26 mobs began to pass the rumor that the two local stamp agents, George Saxby and Caleb Lloyd, were at Fort Johnson with the stamps. After two days of mob threats in the streets of Charles Town to murder the stamp agents if they did not resign, Saxby and Lloyd announced on October 28 that they would not enforce the Stamp Act and would resign in order to "restore and preserve peace." Then approximately 150 Charles Town Sons of Liberty destroyed the stamps.[51] Through these eventful days, Lieutenant Governor Bull was unable to put down the riots because he lacked the troops to take any effective action of resistance. The Sons of Liberty poured onto the streets of Charles Town with their flag, with the word "Liberty" sewed on it, in celebration of their victory. A black slave remarked, "I saw the town illuminated, the guns were fired, and bonfires and other demonstrations of joy shown."

The events of October 1765, in this center of Southern society, revealed the new and profound spirit of resistance to the British.[52] Just after the resignation of the stamp agents, John Laurens (Henry's son) wrote to a merchant in Philadelphia that "A suspension of it [Stamp Act] while it is in force would prove our ruin and destruction," and continued with "We would in one fortnight, if nothing else would do, go down on our knees and pray him to give life to that law. What else, would become of our estates, particularly ours who depend upon commerce?"[53]

In South Carolina the overall view was that to submit to direct taxation by the British Parliament would establish such a bad precedent that their property would ultimately be at the mercy of the British. One South Carolinian expressed his views by saying Americans were like donkeys; if they agreed to the Stamp Act, there was no doubt that "more Sacks, more Sacks" were coming. The fear of tyranny by the imposition of taxation without consent of the Carolina Commons would threaten their last line of defense.[54]

Lieutenant Governor Bull called the local gazette run by Peter Timothy the "conduit pipe" for passing the Northern propaganda about the Stamp Act. It had "poisoned" the minds of the citizens of Charles Town, which led to the violent October. While presenting anti–Stamp Act sympathy, Timothy had not supported the violence of the October riots. In action to calm the violent trends in the nature of events, Gadsden, on his return from the Stamp Act Congress, asked the Assembly to use peaceful methods of resistance as called for in the recommendations of the Congress. Since the Charles Town Sons of Liberty had destroyed the stamps and prevented any further enforcement of the Stamp Act, export trade abruptly terminated since ships could not clear the port without stamped paper clearances. The civil courts and customs house were likewise closed, as the barrels of rice crowded the wharves. The Sons of Liberty were then called out to maintain order as the idled sailors roamed the streets harassing the citizenry.[55]

During the Stamp Act conflict even the western frontier citizens of South Carolina were touched by the events in Charles Town. Lowcountry patriots had indicated to these remote citizens that the British meant them harm and that if actions like the Stamp Act were not resisted, they could see the day when they would lose their cattle, horses and even crops in taxes. This propaganda was successful at uniting the frontier opposition to the British, and it likewise served to foster elements of the Regulator movement in the colony.[56]

The Stamp Act had less impact in Georgia than in any other colony. The colony of Georgia had less justification to complain since it was the newest colony and had been continually subsidized by the British from the beginning. Some four-fifths of the funds to run the colony were supplied from London during the 20 years of its existence. Up until 1775 Georgia received £4000 ($360,000) annually from the British. The Royal Governor Henry Ellis, followed by James Wright, had defended the right of the Parliament to pass the Stamp Act and to have it enforced, even though he did not personally approve of the act. James Wright was American born and served as governor between 1760 and 1775, and later from 1779 to 1782.[57]

The first significant controversy over the Stamp Act in Georgia surfaced in August of 1765 when the text of a pamphlet, *The Claim of the Colonies to an Exemption from Internal Taxes by Authority of Parliament Examined*, written by William Knox, appeared in the *Georgia Gazette*. The pamphlet defended the right of the Parliament to tax the colonies. Knox, who wrote the pamphlet, was the Georgia agent in London, the provost marshal of Georgia, a former Georgia citizen, a plantation owner, and was a friend to Governor Wright and James Habersham. Wright was a successful planter and Habersham a merchant, as well as the secretary and senior councilor to the governor. Knox had been cool to the instructions given to him from the Georgia Commons House of the Assembly to raise objection to the Sugar and Stamp acts, and had decided to publish his infamous pamphlet. For his actions, William Knox was fired as the Georgia agent and the Commons House voted Charles Garth, the South Carolina agent, to represent Georgia. Garth had been elected even though he was already the South Carolina

agent, and, in his role as member of the British House of Commons, had voted in favor of the Stamp Act. Problems developed in the upper house of the Georgia Assembly with the Garth approval, but the motion was carried even though Garth's voucher for payment was not honored.

While the naturalist John Bartram was traveling through Georgia in September 1765, he recorded in his diary that Governor Wright was "universally respected by all the inhabitants. They can hardly say enough in his praise." In less than three months this "universal" favorable view of Wright would no longer be true. The respect and admiration for Wright that had continued for the previous five years would end.

After only slight opposition to the Stamp Act in Georgia, in October 1765 the *Georgia Gazette* began to publish accounts of the wide opposition to the act in the other colonies. In the meeting of the Assembly on the 22nd of October, the Commons House thanked the speaker for the letter he wrote to the Massachusetts Assembly in support of their opposition to the Stamp Act. On October 25, on the anniversary of the accession of George III to the throne, sailors and other patriots showed their allegiance when they carried effigies of the stamp distributor through the streets of Savannah. The same actions occurred on Guy Fawkes Day on November 5.[58]

With the Stamp Act's effective date of November 1 approaching, the Sons of Liberty met at MacHenry's Tavern in Savannah to proclaim that when the stamp distributor appeared in Georgia, they would inform him of the peril of his office. On November 1 there were no stamps in Georgia, no stamp distributor or even a copy of the Stamp Act itself. Since there were no stamps, Governor Wright and his council decided to close the courts and land office, but allowed ships to clear customs with "endorsements" on their papers. Wright received a copy of the act in late November "in a Private way" and he took the oaths as specified. On December 4 the Port of Savannah was closed, and the following day stamps arrived at Fort Halifax in Georgia aboard the British man-of-war, H.M.S. *Speedwell*, under the direction of Captain Fanshaw.[59] With some 60 vessels in the harbor, with many ready to sail, there was still no stamp distributor available to process the paperwork.

On the afternoon of January 2, 1766, Governor Wright, who was the captain of a group of 56 rangers guarding the stamps in Savannah, was informed that a crowd of 200 had already gathered to protest the Stamp Act. Since Wright was afraid that the stamps would be destroyed, he took personal charge of the rangers and confronted the crowd with musket in hand at his gate. Wright was asked if he intended to appoint a temporary stamp distributor. In response he asked if theirs was "the manner to wait upon the governor," and said he would carry out his orders from the king. The crowd then disbanded for the time being. Wright and his rangers then moved the stamps from the storeroom at Fort Halifax, located on the outskirts of the town, to the guardhouse in the center of Savannah with the idea that the stamps would be safer there. Another 40 guards were placed around his home. The rangers guarded the stamps while a local volunteer patrol made up of sailors, clerks and merchants also kept watch over the stamps. The governor was so concerned that he spent several nights fully clothed and ready for action during the standoff.[60]

On the next day the Georgia stamp distributor, the only non–American stamp distributor and an Englishman, George Angus, arrived at Tybee Island. He was quietly brought three days later to Wright's home without incident, where he began to distribute stamped papers to the custom officials. On the 7th of January, the Port of Savannah was opened with vessels receiving clearance using Stamp Act paper. These were the only stamps used in all the Thirteen Colonies. After this initial use of the paper to clear the vessels from the port, there was a general agreement that no more stamps would be used until the issue of a potential repeal of the Stamp Act was known. The stamp distributor Angus soon found it difficult to stay in the town after hearing that as many as 600 men were approaching Savannah to seize the stamps.[61] He headed "into the country to avoid the resentment of the people." Angus later returned for a short visit to Savannah in late March, but then he disappeared from Georgia history forever, and was never heard of again.

In early January rumors of threats of hundreds of patriots heading from the backcountry to Savannah to prevent stamp sales reached the governor. He decided to have his rangers move the stamps to Fort George on Cockspur Island located below the town. The threatened "invasion" scheduled for January 31 did not take place, but the rumors continued. One such rumor indicated that the governor was to be shot if he was not compliant with desires of the Sons of Liberty. Others said those who had supported the governor were in danger. Even James Habersham was warned not to be at home for several nights. The H.M.S. *Speedwell* arrived on the 2nd of February. Wright ordered the stamps to be loaded aboard the ship and removed from the current repository at Fort George, and that the stamps were to leave the colony. The rumored backcountry people arrived late in Savannah with guns, drums and flags flying on February 4. The backcountry group now faced Wright's rangers, 20 armed sailors from the H.M.S. *Speedwell* and some 100 supporters. The patriots reluctantly dispersed, disappointed that the other promised 400 to 500 men from South Carolina had not arrived.

Governor Wright blamed the events surrounding the conflict in Savannah during the Stamp Act on the Sons of Liberty in Charles Town. In fact, Wright blamed most of the ills in Savannah on that neighboring city. The membership rolls of the Georgia Sons of Liberty were never documented, and none of the men were ever identified by the governor or by those who wrote of the events. Another problem in determining the patriot leaders during this period occurred because the colony's only newspaper, the *Georgia Gazette*, ceased publication when the Stamp Act went into effect because stamps were required for the newspaper. The newspaper did not resume publishing until May 21, 1766, with word of repeal.[62]

Because of the common disenchantment with the Stamp Act throughout the colonies, James Otis of Massachusetts proposed that a "Congress" be convened in October of 1765 in New York with representatives from all the colonies. In June of 1765 the General Court of Massachusetts issued the circular letter to all the colonial assemblies calling for the congress. On the first Tuesday, October 7, the "Stamp Act" Congress met at City Hall on Wall Street. This was the first Colonial Congress and it was to establish the precedent for those later infamous gatherings that would form the new nation. In September, even before the event had begun, news of the congress was to reach the British Lords Commissioners for Trade and Plantations with outcries that the movement was a "dangerous Tendency" for the empire. The commissioners drafted a "representation" addressed to the king presenting the news of the upcoming congress and the text of the *Virginia Resolves*.[63] The Lord Commissioners were correct in their concerns.

The body was made up of 28 representatives from nine of the Thirteen Colonies, with only two Southern colonies represented. From South Carolina were Thomas Lynch, Christopher Gadsden and John Rutledge. Representing the Maryland Assembly were William Murdock, Edward Tilghman and Thomas Ringgold. Not present for the South were representatives from North Carolina, Virginia or Georgia. North Carolina's Assembly and Virginia's House of Burgesses were not in session when the invitation came and, thus, could not properly elect delegates. While Georgia also found itself between sessions and had no delegates, Speaker Alexander Wyly of the Commons House invited the members to meet in Savannah to discuss the matter. Sixteen of the 25 members attended the session, but Governor Wright opposed the Stamp Act Congress and would not formally recall the Assembly. Speaker Wyly did write the Massachusetts Assembly that even though the colony would have no delegates present, Georgia was concerned about the plight of all the colonies and would support whatever action they decided upon.[64]

The congress elected a moderate member of the

Massachusetts House of Representatives as the speaker, instead of James Otis, who called the meeting. Gadsden of South Carolina was elected the chairman of the Correspondence Committee to draft the resolutions that would be forwarded to London. The Congress decided to draft three responses; the Declaration of Rights, a petition to the king and memorials to both houses of the British Parliament.

The primary document, which was mainly the effort of John Dickinson of Pennsylvania, presented "declarations of the rights and grievances of the colonists in America" organized in 13 sections. While the document was moderate in overall tone, it presented the case that the people of the colonies were entitled to the inherent rights and liberties of other British subjects and among them the right of direct representation in legislation associated with taxation. It also indicated that there was no such representation in the House of Commons. The petition to the House of Commons spoke of the two essential rights—taxation by consent of the governed and the right of trial by a local jury. It also expressed the "glory in being subjects of the best of Kings having been born under the most perfect form of government."[65]

The Stamp Act Congress concluded its work on October 25, 1765. The products of the Stamp Act Congress met the approval of all the colonial assemblies except that of Virginia. The Virginia House felt that Patrick Henry's *Resolves* and the *Virginia Resolves* had already presented Virginia's position more than adequately before the British.

In reflecting on the profound events surrounding the Stamp Act controversy, it is without much exaggeration to say that if the British had actually tried to enforce the Stamp Act, which they did not, blood would have been shed ten years before Lexington. This probability of bloodshed is well justified after understanding the reactions of numerous parties and groups in Parliament, who were determined to put down the rebellious acts of the colonial "peasantry." The Duke of Bedford headed up such a group, known as the Bedford Party. They urged that the American colonies should be dealt with harshly, saying they would rather "butcher all America" than give up the Stamp Act, even if it came to spilling blood. The Bedfords proposed sending British dragoons with cannons to the Americas to cram the stamps down the throats of the colonists. They wanted to rescind the colonial charters and abolish the colonial assemblies. In the March 17, 1766, edition of the *New Daily Advertiser* in London, the Bedfords indicated the simple issue was whether "American insolence shall rule British councils, or, Whether Britain shall rule an American rabble?"[66]

Almost from the time the Stamp Act took effect there had been talk of repeal in England and in the colonies.

But serious consideration did not surface until the British merchants saw that the American colonial merchants were beginning to boycott British goods. Such activities had occurred during the Sugar Act, especially in New England, but the Stamp Act inspired considerably more action to boycott both in the North and the South because the merchants believed they could face ultimate ruin if legislation like the Stamp Act was allowed to stand. The colonists had a powerful leverage against the British merchants in the form of growing debts, as the existing commercial relationship had yielded over time. To some extent the British merchants were at a greater disadvantage than the American merchants. Debts owed from the colonists amounted to £4 million ($360 million).

On December 6, 1765, the Committee of Merchants of London presented a memorial to the mayor of London pointing out that they would lose property, and trade itself, if the Parliament did not grant "every Ease and Advantage the North Americans can with property desire...." Similar petitions from the leading cities like London, Bristol, Liverpool, Manchester, Leeds and Glasgow, as well as other smaller towns and boroughs around Britain, arrived before the Parliament.[67] Soon reports of expected riots began to appear. It had been reported that the number of unemployed workers was approaching 100,000 in Manchester, Liverpool and Bristol, and they would be marching to London soon to demand the repeal of the Stamp Act. A document, *The Necessity of Repealing the American Stamp Act Demonstrated*, published in 1766 in London, expressed the sentiment of the merchants who said the colonial merchants "will never consent to enrich us while they think we oppress them." The British merchants did not want the Parliament to affect the pocketbooks of the colonists when they had their hands there too.[68] As George Washington of Virginia wrote in a letter to a British correspondent on the issue of the Stamp Act, "I fancy the Merchants of Great Britain trading to the Colonies will not be among the last to wish for a Repeal of it."[69]

On the political front, July of 1765 had seen the close of the George Grenville Ministry. The king dismissed it after Grenville attempted to establish a regency to deal with problems associated with the periods of insanity experienced by King George III.[70] In its place was a party led by the Marquess of Rockingham, a rather young and inexperienced aristocrat. While the Rockingham Party did not have the political influence to drive through the repeal of the Stamp Act alone, they did have support of the "King's Friends," the pro-colonial William Pitt, their elected secretary Edmund Burke, and above all, the recognized distress of the British merchants. The Rockingham Ministry, working with the alarmed London merchants, was successful in generating influential propaganda against the Stamp Act.

The Rockingham Ministry was intent on trying appeasement with the American colonials in contrast with the Grenville approach. They were indeed the most pro–American groups among the Whig establishment in Parliament. In supporting the interests of the British merchants in their current circumstance, they were extremely concerned with the prospect of losing the colonial market. While the landed gentry controlled the Parliament, there was much sympathy for the plight of the merchant community. Even though they believed, as all British subjects did, that they must maintain British sovereignty, they viewed the colonists as "customers rather than rebellious rogues" who, perhaps, deserved a good lashing. They preferred to explain the riots over the Stamp Act as being the "effervescence of liberty."[71]

The matter of repeal was foremost in the minds of the Rockingham Ministry, when the leading members gathered during the Christmas Parliamentary recess at the London home of the Marquess of Rockingham to consider the various options. The king had taken an evasive response in publicly discussing the matter. In his speeches of December 17, 1765, and January 14, 1766, he used phrases like "matters of importance had happened in America," revealing the lack of any specific direction in resolving the Stamp Act controversy.[72]

While William Pitt had not expected that he would support the Whig cause in this matter, he became engaged and publicly said that he rejoiced at America's resistance of the Stamp Act and frustrating the taxation scheme of George Grenville. Pitt felt the colonials could only be taxed if they had direct representation in Parliament, leaving his support with the colonial assemblies to tax their own. Pitt did support the passage of navigation and trade restrictions, and even expressed that he would send the British Navy to the Thirteen Colonies if the colonials began taking up their own manufacturing activities. With Pitt's support, along with that of the Rockinghams and others in Britain, coupled with the continued newspaper articles and speeches to the House of Commons by the well-known Pennsylvanian Ben Franklin, it was still not a given that the Stamp Act would be repealed.

The real showdown over the Stamp Act repeal effort took place in the House of Commons. Grenville supporters refused to accept repeal, feeling that the British military should enforce the act. They accused the Rockinghams of whitewashing the colonial rebellions by calling them "important occurrences," and described the colonial actions as "Tumults and Insurrections of the most dangerous Nature." The House turned to the king for direction of this matter. King George III first desired to have the act modified, but he was told that it must be either enforced or repealed to reach any conclusion on the matter. The king said that repealing the Stamp Act

would "ruin him, themselves, and the nation, by trying for popularity." The issue came down to this: how could English pride be maintained while relieving the British merchants of economic ruin?

The answer finally came in the form of the "Declaratory Act," which dictated that full authority over the American colonies in "all cases whatever" remained and that the colonials were indeed subjects of the British Crown and the Parliament. With this additional act devised, on March 18, 1766, the House of Commons repealed the Stamp Act with 100 votes in support, and the Declaratory Act passed with a unanimous vote. In the House of Lords the Stamp Act repeal passed, and the Declaratory Act was only five votes shy of being likewise unanimous.[73] The Stamp Act was now retired to history.

In England, the repeal of the Stamp Act and the approval of the Declaratory Act, known together as the "Twin Brothers," was met with celebrations, bell ringing and bonfires in joy. All England felt that the Parliament had "saved England from ruin."[74] The American colonials had now been warned that the repeal must be taken with the stern declarations of authority revealed in the other act.

The reaction to the repeal of the Stamp Act across the Atlantic, and indeed in the Southern colonies, was even more spectacular than it had been in England. In Maryland the news of repeal was met with rejoicing and a spirit of reconciliation. Annapolis' citizens gathered in "all patriotic toast" and later in June held a city commemoration sponsored by the mayor. In Queen Anne town, outside Annapolis, numerous gentlemen and freeholders met at the home of Thomas Baker to dig a hole to bury the emblems of "Discord" accompanied by some 23 toasts, according to the *Maryland Gazette*. There were numerous celebrations, and festivals, with illuminations in outlying towns and villages throughout Maryland. The governor's proposal to appropriate £100 ($9,000) to refund the former stamp distributor, Hood, for the loss of his destroyed warehouse was approved by the lower house of the Maryland Assembly.[75]

Westmoreland County of Virginia celebrated the appeal with the commissioning of a portrait of William Pitt to be painted by Charles Willson Peale, who would soon return from London to paint the first portrait of the future rebel commander in his British colonial uniform at Mount Vernon. Other prominent Virginians celebrated this momentous event as they often did with "a ball and elegant entertainment at the Capitol."[76] The Virginia Assembly was also considering erecting a statue to King George III, but as it turned out, the only statue eventually erected was in honor of the first president of the United States. In North Carolina the news brought great joy throughout the colony, as in Wilmington where the gentlemen of the town presented the royal governor with their hearty congratulations.[77]

Even though the king signed the Stamp Act repeal on March 18, 1766, the first news of that occasion did not reach Charles Town, South Carolina, until that May 3. The formal news did not arrive until a month later. Both announcements were met with celebrations. In the spirit of excitement, the Commons House commissioned a statue of William Pitt in honor of "his noble Disinterested, and Generous Assistance" in obtaining a repeal of the hideous act. The body also had their delegates to the Stamp Act Congress sit for portraits to be hung in the State House "as a memorial of the high esteem this House have for their Persons and merit, and the great service they have done their Country." While the repeal was the key focus of all those Carolinians, there was some reaction to the Declaratory Act. Henry Laurens felt the act seemed to be "the last feeble struggle of the Grenvillian party." Laurens was later to write that the principles of the act would make a "platform for the Invincible Reasoning from the mouths of four and twenty pounders."

While the Stamp Act controversy was over in South Carolina, conflict over certain customs activities was not concluded. In the spring of 1767 a new customs collector and former member of Parliament, Daniel Moore, arrived in Charles Town. He began to show a special zeal in strictly enforcing trade regulations with the help of the Royal Navy. Conflict came to a head when an inspection boarding party, sent by Captain James Hawker of the H.M.S. *Sardoine*, was repelled by the crew of a schooner to the cheers of the local citizens on the waterfront. But then, "with the British flag in my hand," Captain Hawker led the party to receive the "highest of insults" along with "cutlasses, axes, stones, clubs, etc." While Moore succeeded in this act, he ran into a significant number of lawsuits and complaints.

But before Moore left for England, he was involved in the most famous pre–Revolutionary period customs event in South Carolina. In an attempt to make an example of a prominent merchant, Moore demanded that his staff seize two plantation schooners owned by Henry Laurens for violation of the regulations requiring all vessels to clear customs before each voyage. While the seizure was technically justified, it was obviously an impractical regulation for these types of small coastal vessels. The trial of the vice-admiralty court, which had no jury, was conducted by Judge Egerton Leigh, who was a personal friend of Laurens and related to him by marriage. Believing he could deal a compromise, Leigh ordered one of the vessels returned to Laurens, and the other forfeited. But Leigh made an error in not presenting that the seizures had been reasonable in light of the regulation, which allowed Laurens to eventually recover losses by

suing for damages. Laurens also sued George Roupell, the customs searcher who had made the actual seizure of Laurens' vessels, and a jury awarded the judgment in favor of Laurens. Roupell was unable to pay, and he then seized another vessel belonging to Laurens, helped by Judge Leigh. Roupell offered to release the vessel if Laurens would drop the demand for the damages, but Laurens initially refused. Eventually Leigh had the vessel released. Laurens was so upset by the way he had been treated in the matter, he vented his outrage in a pamphlet titled *Extracts from the Proceeding of the Court of Vice-Admiralty*. Leigh responded in defense of his actions with his own pamphlet, *The Man Unmasked*.[78]

After hearing the official announcement of the repeal in Savannah, Georgia, the governor of the colony, James Wright, convened the General Assembly on July 16, 1766. He then presented his address to both houses with the words: "I think myself happy that I have the power to congratulate you on this Province having no injuries or damages, either of a public or private nature, with respect to property to compensate, and that you, Gentlemen of the Assembly, have no votes or resolutions injurious to the honor of his Majesty's government, or tending to destroy the legal or constitutional dependency of the Colonies on the Imperial Crown and Parliament of Great Britain to reconsider." Responding, the General Assembly declared, "Permit us, dread Sire, while we endeavor to express our gratitude to the best of Kings for affording us so speedy and necessary relief, to assure your Majesty that we shall, upon all occasions, strive to evince our loyalty and firm attachment to your Majesty's sacred person and government, being truly sensible of the advantages derived to us from the protection of our Mother Country…." (signed by James Habersham, president of Upper House and A. Wyly, speaker of the Commons House of Assembly). Even though the public words were "glowing," Governor Wright did not fail to understand the real condition in the colony of Georgia when he wrote to Secretary Conway of the Assembly's declarations, expressing his belief that many in the Georgia Assembly still accepted "the late avowed sentiments and strange ideas of liberty."[79]

As the full scope of the events of the Stamp Act controversy came to a conclusion, the results would forever establish the foundation for subsequent disputes between Britain and the American colonies. Most of the English believed they had restored their economic and commercial relationships with the colonists by the act of repeal, while their Parliament and king had maintained the political high ground of authority over their subjects through the Declaratory Act. The repeal and its loss of colonial revenue frustrated the backers of the Grenville regime. It would be even harder in the future to "command a single shilling" from the colonies. Not only had the

Stamp Act failed to provide any funds to Britain, it had cost some £631 and 9 shillings to print the stamps, and much more to distribute them. Only the colony of Georgia had actually allowed the stamps to be sold, and those proceeds were very small.

For the colonists, the repeal was generally received with sincere celebration, with a spirit of relief that perhaps conflict with the mother country was over as life returned to normal. But the Stamp Act, the repeal and the Declaratory Act presented a new reality. The colonists saw the "evil" Stamp Act eradicated and the Declaratory Act worthy at best of being essentially ignored. The general outcome in the eye of the Southern colonists was that the local assemblies had the only right to tax them, the royal governors had shown themselves too loyal to their king and Parliament to avoid being hated, and that they had indeed "won" the conflict.

The Sons of Liberty, and their often prominent supporters, believed they had pushed all those sitting on the sidelines to make a stand, and that they had established themselves as the true "organization" of liberty. These "Sons" had shown how weak the British were to counter local resistance. The Southern colonies found their "liberty leaders," like the most prominent, Patrick Henry of Virginia. From this point forward, the colonial citizens would need to consider which camp they would belong to—patriot or loyalist. More than ever the British and the American colonists would focus now on their differences.

The North Carolina governor in 1766 found the people to be "as jealous of any restraint put on their consciences as they have of late shewn for that on their property." Others like dissenters in Mecklenburg County in North Carolina would begin to expand the spirit of resistance and express their distaste for the provincial laws in support of the Church of England as being "as oppressive as the Stamp Act."

The Stamp Act had changed the Southern colonists forever. They would be ever more suspicious of the British, and the British would sense a change also. A loyalist remarked that "Every dirty fellow, just risen from his kennel, congratulated his neighbor on their glorious victory over England." In the words of an Englishman some eight years later on the pages of the March 11, 1774, edition of the London *New Daily Advertiser*, the repeal of the Stamp Act should have been called "a formal renunciation of the legislature of BRITAIN over the COLONIES." The Stamp Act had made the British Parliament the object of colonial contempt. As evidence that the British continued to misunderstand the American mind on the events that had taken place, George III declared after the American Revolution had come to a close that the only thing he regretted was the repeal of the Stamp Act.[80] Without the timely dismissal of the Grenville Ministry and the accession of the Rockinghams to power, the British and the colonists may well have seen the American Revolution begin ten years earlier.

3

ON TO REVOLUTION

Any reason for celebration of the repealed Stamp Act on both sides of the Atlantic was indeed short-lived. Irrespective of the repeal, the struggle for revenue by the Rockingham Ministry was still a stubborn necessity that would not go away. Taxes on houses, windows and lights in Britain, originally passed in 1761, were extended and covered even the most humble abode with graduated rates. Duties on imported liquor and even the public lottery were authorized. There was popular unrest in England, with the multitude of taxes placed on the citizens. Bread riots had been reported. Conditions were deteriorating.[1]

Even with these problems the Rockingham group continued to seek moderation with the colonials, while suffering increasing English opposition. With confidence waning, the king, with support from William Pitt, forced the Rockinghams from power in August of 1766. Pitt had agreed to form a new ministry, but he had lost much prestige when he began to seek membership in the House of Lords. Pitt then became the Earl of Chatham and left the House of Commons for the "Lords." Even this lessened role was further diminished because Pitt suffered so much from gout that he was often away from public affairs seeking a cure.

The earl was seen by his solicitor on a hot August day seated under a shade tree, pale, despondent, a little bewildered and obviously ill, talking with Lady Chatham as he discussed that there was no hope of returning to the political scene. The role of prime minister would now fall to the Duke of Grafton. The duke was a wealthy young man who cared little for work, and cared a great deal about his horses and his mistress, Nancy Parsons. Those who disliked him felt he had fled to his country estate to seek "rural entertainment, lolling in the arms of a faded

beauty."[2] If Grafton had been a worthy follower of Chatham, he might have been able to substitute for Pitt in a pro-colonial ministry and avoid future conflict.[3] But this was not to be.

The only man up to the task, and one who was well liked by his House of Commons peers, was the ambitious, high-spirited, and witty chancellor of the exchequer, Charles Townshend. He had gained some of his popularity from amusing the members by portrayals of his friends and enemies. In the local London clubs he was known as "Champagne Charley."[4] In spite of his reputation for "reckless statesmanship," Townshend came to the forefront to assume the difficult task of finding some way to increase revenues. On February 25, 1767, Townshend proposed to continue the land tax at the war level of four shillings per acre. This was perhaps the most sensitive issue regarding taxation in England and more so ever since the promise had been made by the Rockingham Ministry to reduce that land tax.

The Townshend proposal was defeated and the land tax was reduced to three shillings per acre, even without a way yet devised to make up for the budget shortage. With strong opposition to increasing the taxes of the already overtaxed subjects, Townshend proposed in the spring of 1767 to solve the problem by levying new colonial duties in addition to those provided in the Sugar Act.

At the time some attention had been given to the distinction that Ben Franklin had made before the House in 1766 between internal and external taxation by Parliament. Townshend's comments in the House of Commons in early February were, "I do not know any distinction between internal and external taxes; it is a distinction without a difference, it is perfect nonsense; if we have a right to impose one, we have the other." While looking at the colonial agents in the gallery, he continued, "I speak this aloud, that all you who are in the gallaries may hear me." On June 2, the Committee of the Whole House passed a series of resolutions calling for duties to be collected on imports to America of all glass, red and white lead, painters' colors, paper, paint, and tea. Grenville attempted to add a measure that would force each colonial assembly to declare their formal acknowledgment of the sovereignty of Britain in the spirit of the Declaratory Act, but the measure was voted down. Debate over the Townshend Act received no dramatic opposition as most felt that the new duties were quite fair.

On July 2, 1767, the Townshend Act became law, with an effective date set for November 20, 1767. While the act was expected to yield from £35,000 to £40,000 ($3.15 to $3.6 million) at the time it was passed, it is interesting to note that such an amount was not even one-tenth of the amount that had been given away by reducing the land tax by one shilling per acre. But the Townshend Act was viewed as a good start and favorable direction in having the American colonials contribute to the empire.[5]

Actually the Townshend Act was made up of three measures — the Revenue Act passed on July 2, 1767, covering the new duties, the second intended to pay the salaries of colonial governors and other royal officials and the third calling for strict enforcement of duties in admiralty courts by a new centralized Board of Customs in America.[6] Charles Townshend was out of the political picture before the effective date of his act, as he died in September of a virulent fever.

In June of 1768 the Maryland House of Delegates took under consideration a circular letter from the speaker of the Massachusetts House of Representatives calling for a boycott of British goods until the Townshend Act was repealed. Maryland, like other Southern colonies, reacted with relative dispatch to petition the British king for relief of this unconstitutional taxation, and to form merchant associations to boycott British goods. To the dismay of Maryland's Governor Sharpe, the lower assembly house endorsed the Massachusetts circular letter, indicating that it was "expressive of duty and loyalty to the Sovereign" and "replete with just principles of liberty." The delegates adopted their document expressing an appeal to the king, which upset the red-faced governor because he had recently sent a letter to the Earl of Hillsborough remarking that Maryland had not followed the lead of the rebellious group in New England in this matter.

The boycott actions in Maryland were slow coming, even though the issue had come before court and legislative discussions in Annapolis. The Baltimore merchants did not take action until March 20, 1769, when they signed an agreement after much pressure from merchants in Philadelphia. Later, on May 19, the Baltimore Association met at the courthouse of Anne Arundel County to adopt a non-importation agreement, which became the model for the other counties in the following weeks. In a meeting of 43 "merchants, traders, freeholders, mechanics, and other inhabitants" from all counties, the "delegates" developed a considerable document containing a preamble and nine articles that detailed the common concerns. They declared the Townshend Act violated "the spirit of our constitution" and served to "deprive us in the end of all political freedom."

The document called for boycotting not only the goods covered in the Townshend Act, but included some 125 additional commodities from textiles to hardware. The signers vowed to boycott any individual who imported boycotted goods, or who raised prices on items in stock above the current levels. Those who violated the boycott were considered "as enemies to the liberties of America … and treated with the contempt they deserve." Over time, some had been critical of how slowly the Maryland Assembly leaders had been in boycotting British goods in defiance of the Townshend Act, but evidence indicated that their hope for relief had been with the lord proprietor. After no such support was forthcoming, the colonists moved appropriately.

Evidence of the ultimate resolve of the Baltimore Association occurred in February of 1770 in what was to be known as "The Case of Good Intent." When the brigantine *Good Intent* docked at Annapolis with a cargo worth £10,000 ($900,000) consigned to some of the most prominent merchants on the Western Shore of Maryland, the association took action. The largest consignor of goods aboard the brigantine, the mercantile firm of Dick and Stewart, requested to meet with representatives of each of the three counties to consider the matter of the cargo. The group voted eight to four to force the *Good Intent* to return to England without breaking open or unloading the cargo. The governor appealed the action by showing the committee a letter from Hillsborough promising that there would be a repeal of the Townshend Act soon. But the committee would not yield, and the *Good Intent* sailed back to England on February 27, with significant financial losses to the merchants. The Baltimore Association had shown their resolve to break the act.[7]

During the period between the repeal of the Stamp Act in March of 1766 to the passage of the Townshend Act in July 1767, the Virginia Assembly had been in session with no problem or controversies within the commonwealth. At this time the Virginia royal governor, Francis Fauquier, and the Assembly members were on the best of terms.[8] The Townshend Act brought the Burgesses to pass resolutions vindicating the rights of the colonies with a response to the king over the disapproval of the act. Then the new Virginia governor-in-chief, Lord Botetourt, arrived to continue the conflict. When the House of Burgesses convened in Williamsburg on May 11, 1769, the new governor was intent on impressing the colonials with his position and authority. He rode up in a coach with the vice royalty insignia on the side, pulled by six "milk-white" horses. The coach had been a present of King George III to Lord Botetourt.

Reacting to the actions of the Burgesses, Lord Botetourt addressed the Virginia Assembly on May 18, 1769, remarking, "Mr. Speaker and gentlemen of the house of burgesses, I have heard of your resolves and augur ill of their effects. You have made it my duty to dissolve you and you are dissolved accordingly." The Burgesses then retired to the Apollo Room in Raleigh Tavern on Duke of Gloucester Street where they signed an agreement presented by George Washington, which had been drafted by George Mason.[9] This agreement called for no importation of any British goods into Virginia until the Townshend Act was repealed.[10]

North Carolina was the last of the older Southern colonies to enact a non-importation agreement. In the North Carolina Assembly, Speaker John Harvey presented the Massachusetts Circular Letter of 1767 before the body. The Assembly took no action except to vote to send "an humble, dutiful and loyal address" to the king pleading for repeal of the "several acts of Parliament imposing duties on goods imported into America." The speaker sent the letter to the Massachusetts legislature indicating that North Carolina will "ever be ready, firmly to unite with the sister colonies, in pursuing every constitutional measure for redress of grievances so justly complained of." The Assembly again met in 1769 during October after most of the colonies had already signed non-importation agreements.

In the November 2nd session Speaker Harvey presented the Virginia resolutions, which were adopted without dissenting vote or change. Governor Tryon reprehended the Assembly and declared that it had "sapped the foundations of confidence and gratitude" and that it was his "indispensable duty to put an end to this Session." The members then called for a meeting of an extra-legal body to consider its own separate legislation. This resulting two day session of the new legislative body to draw up a non-importation agreement was the first such legislative body in any colony. The session was attended by 64 of the Assembly's 67 members.

In other activity in North Carolina over the Townshend Act, the merchants of the Cape Fear area, along with Cornelius Harnett, who was the "Pride of the Cape Fear" district Sons of Liberty, attended a meeting during which the parties "meaningfully agreed to keep strictly to the non-importation agreement" and to cooperate with the other colonies.[11]

When the South Carolina Commons met in November, 1768, their new royal governor, Lord Charles Montagu, indicated to the members that he desired that they consider any letter advocating disapproval with the king or the Parliament with the "contempt it deserved." The speaker, Peter Manigault, had received the Massachusetts Circular Letter during the summer and he had offered it to the Commons for consideration. The Commons then told Montagu that it had received no letters challenging the authority of the Parliament.

The merchants of South Carolina were unhappy to see any attempt to suspend imports from Britain. They felt any boycott would unfairly hurt them more than others. Others, including the planters, were less affected. Eventually a Committee of Thirty-Nine was formed by the Assembly with 13 representatives from each of the parties — merchants, planters and artisans. A deal was created to stop all slave imports, as well as suspend importation of most manufactured goods. The push toward the boycotts served to reduce imports of British goods by 50 percent in South Carolina.[12]

The meetings began on July 22, 1769, and for the first time a voice was granted to the working classes by a South Carolina government. But some, like the wealthy planter William Wragg, complained that his "freedom" might be endangered by these actions. William Henry Drayton of Magnolia Plantation near Charles Town declared that men educated in the liberal arts should not have to "consult on public affairs with men who" knew only "how to Cut up a beast … Cobble an old shoe … or to build a necessary house." These men feared any shift in political power from their grasp. Gadsden, likewise, sensed some fear, but felt that it was in his interest to deal with all manner of society. From this day forward in South Carolina, the laboring classes and the elite began to work together, as the colony headed toward the Revolution.[13]

In Georgia, the House considered the Massachusetts Circular Letter and the Virginia document against the Townshend Act. They considered that the petition to the king was proper, being a right of all English people. But Georgia Royal Governor Wright did not take the actions of the Assembly well at all, and promptly dissolved it. During the first half of 1769 the various protests against the Townshend Act were published by the local *Georgia Gazette* with little attention. But on September 6, 1769, the *Georgia Gazette* gave an invitation to the citizens of Georgia to uphold their rights as Englishmen. On September 16 a meeting in Savannah was attended by merchants who promised to cancel existing orders for British goods and to purchase no more taxable goods. A general session was held on September 19 in which resolutions were passed against the Townshend Act for non-importation. Georgia's resolutions were modeled after those of South Carolina, but it embraced no enforcement wording and there were no actions to sign the document.[14]

After Townshend had died in 1767, Frederick, Lord North, the eldest son of the Seventh Baron North from Banbury in Oxfordshire, assumed the office of chancellor of the exchequer and leader of the House of Commons. North, who was born in 1732, was named for his godfather, Frederick, Prince of Wales. Having been born to wealth and position, he appropriately attended school at Eton and then on to Trinity College, Oxford. His family home, Wroxton Abbey, was actually owned by Trinity College, through the generosity of North's forebears. At college, North was known as a rather straight fellow and average student who did little drinking, gambling or horseplay. His peers considered him a pleasant guy, witty, a good dancer and popular.

North took his seat in the House of Commons at age 22, married two years later and settled in to his new career. Beginning his first position as a junior lord of the treasury in 1759, he received some attention by his associates and gradually moved up to assume the Exchequer role at age 35. He had voted for the Stamp Act, against its repeal and for the Townshend Act. He was considered one of the "King's Friends," having impressed the king with his loyalty, conservatism with colonial Americans and his influence with his colleagues in the House. North would remain in this post throughout the American Revolution, leaving in March of 1782.

The conflict over the Townshend Act had reaped the usual rewards to British taxation in the British colonies and in Britain. Lord North took office as prime minister and first lord of the treasury on February 10, 1770, and was able to secure a repeal of most of the Townshend duties on April 12.[15] Lord North urged the repeal, not for the constitutional issue, but because it failed to promote British trade. At the request of George III, the duty on tea was retained in order to maintain some sense of authority by the British to tax the colonies. The British and American merchants were delighted. While the tea duty remained, it was widely evaded and taxes were actually paid on only one tenth of the imported tea after 1770.

After the Townshend crisis, the political conflict between the British and the Southern Assemblies was generally quiet, and rather non-eventful. The next three years would prove to be quite prosperous in the South, while the Anglo-American relationship held at the status quo. As the South had been slow to boycott, they were likewise somewhat deliberate before dropping their agreements. The boycotts did fall with little if any issues in North Carolina, Virginia and Georgia. In Maryland the planters tried to maintain the boycott, but were repelled by the powerful merchants in Baltimore and Annapolis. On December 13, 1770, Henry Laurens presided over a great public gathering in Charles Town to consider the boycott of all British goods in South Carolina.[16] In that session, Thomas Lynch "exerted all his eloquence and even the trope of rhetorical tears for the expiring liberty of his dear country," but the merchants won out over the planters and mechanics in lifting the boycott of British goods except tea or any other taxed goods.[17]

This period after 1770 was surprisingly calm in Maryland, with the only issue of substance being an internal controversy over fees paid to the clergy and officers, largely reflecting the unique proprietary condition of that colony. William Eddis, a newcomer to Maryland, wrote to an English friend that "This is a dead time with us. Politics are scarce talked of." Eddis continued to write of the pleasant life in Maryland.

The fee controversy, as it was called, initiated Governor Robert Eden, age 28 and the second son of Sir Robert Eden of Durham, and the sister of the lord proprietor, Caroline Calvert, into Maryland politics. Eden had taken over the position from Governor Sharpe in 1769. The controversy began with the question before the Assembly of extending the Tobacco Inspection Act of 1747, which expired on October 20, 1770. The question of collecting fees surfaced in the lower house when it was learned that the clerk of the land office had collected fees after the expiration of the act. Since the offending clerk, William Stewart, had violated the British constitution, the house ordered the sergeant-at-arms to take Stewart to the county jail. Governor Eden then released Stewart and eventually dissolved the Assembly when the lower house ordered a committee report that showed the size of several major officers' incomes from fees — the secretary between £1,000 to £1,500 and the clerk of the land office upwards of £1,800. To settle the issue, Governor Eden issued his fee proclamation of November 26, 1770, which took the position of defending the people against high fees, and ordered the salaries reset to the 1733 level of the original act. But the fee proclamation only served to confirm the dissatisfaction of the delegates for the proprietary regime.

In September, 1771, the proprietor, Frederick, the last Lord Baltimore, died without an heir. The terms of all the Assembly representatives were expired, and new elections in the spring would be required. The issue of the fee controversy again was raised. The political landscape was eventually affected when two politically significant individuals in Maryland began to debate the fee proclamation. The debates began in earnest when Daniel Dulany published an article in the first issue of the *Maryland Gazette* in 1773. He discussed the matter in satirical dialogue using the opposing imaginary speakers "First

Citizen," who opposed the proclamation, and "Second Citizen," who defended it. A month later, Charles Carroll, a Catholic politician, answered the article with a positive view for "First Citizen." The writings continued in three long letters with the parties abandoning the pen names for more direct debate. Charles Carroll of Carrollton had returned from college on the Continent and had been interested in the political issues of the day. While abroad he had said that "America is a growing country: in time must and will be independent." These debates not only made the issues widely public, but they gained popularity for the young Carroll, who now dined with the powerful personages of William Paca, Samuel Chase and Thomas Jefferson, all of whom would become state governors and signers of the Declaration of Independence.[18]

Botetourt died on October 15, 1770, at age 53, after an administration of two years. He had attempted to hold the Virginians as loyal subjects of the crown by either persuasion or force at first, but then he became more sympathetic with the people and began to ask the British Ministry to repeal all the taxes on the colonists. Botetourt had become a patron of William and Mary College by giving gifts of gold and silver out of his own funds to deserving students. The Virginia Assembly even erected a statue in his honor. To the ultimate dismay of all Virginians, John Murray, Earl of Dunmore, was transferred from his position in New York to assume the governorship of Virginia.

North Carolina's political landscape had been dominated by the tyrannical administration of Governor Tryon. His oppressive regime had created an atmosphere that not only fostered the Regulator Movement throughout the western counties of the Carolinas, but had left the eastern citizenry weary of his leadership. The hatred of the English tyrant had the effect of nurturing the seeds of discontent in the colony and served the idea of independence well. After the Battle of Alamance in May 1771, which essentially ended the Regulator Movement in North Carolina, Governor Tryon left for his new post in New York.

Tryon was replaced by Josiah Martin on August 12, 1771. Martin was considered to be a rather stubborn, overbearing and tactless man who even provoked his father to be publicly critical of him. His father once said that his son was good for only two things — setting a good table and keeping his wife pregnant. Martin came from a military background, having served for 12 years in the British Army, leaving as a lieutenant colonel two years before being appointed governor of North Carolina. His actions as royal governor in North Carolina would soon serve to further the patriot cause.[19]

The decade of the 1770s opened in South Carolina with the controversy over a member of the Parliament,

John Wilkes, who had been charged with libel for criticizing the king and sent to a London prison. The Assembly looked upon the Wilkes issues as symbolic of their own cause and on December 8, 1769, voted a gift of £1,500 to Wilkes to aid him in his efforts. The royal governor, Lord Charles Montagu, considered the action an insult to the king. He added to the conflict by becoming involved in a dispute with the Commons House when he tried to take away the rights of the colony regarding monetary matters. Henry Laurens took up the cause by declaring that the governor was dealing with "nothing less than the very Essence of pure liberty." The Assembly then refused to transact any business, and Governor Montague promptly dissolved it. The governor became so frustrated with the situation, he left the colony for England and resigned. The Council of Royal Appointees then took over the struggle, continuing to push the concept that the Assembly no longer had sole responsibility for appropriation of public funds. But the Assembly refused and a deadlock situation resulted. Because of the Wilkes controversy, the activities of royal government came to a standstill in South Carolina until 1773.

After the Townshend-inspired boycott had been lifted in Charles Town, trade was quickly revived. By the spring of 1771, the stores in Charles Town were full of imported goods from Britain. Rice prices doubled within two years, and the planters again put their money on increased slave purchases. In 1772 and 1773 some 65 vessels carried over 10,000 black slaves to the wharves of Charles Town. The planters and merchants were increasing their fortunes as the boom time continued. A local merchant remarked in April of 1772 that "The desires of the planters increase faster than their riches."[20]

On February 22, 1771, Georgia Governor James Wright dissolved the Georgia Commons House that had first met in October of 1770 because it refused to enact a tax bill. Since no actions were forthcoming from this body, he called for new elections. In April 1771 the Commons House elected as their speaker a leading member of the Georgia Sons of Liberty, Noble Wimberly Jones, but Wright rejected that action. The body then elected Archibald Bulloch, who was another patriot in defiance of Wright. The governor then dissolved the Assembly on the third day. In July of 1771 Governor Wright left for England where he remained for two years. During his absence, he turned the acting governorship over to his wealthy 58-year-old senior councilor, James Habersham, who continued the trend by dissolving the Assembly in April 1772 over electing a speaker. Finally the Assembly of December 1772 was able to elect William Young as speaker and legislative activities were continued. These were the first acts since 1769 and there would be no more dissolution in colonial Georgia history.

When Governor Wright returned to Georgia in February 1773, he was welcomed by the members of both houses primarily for his successful actions to obtain approval for Indian lands west of Augusta. With the support of the Indian agent, John Stuart, they met in May of 1773 with the five major Southern Indian nations in Augusta and gained the 1,600,000 acres between Savannah and the Ogeechee and 500,000 acres between the Ogeechee and the Altamaha from the Creeks.[21]

The period of stalemated calm in the British colonies came to an end on May 10, 1773, when the Parliament passed a bill, the East India Company Act, to allow the failing British East India Company to ship surplus tea to the colonies without paying the regular English export duty on the tea. The firm was left to pay only the token duty of three pence per pound on tea left from the Townshend repeal action. The company was near bankruptcy with a large quantity of unsold tea, which could now be sold at below the level of the smuggled tea price. The bill was not well received in the colonies as merchants viewed this monopolistic move as offensive and essentially a bribe for consent to pay the tax.

In the autumn of 1773 seven ships came down the Thames River into the open sea loaded with consigned tea from the British East India Company en route to the ports of Boston, New York, Philadelphia and Charles Town. When the ships arrived some seven weeks later at the ports of New York and Philadelphia, the local citizens would not allow the ships to land. On December 2, 1773, the British ship *London* anchored in Charles Town harbor with 257 chests of tea. That day the town's Sons of Liberty passed out handbills along Broad Street calling for the local citizenry to meet the next day in the Great Hall in the Exchange Building to obtain "the sense of the people" on the matter of the tea ship. The meeting was held with representatives from the planters — Charles Pinckney, Charles Cotesworth Pinckney and Thomas Ferguson, the artisans — Gadsden and Daniel Cannon, and the merchants — John Savage, Miles Brewton and David Deas. Those at the meeting appointed a speaker and proceeded to draft resolutions to prevent the landing of the tea, without the support of the leading merchants who already held quantities of tea and desired no boycott. The captain of the ship *London* was threatened later in December that his ship would be burned unless he moved it to deeper waters. Conflict was avoided when the royal officials had the tea moved to the damp cellar in the basement of the exchange, where it remained until it was worthless.[22]

On October 25, 1773, in Edenton, North Carolina, Mrs. James Iredell, Mrs. Hannah Johnston, Mrs. Elizabeth King, Mrs. Penelope Barker, Mrs. Basco and other ladies totaling 51, from five North Carolina counties, pledged themselves not to use tea until the tax was removed. The Edenton Tea Party, as it came to be known, was the earliest known instance of political activity by women in the American colonies.[23]

On Sunday, November 28, 1773, the *Dartmouth* arrived in Boston and tied up at Griffin's Wharf. Being one of four ships scheduled to arrive in the city loaded with tea, the Patriot Committee of Correspondence placed an armed guard at the dock to prevent any tea from being unloaded. The next day a meeting, attended by a crowd estimated at 5000 citizens, was held where it was resolved that "the tea should be returned to the place whence it came." Governor Hutchinson ordered the citizens to disperse, but received only jeers and hissing.

Several weeks later, on December 15, there were now three tea ships under guard at the wharf, with the fourth scheduled British tea ship, *William*, having run aground off Cape Cod. The British customs commissioners indicated that the ships would be seized within 36 hours if the duties were not paid. On Thursday, December 15, as thousands of patriot citizens gathered in the Old South Church, the governor refused to act to have the tea ships ordered out of the harbor, as he retired to his country estate in Milton. A tea consignee was sent to Milton to see if the governor would change his mind, but it was not to be. The news was revealed to the Old South group, which prompted Samuel Adams to rise from his seat and exclaim, "This meeting can do nothing more to save the country." The cheers went up: "Boston Harbor a Teapot tonight"; "Hurrah for Griffin's Wharf"; "The Mohawks are come."[24]

On December 16, 1773, a group of locals, thinly disguised as Mohawk Indians with blackened faces and blankets hiding their clothing, boarded the three ships — *Dartmouth, Eleanor* and *Beaver* — and threw 342 chests of tea worth £15,000 ($1,350,000) into Boston Harbor "making saltwater tea," as they called it.[25] This incident, well known as the Boston Tea Party, was to bring about a major crisis within the British colonies. The patriots were well aware that there would be a significant reaction to this extreme act of defiance. The day after the dumping, Admiral Montagu remarked to the local citizens, "Well, boys, you have had a fine pleasant evening for your Indian caper, haven't you. But mind, you have got to pay the fiddler yet!"[26] Because of the Boston Tea Party, as time would ultimately reveal, not a single chest of tea was sold in America.[27]

On the 17th, John Adams wrote in his diary that "Last Night 3 Cargoes of Bohea Tea were emptied into the Sea.... This is the most magnificent Movement of all. There is a Dignity, a Majesty, a Sublimity in this last Effort of the Patriots, that I greatly admire. The People should never rise without doing something to be remembered, something notable And striking. This Destruction of the Tea is so bold, so firm, intripid and inflexible, and it must have so important Consequences, and so lasting, that I can't but consider it as an Epocha in History."[28] And so it was indeed.

News of the destruction of private property at the "Boston Tea Party" caused a storm of protest in London. The king was prepared to move against Massachusetts immediately with a royal executive order, but the ministers advised the king to let the Parliament act. On January 29, 1774, Benjamin Franklin was forced to endure over an hour of angry lecture from British Solicitor General Alexander Wedderburn over the Tea Party.[29] Lord North met the news with disbelief, since the duty on tea was cheaper than it was before, and he had provided the colonists with "a relief instead of an oppression." He declared that only "New England Fanatics" would have rebelled against the tea. For Lord North and his ministers, the Boston Tea Party had finally revealed that the real issue with the New Englanders was not the tax, but whether the British would indeed have any authority over the "haughty American Republicans."[30]

Because the East Indian Company was carrying out a British law, and backing away from this challenge would be too humiliating to all Englishmen, George III, Lord North and the Parliamentary ministers were in full agreement that the matter must be firmly dealt with. The English now had proof that Boston was "a nest of rebels and hypocrites" and had been "obstinate, undutiful, and ungovernable from the beginning." They were "a canker worm in the heart of America" and a "rotten limb which will inevitably destroy the whole body of that extensive country." Indeed the English believed "it would be best to blow the town of Boston about the ears of its inhabitants, and to destroy that nest of locusts."[31] Unquestionably, the British knew that if they did not assert firm authority here, their authority would be diminished in other cities, towns and villages throughout the colonies.[32]

While many called for blood to be shed in response, Lord North was able to temper the emotions to consider a severe but moderating approach. He proposed that the Boston rebels be starved into submission. On March 25, 1774, the House of Commons passed the Boston Port Act by overwhelming majority to deal with these "Boston mutineers." This act closed the Port of Boston to all shipping until the British East India Company had been compensated for the losses incurred by the Tea Party mob and when the crown had been given evidence of their good intentions. The English rejoiced, as George III declared that England was now united.

News of the Boston Port Act reached Boston on May 11, 1774, and the Committee of Correspondence went into quick action in sending out a circular letter to the neighboring towns calling for a meeting to be held at Faneuil Hall. The Boston Town Meeting met and the patriotic declarations were expressed with passion. The Whigs said that the frontier of American liberty was on the Charles River, and that the Boston patriots must resist the British at all costs. The Port Act, scheduled to take effect on June 1, 1774, was serious and it could not be avoided or ignored. Business in Boston came to an abrupt standstill, and the citizens wondered how they would deal with this new oppression.[33]

On May 6, 1774, the Parliament passed another bill aimed at continuing to punish the patriots of Boston, the Administration of Justice Act. This act allowed royal officials accused of a capital offense in the performance of their official duties to be tried in another colony or in Britain. The British ministers were not finished when they passed, on May 20, the Massachusetts Government Act, which called for the provincial council to be appointive, as in other colonies, rather than elective. This act gave the royal governor more power to appoint or dismiss officers, judges or sheriffs at will. Then, on June 2, 1774, the king gave his royal approval to a new bill, the Quartering Act, which required that proper facilities be provided in the colonies for housing the British Army, rather than the often dilapidated shelter.

These collective acts were known as the Coercive or Intolerable Acts, and served to essentially leave the citizens of Boston and Massachusetts with no other recourse but rebellion. Throughout the 13 Atlantic colonies, most of the liberty associations began to make serious military preparations for the first time.[34] George Washington saw the issue of the Coercive Acts as being a question of whether Americans should "supinely sit and see one province after another fall a prey to despotism."

While not considered as one of the Coercive Acts, Parliament received the king's approval on its final act affecting the colonies on June 22, 1774, known as the Province of Quebec Act. This bill was an extension of the 1763 legislation to include French-speaking settlements in Illinois country and the Ohio Valley under the civil government that had been left out in the Proclamation of 1763. Western land speculation was now a dead issue with this act. Those suffering from this measure were well-known patriots George Washington, Patrick Henry and others who hoped to gain wealth though acquisition of western lands, as settlement by whites was projected to expand over time. Some in Parliament felt that these Canadians, given their religious freedoms, would temper "those fierce fanatic spirits in the Protestant colonies."[35]

Southern reaction to the events in Boston and the Coercive Acts was predictable. In Wilmington, North Carolina, patriot leaders Cornelius Harnett, John Ashe and Hugh Waddell destroyed tea in the open daylight for all to see.[36] The citizens of Annapolis, Maryland resolved on May 22, 1774, that no suits would be brought for debt recovery until the British repealed the Boston Port Act. The *Virginia Gazette* of Williamsburg on April 28 carried an article from Mr. "R" warning George III and Lord North that they would "dye th' Atlantick's verge with noble gore" rather than submit to force of arms.

In Norfolk, at a celebration of Saint Tammany, one man predicted that America would respond to an appeal to arms if required, "And shine sole empress of the WESTERN WORLD."[37] In May, the Virginia Assembly, upon hearing of the Boston Tea Party, set the date of June 1st as a day of fasting. On May 25, Lord Dunmore dissolved the House of Burgesses, leaving the 89 members to retire immediately to the Apollo Room of the Raleigh Tavern, where they adopted resolutions against the use of tea and other East India commodities. Further news arrived from Boston some days after, and on May 29 some 25 burgesses, among them George Washington, remained in Williamsburg to attend a meeting. In this session a circular letter was issued recommending a meeting of deputies in a convention to be held at Williamsburg on Aug. 1.[38]

The Norfolk Public Safety Committee met and wrote, "Our bosoms glow with tender regard for you, and we will support you to the limit of our ability." On June 27 the citizens of Norfolk met at the courthouse to denounce the blocking of the harbor as a "most tyrannick exercise of unlawful power." Late in August, the Norfolk citizens were shaken to hear that nine chests of tea consigned to some of the leading merchants had just arrived in port on the brigantine *Mary and Jane*. The group resolved that the tea must be sent back. The affected merchants agreed with no conflict encountered and received the thanks of those gathered. Thus, a Norfolk "tea party" was averted.[39]

When tea arrived in Charles Town harbor aboard the British ship *Magna Carta* in late June, Captain Richard Maitland told local officials that he would return the tea to England. But on rumors that Maitland planned to sell the tea anyway, angry and unemployed men in the port boarded the ship as Captain Maitland quickly exited to take refuge aboard the British man-of-war *Britannia*. In November the *Britannia*, which carried consigned tea, landed. The Charles Town General Committee ordered the merchants to dump the tea in the Cooper River to avoid mob violence, which they accomplished.[40] Henry Laurens of Charles Town said these new acts were simply the first of perhaps many laws to "Mandate which Ministers Shall think proper for keeping us in Subjection to the Task Master who Shall be put over is."

Tensions between the British and Marylanders had been calm since 1773 until news of the Boston Tea Party and Port Act reached Maryland. The news brought the common cause of liberty to the citizens, as the Assembly leaders considered action. The circular letter from the Massachusetts House, asking for support against the tyranny of Great Britain by passing non-importation and non-exportation agreements, arrived in Baltimore and Annapolis. On May 24, Baltimore merchants gathered and selected a committee to correspond with the neighboring colonies. The next day 80 citizens of Annapolis met and passed resolutions calling for the colonies to support the suffering in Boston as the common cause of America, and to seek a repeal of the Boston Port Act.

As effects of the Coercive Acts took full force in Boston, the Massachusetts legislature on June 17, 1774, called, via circular letter to the other colonies, for a "general congress of the colonies to bring about united action in the emergency." The Congress was to be held in Philadelphia. The first meeting of the Continental Congress was about to make history.

In Annapolis, Maryland, on June 22nd, the first provincial convention was held to consider the cause of Boston's populace.[41] Ninety-six delegates chose their representatives to the Continental Congress, with Matthew Tilghman as their chairman, as well as Robert Goldsborough from the Eastern Shore, and Thomas Johnson, William Paca and Samuel Chase representing the Western Shore. These men would attend and return to "lay before them the measures adopted by the general congress." The provincial convention condemned the Boston Port Act as being "cruel and oppressive invasions of the natural rights of the people of Massachusetts Bay ... now suffering in the common cause of America."[42]

The Massachusetts request for a general congress brought forth a meeting on July 6, 1774, in Charles Town. The session with 104 delegates became "the most general meeting that has ever been known" in Charles Town and "almost every man of consequence" in South Carolina attended. They adopted resolutions of condemnation for the recent British measures, considered the issue of non-importation and selected delegates to the Continental Congress. They chose Henry Middleton, John and Edward Rutledge, Christopher Gadsden and Thomas Lynch to represent South Carolina.[43]

In Williamsburg, Virginia, on August 1, a colonial convention met in a tavern to consider both radical and conservative views toward the issues. Patrick Henry and George Mason and Richard Henry Lee called for ceasing payments on British debts, while the conservatives, led by Paul Carrington and supported by Carter Braxton, Thomas Nelson, Jr., and Peyton Randolph, called for continuing payments and exporting. The resulting agreement of the group called for termination of both importing and exporting, while allowing debt collection. The body elected Peyton Randolph, Richard Henry Lee, George Washington, Patrick Henry, Richard Bland, Benjamin Harrison and Edmund Pendleton as delegates to the Philadelphia congress.[44] The August convention was to mark the beginning of the formal move to the Revolution in Virginia.[45]

When Governor Martin of North Carolina got wind of a meeting to consider sending representatives to the Continental Congress, he refused to call for the Assembly to meet. When Martin's secretary announced the governor's decision, Speaker John Harvey went into a rage and proclaimed that the people would call an Assembly without the governor. A meeting of some members occurred in Wilmington on July 21, where it was declared that it was "highly expedient that a provincial Congress independent of the governor" be scheduled for August 25 in New Bern. This planning session, presided over by William Hooper, with representatives from all the Cape Fear counties in attendance, first considered having the August meeting in Johnston County to avoid the watchful eye of the governor. But the delegates felt it was better to meet right under the nose of the governor in New Bern.[46]

Governor Martin then met with his council to see if there were "any further measures" that could prevent the upcoming convention. But the First Provincial Congress of North Carolina met anyway on August 25, 1774, with 71 delegates from 30 of the 36 counties present. The body elected William Hooper, Richard Caswell and Joseph Hewes to represent North Carolina. This congress was of major significance in North Carolina as it became a practical example of self-government and showed that intercolonial cooperation was possible in defiance of the British royal authority.[47] In the three days the session lasted, the delegates considered issues like the "Charter rights," the *Magna Carta*, criminal justice and even slave trade. They agreed "that we will not import any slave or slaves, nor purchase any slave or slaves imported or brought into this province by other from any part of the world after the first day of November next." The Whig cause was solidified and the patriots of North Carolina moved closer to an understanding of what it would to be to gain independence from the royal government.[48]

Noble W. Jones, Archibald Bulloch, John Houstoun and George Walton invited fellow Georgians to meet at the "liberty pole" at Tondee's Tavern in Savannah on July 27 to consider the Philadelphia congress. The meeting addressed various letters and resolutions from the other colonies. A committee was assigned to draft resolutions to be formally considered in a second meeting planned for August 10. Then, Georgia Governor Wright issued a proclamation against the upcoming meeting, to no avail. The August 10 session included representatives from the parishes in the same number as the Commons House of Assembly. The delegates adopted a number of resolutions, including condemnations of the Boston Port Act, attempts to tax the colonies and moving trials to England and the abolition of the Massachusetts Charter. They also expressed support for the redress of grievances for actions by the British in their sister colonies and affirmed their right to petition the crown for historic British rights, privileges and immunities. Even though there was decided support for sending delegates to the first Continental Congress, it was ultimately agreed that no delegates would be sent because the colony was divided. Many in Georgia were still quite loyal to Britain in 1774. Regardless, the meeting was evidence of the revolutionary spirit gaining in this southernmost Atlantic colony.[49]

The First Continental Congress met on September 5, 1774, in Carpenter's Hall in Philadelphia with 54 delegates from 12 Atlantic colonies. The seaport of Philadelphia was considered a patriot haven, while many patriots felt the colony of Pennsylvania was still a home of too much "Toryism." The delegates were "the ablest and wealthiest men in America" according to Chatham, and "the most honourable Assembly of Statesmen since those of the ancient Greeks and Romans, in the most virtuous Times." John Adams of Massachusetts said they were "one third Tories, another Whigs, and the rest mongrels."

The undercurrent of what was certainly an aristocratic Congress was a struggle of the conservatism against a decidedly radical membership. Peyton Randolph, one of the radical representatives from Virginia, was elected the Congress president. His fellow Virginia delegates Henry, Jefferson and Washington, in cooperation with the radical delegates of Massachusetts, set the radical flavor of the Congress. Even the choice of Carpenter's Hall, the meeting location of the Carpenter's Guild of Philadelphia, rather than the State House for the home of the Continental Congress, was considered by conservatives to be a ploy to gain favor of the city's working class. The leading radical representative from Philadelphia, Charles Thomson, was elected secretary.

While it was expected that the New Englanders would lead in fury the declarations, having experienced the recent ill favors of the British, such was not the case. It was the planter aristocrats of Virginia and the Carolinas who would set the direction and champion the patriot cause. A delegate from Pennsylvania professed, "There are some fine fellows come from Virginia, but they are very high. The Bostonians are mere milksops to them." Patrick Henry, now to be known by all the delegates as a great orator, was the first to speak. He urged that the empire was already dissolved and that essentially the colonies were in a "state of nature." Christopher Gadsden of South Carolina, the man who left "all New England Sons of Liberty far behind," as one Connecticut delegate reported, urged to attack the British forces under General Gage before they could be reinforced.[50] Another South Carolinian, Thomas Lynch, was described as a "man of sense" who "carries with him more force in his very appearance than most powdered folks in their conversation."[51] John Adams called Lynch "a solid, firm, judicious man," and called Richard Henry Lee "a masterly man, sensible and deep."[52] Patrick Henry was later asked, "Who was the greatest man in congress?" and remarked, "If you speak of eloquence, Mr. Rutledge, of South Carolina, is by far the greatest orator; but if you speak of solid information and sound judgment, Colonel Washington is unquestionably the greatest man on that floor."[53]

During the early stages of the Congress, a provocative rumor had spread that General Gage had begun "horrid butchery" in Massachusetts and had destroyed Boston with cannon fire from the British ships in the harbor. This false rumor, later to be known as the "Powder Alarm," almost sent provoked men to Boston looking for revenge. But as it turned out, the real revenge was the passage of the "Continental Association" on September 27, as presented by Richard Henry Lee of Virginia. This "Association" called for no importation or exportation, and even non-consumption. Due to a distrust of merchants, which arose because of the failures of the import boycotts of 1770, the Congress sought to take control with the Non-consumption Agreement and to ask the people not to buy British goods at all. The second agreement called for solid enforcement of the agreement by local committees that would be dominated by radicals. The Non-importation and Non-consumption agreements were scheduled to take effect on December 1, 1774, and would apply to Great Britain, Ireland and the British West Indies.

It was during the discussion of this issue that the original conflict between the North and the South surfaced. Many of the Southern delegates believed, as did John Rutledge of South Carolina, that the Non-exportation Act would certainly ruin the economy of the South, while the Northern colonies would not be seriously hurt. Rutledge declared, "The affair seemed rather like a commercial scheme, among the 'flour' Colonies, to find a better vent for their flour through the British Channel, by reverting, if possible, any rice from being sent to those markets: and, for his part, he could never consent to our becoming dupes to the people of the north." The Virginia delegates pleaded to have the agreement postponed until the autumn of 1776. South Carolina delegates refused to sign the agreement until rice and indigo were excluded, to allow them to continue to ship these staples to European markets. Compromises were eventually reached between the parties by deferring the effective date of the agreement until September 1775, and to allow rice, but not indigo, to be exported.[54]

As the Congress considered the grievances with Britain, Virginia delegates were successful at influencing the other delegates to confine their complaints beginning with the Grenville administration of 1763, and the reign of George III. Tories reported that "Adams, with his crew, and the haughty Sultans of the south, juggled the whole conclave of the Delegates." The radicals were setting the agenda as the Congress considered the conservative proposal and a "Plan of a Proposed Union between Great Britain and the Colonies," from Pennsylvania delegate Joseph Galloway.

This plan called for the establishment of a "Grand Council" that would act like a colonial "House of Commons" to handle local affairs. The proposal also required that acts from Parliament be approved by the Grand Council before affecting the colonies. Galloway's plan was to negotiate with Britain in the hope that a reconciliation could be reached. But Congress rejected Galloway's proposal by a vote of six colonies to five, with one divided, in favor of the Suffolk Resolves on October 8.[55] These resolves declared that there would be no adherence to the Coercive Acts, and that taxes would be paid to the Provincial Congress and withheld from the royal government until the Massachusetts government had been "placed upon a constitutional foundation." They also called for military preparation to defend against the risk of attack by the British Army, and that if a patriot leader would be taken by the British, it would be appropriate to imprison "every servant of the present tyrannical and unconstitutional government."

The loyalists considered the work of the First Continental Congress to be completely depressing because it gave no real consideration to reconciliation. They remarked that the Congress had "erected itself the supreme legislature of North America" in taking power away from the colonial legislatures. The establishment of the Continental Association was viewed as a sure way to bring Britain to her senses. South Carolina delegates warned that "Before nine months millions of people, who depend on America for their daily bread, will curse you with their dying groans." Some felt that Britain would not yield anyway, regardless of colonial actions. John Adams said to Patrick Henry, "I expect no redress but, on the contrary, increased resentment and double vengeance." Henry replied, "We must fight. By God, I am of your opinion."[56]

After development of a formal Declaration of Rights, an address to the citizens of Britain condemning the Parliamentary acts since 1763 and a petition to King George III, the First Continental Congress adjourned on October 26. It was decided that a second congress would meet on May 10, 1775, if there was not a redress of grievances.[57] This Congress had established "the United Colonies" as a legitimate entity, and had essentially declared economic war against England. The economic effects were soon felt. Imports from Britain to the colony of North Carolina dropped 97 percent within one year, from £278,116 to £6,245.[58]

In considering the various documents developed during the First Continental Congress, the great English statesman William Pitt, the Earl of Chatham, remarked, "I must declare and avow that in all my reading and study—and it has been my favorite study—I have read Thucydides, and have studied and admired the master states of the world—that for solidity of reasoning, force of sagacity, and wisdom of conclusion, under such a complication of circumstances, no nation or body of men can stand in preference to the General Congress at Philadelphia."[59]

With the last of the old proprietary legislature sessions ending in March of 1774 after some 138 years, coupled with the First Provincial Convention in June of 1774, Maryland was ready to build the new government with the influential examples set forth by the First Continental Congress. In November a convention met at Annapolis to call for support of the programs developed by the Continental Congress. In addition to supporting the Continental Association guidelines and electing the representatives to the next Continental Congress, the Maryland delegates made plans to deal with probable British military force. They declared that only a "well-regulated Militia" could be "the natural strength and only stable security of a free Government." The delegates called for all Marylanders between the ages of 16 and 50 to form themselves into companies, elect officers to lead them and acquire weapons and ammunition. The funding was to come from a subscription or "other voluntary manner." Maryland Governor Martin, a former British Army member, was said to be shocked to see a former British officer, General Charles Lee, drilling a militia at Annapolis in December.[60]

While the Maryland delegates were meeting in Philadelphia, Annapolis had its own "tea party." Although this event was not as well known as the Boston Tea Party, it was perhaps more dramatic. On October 15, 1774, the brig *Peggy Stewart* arrived at the port of Annapolis with a cargo that included 17 barrels of tea that weighed 2320 pounds. The owner, Anthony Stewart, was now in a difficult situation. He had chartered his ship to an Annapolis firm to sail to England to be sold by his London correspondent, James Russell, for some £550 if possible. As it turned out, Russell was unable to find a buyer, and decided to charter the *Peggy Stewart* to return to Annapolis with tea included in the cargo.

After the customs fees had been paid, the local committeemen were alerted of this violation of the import ban on tea. They called for a meeting of delegates from the counties for Wednesday, October 19, to consider the matter. Stewart requested in a meeting in Annapolis to be allowed to burn the tea publicly and before the representative meeting. But the committee insisted on waiting for the general meeting. During the meeting on that Wednesday, Anthony Stewart, as ship owner and representing the charter firm Williams, gave his apology for "importing the tea" and for "paying the duty thereon." The written apology was signed publicly by Stewart and the Williams brothers, along with their pleas to allow them the opportunity to burn the tea. While there was talk of tar and feathering, and even burning the brig, the committee finally gave them "consent to burn the tea." But Stewart had heard enough. Fearing for his safety and hoping to repair his public image, he decided to burn his own ship. Stewart directed his crew to run the ship aground at Windmill Point. In full view of the witnesses in the town, he gave the ship the torch himself and within a few hours, the *Peggy Stewart* was burned to the water's edge.[61]

In Virginia, brave actions were afoot when George Washington, serving in January 1775 as chair of the Committee of Fairfax County, called for the freeholders to sign up for the militia. Committees in the other counties also took action. Washington was eventually to command some six companies of militia in Virginia. Then, at the request of the General Assembly, on Monday, March 20, 1775, the Second Virginia Convention met at St. John's Church in Richmond to approve the proceedings of the First Continental Congress.[62] It was Patrick Henry who introduced resolutions based on the actions of the Maryland program calling for the colony to "be immediately put into a posture of defense" against Britain.[63] Though some members felt Henry was too premature in his requests, the measures were approved.

On March 23, Henry gave another of his assertive speeches in which he said Britain has no desire for reconciliation, but really desired "war and subjugation ... to force us to submission." He exclaimed, "There is no longer any room for hope. If we wish to be free ... if we mean not basely to abandon the noble struggle in which we have been so long engaged ... we must fight!" Henry continued, "It is vain, sir, to extenuate the matter. Gentlemen may cry for peace, peace, but there is no peace. The war is actually begun! The next gale that sweeps from the north will bring to our ears the clash of resounding arms! Our brethren are already in the field! Why stand we here idle? What is it that gentlemen wish? What would they have? Is life so dear or peace so sweet as to be purchased at the price of chains and slavery? Forbid it, Almighty God! I know not what course others may take; but as for me, give me liberty or give me death!" William Wirt remembered that as Patrick Henry sat down, "The cry, 'To arms!' seem[ed] to quiver on every lip and gleam from every eye."[64]

Henry called for the establishment of two regiments of militia for defense of the colony. While Robert Carter Nicholas knew there were also county militia groups forming, he proposed that the force to defend the colony should be 10,000, or even perhaps 20,000 strong. The convention decided on calling forth as many men as possible and appointed Pendleton, Nicholas and Benjamin Harrison to form the Committee of Defense to handle military planning.[65] In addition to military measures, actions were taken to promote the culture of wool, cotton, flax and hemp and to encourage local manufacturing, which had always been disallowed by the British. The former delegates to the First Continental Congress were reselected for the second, with the exception that Thomas Jefferson was substituted for Peyton Randolph if he was not able to attend.[66]

In March 1775 the Norfolk Public Safety Committee condemned John Brown, a local merchant, for bringing in a number of slaves from Jamaica on the brigantine *Fanny*, which was a violation of the Continental Association. Some weeks later Captain Sampson of the scow *Elizabeth of Bristol* incurred the anger of the committee for taking on a load of lumber, another violation. The committee presented that "We trust the merchants, planters, and skippers of vessels will make him feel their indignation, by breaking off all kinds of dealings with him." Other violations were found out, like that of the local firm Elilbech, Ross & Co., which was forced to send back to England the ship *Molly* without offloading any of her cargo.[67]

Early in 1775 hundreds of men in Anson, Guilford, Rowan and Surry counties of North Carolina had signed pledges of loyalty to Britain and had sent them to Governor Martin. Martin hoped to keep the colony out of revolutionary furor with these and other supporters. Martin asked General Gage for arms and ammunition to equip the loyalists. But resistance was building. In New Hanover County, Colonel John Ashe was drilling men through maneuvers, as was Colonel Robert Howe in Brunswick. When some citizens in Wilmington displayed their reluctance to join the boycott of British goods, Colonel Ashe appeared in the town with a "public" showing of 500 men to dissuade such thoughts.[68]

On April 3, 1775, at New Bern, North Carolina, the Second Provincial Congress met as directed by Speaker John Harvey and agreed "to act in union with our neighboring colonies" and elect the delegates to the upcoming Congress. Harvey had set the session to precede the Assembly session called by Governor Martin. Martin was upset with Harvey and denounced him in two different proclamations. But the Provincial Congress met anyway

at 9 A.M. for business, and at 10 A.M. in the same hall where the Royal Assembly met. Both governments were administered by the same man, Speaker Harvey.[69]

At the first session, the Provincial Congress, the same delegates were elected to the Second Continental Congress. The body also passed resolutions enunciating the right of the people to hold meetings and petition the king for redress of grievances, approved the Continental Association, and endorsed the establishment of the committees of safety. The following Royal Assembly meeting accomplished little, and on April 8, 1775, Governor Martin dissolved the last Royal Assembly ever held in North Carolina.

The events in North Carolina were no real surprise to Martin. On January 30, 1772, he had written Lord Hillsborough, the secretary of state for the colonies, complaining about "the propensity of this people to democracy." Writing later to Hillsborough's replacement, the Earl of Dartmouth, Martin stated that the royal authority "is here as absolutely prostrate as impotent, and nothing but the shadow of it is left." Unless "effectual measures" were taken, he wrote, "there will not long remain a trace of Britain's dominions over these colonies."[70]

On November 6, 1774, the South Carolina delegates from the First Continental Congress returned to Charles Town. The General Committee then called for elections to a meeting of the Provincial Congress scheduled for January 11, 1775. At the meeting, the issue of rice exports was raised. Christopher Gadsden expressed his belief that the Congress should go beyond the Association requirement and agree not to export rice at all. The indigo planters were unhappy with the actions from the Continental Congress. In order to aid them, the group agreed upon a plan to compensate the indigo planters, and planters of other crops, with one-third of the rice crop income. The Congress also established a secret committee to obtain arms and ammunition for resistance. The delegates to the next Continental Congress were also elected. The actions of this Congress were strongly enforced, with confiscated goods imported from Britain put up for public auction. In South Carolina there were numerous contributions of goods and supplies to the embargoed citizens of Boston as a symbol of their care for their fellow Northern patriots.[71]

Georgia Governor Wright reported in late 1774 that things were tolerably quiet, but he did expect troubles would surface. He was correct. In December, the *Georgia Gazette* published news of the actions of the First Continental Congress. On December 3, a group in Savannah called for a Provincial Congress to meet in January. Thus, on January 18, 1775, in Savannah, the day following the regular Assembly meeting, the Provincial Congress met with delegates from five of the 12 parishes. The delegates elected Archibald Bulloch, Noble W. Jones and John Houstoun to be the delegates to the Second Continental Congress, but it was decided that since the Georgia citizenry were divided on the issue and with only five parishes represented, they would not attend. They did send a document expressing that there were men in Georgia who indeed supported the patriot movement. The Congress did approve a "watered-down version" of the Continental Association, and adjourned on January 25.[72]

Merchants in Savannah did not adhere to the ideals of the association. They continued to trade as usual, stealing business from their neighbors in Charles Town. They ignored the action of the "General Committee" in Charles Town that forbade all commercial interface with Georgia. Georgia Governor Wright also hoped to keep his colony out of the patriot movement if possible. But the fragile nature of his hold was evidenced by an incident on February 15, 1775, when customs officials seized a shipment of smuggled molasses and sugar, and placed it aboard the schooner *St. Johns*. At midnight a mob of 20 black-faced men boarded the schooner, tarred and feathered one of the crew, and threw the other two crew members and seized goods into the water. The mob then prevented one of the men in the water from coming ashore and the poor man drowned. Soon the move to Revolution would be as active in Georgia as in the other colonies.[73]

As the Southern provincial conventions were engaged in organizing for action, the British Parliament was taking the unwise course of rejecting the colonial petitions and addresses from the Continental Congress, the colonial congresses and even from some British merchants. William Lee of Virginia, who was now in London, wrote on April 3, 1775, that the conflict between Britain and the colonies "must now come to a final decision, and in my opinion, it will end in absolute independence of the colonies."[74] By mid–April, the Southern colonies, as in all the Thirteen Colonies, were ripe for an event to push the people over the cliff to pure revolt against the British. The potential for armed conflict was in the air, and there seemed to be no serious chance that positive reconciliation between the British and the American colonists could occur. Patrick Henry was right in March of 1775 when he said, "Gentlemen may cry for peace, peace, but there is no peace. The war is actually begun!"

While the seeds of a Revolution were present from the beginning, these 12 years, from 1763 to 1775, shaped the form of dissolution of the British North American colonial experience. The British contributions to failure were aristocratic and legislative arrogance, a false set of mercantile rules, the reign of George III, the English debt and a total misunderstanding of the American views. For the American colonists the contributions to dissolution were a love of local liberties, an incredible economic success, the spirit of self-reliance, a legacy of colonial assembly, highly cultivated society, and the actions of great leaders in each of the colonies. There was no serious hope of reconciliation now. The end of the British American Colonies had come. It was time for an American Revolution.

4

THE REVOLUTION BEGINS

The American Revolution began just after 5 A.M. in the morning air of Wednesday, April 19, 1775, on the Common at Lexington Green in Massachusetts. Having received instructions from Lord Dartmouth for spirited action against the patriots, General Thomas Gage, the commander of all British forces in North America, decided to send a force of around 800 men under Lieutenant Colonel Francis Smith to march "with utmost expedition and secrecy to Concord, where you will seize and destroy all the Artillery, Ammunition, Provisions, Tents, Small Arms, and all military stores whatever."

On that famous morning, the forward units of Major John Pitcairn's Royal Marine light infantry of the British 4th and 10th Foot approached Lexington Green, with Lieutenant Jesse Adair at the head. The British force of approximately 250 men moved on to the Common to confront a line of some 70 men of the Lexington Militia under Captain John Parker. With much shouting, including a British officer's shout, "Throw down your arms, you damned rebels!" Captain Parker ordered his men to disperse. As the militia began to disperse, an unknown shot rang out which caused Lieutenant Adair's men to fire at the ranks of the Lexington Militia. The War of Independence was begun.

The news of fighting at Lexington and Concord moved rapidly by colonial standards, as relay riders and sea-borne "reporters" went north and south armed with reports. Knowledge of the event reached Baltimore and Annapolis, Maryland, on April 25, 1775, by relay riders.[1]

When the news reached the Third Maryland Convention, which was in session in Annapolis, it sent a thrill through the town. William Eddis, a minor British official in Annapolis, wrote upon hearing the news "at a place called Lexington" that "With the most dreadful anxiety we are now waiting for further and more circumstantial intelligence."

At the advice of his Council of State, Governor Eden kept the harmony with the patriot factions by agreeing to "commit the care of the arms to the custody of such gentlemen of the militia as they most place confidence in." As he revealed to his brother, "They expressed great satisfaction with this." Reacting to the governor's actions in giving up arms to the provincials, Eddis expressed his understanding with his words, "In these turbulent times something must be yielded to the clamor of an infatuated multitude."[2]

News reached Williamsburg, Virginia, late at night on April 28 by rider.[3] The Williamsburg *Virginia Gazette* published a heavy-worded assault on the British and printed, "The Sword is now drawn, and God knows when it will be sheathed." But Lord Dunmore had already aroused and inflamed the patriot countryside in Virginia. On the night of April 19, British sailors were quietly quartered in the Governor's Palace in Williamsburg. Under English ministerial orders and sanctioned by Lord Dunmore, the sailors sneaked out before dawn on the 20th, under the command of Captain Henry Collins, and clandestinely seized all the powder from the Williamsburg Magazine they could carry in the governor's wagon. Then they transported the powder to the British man-of-war *Magdalen*.[4]

Expecting trouble, Lord Dunmore armed his servants with muskets, loaded and ready for action. Only through the actions of leaders like Speaker Peyton Randolph and Treasurer Robert Carter Nicholas was the Governor's Palace not stormed and Governor Dunmore not seized as the population learned of the event. The

Council of Williamsburg called for Dunmore to return the powder. Dunmore replied by indicating that the powder had been removed due to some intelligence of a possible slave insurrection in Surry County, and gave a weak promise to return the powder.[5] The militia became more active, and on April 22, Dunmore sent a message to Dr. William Pasteur, mayor of Williamsburg, that if any harm came to Captain Collins of the *Magdalen* or his secretary, Captain Foy, he would "proclaim liberty to the slaves and reduce Williamsburg to ashes." There had been no reports of indignities to either Collins or Foy. If Lord Dunmore had possessed any units of British regular troops (which he did not — only sailors) and moved against the patriots at this point, there would have been another Lexington in Virginia.

When the news of Lexington reached the countryside of Virginia, the patriot militias were already forming to counter the events in Williamsburg. Seven hundred militiamen, mostly cavalry, gathered at Fredericksburg, Virginia, with plans to move on Williamsburg. In order to determine the latest situation in Williamsburg, Mann Page was deputized to ride to Williamsburg to inquire on the status of the powder. Page made the 100-mile ride in 24 hours. Peyton Randolph advised against violence at this point. George Washington, now outside Fredericksburg and awaiting Randolph to accompany him to Philadelphia for the Second Continental Congress, also concurred with Randolph. The 102 deputies appointed by the militia voted down the motion to march on Williamsburg by only one vote.[6]

Militia were moving from almost every corner of Virginia, including Bowling Green, Frederick, Berkeley and Dunmore counties. The Committee of Safety in Hanover County called for reprisals against the king's property if the powder was not returned or paid for. Meeting in Newcastle, the Hanover citizens, along with Patrick Henry, called for action. Captain Henry was elected to command the militia, which headed off to Williamsburg. Ensign Parke Goodall with 16 men was sent to Laneville in King and Queen County to obtain £330, the estimated value of the Williamsburg powder that had been seized, from the king's deputy receiver-general, Richard Corbin. When the group reached Laneville around midnight, they placed a guard at Corbin's home. At dawn Mrs. Corbin told Goodall that funds were only kept in Williamsburg, where her husband was currently located.

The news of Henry's march to Williamsburg spread like wildfire. Alarmed about what would happen next, patriot and burgess member Colonel Carter Braxton recommended that Henry not enter the town. Lord Dunmore had placed marines from the British man-of-war *Fowey* and cannons around his palace and threatened to fire on the town if Henry's force entered Williamsburg.

Captain Henry with his 150 men stopped the night of May 3 at Doncastle's Ordinary located 16 miles outside Williamsburg to meet with Braxton. Braxton was able to soften Henry's bloodthirsty mood, in his appeal not to risk bloodshed for such a small sum. On May 4, Henry received the £330 from Corbin as compensation for the seized powder. Two days later Dunmore issued a proclamation indicating that a "certain Patrick Henry, Jr., of Hanover, and a number of deluded followers," were charged with extortion of £330 from the king's receiver-general. The proclamation also forbid all persons to aid or abet "the said Patrick Henry, Jr.," or his confederates. Henry then headed off to the Second Continental Congress in Philadelphia with an escort of three volunteer militia companies in full dress to Hooe's Ferry on the Potomac with the praises and "applause of the countrymen."

Threatened by the possibilities of hostilities, Lady Dunmore and her children fled to Yorktown and the protection of Captain Montagu's man-of-war *Fowey*. Dunmore stayed in his palace, reinforced with sailors from that warship. Lady Dunmore and family had returned from the *Fowey* to the palace as a gesture of good will when the conciliatory proposition from Lord North arrived.[7] On May 12 Lord Dunmore issued a call for a meeting of the General Assembly to consider the proposals of Lord North. When Peyton Randolph heard of these events, he immediately resigned as president of the Second Continental Congress and rushed to Williamsburg to take up his role as speaker of the House of Burgesses, which had planned to meet on Thursday, June 1. After meeting for a week, on June 8 with Lord Dunmore in attendance, the burgess delegates learned that Lord Dunmore, his wife the countess, three boys, three girls, one infant, Reverend Gwatkin, several servants and Captain Edward Foy were now in residence aboard the *Fowey*, having fled the Williamsburg palace undetected at 2 A.M.[8] Dunmore wrote to England of the event indicating that "My house was kept in constant Alarm and threatened every Night with an Assault."[9] The House of Burgesses rejected the proposal from Lord North as it still allowed the British Parliament to be involved in the affairs of the colony.[10]

Dunmore's flight from the palace "brought consternation and anger" to the Virginia burgesses. Few people actually believed that Dunmore had feared for his life, since he had crossed the town the evening before to meet with Attorney General John Randolph. The appearance of the H.M.S. *Otter* and the schooner *Arundel* in the York River raised the possibility that his departure had coincided with a planned invasion. The effect of Dunmore's move tended to harden the political sympathies against the British in Virginia. Now political moderates were faced with difficult choices, as the royal government abandoned them.

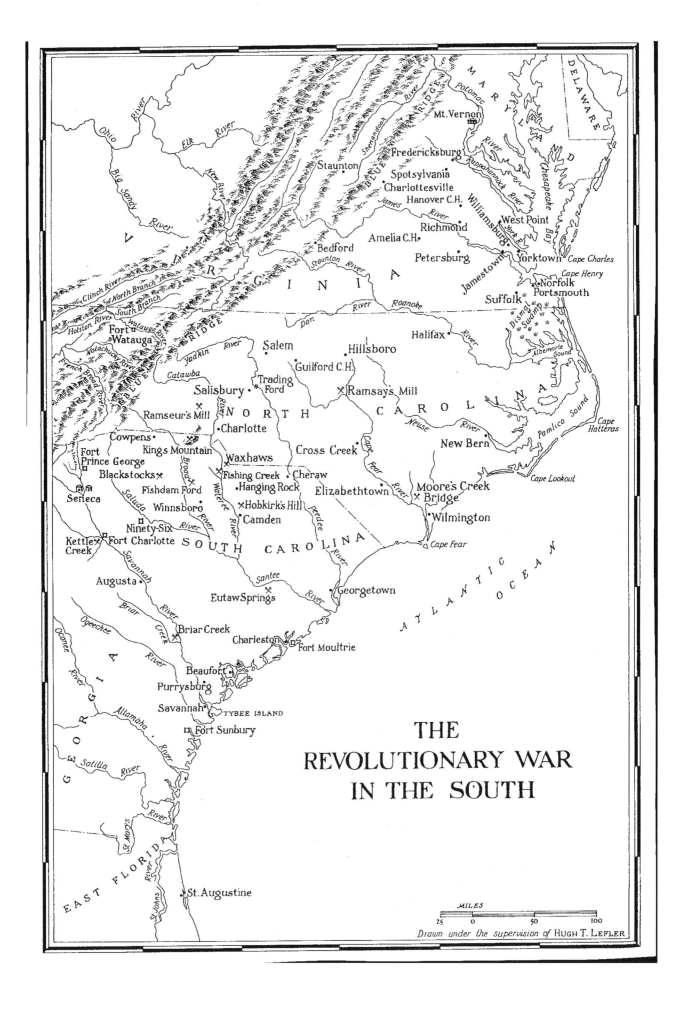

THE
REVOLUTIONARY WAR
IN THE SOUTH

Drawn under the supervision of HUGH T. LEFLER

MILES

25   0   50   100

On news of Dunmore's retreat and the expected invasion, some 200 armed men gathered in Williamsburg to protect the town. These young men "appear rather invited to feast then fight," one observer wrote. The elected officers of the troops were unable to control their men, and the number of incidents began to increase. On June 2, a group led by Theodorick Bland Nicholas, broke into the governor's palace and took some 200 pistols and muskets.[11]

At the close of the session, the assembly asked Dunmore via message to attend the adjournment at the capital according to usual custom. Dunmore invited the representatives to join him aboard the *Fowey*. The assembly was not interested. The last "governing" session of the House of Burgesses closed its proceedings on Saturday, June 24, 1775.[12] With the illusion of a functioning royal government continuing in Virginia, the final official session of the Burgesses was held on May 6, 1776, with these words of record, "SEVERAL Members met, but did neither proceed to business, nor adjourn as a House of Burgesses. FINIS."[13]

The Lexington news arrived in North Carolina at New Bern on May 3 by ship from Newport, Rhode Island, and in Wilmington on May 8. Upset by the events in Lexington, a dissolved assembly, the actions of the various county Committees of Safety, and rumors of a plan by patriots to seize his palace in New Bern, Governor Martin fled on May 24 to Fort Johnston, located near the mouth of the Cape Fear River.[14] Newspapers from London received about this same time reported that Parliament had declared Massachusetts to be in a state of rebellion.[15] Virginia publisher Alexander Purdie wrote in his daily news that "Lord Dunmore and governor Martin have certainly compared notes."[16]

While Governor Martin of North Carolina was fleeing to Fort Johnston, the Mecklenburg County Committee of Safety was meeting in Charlotte to consider the recent events. This patriotic group drafted 20 resolves to present to the Continental Congress. The resolutions, first published in the New Bern–based *North Carolina Gazette* on June 16, 1775, declared that all royal and Parliamentary laws and commissions were now suspended, and that they intended "for the better preservation of good order, to form certain rules and regulations for the internal government of this county until laws shall be provided for us by the Congress." The committee then called for the formation of nine military companies, named two citizens to settle disputes and established that 18 "selectmen" would manage the county government with the power to collect taxes and expend funds. On April 30, 1819, these Mecklenburg Resolves became known as the Mecklenburg "Declaration of Independence" when the *Raleigh Register* published recollections of some elderly Mecklenburg citizens. These citizens recalled that a true declaration document, drafted on May 20, 1775, had existed but had been destroyed in a house fire in 1800. Regardless, these resolves were never presented to the Continental Congress.[17]

News reached Charles Town, South Carolina, by ship on May 9.[18] Arms and powder had already been seized from the local Charles Town magazines on the night of April 26, and placed in homes around the city, as directed by the Provincial Secret Committee of Five.[19] The word of fighting in Massachusetts induced the general committee to call for a Provincial Congress for June 1. The 172 delegates to the Provincial Congress, with Henry Laurens as president, were especially efficient in establishing a 13-member Council of Safety to assume executive rule, authorizing paper currency, raising troops, and setting the next session for December 1. They also expressed their passion with a formal signed "Association" document, drafted by the radical William Henry Drayton. They pledged to "UNITE ourselves, under every tie of religion and honor" in defending America and, if required, "to sacrifice our lives and fortunes to secure her freedom and safety."[20]

Even with moderate leaders like Laurens in place, it was difficult to hold back the people. Laurens was concerned over the rage of the people and especially "persons not possessed of any visible Estates" who will have the power to determine the fate of "Men of property, Rank and respectable character." He continued with comments: "Some are Red-Hot and foolishly talk of arms and there is another extreme who say that implicit Obedience is the Surest Road to redress of Grievances, the great majority of members lie between, and are men of wealth and consideration." A British official observed that "the Opulent and Sensible" representatives "wish to avoid ... desperate measure ... but they are powerfully opposed by a numerous body of the Low and Ignorant, led by a few desperate Incendarys, who have nothing to lose, and some hot headed Young Men of fortune."[21]

When the new royal governor for South Carolina, Lord William Campbell, arrived on June 18, he was confronted with a provoked citizenry when rumors surfaced that he had brought arms for slaves and Indians with him. Campbell commented, "The cruelty and savage barbarity of the scheme was the conversation of all Companies."[22] During May the king's agent for Indian Affairs in the South, John Stuart, had seen the problems coming and fled from his Orange Street mansion in Charles Town to St. Augustine to avoid harm, as he found he could not convince the Southerners that he was not inciting the local Indians. The old fears of a slave revolt again surfaced. A British official in Charles Town reported that "Massacres and Instigated Insurrections, were words in the mouth of every Child." Another official declared the "the King's Friends … are … expecting every moment to be drove from their Occupations, and Homes, and plundered of all they have." The Council of Safety issued a warning against "instigated insurrections by our negros" and devised a special committee "to secure the Province against an insurrection of slaves or counter-revolutionary moves." The Congress recommended that citizens attending church should "take with them their Fire-Arms & Ammunition."

Violence was in the air. During the Provincial Congress a report was given to the Secret Committee of Five that two loyalists, Laughlin Martin, a merchant, and James Dealy, had expressed their delight in the rumors that slaves, Catholics and Indians were to receive British arms. They were seized, stripped, "tarred, feathered, and carted through the streets of Charles Town." The city erupted with a mob in the streets taunting the "two poor wretches." A British official, Alexander Innes, wrote to London that "the Herd which has been led on from one step to another and now … there is no drawing back as they have gone so far." He continued that the citizens were at the mercy of "Lawless vindictive Ruffians," among them "desperate, … Violent, who are in general the needy, drove at desperate measures … might in the struggle mend their situation."

After the tar and feathering of Martin and Dealy, the provincial government seized some blacks that were suspected of insurrection, but most were released for lack of evidence. Gabriel Manigault wrote to his son in early July, "We have been alarmed by idle reports that the Negroes intended to rise, which on examination proved to be of less consequence than was expected." But one black, Thomas Jeremiah, was detained. Jeremiah was a unique and successful black, who owned over £1000 sterling in property, owned several slaves, and was "one of the best" of a skilled and licensed group of black harbor pilots. The royal governor said he was "a fellow in affluent circumstances." The case was built around the testimony of two slaves, Sambo and Jemmy. Sambo testified that months earlier Jeremiah told him there was going to be a "great war to help the Poor Negroes." He was told to set his schooner on fire and to "jump to ashore, and join the soldiers." On June 16 Jemmy testified that Jeremiah had asked him "to take a few guns" to a runaway slave, Dewar, to "fight against the inhabitants of this Province."

There was the possibility that these slave testimonies could have been coerced, since Jeremiah was the type of black that would have fostered resentment among the poor whites of Charles Town. Governor Campbell believed that Jeremiah was innocent, but when he suggested to the provincial government leaders that he grant Jeremiah a pardon, a wealthy citizen warned that such a move "would raise a flame all the water in the Cooper River would not extinguish." The trial that began on August 11 ended with a conviction of Jeremiah under the provisions of the Negro Act of 1740. Jeremiah was to be "hanged and burned to ashes, on Friday the 18th." The sentence was carried out as directed. The royal attorney general wrote, "The story of this horrid Conspiracy, which … [n]ever had any foundation in fact, was industriously propagated, by the Designing, & was credited by and terrified the Weak."[23]

News of the Lexington battle arrived in Savannah, Georgia, in the evening of May 10, 1775. On the next day, the local underground public powder magazine at the eastern extremity of Savannah was opened by a mob and 600 pounds of gunpowder were removed. Some of the powder was sent to Beaufort, South Carolina, and the rest was hidden in cellars of local homes of the militia. There were reports that some of the powder was sent to Cambridge, Massachusetts, and used at the Battle of Bunker Hill. Governor Wright immediately issued a reward of £150 for apprehension of the offenders. No information was forthcoming.

On June 1, many patriotic citizens of Savannah, who had been moved deeply by the plight of their fellow Boston patriots, shipped out 63 barrels of rice and £122 in specie aboard the ship *Juliana*, under Captain Stringham, for relief. They expressed their disdain for the "late acts of a cruel and vindictive Ministry."[24]

On June 2, at the Battery in Savannah, 21 cannons were spiked and thrown off the bluff in order to prevent them from being used during the upcoming celebration of the king's birthday. But some of the cannons were recovered, drilled out and used in the celebrations that were held anyway. On June 5 the governor, council and local gentlemen drank to the king's health under the flagpole. The same day, Savannah's patriots erected the first liberty pole in Georgia and drank toasts, first to the king, second to American liberty, then toasts for no taxation without representation and speedy reconciliation between the English and colonists on constitutional principles.[25]

News of Lexington first reached Britain on May 27 aboard the *Quero* at Southhampton. The news was already published before the official dispatches from General Gage arrived some two weeks later.[26]

While dramatic events of the initial moments of the American Revolution were unfolding, the Second Continental Congress was underway in Philadelphia. The

Congress began on May 10, 1775, with essentially the same delegates present as attended the First Congress. As in the First Congress, Peyton Randolph of Virginia was unanimously chosen as president and Charles Thompson as secretary. The first topic of interest was the information on various reports of hostile events throughout the colonies. On May 18 Randolph informed the delegates of the taking of Fort Ticonderoga on Lake Champlain by militia led by colonels Ethan Allen and Benedict Arnold. To the British Captain La Place, Colonel Allen answered his question regarding who had authorized the taking of the fort "By the Great Jehovah and the Continental Congress."

Before moving to the issue of military preparations, the Congress adopted measures to appeal to the king in an expression of continued devotion to his person and the deep regret that the circumstances were degrading their relationship. The military acts were presented as being totally defensive in nature, and were prompted and justified by the acts of oppression of the Parliament. They declared that "While we revere the memory of our gallant and virtuous ancestors, we never can surrender these glorious privileges for which they fought, bled, and conquered—your fleets and armies can destroy our towns, and ravage our coasts; these are inconsiderable objects—things of no moment to men whose bosoms glow with the ardor of Liberty. We can retire beyond the reach of your navy, and, without any sensible diminution of the necessaries of life, enjoy a luxury, which from that period you will want—the luxury of being free."

On May 19, John Hancock of Massachusetts was elected to replace Randolph as president of the Congress, while Randolph returned to Virginia to preside over the House of Burgesses. The Congress took up considerations of military matters of the colonies. They established the formal Continental Army to be made up of various militia and volunteers from the colonies. They voted to issue paper currency in the amount of three million dollars to fund the army. On May 15 the Congress adopted a resolution "That a general be appointed to command all the Continental forces raised for the defense of American Liberty," and "five hundred dollars per month be allowed for the pay and expenses of the general." Although it was a delicate matter as to who would assume this critical role, John Adams of Massachusetts proposed that the provincial troops of Boston be designated as "Continental Army" and expressed his intention to propose a member of Congress from Virginia for the office of commander-in-chief. All present understood that person to be George Washington.

On June 1, 1775, Thomas Johnson of Maryland nominated Washington. Washington was unanimously elected. The next day on convening the Congress, Hancock communicated formally the election results to Washington, who stood and delivered "Mr. President—Though I am truly sensible of the high honor done me, in this appointment, yet I feel great distress from a consciousness that my abilities and military experience may not be equal to the extensive and important trust. However, as Congress desires it, I will enter upon the momentous duty, and exert every power I possess in their service and for the support of the glorious cause."[27]

On June 16, General Washington assumed command of the Continental Army and drafted a plan of organization for the army calling for two major generals, five brigadier generals, one adjutant general, one commissary general, one quartermaster general and one paymaster general. To ensure support in both the North and the South, Washington proposed the two major generals be Artemas Ward of Massachusetts and Charles Lee of Virginia. Congress named two additional major generals to the plan—Philip Schuyler of New York and Israel Putnam of Connecticut. On this same day, under orders from General Ward, a force of 1000 militia headed for Bunker Hill and Breed's Hill, opposite Boston, to take up positions. On June 17, fierce battles occurred there between British forces and the American militia, resulting in the taking of Bunker Hill by the British at heavy losses of 226 dead and 828 wounded. Americans, retiring only after their ammunition ran out, lost 140 dead and 271 wounded. The British were demoralized at having lost 48 percent of their attacking force, as their vulnerability was in evidence. On June 23, Washington, having already received his orders, left Philadelphia for Boston with much ceremonial fanfare from the citizens and the delegates of the Second Continental Congress. The American colonies now had an army and a leader.[28]

The Southern colonies continued to take serious actions to formalize their new governmental organizations and make military plans. On Monday, July 24, 1775, a convention was held in Richmond to consider the defense of Virginia. Up to this point the militia units that had been formed in Virginia were only called upon for emergencies. It was now time for the establishment of a permanent military force. On August 17, the convention organized an eleven-member Committee of Safety to take over administration of the colony. The Eastern Tidewater group of six members, with three from south side, one from the Piedmont and one from the west, dominated the committee. The committee established two regiments of regulars and a number of riflemen for border defense. Patrick Henry was elected colonel of the First regiment and William Woodford, a meritorious leader during the French and Indian War, was given the Second regiment. By September 20, troops had been recruited and Colonel Henry's regiment was encamped at the College of William and Mary. Having no money in the Virginia treasury to fund the military or pay delegates to the Continental Congress, the committee voted to issue £350,000 of treasury notes to ultimately be paid for with taxes on the property of the colony, and other special taxes.[29]

On June 21, a call went out to the inhabitants of Savannah, Georgia, to meet the following day at 10 A.M. at the Liberty Pole for the purpose of selecting a committee to form a union with the other colonies in the cause of liberty. The first act of the session was to establish a Council of Safety with 15 leading members of the colony, and a secretary. The council was instructed to correspond with other councils of safety, the Continental Congress and other committees in Georgia. A number of resolutions were considered at this meeting, including one providing that Georgia would not become an asylum for those who were escaping censure in other colonies. One young man named Hopkins spoke openly against this measure. He was later arrested, tarred and feathered and was displayed on a cart through the streets of Savannah for four to five hours. After the meeting, the union flag was hoisted up the Liberty Pole and two cannons were posted at its base. The council then adjourned and many retired to Tondee's Tavern for dinner, where 13 toasts of patriotic salute for the Thirteen American Colonies were delivered, each followed by cannon fire.[30]

On July 4, 1775, the Second Provincial Congress of Georgia met at Tondee's Tavern in Savannah with delegates from all except two of the parishes. The first item on the agenda was essentially a sermon by the Reverend John Zubly on "The Law of Liberty." Then, the Congress passed a petition to the king, followed by a variety of resolutions stating the rights of Americans, using much of the same language as presented by the other colonial bodies. They adopted the Continental Association and elected delegates to the Second Continental Congress already meeting in Philadelphia — Archibald Bulloch, Dr. Lyman Hall, John Houstoun, Noble W. Jones and Reverend John J. Zubly. The Congress also issued £10,000 in certificates for expenses, and formed the Council of Safety to serve as the executive body when the Congress was not in session. The Congress adjourned on July 17, having taken Georgia down a new path toward independence. The Georgia delegates Bulloch, Houstoun and Zubly attended their first meeting with the Second Continental Congress on September 5, along with Dr. Lyman Hall, who was already in attendance representing Georgia's St. John's Parish.[31]

On July 5, 1775, a dispatch from Whitehall from the Earl of Dartmouth advised Georgia Governor Wright that "Advices received from every quarter contain evidences of an intention in all the Colonies to the northward to take up arms against the government of this Kingdom." He continued with:

It is the King's firm resolution that the most vigorous efforts should be made both by sea and land to reduce his rebellious subjects to obedience; and the proper measures are now pursuing not only for augmenting the army under General Gage, but also for making such addition to our Naval strength in North America as may enable Admiral Graves to make such a disposition of his fleet as that besides the Squadron necessary for the New England station there may be separate squadrons at New York, within the Bay of Delaware, in Chesapeake Bay, and upon the coast of Carolina.

Wright's requests for support had never reached their destination due to the efforts of the Charles Town Council of Safety. The patriots had replaced the intercepted correspondence with dispatches reporting the Province of Georgia as being quiet and in no need of troops or war vessels.

The South Carolina Council of Safety was alerted that a ship had sailed for the port of Savannah carrying a large supply of powder for use by Indians and loyalists. Beaufort captains Barnwell and Joyner were directed to seize the expected ship and cargo. With 40 men loaded on two barges, they proceeded to the mouth of the Savannah River at Bloody Point off Tybee Island, in view of the lighthouse. The Provincial Congress of Georgia agreed to provide all assistance, as the South Carolina and Georgia forces cooperated in attempting to capture the British schooner stationed in the river. A schooner, placed under the command of Captain Bowen and Joseph Habersham by the Georgia Congress, headed for the British station schooner. The British schooner then weighed anchor and departed out to sea. At this point the Georgia schooner took up a position behind a sandbar as lookout. After only a few days, on July 10, the predicted British ship from London under Captain Maitland approached Tybee Island inlet. Seeing the schooner and sensing conflict, Captain Maitland kept his ship just out at sea. The Georgians under Captain Bowen, with support from the Carolinians, pursued Maitland's ship and eventually boarded it and took possession. Georgia kept 9000 pounds of powder, and the remaining 5000 pounds was transported to Philadelphia for the Continental Congress. This Georgia schooner was the first vessel commissioned for naval warfare in the Revolution, and it was the first capture of a British vessel in the war.[32]

The Fourth Maryland Convention met at Annapolis in July of 1775 to take the most dramatic steps toward independence yet in that colony. Convention delegates drafted an "Association of Freemen of Maryland," which pledged all signers "to repel force by force." Copies of the document were sent to all the counties in Maryland for signatures. The words of the association were to undertake the "maintenance of good order and the public peace, to support the civil power in the due execution of the laws … and to defend, with our utmost power, all persons from every species of outrage to themselves or their property." The association called for a 16-member (eight from each of Maryland's shores) Council of Safety to assume military and administrative power over the colony when the Convention was not in session. The Convention also issued $264,666 in paper currency for expenses. William Eddis, a resident minor British official in Maryland, observed after the Fourth Convention that "It seems but yesterday that I considered my situation permanent. Every flattering prospect appeared before me…. Alas! my brother, how cruelly the scene is reversed." Eddis was forced to take up residence with Maryland Royal Governor Eden for protection. Maryland was now under the control of the association.[33]

As called for after the First Continental Congress, North Carolina had established committees of safety in 18 of its counties and in four borough towns. The Wilmington–New Hanover Committee of Safety was most active as it totally regulated trade, and took overt steps to prepare the citizens for armed service. Governor Martin remarked over the smuggling of arms from the West Indies and asked for "three or four cruisers to guard the coast, for the sloop stationed at Fort Johnston is not sufficient to attend to the smugglers in the [Cape Fear] river alone." The Halifax County Committee of Safety would have "no commerce or dealing" with a key merchant in Halifax who refused to sign the Continental Association. The Chowan County Committee of Safety called three merchants in Edenton, who imported goods in defiance of the association, to publicly acknowledge their error and promise future compliance. All who refused to sign the association in Craven County were disarmed. Governor Martin wrote from his refuge at Fort Johnston to the Earl of Dartmouth on June 30 that the people "freely talk of Hostility toward Britain in the language of Aliens and avowed Enemies." Shortly afterward he wrote that he attributed this attitude to "the influence of Committees," that have "been so extended over the Inhabitants of the Lower part [Cape Fear area] of this country … and they are at this day to the distance of an hundred miles from the Sea Coast, so generally possessed with the spirit of revolt."[34]

On June 19, 1775, the North Carolina delegates to the Second Continental Congress sent an address to the town and county committees of safety in North Carolina calling for support of the Revolutionary movement and declaring that "The fate of Boston was the common fate of all." On July 18, Governor Martin so feared that the local Wilmington Committee of Safety was about to attack Fort Johnston that he fled to the British ship, *Cruizer*, which was just offshore. When Colonel John Ashe and

his militia arrived at Fort Johnston, they found "this nest of fresh water fled, [and] immediately set fire to the fort…." The gun carriages were taken from the fort and sunk in a local swamp to prevent any future use by the British.[35] Martin's proclamation of August 8 denounced the safety committees, especially the Wilmington Committee of Safety, for circulating "the basest and most scandalous Seditious and inflammatory falsehood," and for their efforts intended to "alienate their affections from His Majesty."

On August 20, the Third Provincial Congress of North Carolina met at Hillsborough, attended by 184 elected delegates from all areas of North Carolina except five counties and four towns. Samuel Johnston was elected president. The Hillsborough Congress went to work by establishing a Committee of Secrecy to procure arms and ammunition. Another committee was created to confer with the Highland Scots who had recently settled in the colony. The committee was tasked "to explain to them the Nature of our Unhappy Controversy with Great Britain and to advise and urge them to unite … in defense of those rights which they derive from God and the Constitution." Another like committee was formed to talk with the Regulator faction for support against the British. On August 25, the Congress responded to Governor Martin's proclamation by stating "that the said Paper is a false, Scandalous, Scurrilous, malicious and sedicious Libel, tending to disunite the good people of this province, … and highly injurious to the Characters of several Gentlemen of acknowledged Virtue and Loyalty…"[36]

The Hillsborough Congress created its first permanent colonial army by authorizing two regiments of 500 men each. The regiments were to be commanded by colonels James Moore and Robert Howe, and to be manned and equipped according to the same standards as the Continental Army. The Congress also called for the establishment of six new regiments of 600 men each, one for each of the newly established six military districts. The Congress also issued $125,000 in bills of credit for expenses. The Congress now turned to consider the plan for colonial government. A committee undertook the work between August 24 and September 9, and defined a government under a supreme Provincial Congress, a Provincial Council, six district Committees of Safety and local Committees of Safety. The Provincial Council of 13 members took the role as the chief executive and judicial authority in North Carolina. North Carolina was now organized to try to deal with significant threats to its survival in every direction; in the east Governor Martin was organizing the Scots and Regulators; to the north in Virginia Governor Dunmore was encouraging slave insurrections in the Albemarle area; to the south a band of loyalists called Scovelites was threatening the southern border; and to the west British agents were influencing the Cherokee Indians for possible action.[37]

Under orders from the South Carolina Council of Safety, patriot militia seized arms and ammunition on July 12, 1775, at Fort Charlotte, located 30 miles southwest of the small settlement of Ninety Six on the Savannah River. Major James Mayson moved a portion of the arms and ammunition to Ninety Six. Loyalists from the Upper Saluda Militia Regiment, led by the subordinates of Colonel Thomas Fletchall, led 200 men and retook the ammunition, and arrested Major Mayson. The Charles Town Council of Safety was alarmed and sent two ministers, two German-speaking men and William Henry Drayton as representatives in an attempt to influence the loyalists. Drayton concluded that the Council of Safety should arrest the opposition leaders. He then established his headquarters at Ninety Six, and began to recruit local patriotic militia. On the second week of September, two forces of 1000 men each under Drayton and Fletchall faced each other across the Saluda River. After negotiations, on September 16 Fletchall agreed on a treaty of neutrality.[38]

Back in Charles Town, rumors were rampant that South Carolina Governor William Campbell was planning to arm the backcountry loyalists to attack the Lowcountry. Fearing for his life, Governor Campbell fled his residence on September 15 and boarded the 14-gun British sloop H.M.S. *Tamar* in the harbor. The *Tamar* was in such poor condition that Admiral Graves had been planning to withdraw it from service. That same day the Council of Safety ordered Colonel William Moultrie and his men to seize Fort Johnson, which guarded the southeastern approach to the city. The Charles Town Council of Safety asked Campbell to return, but he declined on September 30, writing the Council that it had no legal authority and that he considered its existence an "actual and open rebellion against their Sovereign." He continued that he would never return until he was able to "support the King's authority, and protect his faithful and loyal subjects." Royal government in the colony of South Carolina was dead and control was now in the hands of the Council of Safety.[39]

The new governing body for the colony held the Second Provincial Congress at Charles Town on November 1. William Henry Drayton, who had just returned from the backcountry, was elected president by conservatives who hoped to avoid war with England. But Drayton was intent on taking action against the British. On November 11, he supervised the scuttling of various hulks in the Cooper River to prevent the city from being shelled from that direction. His actions drew fire from the British warships *Tamar* and *Cherokee*. These were the first shots fired in anger in the Revolution in South Carolina.

There was much fear in Charles Town of British invasion and cannonading. The prominent citizen Eliza Pinckney wrote in late November, 1775, that a "heavy cloud hangs over us ... almost all the Women, and many Hundred Men have left town." Henry Laurens wrote his son that "I am ... sitting in a House stripped of its furniture & in danger of being knocked down ... by Cannon Ball." The Council of Safety now took action to defend the city. To defend the sea entrance to Charles Town, a fortification of a 20-foot-high fort of "Mud & Sand, faced with Palmetto Tree" was under construction on the southern tip of Sullivan's Island. It was ordered by the Council of Safety that "all able-bodied Negro men be taken into the public service ... and employed without arms for the defense of ... Charles Town." A fire brigade was established. Men were recruited for the militia. Local schooners were outfitted with guns for coastal defense. Charles Town had been transformed into an armed camp. It was said that "half the best Houses were empty."[40]

Another loyalist in South Carolina, Patrick Cunningham, now began to recruit supporters to help him rescue his brother Robert from jail in Charles Town. Robert had been jailed on charges of sedition leveled by Captain Caldwell of the Rangers at Ninety Six on October 23. On November 3 Cunningham's group of 60 captured a wagon train at Mine Creek delivering gunpowder to the Cherokees for the Provincial Congress. A patriot major, Andrew Williamson, heard of the capture and called out his militia to recapture the gunpowder. Finding his force outnumbered, Williamson retreated on the advice of Mayor Mayson from Long Canes to Ninety Six, South Carolina. Williamson's band was attacked there for three days by Major Joseph Robinson beginning Sunday, November 19. The first blood of the war had now been shed in South Carolina. A mutual truce was called on November 22 because Williamson's men were down to two cartridges per man and Robinson feared the arrival of patriot reinforcements.

On word of the wagon train capture, the South Carolina Provincial Congress directed Colonel Richard Richardson, with his 2500 men quartered at Camden, to recapture the gunpowder and seize the loyalists. With help from some North Carolina units, Richardson captured Colonel Thomas Fletchall and other loyalist leaders on December 12. Richardson's force then proceeded southwest from the Enoree River toward Ninety Six. An estimated 130 loyalist men fled into Cherokee country and set up camp on the Reedy River. Richardson's force pursued them, attacked, killed many and seized the rest. As Richardson's force was retiring it began to snow. The patriot units suffered through the snow, sleet and rain for two weeks heading back to their homes. This infamous "Snow Campaign," as it was known, was successful in putting down the loyalists in the backcountry until the British later took Charles Town.[41]

Military action first occurred in Georgia on January 18, 1776, when three British men-of-war arrived off Tybee Island hoping to purchase provisions. The Council of Safety would not allow any dealing with the British. They arrested Governor Wright and other loyalists and called out the militia. In February new vessels arrived with 200 troops. On the night of February 11, Governor Wright and his council broke their paroles by leaving the governor's mansion and escaped to Bonaventure Plantation, where a friend, John Mullryne, lived. A waiting boat then took them through Tybee Creek to board the warship *Scarborough* at Cockspur Island at 3 A.M.[42] The British desired to obtain rice from vessels just up river from Savannah. After waiting over a month for supplies, on March 2 they sent troops up the Savannah River to board boats loaded with rice. Patriots, with support from South Carolina, attempted to release the boats, and burned several boats. The British captured some men. Shots were exchanged with the escaping British aboard the rice boats from the bluffs at Savannah, but the distances were too great to inflict any damage. The British also sailed some boats behind Hutchinson's Island. They had escaped with 1600 pounds of rice, along with Georgia Governor Wright and loyalist supporters. Now all royal authority was absent from the colony of Georgia.[43]

From Maryland to Georgia, the Revolution in the South was a reality as conventions and Committees of Safety took charge of their destiny. The royal governors were now without authority, and, at best, hanging on in hope of military force reinforcement from England. The local militias were gathering and organizing their units under individual control of each of the Southern colonies. Loyalist elements were being engaged. The Continental Army and a new nation were forming, but they had not established a role to play yet in Southern events up to this point. Blood had been shed on Southern soil and the American Revolution had begun in earnest.

5

NORFOLK

The message left for the House of Burgesses on Thursday, June 8, 1775, by John Murray, fourth Earl of Dunmore, royal governor of Virginia, declared, "Mr. Speaker, and Gentlemen of the House of Burgesses, Being now fully pursuaded that my Person, and those of my Family likewise, are in constant danger of falling sacrifices to the blind and unmeasurable fury which has so unaccountably seized upon the minds and understanding of great numbers of People, and apprehending that at length some of them may work themselves up to that pitch of daringness and atrociousness as to fall upon me, in the defenceless state in which they know I am in the City of Williamsburg, and perpetrate Acts that would plunge this Country into the most horrid calamities, and render the breach with the mother Country irreparable, I have thought it prudent for myself, and serviceable for the Country, that I remove to a place of safety; conformable to which, I have fixed my residence for the present on board his Majesty's Ship the *Fowey*, lying at York." Thus began the events that would eventually lead Lord Dunmore in bloody conflict with the patriot forces in Virginia before the year was concluded.

At the time, there were a number of explanations given as to why Lord Dunmore had chosen such a curious time to flee Williamsburg. One rumor even explained that Lady Dunmore had demanded it for her newly christened daughter. It was true that the palace was indefensible if conflict erupted and his only safe haven was under the protection of the British Navy and the Tidewater Virginia geography. Apparently he had already communicated to London his ultimate intentions to depart Williamsburg at some point. On June 10, the *Virginia Gazette* published maritime news that the 14-gun sloop-

of-war *Otter* was in Hampton Roads, and that the *Cerberus* had arrived from Boston. Aboard the *Otter* was a letter from General Gage pointing out that military forces were on their way to him. The military support would come from 60 men of the Fourteenth Regiment of Foot from St. Augustine, and another company of the same regiment from the island of Providence. The *Otter* dropped anchor in the York River on Saturday, June 10, and at 11 A.M. Lord Dunmore was received aboard to a 15-gun salute.[1]

When Dunmore arrived in Virginia in September of 1771, there was no indication that this 39-year-old man with auburn hair, brown eyes, and a sharp long nose, who often wore kilts with his dress uniform, would be the tyrant he turned out to be. As a man who comfortably lived his role as a true aristocrat and descendent of the royal Stuarts, he had every reason to fit in with the Virginia aristocracy who dominated the political scene. Who else could better represent the majesty of the British in this most distinguished Southern colony? Even as Dunmore had dissolved most sessions of the House of Burgesses since 1772 for revolutionary sentiments, he showed a grudging respect for these Virginians. On the evening of the day that the Burgesses passed the resolution calling for the Continental Congress, Lady Dunmore hosted an elegant ball at the Governor's Palace.[2] But the British government in Virginia and Dunmore's royal governorship was ended.

Hidden behind the polite society, Dunmore was a frustrated man. He had strived for 20 years for advancement in England. His first efforts were in the army and then in politics. To improve his lot in life, he had accepted foreign assignments. Though he received some £3000 each year from his estates in Scotland, he would eventually support 11 children. Through his powerful friends like the Earl of Shelburne, Lord Bute and the Duke of Bedford, Dunmore would finally obtain the treasured post he desired, first in New York in 1770. In Virginia a year later he would begin serving as colonial governor through the marriage of his wife's sister to Earl Gower, who served under Lord North.

From the start Dunmore had the mark of a tyrant and a fiery Scot, being rather arrogant and a drunkard too. He possessed the culture of the English nobleman of his day, having brought one of the largest libraries in the colonies to his palace, numerous musical instruments, and an art collection. He seemed more at home with the outdoors and military men and was known to have dined and attended the theater with the likes of George Washington. Dunmore hoped to gain his fortune, like many other Virginians, by speculating in western lands. Though the Proclamation of 1763 forbade the settlements across the Appalachian Mountains, Dunmore's policy was to ignore these instructions in this regard. Eventually the imperial reprimands started coming in with "his Majesty's just Displeasure."

When the Shawnee Indians became hostile in 1774 in the West, Dunmore requested the House of Burgesses to provide troops to put down the uprising. The burgesses refused to support him, and he raised a western militia to counter the threat. Dunmore departed Williamsburg in early July, and returned in early December in triumphant celebration of his successful campaign. An officer who accompanied him wrote, "The news is that all the Country is well pleased with the Governors Expedition."

On his return to Williamsburg, Dunmore immediately composed a lengthy 50-page report to Lord Dartmouth on the situation in Virginia, dated Christmas Eve, 1774. Unfortunately, he devoted most of the text defending his policy in the West, and spent few words on the instability in the colony. Dunmore did relate that he felt most of the Virginia citizens were loyal, and that the rebel organizations were intimidating the locals more than anything. When Dartmouth read the report, with other reports of problems in the American colonies, he wrote in shock to Dunmore:

> The steps which have been pursued in the different Counties of Virginia to carry into execution the Resolutions of the General Congress are of so extraordinary a Nature, that I am at a loss for words to express the criminality of them, and my Surprise, that, the people should be so infatuated as tamely to submit to Acts of such Tyranny and Oppression.

The leading citizens of Virginia had impractical expectations that Dunmore would be on their side, and serve to influence the British leaders to make concessions to the American colonials. Jefferson felt that Dunmore had actually deceived the Ministry in thinking that American opposition represented only a small group of rebels. Regardless, Dunmore did not, or perhaps could not, change the movement towards revolution in Virginia.[3]

The last "governing" session of the House of Burgesses ended on Saturday, June 24, 1775, with no signatures from the "absent" Lord Dunmore on the bills that had been approved by the House in session for three weeks. The next scheduled session was planned for October 12. The delegates left the capitol building without jubilation, as Richard Henry Lee of Westmoreland County, in company with two colleagues, scribbled out the opening words from the play *Macbeth* on the white plastered pillars, "When shall we three meet again? In thunder, lightning, or in rain? When the hurly-burly's done, When the battle's lost and won." Unaware of the adjournment, Lord Dunmore was expecting to receive the bills for signature the following Monday aboard his ship.

On Sunday, Dunmore wrote to the secretary of state that "last night the 24th of June, a considerable body of men violently forced into the Governor's house ... and they carried off all the Arms they could find to the number between two and three hundred stand, which has been always kept in the Hall of this house...." On Thursday, June 29, the citizens of Yorktown watched the well-liked Lady Dunmore and family leave Virginia for England aboard the *Magdalen*. The citizens rejoiced when Lord Dunmore, aboard the *Fowey*, also departed Yorktown that day, but he had just decided to see his family off from the Virginia Capes and later returned to port.[4]

Dunmore had been able to gain passage for his family by persuading Captain Montagu to countermand orders from Admiral Graves sending Lieutenant Collins and the *Magdalen* to Delaware Bay. Dunmore had given his excuse that he badly needed a dispatch sent directly to London explaining his reasons for his flight from Williamsburg. The admiral was unimpressed and threatened to court-martial Montagu. After a relatively short ocean voyage of 29 days, the governor's message, and family, arrived at Portsmouth, England. Two weeks later, on July 12, Captain Foy, who was Dunmore's aide and recent detractor, took the opportunity of rotation of the H.M.S. *Mercury* for the H.M.S. *Fowey*, to return with his wife to New York, and from there to England. Foy remarked that "Lord Dunmore's is not a character from which in any difficult times, I should hope for any great advantage ... at the same time that I should not fail to bear more than my share of all disgrace attending his proceeding." As Captain Foy left Virginia by sea he wrote, "I am no longer interested in the fate of Lord Dunmore."[5]

On July 14, Lord Dunmore's residence, the *Fowey*,

upped anchor at Yorktown and sailed down river with the *Otter* and *Mercury* to Portsmouth. Portsmouth was across the Elizabeth River from Norfolk. There Lord Dunmore had decided to take up residence since Admiral Graves ordered the *Fowey* to proceed to Boston and no suitable vessel was available to his lordship. Norfolk, a seaport town of 6000, was the key commercial and trading center in the colony. The presence of Lord Dunmore, with his small fleet, was not a favorable circumstance for this town or the surrounding area, as events would soon reveal.[6] Admiral Graves had been ordered to station warships in the Chesapeake Bay "to prevent any Commerce between the Colonies … and any other Places than Great Britain or Ireland or … the [British] west Indies." Graves was ordered to stop and search all vessels bound to and from North America and to seize all contraband arms, ammunition or letters intended to aid the patriots. For most of the summer of 1775, the British men-of-war *Otter* and *Fowey* were stationed at the mouth of the bay.

Dunmore was not only frustrated with the patriots of Virginia, but he even quarreled with some of his own. On July 17 Dunmore composed a letter from his residence aboard *Otter* in Hampton Roads to Vice Admiral Samuel Graves:

> As I have received every Assistance from Captain Montagu which it was possible to expect from Zeal and Assiduity, it is particular unfortunate to his Majesty's Service that Gentlemen should be succeeded in the Command of his Majesty's Ships here by Captain [John] Macartney who seems to be actuated altogether by Principles totally different, and to have principally at heart the making Friends among his Majesty's greatest Enemies in this Country. Hitherto instead of aiding me, he has very much prejudiced all the Measures which I have thought requisite to adopt for restoring his Majesty's lost Authority in this Government; and his Conduct has been of such a Nature that I foresee it will be impossible for me ever, with property to apply to him for any Assistance if I should require it of him; and as I think him utterly unfit for such a Command, I hope therefore you will by the most speedy means relieve him or send a different Person for the Command.[7]

Rumors began to circulate that a group was being formed in Norfolk to oppose patriot moves. A correspondent on July 22, 1775, responded in the *Virginia Gazette* that "Nothing could be more false than this. It is true their local situation will not admit at present of offensive measures, but … they are not neglectful of military discipline, and preparations for defense, at the same time that they are forwarding the welfare of the country, equal with its most useful inhabitants, by their industry and attention to its commercial interests." Because Norfolk was a haven of merchants, and others dependent on commercial interests who faced ruin if trading conditions did not improve, there was every reason for their support for maintaining the British relationships. Articles had been published in the *Virginia Gazette* about merchants and shipping firms engaging in the import of banned goods from England or its territories, which tended to make any negative rumors seem more legitimate. Whether entirely true or not, Norfolk was tagged as a Tory haven.[8]

Norfolk had always been a town apart from the rest of Virginia. Even the founding of Norfolk was unique. In June 1680, Governor Culpeper announced to the House of Burgesses that the king "is resolved as soon as storehouses and conveniences can be provided, to prohibit ships trading here to load or unload but at certain fixed places." The British government disliked the idea of the large planters shipping directly from their own plantation docks to London or other destinations. An act was thus passed to purchase 50 acres for the town of Norfolk to be located "on the Eastern Branch on the Elizabeth River at the entrance of the branch." The town was divided into lots of one-half acre each and was granted to those who would build a dwelling or warehouse for 100 pounds of tobacco.

As the town grew as a busy agricultural seaport, the citizens had more in common with their counterparts in Boston and Philadelphia than they did with other Virginians. Norfolk citizens lacked the philosophical view and political life that came from the plantation environment. They were merchants, not farmers. In 1728 William Byrd visited Norfolk and wrote that he felt himself in strange surroundings. This town filled with crowded warehouses, wharves loaded with boxes and barrels, was quite different than all the other Virginia towns. It was this separateness that led to the clash at Norfolk.

The Scotch merchants in Norfolk had no use for the Revolution because it interfered with commerce. Colonel Robert Howe of North Carolina remarked that it was doubtful that any Norfolk merchants "could feel any strong prepossession in favor of America, or its cause, suspicious friends therefore at best." One of Dunmore's officers wrote that the Norfolk Scotch "to a man are well-affected to the [British] government." In July of 1775 the Norfolk Committee of Public Safety wrote to the Virginia Convention protesting trade restrictions. The committee wrote that the merchants "have made large contracts for the articles, so prohibited and have now on hand considerable quantities of these perishable commodities…. They have had no opportunity to regulate their trade agreeably to this unexpected resolve, but are suddenly prohibited from commerce in the midst of their engagements."[9]

On Monday, August 3, 60 soldiers of the Fourteenth Regiment of Foot from St. Augustine arrived. Forty more were expected to arrive soon, but had been detained in

South Carolina. The troops were reviewed at Gosport, Lord Dunmore's headquarters above Norfolk. On arrival Dunmore had no quarters for them. He requisitioned a house from Gosport's leading merchant and proprietor of the Gosport Navy Yard, Andrew Sprowle. Sprowle's home was a three-story "large, well finished Dwelling House situated upon the River." He owned the tallest structure in the lower Chesapeake, a stone warehouse 91 feet long, 41 feet wide and five stories high. He also possessed three other warehouses, a smith's shop, wharves, slaves, cattle, miscellaneous buildings and much land in Gosport and Portsmouth.[10] The Norfolk Committee of Safety determined that Sprowle had not been evicted from his home, but he had actually agreed to allow British troops to occupy it. Sprowle was ordered to appear before the committee on August 21, but he replied to the group that he could not because the British troops required that he be escorted, which would have caused a conflict. Sprowle could not deal with abandoning his property, like many other loyalists likewise caught up in this type situation. He and his family were eventually evacuated aboard a British ship and left Virginia.[11] This and other similar events revealed the dilemma for anyone who did show any loyalist tendencies in public.

As for Lord Dunmore, by the end of August his situation was more comfortable, with troops arriving and his being protected by his small, yet adequate, fleet. He had two companies of 80 men from the Fourteenth Regiment, and about 100 ill-trained blacks and 30 loyalist volunteers. His ships included the Jamaican merchant ship *William*, which had been converted to a flagship and residence for his lordship, two vessels seized from Norfolk merchants, the frigate *Elibeck* and brig, the *Otter*, commanded by Captain Squire, and the *Mercury* under Captain Macartney.[12] On August 23, King George III declared that Virginia and her sister colonies were in rebellion and called on all loyal subjects to aid in the suppression of the insurrection. While the proclamation was not published in Virginia until November 10, it stated the reality of the Tidewater circumstance.[13]

The citizens on the Peninsula and throughout southeastern Virginia were concerned about Dunmore's intentions now that more troops were beginning to surface in Virginia. They had been concerned from the moment on June 8 when Lord Dunmore left his palace for shipboard residence. Previously, the lack of any ground military force, except a handful of Royal Navy crewmembers and marines, had always been a major constraint for Dunmore in attempts of coercion or enforcement of dictates. The *Virginia Gazette* in Williamsburg reported that Dunmore would likely "pay us a visit in this city, although he cannot expect the same cordial reception as on former occasions, but will probably be received with such illumi-

nations &c. as may make him forget his way to the palace."

Black slaves were escaping from their masters and coming to Dunmore's units to join his army. While Lord Dunmore's officers continually voiced to concerned planters that they had not provided any encouragement, the blacks came anyway. By mid–August some slaves were even being returned as the space aboard Dunmore's vessels was strained. The local presence of Dunmore's forces at Norfolk caused significant stress among those patriot and loyalist citizens. British loyalists who wanted to show their support were concerned about the risks they were taking. Rumors reporting exaggerated troop strength and attacks by Lord Dunmore's forces were everywhere. On August 26, the *Virginia Gazette* speculated that the ships were to support "infernal depredations in the rivers, and on the coast." What was Dunmore planning?

While Dunmore was preparing for a war, events in England were unfolding. While some Americans were anticipating, or more accurately "hoping," that the British would consider reconciliation, King George was busy issuing a proclamation that the Americans were rebels and that "such Rebellion hath been much promoted by the traiterous correspondence, councels, and comfort, of divers wicked and desperate persons within this realm." Only those in Britain who were in the government, or those who had commercial relationships with the American colonies, showed any real interest in the events of the times. Likewise in Virginia many of the locals had little wish to become involved in this inconvenient war. It was the hottest period of the year and dealing with the weather was more eventful than the British conflict in late August 1775.

On Saturday, September 2, the weather did become eventful. By noon on that day hurricane winds reached Norfolk. The *Norfolk Intelligencer* would report that storm as the worst "within the memory of man." When the storm let off by midnight, some 24 ships were driven ashore at Norfolk and Hampton Roads. The *Mercury* had been dragged up the Elizabeth River and grounded at Portsmouth Point, with three feet of water in the ship. In attempts to lighten the ship, the crew threw overboard 2100 pounds of bread, 930 gallons of beer, 216 gallons of rum, 130 pieces of beef, 230 slabs of pork, and 620 pounds of butter. The *Otter* and *William* had escaped without damage. The *Virginia Gazette* reported "that the devastation at Norfolk is inexpressible." It took ten days to refloat the *Mercury*, and on September 25, the ship left for Boston with Captain Macartney.

There was speculation that Governor Martin had not survived the same storm aboard the *Cruizer* standing off the Cape Fear River in North Carolina, but the rumor was unfounded. There was much destruction there. At least 37 ships had been lost or severely damaged in the colony of North Carolina. On September 22 the hulls of the *Minerva* and the *Hibernia* were put up for sale where they lay "on the Beech, within 10 miles of Currituck."

During the storm, Lord Dunmore's sloop tender with Captain Squire aboard, which was used to patrol the bay, was grounded near Hampton, and immediately burned by the citizenry. Villagers captured the eight-man crew of the tender, but the upset captain managed to escape into the woods until the winds subsided. Captain Squire then borrowed a canoe from a black man and paddled back to the *Otter*. The crew was taken before the Hampton Committee of Safety for questioning. Two sailors testified that they had carried three Negroes and a mulatto aboard. Two of the Negroes were captured on that Sunday and returned to their owner. The owner wrote a letter to Captain Squire on September 8 thanking him "for his very kind and hospitable treatment of my two slaves...." Two days later the bodies of the remaining two slaves washed ashore with remains of the wrecked tender. The Hampton committee accused Captain Squire of illegal activities and demanded that the king's ship stop molesting boats and persons passing to and from the town. The committee also demanded that they should return the vessels that had been seized in addition to returning all slaves who had sought sanctuary with the British.

Throughout September, Captain Squire continued to take out his frustration on the citizens around the bay. Just before the 15th, Squire seized three passage boats with black crews. On September 17 he seized a man coming from the eastern shore whom Captain Squire had called "a great Rascal." This man had been identified at Hampton and Yorktown "raising men to fight against the King...." The man was forced to serve aboard the *Otter*. Several days later a packet boat from Richmond was boarded in Norfolk harbor, with baggage rifled and some items robbed. Another ship just arrived on the 15th, the *Kingfisher*, was involved in seizing a vessel carrying Joseph Middleton and his family. Middleton went aboard the *Kingfisher* complaining that he had been simply visiting his relatives and had his possessions with him. The captain, James Montagu, according to Middleton, "damned him for a rebel, and said, had it not been for his wife and children, he would have him sent to Boston in irons, pointing to some that were lying upon deck."[14]

The first real aggressive act of Dunmore occurred as a result of the publication of personal attacks on Captain Squire and other British by John Hunter Holt, publisher of the *Norfolk Intelligencer*. Dunmore called Mr. Holt's paper "The Public press of the little dirty Borough of Norfolk." He accused Holt of being "wholely employed in exciting in the minds of all Ranks of People the Spirit of Sedition and Rebellion by the grossest misrepresentation of facts both public and private." Holt's paper had indeed taunted the British. On September 6 Holt's paper published the following inflammatory comments:

> Is it not a melancholy reflection that men who effect on all occasions to style themselves "his Majesty's servants" should think the service of their Soverign consists in plundering his subjects and in committing such pitiful acts of repine as would entitle other people to the character of robbers?

Captain Squire responded to "the Printer of the Norfolk Paper" three days later:

> Sir, You have in many papers lately taken the freedom to mention my name, and thereto added many falsities. I now declare, if I am ever again mentioned therein with any reflections on my character, I will most assuredly seize your person and take you on board the *Otter*.

To this Holt answered the charges with "he [Holt] does not conceive that his press is to be under the direction of anyone but himself, and while he has the sanction of the law, he shall always pride himself in the reflection that the liberty of the press is one of the grand bulwarks of the English constitution."

On Saturday, September 30, at 2 P.M. Dunmore sent a small party of 14 marines and sailors with seven grenadiers ashore at the county wharf from Captain Squire's sloop *Otter*. They marched up the main street of Norfolk to the printing offices of the *Norfolk Intelligencer* and then proceeded to remove all type, ink, paper, part of the press itself and two press workers. While several hundred locals watched the proceedings, no action was taken against the British. The troops loaded the material aboard their boats and returned to the ships offshore. Lord Dunmore with delight had watched the hour and fifteen minute event through his spyglass aboard his ship. The British took a bookbinder and a journeyman as captives. They departed the wharf giving three cheers. Happily for the patriots, the publisher Holt had escaped the print shop during the proceedings.[15] Patriots in Williamsburg criticized the Norfolk citizens for letting the British have their way, but with British warships off shore, it was not practical to create a conflict and hope to survive. Regardless, the image of Norfolk as a Tory haven was again demonstrated before the populace of Tidewater Virginia.[16]

Upset that the citizens of Norfolk had not answered the call to arms against the British incursion to Norfolk, the militia leader, Colonel Matthew Phripp, resigned. The Norfolk civil government called an immediate session in the Common Hall and developed a firm response to Dunmore:

> We his Majesty's faithful Subjects the Mayor, Aldermen and Common Council of the Borough of Norfolk in

Common Hall assembled, beg leave to represent to your Lordship, that on this day a Party of Men under the command of Captain [Matthew] Squire of the *Otter* sloop of War ... landed in the most public part of this Borough in the most daring manner, and in open violation of the peace and good order, Seized on the Printing-Utensils belonging to an Inhabitant of this Town as also the Persons of two of his Family.

We beg leave to represent to your Lordship, that this Act is both illegal and riotous, and that together with a Musket-ball fired into the Town yesterday from on board the King Fisher has greatly alarmed and incensed the Inhabitants, and has occasioned a great number of the Women and Children to abandon this Borough....

We my Lord as Men ... do most earnestly entreat you Lordship ... will interpose your Authority to put a final Stop to such violent infringments of our rights, and to order the Persons Seized on by Captain Squire to be immediately put on Shore, and the property to be replaced from whence it was taken.

Dunmore replied to the Norfolk address with "I do really think they could not have rendered the Borough of Norfolk ... a more essential Service than [to] deprive them of the means of poisoning the minds of the People, and exciting in them a Spirit of Rebellion and Sedition, and by that means drawing inevitable ruin and destruction on themselves and Country."[17]

The taking of the printing press only added fuel to the fire of the patriot cause, and began to harden positions throughout Virginia. In Williamsburg on October 19, the *Virginia Gazette* printed a scathing and unsubstantiated attack on his lordship with charges:

But how will your breasts glow with just resentment, and honest indignation, when I tell you he had dared offer violence to the chastity of a poor innocent girl? This unhappy victim to his lawless lust, whose beauty had stricken him, was by him, or by some of his minions, torn from the poor-house in Norfolk, from the few friends which poverty could procure her, carried on board his ship, and forced to become an instrument of pleasure to him who had degraded himself far beneath the most groveling of the brute creation.

Lord Dunmore now was painted with the personal face of evil. On October 13, John Holt had published an advertisement indicating that he would be in business soon as he acquired new printing equipment so as to keep the citizens apprised of "the machinations and black designs of their common enemy." Holt also had a letter to Lord Dunmore published in the *Virginia Gazette* "to inform him that he has as a partial retaliation for the loss he sustained by his lordship's seizure of his types, and other effects, taken possession of several of his lordship's horses." The forces for liberty were now focused on this local evil party in there midst.[18]

On October 12 began the active operations against the local patriots. On that day the Fourteenth Regiment of Captain Samuel Leslie carried out a series of raids as they successfully destroyed 70 pieces of field ordnance hidden in Norfolk County.[19] On Tuesday, October 17, 1775, Lord Dunmore led his force of some 140 men to the village of Kemp's Landing, the county seat of Princess Anne County, located some ten miles southeast of Norfolk up the East Branch of the Elizabeth River. Dunmore's troops broke open a blacksmith's shop and destroyed some 50 muskets awaiting repair. The chief reason for the attack was to seize artillery rumored to have been there. Fortunately, the militia had removed the powder before the British arrived. Two officers and four privates were taken in the engagement. There was little resistance even though there were some 250 patriot minutemen reported to have been in the area. When Dunmore's troops arrived, they fled to the woods.

On the night of October 19, the British again returned and brought back six guns after they destroyed ten others. Two nights later they captured six more guns, and on the 21st they made their largest haul seizing ten guns, 50 small arms "and a great quantity of Ball of all Sorts and Sizes." Dunmore had captured all the known rebel military stores believed to be in the area, along with seven prisoners, including Captain Mathews and delegate Robinson. The Princess Anne County Militia under Colonel Joseph Hutchings was preparing for battle with Dunmore when his lordship had surprised them before they were ready. After a council of war, they decided not to fight. Captain Mathews had given the order to disperse, but had been captured.[20] By November 1, Dunmore had captured some 77 pieces of ordnance from the militia, rendering most of Norfolk County defenseless.[21]

After the "defeat" of the rebels at Kemp's Landing, the loyalist morale had risen significantly. There were expectations that more troops would be arriving soon to support the governor. But loyalist and patriot citizens were leaving Norfolk and the surrounding area in greater numbers than ever, in expectation of future battle, and out of fear of reprisals. A Mrs. Ross of Norfolk had testified that Colonel Hutchings had threatened "to set fire to the Town and burn the scoundrels Out of it." The lady had been "frighten'd almost to death at hearing of it, and hastened to Abandon her house & her business." With the printing press raid and the Kemp's Landing action, escalation was probable. A correspondent wrote his friend in Williamsburg from Norfolk "the carts have been going all this day."

Lord Dunmore and Captain Squire now turned their attention to the small port of Hampton, just across the bay from Norfolk. This was the customs office for the Lower James River and a strategic location for the Williamsburg patriots who had access to the Chesapeake Bay. The town with 30 buildings was garrisoned by some 400 patriot militia under the command of Captain George Lyne, head of the King and Queen County militia. He had been sent from Williamsburg on October 7 to take over the leadership of the forces there. The first true fighting skirmish between opposing forces of British and patriot forces in Virginia in the Revolution occurred on the morning of October 26 at Mills Creek, just east of Hampton.

The previous night a raiding party from Captain Squire's unit went ashore at Mills Creek and looted several houses. When the news arrived at dawn, Captain Lyne immediately mounted his horse and headed off to get a closer look. When he arrived at the west bank of the mouth of the creek at a windmill, he saw British tenders still lying offshore in the channel behind a sand bar. Lieutenant Smith and 30 militiamen arrived shortly and began firing at the tenders. Soon another 25 men arrived and the firing continued for most of the day. Hoping to draw the British to follow him, Lyne and his force eventually departed around 5 P.M. But the British tenders then came to shore and troops burned the home of Edward Cooper.[22]

Shortly before midnight on October 26, a request for assistance reached Chairman Edmund Pendleton in Williamsburg. He immediately ordered Colonel William Woodford of the colony's Second Regiment to proceed with a company of Culpeper County riflemen to Hampton. Woodford was given an independent command under the direction of the Committee of Safety. This act of selecting Woodford was the beginning of a period of conflict with Virginia's commander-in-chief, Patrick Henry. As Woodford marched under his independent command, Henry fumed in his tent back on the campus of William and Mary in Williamsburg. Woodford's orders were:

> to use your endeavors for protecting and defending the persons and properties of all friends to cause of America, and to this end, to attack, kill, or captivate all such as you shall discover to be in arms for the annoying of those persons, as far as you shall judge it prudent to engage them.
>
> You will use every means in your power for stopping all communications of intelligence and supplies of provisions, to the enemies of America in Norfolk or Portsmouth.
>
> There may be many persons afraid in their present situation, exposed to the vengeance of the Navy, to declare their real sentiments. We think, therefore, that all those who will continue peaceable, giving no assistance or intelligence to our enemies, nor attempting to annoy our troops, or injure our friends, may for the present remain unmolested; those Tories and others who take an active part against us, must be considered as enemies; your own humanity and discretion will, however, prevent the wanton damage or destruction of any person's property whatsoever....

Woodford found borrowed wagons for the Culpeper County riflemen, and he with the unit rode toward Hampton in the rain at night, a distance of 30 miles. Woodford arrived at Hampton at 7:30 A.M. on October 27. He rode to the river on reconnaissance, where he noted five tenders at anchor. He then rode to the home of Colonel Wilson Miles Cary, a former naval officer for the British Customs in Hampton. Cary was now an enemy described by Dunmore as "one of the most active and virulent of the Enemies of Government." As Woodford sat down for breakfast at Cary's home, the British began firing on the town. Woodford immediately proceeded to the wharf, where he observed that the militia had abandoned their "Breast Work" and the citizens fled the town.[23]

Captain Lyne's forces were under cannon fire from five British vessels commanded by Captain Squire. While many felt the town could not be defended, Colonel Woodford took charge and ordered the riflemen to take positions among the houses with the best opportunity to fire on the tenders causing the cannonade. Lyne's men were ordered to defend the west crossroads of the town. The accuracy of the riflemen was so good that the British gunners had trouble loading their cannons without exposing themselves to rifle fire. The cannonade began to slacken some. Seeing what was happening, Captain Squire ordered his men to retire. The bullets were hitting home with much accuracy, so much so that "if the men went aloft to hand the sails, they were immediately singled out." The tender *Hawke* under Lieutenant Wright simply drifted ashore and the crew and vessel were captured. Eventually the British vessels, except the lost *Hawke*, were out of gunshot range and heading away from Hampton. It was an important first battle and a first victory for the Virginia patriots.[24]

The newfound confidence of the patriots led some of the militia to send Captain Squire a message: "The riflemen and soldiers of Hampton desire their compliments to captain Squire and his squadron, and wish to know how they approve the reception they met with last friday." A correspondent of Pinkney's *Virginia Gazette* of Williamsburg printed on November 2 that "In those 2 different actions, Mr. Printer, officers and soldiers of the regular, minute, and militia, acted with a spirit becoming freemen and Americans. And must evince that Americans will die, or be free!" The editor of the paper commented in print, "Lord Dunmore may now see he has not cowards to deal with."[25]

As troops were assembling in Williamsburg, and the afterglow of the Hampton victory was in evidence, Lord Dunmore was concerned with the potential for ferry crossings of patriot forces. Thus, he ordered a small squadron to patrol up the James River to block such militia movements. Off Jamestown Island some shots were exchanged between the British and patriots. Having Dunmore's ships only ten miles from Williamsburg was a bit disconcerting to the locals.

On Sunday, November 5, a hundred men from Chesterfield County arrived at Williamsburg to join their fellow militia, assembled. There was now an adequate number of men to begin the trip toward Norfolk. Dunmore's small squadron was most formidable, with the *Kingfisher* and three large tenders. The day before a thousand patriot men had crossed the river at Jamestown. The *Kingfisher* arrived at Burwell's Ferry, six miles downriver from Jamestown on November 9, but it was still too far off from the Jamestown crossing to stop the troop movements heading to the encampment at Cobham Landing. Captain Montagu of the *Kingfisher* engaged a small Virginia boat at Burwell's Ferry, where shots were exchanged.

Woodford's orders from the Virginia Committee of Safety were to "march towards Norfolk…" with his regiment and five companies of men from the Culpeper battalion and to avoid any major engagement, yet make an obvious attempt to show the local populace their military strength and resolve. With Woodford beginning to move troops across the James, and Captain Montagu trying to stop the crossings, Lord Dunmore was becoming concerned over the patriot moves. On November 14, Dunmore learned that some 120 rebels had just crossed into Virginia from North Carolina, and were camping at Great Bridge, located 12 miles south of Norfolk on the Elizabeth River. He decided to go with "109 Rank and file, with 22 Volunteers from Norfolk" to Great Bridge that night by boat.

When the governor reached his destination, there were no Carolina forces there. While there he did learn that there were between 200 and 300 rebels at Kemp's Landing. Dunmore ordered Lieutenant Batut to build a defensework at the north of the causeway leading to Great Bridge, as he departed with Captain Leslie's men toward the rebels. When they came within a mile of Kemp's Landing, they came under heavy gunfire from the surrounding woods. Leslie's troops moved into the woods firing and chasing the patriot men, killing at least five, two having drowned while crossing a creek. A Mrs. Maxwell, an elderly lady at Kemp's Landing, saw what happened, as she recounted: "When they saw the British coming, with colors flying, arms shining, and drums beating, they all took to their heels and ran away as fast as their horses and legs could carry them, without staying to fire a single shot."

As Lord Dunmore descended upon Kemp's Landing, he hoisted up his royal "pair of Colours" and read a proclamation that would live in the minds of many landowners throughout the Virginia area for some time.

Known as Dunmore's "Emancipation Proclamation," his lordship declared martial law and asked for the support of all citizens. He continued "I do further declare all indentured servants, negros, or others free, that are able and willing to bear arms, they joining his Majesty's troops as soon as may be, for the more speedily reducing this colony to a proper sense of their duty to his Majesty's crown and dignity." Lord Dunmore had hinted at just such a declaration when the patriots at Williamsburg were upset over the taking of the powder the previous April. This most feared and hated move immediately created enemies of all slave owners in Virginia. The proclamation had actually been written aboard the *William* on November 7, and printed on the press equipment taken from Mr. Holt in Norfolk.

The patriot reaction to Dunmore's action was predictable. The most formal reply came in the *Virginia Gazette* which aimed its comments at "two sorts of people"—those colonists who were leaning towards support of the British, and those who Lord Dunmore had offered freedom. The evil acts of 1775 were reviewed, including the attacks on property of peaceful citizens. The paper called the British authority "usurped and arbitrary power," and declared, "To preserve the rights they have reserved is the duty of every member of society, and to deprive a people of these is treason, is rebellion against the state." The presentation of the message to those seeking freedom and the position of the slave owner was most accurately explained as in the following:

> They have been flattered with their freedom, if they be able to bear arms, and will speedily join Lord Dunmore's troops. To none of them is freedom promised but to such as are able to do Lord Dunmore service. The aged, the infirm, the women and children, are still to remain the property of their masters, of masters who will be provoked to severity, should part of their slaves desert them. Lord Dunmore's declaration, therefore, is a cruel declaration to the Negroes. He does not pretend to make it out of any tenderness to them, but solely upon his own account; and should it meet with success, it leaves by far the greater number at the mercy of an enraged and injured people. But should there be any amongst the Negroes weak enough to believe that Lord Dunmore intends to do them a kindness, and wicked enough to provoke the fury of the Americans against their defenceless fathers and mothers, their wives, their women, and children, let them only consider the difficulty of effecting their escape, and what they must expect to suffer at the hands of the Americans.

The *Gazette* continued with comments on how the British had continued the slave trade when many in Virginia opposed it. It proposed that the British might return to ship the Negroes back to the West Indies "where every year they sell many thousands of their miserable brethren, to perish, either by the inclemency of weather, or the cruelty of barbarous master."[26]

At Kemp's Landing, Lord Dunmore took up residence at the home of Mrs. George Logan. The widow Logan was one of the leading citizens of the village, and all indications were that she enjoyed having his lordship there. A Helen Maxwell and her sisters had left Kemp's Landing for safety when the troops arrived. She had been approached by an "ugly Negro man, dressed up in a full suit of British regimentals, and armed with a gun," and asking if she had any "dirty shirts." Dirty shirts were the name given to the patriot men. The term "shirtmen" was also a popular name given to riflemen of the Piedmont area militias, referring to the non–European style of long hunting frocks they wore.[27] Mrs. Maxwell was so upset, she returned to Kemp's Landing to confront Lord Dunmore, who surprisingly agreed to see her. After listening to her complaint, he remarked, "Why, madam, this is a provoking piece of insolence indeed, but there is no keeping these black rascals within bounds. It was but the other day that one of them undertook to personate Captain Squire, and actually extorted a sum of money from a lady in his name. But we must expect such things whilst this horrid rebellion lasts." When Mr. Maxwell eventually returned home, his wife was horrified to see her husband wearing a red strip on his shirt, revealing that he had taken an oath of support to the British. Mr. Maxwell explained that "Phast! do you think it has changed my mind? Don't you see how Dunmore is carrying all before him, and if I can save my property by this step, ought I not in common prudence to wear it, for your sake and the children?" Such was the dilemma of many who took oaths to King George, but had no intention of fighting for the king, or indeed for the Americans either if they could avoid it. Such were the times for the property owners of Virginia in 1775.

Meanwhile, Lord Dunmore returned to Norfolk on the afternoon of November 16, hoping to repeat the flag raising ceremony there the following day. The citizens were coerced to take the "red cloth" oath against the "Committees, Conventions and Congresses," and to bear allegiance to His Sacred Majesty, George III, while agreeing to defend the entries into the country with the last drop of their blood. In the first gazette published on November 25 aboard the *William* with the stolen press, Dunmore told of the great support by citizens of Norfolk and Portsmouth and surrounding areas for the oath, declaring that there were "now upwards of 3000 men determined to defend this part of the country against the inroads of the enemies to our King and constitution." In Lord Dunmore's letter to the secretary of state, with this first issue of his gazette included, his lordship indicated that even though some 3000 had taken the oath, only 300

or 400 were capable of bearing arms. Blacks were indeed beginning to escape their masters, urged on by Dunmore's proclamation. Some 11 were then in the Williamsburg jail, caught trying to escape by boat. Accounts of Negro uprisings and looting were everywhere now. The feared black rebellion was now possible.

Throughout November, Captain Montagu aboard the *Kingfisher* and his little fleet of tenders remained in the middle of the James River trying to control the river crossings by patriot forces. Montagu's attempts to actually control the situation had been inadequate and most actions by him had not been successful. On November 24, Colonel Woodford gathered his forces at Sandy Point, located eight and a half miles above Jamestown, to attempt to cross the James. Woodford had received a dispatch that Dunmore was marching on Suffolk, and was expected there by the 21st. Even though a British sloop arrived to block them, he felt he had to get his men across to counter Dunmore's moves. Woodford decided to have his boats, loaded with Virginia riflemen, directly confront the sloop sitting in their way. As the boats headed toward the sloop, the British sloop skipper immediately realized his predicament, and he tacked away to the safety of his sister ships. Unable to do anything constructive as Colonel Woodford's militia forces crossed the James, Captain Montagu shelled Jamestown out of frustration. His location is appropriately known today as "Sloop Point." The next day Captain Montagu withdrew his tender fleet from the Jamestown area and returned to Gosport in essential failure.

On November 25, Colonel Woodford's forces arrived at Suffolk and were relieved to find that Lord Dunmore was not there. At Great Bridge, British Lieutenant Hill Wallace was hurriedly building a fort there to defend the approach to Norfolk. This fort, called Fort Murray on maps of the day, was of timbers built on a marshy promontory. To take it one had to attack over the wooden bridge, whose planking had already been removed. When Colonel Woodford was at Suffolk, Colonel Scott arrived at the village of Deep Creek, just seven miles from Great Bridge. Scott reported to Woodford that the fort was defended only "by Tories & Blacks" and asked for permission to attack. Woodford told Scott to hold until he arrived.

Woodford reported to Edmund Pendleton from Suffolk that Dunmore had pulled his troops out of Gosport and Portsmouth, and had concentrated all his forces around Norfolk. He continued that "Several of the princable Scotch Tories in Norfolk I'm told command Black Companys, & speak with great confidence of beating us with the odds of five to one." The entire Princess Anne County was reported to have taken up arms with the British and he explained, "But I'm told they are falling off upon our arrival & few or none of them it is expected will

Fight." Woodford also indicated that he expected several hundred militiamen from North Carolina, offered by that colony's Committee of Safety, and that these men were at Currituck just a day's march from Great Bridge.

As the Virginia patriot forces approached conflict with the British, the citizens of the Norfolk area were getting nervous. As events began to unfold, rumors that the patriots would burn the home of all loyalists were discussed. To help to keep the citizens of Norfolk from feeling they were put into a corner, Woodford let it be known that regardless of having taken the red cloth oath of Dunmore, his forces would take only their arms "as these are articles I think such Folks should not be trusted with." Colonel Scott's militia moved forward to Great Bridge and began to build breastworks at the northern end of the village to protect his men from fire from Fort Murray. The first skirmish at Great Bridge occurred when patriot militia was instructed to empty their shot using the "damp powder" at the fort, so as not to waste it. Even though Scott was under orders not to engage, this little skirmish turned into a lively exchange of two hours, resulting in the death of colonial Corporal Davis and an unknown number of British supporters at the fort.

As November came to a close, Colonel Woodford's forces, still divided between Great Bridge and Suffolk, consisted of approximately 900 men. Dunmore was not in such good shape. He had half his force made up of ill-trained former slaves and reluctant volunteer loyalists. On November 30, Dunmore wrote to General Howe in Boston, who had replaced General Gage as commander of all British forces in North America. His lordship requested the rest of the Fourteenth Regiment and he asked for the loan of the Sixty-fourth. Dunmore wrote, "Had I but a few more men here, I would march immediately to Williamsburg … by which I would soon compel the whole colony to submit." But for now Colonel Scott's forces were staged across the causeway from British Lieutenant Wallace and his fortressed men at Great Bridge in the damp air as the rain fell.

Colonel Woodford and men reached Great Bridge to join Colonel Scott's forces on December 2. With the defenses and breastworks prepared, Woodford considered two options — to wait for artillery from Colonel Howe of the North Carolina militia, or to cross the river and marsh downstream to outflank the British. He prepared for both options. He ordered the batteries to be raised next to the village to allow more firepower from the village toward the fort, and he sent out a night unit to see if a flanking action was possible. Woodford ordered Captain Taliaferro to take 60 men and go to an expected crossing five miles downstream. But Taliaferro's group was unable to acquire a boat to use, so they missed that night's mission. On this night, though, Lieutenant Wallace sent out a sortie from the fort and set fire to five buildings. The patriots were entirely surprised by the action, and were unable to stop the destruction of the buildings, which had served as cover for riflemen. The militia killed a single black soldier.

The Virginia Convention first convened on December 1, 1775, in Richmond, but after feeling that it was safe and advantageous to be closer to the action, moved back to the capital at Williamsburg on December 5. The convention was dealing with complaints from Patrick Henry that he had not been kept informed as the Virginia commander-in-chief. As Pendleton and the others dealt with these tidings, Woodford was busy at Great Bridge. Woodford had Taliaferro's group augmented by 42 men of Captain Nicholas' militia to set out to again look into the outflanking action. He put Colonel Stephen, a militiaman, over the combined group. The force of 100 men was able to cross the branch; to reach a small British guardpost manned by "26 Blacks & 9 Whites." A firefight ensued for 15 minutes, with one black killed by gunfire, one killed by a fire, two taken as prisoner, and the house burned.

Report of these events from Colonel Stephen was distressing for Woodford. News from North Carolina was also bad. The promised cannons were not mounted; there was little powder and no swabs, worms or rammers for the cannons. Woodford sent this news and an actual "slit bullet" musketball to the Virginia Convention in report. The slit bullet was designed to break into four pieces and create significantly greater body damage in those hit. Woodford sent the ball as evidence of the outlaw nature of these barbaric British. On December 6, Colonel Scott sent out another flanking party with 150 men. The force ran into a cart being guarded by four men, who gave the alarm to the garrison of 70 that promptly fled. This engagement yielded one white and four blacks killed, three blacks captured, along with six muskets and three bayonets. No patriot men were seriously hurt. This was another uneventful skirmish.[28]

The Williamsburg convention sent Woodford additional forces that arrived on December 7. Woodford received three companies of the First Regiment, without their commander, Patrick Henry, with 1500 pounds of lead and 500 pounds of powder. Six more companies from Southampton and Amelia counties were ordered to proceed to Great Bridge with haste. The stalemate was expected to continue until something changed on either side of this situation. Henry's men charged that they were not welcomed by the other Virginia troops or officers. The detachment officer reported to Henry that "Our reception at the Great Bridge was to the last degree cool, and absolutely disagreeable. We arrived there fatigued, dry and hungry, we were neither welcomed, invited to eat or drink, or shown a place to rest our weary bones…."[29]

At dawn on December 9, 1775, Woodford's forces were surprised to see the British lying planks back on the bridge, and forming up for action. The force, which Woodford had believed to be around 140, had now swelled to some 500 or so. Woodford could not believe that the British were about to attack him. Why would they leave their solid fortifications to advance in the open across this bridge? As it unfolded, Captain Leslie marched out of Norfolk at the head of his full detachment of the Fourteenth Regiment to join the "Blacks & Tories" of Lieutenant Wallace at Great Bridge, at some 12 miles distance. Although it was supposedly stated in Leslie's orders that he should send a force across the branch to create a diversion at the rear of the rebels, Leslie did not take this advice. Woodford's men manned their defenses in preparation for the bridge crossing.

Leslie's force arrived at the fort at 3:30 A.M. and rested for action. The first group to advance from the fort was Lieutenant Batut with two field guns. Batut's party crossed the bridge, set up at the end of the causeway and began firing on the breastwork. The several patriot sentries had fired a few rounds and quickly fled. Batut's men now set fire to the remaining buildings on the "island." Next came the red-coated grenadiers led by Captain Fordyce, six abreast, marching smartly with incredible precision through the mud. Behind the grenadiers were some 230 of the loyalists and black volunteers and the remaining regulars of Captain Leslie. Batut's men provided flanking fire with cannon chain shot to rake the streets. The patriots had 25 militiamen under Lieutenant Travis at the breastwork, with others frantically assembling their gear to support Travis.

Captain Fordyce and his grenadiers continued toward Woodford's breastwork, crossing the last stretch of 160 yards of the causeway. There was no natural protection of any type as Fordyce continued across this dangerous ground. After the first volley, Travis had his 25 men hold their fire waiting for the British to come closer. Another volley came from the 25 men targeted at Captain Fordyce. The first six men in the ranks fired at 50 yards. With this volley, Fordyce went down with a bullet in the knee. Fordyce wrapped a handkerchief around his wound, stood up and rallied his men forward again. The next volley rang out in the smoke. As the shots continued, many tearing into the falling Fordyce and first rank, the British continued to advance. As Fordyce finally fell, his grenadiers stopped, broke their columns and ran back across the causeway in retreat. Meanwhile Woodford had reinforced the breastwork and Colonel Stephen and his Culpepper riflemen had moved to the west to fire at the flank of the British forces. Captain Leslie held on with his bleeding forces, penned down on the causeway before the bridge, for another 15 minutes under fierce fire after Fordyce's men had been routed. He finally had his forces retreat back over the bridge, dragging the cannon with him. The 30-minute battle of Great Bridge was over.

The costs of the Great Bridge battle were totally one-sided. The patriot forces had only two wounded, one in the hand and another in the thigh. The British had three officers killed and one wounded, three sergeants and two drummers wounded, 14 privates killed and 43 wounded. The brave Captain Fordyce had taken 18 bullets. Lieutenant Batut had a shot through his leg. The bodies of the British lieutenants William Napier and Peter Leslie were carried back to the fort. A Virginian who had taken part in the action later wrote, "I then saw the horrors of war in perfection, worse than can be imagin'd; 10 and 12 bullets thro' many; limbs broke in 2 or 3 places; brains turned out. Good God, what a sight!" Under a flag of truce, the dead men were buried, and the wounded collected. At seven o'clock that night the British departed undetected away from Great Bridge and their fort. This was a major blow to Lord Dunmore's hopes of defending Norfolk and of gaining eventual control of the colony of Virginia.[30]

Hours later the British returned to Norfolk with the wounded crying out for water, as the wagons bounced over the rough streets. The town was in a panic. When Dunmore learned of the defeat, he "raved like a madman" and it is said he threatened to hang the boy who brought him the bad news. The troops, with the Ethiopian Corps following, marched down to the wharves, and rowed out to the ships. The loyalists, who expected little mercy from the "shirtmen," packed up what property they could, loaded it aboard their own schooners, and sailed to the protection of the British warships. Entire families, including many who knew every luxury, gave parting glances toward their homes as they headed to live in the dark hold of a British warship, surrounded by hogsheads of tobacco and barrels of rum.[31]

After the loyalists in Norfolk and Princess Anne County learned of the British defeat, having backed the wrong side, they predictably fled to the countryside or boarded ships that were available for such a purpose. Only a few citizens remained in Norfolk, awaiting the arrival of Woodford's units. Many wondered why Woodford's militia had not more actively pursued the British into Norfolk. On December 10 the major reinforcements of 250 men from North Carolina finally arrived. They were a motley bunch of men with only 15 cartridge rounds per man. On the 12th, Colonel Howe arrived with another 340 men from North Carolina who were likewise poorly armed. On December 11, Woodford had issued a proclamation calling on the people of Princess Anne and Norfolk counties to come out and give aid to the patriot forces, in exchange for their protection. On December 14, Woodford's patriot army of 1275 men, with Woodford in the lead, entered Norfolk with no resistance. Those Norfolk citizens that remained in town sent Woodford and Howe a petition:

> The humble petition of the poor Inhabitants of the borough of Norfolk & Colony aforesaid humbly sheweth That your poor unfortunate petitioners have at all times wished for Liberty and have upholded the same as far as their ability lay…. Therefore your poor petitioners humbly craveth your protection & advice so that we may remain in safety as truc Sons of Liberty…."[32]

Most patriots were not at all convinced.

When the patriot troops entered Norfolk, many were upset. Colonel Scott said he felt Norfolk was "the most horrid place I ever beheld." Colonel Howe remarked that he had hoped there was some resistance so the populace could get what they deserved. Howe commented that "Had I not pass'd thro' Princess Anne & Norfolk counties I could not have believed that a colony so truly Respectable as this in every other Part, could have belonging to it, so contemptible a lot of wretches."

While the occupation of Norfolk went unopposed, some shots were fired, and three men were wounded. British Captain Squire was likewise so concerned that shots had been fired in the direction of the *Otter* on December 14 that he sent a midshipman to talk with Woodford and Howe to complain. They responded that they had given no such orders to fire on the British ship. There was now an uneasy and uncomfortable peace between the British, with their loyalist and black guests aboard ships off Norfolk, and patriot occupation army ashore, now shivering in the cold and snow that had fallen. Lord Dunmore commented that "It was a melancholy sight to see the numbers of Gentlemen of very large property with their Ladies and whole families obliged to betake themselves on board of Ships, at this Season of the year, hardly with the common necessary of Life, and great numbers of poor people without even these, who must have perished had I not been able to supply them with some flour, which I had purchased for His Majesty's service some time ago."[33] It was reported that conditions aboard the Dunmore's ships off Norfolk were poor. With the crowded circumstances aboard and some disease noted, corpses were often seen unceremoniously thrown overboard.[34]

The day after the arrival at Norfolk, the patriot military chain of command changed. Colonel Robert Howe of North Carolina was deemed the senior colonel based on examination of their commissions, and he, therefore, took over command of all forces from Colonel Woodford. Howe intended to take a tough position with Dunmore.

When his lordship tried to propose a prisoner exchange on a one-for-one swap, officer-for-officer and private-for-private, between the British and patriot men, Howe declared that he "could by no means submit to place the officers and soldiers of the army, who have been taken in battle, upon a footing with those officers of militia and the peasants that you have thought proper to deprive of their liberty." Howe responded with a proposal to swap the British warriors for loyalists of similar station. The negotiations dissolved. The British and the patriot sentries continued to watch each other.[35]

The British so-called fleet offshore continued to send small boats attempting to obtain supplies in and around Norfolk. Captain Squire had asked if it was the patriot intention to deny His Majesty's ships necessary supplies. Howe responded that he wished no contact between the ships and the port. A town meeting had even called to discuss the requests for supplies for the offshore "band," with a motion forthcoming to indeed allow these vessels to trade. But this motion did not pass.[36]

On December 17, Colonel Howe's men took some action against the British when the *Otter* and *Kingfisher* set sail toward the distillery where they expected to protect the recently seized brig *Snow* loaded with 4000 bushels of salt heading toward the fleet. A boatload of 15 sailors from the *Kingfisher* headed toward the *Snow* that had been somewhat slow to get underway. The patriot shore unit warned the sailors to turn back, or they would be fired on. The British returned to the ship. The militia then ordered the *Snow* back to the wharf. The next day Captain Squire sent a message to Howe indicating that the *Snow* was a prize of the king, and that it should be released. He also said that if the men in an upcoming retrieval boat were fired on, he would "most assuredly fire on the town." Howe then rejoined that he would "give orders to fire upon any boat that attempts to take her away."

On December 21 the man-of-war *Liverpool* under the command of Captain Henry Bellew arrived to join Dunmore's fleet, accompanied by a store ship loaded with arms, ammunition and 400 British marines. Lord Dunmore ordered the *Liverpool* to position off the central wharves at Norfolk, the *Kingfisher* to station off the southern end with the *Otter* located between them. The *Dunmore* anchored at the northern end. These four ships of war were now an even more visible show of force than they had been. What would happen next?

Captain Bellew, as the latest arrival and having not been directly associated with the other military exploits of Lord Dunmore, tried to change the course of probable conflict with the rebels. He asked Colonel Howe if he could be provisioned with supplies. Howe was unsure whether he should make the decision, so he deferred the decision to the Virginia Convention. The delegates had noted

Bellew's remarks that "the effusion of the Blood of the Innocent and Helpless" was most distant from his desires. The convention responded that they would need assurance that "he had come to Virginia on a friendly errand, he might depend on proper respect and attention; if, on the contrary, his design was to aid schemes and efforts inimical to the Colony, he must not blame the inhabitants of Virginia for totally declining to contribute towards their own destruction." No goods were supplied. Colonels Howe and Woodford, and all at the convention, now expected the bombardment of Norfolk could begin at any moment.[37]

With the British warships moored for action off Norfolk, a great exodus began. Wagons, carts and carriages were being loaded at the finest homes on Main, Church, and Talbot streets with all manner of household goods. As the owners watched, the black men and women went to and from bringing beds, chairs, tables, linen, dishes, silver and food to the waiting transports. The women and children took their positions up front with the driver in the wagons, with the slaves following on foot. These citizens, along with inventory of the shopkeepers and merchants, moved out of Norfolk. The tragic processions moved over the Princess Anne Road and on to Portsmouth, Suffolk, and other parts of lower Tidewater Virginia and even into North Carolina.[38]

Christmas passed and on December 30 Captain Bellew wrote the following to Colonel Howe:

> As I hold it incompatible with the Honor of my Commission to suffer Men in Arms against their Soveriegn and the Laws, to appear before His Majesty's Ships I desire you will cause your Centinals in the Town of Norfolk to avoid being seen, that Women and Children may not feel the effects of their Audacity, and it will not be imprudent if both were to leave the Town.
>
> I am, Sir, your most able Servt
> Henry Bellew

Colonel Howe replied late that same day with:

> Sir, I am too much an Officer to wish you to do anything incompatible with the Honor of your Commission, or to recede my self from any point which I conceive to be my duty. Under the force of reciprocal feelings consequences may ensue which each of us perhaps may wish to avoid.

Howe also indicated that the sentries would not be withdrawn, and he asked that the citizens have time to leave with their effects. It was now Sunday, New Year's Eve. What would happen to this city that had taken a century to build?[39]

On January 1, 1776, at 3:15 P.M., after a short rattle of drums onboard, the four British men-of-war opened fire on Norfolk with over 100 guns. Under the cover of this terrible cannonade that lasted the rest of the afternoon and evening, British marines came ashore in small boats at various locations and set fire to a number of houses at the waterfront. The patriot sentries fought off the landing parties, but not before enough of the wooden houses had been set fire to create a significant blaze at the waterfront. While the militia fought off the British, they made no moves to extinguish the fires. In fact, many of the men began to engage in widespread breaking and looting of rum shops and warehouses. Soon these men formed drunken groups and went from house to house breaking open doors, taking out household goods and torching some of the furnishings. The British cannonade, along with the fury of burning houses and shops, was a terrifying sight. The women and children still in the town rushed to seek cover and safety. Several were killed. The last remaining citizens now fled from the burning town to homes in the suburbs, or on to the roads to adjacent counties for shelter. Patriot troops gave some assistance by driving some of the women and children out of the danger. Woodford wrote, "How they will be removed further, it is not in our power to say."[40]

When the ships stopped firing on January 2, these out-of-control men continued their destructive work without any interference from the officers. By the third day Colonel Howe put an end to the militia actions by forbidding the burning of houses under threat of a severe penalty. By this point, over one-third of Norfolk was in ashes. In February, under the orders of the convention, the rest of Norfolk was ordered destroyed to deprive Lord Dunmore of potential cover. It was an incredible and sad sight. Norfolk was no more.

The circumstances of the destruction of Norfolk were a controversial issue for some time after that early 1776 period in Virginia. While there were conflicting testimonies on the events of those infamous three days, the most substantial evidence was established when a commission appointed by the Virginia government investigated the matter in 1777. The commission report revealed that Lord Dunmore's men burned only 19 houses on January 1, while the patriot militia ultimately destroyed 863 houses. The convention had authorized the destruction of an additional 416 that February.[41] The estimated total loss of the property at Norfolk was $1,300,000 (1775 funds).[42] The men who were present at Norfolk perceived these acts of destruction by the militia forces against the loyalist haven of Norfolk with general satisfaction. Colonel Howe felt the burning of Norfolk was beneficial to the public. He indicated that it would have continued to be a place that the British could seize at any time, supported by loyalist citizens that had no devotion to the American cause. The *Virginia Gazette* recorded, "They have destroyed one of the first towns in America, and the only one in Virginia, which carried on anything like a trade.... They have done their worst, and ... to no other purpose than to give the world specimens of British cruelty and American fortitude, unless it be to force us to lay aside that childish fondness for Britain, and that foolish, tame dependence on her."[43] The frustration and revenge that both the British and patriot colonial militiamen felt was now in evidence for all to see.

Woodford and Howe received orders from the Virginia Convention to make Dunmore's position untenable. Since arriving, the British fleet was being supplied from a distillery, several local mills and bake houses on the right bank of the Elizabeth River and from buildings and wells at Gosport. While Norfolk was still burning, a detachment was sent out at night to set fire to the distillery. Several days later the troops returned, gave notice to the residents, and destroyed the wells and remaining property. The British tried to protect the buildings, but their efforts were in vain. At Gosport another patriot unit burned the warehouses, pumps and a windmill. Small units patrolled along both sides of the river from Tanner's Creek to Craney Island driving off landing parties.[44]

The destruction of Norfolk was an incredible strategic mistake on Lord Dunmore's part. In taking his anger out on the city of Norfolk, he had eliminated the best loyalist port and community in the whole of the colonies. The personal assets and property of his colonial supporters in Virginia were now in ruins. The British had probably destroyed their best staging area for future operations against the Americans at the strategic center of the Thirteen Colonies. Colonel Howe had previously written the Virginia Convention of the importance of Norfolk, remarking that the British could "so conveniently barrack almost any number of troops, is well calculated for defense, situated between two colonies, so that the same troops could execute their purposes upon both, and from which their shipping could convey their men to any part of this colony."[45] Incredibly, Dunmore's actions had no real military potential for success from the very beginning, since cannonading the city with no army to follow up in taking possession was rather pointless. In London the Duke of Richmond declared in Parliament that the British officer's attack was a "barbaric rage" as they "reduced the loyal town of Norfolk to ashes."[46] His lordship had shown all that he was certainly no military strategist.

Two decades later, Rochefoucauld smiled when informed that patriots had burned the town, remarking, "You recall that the Jacobins of France said that the aristocrats burned their own chateaux.... Party heat gives rise to the greatest absurdities, men are the same everywhere." But English of established reputations blamed Dunmore for Norfolk's destruction.[47]

After the burning of Norfolk, the two opposing forces were essentially in the same relative positions they had been before. The British continued to send occasional landing parties to shore, as the militias fought them off. On January 21, the *Otter* and *Liverpool* opened fire to cover a shore party setting fire to a few of the remaining houses that had not already been destroyed. The houses were destroyed as the British and militia traded gunfire. The skirmish ended with a number of men killed or wounded on both sides. On February 6, 1776, the provincial army abandoned the ruins of Norfolk and headed to better locations for provisioning and quarters at Great Bridge, Kempsville and Suffolk. A few days later Lord Dunmore received the frigate *Roebuck*, which carried needed additional troops. At this point Dunmore seized the village of Portsmouth for his new base of operations, where he continued to raid area plantations and take American vessels as prizes throughout the Chesapeake Bay region for months.

A curious event occurred in February involving Richard Corbin, the president of the Council of Safety of Virginia. Dunmore sent Corbin a message asking him to act as a mediator between the colony and his lordship. Corbin declined to take him up on his proposal, but he did consult with the council on the issue. Corbin was given permission to visit Dunmore's ship for the purpose of inducing Dunmore to commission the president of the Virginia Convention as the acting governor. Dunmore predictably declined to grant the commission. Even with the burning of Norfolk and the numerous events of military conflict during the previous half-year, there was still some conservative sentiment on the part of many Virginians to save some form of the colonial constitution.[48]

When Major General Charles Lee of the Continental Army arrived in Williamsburg on March 29, 1776, to take command of all forces in Virginia, he took immediate steps to better organize the local troops and prepare to "evict" Lord Dunmore from Virginia. Detachments were maintained at Great Bridge, Kemp's Landing, Ferry Print, Tanner's Creek at Newton and other locations. West of Portsmouth at Tucker's Mill, Dunmore set up a camp under the cover of the British warships *Liverpool* and *Otter*. The British built an entrenchment with a ditch eight feet deep, extending a quarter of a mile in length. Several remaining regulars conducted military drills with the local loyalists and several hundred blacks.

Although the British and loyalists were relatively safe from attack, they were becoming increasingly uncomfortable. While they built a few wells for water, food was very scarce and fever was raging. To aid the British, loyalists rowed out to the fleet in darkness with bread, wheat and corn. On April 10, 1776, the Committee of Public Safety ordered "all the inhabitants of Norfolk and Princess Anne counties, at present residing between the enemy, and our posts at Great Bridge and Kemp's Landing, and in a direct line from Kemp's Landing to the ocean, be immediately removed to some interior parts of this colony." Ordering some 5000 folks to leave their homes and fields, and to live among strangers, was a difficult matter.

General Lee continued to tighten the lines around Dunmore at the Elizabeth River to cut off communications with the loyalists and the fleet. Patriots occupied Portsmouth to watch the British at Tucker's Mill. Lee had ordered the citizens to leave, and now the troops confiscated the goods of the leading loyalists, including Andrew Sprowle, Niel Jamieson, John Goodrich and Robert Spedding. The homes of these loyalists were torched. An attempt was made to set fire to merchant vessels off shore at Norfolk, but the warship *Dunmore* fought these troops off.

When General Lee felt the men were prepared sufficiently, as occurred on May 20, he moved to Norfolk and fought with Dunmore's ships with his shore-borne forces. A few days later, Lord Dunmore's fleet left the Norfolk area with some 100 vessels—brigantines, schooners, sloops—all loaded with troops, blacks and whites loyalists.[49] Dunmore's fleet sailed to Gwynn's Island off the Gloucester shore. Dunmore landed his "disease-stricken crews" and built some fortifications there. On June 1, Pendleton wrote Jefferson that "Dunmore with 400 half starved motley soldiers on Gwynn's Island, and 2000 of Our men on the Main are looking at each other...." The next Dixon and Hunter *Virginia Gazette* reported: "It is an undoubted fact that all the Tories who were in Lord Dunmore's service have left him, there not being half the fleet now at Gwynn's Island; where they have gone to is uncertain. This, it is imagined, was occasioned by a fever which has raged with great fury amongst them for some time past, and from the funeral processions that have been seen there, very probably has proved fatal to some persons of distinction."

On June 10 Captain Hammond wrote Commodore Sir Peter Parker:

> The Island is certainly much too large for us to defend in our present weak situation, if the enemy should make any Serious attack upon us, but if we had a body of 200 Troops more, I do not think it would be in the power of the Rebels to disposess us, and I confess now that we are here, I am very desirous of keeping it; As I don't know a better place in Virginia for the head Quarters of a fleet and an army.... If you can send us any small Guns, Cohorns or Howitzers, they will be of the utmost use to us.

Dunmore sent the *Fowey* to Annapolis to pick up Maryland's governor, Robert Eden, who was also under great pressure by this time. Eden had been a rather respected leader in Maryland, but the Maryland patriot convention required that he either "execute the instructions of administration" or he must "leave this province, and that he is at full liberty to depart peaceably with his effects." The *Fowey*, under Captain Montagu, was sent with orders to "use utmost expedition on this Service, & remain no longer at Annapolis than is absolutely necessary to receive the Governor and his people on board." The *Fowey* and Eden returned to Gwynn's Island on June 29.[50] Now two failed British royal governors were present on Gwynn's Island.

Dunmore had left his ships within easy cannon range of the mainland, and on July 9 at 8 A.M., militiamen under the command of Brigadier General Andrew Lewis opened fire on the island fortifications and the ships offshore. The first shot fired by Lewis himself passed through the warship *Dunmore*. A nine-pounder fired next and entered the ship at her quarters, which smashed the china, splintered a large timber, and wounded Lord Dunmore himself. His lordship yelled, "Good God, that ever I should come to this."[51] Purdie's *Virginia Gazette* reported "a furious attack upon the enemy's shipping, camp and fortifications, from two batteries, one of five 6 and 9 pounders, the other three tenders, one mounting two 18 pounders.... In the haven were three tenders, one a sloop [the *Lady Charlotte*] mounting six carriage guns, a schooner of two carriage guns, six swivels, and a cohorn, and a pilot boat, badly armed; who had orders from capt. [Andrew Snape] Hammond, of the Roebuck, to prevent our boats passing over to the island, and to annoy the rebels by every means in their power." The cannonade was so intense that Dunmore's force quickly loaded and the ships dropped anchor. When General Lewis landed on the island the next day, he found that the British had departed and that he was "struck with horrour at the number of dead bodies, in a state of putrefaction, strewed all the way from their battery to Cherry Point, about two miles in length, without a shovelfull of earth upon them..."[52]

Dunmore's fleet then headed to St. George's Island off Maryland, arriving on July 14. But the local militia again thwarted him. He continued to plunder plantations along the Potomac and tried another time to land at St. George's Island with no success. Being totally frustrated in finding a new base of operations in the Chesapeake Basin, on August 7, 1776, Lord Dunmore and his fleet sailed out of the Virginia Capes and Virginia history.[53] Purdie's *Virginia Gazette* reported on Dunmore's departure that he "took leave of the Capes of Virginia, where he has, for more than a twelvemonth past, perpetuated crimes that would even have disgraced the noted pirate BLACK BEARD." His embarked followers sailed for Florida and the West Indies, and Lord Dunmore headed for refuge in New York, landing on August 15 with 25 sails. Later in 1776 Dunmore left for England.[54] Dunmore remained an obscure member of the House of Lords until 1790 when he returned to public office as the governor of the Bahamas.[55]

Those Norfolk citizens who stayed in Virginia suffered. One such woman wrote,

> I shall not attempt to describe what we have suffered within these last three years. [We all] live together on dear deceased Mr. Aitchinson's plantation. It is a small house for two families that have been used to be better accommodated, but we are very thankful for such an asylum. Many of the poor inhabitants of Norfolk are greatly distressed for any house at all. We spin our own clothes, milk, sew, raise poultry.... Everything has got to such prices here that we buy nothing that we can do without. Our girls are all dressed in their own spinning, even little Molly.... I am sorry our present circumstances prevents them from improving themselves by reading, writing, keeping polite society, etc.

After the war, those Norfolk citizens who could prove they were not loyalists received some compensation for their loss of their homes.

On the ruins of Norfolk, the new town of Norfolk slowly rebuilt, initially by loyalists who returned. In November 1779, Miss Jenny Stewart visited "that once agreeable place" and described Norfolk as having "a great many small huts built up in it." Commercial shipping returned to the region almost immediately, despite the activities of the British frigates and loyalist privateers. French ships called on the wharves at Portsmouth, Gosport, Suffolk and Norfolk, unloading French goods, and taking on tobacco, tar, pitch, turpentine and pork. Virginia ships sailed to Nantes, France, with tobacco, trading for necessary supplies for the citizens of Virginia. No town in America suffered more than Norfolk — its buildings burned, citizens scattered, slave population carried off, and trade ruined, her vessels captured or destroyed.[56]

6

MOORE'S CREEK BRIDGE

In 1745, a tall, slender, redheaded 24 year old, Charles Edward Stuart, landed in Scotland with a few supporters in hopes of raising an army to invade England. While he was successful at raising an army of Scottish Highlanders, they were defeated at Culloden Moor in the rain and hail by the "Bloody Duke" of Cumberland. The Bonnie Prince Charles now became a fugitive as he fled to the Hebrides, attempting to avoid the British who were looking to capture him.

With a bounty on his head of £30,000, Prince Charles continued to evade as he came to the Isle of Skye, where Flora MacDonald lived. This young girl on June 21 agreed to help Prince Charles hide, using the disguise of dressing him up as a girl. The prince was able to escape and eventually left Scotland by ship for France and his home for life in exile. Sadly, Flora was captured, taken to London and kept for a time as a prisoner in the Tower of London. After her release, Flora returned to Skye and married her distant cousin Allan.[1]

After the defeat, the British Parliament abolished the clans, with their proud tartan traditions of kilts and bagpipes. Feudal control was gone in Scotland. The economic situation changed for the worse as rents doubled and food became scarce. Many in Scotland began to consider the opportunities that existed in America where, as the *Edinburgh Advertiser* declared, men were "more valued in proportion to their abilities than they are in Scotland."

After Allan lost 300 horses and cattle to a murrain, Allan and Flora MacDonald, with their sons Alexander and James, immigrated to the colonies in the ship *Baliol* from Campbeltown, Kintyre. They landed at Wilmington, North Carolina, in the fall of 1774 with 14 indentured servants and valued baggage.[2] The MacDonalds,

in company with her daughter's family, the McLeods, headed up the Cape Fear River through Cross Creek to settle on a 475-acre farm. They named the farm, which was located 25 miles from town at Cheek's Creek in Montgomery County, Killiegrey. The McLeods settled at Glendale on Wad's Creek. As they began to establish themselves in this new land, they were confronted with the serious issue of whether to choose between supporting the British Crown or the rebel patriots.[3]

In a letter dated June 30, 1775, the royal governor of North Carolina, Josiah Martin, wrote the Earl of Dartmouth, the secretary of state for the colonies, offering his services in raising a battalion of 1000 Scottish Highlanders and requesting that his previous rank of lieutenant colonel be restored.[4] Soon Alexander McLeod, Allan MacDonald's son-in-law, approached Allan with the news that he had been made the liaison officer between the governor, who was living on the *Cruizer* in the Cape Fear River, and the Highlanders of the Upcountry. The governor would make Allan, who was on British Army half-pay and the husband of the famous Flora MacDonald, an offer of a commission as his recruiting officer. Flora and Allan made their decision to support the loyalists. How could a rag-tag militia of the Lower Cape Fear defeat the orderly British establishment that had crushed the Scots at Culloden Moor? For them it was an easy decision.

On July 5, 1775, McLeod and MacDonald traveled to see Governor Martin at Brunswick. Cornelius Harnett, head of the Committee of Safety, got wind of the trip and attempted to capture the Scots, with no success. The committee, in failure, wrote to Allan asking whether his intention was "to raise troops to support the arbitrary measures of the Ministry against the Americans in this

Colony." But on this trip Allan MacDonald and Alexander McLeod accepted their rank as captains in the governor's new Royal Highland Emigrant Regiment.

Governor Martin was excited about the prospects of retaking control of the colony with his Highlanders. In August he wrote to Dartmouth, "The people are in general well affected and much attached to me." He estimated that at least two-thirds of the 30,000 fighting men in the region would stand behind the king. Based on these estimates, General William Howe in Boston sent a seasoned officer, Major Donald MacDonald, to North Carolina to take charge of military operations in the colony. Also accompanying MacDonald was Captain Donald McLeod. The king was so impressed with Martin's initiative that he decided to send seven regiments and two batteries under Lord Cornwallis. Major General Henry Clinton would sail down from New York with 2000 redcoats. Cornwallis and Clinton would meet at the lower Cape Fear with a combined fleet of 53 ships to join with the local forces. The campaign would take control of the Cape Fear valley all the way up to the mountains, separating the Northern colonies from the Southern colonies. What a grand plan![5]

The arrival of Major Donald MacDonald and his adjutant, Captain Donald McLeod, in New Bern raised the suspicions of the Committee of Safety there. Soon after they arrived, the committee called them in to determine why they had come to North Carolina. They explained that they had come only to see friends and relatives, and not for any purpose associated with the British Army. They were then released. Both these men had much in common with the Highlanders of North Carolina, and were ideal choices to lead the recruiting effort.[6] They both were Scottish and could speak Gaelic. Both had also received minor wounds at the Battle of Bunker Hill. Donald MacDonald was a veteran of the Culloden Moor battle of 1745 and a cousin to Allan MacDonald.[7]

At this point, the governor's mission was to ensure that he could raise the large forces that he had been given to believe he could. He instructed a loyalist lawyer, Alexander McLean, to travel to the interior of North Carolina to survey the prospects among the Highlanders, Regulators and others sympathetic with the British cause. In December 1775 he returned with news that some 5000 Regulators were expected to support the governor's call for arms.[8] With this news of support, Governor Martin issued 26 commissions to these loyalists. The commissions gave the recipients the power to appoint a captain, a lieutenant, and an ensign for every 50 men, and required that they must "concert a place of general rendezvous for your forces, thence to march in a body, by such route as you shall judge proper, to Brunswick" such that they would arrive no later than February 15, 1776.[9]

The British government also promised all Highlanders who supported the effort 200 acres of land, a remission of arrears in quitrents, and 20 years of tax exemption.[10] Christmas on the Cape Fear aboard the *Cruizer* was indeed a happier time of great expectation for the governor. Having received the governor's commissions, Alexander McLean headed to Cross Creek to hand out the commissions and meet with Highlander leaders William Campbell, Neil McArthur and Captain Donald McLeod. At that meeting it was decided that circular letters would be written to urge all the king's supporters to gather on February 5, 1776 "at a friends House and determine on our future Proceedings."

On the day of the scheduled meeting all the Highland Scot commissioners of Cumberland and Anson were present, but only four Regulator officers appeared. The Highlanders wanted to gather their forces only when the British troops arrived off North Carolina, and they expected this event to occur around March 1. The attending four Regulators from the Upcountry were less conservative and "insisted upon taking up Arms immediately." The Scots yielded and agreed to assemble their men after they had been assured that the Regulators could get their men gathered. The Scots also indicated that they could only raise "above Six or Seven Hundred Men." The Regulator officers bragged that they could raise 5000 men, as they already had 500 formed at present under James Hunter and the Field brothers. Being somewhat skeptical of the boasts, Captain Donald McLeod, "being an Experienced Officer, should go with the Gentlemen Loyalists then present, and put and keep them in the best order possibly he could," as he determined if a real unit existed. It was also agreed that McLeod would be followed in three days by William Campbell, Captain Allen Stewart, Captain Nicol and Alexander McLean to assist Captain McLeod in conducting these men to Cross Creek at the appointed rendezvous.

On February 8, the Regulators and McLeod set out from Cross Creek. After traveling 12 miles, Captain McLeod was informed that the unit of 500 men had dispersed. He was left to find his own way back to Cross Creek, being unable to find a guide. Despite the disappointing news, Campbell and Alexander McLean "pursued their journey 40 Miles further" and on the next day sent a message to Hunter and Fields "expressing their surprise at their behavior and entreating them in the most Anxious manner for sake of their Honour & the Kings cause not to fail in calling their Men together and that they only wanted their Answer to join them." The messenger who had traveled to Guilford to deliver it found out from neighbors that "they were Skulking & hiding themselves through Swamps & such concealed places." After hearing this news Campbell and McLean returned to Cross Creek on February 10.[11]

While the precise reason for the desertion of many of the ex–Regulator loyalists is not known, it was true that the Regulators after the Battle of Alamance had not seen much in the way of the reforms promised in North Carolina. There is also evidence that the Regulators were not at all happy having to deal with these newly immigrated Highlander Scots who could barely speak English, and strode about with their tartans and loud bagpipes.[12] The king's cause was not that important to most of the ex–Regulators for they had suffered under the British regime for years.

On February 10, at Cross Hill, upriver from Cross Creek, gathered the now elevated Brigadier General Donald MacDonald, and other officers including Captain Alexander McLeod, Captain Allan MacDonald, Alexander McLean, William Campbell, Captain John Martin, the surveyor of Anson County and a wealthy planter, Colonel James Cotton, and some 500 Highlanders. Meeting at the home of Dr. Alexander Morrison, they determined "as so many Men were embodied at Crosshill, to keep them together & endeavour as formidable a Body as possible." William Campbell was sent ahead to Cross Creek "to influence the friends of Government to stand firm." Colonel Thomas Rutherford assured him that "he would stand by him & others of his Loyal friends to the last." On February 12, Brigadier General MacDonald, Captain Allan MacDonald, Captain Alexander McLeod and Colonel Cotton's men marched to Cross Creek with the sound of bagpipes. Captain Donald McLeod and McLean were sent Upcountry again to gain support. When they had gone some 35 miles, they met Dr. Pyle with 40 men, where they dispatched express messages to the loyalist friends Upcountry. Now this group of an additional 130 loyalists were heading for Cross Creek.[13]

On February 15, a reported 3500 Highlander and Regulator men assembled at Cross Creek. As each day passed, the number of assembled men was reduced by many desertions. Some of the loyalists had been told that they would be met at Cross Creek by as many as a thousand regular British troops who were to escort them to Brunswick. Instead, they found that they were to be sent to Nova Scotia for enlistment in the British Army. They would be required to fight their way to Brunswick, against their neighbors and friends in the Provincial force. So, on February 18, when the loyalist forces marched out of Cross Creek, they had only 1300 Highlanders and 300 Regulator loyalists in company.

While the loyalist forces were being recruited and assembled, the president of the North Carolina Provincial Congress and commander-in-chief, Cornelius Harnett, and his forces were scrambling to counter the governor's loyalists' schemes. In Wilmington on February 9, Harnett had received word of the loyalist gatherings in the area of Cross Creek. The North Carolina patriot militias and Continentals had been training in one form or another for a year. In October of 1775, the Continental Congress had assigned a quota of 1000 men for the colony of North Carolina. The Provincial Congress then elected James Moore as the colonel of the First Continental Regiment of North Carolina, by one vote over John Ashe.

In addition to this unit were the various militia units under the committees of safety. Wilmington's militia battalion was under Colonel Alexander Lillington. The New Bern Committee of Safety elected Colonel Richard Caswell for their militia.[14] Colonel Robert Howe of North Carolina and his forces were then in Tidewater Virginia supporting the Norfolk campaign. Colonel John Ashe, the "out-voted" leader of the First Continentals, now commanded 100 Partisan Rangers.[15] The patriot units of North Carolina were formed and ready for action. The recruiting efforts and preparation of Moore, Ashe, Lillington, Howe and Caswell would now pay off for the patriotic cause.

On February 15, Colonel Moore's 650 First North Carolina Continentals marched out of Wilmington and camped that night on the banks of the Rockfish Creek, only seven miles from the encampment of Brigadier General Donald MacDonald's Highlander Emigrant Regiment and attending loyalist forces. Moore's primary mission was to prevent the loyalist forces from reaching Brunswick, and his secondary mission was to take Cross Creek. Learning of Moore's presence, MacDonald sent a letter to Moore under flag of truce ordering him to lay down his arms or "suffer the fate of an enemy of the Crown." He had also included a copy of Governor Martin's proclamation. Moore answered with a requirement that they should "Take oath to support the Continental Congress or be treated as enemies of the constitutional liberties of America." The General studied his maps and considered his next move. Moore's forces were in his way, so he decided to return to Cross Creek where boats were available to cross the Cape Fear. This path would take his men through marshes and across rivers running into the Cape Fear River. With this approach, they could use a road to Wilmington that crossed the South River by bridge, the Black River by ferry and then across the Widow Moore's Creek Bridge, which would place them only 18 miles from Wilmington. This would be his plan to reach Governor Martin.

During these tense days waiting for news of the activities in the Upper Cape Fear, Cornelius Harnett and Governor Martin sent daily couriers trading messages between Wilmington and the British *Cruizer*. Harnett had complained about the British use of Fort Johnston: "built by the People at a great expense for the Protection of their

Trade and made use of for a purpose the very reverse … and to crown all, you Sir, have brought up the *Cruizer* to cover the landing of an army composed of highland banditti; none of whom you will ever see unless as fugitives imploring protection." Martin replied that he did not like being addressed by "a little arbitrary Junto under the Traitous Guise of a combination unknown to the laws of this Country: the Revilings of Rebellion, and the gasconadings of Rebels are below the contempt of the Loyal and faithful People [Scots] whom I have justly stiled Friends of Government." The governor even made threats that if he was not supplied food from the town of Wilmington he would attack. Indeed he did move the *Cruizer* off Wilmington to apply more coercion.

February 20 saw General MacDonald head his forces back to Cross Creek, ferry his troops to the east bank of the Cape Fear, and sink his own boats to prevent Moore's men from using them. At this time Colonel Caswell was coming from New Bern with 800 militia. From Wilmington to Rockfish Creek had come 100 independent Partisan Rangers under Colonel John Ashe and Colonel Alexander Lillington's force of 150 minutemen. From the west, with patriot militia from Orange and Guilford counties, came colonels James Thackston and Alexander Martin. Colonel Moore estimated that the loyalist forces could move ten miles per day, and that the best place for all the three columns to converge was Corbett's Ferry on the Black River. He ordered Thackston's and Martin's forces to occupy Cross Creek, while Caswell, Ashe and Lillington were to head for Corbett's Ferry to support Caswell's forces. Moore and his Continentals would drop back 35 miles to Elizabethtown, where he planned to cross the Cape Fear and attack Brigadier MacDonald from the rear. Moore was kept at Elizabethtown an extra day, February 25, waiting for supplies.[16]

On February 23, Brigadier MacDonald's forces marched down the east bank road following high ground between the South and Black rivers. Captain Donald McLeod's cavalry force of 100 Highland Scots were ahead of the main force to reconnoiter the countryside. Next McLeod sent word to MacDonald that Caswell's forces were only four miles ahead of him at Corbett's Ferry. With Caswell's forces ahead, MacDonald assumed he had no other recourse but to fight. A volunteer force of 100 men under Captain John Campbell, armed with their favorite weapons of the Highland Scots — broadswords (called claymores) — were placed in the center of the formation. With these 35-inch, single-bladed swords with their basket hilt and fishtail grip in the hands of these Scots, urged on by the music of their bagpipes, the patriot men would be terrified. Just before the battle was expected, MacDonald learned from McLeod's cavalry that a black man had pointed out to them that there was a sunken flatboat which could be raised and used to cross over the Black River five miles above Corbett's Landing. They could then pick up the road to Moore's Creek Bridge without engaging Caswell's men.[17]

The presence of Caswell's forces at Corbett's Ferry was also confirmed by a wagon train captured by Brigadier MacDonald himself with a mounted detail. The train contained 21 bullocks and two wagon loads of meal bound for Caswell's camp. The drivers confirmed the patriot entrenchment on the west side of the Black River. MacDonald sent a few men and two officers, McLean and Frazier, to create a diversion near Caswell's camp with drum, pipes and musket fire to make them think the loyalists were still there.[18] McLeod's cavalry went across the Black River first to scout ahead, with the remaining rear echelon forces crossing shortly after daybreak on February 26.

Colonel Caswell was completely surprised to find out that MacDonald's forces had escaped upriver. From the Black River to Moore's Creek Bridge was high ground that eventually narrowed with marshes on both sides. When Moore at Elizabethtown was informed of the situation at Corbett's Ferry, he ordered Lillington and Ashe to Moore's Creek Bridge, and asked Caswell to reinforce them as soon as possible. The patriot troops of Caswell, Lillington and Ashe arrived at Widow Moore's Creek Bridge on the afternoon of Monday, February 26, ahead of the loyalists who now approached from the northwest. Moore's troops were marching as fast as they could in an attempt to support the patriot forces against MacDonald. They would not arrive in time.

Lillington, Ashe and Caswell were well positioned for a defensive operation. Moore's Creek was a tributary of the Black River that twists through a dense swamp. At Moore's Creek Bridge, the dark stream, home of many Venus flytrap plants, was five feet deep and 50 feet wide. The creek had flowed through one of the early Moore plantations on this coastal plain at a slow two miles per hour. Arriving first, Ashe and Lillington built entrenchments on the east side of the bridge. Caswell initially had his men begin to entrench the west side, but then decided that the east position was better. About half of the wooden planks of the bridge were removed and used as a superstructure for the embankments. Lillington's forces had brought along their two light artillery pieces which they now mounted and aimed toward the bridge. The bridge stringers, where the planks had been removed, had been smeared with soap and bear's grease. The patriot troops were ready and conflict was imminent.[19]

Always trying to avoid a frontal assault, Brigadier MacDonald sent his secretary, James Hepburn, under a flag of truce, to the patriot camp before nightfall on February 26 demanding that Caswell's men surrender. Actu-

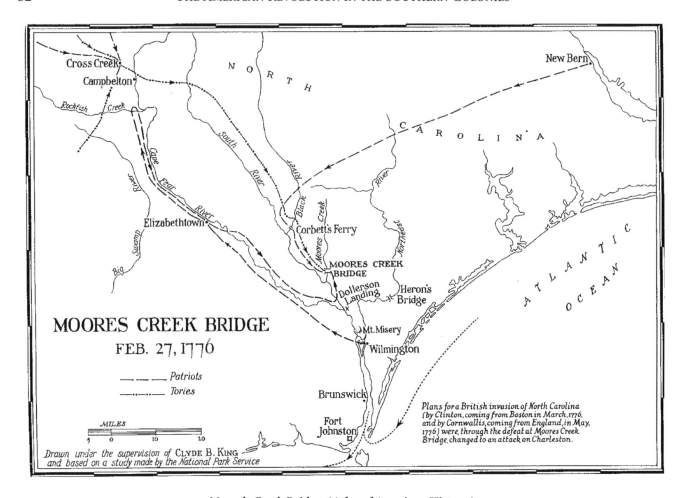

MOORES CREEK BRIDGE
FEB. 27, 1776

——— · —— · Patriots
——— ·· —— ·· Tories

MILES
5   0   10   20

Drawn under the supervision of CLYDE B. KING
and based on a study made by the National Park Service

Plans for a British invasion of North Carolina
(by Clinton, coming from Boston in March, 1776,
and by Cornwallis, coming from England, in May,
1776) were, through the defeat at Moores Creek
Bridge, changed to an attack on Charleston.

Moore's Creek Bridge. (*Atlas of American History.*)

ally, Hepburn had been sent to survey the defense of Caswell's forces. Hepburn made an error and reported to MacDonald that patriots had taken up places on the west side of the bridge, which would have meant the patriots would have to fight with Moore's Creek at their back.

Another major circumstance took place that would hurt the cause of the loyalists. Brigadier MacDonald had become ill and he was now in bed at a farmhouse. A council of officers was called to consider the next move. The older officers who had fought at Bunker Hill wanted to wait until daybreak to make sure there were no entrenchments of the east side of the bridge. The younger men wanted an immediate attack. Young officer Captain Donald McLeod offered to lead the advance guard to the bridge, with the same offer coming from Captain John Campbell. Against their better judgment, the older officers gave in. McLeod and Campbell would lead the attack the next morning with 80 handpicked men in long socks and kilts, armed with claymores and dirks, under cover of bagpipes. At 1 A.M. on Tuesday, February 27, the loyalist force of 1600 men broke camp and plodded six miles through the unfamiliar swamps for two hours to the tune of "King George and Broadswords" until arriving at

Moore's Creek Bridge. With 80 men out front in kilts, they marched through the unfamiliar swamps. Incredibly, only 500 of the 1600 loyalists had firearms.[20]

When the loyalists arrived before daybreak, they came to point on the west bank, facing an open area on the edge of the woods. The road to Wilmington and the bridge were just ahead. They immediately formed a battle line. McLeod and Campbell in the half light saw that many of the bridge planks had been removed, but to the signal of three cheers, drums and the bagpipes McLean and 40 men advanced to the bridgehead. In this dawn light a Provincial sentry called out a challenge. McLean answered in Gaelic, but there was no reply. Colonels McLeod and Campbell, with 80 broadswordsmen, reached the bridgehead and began to cross. Some of the men fell off the greased stringers, but most reached the other side.

Meanwhile, Caswell and Lillington steadied their men. When the Highlanders had advanced to within 30 paces of Lillington's breastworks, the entire patriot group fired in a hail of musketfire and artillery into the center of the formation. A patriot newspaper later reported that "they were received with a very heavy fire, which did great execution." McLeod and Campbell fell mortally wounded. McLeod had 20 bullets in him. The Scots swung their claymores in a futile search for someone to kill. The loyalists immediately retreated. Many fell and some even drowned in the creek. The remaining body of Scots and Regulators were still firing from the west bank at the patriots with no effect. As the loyalists retreated back toward their camp through the swamps in defeat, the patriot forces did not pursue them. It was not until Colonel Moore and his units arrived several hours after the battle that a pursuit was organized.[21]

The battle had lasted only three minutes. Colonel Donald McLeod, Captain John Campbell and 48 other loyalist men died in the smoke and action. The only Provincial militiaman to die was John Grady of Duplin. He was the first North Carolinian patriot to be killed in the American Revolution. The patriot forces now in pursuit captured the entire loyalist camp without opposition. Brigadier MacDonald was captured in his bed. The captured loot included 350 guns, 1500 muskets, 150 swords and dirks, 13 wagons and £15,000 in Spanish gold. For the next two weeks Moore's men rounded up most of the loyalist army that had opposed them at Moore's Creek Bridge.

At the junction of the Little River and the Cape Fear rivers, 800 privates and subalterns were paroled after taking an oath never again to take up arms against the patriot cause. Among the captives not released and being held in jail at Halifax were Captain James Hunter, a Regulator who had fought against Tryon at Alamance, Reverend George Micklejohn, who had once advised Tryon to hang 20 Regulators, Allan MacDonald and his two sons, Brigadier MacDonald, Dr. Alexander Morrison and his son, Captain James Muse, William Garner, John Pile, David Jackson and William Catlett. Alexander McLeod and Alexander McLean escaped after the battle and made their way to the British. On the prisoners' trip from Halifax to Philadelphia, Muse, Garner, Pyle, Jackson and Catlett managed to escape and return home. James Muse continued for some time to be a troublemaker for the Wilmington Council of Safety. Once he was rounded up and asked to take an oath of allegiance to the new state, but he refused.[22]

News of the Battle of Moore's Creek Bridge reached the Lower Cape Fear that same day. McLean and McLeod, traveling the entire night, reached the governor aboard the *Cruizer* on February 28. McLean told Governor Martin of the battle and tried to put a positive spin on the events by saying that the North Carolina people "would assemble upon seeing a proper military force." Martin reported to London that "the little check the loyalists have received will not have any extensive consequences. All is reversible by a body of troops penetrating into the country." The Ministry at London seemed to accept the glossing over of the defeat at Moore's Creek.[23] The British press also downplayed the significance of the battle. In London, *The Gentleman's Magazine* said "they only reduced a body of their own, supported by not one company of regular troops." The *Annual Register* gave a more favorable presentation indicating that the Whigs "had encountered Europeans and had defeated them with an inferior force."[24]

The success at Moore's Creek Bridge had a profound effect on the morale and confidence of the patriots of North Carolina. The news reached all along the Atlantic coast. One North Carolinian wrote to a Northern friend saying, "You never knew the like in your life for pure patriotism." In the *Remembrancer* another reported, "Since I was born I never heard so universal an ardor for fighting prevailing, and so perfect a union among all degrees of men."[25] *The New York Packet*, a patriot newspaper, declared that "this, we think, will effectively put a stop to Toryism in North Carolina."[26]

In considering the tactical military action at Moore's Creek Bridge, it was obvious that Brigadier MacDonald's forces had no real chance to succeed. Their commander was unfamiliar with the terrain, unlike Colonel Moore's forces, had less than one-third of his men with firearms, possessed no artillery, lacked the element of surprise in their attack, and did not have control of the battlefield. The patriot forces of Colonel Moore knew where MacDonald was going and could, therefore, select when and where they wanted to fight. The loyalists were doomed.

The sentiments of the patriots after Moore's Creek were more pronounced than ever against the loyalist faction. William Kenan of Wilmington wrote that the "real distress and usual complaint of the commonalty is artfully heightened and invigorated by the cursed Scottish race." Loyalists were required to take an oath of allegiance and if they refused, they were to give a bond and security to depart the state within 60 days. Most Scots refused to take the oath "almost to a man." Many Scottish families were robbed and their homes pillaged by their neighbors. There were reports of men going "Tory hunting" in the inland counties.

The desire to flee from these injustices was nearly universal among the Scots and other loyalist groups. Those who did stay in North Carolina lived in a continual state of terror for their lives and property. Allan MacDonald and his family were one of those Scottish families who suffered heavily. Allan and his son were transported as prisoners to Philadelphia in late April 1776, after having spent over two months in jail at Halifax, North Carolina. Allan was paroled at Reading, Pennsylvania, and in August, 1777, was permitted to travel to New York "to negotiate an exchange for himself and his son, a lieutenant in the same service." That fall, Allan joined the British Royal Highland Emigrants in Halifax, Nova Scotia.

His wife Flora had also endured a rough time in America. She was forced from her home on Cheek's Creek in Montgomery County and lost all her possessions except "sundry articles" she had been able to hide. Because of her "seditious conduct," she was brought before the Council of Safety for the state where she exhibited "Spirited behavior" before the body. Captain Alexander MacDonald wrote Allan that he did not "doubt but She and Other Gentlewomen there will be solely oppressed by the Savage Cruelty of those Wretches who at present has the Upper hand of them Tho' they may Sorely repent it before this War is at an End." Allan had referred of this wife's condition in a petition to Congress in July of 1777, describing her as being "in North Carolina 700 Miles from me in a sickly tender State of health, with a younger Son, a Daughter, & four Grand Children."

Flora had lived with a Kenneth Black in Moore County after she was evicted. She lived there until the spring of 1778 when she and the other wives were allowed to leave the country. She and her children left Wilmington to join her husband Allan in New York. From there they sailed to Halifax, Nova Scotia. In October of 1779, Flora MacDonald departed Halifax aboard the *Lord Dunmore* and arrived in the Thames River in London in December.[27] Flora returned to her original home at Skye at age 56 to live out her life.[28] Thus passed, in full circle, the life of the renowned Flora MacDonald and family through the history of North Carolina.

On the backs of the Moore's Creek Bridge success, Cornelius Harnett called for the meeting of the Fourth Provincial Congress of North Carolina for April 4, 1776, at Halifax. The village of Halifax, located near the Virginia border, was selected over New Bern and Wilmington as the site of the Provincial Congress to avoid being vulnerable to the British fleet now gathering in the Cape Fear. It was also a location suitable to both coastal and inland delegates. While there was still some sentiment to not break the remaining ties with Britain in the hopes of future restoration of peace, the efforts were hard to reconcile with the desire for independence. The presiding officer, Samuel Johnston, showed his feelings with his remarks, "All our people here are up for independence." Colonel Robert Howe had the same emotions when he declared that "Independence seems to be the word. I know not one of the dissenting voice."

April 8 saw Harnett appointed to head a committee of seven "to take into consideration the usurpations and violences attempted by the King and Parliament of Great Britain against America, and the further measures to be taken for frustrating the same, and for the better defence of this Province." On April 12, the committee's report was unanimously adopted by the 83 delegates then present, from the 148 elected from the 34 counties and eight bor-

ough towns. The last paragraph of this document, know as the Halifax Resolves, read:

> Resolved, That the delegates for this Colony in the Continental Congress be impowered to concur with the delegates of the other Colonies in declaring Independence, and forming foreign alliances, reserving to this Colony the sole and exclusive right of forming a Constitution and laws for this Colony, and of appointing delegates from time to time (under the direction of a general representation thereof), to meet the delegates of the other Colonies for such purposes as shall hereafter be pointed out.

North Carolina was the first American colony to officially declare independence, and it was also the first to recommend to the Continental Congress that independence should be declared by all the colonies.

The day after the Halifax Resolves were adopted, the Provincial Congress of North Carolina formed a committee to look into drafting a temporary civil constitution. But by April 30, the Congress had decided not to adopt a state constitution at this time, but "to form a temporary form of government until the end of the next congress." The Council of Safety was to have "full power and authority to do and execute all acts and things necessary for the defence and protection of the people of this colony." Since Cornelius Harnett was the president of the Council of Safety, he was essentially acting as the first governor of North Carolina. A copy of the Halifax Resolves was sent to Joseph Hewes in the Continental Congress. The reaction was favorable to all. Elbridge Gerry of Massachusetts called it a "noble and decisive measure."[29] Sam Adams wrote in Philadelphia: "The convention of North Carolina has revoked certain instructions which tied the hands of their delegates here. Virginia will follow the lead … the hostilities committed in North Carolina have kindled the resentment of our Southern brethen, who once thought their Eastern friends hot-headed and rash."

On May 15, the Virginia Congress instructed its delegates to the Continental Congress to "move for independence," and on June 7, Richard Henry Lee declared in Philadelphia "that these United Colonies are and of right ought to be free and independent States…." After much consideration and discussion, the Continental Congress adopted the resolution on July 2, and on July 4, 1776, the final draft of the Declaration of Independence, written by Thomas Jefferson, was passed. News of the American Declaration of Independence reached the North Carolina Council of Safety still meeting in Halifax on July 22. Cornelius Harnett was carried on shoulders through a happy crowd.[30] The delegates immediately adopted a resolution that the "good people" of the colonies "were absolved from all Allegiance to the British Crown." The Council of

Safety ordered that an election be held on October 15 at Halifax to choose delegates to the Fifth Provincial Congress. The delegates would be required "not only to make Laws for the Good Government of, but also to form a Constitution for this State...."[31] It was a heady time in North Carolina, as elsewhere in the new "United States of America."

Back on January 20, 1776, Major General Henry Clinton, second in command to Major General William Howe, had sailed from Boston with two companies of light infantry. While General Howe had resisted giving up any of his troops, he was overruled by London. The good part of the Cape Fear Plan was that he could get rid of Clinton, since he could not stand the "thin-skinned and touchy" man.[32] On February 13, 1776, 2500 troops from seven regiments under Major General Lord Charles Cornwallis were loaded aboard 30 transports and set sail from Cork, escorted by 11 warships under Admiral Sir Peter Parker.[33] They were supposed to have sailed in December, but they were delayed by a series of almost humorous situations. "The transports had drawn too much water for effective loading, and their masters had crammed them so full of supplies to sell on their own in America that the cavalry horses could not be reached at feeding time," wrote Cornwallis. On the day planned for departure, December 1, 1775, the circumstances revealed, "no detailed instructions issued to the commanders, the naval convoy force not ready, the transports not finally fitted, the ordance stores still to load, and the composition of the force not finally decided."[34]

News of Sir Peter Parker's fleet movement and intentions reached General Washington even before his fleet had reached the Southern coast. A letter from the secretary of war, dated Whitehall, December 23, 1775, had been intercepted. The letter indicated that a fleet of frigates and small ships with seven regiments aboard were to proceed to the Southern colonies; first to North Carolina, and then to either Virginia or South Carolina depending on circumstances.

The first day on the voyage saw nine ships vanish, being blown back to England. Three weeks later only 14 ships remained in the task force, six of them transports. Cornwallis complained of the harsh voyage, with "almost always contrary" wind and the "constant and most violent gales." On April 18, the first of Cornwallis and Parker's ships arrived off Cape Fear, but the earl and admiral did not arrive until May 3, 1776. Clinton's first stop after leaving Boston was Sandy Hook, New York, which he reached on February 4. Clinton had decided to call at New York to talk with Governor Tryon of New York. While there, he met with Lord William Campbell, governor of South Carolina, and Governor Martin of North Carolina. Carrying Governor Martin and Governor Campbell, Clinton's small fleet of ships reached the Cape Fear on March 12. Clinton was upset to learn that loyalists have been defeated at Moore's Creek Bridge and in South Carolina. He offloaded his two companies and toured the countryside along the Cape Fear waiting for Cornwallis and Parker to arrive. He attacked Brunswick, some 15 miles upriver, and dispersed the militia garrison there.[35] Clinton's force lacked beef and salt, and while they captured some molasses from a passing French schooner, they mostly survived on pilfered local fish, oysters and cabbage consumed along with their own stale biscuits.

When Cornwallis arrived in his 50-gun ship *Bristol*, his forces were in rough shape from the three month ordeal at sea. Clinton's forces were likewise half-starved and weakened attempting to live off the land. It was not a happy homecoming.[36] Governor Martin had already taken up residence aboard Clinton's flagship. Cornwallis deployed his seven regiments as best he could. He put one regiment in camp on Baldhead Island, and five regiments at the ruins of Fort Johnston. Cornwallis issued a proclamation giving amnesty to all North Carolinians, except Cornelius Harnett and Colonel Robert Howe, if they would support the British in North Carolina. On May 12, Cornwallis landed 900 men at Orton, and burned and pillaged Colonel Howe's house with outbuildings at his Kendall Plantation, leaving with 20 of his cattle. Since Harnett's home at Hilton was out of reach, no action was taken against his residence by the British in revenge. Later Cornwallis had Russellboro and Belfont burned.

While these actions served at least some measure of usefulness in restoring British egos, the British forces gathered on the Cape Fear were not well situated or compelled to launch a major and protracted campaign up the Cape Fear. Governor Martin's promised loyalist forces, expected to number in the thousands, had not materialized, and the ones that had been recruited had been soundly defeated three months earlier. Seeing the full and up close perspective of their current situation, the British commanders Clinton, Cornwallis and Parker were not impressed by the pleadings of Governor Martin to begin a campaign. Clinton, now in overall command, agreed with Parker and Cornwallis to abandon the Cape Fear campaign. Influenced by Howe's letter received in late May, and with the urging of Admiral Parker, who had received favorable scouting reports from some of his junior officers of the fortifications at Sullivan's Island guarding Charles Town, Clinton decided to attack there. Their last act of revenge in North Carolina involved landing troops and setting fires to Brunswick and St. Philip's Church. With Brunswick burning, the British fleet sailed out of the Cape Fear River with 63 cows and the last royal governor of North Carolina.[37]

Without question the victory at Moore's Creek Bridge saved the colony of North Carolina from being taken by the British in 1776. The loyalist movement in the colony was now dead, and any real hope of its resurrection was but a fleeting thought. After arriving back in North Carolina from the Continental Congress, John Penn wrote: "The recent events in the colony have wholly changed the temper and disposition of the inhabitants that are friends of liberty; all regard or fondness for the king and nation of Britain is gone. A total separation is what they want. Independence is the word most used. They ask if it is possible that any colony after what has passed can wish for reconciliation. The convention have tried to get the opinion of the people at large. I am told that in many counties there was not one dissenting voice." William Hooper, writing from Congress in Philadelphia, said "it would be Toryism to hint the possibility of future reconciliation."[38] At a time when men were deciding whether they were patriots, loyalists or even neutrals, the victory at Moore's Creek Bridge had set the deciding tone for North Carolina's future. The character of that tone was expressed on March 2, 1776, when General James Moore presented the following to the North Carolina Provincial Council at Wilmington, North Carolina:

> Thus, sir, I have the pleasure to inform you, has most happily terminiated a very dangerous insurrection and will, I trust, put an effectual check to Toryism in this country.[39]

7

SULLIVAN'S ISLAND

The Lowcountry coast of South Carolina is made up of a series of white-sand islands separated from the mainland by marshes, sandbars and tidal inlets. These islands during the period of the Revolution were covered with palmettos and myrtle, with an occasional live oak here and there.

In the summer of 1776 one of these Lowcountry islands of South Carolina became the scene of one of the most significant battles of the early American Revolution in the South. Charles Town is located on a peninsula formed by the Ashley River to the west and the Cooper River to the east. At the entrance to the harbor of Charles Town are two of these coastal islands that formed natural fortresses. The island of interest in 1776 was Sullivan's Island. Located on the northern entrance of the harbor, the island stretches for four miles up the coast, with a width at its widest point of just a few hundred yards. Above it is a similar island, which extends for some seven miles, Long Island, separated from Sullivan's Island by a narrow inlet, better known as Breach Inlet. Above Long Island is Dewees' Island.

On May 31, 1776, the South Carolina Provincial Congress president, John Rutledge, was informed that a large fleet of British vessels was seen off Dewees' Island, some 20 miles northeast of Charles Town. On June 1, the joint British naval expedition of Henry Clinton and Admiral Sir Peter Parker, sailing from Cape Fear, dropped anchor outside the Charles Town entrance bar with 50 vessels. Any previous doubts as to British intentions regarding Clinton's forces were no longer in question.[1]

While the full expectations of Clinton's expedition to Charles Town is not absolutely confirmed, information indicates that Clinton intended to take the fort at Sullivan's Island in order to control the harbor entrance, to seal up the harbor from all shipping, and serve to facilitate a base of operations for eventual military actions against Charles Town. In Clinton's letter to Lord Germain dated July 8, 1776, he declared, "I say immediate, My Lord, for it never was my intention at this season of the year to have proceeded further than Sullivan's Island without a moral certainty of rapid success." In the margin beside that quote Clinton had written, "to get possession of Sullivan's Island without which no fleet could lay in safety; to hold it till the proper season for operations in that climate."[2]

The intelligence Clinton had received indicated that the defenses were not completed on Sullivan's Island, and that, once taken, the island could be maintained by a small British infantry and artillery force with a few frigates. To actually take Charles Town would have required a larger force than Clinton had at his disposal. Considering the information available as Clinton lay at anchor off Sullivan's Island, the general's plan seemed to make strategic sense.[3]

When Henry Clinton left the besieged Boston on January 20, General George Washington was concerned over where Clinton would travel. Earlier Washington had warned the Continental Congress that he believed Clinton would head to New York, but he could not discount the potential of a Virginia visit. Washington immediately dispatched his second-in-command, Major General Charles Lee, to go to New York and strengthen the defense of that city. The day Lee arrived in New York was the very day that Clinton was standing off New York at Sandy Hook. The citizens of New York were in panic as to the intentions of Clinton's forces, but he solemnly promised that he was only there to confer with Governor Tryon. Lee made a masterful survey of the possible defenses, and submitted the report to the Continental Congress. He had called for some temporary measures, but had also warned the congress that the city could not be totally defended from a British landing force. The delegates of the Continental Congress would not take his advice.[4]

As General Lee was about to head north to assume command of the Northern District, succeeding Philip Schuyler, the Continental Congress changed its mind and assigned Lee to the Southern District. Though the commander-in-chief of the Continental Army was General Washington, he was not consulted in this matter. Somewhat reluctantly, Lee began his travel south on March 7 to Williamsburg, where he stayed in the governor's former mansion to consider his next move. He complained in a letter to a friend that "I know not where to turn. I am like a dog in a dancing school."[5] While in Virginia, a privateer ship captain, James Barron, had captured a British dispatch carrier with a letter from Lord Germain to Maryland Governor Robert Eden with information on the Cape Fear Plan of a joint operation of Clinton and Parker in North Carolina. Lee then moved on to Wilmington, North Carolina, with some 1900 Continental soldiers from Virginia and North Carolina.[6] When Clinton and Parker left the Cape Fear, Lee and his Continental soldiers departed Wilmington on June 2, and rushed to Charles Town.[7]

General Lee was an odd man in many ways, yet a brilliant officer. Lee was born 16 days before George Washington in England in 1732 to a British colonel. At age 12, the young Charles Lee was studying in Switzerland and already held a commission as ensign in the British Army. Lee fought beside Braddock in America beginning in 1755 during the French and Indian War. While passing through the Mohawk territory during the war, he married the daughter of Chief White Thunder. The Mohawks gave the curious name "Boiling Water" to Lee based on the way he stode through their camp always talking. In 1763, Lee went to Poland as an aide to King Stanislas II, where he rose to the rank of Polish Major General. While in Europe as a soldier of fortune, he fought with the Turks, commanded Russian Cossacks, and talked with Frederick the Great. For carrying a message from King Stanislas II to King George III of England, he was granted an interview with the king. Having expected King George to offer him a military position in the British Army for his services to a British ally, and having been turned down, Lee had actually been so abrupt as to cut the king off in mid-sentence with the remark, "I will never give Your Majesty an opportunity of breaking your promise to me again."

Already allied with the British Whig cause, Lee settled in America in 1773, and soon became friends with Richard Henry Lee, of the famous Lees of Virginia. John Adams once remarked to friends that they must overlook Lee's flock of dogs, which he loved dearly, and his violent temper, because he was so dedicated to the cause of liberty. In December 1774, Lee was a house guest of George Washington at Mount Vernon for five days. They had once been comrades in Braddock's army. When Lee's name came up for commission as a major general in the Continental Army the next year, Washington personally requested the appointment over the challenges of John Hancock and others in Massachusetts. Charles Lee in 1776 was a tall, skinny and ugly man of 44, with a bony nose. His arrogance, extreme temper, vanity, coarseness, and egotistical nature made him a difficult man to tolerate, but Washington and other patriots hoped his vast military experience would serve the patriot cause well.[8]

Major General Charles Lee arrived at Haddrell's Point outside Charles Town Harbor, on the mainland opposite Sullivan's Island, on June 4, 1776. He was accompanied by the now Brigadier General Robert Howe of North Carolina and other officers. Lee set about to inspect the local defenses in and around Sullivan's Island. Actually, preparations for the defense of Charles Town had begun on Sullivan's Island back on January 10, when patriots started the construction of a fort on the southern tip of the island under the direct supervision of Captain Ferdinand de Brahm, who was a military engineer attached to the Charles Town garrison.[9] Fort Sullivan was built of porous, soft and spongy palmetto tree logs laid one on the other, in two parallel rows, to a height of 20 feet, and bound together with timber dovetailed and bolted to the logs. Between the logs the spaces were filled with 16 feet of packed sand and marsh. The design was essentially a square with a bastion at each angle, with platforms supported by brick pillars. The fort was built to hold up to 1000 men and their artillery.

The fort was not completed on the southwest curtain and bastion, and on the northeastern curtain and bastion the logs were only up to the seven-foot mark. The completed platforms were on the southeastern front and on the southwestern side. On these platforms were mounted a total, on each side of the fort, of 31 guns of various sizes, including six-, nine-, 12- and 18-pounders. Only 25 guns could actually fire in any one direction from the fort. Out from the fort, at right angles to the rear walls, were the cavaliers which were hastily constructed sideworks used to provide some protection to troops. On the southeast bastion was mounted the flagstaff flying a dark blue flag, with a silver crescent in the upper left corner, and the word "Liberty" emblazoned in the center field.[10]

The fort's location was at the strategic point where any ships entering the harbor had to proceed northward from Five Fathom Hole, an anchorage off shore, in a U-shaped course between Sullivan's Island and a treacherous shoal called the Middle Ground, then turning westward

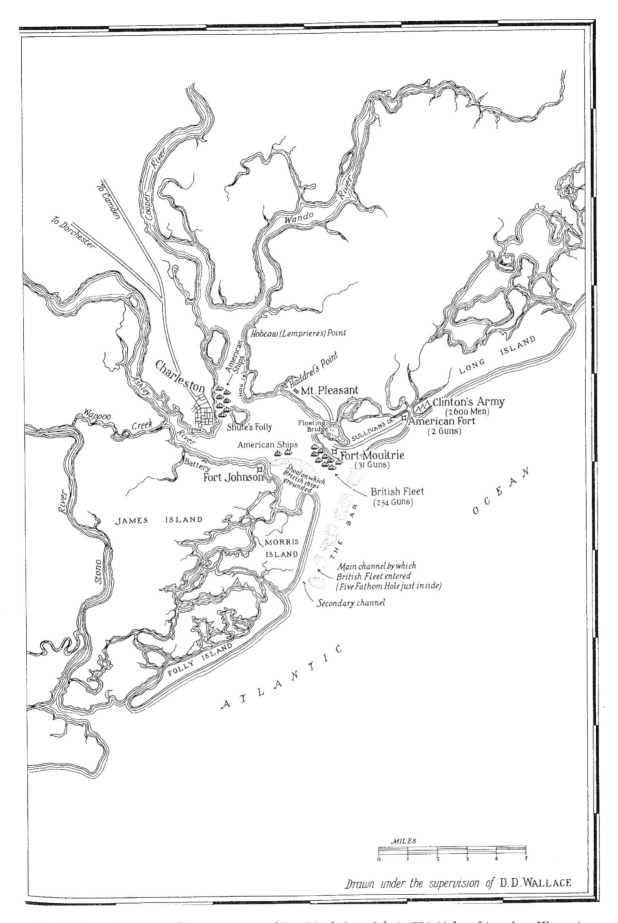

Charles Town 1776. Fort Sullivan was renamed Fort Moultrie on July 4, 1776. (*Atlas of American History*.)

into Charles Town harbor. The fort could bring its guns to bear on the ships that sailed past it with an incredibly deadly force, soon to be experienced by the British. The guns at Fort Sullivan could fire smoothbore, flat trajectory cannonball fire, at the waterline of the wooden ships to open them up to sinking. In addition, chain shot — two cannonballs connected by chain — could be fired from a single cannon at the sails and rigging to keep the ship in the deadly envelope. Another practice was to heat cannonballs to a cherry-red color in an oven and fire them with wet wadding to attempt to set the ships on fire. But the most awesome artillery fire was from grapeshot, which was composed of several small balls clustered around a wooden core. On impact, these balls would break loose as shrapnel in all directions, with terrible destructive power.[11] Going in harm's way against a well-gunned fort, even in the days of the American Revolution, was not a safe exercise.

The commander of Fort Sullivan since early that March of 1776 was Charles Town's own Colonel William Moultrie, who had moved to the island after he received his orders from South Carolina President Rutledge. Moultrie was born in South Carolina in 1730. He had gained some military experience and reputation as a leader of militia during Indian fighting in the 1760s, and was appointed as colonel of the Second South Carolina Regiment by the Provincial Congress in 1775.[12] Moultrie now commanded a garrison of his Second South Carolina Regiment of 413 men, and a detachment of the Fourth Regiment's artillery with 22 men. He had approximately 10,000 pounds of gunpowder, which was not sufficient for a prolonged cannonade engagement.[13]

Across the harbor on James Island was Fort Johnson, which was commanded by Colonel Christopher Gadsden with 20 heavy cannon, of the 18- and 26-pounder variety. The garrison was composed of 380 men from the First South Carolina Regiment of Infantry and a detachment of artillery. Closer toward Charles Town, on the shore of James Island, were some 12 heavy guns with a small battery of artillerymen under Captain Thomas Pinckney.[14]

General Lee's inspection of Fort Sullivan left him very concerned. With the western and rear walls of the fort barely seven feet high, there was little protection from cannon fire from any British ship that could sail into the cove behind the island, or from attacking British troops over land. Lee urged Moultrie to withdraw his troops to the mainland, but Moultrie indicated that he could defend the fort and resisted Lee. Moultrie wrote of Lee that "When he came to Sullivan's Island, he did not like the post at all ... nay, he called it a 'slaughter pen.'" Lee's tactical logic seemed justifiable. Even though Fort Sullivan was in a strategic position to intercept the at-

tacking fleet, the British would have as many as 100 naval guns to bear on the fort at any one time.[15] Lee also proposed to President Rutledge that the fort be abandoned, but Rutledge rejected it outright, and declared that he would cut off his right arm before he would write such an order.[16] So the patriot garrison intended to stay and fight.

From the time the British fleet had sailed into the area off Charles Town bar, the people of Charles Town were alarmed and preparing to resist the British as best they could. While the fleet took soundings off the bar, laying marker buoys in the channel, and on June 7 crossed the bar to their anchorage at Five Fathom Hole, the patriot citizens were busy. Parker's two largest ships, the *Bristol* and *Experiment,* had difficulty getting over the Charles Town bar, and were forced to unship their guns to lighten the ships to get over it. Their guns were then reshipped.[17]

The stores and warehouses on the harbor wharves were leveled to the ground to give room for cannon fire from earthworks along East Bay. Considering that these warehouses handled the goods of as many as 300 vessels in its harbor at one time, it was a significant step to destroy property of that value. Since lead for musketballs was so scarce, weights were removed from the windows of houses in Charles Town for casting. Defensive works were constructed hastily across the streets to stop the potential of raking fire from the British. Batteries and defensive works were established on the Charles Town peninsula just south of Corning's Point on the Ashley River, and stretched along East Bay and South Bay to Gadsden's Wharf on the Cooper River.[18] The printing presses and public records of the town were removed to a place of safety. The gazettes were thus suspended from printing during the period of June 1 to August 1. Even though it must be said that not all Charles Town's citizens were totally committed to resisting the British, they were also not agreeable to absolute submission either. Rutledge asked that for the duration of the siege all gambling and horse racing be suspended.

On the 7th, a boat was seen with a flag of truce coming from the British fleet towards Sullivan's Island. Not being familiar with the protocol, the sentry fired on the boat and it returned at once. Colonel Moultrie reported the incident to President Rutledge, who then ordered that a militia officer explain the unfortunate incident to the commanding officer of the British fleet. Moultrie sent Captain Francis Huger under flag of truce with a letter of explanation, which was accepted. The next day, a second messenger boat from the fleet carried Clinton's communication. President Rutledge and Colonel Moultrie were disappointed to learn that the communication was not related to the issue of the pending engagement, but was a proclamation warning the citizens of the dire consequences of continuing the civil conflict. Apparently no effort was made to respond to the message.

On June 8, General Lee assumed command of operations on Sullivan's Island without consulting Rutledge. At this point the troops under Colonel Moultrie were under the control of the South Carolina provisional government and had not been part of the Continental Army organization. While somewhat irritated with the manner Lee had taken, President Rutledge announced on the 9th that the command of all forces, Continental and militia, was being placed under General Lee to avoid any conflict over authority in the coming campaign.[19]

The tactical plan created by Clinton for taking Sullivan's Island and the fort was, at face value, a practical one. Clinton's thoughts paralleled with the observations that General Lee had made regarding the weakness of the Sullivan's Island defenses. He planned to land his redcoats on Long Island first, to avoid a hostile landing and the heavier surf of Sullivan's Island, and then wade across the shallow inlet to attack the fort from the rear. Clinton had been told that Breach Inlet was only 18 inches deep at low tide and would be easy to cross. His naval forces would simultaneously bombard the fort from the channel, and if possible from the cove behind the island. It seemed like an excellent British plan of attack.[20]

On June 8, Major General Henry Clinton, accompanied by Major General Lord Cornwallis and Brigadier General Vaughn, began to land a force of 2200 redcoats on Long Island from the British transports just off the island. At 6 A.M., upon learning of the troop landing, General Lee sent orders to Moultrie to reconnoiter the landing from the northern end of Sullivan's Island, and based on the information he gained, to reconsider retreating to the mainland. The nature of Lee's comments showed his misunderstanding of the local terrain. In order for Moultrie to attack from the mainland meant crossing miles of marshes.

By 8 A.M. Lee understood the impracticality of such a movement, and he ordered Colonel Moultrie to detach 780 men under Colonel William "Danger" Thomson of the Third Regiment of Rangers with Colonel Sumter's Sixth Regiment, and the companies of captains Alston, Mayham and Couturier to attack Clinton and dislodge the British from Long Island. Lee was insistent that they must keep the British off Sullivan's Island at all costs, and encouraged Moultrie to move two field guns up to command the inlet. Moultrie did not receive Lee's orders until 7 A.M. on June 10. Moultrie obeyed the orders immediately but by that time it was found that all the British troops had been landed.

Lee was still concerned about the real possibility of eventual need for retreat, and he proposed that a bridge be built from Sullivan's Island to Haddrell's Point on the mainland. The idea of a bridge was met with several objections, including that there was no time left to build a bridge, and even if one could be constructed, it could be disabled by a few shots from one of Clinton's warships. Since there was no time for a proper bridge, an improvised one of planks floated on empty hogsheads and anchored boats across the cove was constructed. This bridge was soon proven to be of no value when Lieutenant Colonel Clark with 200 North Carolina troops, heading to reinforce Colonel Thomson, tried to cross it. The bridge sank before the men were even halfway across. The patriots would have to use boats from now on. Colonel Moultrie later wrote, "I never imagined that the enemy could force me to the necessity (of retreating). I always considered myself as able to defend the post against the enemy."

General Lee was still obsessed with the potential for a British movement that could not be countered by his forces, even if the movement was in conflict with the reality of the terrain. Now Lee feared that Clinton would send troops from Long Island across to the mainland and seize Haddrell's Point, and attack the city. He did not understand the futility of the British trying to cross two miles of marsh in the mud, but he decided to reinforce Haddrell's Point with Continental troops under Brigadier General Armstrong. Lee also ordered that an earthen defensive barrier, known as a fleeces, and screen be built on the rear flank of the fort for better protection to the troops from a rear naval attack. General Lee's orders for these works were not heeded, and they were never built. Lee was contemplating removing Colonel Moultrie for failing to make all necessary precautions for the fort. On the night of June 27, Lee directed Colonel Nash of the North Carolina Continentals to report to him on the next morning to take command of Fort Sullivan. The events of that next morning would cause the command to remain in the hands of Colonel Moultrie.

Lee was not altogether wrong to consider censure of Colonel Moultrie for his failure to carry out his orders with loyal support. Moultrie was known to be somewhat careless in the performance of his duties, a poor disciplinarian at times, and did not maintain the punctuality normally expected of a military officer. It is important to note that Moultrie did suffer from gout before and during the campaign, which represented an extenuating circumstance. Regardless of the total character of this officer, Colonel Moultrie was a gallant officer in battle, as history would soon record.

By the night of June 27, the entire patriot forces assembled in the Charles Town area were some 6522 men, including 1400 North Carolina Continentals, 1950 South Carolina regulars, 500 Virginia Continentals, 700 Charles

Town militia and 1972 country militia. At Fort Sullivan were the 435 men under Colonel Moultrie. On the northeastern point of Sullivan's Island, behind two defensive works built by the colonial engineer Captain de Brahm, were the 300 Rangers of Colonel Thomson's Third Regiment, 200 North Carolina regulars under Lieutenant Colonel Clark, 200 South Carolina troops under Colonel Daniel Horry, the Raccoon or Foot Rover Company of 50 Peedee, Waccamaw, Cheraw and Catawba Indian riflemen, with a small detachment of militia. On James Island were the 380 men under Christopher Gadsden of the First South Carolina Regiment of Infantry, with artillery detachment. It was an impressive defensive force, but would they rule the coming engagement? Clinton's forces consisted of the 2200 British regulars on Long Island, and a naval fleet of two 50-gun ships, five frigates, and four other vessels for a total of 270 naval guns.

On the morning of June 28, 1776, Colonel Moultrie and "Danger" Thomson were riding together on the northern end of Sullivan's Island when they noticed movement of the British boats behind Long Island, and saw the warships off Long Island loose their topsails. These being signals for getting under way, Moultrie hurried back to the fort and immediately ordered the long roll of the drums to bring his officers and men to their posts. The battle alarm was now sounded. By the time the guns were fully manned and powder distributed between 10 and 11 A.M., the British ships were under sail bearing down on Sullivan's Island. The bombship *Thunder*, in company with the 22-gun *Friendship*, anchored a mile and a half off the island and began to shell the fort with its 13-inch shells. With a strong tide and active winds from the southwest, the 28-gun *Active*, the 50-guns each of the *Bristol* and *Experiment* and the 28-gun *Solebay* ships came into range of the fort's cannon fire. The *Active* was located off Sullivan's Island at 400 yards, with the *Bristol*, *Experiment* and *Solebay* coming up the rear of *Active*, separated at intervals from each other.

The cannon battle was intense. Many of the shells of the fleet landed in the fort, but did no damage as the shells buried themselves in the loose sand in the fort. General Lee had predicted that the fort would be lucky to endure 30 minutes of a fierce engagement. He was supported in his observation by a Captain Lempriere who had served in action at St. Augustine the year before, taking powder while serving as the master of a man-of-war. Now Lempriere captained a privateer vessel for the colony. Surveying the fleet with Colonel Moultrie, Lempriere commented, "Well, Colonel, what do you think of it now?" Moultrie replied, "We should beat them." Lempriere responded with his prediction that "Sir, when those ships (pointing to the men-of-war) come to lay alongside of your fort, they will knock it down in half an hour."

Colonel Moultrie then declared, "We will lay behind the ruins and prevent their men from landing." Now the reality had come to all. The British had 270 guns firing at Fort Sullivan, plus the shells of the bombship *Thunder*. The patriots had a mere 25 guns firing back.[21] Colonel Moultrie was still confident. The men of the fort continued to maintain a slow and steady cannon fire from the southeast and southwest bastions and curtains, with supporting six 12-pounder fire from the flanking cavaliers.[22]

As soon as the fleet began the bombardment of Fort Sullivan, Major General Henry Clinton began his attempt to cross Breach Inlet and attack the fort from the rear. With his 2200 redcoats, he marched down from his camp on Long Island to the edge of the inlet. His force was flanked by the armed sloop *Lady William* on his right and on this left a group of small longboats. Colonel Thomson had his force of 750 troops and an 18- and a six-pounder cannon. Thomson's men were expert riflemen, but as Rangers they had never fired a cannon before. Clinton's small boat flotilla advanced toward Thomson's men, cheered on by the British troops at the inlet. Colonel Thomson's men opened fire on the flotilla, raking their decks with grapeshot from the cannon and rifle fire. The flotilla dispersed in response to the heavy, deadly fire. Clinton and his men looked on in quiet disbelief and frustration. Clinton, surveying the perilous situation, decided to take no action. It was now totally up to the fleet to decide this engagement.

The excuse that Clinton gave for not crossing Breach Inlet to attack Colonel Thomson was that the inlet was not fordable, being deeper than the 18 inches expected, and that he had no boats available for his troops. The passage was at that time made more difficult than usual due to an easterly wind that had increased the tides around Long Island. Regardless, news of Clinton's aborted attack was not received well in London. There was suspicion that Clinton's heart was not in this action, as it was difficult to believe that Clinton would spend 19 days on a small island and not test the depth of the inlet his entire attack plan depended on. In *St. James Chronicle* an epigram appeared under the title "A Miracle on Sullivan's Island" with the phrase "Though Clinton's troops have shared a different fate, 'Gainst them, poor men! Not chosen sure of Heaven, The miracle reversed is still as great — From two feet deep the water rose to seven."[23] The *Annual Register* published this scathing critique, "To suppose that the Generals, and the Officers under their command should have been nineteen days in that small island, without ever examining until the very instant of action the nature of the only passage by which they could render service to their friends and fellows, fulfill the purpose of their landing and answer the ends for which they were embarked in the expedition would seem a great defect in military prudence and circumspection."[24] At 5 P.M. Colonel Thomson was reinforced from Haddrell's Point with an additional 700 Virginia and South Carolina Continentals under command of Colonel Peter Muhlenberg.[25]

Meanwhile, the cannonade of the fort continued. The heavy British fire gave the naval forces confidence that they would prevail. But the men of Fort Sullivan were undaunted. The British had great expectations of the damage that would be done by the *Thunder*. But as it turned out, she had anchored too far off Sullivan's Island and had overcharged her mortars to compensate. The recoil from the shipboard mortars shattered the beds, and soon the *Thunder* was out of action. The legend says that the only fatalities from the *Thunder* were three ducks, two geese and one turkey.[26] The principal fire continued from the *Bristol* and *Experiment*, with their 50 guns each. The *Syren* and *Friendship* also engaged the fort in the afternoon, with the *Active* and *Solebay*.[27]

At around noon, Sir Peter Parker ordered the three ships, *Sphynx*, *Acteon* and *Syren*, to pass the fort and attempt to enter the cove behind the fort, as General Lee had feared. To complete the movement in the channel, the British ships, with native black pilots at the helm, directed the frigates too close to the shallow Middle Ground shoal. All three ships ran aground on the shoal. The *Syren* and *Sphynx* were able to get off the shoal without their bowsprits, but the *Acteon* was lost and abandoned.[28] This was yet another fortunate event for the patriot cause.

The battle raged on. The fort and its men were taking their punishment. The first South Carolinian killed in the fort was a corporal of grenadiers. The men of the gun crew vengefully threw his dead body off the platform and continued firing their cannon in defiance. A sergeant named MacDonald in Captain Frank Huger's unit was severely wounded by a round. As he lay dying, he urged the men on by asking them to not let liberty expire with him. The greatest reported act of heroism came when the flagstaff at Fort Sullivan was shot away midway in the battle. The brave old Sergeant William Jasper shouted to Colonel Moultrie that they should not fight without a flag, and promptly mounted the parapet being pounded by British cannon, to place the blue flag to a gun sponger on the merlon of the bastion closest to the British. After the battle on the 4th of July, Jasper was publicly recognized by President John Rutledge, who presented him with his own sword. Sergeant Jasper was later killed in 1779 during the attack at Savannah when he fell mortally wounded bearing the colors of the Second South Carolina Regiment defending against a frontal assault at Spring Hill redoubt. Not surprisingly, monuments to Sergeant Jasper were later erected at Charles Town and Savannah.[29]

As the battle continued, General Lee had issued orders to Colonel Moultrie indicating that he was to spike his guns and retreat with all order possible if he ran out of ammunition. Moultrie was determined not to be forced into retreating from the fort and leaving Colonel Thomson stranded on the northern end of the island with Clinton. Colonel Moultrie decided to slow down his cannon firing in order to last as long as possible. The intervals between firing from the fort were so long, at some ten minutes at times, that between 3 and 5 P.M. the British thought several times that the fort had been silenced. Eventually Fort Sullivan ran short of powder. Rutledge then sent 500 pounds to the island by small boat. With the powder, he instructed Moultrie to make free with his cannons, but to stay cool and do mischief. At one point during the battle, General Lee made the only command visit to Fort Sullivan, where he ascended a platform, fired a cannon and left for Charles Town. After his 15-minute visit, Lee remarked to Moultrie, "I see you are doing very well here — you have no occasion for me — I will go up to town again." Lee retired to Haddrell's Point.[30]

The battle raged in the summer heat of June as the defenders shed their uniform jackets and shirts. Some of these articles of clothing had been placed on trees inside the fort perimeter, and were mistakenly interpreted by the British lookouts stationed on mastheads as members of the garrison being hanged for desertion in battle. The fort was enduring the brutal assault of the naval gunfire. While the structure would quiver when three broadsides would hit at one time on the walls, the spongy log walls would absorb the cannonballs with no surrounding damage to men or fort. To relieve the summer thirst during the battle, grog, which was a combination of rum and water, was served in fire buckets around the fort. Colonel Moultrie, who fought and drank on occasion with his men, later recalled that he never had a more agreeable draft than the one he took in the middle of a battle from a fire bucket.[31]

Around 7 P.M., with the sun slowly setting, the cannon firing slackened off. At half past 9 P.M. all firing ceased. The implausible nine-hour battle was over. At 11 P.M. the British ships slipped their cables without noise and returned with the ebb tide to their previous anchorage near Five Fathom Hole. It was an incredible victory for the American forces on Sullivan's Island. Colonel Moultrie had lost 12 men and had 25 wounded. The slaughter aboard the British ships was most terrible, and if Moultrie had not run low on powder, the carnage would have been even worse. Aboard the *Bristol*, 64 were killed and 161 wounded. Captain Morris lost his arm and later died. Captain Scott of the *Experiment* likewise lost his arm, as 57 died and 30 were wounded. The *Solebay* lost 12 killed and wounded, and the *Active* seven.[32] The British had expended 34,000 pounds of powder, and the Americans only 4766. After the battle, some 7000 British cannonballs were recovered at Fort Sullivan.[33] Even Admiral Sir Peter Parker was wounded, having suffered the personal indignity of having his pants split in the rear by a passing round. It was a clear defeat for the British.

Captain James Murray of the Fifty-seventh Regiment commented that he looked on with amazement at the efforts at Fort Sullivan: "After the first hour we began to be impatient and a good deal surprised at the resistance of the battery. But [after] 4 hours the fire grew every moment hotter and hotter we were in wonder and astonishment." The fire at the *Bristol* and *Experiment* was brutal. Moultrie's men fired chain shot at the masts, and grapeshot to kill the crew. A British officer aboard the *Bristol* later wrote that "During action no slaughter-house could present so bad a sight with *Bristol* blood and … lying about." A sailor on Clinton's flagship wrote, "I was on board during action and suffered much from the sight of so much slaughter. I am … satisfied with what I have seen of civil war and devoutly wish that impotence would arrest the progress of the destroying angel…."[34]

The morning of June 29 found the fleet of Admiral Sir Peter Parker at anchor off Morris Island licking its wounds, with the admiral's flagship flying his broad pennant on a jury mast, since he no longer had a mainmast. The British ship *Acteon* still lay a mile off Fort Sullivan on the shoal. At Fort Sullivan the blue flag with crescent and liberty words was still flying from the sponge staff set by Jasper. The garrison of Fort Sullivan was occasionally firing toward the *Acteon*, with Captain Atkins returning fire. Atkins set his vessel afire and loaded her crew aboard small boats as he departed. A party under Lieutenant Jacob Milligan of the Carolina ship *Prosper* boarded the *Acteon* while it was afire, and fired three guns at the Admiral. Milligan carried off the colors, ship's bell, sails and stores. Just after Milligan's party left the ship, the *Acteon* blew up with an awesome explosion.[35]

On June 30, in the afternoon, General Lee and his staff reviewed the garrison at Fort Sullivan, and thanked them for their defense. On July 4, President Rutledge visited the garrison for formal victory ceremonies. William Moultrie was promoted to general, and the fort was renamed Fort Moultrie. A battery there was named for Sergeant Jasper. Jasper was offered a commission, but declined it, indicating that he lacked education, as an illiterate.[36] William Logan of Charles Town sent his compliments to General Moultrie and his staff and begged them to accept a hogshead of Antigua rum. Moultrie reported that his gift was gratefully received and forthwith enjoyed.[37]

Clinton stayed on Long Island until early July, when most of Parker's fleet embarked his troops and headed North to New York to rejoin General Howe. On August 1, 1776, Clinton sailed into New York harbor, which Howe called a "very fine appearance" and "an agreeable circumstance." The two largest ships remained at anchorage at Five Fathom Hole just out of range undergoing repairs until August 2, when they floated over the Charles Town bar and sailed to New York.[38]

In England there were many recriminations against both Clinton and Parker for the fiasco, even though official statements downplayed the events at Sullivan's Island. Friends of Clinton had Lord Germain sign a statement that Clinton was not at fault, but Clinton became angry when Germain refused to have the statement published. Clinton was even more upset when Admiral Parker's opinions began to appear in print. So distraught, Clinton got a leave of absence from Howe to return to England, where it was widely reported that he intended to have a pistol duel with Lord Germain. But Lord Germain was able to avoid the duel by bestowing Clinton with an Order of the Bath, making him Major General Sir Henry Clinton, K.C.B. General Howe was furious with the news.[39]

The circumstances of the defeat of the British at Sullivan's Island were indeed worthy of analysis and at least some degree of blame. Admiral Sir Peter Parker later stated that he had fired at the fort at 450 yards or less during the battle, but he admitted that this distance was too great to be effective against the low-lying fort. If Parker had used grape or canister shot at Moultrie's men on the open gun platforms, the battle might have gone in a different direction. But this type shot was well out of range at the distances from which Parker fired. Clinton claimed that Parker's ships were positioned between 400 and 800 yards of the island, and that gunshots from the upper decks of the larger ships sailed over the fort's walls. Clinton also felt Parker's inability to bring the three frigates around to the cove to fire on the fort from the rear sealed their fate. Of course, Clinton failed to accept that his failure to successfully cross to Sullivan's Island and attack the fort was a major factor contributing to the ultimate British defeat.[40]

The patriot victory over the British at Sullivan's Island was one of the most decisive and pure victories in the South and in the entire American Revolution. Here Southern militia and Continental troops defeated both royal army troops and the often-feared British Royal Navy. The expedition to establish a foothold in the South had failed, and the Southern colonies would remain invasion free for another three years as a result. The Americans had not just resisted the British, they had utterly defeated them. For the patriots of South Carolina, who would always remember this battle on Palmetto Day, it was a brilliant victory. Certainly, if General Lee had prevailed, the battle at Fort Moultrie probably would not have occurred, and the British could have occupied the controlling entrance to Charles Town beginning in the summer of 1776. But due to the defiant attitude of Colonel William Moultrie and bravery of his men, coupled with the political and moral support of South Carolina President John Rutledge, the British would gain a new respect for the military forces of the Southern colonial forces.

The lesser-known, yet great, Revolutionary victory was a significant omen of what was to come for the British, as they attempted to engage those bent on seeing liberty and freedom prevail in the South, and throughout the Thirteen Colonies.

8

SAVANNAH

At 2 P.M. on October 17, 1777, the British forces under General John Burgoyne marched from their fortifications at Saratoga, New York, to the beat of drums as they surrendered to the superior forces under American General Horatio Gates. After the surrender ceremony, the two commanders and their immediate staffs ate lunch together during which General Burgoyne, to everyone's surprise, proposed a toast to General Washington. General Gates responded to the gesture by toasting King George III.[1]

The news of the surrender at Saratoga arrived in London on December 2. The British administration was suddenly confronted with what they believed to be a crisis regarding the future of the war against the American colonies. The reaction of George III to the news was to indicate that Britain would now have to "act only on the defensive in America." The time had unfortunately arrived for a thorough re-examination of the military policies and strategies of this war. Even though there was much reason to deal with this issue with great urgency, the Parliament adjourned for their six-week Christmas recess.

When the government took up the issue in mid–January, the atmosphere was now even more controversial regarding war policy. Evidence of the near disintegration of the British-seating Ministry was beginning to appear. In Parliament there was now talk of asking for the resignations of General Howe and Lord George Germain over the military failures. Indeed, Howe's resignation was accepted on February 4. The undersecretary in the American Department, Christain D'Oyley, resigned his post within ten days, followed by an announcement on February 16 that the lord chancellor, Lord Bathurst, desired to retire from the cabinet. Rumors of Lord Germain's potential resig-

nation were received with little surprise. George III wrote to Lord North that "I think Lord G. Germaine's defection a most favorable event; he has so many enemies, that … [he would have been] an heavy load whenever the failure if the expedition under Lt. G. Burgoyne came to be canvassed in Parliament." But the issue of Lord Germain's resignation was quietly averted.

Meanwhile, on February 6, 1778, His Majesty Louis XVI of France signed secret treaties which recognized the independence of the United States, created a Franco-American defensive alliance and supported the concept of a joint effort to prosecute a common war with Britain. In addition, France forever renounced all claims to North America east of the Mississippi. The United States agreed to help the French defend their West Indian possessions against attack.

The Continental Congress formally ratified the treaty with France on May 4. The British were officially notified of the treaty signing in March, and the French received naval gunfire as a response.

Naval actions between the two nations began immediately from the English Channel to the Mediterranean, in west Africa, in India and the West Indies. A powerful French fleet headed to North America under the command of Admiral Charles-Henri, Compte D'Estaing, with some 4000 French troops. It departed Toulon, sailed through the Strait of Gibraltar and on to the Delaware Capes to confront Admiral Richard Howe.[2] Now the American colonies had a major ally with which to fight the British.

With Germain's status resolved, the new topic for the English was whether the head of the Ministry, Lord North, should resign. On January 29, North discussed the issue with George III. The king felt North was too dismal in his assessment of the situation, and refused to accept his resignation. By the end of March though, Lord North was again discussing the request since he was convinced that Britain was "totally unequal" to a war with both the colonies and the "House of Bourbon." North remarked that "peace with America and a change in the Ministry are the only steps which can save this country." The crisis was now real and change was required to avert disaster.

With the prosecution of the colonial war in question, coupled with the continuing financial burdens and entry of the French to the war, the North Ministry desired to take a conciliatory position with the colonies. On February 17, 1778, Lord North laid before the House of Commons proposals for "removing doubts" concerning colonial taxation and for enabling His Majesty to appoint a peace commission. Parliament also considered military assumptions as set forth by Lord Amherst that unless at least 30,000 troops were sent to the colonies to carry on an effective "offensive land war," future operations must be "principally naval, to distress their trade and prevent their supplies from Europe." After Lord Amherst refused to accept Howe's command, the choice fell to Sir Henry Clinton by default.

On March 8, Lord Germain signed the final instructions, as directed by general agreement of the British cabinet, for General Clinton's future military operations against the colonies. The instructions called for offensive operations "upon a different plan from that it has hitherto been carried on." Clinton was told that it was impractical to bring Washington's forces to a "decisive action early in the campaign," and that he should relinquish the idea of carrying on a land offensive there. He was instructed to attack rebels on the coastal areas between New York and Nova Scotia, including destroying wharves and shipbuilding materials, seizing ships, and curbing American attacks on British trade, which had already been "so much annoyed."

The key directive to Clinton included the following: "When these operations on the sea coasts of the Northern Provinces are concluded, which it is supposed they will be before the month of October, it is the King's intention that an attack should be made upon the Southern Colonies, with a view to the conquest and possession of Georgia and South Carolina." The Southern loyalists were expected to play a significant role in these operations in the South, and Clinton was to provide a large supply of arms for their use. The loyalists would have the option to join the regular British army or to be formed into militia, which would be "officered by their own countrymen."

Germain proposed that the method of attacking the South be through Georgia. He declared that a detachment of 2000 men should be dispatched from New York to capture Savannah, assisted by forces under General Augustine Prevost. Prevost was to travel from his St. Augustine location in East Florida to join with the New York forces via land. With the added support of frontier Indians, through the Indian superintendent, John Stuart, as well as other backcountry loyalists, they "would probably avail themselves of the communication being opened." Germain felt they could easily capture Augusta, and with forces totaling some 5000, they would be ready to attack Charles Town, South Carolina. He predicted that the Lowcountry planters would come to immediate terms with the show of such a substantial force. Germain even asked, "Could a small corps be detached at the same time to land at Cape Fear … It is not doubted that a large number of inhabitants would flock to the Kings Standard, and that His Majesty's government would be restored in that province also."

Germain continued his proposal that if there were any troops remaining, he should deploy them in Virginia and Maryland in a diversion. The idea was to make it impossible for the rebels to send reinforcements to aid Georgia or South Carolina. While Clinton was told that the king considered the conquest of the Southern colonies "an object of great importance," he was not to interpret the instructions as specific orders. This note was included to make it look like the Ministry was not actually encumbering the British commanders in America, which had already been leveled against Germain in the Burgoyne Campaign. But, oh, what a grand plan it was. The British strategy had turned the focus of the war effort to the South, where it would remain until the end of the Revolution.

Along with his instructions, Clinton was notified by letter dated March 8, 1778, of his appointment as the commander-in-chief of all British forces in North America. Also included were assurances from Germain that he would receive an army equal to that given to the previous commander, General Howe. Information was also provided regarding a peace initiative, known as the Carlisle Peace Commission. This commission consisted of three members — the Earl of Carlisle, William Eden and George Johnstone — who were empowered to offer rather liberal terms, except independence, to the colonies to restore relations.

The commission left England for America to join Clinton in April 1778. Germain was not impressed with the prospects of the commission making much headway and he indicated that "His Majesty does not think fit to slaken any preparation." The commission was really doomed from the start since before they could begin negotiations the Continental Congress had already ratified the French Treaty and Clinton had begun the evacuation of Philadelphia. The Continental Congress demanded recognition of independence or evacuation of the British army from America before any negotiations would be considered. The commission was frustrated in their efforts and finally left America for London in December.[3]

Sir Henry Clinton was not totally happy with his assignment as commander-in-chief of His Majesty's army in the American colonies, as he complained, "The great change which public Affairs had undergone, in Europe as well as America … had so clouded every prospect of a successful issue to the unfortunate contest we were engaged in that no officer who had the least anxious regard for his professional fame would court a change so hopeless as this now appeared likely to be. For neither honor nor credit could be expected from it, but on the contrary a considerable portion of blame, however unmerited, seemed to be almost inevitable."[4] His words were not without merit.

Previously, on the day after the British were engaged by loyalists at Concord, Major General Henry Clinton, accompanied by major generals John Burgoyne and William Howe, embarked aboard the British frigate *Cerberus* heading for Boston. At age 37, Clinton was quite familiar with the colonial world, having been raised in New York while his father, Admiral George Clinton, served as royal governor from 1741 to 1751. The young Clinton had returned to England with his father and became a lieutenant in the Coldstream Guards. In 1758 he was promoted to lieutenant colonel in the Grenadier Guards. Clinton served in the Seven Years' War as the *aide-de-camp* to the Prince of Brunswick, and was wounded at Johannesburg in August of 1772. Cited for gallantry, Clinton returned to England at the end of the war at age 25 to be given several rather boring assignments.

In 1772 he was promoted to major general and was elected to the House of Commons with the support of his cousin, the second Duke of Newcastle. Clinton took this peaceful decade to continue to improve himself in his chosen profession. As a shy man who tended to conceal his natural characteristic of "stubborn assertiveness," Clinton occasionally found himself in conflict with his seniors, naval colleagues and subordinates. The death of his wife in August of 1772 left him upset, but he was able to eventually pull himself out of his despair. Now the weight of the American conflict was on his shoulders to solve.[5]

To the surprise of Clinton, on March 21, 1778, he received revised orders to prepare an expedition to attack the French island of St. Lucia. These new instructions had been the reaction to the official intervention of France in the war on March 13. With 5000 troops, Clinton was to take possession of St. Lucia, and hold it with adequate troops, and then to deploy the remaining troops among the other islands of the British West Indies as sufficient. He was also instructed to send an additional 3000 troops to Florida, to be equally deployed between St. Augustine and Pensacola.

The last minute decision to send troops to the Caribbean was seen as an over-reaction by the British Ministry, and quite a pessimistic signal. To send 8000 troops to the West Indies and Florida would significantly impact the American war effort, to the point where there was consideration of the possibility of withdrawing all British troops from the Thirteen Colonies. As it turned out, the revised instructions were never carried out. No troops were sent to the West Indies and Florida was not reinforced. Clinton's withdrawal from Philadelphia had not come off well, and the appearance of the French fleet ended all hope of focusing on Caribbean possessions. Loyalists feared that Clinton would abandon them on the mainland in favor of the Indies, yet Clinton seemed to understand their concerns as he later wrote in his *Narrative*, "[I] called forth my utmost exertions to ease their minds…. For I readily saw that the very worst consequences were to be apprehended from such an idea laying hold of them, as the number and zeal of those colonists who still remained attached to the sovereignty of Great Britain undoubtedly formed the firmest ground we could rest out hopes on for extinguishing the rebellion."[6]

The British strategy to begin offensive operations in the South was in some ways a curious decision. The military situation in the North was indeed a stalemate after three years of war. Howe's strategy had not worked, and without some new approach, there was no reason to believe that better days were coming. There was pressure from the British former royal governors to focus more assets on the South. Back on August 27, 1777, former governors Lord William Campbell of South Carolina and Sir James Wright of Georgia submitted a well-written appeal to George Germain on the practically of reducing South Carolina and Georgia "to His Majesty's obedience." The document focused on the testimony of returned loyalists and royal officials that there was still much support for Britain in Georgia and South Carolina and that loyalty would come forth if only they would send an immediate expedition there. The appeal document urged, "From our particular knowledge of those Provinces, it appears very clear to us, that if a proper number of troops were in possession of Charleston … or if they were to possess themselves of the back country thro' Georgia, and to leave a garrison in the town of Savannah, the whole inhabitants in both Provinces would soon come in and submit."[7]

Even though British political and military leadership always seemed to believe that operations in the South could yield positive results, it was not an ideal situation for them. From a military view, engaging the South would disperse the British resources even more than they already were, and troop levels were not being radically increased. The French fleet was now in the picture and the Americans had shown no desire to retreat from their militant position. Even the defeats suffered in the South at Norfolk, Moore's Creek Bridge and Sullivan's Island had not dissuaded the British from looking South yet again. The British Ministry, under Lord George Germain, was under pressure to save face after three years of North American war and some type of change was necessary to gain at least some level of support for the colonial war.

The justification for a move to the South was additionally melded in the perpetual hope of collateral support from Southern loyalists, a view continually encouraged by the former Southern royal governors and various other loyalists. These were the circumstances as Clinton weighed his alternatives in the spring of 1778. With D'Estaing heading for America, available to strike the West Indies or the North American coast at any time, and with troop levels at only 12,000 men, Clinton was not interested in carrying out the West Indies expedition or to support Florida, but was considering when to attack the South.[6]

On the afternoon of June 28, 1778, a British packet boat reported that it had sighted D'Estaing's fleet heading for the Virginia coast. The French admiral arrived in Delaware Bay on July 8 aboard his 90-gun flagship *Languedoc*, accompanied by 11 other ships of the line and four frigates. The admiral sent one frigate to convey Louis XVI's emissary, Conrad Alexandre Gerard, and the former Commissioner Silas Deane to Philadelphia, and then detached two messengers to Washington "to offer to combine my movements with his own." His letter to the president of Congress indicated that he had arrived and wished to join Washington "immediately and without delay, to act in concert for the benefit of the common cause." D'Estaing then sailed north and anchored four miles east of Sandy Hook at New York on July 11.

British Vice Admiral Howe knew he did not possess a fleet that could defeat D'Estaing at sea. Thus, he took up a brilliant defensive position inside Sandy Hook with his ships using spring cables to keep them in a perfect anchored position to rake the French men-of-war if they crossed the channel bar. They wished to deliver a broadship of fire at the French ships at a short range. The day that D'Estaing arrived at New York, Congress had informed Washington at his Paramus, New Jersey, headquarters that he should cooperate with the French admiral "in execution of such offensive operations against the enemy as they shall mutually approve." Washington then sent an aide, Lieutenant Colonel John Laurens, the son of the president of the Congress, along with a few officers who spoke fluent French, to greet D'Estaing. A few days later Washington moved his headquarters to White

Plains, New York, and had his troops moved up the Hudson River to better threaten Clinton in New York.

The first joint operation between French and Continental forces, as planned by General Washington and D'Estaing, was to attack Clinton in New York. The plan was abandoned as D'Estaing reconsidered how well prepared Vice Admiral Howe's forces were, with his land support batteries there. On July 15 Washington wrote Major General Sullivan at Providence, Rhode Island, that the first joint French-American operation would be against the British forces under Major General Sir Robert Pigot at Newport on Aquidneck Island. Washington also authorized Sullivan to call up 5000 militia from the surrounding colonies, and directed him to begin to gather boats for an amphibious assault. Instead of immediately moving to Newport, D'Estaing continued to consider the possibility of getting safely over the bar to attack New York. Even on July 22, with the "fresh northwest wind … to give the highest possible water over the bar," D'Estaing, with agreement from the American assigned harbor pilots, determined that it was still too dangerous to attempt to cross the bar.

This delay in heading for Newport served the British cause as Clinton sent five battalions via Long Island Sound to reinforce Pigot's Newport garrison, as well as to put 4000 regular troops on alert to embark at a minute's notice. The British were anticipating a difficult battle at New York with their enemies. "We … expected the hottest day that had ever been fought between two nations. On our side, all was at stake. Had the men-of-war been defeated, the fleet of transports and victuallers must have been destroyed, and the army of course, have fallen with us. D'Estaing, however, had not spirit equal to the risk; at three o'clock we saw him bear off to the southward, and in a few hours, he was out of sight." Washington wrote D'Estaing expressing regret that "the brilliant enterprise was frustrated by physical impossibilities."

One week later D'Estaing's fleet arrived off Point Judith. He ordered two of his men-of-war to move into Narragansett Bay to anchor off Conanicut Island, and two other frigates to operate in Sakonnet Passage to the east of Aquidneck Island. Pigot's forces were now surrounded by the French fleet, and were not optimistic about their situation. But the British forces were saved by the actions of Vice Admiral White Richard Viscount Howe, R.N., and the good fate of timing. As D'Estaing prepared to work with the land forces under General Sullivan to operate against the British around Newport, Howe's British fleet was receiving reinforcements from "Foul-weather Jack" Byron's squadron that arrived in American waters after sailing from England on June 9. Since Byron's ships had been scattered "from Nova Scotia to the West Indies" during gale force winds during the Atlantic voyage, these reinforcement ships were arriving in small numbers to support Howe. With increasing fleet strength, Howe moved his men-of-war to confront D'Estaing, and anchored at Point Judith on August 9. By this time Sullivan had crossed over to the north end of Aquidneck Island and entrenched. All was now ready for a decisive battle involving the American and British armies, and the French and British fleets.

D'Estaing called a Council of War to discuss options regarding the upcoming battle. The decision was to move his units further into the harbor and take up positions near the entrance to engage the British Fleet. On August 11 the French Fleet maneuvered for advantage as a violent gale hit both fleets. During the next several days the ships took quite a beating. D'Estaing's flagship lost all her masts, rigging and rudder. The 80-gun *Tonnant* lost all her masts. The British ships had also been severely damaged, and Admiral Howe moved his fleet back to New York for repairs. With his crippled fleet D'Estaing called a conference and reached the unanimous opinion with his officers to abandon the Newport operation and sail to Boston for repairs. D'Estaing wrote his Marine Ministry that "All the opinions, very many arguments and the dictates of reason itself urged me to steer to that port [Boston].... But my duty before all else was, to prove to the new allies of His Majesty that we are ready to sacrifice everything in order to keep a promise that we had once made. Our need of water, and the uncertainty as to what might happen, could not release us from a fixed engagement, and I felt that I must inform General Sullivan and assist him, by the presence of the fleet, either to conquer or to retreat."

The next day D'Estaing announced his intention to proceed to Boston for repairs. General Sullivan, along with Washington's major generals Nathanael Greene of Rhode Island and the young French volunteer, the Marquis de Lafayette, appealed D'Estaing's decision and asked him to refit at Providence, as well as Boston, and said that all supplies would be provided. But D'Estaing was not convinced. A loyalist resident of Newport wrote the *New York Royal Gazette* that "the monsieurs and the rebels are likely to come to blows on account of the late movements in Rhode Island."

There was much resentment over D'Estaing's decision not to further support the Newport operation. Sullivan did nothing to conceal his resentment, and Greene wrote Washington that the departure of the French fleet had "struck such a panic among the Militia and Volunteers that they began to desert by shoals." Sullivan's army of 9000 had now shrunk to nearly one-half its former size. Even though abandoned by the French Fleet, General Sullivan attempted to continue the fight, but with the recommendation of Greene, he retired to the mainland during the night of August 28 and on August 30 withdrew to Tiverton and Bristol.

Two days later Clinton arrived at Newport with transports loaded with 5000 reinforcements. The words of disappointment and resentment continued in an American reaction to D'Estaing's move. In words to General Sullivan, Washington gave his advice on how to deal with the disappointment:

> I will just add a hint, which, made use of in time, may prove important and answer a very salutary purpose. Should the expedition fail, thro' the abandonment of the French fleet, the Officers will be apt to complain loudly. But prudence dictates that we should put the best face upon the matter and, to the World, attribute the movement to Boston, to necessity. The Reasons are too obvious to need explaining. The principal one is, that our British and internal enemies would be glad to improve the least manner of complaint and disgust against and between us and our new Allies into a serious rupture.[7]

After a short refitting of his ships in Boston, D'Estaing's fleet, on November 3, 1778, departed for the French West Indies. The prestige of the French was damaged and Admiral D'Estaing's reputation was now blemished. The situation of the New York and Newport operations with the French had actually hurt the patriot cause. Could this emotional break in spirit of allied Franco-American relations be repaired?

Even though the French had won no naval victories yet, General Clinton realized that he must now heavily consider the presence of the French Navy in the Thirteen Colonies in all his planning. While he was continually harassed by Washington's forces around New York, Clinton felt relatively safe there to maintain a campaign of wearing down the American resistance, seeking loyalist support, controlling shipping lanes, ravaging the coastal shores, and occupying strategic points along the coastline. With D'Estaing in the West Indies and with full control of New York, Clinton resolved that it was time to undertake operations in the South.[8]

After several frustrating delays, Lieutenant Colonel Archibald Campbell sailed from New York with over 3500 troops from the 71st Regiment, the Wessenbach and Woellwarth Hessian Highlander regiments, and four provincial loyalist battalions, with a fleet commanded by Commodore Hyde Parker. One of the battalions was the Volunteers of Ireland, formed in Philadelphia by Lieutenant Colonel Lord Rawdon, and made up of deserters of Washington's army.[9] They arrived off Tybee Island, Georgia, on December 23, 1778.[10] The target was Savannah.

This man, Archibald Campbell, who had been chosen to lead the Georgia attack, was a member of Parliament representing the Stirling burghs of Scotland. He was the son of the commissioner of the Western Isles, and was known as a true Scotsman. He had served in the Seven

Years' War in Canada with the Fraser's Highlanders and was wounded at the Battle of Quebec in 1759. Campbell served in India, and came to America to serve again with the Fraser Highlanders as the commanding officer of the second battalion. Campbell landed in Boston and was captured, but later released in exchange for Ethan Allen.[11] He was not new to combat in America.

The situation in Georgia was not ideal for the patriot cause. Prior to December 1778, the patriots had tried three times to make Georgia more secure by attacking British Florida. In 1776 Charles Lee had tried but had seen his troops falter with yellow fever and malaria in the hot marshes and swamps of the Ogeechee River. In 1777 the Georgia Provincial Congress had made a second attempt at attacking St. Augustine, but the mission failed largely due to bickering between two officers over who was in command. The third attempt at putting Florida down had occurred in 1778 under the North Carolinian, Major General Robert Howe, then appointed to head the Department of the South. This attack, likewise, failed for command reasons. Howe wrote, "The situation of this country is a circumstance of exceeding anxiety for me. It is a melancholy truth that our regulars do not exceed 550 effectives." Due to the ill-fated campaign, Major General Benjamin Lincoln of Massachusetts was selected by the Continental Congress to replace Howe as the head of the Southern Department in September of 1778. On hearing the news, General Howe wrote to Henry Laurens, the president of the Congress, "Think, Sir, the underserved mortification I must feel on an occasion like this."[12]

The issue of command conflict, which had led to the removal of Howe from the leadership of the Southern colonies, was not an unusual situation. Most governors and state military leaders tended to look upon the Continental Army as "outsiders" and they desired to act independently in military operations. While the state officials had no part to play in selection of the Continental line officers, they continued to exercise control of their own militia, thereby complicating matters. Adding to the conflict was the situation of recruiting and pay. Continental soldiers were required to serve for at least three years, while state militia had only to serve for one year. The militia enlistees usually received financial incentives, which compared rather favorably with pay received by their Continental brethren. The situation of command conflict required that each successful Continental officer possess great skills of negotiating to bridge the vast bureaucratic barriers and local egos. Apparently, General Robert Howe did not possess enough diplomatic skill to succeed.

Hearing that Major Mark Prevost, the younger brother of Augustine Prevost, was collecting cattle and supplies in the Newport and Midway areas of Georgia,

General Howe marched his troops out of Charles Town on November 18, 1778, heading towards Savannah. On November 27, Howe's men reached Zulby's Ferry on the Savannah River, 30 miles upstream from the capital. An observer of Mark Prevost's activities reported to Howe that they "destroy everything they meet in their way. They have burnt all the houses on the other side of Newport Ferry."

Campbell had learned from the locals that the city was under the command of Major General Robert Howe of North Carolina, and that he had just returned from an expedition in East Florida. These informants estimated that Howe had some 1500 troops, but that reinforcements were expected. Acting on this information, Campbell decided to strike immediately. He was well aware that he was under orders to coordinate the campaign with Major General Augustine Prevost coming up from East Florida with his force, but he was convinced that swift action was warranted. Campbell re-embarked his troops into their transport vessels and sailed upriver to land closer to town.[13]

The town of Savannah, consisting of 450 houses situated on bluffs above the river, had been alerted to the presence of the British. General Robert Howe of the Continental Army was now in Savannah with 600 soldiers to defend the town, made up almost equally of South Carolina troops under General Isaac Huger and Georgia troops under General Samuel Elbert. The local Georgia militia of 100 men, under Governor Houstoun and commanded by Colonel George Walton, had been reluctantly placed under Continental authority on Christmas Eve. How would the Americans defend Savannah?[14]

On December 29, 1778, Campbell began putting troops ashore on the right bank of the Savannah River at Girardeau's Landing. This small piece of firm ground, a causeway, was bordered by rice plantations and put the force about two miles from the town. This was the main road to Savannah. Howe had placed Colonel Huger and his troops to guard the road that ran from Thunderbolt to Savannah, which included Girardeau's Landing, at Fair Lawn Plantation, just outside Savannah. Although Howe was informed by Colonel George Walton that a private road existed through a swamp that might be used by the British, he ignored the warning and failed to send any troops there.

At this point a local male black slave named Quamino Dolly wandered into the scene and informed Campbell of the private path through the swamp. Campbell immediately hired him as a guide. As Campbell's troops traveled down a path towards a low hill, they came under fire from American troops. Leading the British advance were the Highlanders, who in their usual manner were brandishing their large claymores in a frightful fracas. In reaction to the sight of the Highlanders, the Americans fled quickly from the hill.[15]

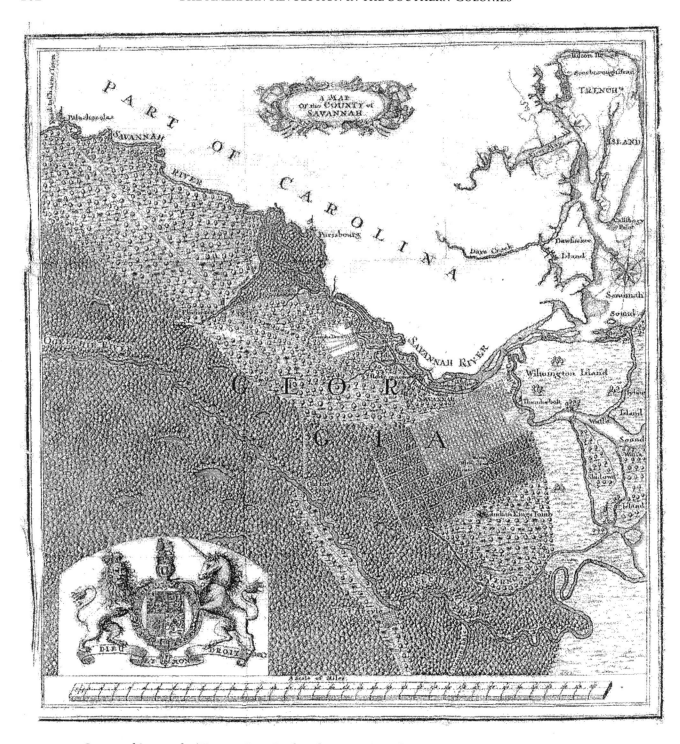

County of Savannah. (Hargrett Rare Book and Manuscript Library, University of Georgia Libraries.)

As Campbell advanced, he noted the main body of the rebels was positioned ahead and along the road. General Elbert's Georgia troops faced him on his left flank, with Colonel Walton's men on his right flank.[16] With rice fields bordering the river, stretching as far as he could see on his left and a wooded swamp on his right, Campbell was looking for a way out. Campbell now realized the significance of the information from his black slave guide. On either side of the road was a trench, which protected their two field guns. In front they were somewhat protected by a marshy rivulet that ran parallel with the trench. Even though nearly half of his troops were still aboard the transports, Campbell ordered his main force to retire behind a fold in the ground to conceal them from view of the Americans. He directed his main body of troops to make a deceptive pretended attack on his left flank to mislead Howe. The British commander of the 71st Regiment, Sir James Baird, was directed to lead his light infantry troops around behind the American positions using the unguarded path on the right through the swamp.[17]

Colonel Walton's militia was totally surprised when Baird's troops burst out of the swamp and fell upon them. They retreated in horror. Up to this point Campbell had kept his field guns hid in front. When the rear British troops were in position, Campbell ordered the guns forward, on to a mound, and issued a general advance, opening cannon fire on the Americans. Attacked from the front and rear, the Americans panicked. A retreat was sounded and the Americans, in total disarray, fled as best they could toward Savannah. The Georgia Continentals became confused when General Elbert ordered them to alter their march, and they dashed through the streets of Savannah, pausing briefly at the courthouse, and then scattered toward Musgrove Creek just west of the town. They had been told earlier that if they were forced to retreat, they would be able to cross a bridge to safety at Musgrove Creek, but the reports were false. No such bridge existed across the cold waters. Led by General Elbert, his troops jumped into the murky chilled waters and attempted to swim to the other bank. By 3 P.M. the British captured most of this force. One of the prisoners later wrote of the capture at the creek recalling, "being caught, as it were, in a pen, and the Highlanders keeping up a constant fire on us, it was thought advisable to surrender ourselves, which we accordingly did, and which was no sooner done than the Highlanders plundered every one amongst us...." Many had fled without even having a chance of firing a shot. It was not really a battle, it was a rout.[18]

Howes forces had suffered a major defeat, with 83 killed, 11 wounded and 453 captured.[19] American prisoners indicated that some 30 men had lost their lives in the swamps trying to escape. The British had only seven killed and 19 wounded. They had captured 48 cannons, 23 mortars and 94 barrels of gunpowder. Worst of all, the patriots had lost the capital of Georgia. The Georgia militia under Colonel Walton received the worst of the attack by Sir James Baird's forces. Colonel Walton was wounded, fell off his horse and captured. Campbell reported to Lord Germain with pride that he had defeated the Americans and that the capital "fell into our possession before it was dark...."

Campbell had shown that he was a bold officer, unlike many British officers of his day. He wrote to Germain of the operation, "I thought it expedient, having the day before me, to go in quest of the enemy rather than give them an opportunity of retiring unmolested."[20] Captain John Jervis, a friend to Clinton, wrote to Clinton,

"your coup in Georgia, and the repulse of D'Estaing in his attempts upon St. Lucia have preserved the nation from despair and the Ministry from perdition. There never was a thing so well timed, as the Georgia business, which arrived on the eve of the opening the Budget, and of the arrangement of measures, and impeachment of men." Alexander Innes, who carried the news of victory to England, reported to Clinton in a letter dated February 20 that the positive events "had an astonishing effect" in London.[21] Finally, Clinton and the Germain administration had possession of a Southern port, and had won a victory.

Howe, now with only 150 remaining of the original 700 troops under his command, led his frazzled group northward to Cherokee Hill, located some eight miles from Savannah. There he waited for stragglers. He then sent orders to Lieutenant Aaron Smith, who commanded the Third South Carolina Regiment at Ogeechee Ferry, and to Major Lane at Sunbury, to evacuate their posts and join up with him as soon as possible. Smith obeyed orders and returned with 20 men, but Lane was persuaded by the local citizens of Sunbury not to leave. Later Lane was captured by General Prevost, and exchanged for a British prisoner. Lane was court-martialed and dismissed for disobeying his general's orders.

During the next two days Campbell had Sir Hyde Parker, commander of the British fleet, to move his ships up to the town, where rebel prisoners could be loaded aboard. The heat was so bad that many prisoners died. In this operation, Parker captured 126 prisoners, three ships and eight smaller vessels, with the loss of only one British seaman killed and five wounded. Campbell continued his advance upriver even though his ships carrying his horses had not arrived. His men were forced to drag their guns and carts cross country with the help of the few animals they could round up. A number of locals volunteered to help Campbell, and they were organized into militia. Small groups of Americans were encountered and overpowered. Colonel Campbell reached Cherokee Hill on January 1, 1779, shortly after General Howe had departed across the Savannah River into South Carolina.

At Ebenezer, loyalist Reverend Christopher Triebner, the minister of the village who had taken an oath of allegiance to the king and accompanied Campbell's troops into the Ebenezer, joined Campbell. Others of Salzburgers' Church joined the British. These loyalists even organized marauding parties, and they started on a campaign of burning and pillaging every farm and plantation whose owners were believed to be patriot. Campbell stationed a company of troops at Ebenezer, and set up the Salzburgers' Church as a hospital. Prisoners that had been rounded up were taken to Savannah under a guard of ten soldiers. On the way to Savannah, two patriots, Sergeant William Jasper and his friend Sergeant Newton, waited by a spring and attacked the British guards. Two British soldiers were killed and the other eight were taken to the Americans' camp across the Savannah River. The spot was later named Jasper Springs.

Now that Campbell had possession of the countryside around Savannah, he intended to head toward Sunbury, but learned that General Augustine Prevost had already taken it. A thousand citizens of Sunbury watched as Prevost's men destroyed the town, burned the church and laid the crops to waste. Many locals retreated into South Carolina as refugees.[22] Fort Morris at Sunbury, under patriot command of Major Joseph Lane, had tried to defend the fort with but 200 men. General Prevost, being delayed in arriving from East Florida, had sent his brother, Lieutenant Colonel James Mark Prevost, to attack, which he did on January 6, with some 2000 men. When the British moved up artillery to bombard the fort on the 9th, Lane surrendered the fort. Lane had suffered 11 casualties, and Prevost only four. [23] Besides the 212 prisoners taken, the patriot forces gave up 40 guns with ammunition and supplies.[24]

On January 10, Campbell returned to Savannah, and on the 17th he was finally joined by General Augustine Prevost, who had endured a difficult march from East Florida. Augustine Prevost, who was born in Geneva, Switzerland, had joined the British Army in 1756 and served in the French and Indian War, where he suffered a serious wound in the Battle of Quebec. In 1775 Prevost had been placed in command of British East Florida.[25] Now in command of all Southern British forces at Savannah, he too was without horses and his men were barely surviving on oysters as they came up through the swamps of Georgia. With forces now joined and working from the base at Savannah, Prevost sent Campbell to take Augusta.[26]

On January 22, Campbell set out from Ebenezer for Augusta, some 100 miles up the Savannah River to the northwest. In a letter to Germain, Campbell wrote, "I need not inform Your Lordship, how much I prize the hope of being the first British Officer to rend a Stripe and a Star from the flag of Congress."[27] On the march Campbell's troops were joined by a number of loyalist militia. Even though the forces of General Lincoln and Moultrie were located just across the Savannah River from Campbell at Purrysburg, they did not have the sufficient strength to attack him. General Lincoln did send General Elbert with his Georgia troops to the upper part of South Carolina to stop Campbell from taking Augusta. Elbert's troops skirmished with Campbell's army at Briar Creek, but were unable to stop their movement toward the town. On January 29, Campbell took Augusta without opposition. The British now occupied the seat of the Georgia government, which had moved to Augusta in 1776.

Just ten days before the fall of Savannah, December 19, 1778, Major General Benjamin Lincoln arrived in Charles Town to take over the Southern Continental Army from General Robert Howe, who was in Savannah. Lincoln, formerly a farmer from Hingham, Massachusetts, was a tubby, genial man who was known for having a sharp mind.[28] Lincoln, born in 1733, had worked hard and moved up the ladder of success to prominence. He had served as town clerk, justice of the peace and as a militia officer for a Suffolk County regiment. As the Revolution approached, he served on the Hingham Committee of Correspondence and in the Massachusetts Provincial Congress. As a militia lieutenant colonel when the war started, he rose rapidly to major general in the Continental line by early 1777, with Washington's support.[29]

At the time only 1500 troops were available to march in relief to Savannah, but after urgent pleas for local militia, Lincoln's force grew to some 3500 troops. He departed for Purrysburg, South Carolina, which was located just across the river from British-held Ebenezer.[30] Shortly after arriving, Lincoln's forces captured a company of loyalists on their way to join Campbell in Augusta. Lincoln brought 70 of these men before a court under charges of treason. Five of these men were ultimately hanged. There appeared to be little sympathy for those who took up with the British at this point.[31]

On February 3, British Major Gardiner, with 200 troops, made an amphibious landing on Port Royal Island supported by a naval squadron from Commodore Hyde Parker. General Lincoln sent General William Moultrie and Brigadier General Stephen Bull, with 300 South Carolina militia, to drive the British off the island. With Moultrie's three field guns, 300 troops and 10 Continentals, he occupied Beaufort, placing his men on both sides of the road that Gardiner's troops would approach on. When Gardiner's men arrived, Moultrie fired a cannon blast that sent the British running for cover in the woods. After an hour of fighting, the Americans ran out of ammunition, but fortunately the British appeared to be retreating. American dragoons made chase, but only a few British prisoners were taken. Moultrie suffered 30 casualties, with British losses unknown. The battle distinguished the Charles Town Battalion of Artillery unit under Major Thomas Grimball, and the two companies under captains Thomas Heyward and Edward Rutledge, both signers of the Declaration of Independence. This unit had been organized by Christopher Gadsden from the best families of Charles Town.[32]

In the meantime, loyalist Colonel John Hamilton, a well-respected Scottish patrician of large fortune with high social standing and a veteran of the Battle of Culloden, had been sent by General Prevost upriver towards

Augusta, with some 200 mounted infantry, to show the flag and urge support of the British. At Carr's Fort, Georgia, on February 10, the combined force of 350 men from Colonel Andrew Pickens' South Carolina Militia and Captain John Dooley's Georgia Militia attacked Hamilton's loyalist infantry. As the battle ensued, with the Americans winning, news arrived that another loyalist militia force of 700 men from North Carolina under Colonel Boyd was heading South to join Hamilton. Pickens broke off the engagement and began the march to attack Boyd.[33]

Andrew Pickens was a dour Presbyterian elder who had grown up in an "atmosphere of rifle and religion." Born in 1739 in Bucks County, Pennsylvania, his family had moved to the Shenandoah Valley of Virginia, and later southward, along with other Scotch-Irish, to the Waxhaw community in upper South Carolina. In the 1760s, Pickens had settled and married in the Long Canes district of South Carolina, located some 22 miles west of Ninety Six. Pickens prospered in Indian trade and soon became such a successful merchant that he built a warehouse across the Savannah River from Augusta to hold the goods acquired for sale downriver. Like most of the backcountry wealthholders, Pickens sided with the patriot cause because he shared the common economic values of the coastal plantation owners of the Carolinas and Georgia. Pickens was a determined patriot who desired to protect his holdings and way of life.[34]

On February 13, Colonel Boyd's forces crossed the Savannah River and camped at a farm on the north side of Kettle Creek, located some 50 miles northwest of Augusta. Unaware that Pickens' forces had made a complete circle, crossed the river and moved in behind them, they turned their horses loose to allow them to graze, as they slaughtered cows and parched corn. Based on a favorable scouting report from Captain Hugh McCall indicating that Boyd's troops were not aware of the American patriot forces' presence, Pickens launched his surprise attack the next day from three directions simultaneously. When the Americans advanced, the alarmed loyalists quickly formed a line behind a fence, and returned fire. After nearly an hour of fighting, Boyd's forces were eventually driven back. As the loyalists retreated, Colonel Boyd was struck by three cannonballs, two of which passed through his body. Boyd's troops fled across the creek and into a swamp, leaving their horses, baggage and arms behind. Pickens led his forces through the swamp and continued the battle on the other side of Kettle Creek. Finally the battle ended, with 70 loyalists dead, and another 75 either wounded or captured. Pickens' forces suffered only nine killed and 23 wounded in the battle.

Pickens, who had known Boyd before the war, found his mortally wounded foe and ordered that he receive all possible medical attention. Boyd thanked Pickens for his chivalry and asked him who had won the battle. When he was told that the patriots won, Boyd remarked that the outcome would have been different if he had not been wounded. He then asked Pickens to bury him, and also asked Pickens if he would send his wife his brooch he had worn and tell her of his death. Pickens agreed and the dying officer's wishes were carried out. The Battle of Kettle Creek was a significant victory for the patriot forces, and put added pressure on Campbell's forces in Augusta. The battle had scattered the loyalists, as some fled to Florida. Others returned to their homes to ask for mercy. Approximately 200 retreated to Augusta to join Campbell. The loyalist prisoners were taken to South Carolina, where they were tried for treason and most pardoned. Five were executed.[35]

With Lincoln's forces eager to engage the British, he sent a sizable force under Major General John Ashe to retake Augusta from the British. With 1400 North Carolina militia, 100 Georgia Continentals and 200 light-horse militia, General Ashe headed for Augusta. With Ashe approaching, Lieutenant Colonel Campbell decided to retreat from Augusta, leaving on February 14. The local Anglican priest, Reverend James Seymour, who had only two weeks before celebrated the arrival of Campbell's troops in Augusta, was sadly lamenting the scene before him as the British marched into the thick woods. He remarked, "Our feelings at first on that Occasion cannot be easily described. We expected to be plundered of everything we had, and even that our Lives were in danger."[36]

Campbell withdrew across Briar Creek, stopping to burn the bridge there. On March 3, 1779, while troops from General Ashe's units were in the process of rebuilding the bridge, a force of some 900 infantry, grenadiers, dragoons and militia from General Mark Prevost's forces began to cross the creek above Ashe's camp, in an attempt to get behind the patriot forces. As the British attack began, Ashe's Continentals opened fire, which alarmed the militia, who immediately began to scatter. Then, the Continentals, realizing their situation, also retreated in disorder. The American retreat found many men throwing down their weapons and heading for the river. The shameful defeat left over 150 American dead, with the British capturing 11 officers and 162 other troops. The British also captured seven cannons with other ammunition and supplies. General Prevost suffered only 16 casualties. Of the defeat, the British publication *New York Gazette and Weekly Mercury* declared, "The panic occasioned by the terror of the bayonet, left them no alternative but that of plunging into the water ... few would have escaped if night had not come on soon."[37]

While the Battle of Briar Creek was a worthy British victory, the result was that the Americans had at least regained Augusta, and the British had not shown any degree of firm control of the backcountry, which was so important to gaining loyalist support.[38] When General Moultrie heard of the defeat at Briar Creek, he said it was nothing but a total rout, and one that would serve to lengthen the war by a year in his opinion. It was an unfortunate event, and it allowed the British more freedom of action than might have been the case if the patriot forces had won at Briar Creek. Another result of the defeat was that many volunteers, who were on their way to join General Lincoln, turned around and went back home with the sense that the patriot cause was lost. While South Carolina was indeed in more peril than before, the real gloom was felt by the citizens of Georgia, who were now under total British control.[39]

Following the defeat at Briar Creek, on April 20 General Lincoln commenced a march up the Savannah River towards Augusta with about 2000 of his army, leaving General Moultrie behind at Black Swamp—located 25 miles from Purrysburg. Moultrie's force consisted of two regiments, the Second and Fifth, with another 220 men under Colonel McIntosh and Colonel Maurice Simon's brigade of Charles Town Militia, all totaling some 1200 men. Moultrie was instructed to hold Purrysburg as long as possible, but if the British headed for Charles Town, to delay them long enough to give Lincoln time to return. On April 22 Lincoln wrote to Moultrie ordering all Continental troops to join him except for the Second and Fifth regiments. Lincoln did receive intelligence on April 24 that the British intended a movement into South Carolina, but he discounted it as an attempt to draw him back from Georgia. Seeing a real opportunity that Lincoln's absence had afforded, Lieutenant Colonel Mark Prevost took 2000 men across the Savannah River on April 28 and marched towards Charles Town. The garrison at Purrysburg under Lieutenant Colonel McIntosh retreated immediately and moved to Coosahatchie, where General Moultrie joined him. Moultrie sent dispatches immediately to General Lincoln, South Carolina Governor Rutledge at Orangeburgh, and to Lieutenant Governor Thomas Bee in Charles Town notifying them of the situation.

On May 1, Moultrie moved his troops to Tullifiny Hill, leaving a rear guard of 100 at Coosahatchie. Moultrie sent out horsemen in every direction to reconnoiter for the British. On May 3, Colonel John Laurens joined Moultrie and asked for an opportunity to serve. Moultrie agreed and placed some 350 men under Laurens, with orders to move the rear guard down to Moultrie's position. In his zeal to make an impact, Laurens exceeded his orders to bring up the rearguard and crossed the river to the east side and engaged the British. After losing a number of men, the force retreated and marched in good order to Salkehatchie Chapel that night.

The British were encamped at Pocotaligo, some five miles in Moultrie's rear. Moultrie continued his retreat, while destroying the bridges as he passed as best he could. Messages to Lincoln about the retreat did not persuade Lincoln of the peril. The May 6 message to Lincoln urged that he return to Charles Town immediately. Moultrie estimated incorrectly that Prevost's forces were 4000 strong. Lincoln now yielded somewhat and sent word that he was moving down the Savannah River to draw off the British. Moultrie hoped to hold at Ashepoo, but he found his force diminishing, as his troops left to look after their families and property. On May 7, Moultrie halted at Dorchester, just 24 miles from Charles Town. While he had left Purrysburg with 1200 men, Moultrie now had only some 600 men heading into Dorchester to join five separated military units gathered there. Forces of Prevost were in hot pursuit of Moultrie toward Charles Town.

Patriot forces were now all heading toward Charles Town. General Lincoln's forces were marching now, slowly, towards Charles Town, as Governor Rutledge's militia of 600 rushed home. Colonel Harris of Georgia, with his detachment of 250 Continentals, was likewise on the way. Moultrie's 600 men marched into Charles Town on May 9, at about the same time as Governor Rutledge's and Colonel Harris' militias. A small party of cavalry from General Washington's army under Brigadier General Pulaski had come over from Haddrell's Point on May 8, followed on May 11 with his infantry force of 125. Could the patriot forces stop Prevost from taking Charles Town?

Charles Town, situated on a narrow neck of land between the confluence of the Cooper and Ashley rivers, was not entirely prepared for an attack. The city had done some defensive construction, including fortifications from the rear land entrance to the city. A large number of black slaves had been put to work to build works with walls only three to four feet thick at the strongest points across the neck of land. Here, on May 10, patriot forces were deployed. The Charles Town Militia was placed along the line running from the Cooper River at a battery to the center of the fortification. Also, on the right was the Charles Town Artillery, with the artillery of the Fourth Continental Regiment, under the command of Colonel Roberts, on the left. The Fifth Regiment of Colonel McIntosh's was located on the redoubt on the right line, with 100 men of the Second Regiment under Lieutenant Colonel Marion on their left. Colonel Harris' detachment was on the left on a redoubt, with the remainder of the Second Regiment with General Pulaski's infantry occupying the center of the line. General Moultrie reported that there were 3180 troops ready to defend Charles Town.[40]

Fording rivers with pontoon bridges, and plundering homesteads as they passed, Prevost and his forces reached Ashley Ferry in the evening of May 10, just seven miles above the city. Prevost's men crossed the Ashley River and appeared before the lines the next morning. In an effort to slow the advance of the British force, Brigadier General Pulaski, with his infantry and some of the militia, engaged the forward guard of Prevost's forces. The skirmish occurred near Nightingale Race Course, near the present Line and Meeting streets. His unit was overpowered, and he lost most of his infantry — either killed, wounded or taken prisoner. With some difficulty Pulaski's retreating troops got back into the lines. The skirmishing continued with little result until, by afternoon, the full British force reached the location where Pulaski's men had fallen. At this point, Moultrie opened fire at the British with cannon, which stopped their advance.

The evening of May 11 saw a tragic event that served as a stark and horrible reminder of the confusion of command authority that continued to plague the American forces in every campaign to date in the Revolution. At around 10 o'clock in the dark night, some men on the right thought they saw the enemy approaching, and fired a few shots in the direction of the supposed British. Immediately the entire line of defenders opened fire with cannon, field-pieces and muskets. Unfortunately, Major Benjamin Huger was killed by mistake, along with 12 others who were either killed or wounded. Huger, a brave and able officer and well-respected citizen, had been sent out from the lines to stop a gap that had opened through the abatis. An "abatis" is made up of sharpened stakes embedded at an angle in the ground toward the enemy. The confusion had come over the command of the militia serving with the Continental Army units. The militia had been told to obey orders from the governor, Moultrie or the Privy Council. Moultrie had earlier remarked to one unit that the Privy Council's orders must not be obeyed, which appears to have been the case that killed Major Huger. The governor and General Moultrie had given no such order to send Huger out from the lines.

On the tragic event, General Moultrie addressed the governor and council: "Gentlemen, this will never do; we shall be ruined and undone if we have so many commanders; it is absolutely necessary to choose one to command: if you leave the command to me, I will not interfere in any civil matters you may do with the enemy, such as parlays, capitulations, etc. I will attend only to the military department." The governor and council unanimously chose Moultrie to command. Thus, the command of the defense of Charles Town was arrived at only after they had killed some of their own men, and when the British were at the gates to the city, a few hundred yards away.[41]

The presence of Pulaski in Charles Town at this moment was a mixed blessing for General Moultrie. Kasimir Pulaski, who was born in Poland in 1747 to a noble family, had fought with his father's troops against the Russians and served in the Turkish Army. In Paris he had became a friend to Ben Franklin, who encouraged him to come to America. With Franklin's recommendation to Congress in hand, he arrived in America in 1777. He became an aide to General Washington at the Battle of Brandywine, and based on a suggestion from Washington, Congress offered Pulaski a commission as brigadier general of a newly authorized cavalry unit. After ineffective efforts at Germantown, he spent the winter with Washington at Valley Forge. He, like many of the European mold, was highly egotistical and difficult to get along with. He was known to quarrel with his American subordinates, and once brought up his second-in-command for not showing proper respect to him, as a noble Pole. He resigned from his cavalry unit in 1778 and was allowed to raise his own "elite" corps, made up of former British deserters and prisoners. His Pulaski Legion had not shown any success so far, and the events at Charles Town in May of 1779 did nothing to increase the war record of Pulaski's units.[42]

That night, at around 3 A.M. on May 11, Moultrie was summoned to meet with Governor John Rutledge. Moultrie rode to the governor, where he was asked "whether we had not best have a parley with the enemy; and whether we were able to resist their force." Moultrie told the governor that he estimated his troop strength at around 2200 men at least. The governor replied that he felt they had only 1800 men at best, and that the enemy strength was between 7000 and 8000. The governor reminded Moultrie that if they forced through the lines, a great number of citizens would be put to death. The governor spoke of the state's engineer, Colonel Senfs, and reported that their lines were indeed weak. After some discussion the governor proposed that they determine, under flag of truce, what terms they would receive from Prevost. Moultrie remarked that he felt they could hold, but he indicated that he would deliver the message if the governor would call the council together to consider the matter. Thus, under Moultrie's own name, the message was passed to Prevost by Moultrie's aide, Mr. Kinloch. The delivered message read:

> General Moultrie, perceiving from the motions of your army that your intention is to besiege the town, would be glad to know on what terms you would be disposed to grant a capitulation should he be inclined to capitulate.

Under the signature of Lieutenant Colonel J.M. Prevost, the brother of General Prevost, the general returned his answer at 11 A.M. on May 11 as follows:

> Sir, The humane treatment which the inhabitants of Georgia and this province, have hitherto received, will, I

flatter myself, induce you to accept of the offers of peace and protection, which I now make by orders of General Prevost; the evils and horrors attending the event of a storm, (which cannot fail to be successful) are too evident, not to induce a man of humane feelings, to do all in his power to prevent it: you may depend, that every attention shall be paid, and every necessary measure be adopted to prevent disorders; and that such of the peace and protection, may be received as prisoners of war, and their fate decided by that of the rest of the colonies. Four hours shall be allowed for an answer; after which, your silence or detention of the bearer of this, will be deemed a positive refusal.

When Moultrie received Prevost's reply, he showed it to the governor. Immediately the governor summoned the council to meet at his house. General Moultrie ordered Colonel Cambray to work on the left lines as fast as possible and ordered ammunition brought up from the city to the lines. In attendance at this critical meeting were Governor Rutledge, Moultrie, Lieutenant Governor Bee, Colonel Charles Pinckney, Christopher Gadsden, Roger Smith (the governor's brother-in-law), Thomas Ferguson (Gadsden's brother-in-law), John Edwards, John Neufville, Colonel Isaac Motte, John Parker, Count Pulaski and Colonel Laurens. Prevost's letter was read and the issue of giving up the city was discussed in earnest. Moultrie, Laurens and Pulaski recommended against capitulation. When asked how many troops they had, Moultrie indicated that he had 3180 men, which was immediately disputed by the governor, who felt sure there were only 2500 men at most. During the continued discussion, Captain Dunbar of the Second Regiment with much haste approached General Moultrie with a message that Prevost had asked for the work on the lines to cease immediately. Moultrie agreed to stop the work. Moultrie then asked the governor and council for a decision. Finally the following day this message was sent to Prevost:

Sir, I cannot possibly agree to so dishonorable a proposal as is contained in your favor of yesterday; but if you will appoint an officer to confer on terms, I will send one to meet at such time and place as you fix on.

Prevost refused to negotiate as requested, and the council was again summoned to consider the next action. After much consideration the following message was sent:

To propose a neutrality during the war between Great Britain and America, and the question whether the State shall belong to Great Britain or remain one of the United States, be determined by the treaty of peace between those two powers.

The message was delivered by Colonel McIntosh and Roger Smith, after Colonel Laurens refused, and Moultrie "pressed them into a compliance." Many in attendance during the considerations with the governor and council were openly upset. According to Moultrie, John Edwards "was so affected as to weep, saying, 'What! are we going to give up the town at last?'" Even though the proceedings of the council were considered secret, Christopher Gadsden openly discussed the decision with other citizens. This decision to seek neutrality was considered a disgrace by many South Carolinians. Regardless, McIntosh and Smith met with Colonel Prevost for a conference a quarter of a mile from the city gates, in sight of the lines. Lieutenant Colonel Prevost indicated "that they did not come in a legislative capacity, but if Colonel Smith pleased, he would show the proposal to the General." A second meeting at 12 o'clock was held when Colonel Prevost remarked "that he had nothing to do with the Governor, that his business was with General Moultrie, and as the garrison was in arms they must surrender prisoners of war."

The governor, Moultrie and the council now considered this situation. After a short pause, Moultrie declared, "Gentlemen, you see how the matter stands; the point is this: I am to deliver you up prisoners of war or not." Some indicated a hearty, "Yes!" Then Moultrie continued, "I am determined not to deliver you up prisoners of war. We will fight it out." Colonel Laurens jumped up and declared, "Thank God, we are on our legs again." As Moultrie departed, Gadsden and Ferguson followed him and said, "Act according to your judgment and we will support you." Moultrie immediately ordered the flag to signal that the conference be at an end. After confusion on the British part on the meaning of the signal, Moultrie sent out Mr. Kinloch to tell Prevost that he "was very sorry they should be detained so long—that his flag had been waved some time ago, and that all conference was at an end."

Incredibly, the next morning at daybreak, on May 13, the citizens of Charles Town awoke to great joy as many cried out; "The enemy is gone!" And so they were. As it turned out, the main body of Prevost's forces had begun to depart just after the conference had ended. Some light infantry had been left behind to make sure Moultrie did not move as the main force retreated under the cover of night. Pulaski proceeded to follow the British with his cavalry, but the British had already crossed the Ashley River before he could reach them. Charles Town was saved!

Back on May 8, 1779, General Moultrie sent a report to Lincoln updating him on the status of his activities, including the fact that he had reached Charles Town. This report reached General Lincoln at 4 P.M. on May 10, and he immediately dispatched a reply within the hour. Unfortunately, Lincoln's reply letter was taken by the British near the battle lines at Charles Town. Thus, Lincoln was within a 24-hour communications ride from his location to Charles Town on May 10, and on the afternoon of May 12, Lincoln was 65 miles away from the city and 35 miles from Wort's Ferry on Edisto. Lincoln commented that "We are now making and shall continue to make every exertion for the relief of Charlestown. The baggage will be left … the inability of the men only will put a period to our daily marches." But in fact Lincoln was not making a truly rapid movement to Charles Town as he had written. Had Lincoln exerted real haste in attempting to reach the city, it is most likely that Prevost's forces would have been defeated. But, as it turned out, Prevost was able to escape.

General Lincoln's force of over 5000 men reached Dorchester on May 14, which was the day after Prevost's army had crossed the Ashley River. Prevost had remained just across the river from Ashley Ferry for several days, and then, as Lincoln approached, he moved to the southwest to take possession of John's Island. John's Island is separated from the mainland by the Stono River. There, on the mainland eastern shore, General Prevost had three redoubts constructed for defense and set up garrison of some 1500 under Lieutenant Colonel Prevost. On May 31, Lincoln detached General Isaac Huger with 1000 militiamen, plus the horse units under Pulaski and Horry, to attack the British outpost at Stono River. After Pulaski's men conducted reconnaissance to report that the British force was too strong and well entrenched to attack, the patriot force was withdrawn.

As might be expected, General Lincoln came under much criticism by this time in May of 1779. His decision to head out to Augusta with most of the available troops and leave Charles Town with limited support was the chief point of discontent. Lincoln's slow progress at returning his forces to Charles Town in their moment of need was but another complaint. Comments regarding the withdrawal of the attack at Stono River were, likewise, negative. The displeasure with General Lincoln was held not only by many of the citizens of the area, but was in evidence with many of the officers in his own command. Lincoln had been aware of his unpopularity and had requested permission to retire for health reasons. On May 13 the Continental Congress gave him permission to retire and had "resolved that Brig. Gen. Moultrie be commander in the absence of Maj. Gen. Lincoln of the Southern army during its continuance, to the southwest of North Carolina, with the allowance of a Major General on a separate command until the further order of Congress." Moultrie responded to the affair with a sense of loyalty

and respect for Lincoln by urging Lincoln not to retire. Lincoln then responded to Moultrie on June 10 that he would continue to render service to the state as long as his health held out. Lincoln told Moultrie that he knew that the people had a great attachment and confidence in Moultrie, and that he knew that Moultrie would command with honor to him and the country. But, after receiving his permission to retire and with the knowledge of his current unpopularity with many, Lincoln did not relinquish his command after all and the issue was dropped.[43]

So it was that on June 1, 1779, the majority of the patriot forces in the lower South were positioned around Charles Town under the command of Major General Benjamin Lincoln, while the British forces, under General Augustine Prevost, held Savannah and those environs. From these two Southern towns, located only 100 miles apart, were these opposing armies, each making plans to overwhelm the other in some future campaign. While Prevost's attempt to take Charles Town had shown great daring, it was not universally considered as an appropriate move. Sir Henry Clinton wrote Prevost that he had considered the effort to be reckless based on his understanding that he would not conduct major offensive operations without reinforcements from New York. Clinton had made no commitment to send additional troops to Georgia or South Carolina at this point. In his private correspondence Clinton revealed that the Charles Town offensive only served to inflame the patriot spirit when there was no justification or advantage.[44]

The surrender of Savannah to the British after a total rout, and the near capitulation of patriot forces at Charles Town at the hands of General Prevost and his brother were severe blows to the patriot psyche. To the loyalists, who had flocked to support Campbell and Prevost, the events gave some hope for restoration of British rule in the Southern colonies, after three lonely years without the comfort of a British presence. The damaging revelation that the leaders in Charles Town had considered neutrality was now an incredible embarrassment to all Southern patriots. Even after the Southern victories at Norfolk, Moore's Creek Bridge and Sullivan's Island, the loss of Savannah and the colony of Georgia to the British was difficult to accept. With Clinton and Germain now riding this newfound success of the Southern strategy with satisfaction in the halls of Parliament, and within the inner circles of British government, what new plans would they make to further the pain of the patriot South? A new low point in patriot morale had been reached.

9

D'Estaing and Savannah

General Benjamin Lincoln was determined to regain the offensive to drive the British out of the Lowcountry and Savannah. On June 15, 1779, General Lincoln traveled from his camp at Stono River to Charles Town to consult with the South Carolina governor and his council. Lincoln then presented his plan to carry out a major attack on the British force of 1500 men at Stono. With Lincoln's force of over 5000 men, supported with the strong detachment from the Charles Town area, there was every belief that the patriot forces could gain a victory. The governor and council agreed to let Lincoln take 1200 men from the Charles Town force for the attack. Lincoln told General Moultrie to hold the garrison in Charles Town in readiness to move at a moment's notice.

Lincoln had much concern with his ever-continuing problem of keeping his forces from deserting the cause. The South Carolina Militia, commanded by General Williamson, was disappearing one man at a time, and Colonel Kershaw's Regiment even lost an entire company of 27 privates and two officers. Also of great concern was that the North Carolina Militia was coming to the end of their enlistment period in a few days. Given the situation with his ever diminishing force and the need to overwhelm the enemy, Lincoln was motivated to move quickly.

The next day, June 16, Lieutenant Colonel Prevost left Stono Ferry by boat for Savannah with the majority of the British force, including the grenadiers of the Sixteenth Regiment. In addition, he took along all the vessels that had served the British to maintain a "bridge" from his post on the eastern shore of John's Island across to James Island. Prevost left behind Lieutenant Colonel John Maitland to defend the British rear with some 900 men of the First Battalion of the Seventy-first Regiment,

loyalist militia and Hessians. Maitland's force spent the days from June 17 to June 19 transporting the sick and wounded, blacks and Indians across the inlet with the baggage and horses of the garrison. Maitland also ordered the unnecessary buildings of the force destroyed in preparation for defense of the post.

On June 19 Lincoln ordered Moultrie to move on to James Island across from Charles Town as a show to the British on John's Island. Lincoln's plan was to have Moultrie take his boats up to Wappoo Cut to be in position to head off any retreating British and support action from Lincoln at Stono Ferry. Unfortunately, General Moultrie did not follow Lincoln's orders with speed. When Lincoln began his attack on Maitland at seven o'clock the morning of June 20, Moultrie had only half of his force on James Island. Moultrie's force did not reach Wappoo Cut until the battle was over.

Lincoln's forces arrived at the British defensive works about an hour after daybreak on the 19th after traveling the 18 miles from the Ashley River. Lincoln's army was positioned in the center, with the flanks covered by two battalions of light infantry led by Lieutenant Colonel Henderson and Colonel Malmedy. On the left of the line was positioned the Continental troops under General Huger. On the right was the brigade of North Carolina and South Carolina militia commanded by General Jethro Sumner of North Carolina. Behind this brigade was a small group of Virginia militia under General Mason. Pulaski's cavalry unit was on the far right, with a small unit of North Carolina horsemen commanded by William Richardson Davie.

The British forces of Lieutenant Colonel Maitland had the North and South Carolina Provincial Regiment under Lieutenant Colonel Hamilton in the center, with the Highlanders of the Seventy-first Regiment on the right and the Hessian Regiment on the left.

The American forces were positioned along a line 700 yards long, advancing in two lines through a scant pine forest. British pickets first met gunfire from the Americans. Two companies of the Seventy-first Regiment were sent out to meet Lincoln's troops. After moving out about a quarter of a mile they engaged the Continental troops on Lincoln's left. The Highlanders fought bravely and did not retreat until all their officers were killed or wounded, and only 11 remained. The British officers decided to hold back their fire and wait for the Americans to approach their works. At 60 yards from the abatis, Lincoln's men received full volleys from the artillery and infantry. Lincoln's men returned fire against the orders of Lincoln. On the British left the Hessians began to break under the onslaught of the Carolina militia under General Sumner. But immediately, Maitland moved the 71st Regiment to the left and stopped the Sumner advance. The Hessians rallied with the 71st and fierce fighting continued with Lincoln's Continental and militia troops.

Lincoln orchestrated a charge, but the troops could not advance past the British defenses. Lincoln, seeing his forces being cut down without mercy, ordered a retreat. The cavalry, with Pulaski absent, charged the British force defiantly, but Maitland's troops closed ranks as the horses approached, returning an incredible barrage of musketfire. As Lincoln's men retreated, General Mason's Virginia brigade advanced with heavy fire which served to stop the British advance. Lincoln's main forces retired, and the battle at Stono Ferry was over at 8:30 A.M. Lincoln's retreating forces returned to Charles Town.[1]

Casualties were heavy on both sides, as the British suffered 26 killed and 103 wounded or missing. The patriot forces lost 34 killed and 113 wounded. Among the casualties was Colonel Owen Roberts, the commander of the Fourth Continental Regiment of South Carolina, who while in the process of dying in the hands of his own son, declared, "I rejoice, my boy, once more to embrace you. Receive this sword, which has never been tarnished by dishonor, and let it not be inactive while the liberty of your country is endangered. Take my last adieu, accept my blessing, and return to your duty." Major Ancrum and newly promoted Brigade Major of Cavalry William R. Davie were both severely wounded. Davie had only been saved by the bravery of one of his men who grabbed Davie on his own horse on the field of battle to escape. General Isaac Huger over the Continentals was wounded slightly, while Hugh Jackson, the brother of future President Andrew Jackson, died after the action of fatigue.[2]

While there were numerous decisions that could have affected the outcome of the battle for the patriot forces, the most significant failure was the missing forces under Moultrie. Had General Moultrie followed orders from Lincoln and moved his men up to support Lincoln's attack at Stono Ferry, his force of 700 men, which nearly equaled to the entire British force, would have destroyed the British. The hero of Sullivan's Island and the defense of Charles Town now had his honor tarnished. On June 22 Moultrie sent three galleys through Wappoo Cut to hit at the British communications. The galleys received fire from field pieces and small arms in a skirmish that lasted three-quarters of an hour. After taking a British schooner, they proceeded upriver and attacked another gun battery on a bluff with three pieces and silenced them. As the tide ran out, Moultrie's galleys returned downriver with their captured schooner. Moultrie had lost six men killed and several wounded.[3]

On June 24, having accomplished his mission of protecting Prevost's movement to Savannah, Maitland evacuated his post at Stono Ferry and marched southward along the seacoast, from island to island, to rejoin Prevost at Beaufort, on Port Royal Island on July 8. General Prevost then departed Beaufort for Savannah leaving Lieutenant Colonel Maitland in command of a garrison of some 900 troops. The British could use Beaufort as a forward base of operations into the Lowcountry.[4] The British offensive campaign into South Carolina was now at an end.

The British plunder of some of the richest areas in South Carolina was significant and disturbing. Some 3000 black slaves were believed to have been taken by the British leaving South Carolina. Many slaves were shipped off to the West Indies and sold. Thousands of other slaves who were left behind suffered terribly under the British. During the retreat of the British Army, many blacks would cling to the sides of the boats. In attempts to prevent danger to their boats, British soldiers were posted with cutlasses and bayonets to keep them at bay. Many blacks had their hands cut off in this way. Hundreds died of disease. Sadly, other blacks died in the woods and marshes, being unable to return home for fear of a certain death, with disease all around them in a condition of being destitute without food or shelter, under the horrid heat and humidity of the Carolina summer.[5]

Prominent Lowcountry planters saw major destruction, like Eliza Lucas Pinckney at Belmont, who had her furnishings smashed; the Bull family's Ashley Hall was looted; Major Thomas Pinckney's home at Ashepoo had 19 slaves taken, along with their prize horses, sheep and poultry and the dwelling house burned.[6] Even with the aid of stolen horses taken from planters, the British could barely transport all the loot from the Lowcountry homesteads. More wealth was actually destroyed than was taken out by the British. Large livestock were cruelly shot down, rice barrels filled with plates and furniture were stolen, some homes burned, chinaware was dashed to pieces, featherbeds were ripped open, jewelry and money was taken, and other personal treasures were destroyed. The barbaric behavior toward the slaves, with the plundering of the Lowcountry, was truly a British disgrace, not to be easily forgotten by the inhabitants.

Just after the attack at Stono Ferry, the patriot command had to deal with the men who wanted to return home, having reached the end of their enlistment periods. On July 3, 1779, General Moultrie wrote South Carolina Governor Rutledge with word that General Williamson felt that he could not keep the South Carolina Militia in the field any longer without replacements. There were no replacements. The usual excuses for abandoning the effort began to surface. Included in these excuses, beyond the issue of enlistment periods, were the rumors of Indian or loyalist forces moving toward their homes. The governor issued an order dated July 8 for the return of the militia. The governor wrote, "I know they would go without my leave, had I not done it." The men, from North Carolina and Virginia of Colonel Pickens' militia promptly departed, as their enlistment term expired. Lincoln was now left at Sheldon in the heat of the summer with about 800 Continental troops to watch the British forces at Beaufort, just 15 miles away.[7]

On July 14, 1779, Royal Governor James Wright, Lieutenant Governor John Graham and Chief Justice Anthony Stokes returned to Savannah, from England, to take up duties and restore the formal British civil government in Georgia. Actually the move to re-establish the British civil government in Georgia had begun in January when Germain directed that they return to Savannah. Germain pointed out that "The presence of these Officers will serve to prove to the people of Carolina that it is not intended to govern them by Military Law."[8]

When they arrived the situation was troublesome. Governor Wright was concerned about the inadequate number of British troops in and around Savannah to defend it. In a letter to Germain dated July 31, Wright declared, "I shall look with the utmost Anxiety and Impatience for the Troops from New York and hope they will be in our Neighborhood early in October, for till then, as the Troops that were here are so much Scattered about, I shall not Consider this Province as safe." The reference to the month of October is significant because that was the most likely point when the French fleet under D'Estaing might appear off the Georgia coast, being the end of the hurricane season along the Atlantic seaboard. Clinton had admitted that he "had not received any accounts of the French fleet's operations on the American coast."[9]

Later on August 9, Governor Wright wrote to Germain, "The more I am able to see into the state of affairs here, the more I am convinced of the wretched situation this Province is in, and how nearly it was being totally lost while the army was carrying on their operations in South Carolina; and now, my Lord, the Rebels who went from hence into Carolina on the arrival of Colonel Campbell, with other Rebels of Carolina and this Province, are possessed of the Country at and about Augusta, and all above it, and I have the honor to inclose your Lordship the information I received from three Back Country People by which it appears that almost the whole settlements down to Brair Creek are broke up, or the inhabitants skulking about to avoid the Rebel Partys, and that the Rebels have collected upwards of 600 men and are going to establish a post with them somewhere in St George's Parish."[10]

Governor Wright had other concerns in Georgia. Wright, who had always been suspicious of the reliability of the those locals who had taken the oaths of allegiance to the British after Savannah fell, found that the people were not ready for an assembly. Trade restrictions had only been lifted in Savannah, where some level of normalcy had returned. Due to the pressure exerted by British creditors desiring to collect debts from the citizens in South Carolina and Georgia, the Ministry directed General Prevost to restore commercial relations "as your situation will admit." The British Peace Commissioners likewise issued a blank proclamation for use by Prevost to suspend the Prohibitory Act if possible. While the expectation of regaining full and effective civil governmental control of the recaptured colony of Georgia was present when Campbell won his easy victory at Savannah in the beginning, the British weakness in regaining civil management was a continual problem throughout the Revolution.[11]

With serious reflection of their perilous American situation in the Southern States in attempting to drive the British out of the Lowcountry and Savannah, Governor Rutledge, General Lincoln and the Monsieur Plombard, the French consul at Charles Town, wrote letters to Admiral D'Estaing at Cape Francois in Hispaniola pleading him to come to the aid of the patriot forces at Savannah.[12] Another French supporter, a colonel and Marquis de Bretigny, who was stationed at Charles Town, also urged the admiral to come to the Carolina coast. The Colonel wrote to D'Estaing that "All here is in frightful confusion; very few regular troops, no help from the north, a feeble and badly disciplined militia and the greatest friction among the leaders." D'Estaing indicated that he had been told that the "American cause was in peril and all hopes were based on my early arrival."[13]

Admiral D'Estaing had been rather successful in his expedition against the British in the West Indies. His fleet had captured the island of St. Vincent in June, took Grenada in July, and defeated a British admiral, the Honorable John "Foul Weather Jack" Byron, in a major naval engagement during this 1779 summer. Coming off his victories in the Caribbean, and with the pleas from the Southern patriots, D'Estaing saw an opportunity to increase his reputation and come to the aid of the American cause in retaking Savannah.[14]

Admiral Charles Hector Theodat D'Estaing was born in 1729 in Auvergne, France. He started his military career early and by age 16 he was a regimental colonel. By age 26 D'Estaing became a brigadier. He served in the East Indies beginning in 1757, and in 1759 was captured by the British at the siege of Madras. In violation of his parole by leading naval operations against them, the British again captured him in 1760, causing him to spend a short while in a prison in Portsmouth. Moving up the ranks, D'Estaing became a lieutenant general in the French Navy in 1763. A year after he was promoted to vice admiral in 1777, D'Estaing was given the fleet command assignment to support the colonists.[15]

Putting aside the threat of fleet destruction at the height of the hurricane season, D'Estaing's fleet departed Cape Francois on August 20 by the windward passage. The admiral dispatched two ships of the line and three frigates to Charles Town to communicate his intentions to General Lincoln. The advance vessels were spotted by the British off Tybee Island, Georgia, on September 3. On the next day, Viscount De Fontanges, the adjutant-general of the army, arrived aboard the French frigate *Amazon* in Charles Town with dispatches for Lincoln. These dispatches revealed that the French fleet was then off the Savannah bar, with a fleet made up of 21 ships of the line, eight frigates, and five smaller armed vessels. Aboard the fleet were 5000 men, including troops, marines and seamen. The dispatch also indicated that while the admiral was ready to cooperate with the Americans to retake Savannah, he urged that actions be taken with much dispatch, as he was concerned about remaining too long on the coast during this hurricane season.[16]

The news of the presence of the French fleet caused great excitement. The South Carolina legislature, which was in session working on issuing paper money, raising taxes, regulating auctions and establishing embargoes, immediately adjourned to consider the military issues.[17] Boats were immediately sent to assist the French in landing troops, ordnance and stores. Lincoln ordered his aid, Colonel Thomas Pinckney; Colonel Cambray of the engineers; Captain Gadsden and several other intelligence officers to return with Viscount De Fontanges to support D'Estaing with the Georgia landing operation. An initial plan of action was developed and agreed upon. At Ossabaw Sound, D'Estaing was to be joined by Colonel Joseph Habersham to advise the admiral on the ideal location to debark his troops.[18] There was a sense

of exhilaration among the patriot forces in Charles Town.

The British were totally shocked at the arrival of the French fleet off Savannah. Royal Governor Wright exclaimed that nobody "could have thought or believed that a French fleet ... would have come on the Coast of Georgia in the month of September."[19] On September 4, a dispatch was sent from General Prevost in Savannah to Lieutenant Colonel Maitland at Beaufort ordering him to keep his detachment in readiness to march to Savannah at short notice, since it was possible that the French fleet might attempt to cut off communications by going into Port Royal Bay. Maitland was ordered to move over to Tench's Island, a promontory of Hilton Head Island, where he was to proceed toward Savannah if not receiving other orders along the way. On the evening of August 4, the French fleet disappeared from view off Tybee Island, which prompted General Prevost to issue countermanded orders for Maitland to hold his force at Beaufort. Maitland was instructed to have his heavy baggage embarked, and if he had other intelligence that was more accurate, he was to use his own judgment in taking no risk and return to Savannah.

Lieutenant Colonel Cruger was ordered to evacuate Sunbury and march by land to Savannah. The sick and invalids were to embark in small armed vessels and to proceed by the inland navigation to Savannah under the care of Captain French. Due to headwinds, Captain French's vessels could not reach the pass until the French forces had already taken possession of it. Captain French then sailed up the Ogeechee River, but finding the land occupied by the Americans, he landed and fortified a camp just 15 miles south of Savannah. French fortified his camp with his four armed vessels up front, each equipped with one 14-pounder and three four-pounder guns. With 40 able seamen, and 111 regular troops who were mostly invalid, French set about to fight off the Americans. Captain French and his force did not reach Savannah.

On September 6, the French fleet reappeared off the Savannah bar at Tybee. Prevost decided that it was necessary to strengthen the works at Fort Tybee, and increase the number of troops there. He ordered Captain Moncrief to reinforce the post with 100 infantry. Prevost was now aware of the size of the French fleet and the danger he and his forces were in. He ordered Maitland to march to Savannah with haste, and he assigned alarm posts at the appropriate locations to ensure communications of any approaching attack.[20]

The French fleet had become somewhat scattered by rough seas and high winds, and they did not reunite until September 4. On September 9, Admiral D'Estaing arrived off Tybee Island aboard the *La Chimere*, accompanied by three frigates. D'Estaing with his four vessels then forced their way across the Savannah River bar. With the entire French fleet now off Tybee Island, the British warships *Rose, Fowey, Keppel, Germain,* and the *Comet,* along with a galley and several smaller vessels lying in Tybee Roads, weighed anchor and sailed to Five Fathom Hole and immediately anchored. The British at Fort Tybee opened fire on the French squadron offshore. Fort Tybee, located near the lighthouse on the northern edge of Great Tybee Island, had been built to guard the entrance to the Savannah River. The fort contained one 24-pounder gun and an eight-and-a-half-inch howitzer, now manned with British troops under Captain Moncrief. After having no effect upon the French fleet operations off Tybee and recognizing their hazardous position, Moncrief ordered the guns spiked, and the entire British garrison at Fort Tybee to abandon it, escaping from the island the next morning.

On September 11, the 36-gun French frigate *Amazon,* commanded by the famous navigator Perouse, was successful at capturing the 24-gun British warship *Ariel* after a gallant resistance by the British captain. The *Ariel* had been patrolling along the Atlantic coast out from Charles Town in complete ignorance of the presence of the French. Two weeks later the British 50-gun warship *Experiment* was on a passage from New York to Savannah, having lost her bowsprit and masts in a gale wind. She was accompanied by the navy victualer *Myrtle* and the storeship *Champion.* Likewise, unaware of the French navy, the *Experiment, Myrtle* and *Champion* were captured by the French.[21]

On September 5, Lincoln ordered all officers and men to join their regiments. American patriots joined forces with General Lincoln's, garrisoned at Sheldon, some 15 miles from Beaufort. That same day General Lincoln sent a dispatch to General Lachlan McIntosh in Augusta declaring, "You will excuse my pressing the matter in such strong terms — I do not mean to call into question your zeal and dispatch, but to convey my own ideas how necessary I take the measure — Saturday next (the 11th) I have engaged that the Troops shall be collected near Ebenezer — the good of my Country and my own honor demand from me a fulfillment of the engagement." After the battle at Stono, Brigadier General Pulaski had been sent with his cavalry to a post located 50 miles northeast from Augusta for forage and provisions and to be at Augusta and Charles Town for required support operations. Pulaski was now ordered to join General McIntosh at Augusta. McIntosh was ordered to Ebenezer as discussed.[22] McIntosh advanced past Ogeechee Ferry, and proceeded to Millen's Plantation, three miles from Savannah, waiting for General Lincoln's force to join him.

On Saturday, September 11, 1779, D'Estaing's fleet rendezvoused in Ossabaw Sound. At 9 P.M. the next evening, D'Estaing landed 1200 French troops at Beaulieu

Plantation on the Vernon River, some 14 miles from the Georgia capital. Ossabaw Sound is an inlet a few miles south of the Savannah River entrance to the sea. The British had positioned a small unit at this place, formally the residence of Colonel William Stephens, with two field guns. On the appearance of the French landing, the small force of British fled. Thus, the landing was entirely unopposed. The initial 1200 troops moved from Beaulieu to camp three miles from Savannah. The remaining troops, with artillery, ammunition, provisions and entrenching tools were landed over a period of days until September 15. During the French disembarkment, high winds, including a gale, had delayed the efforts. Several vessels slipped their cables and sailed out to sea in an attempt to avoid damage. Several vessels sustained severe damage, and it was not until the 15th that the winds calmed enough to complete the operation. D'Estaing's force, totaling over 3000 French troops, was now encamped three miles southeast of Savannah in three groups, with the admiral in the center, on the right was Count de Dillon, and to the left was Viscount de Noailles.[23] As the French had moved up to their encampment, they had confiscated 13 steers, ten cows, five sheep, 39 hogs, 50 fowl and 20 gallons of Jamaican rum from the Georgia citizenry.

On the way toward Savannah, Pulaski ran into some of the forward piquets, killing and wounding five men, and capturing five privates and a subaltern. Pulaski's cavalry pressed on toward Beaulieu in a driving rain to join D'Estaing. Pulaski was looking forward to joining up with the French, since he had come to find the Americans without Continental culture.[24] When Pulaski arrived at Beaulieu, D'Estaing "cordially embraced and expressed mutual happiness at the meeting." Pulaski was then informed by the admiral that he intended to move on Savannah without waiting for Lincoln's force to arrive, and that "he counted on his Legion to form his van." Captain Bentalou recorded that "In pursuance of this wish, we set out immediately and reached Savannah some time before D'Estaing, where we engaged and cut off an advanced picket of the enemy's infantry."

During the days September 12 and 13, General Lincoln's forces were involved in crossing over the Savannah River at Zubly's Ferry. The effort was hampered by the lack of boats, which had been earlier destroyed or taken by the British. By the afternoon of the 13th, advance parties of Lincoln's troops had joined up with General McIntosh. On September 15, the united forces of Lincoln and McIntosh were encamped at Cherokee Hill.[25] This force of some 3000 troops was made up of the Continental regiments from South Carolina and Georgia, and every militia unit that could be rallied. In the suffocating heat, with temperatures reaching to 100 degrees, an interesting and diverse array of patriot men marched down the road toward Savannah. There were so many different styles of "uniforms" that one officer commented, "Makes them appear more like wild savages than soldiers." Stretched out for miles was this patriot army, which included not only generals Lincoln and McIntosh, but also the soon to be renowned "Swamp Fox," Francis Marion; John Laurens and his regiment; Charles Cotesworth Pinckney; Thomas Heyward, Jr., a signer of the Declaration of Independence; and the Huguenot leader, General Isaac Huger.[26] It would soon be time for an attack on the British.

Meanwhile, in Savannah, the British were making preparations for the eventual attack on their positions. When the French had first arrived off Tybee Island, the British had only 23 cannons mounted on the works around Savannah. On the first day of the actual American and French assault, there were 100 more cannons deployed. Since the capture of Savannah back in December, 1778, the British had not materially strengthened the works around Savannah. The works built by the Americans originally were intended to protect the southern, eastern and western exposures of the town. To upgrade the works around Savannah, Prevost put some 400 to 500 black slaves to work on the lines.[27] Moncrief ordered the construction of a semi-circular line of fortifications about 1200 feet long on the level plain south of the town. A British seaman wrote "The General, ever attentive to increase the defenses of the town, with Captain Moncrief, our principal engineer, was now, indefatigably, night and day, raising new works and batteries." The barn and other agricultural buildings on Governor Wright's plantation just outside Savannah were dismantled and the lumber used for cannon platforms. Houses were destroyed at the edge of the town to prevent the attackers from having any place to cover them as they approached across an open area of several hundred yards.[28]

Beginning on September 11, the British warships were stripped of most of their cannons, as they were deployed along the earthen works. The British ended up with 13 substantial redoubts and 15 gun batteries. Batteries were manned by sailors and marines from the vessels *Fowey, Rose* and *Keppel*. In addition to the gun batteries from the warships, field pieces were fixed at intervals. The British ships *Rose* and *Savannah*, with four transports, were sunk in a narrow channel of the river at three miles below the town to prevent any French or American vessels from getting close enough to the town for direct support of infantry operations. Above the town, small craft were sunk and a boom was stretched across the river to stop any vessel from passing up the North River, around Hutchinson's Island, to attack from the northwest. Entrenchments were also dug to cover the British regular and reserve troops. The strengthening of the Savannah fortifications was an impressive undertaking, and

worthy of significant praise for the engineering officer in charge, Captain James Moncrief.[29]

In Savannah were civilians and General Prevost with his garrison of 1700 men. Colonel Maitland's force of 800 men was now heading toward Savannah. On September 10, Lieutenant Colonel Cruger had arrived in Savannah with his detachment from the fort at Sunbury. On September 15, the British in Savannah were in no shape to hold off an attack from both D'Estaing's 4000 French troops, now outside Savannah to the southeast, and General Lincoln's troops totaling some 2500 men coming up to join in the attack on Savannah from the northwest.[30] Without Maitland's forces, even the superior defensive fortifications now constructed could not prevent a patriot victory.

Having encountered no opposition to his landing or his move up to Savannah, and with supreme confidence in his situation, Admiral D'Estaing decided not to wait for General Lincoln before engaging the British. On September 16, D'Estaing sent a summons to General Prevost as follows:

> Count D'Estaing summons his Excellency General Prevost to surrender himself to the arms of his Majesty the King of France. He admonishes him that he will be personally answerable for every event and misfortune attending a defense demonstrated to be absolutely impossible and useless from the superiority of the force which attacks him by land and sea. He also warns him that he will be nominally and personally answerable henceforth for the burning, previous to or at the hour of attack, of any ships or vessels of war or merchant ships in the Savannah River, as well as of magazines in the town.
>
> The situation of the Morne de l'Hospital in Grenada, the strength of the three redoubts which defended it, the disproportion betwixt the number of the French troops now before Savannah and the inconsiderable detachment which took Grenada by assault, should be a lesson for the future. Humanity requires that Count D'Estaing should remind you of it. After this he can have nothing with which to reproach himself.
>
> Lord Macartney had the good fortune to escape in person on the first onset of troops forcing a town sword in hand, but having shut up his valuable effects in a fort deemed impregnable by all his officers and engineers, it was impossible for Count D'Estaing to be happy enough to prevent the whole from being pillaged.
>
> Camp before Savannah, September 16, 1779. D'ESTAING.

In an attempt to delay D'Estaing until Maitland's force reached Savannah, General Prevost responded as follows to D'Estaing's demand for surrender:

> SIR, I am just honored with your Excellency's letter of this date, containing a summons for me to surrender this town to the arms of his Majesty the King of France, which I had just delayed to answer till I had shown it to the King's Civil Governor.

I hope your Excellency will have a better opinion of me and British troops than to think either will surrender on general summons without any specific terms.

If you, Sir, have any propose that may with honor be accepted of by me, you can mention them both with regard to civil and military, and I will then give my answer. In the meantime I will promise upon my honor that nothing with my consent or knowledge shall be destroyed in either this town or river.

Then, D'Estaing countered with another message.

SIR, I have just received your Excellency's answer to the letter I had the honor of writing to you this morning. You are sensible that it is the part of the Besieged to propose such terms as they may desire, and you cannot doubt of the satisfaction I shall have in consenting to those which I can accept consistency with my duty.

I am informed that you continue entrenching yourself. It is a matter of very little importance to me. However, for form's sake, I must desire that you will desist during our conferences.

The different columns, which I had ordered to stop, will continue their march, but without approaching your posts or reconnoitering your situation.

P.S. I apprize you Excellency that I have not been able to refuse the Army of the United Sates uniting itself with that of the King. The junction will probably be effected this day. If I have not an answer therefore immediately, you must confer in future with General Lincoln and me.

To this new message, Prevost responded:

SIR, I am honored with your Excellency's letter in reply to mine of this day. The business we have in hand being of importance, there being various interests to discuss, a just time is absolutely necessary to deliberate. I am therefore to propose that a cessation of hostilities shall take place for twenty-four hours from this date: and to request that your Excellency will order your columns to fall back to a greater distance and out of sight of our works or I shall think myself under the necessity to direct their being fired upon. If they did not reconnoitre anything this afternoon, they were sure within the distance.

Without any consideration for the importance of his decision on future events, or for the advantage it gave General Prevost and the British, Admiral D'Estaing agreed to a truce for another 24 hours. As history would soon reveal, this decision to allow for the delay would turn out to be a fatal error.

SIR, I consent to the truce you ask. It shall continue till the signal for retreat tomorrow night, the 17th, which will serve also to announce the recommencement of hostilities. It is unnecessary to observe to your Excellency that this suspension of arms is entirely in your favor, since I cannot be certain that you will not make use of it to fortify yourself, at the same time that the propositions you shall make may be inadmissible.

I must observe to you also how important it is that you should be fully aware of your situation as well as that of the troops under your command. Be assured that I am thoroughly acquainted with it. Your knowledge in military affairs will not suffer you to be ignorant that a due examination of that circumstance always precedes the march of the columns, and that this preliminary is not carried into execution by the mere show of troops.

I have ordered them to withdraw before night comes on to prevent any cause of complaint on your part. I understand that my civility in this respect has been the occasion that the Chevalier de Chambis, a lieutenant in the Navy, has been made a prisoner of war.

I propose sending out some small advanced posts tomorrow morning. They will place themselves in such a situation as to have in view the four entrances into the wood in order to prevent a similar mistake in future. I do not know whether two columns commanded by the Viscount de Noailles and the Count de Dillon have shown too much ardor, or whether your cannoniers have not paid a proper respect to the truce subsisting between us: but this I know, that what has happened this night is a proof that matters will soon come to a decision between us one way or another.[31]

The joining of General Lincoln's forces with Admiral D'Estaing's troops occurred before the lines around Savannah before the end of the day on September 16. The Americans were in high spirits as they took their positions.

On the evening of the 16th, Lieutenant Colonel Maitland arrived at Dawfuskie Island. The French had positioned ships outside the mouth of the Broad River, which separates Port Royal Island from Hilton Head Island. Since no ships were stationed behind Hilton Head Island, Maitland's force of 800 were thus able to cross into Callibogue Sound in small boats and on to Dawfuskie. Due to the shortage of small boats, the ships and galleys under Captain Christian of the Royal Navy were left behind with some of the Beaufort garrison on Dawfuskie, erecting shore batteries. His force was so strong that neither the French nor Americans attempted to engage his defensive forces during the entire siege of Savannah.[32]

From their location on Dawfuskie, Maitland could see the masts of the French warships in the entrance to the Savannah River. All seemed to be lost until a black Gullah fisherman told Maitland about a narrow passage marsh called Wall's Cut behind Dawfuskie Island, through Skull Creek, that emptied into the Savannah River upstream of the French ships. Maitland, who was fatally ill with bilious fever, led his men through Wall's Cut at high tide, in places wading up to their waists and dragging their boats through the mud. The tide and the thick fog had made the passage secure.[33]

Maitland's force reached the shore of the Savannah River, in sight of town across the river on the Southern shore, on the morning of the 17th. Using 14 boats, Maitland's force crossed the river to the town. By midday the entire force had disembarked. "The acquisition of this formidable reinforcement," said a Captain McCall, "headed by an experienced and brave officer, effected a complete change in the dispirited garrison. A signal was made and three cheers were given, which rung from one end of the town to the other."[34] A loyalist woman explained, "Our men ... suffered from fatigue and want of rest, but in the height of our despondence Colonel Maitland effected a junction in a wonderful manner ... thus giving new life and joy to the worn-out troops."[35]

Bolstered by the arrival of Maitland's force, General Prevost sent the following letter to Admiral D'Estaing on September 17:

> SIR, In answer to the letter of your Excellency which I had the honor to receive about twelve last night, I am to acquaint you that having laid the whole correspondence before the King's civil Governor and the military officers of rank, assembled in Council of War, the unanimous determination has been that though we cannot look upon our post as absolutely impregnable, yet that it may and ought to be defended: therefore the evening gun to be fired this evening at an hour before sundown shall be the signal for recommencing hostilities agreeable to your Excellency's proposal. I have the honour to be, &c.
>
> A. Prevost

There was general disappointment in the American ranks that the British had not taken the road to surrender. Having let the British have enough time to parley and, thus, reinforce Savannah had proven to be a key mistake on D'Estaing's part. Some British officers had indicated that the town could have been taken with little or no bloodshed, without artillery, in ten minutes if the French admiral had moved at the first opportunity. In D'Estaing's defense, he was not provided with the necessary intelligence information to have made such a judgment earlier in the operation.[36]

With the idea of an all-out direct assault on Savannah now considered foolhardy, D'Estaing resolved to approach the taking of Savannah gradually by siege. The French frigates moved up within gunshot of the town, as the British ships took shelter under the battery. D'Estaing's and Lincoln's forces moved up to surround Savannah and were situated within 1200 yards of the English. Both sides were busy making preparations of the upcoming battle. Savannah is situated on the southern bank of the river of the same name, thus, securing the northern front. To the west was a thick swamp and woody morass. The south and east were open ground with few trees for some distance from the town.[37]

American troops, numbering some 2127 men under General Lincoln, were on the western front, resting on the swamp which bordered the town. They consisted of 1003 Continental troops, including the Fifth Regiment of the South Carolina Infantry, 65 men from Heyward's Artillery, 365 men of the Charles Town Volunteers and Militia, 212 troops from General Williamson's Brigade, 232 men of the Georgia Militia regiments under colonels Twiggs and Few, and the 250 men of the cavalry of Brigadier General Count Pulaski.

On the Americans' right came the division of M. de Noailles with 900 men of the regiments of Cambresis, Auxerrois, Foix, Guadeloupe, and Martinique. To Noailles' right, in the direct southern front of the town, was D'Estaing's division of 1000 men of regiments of Cambresis, Hainault, the volunteers of Berges, Agenois, Gatinois, the Cape, and Port au Prince. On the eastern front on D'Estaing's right ready to attack were the forces of Dillon's division comprising some 900 men of the regiments of Dillon, Armagnac, and the Volunteers' grenadiers. On Dillon's right were the powder magazine, cattle depot, a field hospital and the quarters of the 50 dragoons of Conde and of Belzunce, under command of M. Dejean. On their right were the dragoons of M. de Rouvrai with the 750 men of the Volunteer Chasseurs. To their right and in advance some 200 yards were the 156 Grenadier Volunteers with another 200 men of mixed regiments under M. des Framais. The total French forces at Savannah, including an estimated 500 sailors and marines from off the ships, came to 4456 men.[38] This combined French and American force of some 6583 fighting men now enclosed the entire semi-circle around Savannah, the loyalist citizens and the British, from west to east.

The British forces of some 2500 men were deployed behind the substantial defensive works that had been under construction for some time. There were a line of works, with the right and left defended by redoubts and in the center by seamen's batteries. The entire works were surrounded with abatis. On the right toward the swamp were three redoubts, manned in the center by two companies of militia supported by the North Carolina loyalist regiment under Lieutenant Colonel Hamilton. On their right were the South Carolina King's Rangers under captains Raworth and Wylie. Captain Tawse commanded the dismounted corps of provincial dragoons on the redoubt on Hamilton's left known as the Spring Hill redoubt. South Carolina loyalists under Lieutenant Colonel Thomas Browne supported Tawse.

Between the Spring Hill redoubt and the center of the British lines were batteries under the command of Captain Manby, with Lieutenant Colonel Glazier's Sixteenth Regiment grenadiers and the marines from the ships. The entire force on the right, which would be forced to take the brunt of the attack, was under the command of Lieutenant Colonel Maitland. The left lines were defended by

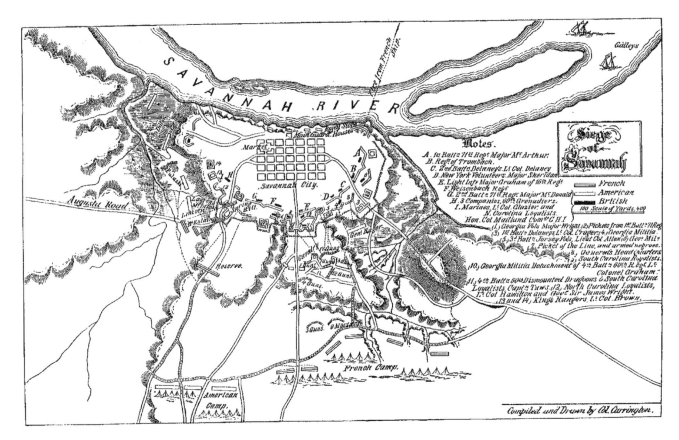

Siege of Savannah. (*Battles of the American Revolution.*)

two redoubts which were strongly constructed of heavy green and spongy palmetto trees filled by sand, with heavy cannons deployed. Lieutenant Colonel Cruger and Major James Wright with his Georgia loyalists each commanded a redoubt. Behind these defensive works were impalements and transverses in the center with two regiments of Hessians, two battalions of the Seventy-first Regiment, the New York Volunteers, a battalion of Skinner's Brigade, a battalion of DeLancey's and the light infantry unit under Major Graham.[39] The British were now ready for the promised attack on their positions and the town of Savannah.

Savannah had always been considered to be a healthy town from its earliest days of settlement. Savannah, like Charles Town, was a refuge during the summer and autumn months from the fevers incident to the swamps for rice planters from the nearby Lowcountry. The dense forests on Hutchinson's Island and to the east and west of the town had once shielded the citizens from "the noxious vapors and malarial influences" of the Lowcountry rice fields. But after the trees had been cut down to convert more land for rice plantations, the town was now more susceptible to the winds from the east and north carrying unhealthy ill vapors to the inhabitants. In 1779 Savannah was a town of some 430 mostly wooden houses built out from the river's wharves and bluffs. The wharves below

the bluffs had been well constructed according to a design provided by the Surveyor-General DeBrahm in 1759. De-Brahm recommended "to drive two Rows of Piles as far asunder as he desired his Wharf to be wide, and as far towards the River as low Water Mark; secure their tops with plates, and to trunnel Planks within on the Piles; this done, then brace the insides with dry Walls of Stones intermixed with willow Twigs, and in the same manner to shut up the Ends of the two Rows with a like Front along the Stream; to build inside what Cellars he had occasion for; then to fill up the Remainder with the Sand nearest at hand out of the Bluff or high shore of the Stream under the Bay." Now this well constructed town of Savannah was under siege, which could mean its possible destruction.

On September 22, Savannah was completely isolated on the land side. The French frigate *La Truite* armed with nine-pounder guns and two galleys with 18-pounders moved up within cannon shot of the town. To ensure all communications routes were blocked, the frigate *La Chimere* and storeship *La Bricole* were posted before the river islands. Both armies were now ready for the final struggle. The French fleet offloaded their naval guns at Thunderbolt and transported them to their batteries outside Savannah.[40] September 23 saw the allied forces making fascines and building batteries at their positions opposite Savannah. During 12 days some 53 artillery pieces and 14 mortars had been moved up and mounted for the siege.[41]

On Wednesday, September 22, M. de Guillaume, of Noailles' division, with 50 handpicked men, set out to capture an advanced British position, but were forced to turn back by heavy musket and artillery fire. At 3 P.M. the next day, the French had opened a trench to a point only 300 yards from the British lines. After the fog finally lifted the next morning, the British became aware of the new approach and sent a sortie at 9 A.M. of three companies of light infantry under Major Graham to capture it. With a loss of 21 men killed or wounded, Graham retreated with two columns of French on his heels. The French were finally drawn off when they had come close enough to British batteries to receive accurate firing.[42] The French loss was 48 killed or wounded.[43]

On September 25 at 7 A.M., a French artillery officer, M. de Sauce, opened fire on the town with his two 18-pounder guns from a newly erected battery. On inspection D'Estaing ordered the battery re-configured and armed with twelve 18- and 12-pounder guns, and called for construction of another battery just to the right of the trench to contain thirteen 18-pounders. Other batteries erected were a battery holding six 16-pounder guns manned by Americans, and a bomb battery 200 yards to the left of the trench with nine mortars. D'Estaing ordered that no more firing would occur until these artillery batteries were completed.

While the allied armies were in final preparation for a grand assault on the British works at Savannah, the French sailors of the 32-ship fleet were enduring much suffering at anchor offshore. According to the journal of a French naval officer with D'Estaing's fleet at Savannah, published in Paris in 1782, the conditions of the fleet were miserable. The officer told of being anchored offshore at the mercy of southeastern winds driving the ships ashore causing damaged rudders, lost anchors, and crippled rigging. The poor sailors suffered from scurvy, no refreshments for the sick, little adequate clothing or shoes, no linen, and little to eat except salt provisions which created severe thirst. The bread, having been stored for two years, was decayed and worm-eaten, and so inedible that even the domestic animals would not touch it. Food was rationed severely as it was felt the engagement might last for a significant period. The naval officer told of having to throw overboard an average of 35 dead French sailors on a daily basis. Those sailors who did survive were almost too weak to complete any simple shipboard tasks. With the French admiral's attention on the siege, there seemed to be no compassion for the average sailor of the French naval force.[44]

On the night of the 27th British Major Archibald

McArthur with a detachment of the 71st Regiment attempted to sortie against an allied battery where heavy cannon was being mounted. After a vigorous attack, McArthur's men retreated suddenly and with great silence. Confusion between the French on the right flank and the Americans on the left resulted in several friendly-fire casualties for the allies.[45] The French account of the incident had revealed that twice during the night the troops in the trenches had believed they had seen the enemy on the approach, and had presented heavy fire by mistake on the working parties. Seventeen men were reported to have been killed or wounded.[46]

The next day, September 28, the French frigate *La Truite* moved up and anchored in the north channel. The ship fired several cannon shots toward the town with little effect. On the next day General McIntosh asked General Lincoln for permission to send a flag of truce to General Prevost to request that his wife and family, and any other women and children as might desire, leave the besieged town before the battle. Lincoln agreed, and Major John Jones who was an aide to McIntosh took the flag and request to Prevost. But the request was refused by General Prevost who felt that the presence of McIntosh's family would tend to restrain the shelling on the town.[47] This was not to be the case.

A rather interesting and brave event occurred on the night of October 1, when Colonel John White, with captains George Melvin and A.C.G. Elholm, a sergeant and three privates set out to reconnoiter the position of Captain French. Captain French and his 111 regular troops, with five vessels and crew, had been cut off from reaching Savannah and had taken refuge in the Great Ogeechee River. Approaching French's camp on the left bank of the river, White had a number of fires built to give the impression that a large force was in the area. Colonel White summoned Captain French to surrender his forces. Thinking he was outnumbered, French complied with White's summons. The British were disarmed of his stand of 130 weapons and the troops were marched to the allied camp.

On October 2 the frigate *La Truite* and two armed American galleys positioned in the north channel opened fire on the southeastern end of the town. The shelling prompted the British to build a new battery and to strengthen this defensive works on that side of the town. Having completed all the necessary artillery batteries, D'Estaing ordered the bombardment of Savannah, which began at midnight on October 3, 1779. This initial shelling ceased at two o'clock the next morning after an assessment of the poor accuracy of the cannoneers, who were believed to have been under the influence of too much rum. A French journal recorded that first day's results:

October 4th, Monday. At four o'clock in the morning, the enemy's beat of drum at daybreak furnishes the signal for unmasking our batteries on the right and left trench, and that of the Americans to the left of the mortar battery, and we begin to cannonade and bombard the town and the enemy's works with more vivacity than precision. The cannoneers being still under the influence of rum, their excitement did not allow them their pieces with proper care. Besides, our projectiles did little damage to works which were low and constructed of sand. The effect of this very violent fire was fatal only to the houses and to some women who occupied them.

Protected by their entrenchment, the enemy could not have lost many men, if we may judge the effect of their fire upon our works which had been hastily constructed and with far less skill and care than theirs.

All our batteries ceased firing at eight o'clock in the morning that we might repair our left battery which had been shaken to pieces by its own fire. A dense fog favors our workmen. We open fire again at ten o'clock in the morning and continue it with little intermission until four o'clock after midnight.

The allied bombardment of the 4th had opened up with nine mortars and 37 guns from land and 16 shipboard cannons. This shelling caused considerable damage to the town and some lives were lost.[48] The bombardment of Savannah terrified the occupants. The loyalist chief justice of Georgia, Anthony Stokes, whose house was burned by a shell and his library and manuscripts destroyed, described the events: "I had some distance to go before I got out of the line of fire, and did not know the way under the Savannah bluff, where I should have been safe from cannon balls, and therefore, whenever I came to an opening of a street, I watched the flashes of the mortars and the guns, and pushed on until I came under cover of a house, and when I got to the Common and heard the whistling of a shot or shell, I fell on my face."

Stokes continued, "The appearance of the town afforded a melancholy prospect, for there was hardly a house which had not been shot through, and some of them were almost destroyed.… In the streets and on the Common there was a number of large holes made in the ground by the shells.… The troops in the lines were safer from the bombardment than the people in the town.… In short, the situation of Savannah was at one time deplorable. A small garrison in an extensive country was surrounded on the land by a powerful enemy, and its seacoast blocked up by one of the strongest fleets that ever visited America. There was not a single spot where the women and children could be put in safety, and the numerous desertions daily weakened that force which was at first inadequate to man such extensive lines, but the situation of the ground would not permit the able engineer to narrow them. However, with the assistance of God, British valor surmounted every difficulty."[49]

To avoid the cannonade, Governor James Wright and Lieutenant Governor John Graham moved out of the town itself and stayed in a tent next to Colonel Maitland, located on the right of the British lines. Ensign Pollard of the Second Battalion of General DeLancey's Brigade was killed by a bomb from the allied nine mortar battery. Mrs. Thompson's daughter was killed by a shot. General Prevost's *aide-de-camp*, T.W. Moore, described the shelling as tearing the town to pieces, to the "shrieks of women and children" on every side. He added that "Many poor creatures were killed in trying to get in their cellars, or hide under the bluff of Savannah River." According to Rivington's *Royal Gazette* on October 5th a mulatto man and three Negroes were killed in the lieutenant governor's cellar. That evening Mrs. Lloyd's home near the church was burnt by a shell and seven blacks lost their lives. Also that night a shell fell on Mr. Laurie's house on Broughton Street which killed two women and children.[50]

A patriot soldier recorded the details given by a deserter who told him a stirring account of the shelling of Savannah:

Poor women & children have already been put to death by our bombs & cannon; a deserter is this moment come out, who gives an account that many of them were killed in their Beds and amongst others, a poor woman with her infant in her arms was destroyed by a Cannon Ball; they all got into Cellars but even there they do not escape the fury of our Bombs, several having been mangled in that place of security.[51]

The shelling of Savannah on the 6th was rather weak, with long intervals between firings. At 1 A.M. Prevost beat for a parley and the following message was delivered to D'Estaing:

SIR — I am persuaded your Excellency will do me the justice to believe that I conceive in defending this place and the army committed to my charge I fulfil what is due to Honor and Duty to my Prince. Sentiments of a different kind occasion the liberty of now addressing myself to your Excellency. They are those of Humanity. The houses of Savannah are occupied soley by women and children. Several of them have applied to me that I might request the favour you would allow them to embark on board a ship or ships and go down the river under the protection of yours until this business is decided. If this requisition you are so good as to grant, my Wife and Children, with a few servants, shall be the first to profit by the indulgence.

The response was returned as follows:

SIR — We are persuaded that your Excellency knows all that your duty prescribes. Perhaps your zeal has already interfered with your judgement.

The Count d'Estaing in his own name notified you that you alone would be personally responsible for the consequence of your obstinacy. The time which you informed him in the commencement of the siege would be necessary for the arrangement of articles, including different orders of men in your town, had no object than that of receiving succor. Such conduct, Sir, is sufficient to forbid every intercourse between us which might occasion the least loss of time. Besides, in the present application latent reasons might again exist. There are military ones which, in frequent instances, have prevented the indulgence you request. It is with regret we yield to the austerity of our functions, and we deplore the fate of those persons who will be victims of your conduct, and the delusion which appears to prevail in your mind. We are with request, Sir, Your Excellency's most obedient Servants, B. Lincoln. D'Estaing.

The next several days of engagement at Savannah were recorded in a French officer's journal:

> 7th, Thursday. A very lively cannonade. We bombard and throw carcasses into Savannah, which set the town on fire for the third time.
>
> 8th, Friday. We cannonade and bombard feebly. The enemy does little more. He seems to be husbanding his strength for the anticipated attack. Informed of all that transpires in our army, he is cognizant of the trifling effect produced by his fire upon us in our trenches.

Another Frenchman observed that the British had built defensive works "which were more easily repaired than damaged." General Lincoln remarked, "I am fully of the opinion that a more determined mode of attack must be adopted before Savannah is ours." Such was the situation regarding the continual siege of Savannah by October 8. D'Estaing was likewise frustrated with the slow progress at breaking down the British by cannonade. Having been on the Georgia coast for over a month, with his naval forces in poor condition, and with disease now in the French camps, an appearance of the British fleet always possible at any point, a continuing threat of hurricanes coming up the coast, and with little hope of inflicting greater cannon damage on the British at Savannah, D'Estaing, with support of Lincoln, was convinced that it was indeed time to begin the attack.[52]

On the evening of October 8, 1779, General Lincoln issued the orders for the allied attack on Savannah. The time of the attack was set for four o'clock the next morning. The specific details of Lincoln's attack orders were:

> Watch word — Lewis.
> The soldiers will be immediately supplied with forty rounds of cartridges, a spare flint, and their arms in good order.
> The infantry destined for the attack of Savannah, will be divided into two bodies: the first composing the light troops [South Carolina regiments] under the command of colonel Laurens: the second, of the continental battalions [1st and 5th South Carolina Regiments, and some Georgia Continentals all under General Lachlan McIntosh] and the first battalion of Charleston militia, except the grenadiers, who are to join the light troops. The whole will parade at one o'clock, near the left of the line, and march by the right, by platoons.
> The guards of the camp will be formed by the invalids, and be charged to keep up the fires as usual in the camp.
> The cavalry under the command of count Pulaski, will be at the same time with the infantry, and follow the left column of the French troops, and precede the column of the American light troops: they will endeavour to penetrate the enemy's lines between the battery on the left of the Spring-hill redoubt, and the next toward the river. Having effected this, they will pass to the left toward Yamacraw, and secure such parties of the enemy as may be lodged in that quarter.
> The artillery will parade at the same time; follow the French artillery, and remain with the corps de reserve, until they receive further orders.
> The whole will be ready by the time appointed, with the utmost silence and punctuality, and be ready to march the instant count D'Estaing and general Lincoln shall order.
> The light troops who are to follow the cavalry, will attempt to enter the redoubt on the left of the Spring-hill, by escalade if possible; if not by entrance into it. They are to be supported, if necessary, by the first South-Carolina regiment: in the meantime, the column will proceed with the lines to the left of the Spring-hill battery.
> The light troops having succeeded against the redoubt, will proceed to the left and attempt the several works between that and the river.
> The column will move to the left of the French troops, taking care not to interfere with them.
> The light troops having carried the works toward the river, will form on the left of the column.
> It is expressly forbid to fire a single gun before the redoubts are carried, or for any soldier to quit his ranks to plunder, without an order for that purpose; any who shall presume to transgress, in either of these respects, shall be reputed a disobeyor of military orders, which is punishable with death.
> The militia of the first and second brigades, general Williamson's and the first and second battalions of Charlestown militia, will parade immediately under the command of general Isaac Huger, after drafting five hundred of them; the remainder will go into the trenches and put themselves under the command of the commanding-officer there. With the five hundred, he will march to the left of the enemy's lines and remain as near them as he possibly can, without being discovered, until four o'clock in the morning, at which time the troops in the trenches will begin the attack upon the enemy: he will then advance and make his attack as near the river as possible; thought this is only meant as a feint, yet should a favorable opportunity offer, he will improve it and push into the town.
> In case of a repulse, after having taken the Spring-hill redoubt. The troops will retreat and rally in the rear

of the redoubt: if it cannot be effected that way, it must be attempted by the same route, at which they entered.

The second place of rallying, or the first if the redoubt should not be carried, will be at the Jews' burying ground, where the reserve will be placed: if these two halts should not be effectual, they will retire toward camp.

The troops will carry on their hats a piece of white paper, by which they will be distinguished.[53]

Unfortunately the actual details of the attack were given to British General Prevost on the night of October 8 when James Curry, a sergeant major of the Charles Town Grenadiers, deserted to the enemy. Prevost and his forces at Savannah were now well prepared for the upcoming attack. With the new intelligence, Prevost moved many of his troops from the left works to the right works near Spring Hill redoubt under Lieutenant Colonel Maitland.

The French troops were to form in three columns, with two attacking and one held in reserve. The first column under M. Dillon would be commanded by Admiral D'Estaing himself. The second column would be commanded by the colonel of the infantry, M. de Steding. The third column of French reserves was under Viscount de Noailles.[54] Now all were in position for the fateful attack.

Any hope of starting the attack at 4 A.M. was lost when the guides provided to General Lincoln got lost in a dense fog. The marsh near the Spring Hill redoubt confused the attackers and they lost their way and fell behind schedule. Another factor in the delay was caused by the rigid French military etiquette which stipulated that the placement of regiments in the line of troops moving into battle must conform to the date of each regiment's establishment.[55] At the appointed hour of attack and after wading through rice fields for half a mile on the east of the town, General Huger's forces began their assault. Under heavy cannon and musket fire, Huger's units lost 28 men and retreated. His units took no further part in the engagement. Attacks on the center of the British works from trenches by troops commanded by M. de Sabliere, supported by the Chasseurs of Martinique, was too weak, and Lieutenant Colonel Hamilton's North Carolina loyalists' regiment easily fought them off.

A French officer's personal journal documents the entire French attack on the enemy's right:

By three o'clock in the morning all our dispositions had been perfected.... We commenced marching by the left to attack the city on its right where its western side, as we have before intimated, is fortified by three redoubts located triangularly.... At five o'clock in the morning, the three columns, which had observed a similar order of march, arrived within about eighty toises (160 yards) of the edge of the wood which borders upon Savannah. Here the head of column was halted and we were ordered to form into platoons. Day begins to dawn and we grow impatient. This movement is scarcely commenced when we are directed to march forward, quick time, the vanguard inclining a little to the right, the column of M. de Steding to the left, and the column of the General (D'Estaing) moving straight to the front. M. de Noailles, with his reserve corps, proceeds to a small eminence from which he could observe all our movements and repair to any point where the exigencies might demand his presence.

At half past five o'clock we hear on our right, and on the enemy's left, a very lively fire of musketry and cannon upon our troops from the trenches who had commenced the false attack. A few minutes afterwards, we are discovered by the enemy's sentinels, who fire a few shots. The General now orders an advance at double quick, to shout Vive le Roy, and beat the charge. The enemy opens upon us a very brisk fire of artillery and musketry, which, however, does not prevent the vanguard from advancing upon the redoubt, and the right column upon the entrenchments. The ardor of our troops and the difficulties offered by the ground do not permit us long to preserve our ranks. Disorder begins to prevail. The head of the columns penetrates within the entrenchments, but, having marched too rapidly, it is not supported by the rest of the column which, arriving in confusion, is cut down by discharges of grape shot from the redoubts and batteries and by a musketry fire from the entrenchments. We are violently repulsed at this point. Instead of moving to the right, this column and the vanguard fall back toward the left. Count d'estaing receives a musket shot when almost within the redoubt, and M. Betizi is here wounded several times.

The column of M. de Steding, which moved to the left, while transversing a muddy swamp full of brambles, loses its formation and no longer preserves any order.... Firing is very lively; and, although this column is here most seriously injured, it crosses the road to Augusta that it may advance to the enemy's right which it was ordered to attack. On this spot nearly all the volunteers are killed. The Baron de Steding is here wounded.

The column of M. d'estaing, and the repulsed vanguard which had retreated to the left, arrived here as soon as the column of M. de Steding, and threw it into utter confusion. At this moment everything is in such disorder that the formations are no longer preserved. The road to Augusta is choked up.... We are crowded together and badly pressed. Two 18-pounder guns ... charged with canister and placed at the head of the road, cause terrible slaughter. The musketry fire from the entrenchments is concentrated upon this spot and upon the swamps. Two English galleys and one frigate [the armed brig Germain] sweep this point with their broadsides, and the redoubts and batteries use only grape shot, which they shower down upon this locality. Notwithstanding all this our officers endeavor to form into columns this mass which does not retreat, and the soldiers themselves strive to regain their ranks ... the General orders the charge to be beaten. Three times do our troops advance en masse up the entrenchments which cannot be carried. An attempt is made to penetrate through the swamp on our left to gain the enemy's right. More than half of those who enter are either killed, or remain stuck fast in the mud.... Standing in the road leading to Augusta, and at a most exposed point, the General, with perfect self-possession, surveys this slaughter, demands constant renewals of the assault, and, although sure of the bravery of his troops, determines upon a retreat only when he sees that success is impossible.

We beat a retreat.... At this juncture the enemy show themselves openly upon the parapets and deliver their fire with their muskets almost touching our troops. The General receives a second shot.... Towards eight o'clock in the morning the army was again in camp, and a cessation of hostilities for the purpose of burying the dead and removing the wounded was proposed and allowed.

The Americans fared no better than the French in their attacks. The American right column under Colonel Laurens, preceded by Pulaski's unit, assaulted the Spring Hill redoubt with much determination, and at one point had planted the colors of the Second South Carolina Regiment on the exterior slope. But the British firing was too heavy, and Laurens' group was driven back. Confusion was caused during the retreat by Pulaski's cavalry passing through the ranks of the infantry also in retreat from hellish fire.

The second column of Americans under General McIntosh arrived at Spring Hill redoubt at a moment of severe confusion as D'Estaing had been wounded in the arm. Although speaking no French, McIntosh was given verbal orders to move his fresh units more to the left and to not interfere with the attempts by the French to rally and attack. In taking that course, the troops were too much to the left and ended up in the wet, boggy Yamacraw Swamp, where they received cannon grapeshot from the British galley deployed there. With Spring Hill redoubt fighting off all the attackers, and with the grapeshot killing his men in droves, McIntosh ordered a retreat.

During the raging attack, Count Pulaski, with the approval of General Lincoln, attempted to take 200 of his cavalry, made up of his Legion accompanied by some Georgia Cavalry, between the British works to penetrate the town and pass behind the enemy's rear to the British camp. Pulaski's cavalry attacked at full speed, but were stopped by the abatis, where they received heavy crossfire from surrounding batteries. Pulaski was wounded by cannister shot in the groin and right thigh, and unhorsed. His men took Pulaski from the battlefield.

After the terrible frontal attack at Savannah, the battlefield was covered with the slain. On the right of the British lines were 80 men dead in the ditch, and at the parapet of the first redoubt attacked were some 93 killed. Many troops were hung in the abatis, along with disfigured men slain by grapeshot everywhere in the open.[56] The gallant attack on the Spring Hill redoubt had seen two American standards planted. But the effort was in vain as the British resistance was too strong.[57] The allied forces were repulsed at every location, and the British prevailed to a hard-fought victory.

D'Estaing reported the allied men killed and wounded at Savannah on August 9, 1779, as 760 French soldiers, 61 French officers, and 312 Americans. General Moultrie reported, "Our troops remained before the lines in this hot fire fifty-five minutes; the Generals, seeing no prospect of success, were constrained to order a retreat, after having six hundred and thirty-seven French and four hundred and fifty-seven Continentals killed and wounded." Because of the attack plan intelligence, incredible defensive works and gallant battlefield behavior, the British suffered few casualties. General Prevost reported 40 killed, 63 wounded, four missing and 48 desertions during the Savannah battle. Captain T.W. Moore, Prevost's aide, estimated the losses in a letter to his to be 163 men, including desertions.[58] Thus, with near one-tenth the losses of the allied French and Americans, the British and American loyalists were able to fight off the attack with brilliant success. It was a patriot disaster.

The sight of the battlefield after the allied attack prompted General Augustine Prevost to write:

> Our loss on this occasion was one captain and fifteen rank and file killed, one captain, three subalterns, and thirty-five rank and file wounded. That of the enemy we do not exaggerate when set it down from 1000 to 1200 killed and wounded. We buried within and near the abatis 203 on the right, on the left 28, and delivered 116 wounded prisoners, the great part mortally. They themselves, by permission, buried those who lay more distant. Many no doubt were self-buried in the mud of the swamp, and many carried off.

The number of well-known military men were among the brave killed or wounded at Savannah. D'Estaing had been shot in the arm and in the calf of his right leg.[59] French Major General De Fontanges, along with colonels de Betizi and de Steding, were wounded. The Americans lost Sergeant Jasper, Lieutenant Gray, and Lieutenant Bush. Majors Pierce Butler and John Jones were aides to Brigadier General McIntosh. The brave Brigadier General Count Pulaski, wounded in the groin and right thigh, was taken aboard the United States brig *Wasp* to head for Charles Town. Forced to remain for several days in the Savannah River due to headwinds, Pulaski was attended by surgeons from the French fleet. In spite of the efforts of the surgeons, Pulaski died as the *Wasp* was leaving the river. Colonel Bentalou reported that Pulaski's corpse was so offensive that they were "compelled, though reluctantly, to consign to a watery grave all that was now left upon earth of his beloved and honored commander."[60] Funeral rites were performed in Charles Town with military honors. On October 25, 1779, the brave and resourceful Lieutenant Colonel Maitland of the 71st British Scots Regiment, and a member of the House of Commons, died suddenly at Savannah from convulsions from over-drinking, one of his bad habits.[61]

General Lincoln urged D'Estaing to continue the siege of Savannah, but the French admiral, having sustained such a devastating loss and with his other problems, decided to break off the engagement. On October 10, D'Estaing ordered the dismantling of the batteries and return of the guns on shipboard. The embarkment location was set for Castion's Bluff, with 292 men detailed from regiments of Armagnac and Auxerrois and the marine unit to guard the retreat, deploying at three points to the east of the town. On the 15th M. de Bretigny arrived from Charles Town to ask D'Estaing if he would send 900 French troops to protect Charles Town. The French admiral refused. Also, on October 15 the militia of Georgia, Virginia and the Carolinas withdrew.

On October 18 at 10 A.M. the tents and camp were placed in wagons and transported to the embarkment point. At 11 A.M. the remaining American forces moved to the left and the French to the right, as the allied force broke off. General Lincoln's forces moved toward Zubly's Ferry, and on to Ebenezer. Lincoln then left his force and headed to Charles Town. The French had only traveled two miles toward Causton's Bluff when the darkness of night overtook them. The next morning at five o'clock, Tuesday the 19th, the French reached the Bluff and began loading. A French journal recorded that "Causton's Creek and all Georgia are evacuated."[62] All was loaded aboard the French fleet by October 20, but adverse winds forced the French to stay until November 1. On that date the French ships passed the bar, and the next day the fleet sailed away from Georgia. Almost immediately D'Estaing encountered a violent gale that dispersed the fleet. It was another displeasure to add to all the other disappointments the admiral had endured in the Southern colonies.

There was much disappointment and near despair in all patriot quarters over the failure of French and Americans to retake Savannah. But General Lincoln had good things to say about D'Estaing. In his letter to Congress he said, "Count D'Estaing has undoubtedly the interest of America much at heart. This he has evidenced by coming over to our assistance; by his constant attention during the siege; his understanding to reduce the enemy by assault, when he despaired of effecting it otherwise; and by bravely putting himself at the head of his troops and leading them to the attack. In our service he has freely bled. I feel much for him; for while he suffering the distress of painful wounds on a boisterous ocean, he has to combat chagrin. I hope he will be consoled by an assurance, and those of America; we regard with high approbation his intentions to serve us, and

that his want of success will not lessen our ideas of his merit."[63]

Most of the blame for the defeat at Savannah went in the direction of D'Estaing. First, he had let the British delay to reinforce with Maitland's force from Beaufort, and, second, he pushed for the frontal attack on the defensive works at Savannah. Perhaps the arrogance that D'Estaing showed at believing that it would be easy to take Savannah tended to taint the whole of his actions and his relationships with the Americans. John Harris Cruger, a loyalist officer, described the lack of Franco-American cooperation, "They came in so full of confidence of succeeding, that they were at some loss where to lay the blame, each abusing the other for deceiving them.... We are all hands sufferers by this unfortunate invasion. The difference is we have acquired glory and our Enemies, Disgrace."[64] It was reported that some French officers informed General Prevost, with their apologies, that the Americans were the blame for not allowing the women and children to leave the town by ship as Prevost had requested.[65] General Lincoln was also deserving of some culpability for his lack of a prompt troop movement to join up his forces with D'Estaing's earlier in the campaign. It was seven days before Lincoln joined the French after D'Estaing had landed. If Lincoln had rushed to the side of the French, it is very likely that the truce would have been rejected and the Savannah taken before Maitland arrived.[66]

While it might be appropriate to place some fault on D'Estaing, it does not diminish the valor and courage that he and his men demonstrated in their attempts to aid the struggling American patriots. One of D'Estaing's naval officers wrote the following about their leader:

Count d'estaing was unable to resist a desire, rising superior to the hazard, to attempt to add new triumphs to those which he had already achieved. If zeal, activity, eagerness, and ambition to accomplish great deeds are worthy of recompense, never will France be able sufficiently to acknowledge, he possesses the enthusiasm and the fire of a man twenty years of age. Enterprising, bold even to temerity, all things appear possible to him. He fancies no representations which bring home to him a knowledge of difficulties. Whoever dares to describe them as formidable is ill received. He wishes every one to view and to think of his plans as he does. The sailors believe him inhuman. Many died upbraiding him with their misery and unwilling to pardon him; but this is a reproach incident to his austere mode of life, because he is cruel to himself. We have seen him, sick and attacked with scurvy, never desiring to make use of any remedies, working night and day sleeping only an hour after dinner, his head resting upon his hands, sometimes lying down, but without undressing.

Thus have we observed Count d'estaing during this campaign. There is not a man in his fleet who would believe that he has endured all the fatigue which he has undergone. When I am now asked if he is a good General, it is difficult for me to respond to this inquiry, He committed much to chance, and played largely the game of hazard. But that he was energetic, adventurous almost to rashness, indefatigable in his enterprises which he conducted with an ardor of which, had we not followed him, we could have formed no conception, and that to all this he added much intellect, and a temper which imparted great austerity to his character, we are forced to admit.

The Georgia General Assembly was so impressed with the service given to their cause that it granted 20,000 acres of land to Admiral D'Estaing and gave "him all privileges, liberties and immunities of a free citizen of the State."[67]

The English savored their new victory. Henry Clinton remarked, "I think that this is the greatest event that has happened the whole war." Governor Wright gave the credit for the victory with his words, "Give me leave to mention the great ability of Captain Moncrief, the Chief Engineer who was Indefatigable day & Night and whose Eminent services contributed vastly to our defense and safety." It was another crowning achievement for Lord North and George Germain's Southern strategy, while it did show the weakness in British sea power in colonial waters. Wright told Germain, "The Southern parts of No. America are now in Your Lordships Power, whereas had the French got Footing here, I fear they wou'd have been Lost."[68]

Regardless of the best of intentions and great bravery on the part of the allied French and Americans to retake Savannah, the British continued to hold Savannah, Georgia. The remaining patriot army had retired to South Carolina and the British continued to re-establish their civil administration. What remained of the Georgia patriot government was now at Augusta. With no present threat to their existence, the arrogant loyalists now demonstrated their cruelty upon those who had supported the patriot cause with more pronouncement than even before the French had landed. The loyalists took to plundering the homes of the defeated. They took black slaves, furniture, stock, clothing and anything of value from the patriot families of Georgia. Being under the protection of the British was of little conciliation to those suffering at the hands of these loyalist activists. General McIntosh's family was reduced to poverty, Colonel Twigg's home was burned and a young man killed, Colonel Elijah Clarke's home was set on fire and his family ordered to leave the state. The obscene language and personal insults were extreme and the cruelties toward these fellow Georgians were beyond that of a civilized people. Savannah and Georgia were still lost.

10

PORTSMOUTH AND CHARLES TOWN

As early as March of 1779, Clinton had started to consider plans for further offensive operations in the South. The two primary obstacles to executing such plans were the arrival of reinforcements from England, and the return of the British forces in the West Indies under the command of General Grant. Clinton wrote his *aide-de-camp*, Major Drummond, that if Grant's forces could return for use against South Carolina before July, he would send what troops he could from New York to support the effort. Clinton wrote, "I know no place where that Corps [Grant's] can act with more probability of solid advantage at this time, than at S. Carolina.... You know I am not apt to be too sanguine; I am clear I am not so, when I say this first part would succeed. If Grant is wanted in the West Indies defensively, I have nought to say, but lament that he is."

Clinton's correspondence during this period of 1779 revealed the indecision he had regarding his next move towards further Southern operations and South Carolina. Two letters written by Clinton on the same day, April 4, 1779, provide the evidence of his near opposing themes. The letter to William Eden said, "that a solid operation in the proper season against Charles Town, and S. Carolina will be of infinite consequence." But the letter to Germain that same day showed a different face, reporting,

> I have as yet received no assurances of any favorable temper in the Province of South Carolina to encourage me in an undertaking where we must expect much difficulty. The force which the present weakness of Genl. Washington's army could enable me to detach, might possibly get possession of Charles Town ... but I doubt whether they could keep it, and in the present stage of the war, I do not

> think such a desultory advantage, in that quarter, would be beneficial to our interests; it might induce a number of persons to declare for us, whom we might afterwards be obliged to abandon; and thus might destroy a Party, on whom we may depend, if circumstances will permit a more solid attempt in a properer Season.

With no troop reinforcements from the British government and feeling a heightened level of real stress under the weight of the colonial mission, Clinton chose to hold back revealing the full measure of his feelings on the subject to the government.[1]

Though he showed a reluctance to immediately take on Charles Town without more troops, Clinton did take some action on the recommendation he received in a letter from Germain, dated January 23, 1779, to attack on the coasts of New England and Chesapeake Bay. The purposes of the expedition to Chesapeake were to keep any available patriot troops from supporting operations in Georgia or South Carolina, to keep Virginia troops from heading to Washington's army, and to destroy the ships and magazines supplying the patriot army in South Carolina. In addition, Virginia and Maryland had been spared from any major engagements so far during the war, which had allowed them to support the American armies in the North with men and supplies. The hogsheads of golden tobacco shipped via the Chesapeake from these two colonies had increased the opportunity for credit among the European governments as aid in the American cause. Clinton had no plans to carry out a major strategic campaign, but wished only to harass the trade and sow destruction throughout the Lower Chesapeake. Tobacco was king along all the Chesapeake Bay and its tributaries, and with it the struggling new nation could acquire guns, gunpowder, and cannons. From the outbreak of the Revolution until 1779, the importance of Chesapeake tobacco trade was greater than it had been before the war. As the Chesapeake campaign approached, Commodore Collier commented on the importance of stopping the trade:

> The most feasible way of ending the rebellion was by cutting off the resources by which the enemy could continue war, these being principally drawn from Virginia, and principally tobacco, that an attack and the putting up and shutting up of the navigation of the Chesapeake would probably answer very considerable purposes and if not of itself sufficient to end the war would drive the Rebels to infinite inconvenience and difficulty especially as [their] army was constantly supplied by provisions sent by water through the Chesapeake....

Orders from Germain confirming the Chesapeake campaign arrived in New York on April 24. On May 5, 1779, the Chesapeake expedition sailed from New York on Commodore Sir George Collier's ships with around 1800 men under the command of Major General Edward Mathew. Sailing along with Collier's flagship *Raisonable* were the *Rainbow, Solebay, Otter, Diligent, Harlem, Cornwallis Galley* and 28 troop transports. The army aboard consisted of detachments of the Guards, the Royal Volunteers of Ireland, Prince Charles' Hessians and others. Nearing Cape Henry on May 6, the fleet anchored off Willoughby Point on May 8. The *Solebay* left the fleet, having been sent to Georgia, and was replaced by several vessels of privateers who asked to accompany the British. The next day the *Raisonable* anchored in Hampton Roads.

Since the draft of the *Raisonable* was too deep to move up the Elizabeth River to Portsmouth, the primary objective, Collier switched his flag to the *Rainbow* and headed out. Collier's journal recorded the action:

> The Commodore led the fleet as high up the Elizabeth River as the tide would permit, but falling calm they anchored. Sir George proceeded up the river in a small army schooner to reconnoiter the Fort and to get information if possible of the Enemy's strength and found rebels had few troops because of the unexpected arrival of Sir George. The ships could not move because of no wind so the division of troops went into flat boats led by Sir George and General Mathew in the *Rainbow* barge and covered in the flanks by the *Cornwallis Galley* and several gunboats carrying a 6- or 9-pounder in their prows.

Collier continued as the sails began to billow forth:

> The sight formed the most beautiful regatta in the world.... When the landing boat was within less than a musket shot of the intended place for landing a signal to halt was made. The galley and the gunboats then advanced and kept up a warm cannonade towards the shore for several minutes which the rebels returned from the

Fort. The most of their shot fell short. On the gunboats ceasing firing the troops pushed ashore at a spot called the glebe, about a mile from the Fort and landed without the least opposition.... It was agreed between the Commodore and the General that a joint attack upon the Fort by sea and land should be made early in the morning.... Everything was prepared for the attack but the Enemy with great cowardice abandoned it in the night and fled, leaving the 13 stripes flying....[2]

Clinton wrote in his narrative about Collier and Mathew as they carried out the operation, "besides the universal terror and alarm which this armament spread in its arrival through every part of the country bordering on that great expanse of water, the loss which the enemy sustained was prodigious — consisting chiefly of provision magazines, gunpowder, and naval stores, about 150 vessels of different sizes (several being of force and richly laden) and a quantity of cannon and ordance stores, together with some thousand hogsheads of tobacco...."[3]

The patriot artillery officer, Major Thomas Matthews, on hearing news of the landing at Portsmouth, immediately spiked his cannon and evacuated his 100 to 150 men from Fort Nelson, taking a brass field cannon with him. He removed the public stores from Portsmouth, and proceeded up the Southern Branch, and then into the Dismal Swamp of North Carolina on several small boats. His actions were found to be without blame in a subsequent court of inquiry held at Williamsburg on June 4.

Captain Kendall, offshore aboard his ship the *Rainbow*, saw the patriot flag come down at Fort Nelson, to be replaced with the English jack, raised in victory. Collier commented on the "astonishing strength toward the river" of the fort, with its "parapet 14 feet high and 14 feet thick ... surrounded with strong timbered dovetail and middle part filled with earth hand rammed...." Collier recorded the continuing operations:

> The town of Portsmouth within one mile of the fort was taken possession of at the same time Norfolk on the opposite shore and Gosport where the rebels had established a very capital marine yard for building ships.... The enemy previous to their flight set fire to a fine ship of war of twenty guns ready for launching belonging to Congress and also to two large French merchant ships one of which was laden with baked goods and the other with one thousand hogsheads of tobacco.... Many vessels for war were taken on the stocks.... The whole number taken burnt and destroyed ... amounted to 137 sail of vessels!... A great deal of tobacco, tar, and other commodities were found in the warehouses and some laden merchantmen were seized in the harbor. Many of the privateers and other vessels fled up the different branches of the river, but as there was no outlet the commodore either captured or destroyed them all.[4]

The British had destroyed the public stores at Gosport, Norfolk and Portsmouth, and later burned

Suffolk. When some 600 British infantry approached Suffolk, most of the citizens fled. Those who stayed were taken prisoner. With hundreds of barrels of tar, pitch, turpentine and rum on fire, the molten mass flowed like a lava field, with winds fanning the fire as gun magazines exploded.[5]

Collier and Mathew had taken Portsmouth, Norfolk, Gosport and Suffolk without opposition. Collier was delighted with their conquests, and strongly recommended that a post on the Elizabeth River be retained, with additional reinforcements from New York. On May 16 Collier wrote Clinton, "Our success and the present appearance of things infinitely exceed our most sanguine expectations, and, if the various accounts the General and myself have received can be depended on, the most flattering hopes of a return to obedience to their soverign may be expected from most of this province." Though Mathew's report was not as enthusiastic, he did express his sense that the locals would support British operations in Virginia. Local loyalist citizens had almost embarrassed Collier and Mathew when they declared themselves and offered all measure of assistance. The British leaders knew they were under orders to return quickly to New York, and these loyalist actions rather complicated their plans. The only flexibility in their orders that might allow them to remain in Virginia was if "motives of extraordinary importance arise."

Clinton was not sympathetic with Collier's request to stay in Virginia. He was concerned over sending any further troops to Virginia when he planned to start a new campaign soon against Washington up the Hudson. Clinton delayed a few days waiting to see if Washington would detach any troops to the Chesapeake. By the time Clinton finally gave permission to stay in Virginia if they could defend the post without additional reinforcements, Mathew had already re-embarked his troops for New York. Mathew felt that the declarations from the Virginia loyalists were not that important to risk upsetting Clinton's other military plans. Collier was most disappointed, believing that the success at Portsmouth, together with the positive declarations from the local loyalists, was enough to convince them to remain engaged. Collier's bitterness was reflected in his report to Germain, which also served to reinforce Germain's feeling that the Virginia loyalists could be depended on. But Clinton made light of this withdrawal from Virginia, conveniently giving the credit for the decision to Mathew, and kept to his consistent feeling that other operations were more worthy of his focus.[6]

The operations on the Chesapeake Bay had been so swift that by the time most of the surrounding inhabitants learned of the attack, the British had already departed. When the citizens of Annapolis and Baltimore heard the news of a landing and prepared to resist, the British were gone. On June 2, 1779, the *Maryland Journal and Baltimore Advertiser* published a letter from Patrick Henry written on May 27 that had been sent to the Congress and dispatched to Maryland Governor Johnson:

> Sir,
>
> The enemy, who lately invaded this State, with a fleet of ships, consisting of the Raisonable of 64 guns, the Rainbow of 40, the Otter of 14, and sundry other armed and unarmed vessels, commanded by Commodore Sir George Collier, together with a number of land forces, amounting to 1500 or 2000, commanded by Major General Metthew [Mathew] evacuated Portsmouth on Tuesday last, after committing ravages and depredations of the most cruel and unmanly sort....

The reporting of the events of the British expedition to the Chesapeake yielded an ever-increasing level of alarm and outrage as time progressed. Thomas Jefferson wrote William Fleming on June 8 that "Some resolutions of Congress came to hand yesterday desiring an authentic state to be sent them of the cruelties said to have been committed by the enemy during their late invasion.... Tho so near the scene where the barbarities are said to have been committed I am not able yet to decide within myself whether there were such or not...." Richard Henry Lee wrote his brother, Arthur, on May 23 speaking of the "murders in cold blood and rapes without end." The *Pennsylvania Gazette* published on May 26 an account to Governor Henry by Colonel Lawson from Smithfield dated May 13:

> I presume your Excellency, by this time, is pretty well informed of the strength and movements of the enemy. From accounts which I have received, the cruel and horrid depredations and rapine committed on the unfortunate and defenceless inhabitants who have fallen within their reach exceed almost anything yet heard of within the circle of their tragic display of savage barbarity!—Household furniture, stock of all kinds, houses, and in short almost every species of perishable property, are effectually destroyed, with unrelenting fury, by those devils incarnate; murder, rape, rapine, and violence fill up the dark catalogue of their detestable transactions!"

Captain Kendall in the *Rainbow* weighed anchor at 3 A.M. and by 8 A.M. noticed that all the troops were re-embarked aboard the transports. The barracks and the fort were destroyed and the fleet moved downriver to Hampton Roads. Collier's flag was moved back to the *Raisonable*, and the next day, May 26, 1779, the major elements of Collier's fleet put to sea. It had been only 20 days since the first sails of Collier's fleet had flown off Cape Henry. The successful Collier/Mathew's Chesapeake expedition was indeed over. Collier reported that the expedition had damaged patriot property and goods worth "upward of a Million Sterling."

To continue some level of harassment in the area, Collier left Captain Richard Creyk and his 14-gun H.M.S. *Otter* and the *Harlem*, with an accompanying array of privateers to roam the Chesapeake Bay region. From May 28 until June 22 the *Otter* and *Harlem* cruised the Chesapeake with privateers *Lord Dunmore, Fincastle, Hamond* and *Lord North* with much success. They captured warehouses and cargoes of tobacco and coal, burned vessels and took their crews prisoner, and created much havoc on the Chesapeake. While the *Otter* and *Harlem* departed on June 22, there were continual raids in the Bay area throughout 1779 and 1780 by privateers and occasional British warships.[7]

Collier and Mathew returned to New York from the Chesapeake expedition on May 29 just as Clinton began his new operation up the Hudson. Mathew's troops were kept aboard Collier's fleet, and the next day Clinton embarked in a following wind and the fleet sailed upriver toward Verplanck's and Stony Point to seize these patriot outposts. Again, with Sir Henry Clinton, as it was during Lord Dunmore's Norfolk operations, the British leadership in America seemed unable to understand the strategic importance of maintaining and controlling the Lower Chesapeake Bay. The third and next significant opportunity in a few years henceforth would reveal to the British the true folly of their decisions in this regard.

Back in England the Germain administration continued to be confronted with an increasing array of issues and problems as 1779 progressed. The good news of the taking of Savannah in February had heightened spirits and gave some new life to the administration. With spirits raised, Germain had promised Clinton 6000 troops and reassured him that Major General Grant would soon be returning to New York from his West Indies operations to aid him. The short, yet successful, Chesapeake expedition had been concluded. On June 1, 1779, Clinton held Fort Verplanck's Point and was fortifying captured Stony Point, giving the British a gateway to the strategic Hudson River Highlands. Clinton was poised to attack Connecticut and Maine. Although Clinton was not receiving the support he desired, he had some reason to be more content with his situation.[8]

But there were storm clouds on the Germain administration even with the positive American events during the first half of 1779. On June 16 the Spanish ambassador brought a declaration to Lord Germain covering a list of grievances, which was interpreted as tantamount to a declaration of war against Britain. After this declaration Lord Cavendish forced a vote for a resolution to have Britain abandon the American war and put all efforts against the French and Spanish. In Parliament the Cavendish vote failed by a 2-to-1 margin, but King George III on June 21 summoned his cabinet and challenged the Ministry to meet the threat of the French and Spanish, as well as defend the war against the American colonies. The king defended his colonial generals in their actions to prosecute the war, reaffirmed his duty to preserve the empire, and declared that God was on his side.[9] The expense of the American Revolution was also a significant burden to the government, and a focus of much discontent.

Not since early 1778, during the crisis over Germain and Lord North, had there been such opposition in Parliament to continuing the war. A serious challenge to the continuation of the American war was now in full swing in the British Parliament. Beginning in November 1778, and lasting until July of 1779, the Howe Inquiry placed this important issue before the British government. The opposition to the Germain administration had attempted every tactic to undermine the Ministry to denounce the war. During various debates before the House of Commons, General Sir William Howe, the former British commander-in-chief in the American colonies, placed a motion to have the correspondence between Lord Germain and himself made public before the Commons. To further the issue, Howe attempted to have various witnesses called to testify before the Commons.

After holding off such testimony for many months, the Ministry was finally forced to allow Howe to call his first witness on May 6. General Howe's second witness, General Charles Grey, struck home the opposition's point that winning an American war was impractical. General Grey testified, in reply to the question regarding whether he believed the colonial war could be won, "I think that with the present force in America, there can be no expectation of ending the war by force of arms. I do not think, from the beginning of June, when I landed at New York, in 1777, to the 20th of November, 1778, there was in that time a number of troops in America altogether adequate to the subduing that country by force of arms." No testimony could have been more damaging to the Ministry. The Ministry's primary witness, Major General James Robertson, defended the administration's policy during four days of testimony by stating that "more than two thirds" of Americans desired peace and that the way to British victory was by "having the people ... armed in their own defense." Robertson continued, "The object of the war was to enable the loyal subjects of America to get free from the tyranny of the rebels, and to let the country follow its inclination, by returning to the King's government."[10]

As July of 1779 came, Clinton was still unhappy with the circumstances of his command situation. That same month Lieutenant General, Earl, Lord Charles Cornwallis arrived in New York without the reinforcements that Clinton had been promised. The disgruntled Clinton almost immediately turned in his resignation, feeling the Ministry had let him down. On August 20 Clinton wrote Germain that his enthusiasm was "worn out by struggling against the consequences of many adverse incidents...." In the same letter Clinton wrote, "I must beg leave to express how happy I am made by the return of Lord Cornwallis to this country. His lordship's indefatigable Zeal, his knowledge of the Country, his professional Ability, and the high estimation in which he is held by this Army, must naturally give me the warmest confidence of efficacious support from him in every undertaking which opportunity may prompt, and our circumstances allow." Soon this warm but strained friendship between them would be dissolved.[11] Clinton also wrote that he wished to "be relieved from a station which nobody acquainted with the condition will suppose to have set light upon me." Clinton urged that Cornwallis take over as American commander-in-chief. In Clinton's letter of October 29 he informed Germain that he was keeping Cornwallis fully informed on all future operations in anticipation of "His Majesty's most gracious acquiescence in his prayer to be recalled." Both Clinton and Cornwallis would not be informed of the decision of the king and the Ministry to keep Clinton in America until March 19, 1780.[12]

Back on August 5, Germain wrote Clinton that "It is from such a conduct [arming the Southern loyalists] we must hope for a speedy issue to this unhappy contest; for not withstanding the great exertions this Country had made, and the prodigious force sent out for subduing the Rebellion, I am convinced our utmost efforts will fail of their effect, if we cannot find means to engage the People of America in support of a cause, which is equally their own and ours." This was indeed the substance of the only hope that the British had, and history would reveal that Americans would not be able to make the British vision "their own." In September Germain wrote Clinton that the proposed offensive operation in South Carolina "is an object of such vast importance that I would not, on any account, suggest the most distant idea of changing it for any other."[13]

On October 8, 1779, Sir Henry Clinton first learned that D'Estaing was on the Georgia coast and a siege of Savannah was underway.[14] When the news reached Germain in London, there was nothing to do but wait for the results. Word that the siege was lifted in a grand British victory reached Clinton on November 19. Clinton immediately made plans to attack Charles Town, as he awaited news of the status of D'Estaing's fleet. One month later Clinton learned the good news that the French fleet had departed the American coast. The critical continuation of the Southern Campaign was about to begin.[15]

In spite of the opposition to sending additional troops to the American colonies, Vice Admiral Marriot Arbuthnot's fleet arrived in New York from England with 3000 long-requested troops to support Clinton. The 68-year-old vice admiral, whose career had been so void of command experience, was deemed the replacement for Commodore Sir George Collier. While Collier had worked so well with Clinton, such would not be the case with Arbuthnot. He would prove to be without vigor and indecisive in the extreme. From the day Arbuthnot arrived at Sandy Hook, he began to show himself, by complaining that his men were inadequate, and in poor condition, for operations. Some complaint may have been justified, most especially regarding the condition of his ships. Most of his ships were in great need of overhaul, and none of them were fully manned. The arriving fleet consisted of two 74-gun, three 64-gun, two 50-gun and two 44-gun frigates accompanied by a dozen smaller vessels. Of Vice Admiral Arbuthnot's professionalism, Clinton thought little, but with his small fleet he could get to Charles Town.[16]

On December 1, 1779, Clinton had 38,569 British troops in America, distributed as follows: 28,756 in and around New York, 3460 in Halifax and Penobscot, 636 in Bermuda and Providence, 3930 in Georgia, and 1787 in West Florida. George Washington's Continental Army consisted of around 27,000 men. With winter operations shut down in the North, the availability of Admiral Arbuthnot's fleet, D'Estaing now in the West Indies, the support of Lord Cornwallis, and the urging from Lord Germain, Sir Henry Clinton decided the time was right to undertake the capture of the prize city of the South, Charles Town. Clinton placed the German Baron Wilhelm von Knyphausen in command of New York.[17] He was now ready to continue with Germain's Southern strategy.

What should have taken some ten days sailing time from New York to Charles Town proved to be a much more untimely ordeal. December of 1779 had been so cold in New York that heavy guns could be taken across the frozen Hudson River. The start of the operation was not promising. Lord Cornwallis' own 33rd Regiment found it challenging just to embark aboard Arbuthnot's fleet, as the wind, high sea conditions and ice hindered operations. December 10 came, when the ships loaded with troops put to sea, only to be turned back by conditions.[18] In company with the fleet's warships on the day after Christmas at 10 A.M., the fleet with troop transports sailed from Sandy Hook. Ice in New York harbor destroyed seven transports at the initial sailing. The fleet consisted of 96 ships, led by Vice Admiral Arbuthnot's 64-gun flagship *Europe*. The men-of-war with the flagship were the 74-gunned *Russell* and *Robust*, the 64-gunned

Raisonable and *Defiance*, the 44-gunned *Roebuck* and *Romulus* and the remaining *Perseus, Renown*, and one other. Clinton was aboard the *Romulus*, with Cornwallis on the *Roebuck*.

Loaded aboard the British ships were 6975 troops. British forces consisted of 1008 grenadiers, 2400 regular troops of the 7th, 23rd, 33rd, 42nd, 63rd, 64th regiments, and 1012 British light infantry. German Hessian troops were 1200 grenadiers, 250 Jagers, 120 chasseurs and 450 of the Regiment Huyn. Remaining troops included 400 New York Volunteers, 35 Althausen Riflemen, 700 Legion troops of Lord Cathcart, 100 guides and pioneers, 150 of Ferguson's Corps and 150 from a detachment of the 71st Regiment. These troops were distributed among some 80 transports. It was a formidable army, deployed aboard a powerful and worthy fleet and all heading to attack the fair city of Charles Town.[19]

On the initial sailing, "The wind was moderate and the cold endurable," according to German Jager Staff Captain Johann Hinrichs aboard the transport *Apollo*. But as the sea voyage continued, everything turned toward being dreadful. The heavy seas and spirited winds were punishing on those ships that could get out of the harbor, and one ship, the *Anna*, which had been dismasted, actually was blown clear across the Atlantic to set anchor at St. Ives, Cornwall. On December 28, the storm began in earnest and the transports began to take on water, pitch and make all life aboard a misery. The storm continued in one form or another until January 20, and drove the fleet far off the coast to the longitude of Bermuda.

Off the Outer Banks of North Carolina the winds were so strong that the sails were generally ripped to shreds, and masts crashed to the decks. The frigate *George* sank. It took over a month before the fleet gathered off Tybee Island, Georgia. Some 16 ships were off Tybee Island on February 1, and the remainder of most of the fleet, including Cornwallis, arrived by late the next day. Aside from the damage to the ships, men lost baggage, clothing, and most of the horses. Cornwallis seemed to endure the voyage better than Clinton, who had never been known as a good sailor. Captain Hinrichs reported that of the 36 days of the voyage, 15 days were with a storm, 25 were with a "contrary wind," during the sailing of some 1851 miles.[20]

As the fleet formed off Tybee, preparations were being made for replenishing of necessary food and supplies. By February 3, ten transports and the man-of-war *Defiance* were still missing. On that day Clinton, Cornwallis and Arbuthnot went to Savannah, as the ship's officers were directed to acquire as much water as they could. Throughout the day boats moved back and forth to 12 miles up the river to land just off Five Fathom Hole. On February 5 the captains were told "to have ten days'

supply of provisions for the troops on board and to have the provision ships make up any shortage."

On the next day Admiral Arbuthnot's agent visited the ships and read a directive from the admiral to the sailors and troops "forbidding them, under pain of severe punishment, to plunder the houses on the landing of the troops." Clinton and the admiral returned to their ships on February 7, and all transports were ordered to procure 30 days' supplies, which indicated that they would sail to their landing point. As the evening of February 8 approached, all the transports received word that they must prepare to sail immediately. The lead units of the fleet weighed anchor the next day at noon and sailed north, with some units stopping at the 10 mile long, pine-covered, Trench Island (Hilton Head Island) to wait for the rest of the vessels to leave the Savannah River and Tybee.[21]

On February 10 the British fleet of 62 vessels was sailing along the South Carolina coast toward North Edisto Inlet. The first dispute between Clinton and Vice Admiral Arbuthnot occurred over where to land the troops. Clinton liked North Edisto, which would shorten the voyage by two days. Arbuthnot wanted the landing at Stono Inlet, but Clinton gained the support of one the British ship captains, Captain George Keith Elphintone, who knew the waters around Charles Town. Arbuthnot finally yielded reluctantly.[22] On February 11, 1780, the fleet came in at North Edisto with the transports anchoring behind Deveaux Bank off Simmons Island (Seabrook Island) in "five and one-half fathoms of water." Part of the fleet was sent around to block the harbor sea entrance while the troops disembarked. Four battalions of light infantry and the grenadiers landed at Simmons Point on Seabrook Island, some 30 miles south from Charles Town, and marched inland across John's Island and James Island. The area was reported to be "desolate and salty, and full of cabbage trees."[23] The remaining troops landed the following day.[24]

With Sir Henry Clinton and Lord Cornwallis in the lead with the light infantry, the British forces advanced to Simmon's House at a bridge "through the woods in swamp and rain." On February 12 these lead units marched "through a wilderness of deep sand, marshland, and impenetrable woods where human feet had never trod!" and reached Wilson's House. Wilson's House was deemed a headquarters, and two companies of grenadiers were ordered to remain there. The going was rough and as Hessian Staff Captain Johann Hinrichs wrote in his diary, "Sometimes we had to struggle, singly or two abreast, through marsh and woodland for half a mile.—What a land to wage war in!" The day ended making camp two miles from James Chapel, which was one and one-half miles from Simmon Bridge and some 25 miles from Charles Town.

By February 14 the British and Hessian force had advanced to the right bank of the Stono River, with the light infantry at Fenwick's and Chisholm's ferries, and the 33rd Regiment and the Hessian Jagers under Major Von Wurmb at Stono Ferry. Reaching Stono Ferry was not a simple task for all. The Jager unit under Lieutenant Colonel Webster captured a black boy who acted as guide. Jager Staff Captain Hinrichs recalled the following:

> We asked him [the black boy] if he knew the way to Stono Ferry; he said he did, and he took us to the river. I must admit that I feel a shudder when I think of our situation; six hundred men on a pebble bar a thousand paces long, bordered on both sides by bottomless swamps; on the opposite bank the enemy, on higher ground and in possession of works, and the river between us a hundred paces wide. Such was our situation! The enemy had no guns. They were dumfounded by our approach, and gave us enough time to withdraw behind the swamps without loss.

The night of February 14 saw two "row-galleys" come up Stono River and anchor between Fenwick's and Chisholm's ferries, in preparation for a crossing. On the next day the generals reconnoitered the works on the enemy side of the river, as well as along the river. Boats were secured and on the morning of the 16th, a battalion of light infantry crossed the Stono at Sucky Staniard's house in several boats, landing at Ingle's Plantation. The patriot forces learned of the crossing and left their posts at Stono Ferry at 9 A.M. using the Wallace and Rantowle bridges, destroying them as they crossed. After more boats came up New Cut Creek and Stono, other units crossed the Stono and advanced above Wallace's Bridge, located 3.5 miles from Stono Ferry. On February 20 British units continued to be brought up as the advance units reconnoitered the John's Island area. Captain Elphinstone was busy attempting to bring the "cannon, ammunition and provisions up the Wadmalaw River, New Cut Creek, and Stono River as far as Wappoo Creek."

On February 19 General Lincoln sent General Moultrie to head for Bacon's Bridge across the Ashley River, some two miles from Dorchester and 24 miles from the city, to create an encampment for the militia. That same day patriot deserters informed the British that the Charles Town forces "were working day and night on the fortifications of the city, that they were firmly determined to maintain their post, and that the detachments posted at Dorchester and Ponpon were one by one approaching the city, leaving behind small parties and observation posts." At dawn on the 21st the light infantry and grenadiers under Major Moncrieff crossed to James Island landing near Hamilton's House from John's Island and advanced to Newtown, New Cut and Fort Johnson. On the afternoon of the next day a British officer and eight men were captured at William Ashley's House by some 20 patriot horsemen on a patrol.

By February 24, the British light infantry had advanced to Wappoo Cut, the British grenadiers were at Newtown New Cut and the Hessian grenadiers were holding Fort Johnson. That morning each of these groups sent out a hundred men to "drive in livestock." Also on this day, Pulaski's former cavalry, "Legion," now under the command of French Major Vernier, waited in ambush on Wallace's Road at a point where two roads were joined between marshes. As the British came down the road with livestock, "without having loaded their muskets," they were met by Vernier's cavalry. The patriot horsemen wounded three fusiliers with their lances before anyone could even load their weapon. Hessian troops happened to be in the area and they came to the rescue of the British just in the nick of time. The British suffered six wounded.

When the Hessian troops had taken Fort Johnson, they had found it abandoned and demolished. The fort, built in a quadrilateral shape of "bricks and palmetto logs," was positioned too high to be effective at damaging shipping traffic once they had passed Fort Moultrie. Out from the fort extended a dominant sand bar that projected all the way to Lighthouse Island. The sandbar forced all shipping to sail close to Fort Moultrie at near point-blank range.[25] On the afternoon of February 28 the patriot frigate *Providence* came down the river at Sullivan's Island and anchored just below Fort Johnson on the left bank and began to cannonade the grenadiers. One Hessian grenadier lost his leg and later died, "another was severely wounded in the arm … and a British gunner was killed." The units at Fort Johnson then decided to encamp farther back. The British erected a hospital on James Island to handle the growing number of sick. By February 29, all was quiet on James Island.

Now the British held the southern side of the Ashley River opposite Charles Town, and they had gotten there without any real patriot opposition. Clinton intended to act slowly and deliberately in classic eighteenth century fashion. Clinton's delay, after forming a camp at Stono Ferry, allowed his army to establish a supply depot and magazines and acquire additional reinforcements. He had sent for more troops from New York and Savannah. Arbuthnot and his fleet of eight frigates carrying 216 guns had moved around to anchor at Five Mile Hole at the entrance of Charles Town Harbor.[26] From atop the newly blackened steeple of St. Michael's Church, Peter Timothy, the editor of the local gazette, could see with his spyglass the smoke rising from the campfires of the British troops and the outline of the ships of the supporting fleet.[27] He could even see Lord Cornwallis and a Hessian general looking over the works at Wappoo Cut.

When first news that the British were off North Edisto Inlet had reached Charles Town, the South Carolina Assembly was in session. They immediately passed sweeping powers for the governor and his council and adjourned, as all officers were ordered to their posts. The power given was "till ten days after their next session … a power to do everything necessary for the public good except the taking away the life of a citizen without a legal trial." Governor John Rutledge then issued a proclamation ordering "such of the militia as were regularly drafted and all the inhabitants and owners of property in the town, to repair to the American standard and join the garrison immediately, under pain of confiscation." Sir Henry Clinton countered the patriot proclamation with one of his own, stating that he offered a free and general pardon for all the treasonable offenses committed, assuring protection and support and warning the citizens of the guilt and danger of refusing his gracious offer.

General Benjamin Lincoln had at the time of the British landing 800 South Carolina Continentals, a detachment of 400 Virginia Continentals under Lieutenant Colonel William Heth who had arrived in December, some 379 cavalry consisting of Colonel Horry's dragoons and the remains of Pulaski's old legion under Major Vernier. In the South Carolina militia Lincoln had about 2000 men, including the Charles Town battalion of artillery, Colonel Simon's Charles Town Regiment and General Lillington's North Carolina Brigade. In total Lincoln had approximately 3600 men to defend the city.

When General Washington learned of Clinton's destination in South Carolina, he ordered General Hogan with his North Carolina Continental Brigade to march to reinforce Lincoln. When the brigade passed Philadelphia they consisted of 700 men, but by the time they arrived in Charles Town, some three months later on March 3, 1780, they numbered 600. Their trip had been quite slow due to the extreme cold and deep snows. Colonel Laurens, Washington's former aide, had traveled from South Carolina, at the request of Lincoln, to appeal to Washington for additional troops to defend the city. Even though Washington had already sent Hogan's brigade, he wrote to Congress asking to send the entire Virginia Army of around 3000 troops to South Carolina. Washington recommended that the troops be transported via the Chesapeake Bay by ship to avoid the fatigue, sickness and desertions that would be expected if the army traveled by land in the inclement weather from New York to Charles Town.

Congress agreed to allow Washington to send the Virginia troops South, and on December 14, 1779, the last rear guard of the force left from New York. The journey was by land to Head of Elk, Maryland, then by water to Williamsburg and on toward South Carolina. Washington wrote General Woodford, "Nothing will make me happier than to hear at all times that the Virginia Line distinguishes itself in every quality that does honor to the military profession. Its compositions excellent, and a strict discipline will always entitle it to vie with any corps in this or any other service." On April 1, 1780, Colonel Washington with his 100 cavalrymen joined up with General Huger's force at Monck's Corner, and on April 6 General Woodford's total force of 750 Continental troops reached Charles Town.[28]

In addition to these Continental troops, Lincoln had been promised support from other circles. North Carolina Governor Caswell would send 1500, and General Rutherford would supply around 500 more. Besides the Virginia Continental troops Washington had promised, Virginia had agreed to send 900 more militia. In all, Lincoln was expecting to see nearly 6600 additional troops to come to the aid of the current 3600 men in Charles Town. But the number of troops promised never arrived. First, most of the South Carolina militia refused to come in from the countryside to the city because of the smallpox outbreak that had appeared. The men were not being overly cautious as smallpox outbreaks in the fair city in 1738 and in 1760 had been severe and most fatal to hundreds. When the 1760 outbreak ended in the month of June, some 730 blacks and whites had died of smallpox, even with the heroic efforts of the 18 physicians in the city to inoculate thousands of citizens.[29] Only a few of the North Carolina militia arrived, and none of the Virginia militia appeared. In all, only 1950 patriot troops came to the aid of Charles Town, and 1350 were those sent by Washington.[30]

Preparations for the defense of Charles Town were now of paramount importance to the patriot forces. Lincoln had assumed that Clinton would attack from the northwest and landed side of the city. Therefore he ordered that the defensive works on the Neck be built. North of Boundary Street slaves were put to work digging a line of trenches. Redoubts for cannons were built of oyster-shell and mortar linking the marshes and rivers on the east and west of the city's peninsula. The primary redoubt, known as the Citadel, was located in the center at the intersection of King and Boundary streets. Ahead of these defensive works was a network of abatis, which were sharpened stakes embedded at an angle in the ground. Beyond the abatis was a deep and wide ditch, which had been flooded with water.[31]

Lieutenant Colonel Banastre Tarleton with Cornwallis wrote in his journal:

> Intelligence was now daily obtained, that the defenses of Charles Town increased very fast, and that the troops who were to maintain them, received hourly additions from Virginia and the two Carolinas. In consequence of this information, the general did not hesitate to make preparations, to assemble in greater force than appeared requisite at the first view of the expedition; in addition,

therefore, to the order conveyed to the northward, commands were forwarded to Major-general Prevost, to send a detachment of twelve hundred men, the cavalry, from the garrison of Savannah.[32]

Clinton had also sent to New York for 3000 additional reinforcements. With the 6975 troops brought from New York, the total number of British troops positioned to attack Charles Town would be over 11,000 men. This was one of the largest concentrations of British forces in the entire Revolution, with only the Philadelphia Campaign being larger.

On February 23 at the patriot encampment near Dorchester, Moultrie had taken command of 606 men, made up of 227 Continental light infantry of Lieutenant Colonel Marion's, and 379 cavalry under Major Jameson. There was no militia to be seen. Marion turned over his force to Lieutenant Colonel Henderson after being ordered to join Lincoln in Charles Town. Moultrie had been directed to blanket the area between his camp and the Stono River and remove all horses, cattle, carriages, boats or other equipment that would be of use to the British. Moultrie gained significant intelligence and wrote to Lincoln that the British were collecting flatboats. By February 25 the message to Lincoln was that some 90 flatboats and canoes had gone down the Stono a few days earlier.[33]

Between February 29 and March 6, according to the diary of the Hessian Major General Johann Christopher Von Huyn, the British built a "bridge over the Wappoo River; headquarters, Peronneau's house, was strongly fortified, and the two redoubts were thrown up…. Also, the necessary abatis," with all of this work taking some "two thousand men a day." On the night of March 6, Lord Cornwallis with his light infantry "crossed the bridge built over the Wappoo River, and at five in the morning the Commanding General [Clinton] followed with the 1st Battalion of British grenadiers."[34] Cornwallis and Clinton had hoped to surprise the patriot cavalry and militia camped at Governor Bull's Plantation on Wappoo [mainland], but they were unsuccessful. The information on their movement had been obtained from a grenadier captain deserter. Captain Hinrichs wrote, "Our plot was betrayed. At half-past two the cavalry retired, and at three o'clock the light infantry arrived in the rear of the plantation only to find that the birds had flown. Today came thirteen Negroes fleeing from Young's Plantation on the Wadmalaw Island. Vernier had crossed New Cut Creek and plundered this plantation."[35]

After Admiral Arbuthnot had protected the disembarkment of the British and Hessian troops at North Edisto Inlet, he separated from his transports and moved his eight frigates carrying some 216 guns to Five Fathom Hole, thus blockading Charles Town harbor. At the entrance of the harbor, between Lighthouse Island and Sullivan's Island, was a sandbar, called the Bar. Through this Bar were five ship channels, the deepest being Ship Channel which had only 12 feet of water at low tide and 21.5 feet at high tide. Even this deepest of channels would not permit a British ship over 40 guns to pass over the Bar unless it was lightened by removing its heavy guns.[36]

When the Continental Congress had been informed of Clinton's move to attack Charles Town, it had sent Commodore Abraham Whipple with nine patriot ships, the largest with 44 guns, to defend the city. General Lincoln had suggested on January 30 by letter that Whipple station his small fleet just inside the Bar, which would serve to keep the British out of the harbor. As it turned out it was impossible to remain close to the Bar under sail "in the face of a rising tide and a strong east wind." Whipple responded to the question, but again on February 12 and on the 26th Lincoln sent letters to Whipple requesting him to station his ships as near to the Bar as possible. Lincoln finally asked Whipple how he intended to secure the harbor entrance. Commodore Whipple, consulting the ships' captains and pilots, responded that it was a better strategy to coordinate the defense with Fort Moultrie on Sullivan's Island in defense of the harbor entrance. But with a Council of War meeting, it was decided that Whipple's squadron could not stop Admiral Arbuthnot's fleet, being out-gunned 152 American guns to 216 British guns. Thus, the squadron sent by Congress abandoned its mission and retreated back toward the city, where the guns were removed from the ships and disposed to the various landed batteries around the city's defensive works. Seven of the patriot vessels were sunk across the Cooper River from the Exchange Building to the opposite marsh.[37]

By the end of the day on March 7, 1000 British and Hessian grenadiers and light infantry had taken possession of land within three miles of Ashley Ferry, which was just 12 miles from Charles Town. This movement was successful at surprising some militia and the drivers of a large number of cattle being held in that area. The speaker of the South Carolina House of Representatives, Thomas Farr, was captured along with his son and several others, and was required to perform the undignified task of driving the cattle for his captors.[38]

When Lieutenant Colonel Banastre Tarleton had reached Tybee Island, before the sailing to North Edisto Island by the main body, he was disappointed to find that all the horses of his dragoons that had been embarked in New York in excellent condition were lost. His horses had been "destroyed, owing to the badness of the vessels employed to transport them, or to the severity of the weather on the passage." Since there were no horses in Georgia, Tarleton headed to Port Royal Island via "some of the quartermaster-general's boats." His mission was "to collect at that place, from friends and enemies, by money or by force, all the horses belonging to the islands in the neighborhood." Tarleton's plan was to link up with Brigadier General Patterson's cavalry from Savannah and join the main forces heading to the Ashley River.[39]

On March 12 the citizens of Charles Town were awakened to find that a British battery had been erected across the Ashley River at Fenwick's Point on Wappoo, in a direct line with the city's Tradd Street. By 7 P.M. the British had deployed heavy cannons on the battery. The British continued the building of batteries on the south bank of the Ashley, and by the 18th one appeared near Old Town. Patriot reconnoitering of the British and Hessian forces continued south of the Ashley throughout the month of March. Vernier's cavalry was seen in various locations in the area, but had not engaged the British.[40]

In mid–March British Brigadier General Patterson crossed the Savannah River with the reinforcements requested by Clinton. His forces, numbering about 1500 men, consisted of the garrison of Savannah including the 71st Regiment under Major McArthur (replacing Maitland on his death), the light infantry of the British Legion under Major Cochrane, Major Graham's light infantry, the American Volunteers of Lieutenant Colonel Ferguson, the New York Volunteers of Colonel Turnbull, Colonel Innes' South Carolina Royalists, Lieutenant Colonel Hamilton's North Carolina Royalists, and a number of dragoons. This force had marched from Savannah on the road toward Augusta for 40 miles, crossing the Savannah at the ferry at Two Sisters. Patterson was heading towards "the Cambayee, through the swamps and difficult passes."[41] On March 13 Colonel Ferguson's volunteers and Major Cochrane's legion were ordered to secure the passes across the river. Working as separate units, these two groups mistakenly engaged each other as the enemy and tragically several were killed and wounded.[42]

On March 14, 1780, Lieutenant Colonel John Laurens wrote the following accurate and insightful letter to General George Washington concerning the tactical situation in Charles Town:

> The enemy's present disposition of his force, and all his late operations, indicate a design to attack Charleston by a siege in form. To complete the investiture, he must introduce his ships of war into the harbour. That it is his intention appears from his fixing buoys on the bar, barricading his ships' waists, and anchoring them in a station where they may embrace the first favorite spring tides to enter. His transports and store-ships have removed from Edisto up Stono River, where they lie contiguous to Wappoo Cut, which is the communication from thence to Ashley River. At a point of the mainland ... he raised, in the course of a night, the 11th instant, a battery of six embrasures. This situation, naturally advantageous, he will probably render very strong and establish in it his de-

posit of military stores and provisions. He then may either force a passage over Ashley River or turn it by a circuitous march, fortify a camp on the Neck and open his trenches. The best communication between his magazines and camp will be across the Ashley River....

> Your Excellency will have learnt that the Commodore and all his officers renounce the idea of defending the passage of the bar; they declare it impracticable for the frigates to lie in a proper position for that purpose. The government has neglected to provide batteries ... so that it has been agreed, as the next best plan, to form a line of battle in such a manner as to make a cross-fire with Fort Moultrie, a shoal called the Middle Grounds being on the right of the ships, and the fort advanced on the left. As it would be the enemy's policy, with a leading wind and tide, to pass the fire of the fort and run aboard of our ships, the Commodore is contriving an obstruction which he thinks will check their progress and allow time for the full effect of our fire.

> The impracticability of defending the bar ... appears to me a great diminution of our means of defence.... The Commodore has destroyed one set of the enemy's buoys, and I hope he will ... order the galleys to give all possible annoyance to the enemy's ships in the act of entering.

> The attention of the engineers has been distracted by the different demonstrations on the part of the enemy, and they have not perfected the line across Charleston Neck.... As the enemy is determined to proceed by regular approaches, all his operations are submitted to calculation, and he can determine with mathematical precision that with such and such means, in a given time, he will accomplish his end. Our safety, then, must depend upon the seasonable arrival of such re-enforcements as will oblidge him to raise the siege. The Virginia line is much more remote than we could have thought it would have been at this moment. Your Excellency, in person, might rescue us all. Virginia and North Carolina would follow you. The glory of foiling the enemy in his last great effort and terminating the war ought to be reserved for you. Whatever fortune attends us, I shall, to my latest moments, feel that veneration and attachment which I always had for your Excellency.[43]

On March 19 Cornwallis received the news in a letter from Germain of the British Ministry's decision regarding Sir Henry Clinton's request to resign his North American assignment. The ministry felt they were "too well satisfied" with Clinton to let him resign, even as they praised the skills of Cornwallis. Cornwallis was discouraged. Up to this point Clinton had consulted and received Cornwallis' input on all key decisions. Now Lord Cornwallis had changed his attitude of cooperation. He informed Clinton that he no longer wanted to be consulted. It was the feeling of Cornwallis that he must distance himself from the responsibility as a near co-commander and decision-maker, and move to establish an independent image. Cornwallis requested a separate command. Clinton reacted with anger.[44]

The showdown between Clinton and Cornwallis occurred in an interview session during which each dredged up old differences and conflicts. The meeting solved nothing. Clinton felt Cornwallis was "unmilitary" regarding the request for a separate command. Clinton was "nearly frantic," as he found out that Cornwallis was having cordial relations with Admiral Arbuthnot. Relations between Clinton and Admiral Arbuthnot had also deteriorated. Clinton had come to believe the admiral was "imperceptive and vacillating" and was essentially plotting behind his back. Clinton wrote of the admiral, "I am sure he is FALSE AS HELL. He swore he would act with me in [everything] … and if he ever did otherwise or deceived me, he hoped he would be damned. The gentleman swears most horribly and I believe will LIE — NAY, I KNOW HE WILL IN A THOUSAND INSTANCES … He forgets all he says and does, and talks nonsense." Clinton summarized with the observation that never again would he serve "with such an old woman."[45] Clinton consulted with his *aide-de-camp*, Major John Andre, on the issue of what to do with Cornwallis. Andre advised Clinton to let Cornwallis have his separate command and to detach him from the main army. Clinton would consider his advice.[46]

Meanwhile the British ships *Renown* of 50 guns, *Roebuck*, 44 guns, and the 44-gun *Romulus* were lightened and passed across the bar without American naval opposition. On March 20 Peter Timothy wrote in his journal, "The crisis of our fate approaches pretty near…. This morning, soon after five, signals were made. At six the admiral's (Arbuthnot's) flag was shifted to the *Raisonable*, and all the men-of-war, except the new admiral's ship, loosed their topsails. They were under way in five minutes; and at half-past seven every one safe anchored within the bar without meeting the least accident."[47] This was a strategic mistake of great proportions.

On March 21, Tarleton joined Patterson and by the 25th they reached Stono Creek. Tarleton's unit of green-clad light cavalry of dragoons and infantry, called the "British Legion," had been recruited and organized by Tarleton from the ranks of loyalists. Soon to become the terror of South Carolina, Banastre Tarleton was born in Liverpool in August of 1754 to a local rich and prominent merchant. Tarleton, a graduate of Oxford, joined the British Army as a coronet in 1775 to fight the rebels in the North American colonies. Tarleton had served at the first Charles Town battle in 1776 at Fort Sullivan, fought in New York, and in 1778 was promoted to lieutenant colonel.[48] On his way to America from London, he had stopped at the Cocoa Tree Club on St. James' Street where it was reported that he tapped his sword on a table and vowed, "With this sword, I will cut off General [Charles] Lee's head!"[49]

On March 23 Tarleton, after crossing the Edisto River, ran into patriot militia at the plantation of Lieutenant Governor Bee. Tarleton's dragoons proceeded to kill 10 militia, took four prisoners and obtained a number of good horses. Three days later Tarleton engaged another cavalry leader, Lieutenant Colonel William Washington, and his force made up the remnants of the cavalries of Bland's, Baylor's and Moylan's Virginia regiment of horses. In this engagement Washington's cavalry fought off Tarleton's cavalry and took several prisoners, including Colonel Hamilton of the North Carolina Royalists and a British surgeon. Lieutenant Colonel Washington almost captured Clinton himself in the battle.[50] General Patterson and Tarleton soon joined up with Clinton near the banks of the Ashley, who was busy "establishing magazines, and erecting works to defend the communications."[51]

As the British consolidated their positions south of the Ashley River, the patriot forces in Charles Town continued to erect defenses and prepare for the battle that would surely come. On March 26 General Lincoln's forces took their positions on the defensive line. The line had been strengthened across the entire neck from the Cooper and Ashley rivers. The main line started on Town Creek, a branch of the Cooper (present day site below the railroad depot on Chapel Street), north to the Liberty Tree, then crossing King Street — the only road to the country — and ended at the creek between Cannonsborough and the city. South of this line on the Ashley were batteries at Coming's Point and at South Bay. In front of the main line was the abatis and a wide ditch filled with water across the neck. The defensive works were the engineering results from two French engineers, Colonel De Laumoy and Lieutenant Colonel De Cambray. Manning the defensive works were Hogan's North Carolina regulars on the right; next were Heth's Virginia battalion, then Lytle's North Carolina corps and on the left the South Carolina regulars at Coming's Point battery. The militia was stationed at South Bay and some other locations in the city. General Moultrie directed the placement and units associated with the artillery around the city. On March 27 a Council of War was held at the headquarters on Tradd Street to consider whether they should vacate Fort Moultrie immediately since the harbor had been abandoned by Commodore Whipple's patriot fleet. The council made the decision not to evacuate.[52]

On March 28, 1780, General Patterson's forces joined up with the rest of the army at Drayton's House along the western bank of the Ashley River, as the orders for immediate march were issued. By evening a number of flatboats and two armed vessels had arrived via Stono Inlet at the mouth of the Wappoo Creek. At daybreak the next morning the flatboats, whaleboats and armed vessels came up to the bank near Drayton's House as the British Army

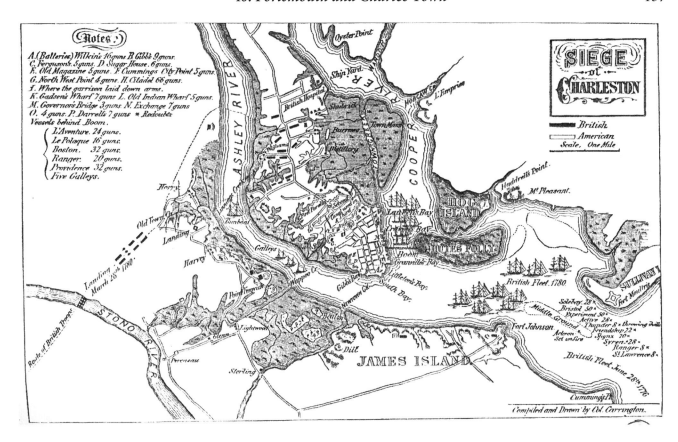

Siege of Charleston. (***Battles of the American Revolution.***)

broke camp. At 6 A.M. the troops began to board the boats under the supervision of Captain Tonken "in the following order: (1) two battalions of the light infantry under General Leslie; (2) the Jager detachment under Major von Wurmb; (3) four battalions of Hessian grenadiers; (4) two battalions of English grenadiers; (5) the 7th and 23rd Regiments, Colonel Clarke; (6) the 33rd and 1st Regiments, Colonel Webster; (7) one troop of the 7th Dragoon Regiment — all these under the command of Lord Cornwallis."[53]

At the point of the intended British Army crossing, the Ashley was only 200 yards wide. The bend in the river shielded the crossing from the patriots.[54] At 7 A.M. the flatboats departed the shore and at 8 A.M. the light infantry and Jagers landed on the eastern bank of the Ashley River at Benjamin Fuller's House, one and one-half mile above Drayton's House. Captain Hinrichs reported that "An enemy cavalry picket stopping between Tom fuller's and Wahnest's house was immediately driven back by several shots from the armed ships." The British were now on Charles Town Neck, some 14 miles from the city. Hessian Captain Ewald recorded the following events after the Ashley crossing:

> Major von Wurmb detached me with twenty jagers to take post on some rising ground half a mile in advance, where I saw a troop of dragoons. I engaged them and they

withdrew. By noon the entire army had crossed the river and taken post in the shape of a crescent, but without guns and equipage except the four light fieldpieces of the light infantry. At noon the army set out to march along the highway. After eight miles they went into camp on the heights one mile from the Quarter-House and six miles from the city…. The night was very quiet, and we saw and heard nothing of the enemy.

As the British moved down the Charles Town Neck on March 29 with no opposition, General Patterson "and his corps, reinforced by Huyn's Regiment, had proceeded to James Island and taken post in the trenches at Hudson's house, and in the redoubts on Fenwick's Point and at Linning's house, in order to cover the communication between the army and the transports which lay in the Stono River." Meanwhile, Tarleton and 200 horsemen advanced toward Dorchester to acquire livestock and capture any patriots they encountered. Lieutenant Colonel William Washington's unit had "received intelligence of the movements, had withdrawn across the Ashley near Bacon's bridge."

On the night of March 29 and the morning of the 30th, cannon, ammunition and baggage was transported across the Ashley and delivered to the forward British units. At 9 A.M. on the morning of the 30th British broke camp and proceeded to march to "Governor's house." Clinton, using this house as a base, wanted "to reconnoitre

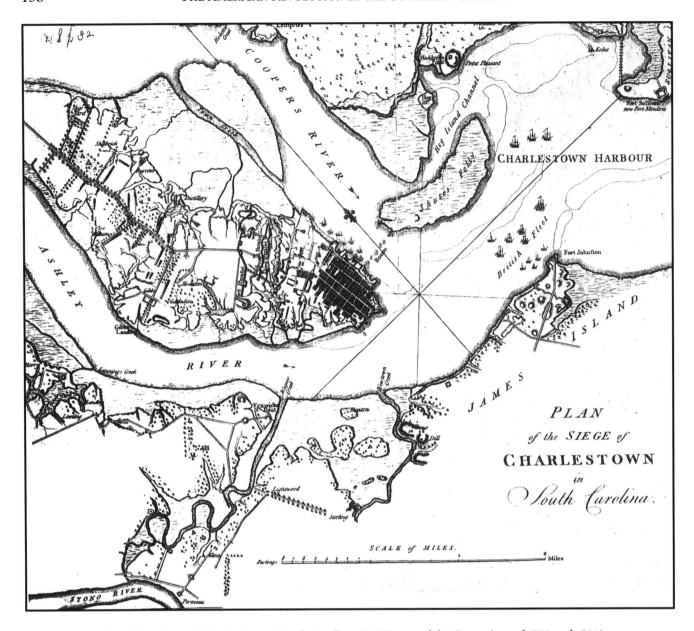

Plan of the Siege of Charles Town, South Carolina. (*A History of the Campaigns of 1780 and 1781.*)

the Cooper River and the right wing of the fortifications of the city." Some small patriot units soon appeared and at noon, as the British advanced forward within two miles of the city, Colonel John Laurens with 200 men of the light infantry attacked up the main road to Charles Town. A Hessian officer reported:

> We had barely gone some hundred paces when several musket shots were fired from the left of the road, one of them inflicting a severe abdominal wound upon Lord Caithness, who was riding in the party of the General.... We immediately deployed to the right and left of the road, attacked them at a quick jager pace and threw them back more than one and one-half miles to their outer work, a fleche in the road protected on both sides by a morass. The enemy had cut up and barricaded all the dams and

footpaths between the road and the Ashley. Between the Cooper and the highway there was no road. We were already in the bog that surrounded their right flank and front as far as the road.... The enemy's force consisted of about three hundred men. Among them were very good marksmen, with whom we exchanged some shots.[55]

Colonel Laurens' unit skirmished for the rest of the day, with reinforcements from Major Lowe including 90 men and two cannons. This engagement occurred in view of both armies, and even some of the ladies of Charles Town came to the works to see the action. During this first encounter of the siege, Captain Bowman of the North Carolina Brigade was killed, with wounded including Major Hyrne and seven privates. In addition to an aide to Clinton, Lord Caithness, several other British men were wounded. As the darkness of March 30 fell on the Neck, Colonel Laurens and his unit fell back inside the lines.[56]

On the afternoon of March 31 the British "broke ground … from ten to twelve hundred yards" from the patriot line. The British and Hessian troops began to build their works, the grand efforts as described by a Hessian officer:

> From this day on hurdles, entrenching tools, and provisions were brought over, as well as disjointed mantelets fourteen feet long and ten feet high that had been built in New York and were being put together at Gibbes', where the engineers and artillery were taking post. This is the finest, easiest, and safest way to build batteries, redoubts, etc., in a sandy soil…. During the night a passageway was cut through the enemy's abatis, which was built of felled trees three thousand feet in front of our camp…. The mantelets were put together, and during the day two brass 24-pounders, … two brass 18-pounders, one 7-inch and one 9-inch howitzer, 12 mortars (royals), and two bell-muzzles with bores from two to four and one-half inches were brought over…. During the night our first parallel was opened, three redoubts having been finished. Every redoubt required sixteen mantelets, which were carried by 400 workmen who were accompanied by another 100 with tools. Thus each face required 125 workmen, which made a total of 500 men per redoubt and a grand total of 1,500 workmen for the night.[57]

That same day General Scott arrived in Charles Town from Virginia, but to the disappointment of the citizens he brought no militia troops as had been promised.[58] Would anyone come to the aid of these American patriots under siege?

The first days of April were taken up with the British building their works, and the patriots engaged in strengthening theirs. General Von Huyn wrote, "From the 31st of March to the 3rd of April some sixty heavy pieces, howitzers, etc., were brought over." The "country around Gibbes' house has been made a park and depot for the siege…." The Americans on the Charles Town main line fired cannons occasionally at the British and Hessian working parties during this period. The British troops guarding the workmen were under the protection of Colonel Abercrombie with the light infantry and units from colonels Webster and Lining.

The night of April 2 recorded some 12 cannon shots, with only a few shots on the 3rd. But on April 4 the patriots opened up with a major cannonade against the British troops, beginning at dawn. The British reported that "by eight o'clock we had already counted two hundred shots." At 8:30 A.M. two patriot frigates, the 36-gun *Queen of France* and the 26-gun *Boston*, weighed anchor sitting close to the city in the Cooper River and sailed "to the flank of our [British] redoubt, and honored me with ten to twelve broadsides." Major Moncrieff had two 24-pounders and one howitzer moved around to face the vessel "four hundred paces behind the redoubt, thus forcing the ships to return to their station." At 6 P.M. the same day an armed schooner came up to the same redoubt, fired eight shots and then "proceeded three miles farther up the Cooper River and anchored opposite the Governor's house."[59]

Meanwhile, on April 2, 1780, General Washington directed the Maryland Line and the Delaware Regiment to proceed immediately to South Carolina. He declared that "Something should be hazarded here … for the purpose of giving further succor to the Southern States." The force was to be commanded by Major General De Kalb. Although Washington had expected Charles Town to fall, he did not want Lincoln's army and all its equipment to be lost. He desired the Continentals he was sending "might assist to check the progress of the enemy and save the Carolinas." De Kalb headed to Philadelphia to meet with the Board of War, where he obtained some supplies and funding. He left the city on May 13 and arrived in Petersburg, Virginia, ten days later. His command army had marched to the Head of Elk, Maryland, and sailed down the Chesapeake Bay, to march into Petersburg several days after De Kalb had arrived. There was some delay leaving southward due to the late arrival of the wagon teams. The last of Major General De Kalb's brigades left Petersburg on June 3, too late to influence the events in Charles Town. [60]

Back in Charles Town on the night of April 5 the patriot forces kept up the cannonading of the British positions on their works, but the British did not return fire until 7 A.M. That evening four British galleys came out of Wappoo Cut. The British on Wappoo Neck opened fire on the city concentrating on the American battery at Coming's Point garrisoned by South Carolina's 3rd Regiment. The British fired with 24- and 32-pounders, and caused some damage, including several shattered homes. A militia grenadier, Mr. Thomas, was killed as he stood in his own doorway on King Street, and General McIntosh lost two horses that were killed on the lot of Mr. Lowndes' residence on Broad Street where the general was staying. During that night the British made a move to make a surprise attack on Colonel Washington's cavalry at Middleton Place located at the head of the Ashley River. When the British force of some 50 horsemen and 500 infantry troops arrived with fixed bayonets, they were surprised to find fires burning but no Americans present. Colonel Washington had gained previous intelligence of their action, and had moved his force to Twenty Three Mile House. As the British departed, Washington's cavalry was able to capture 3 troops in the rear guard.[61]

On April 6 the British and patriot forces continued

to prepare their works and kept up the cannonade of each other. On Friday, April 7, the city was in good spirits as the fine looking and experienced troops from Woodford's Continental brigade of Virginians, along with Colonel Harrington's North Carolina Militia arrived in Charles Town. They had arrived by Hobcaw Ferry and the Cooper River. The patriots "expressed their joy by firing at their batteries at retreat, while the garrison gave three huzzas from the works." At "eight to ten in the evening all the bells in the city rang out." The Charles Town Militia moved to their former position on the line on South Bay from their position on the right to allow room for the newly arrived troops. Woodford's troops had marched 500 miles in 28 days. The only disappointment was that the force consisted of only 750 troops, not the 3000 that had been promised.

On Saturday, April 8 Admiral Arbuthnot and his British warships inside the Charles Town Bar finally received a favorable wind and fog, which allowed them to attempt to pass Fort Moultrie and come into the inner harbor opposite the city. With a strong southerly wind and high tide, Arbuthnot signaled Clinton that he would immediately weigh anchor and come in. Peter Timothy in the steeple of St. Michael's Church at 4:30 P.M. reported that the admiral's ship, *Roebuck*, was receiving and returning fire from Fort Moultrie. The admiral's ship passed, as the frigate *Blonde* also moved past the fort with the loss of her foretopmast. With no apparent damage the 44-gun *Romulus* passed through the fierce cannon fire.

By 5 P.M. the admiral's ship was at anchor near James Island above Fort Johnson, with four other ships. The *Renown* now passed and by 5:30 P.M. all the British fleet was past Fort Moultrie and rested at anchor except for the storeship *Acteus*, which had run aground at Haddrell's Point. Captain Hinrichs wrote, "The enemy suddenly stopped firing and, filled with amazement, saw the proud Briton, the master of the sea, meet and overcome every danger, every obstacle, with scorn and disdain."[62] The garrison at Fort Moultrie under the command of Colonel C.C. Pinckney reported the afternoon of the next day that not a single person had been wounded. The British had landed only ten cannonballs on the fort while the patriot forces had inflicted a British loss of 29 seamen—14 killed and 15 wounded. While the patriot forces at Fort Moultrie had put up a fierce cannonade against the British vessels, they had failed to prevent the British from reaching the inner harbor of the city.[63]

Tarleton wrote in his journal the following regarding the British fleet's passage to the inner harbor of Charles Town:

On the 9th of April [disputed date, in the journals of

three Hessian officers as April 8], the admiral, by signal, discovered his intention to the navy and army, of passing Sullivan's island, on which was constructed a formidable fort, with batteries of heavy cannon. The *Roebuck*, *Richmond*, *Romulus*, *Blonde*, *Virginia*, *Raleigh*, *Sandwich*, and *Renown*, weighed about one o'clock, and exhibited a magnificent and satisfactory spectacle to the royalists, by steadily effecting their passage, under the fire of the American batteries, with the trifling loss of twenty-seven men, killed and wounded: The *Acteus*, a storeship, in following the squadron, grounded, and was burnt; otherwise the navy suffered less than could have been expected from so severe a cannonade. The frigates now taking a position under James' island, blocked up the harbour, and Charles town was barred from all communication with the country, in every point of its circumstance, except in that which faced the river Cooper.[64]

As Sunday, April 9, arrived, the patriots were working with little rest to complete their defensive works, as the city's remaining residents continued their efforts to pile up earthen banks around their homes for protection against the British shelling. There was little shelling on this day, with only 20 shots fired at the British. Hessian Captain Ewald recorded that "In the city they are busy taking people, livestock, and goods over to the left bank of the Cooper River."[65] The British had now completed their "first parallel" works opposite the patriot defenses on the city line, thus, nearly surrounding the city. The only place where it was still possible to communicate with the outside world was by crossing the Cooper River and landing at Haddrell's Point, Lempriere's Point or Hobcaw. Admiral Arbuthnot, having brought his fleet into the inner harbor, arrived at Clinton's headquarters on Charles Town Neck with a warm welcome. Now Clinton, with input from Arbuthnot and Cornwallis, planned the next move.

The night of April 9 remained rather quiet, with no cannon fire. The British and Hessian troops moved to their most advanced positions at daybreak the next morning to "280 shots and ... 10 shells" from the Americans. At around 6 P.M. Sir Henry Clinton sent Major Crosbie under a flag of truce to the American lines carrying a summons from the "Commanding General." The summons read as follows:

CAMP BEFORE CHARLESTOWN
April 10, 1780

Sir Henry Clinton, K.B., General and Commander-in-Chief of his Majesty's forces in the colonies, &c., and Vice-Admiral Arbuthnot Commander-in-Chief of his Majesty's ships in North America &c., regretting the effusion of blood and the distress which must now commence deem it consonant to humanity to warn the town and garrison of Charlestown of the havoc and desolation with which they are threatened from the formidable force surrounding them by sea and land. An alternative is offered at this hour to the inhabitants, of saving their lives and property contained in the town or of abiding by the fatal consequences of a cannonade and storm.

Should the place, in a fallacious security, or its commander in a wanton indifference to the fate of its inhabitants, delay the surrender, or should public stores or shipping be destroyed, the resentment of an exasperated soldiery may intervene; but the same mild and compassionate offer can never be renewed.

The respective commanders who hereby summon the town do not apprehend so rash a part as further resistance will be taken; but rather that the gates will be opened and themselves received with a degree of confidence which forebode further reconcilliation.

(Signed) H. Clinton.
M. Arbuthnot.

Without consultations General Lincoln immediately sent Major Crosbie off with the following reply to Clinton's summons:

GENTLEMEN,—
I have received your summons of this date — sixty days have passed since it has been known that your intentions against this town were hostile, in which time has been afforded to abandon it, but duty and inclination point to the propriety of supporting it to the last extremity.

I have the honor to be &c.
B. Lincoln.
Commanding in the South department.

While General Lincoln had decided that he would not be party to premature surrender of the city, he was concerned that the government leaders must leave the city to ensure the continuation of the administration even if Charles Town were captured. On April 12 General Lincoln brought the general officers to a meeting and obtained their signatures to a letter urging Governor Rutledge and his council to leave. Lieutenant Governor Bee was still in Philadelphia at the Continental Congress as the state's delegate. The local constitution of South Carolina of 1778 provided that on absence from the seat of government or sickness of the governor and lieutenant governor, any member of the Privy Council could be empowered by the governor to act in his absence. Due to the circumstances, Christopher Gadsden was appointed as the lieutenant governor. On April 13 Governor Rutledge, Colonel Charles Pinckney, Daniel Huger and John Lewis Gervais left the city. Staying behind, to represent the government, were Gadsden, and the remaining council, Thomas Ferguson, David Ramsay, Richard Hutson and Benjamin Cattell.

There was little cannon firing during April 11 and 12, but at 9 A.M. on the 13th the British opened up with the much expected and fierce cannonade of the city. This was the first time the British had fired on the city from their newly constructed front lines. They fired bombs, carcasses (combustibles confined in iron hoops), and red-hot cannonballs. With most of the citizenry huddled in their cellars, the cannonade continued with many homes damaged and on fire. To put out fires, an informal fire department was organized, with much danger to their person from being out in the open with shots and shells landing everywhere. Several homes were burned to the ground, and over 20 persons were killed, including a child and her nurse.

To cut off the last point of communications with the city, Lieutenant Colonel Tarleton with his legion had left his camp on April 12 at the Quarter House on the Neck, some six miles from the city. He headed toward Monck's Corner to find and attack Colonel Washington's force. His cavalry, reinforced with Major Ferguson's corps of "marksmen," had proceeded ten miles to Goose Creek. The next day Tarleton was joined by Colonel Webster's force of infantry of the 33rd and 64th regiments. At Monck's Corner was General Huger with his force made up of Pulaski's old legion, the remainder of Horry's cavalry, and some recently arrived Virginia horsemen. Also there was Colonel Washington's infantry which had moved there after the attempted British surprise attack at Middleton Place. From this location at the head of the Cooper, Huger and Washington commanded the "forks and passages of that river," which allowed the city to communicate with the outside world through the parishes of St. John's Berkeley, St. Thomas, and Christ Church to Hobaw and Haddrell's Point on the eastern shore of the Cooper.[66]

Lieutenant Colonel Tarleton's journal recorded the following about the events at Monck's Corner:

Tarleton again moved on in the evening, with his own and Ferguson's corps, toward Monk's Corner, as had been previously concerted with the commander in chief, in order, if possible to surprise the Americans encamped at that place: An attack in the night was judged most advisable, as it would render the superiority of the enemy's cavalry useless, and would, perhaps, prevent a favourable opportunity of getting possession of Biggin bridge, on the Cooper river, without much loss to the assailants. Profound silence was observed on the march. At some distance from Goose creek, a negro was secured by the advance guard, who discovered him attempting to leave the road. A letter was taken from his pocket, written by an officer in General Huger's camp the afternoon of that day, which he charged to convey to the neighbourhood of Charles town: The contents of the letter … and the negro's intelligence, purchased for a few dollars, proved lucky incidents at this period:… It was evident, that the American cavalry had posted themselves in front of Cooper river, and that the militia were placed in a meeting house, which commanded the bridge, and were distributed on the opposite bank.

Led by the captured Negro, Tarleton's forces set out at 3 A.M. toward Monck's Corner. Tarleton's mounted Legion attacked with such speed and surprise that the American cavalry forces were totally overwhelmed immediately in the assault. British Major Cochrane led the British infantry forces against the patriot militia at the meetinghouse at Biggin's Bridge, charging the patriots with fixed bayonets. The attack was over in short order with much loss to the Americans. Major Vernier of Pulaski's Legion was killed, along with three captains, one lieutenant and 10 privates. American wounded included three officers and 15 privates. General Huger, Colonel Washington and Major Jameson, with other officers and men, fled on foot through the swamps and escaped. The British lost only one officer and two men wounded, along with five horses killed or wounded. Tarleton's forces were able to capture some 400 prime American cavalry horses, "together with fifty wagons, loaded with arms, clothing and ammunition...."[67]

When Lieutenant Colonel Webster, who had been put in charge of the command of 1500 men, arrived at Biggin Bridge along with two regiments, he directed Tarleton to seize the boats and take Bonneau's Ferry on the eastern branch of the Cooper River. The British then advanced into St. Thomas and Christ Church parishes using the Wappetaw Bridge on the Wando, to a position some six miles from Lempriere's Point. Now Charles Town was cut off. Even though Colonel Webster was in position to stop most travel to and from the city, Clinton was still concerned over locking out any support for Charles Town. With the 3000 troop reinforcements under Lord Rawdon who had arrived on April 12, Clinton was now able to consider his next move to take further steps to secure all northern approaches to the city.

Meanwhile Clinton's forces on the Neck were steadily advancing toward the city. A continuous mortar, cannon and small arms fire was kept up on April 13 and 14 by the British on Charles Town, and by the 15th a new battery with two guns was opened up from "Stiles" Place on James Island, only one mile away. This new battery, known by the citizens as the "watermelon" battery, continued firing on the city and on April 16 struck St. Michael's steeple and carried off the arm of the statue of Pitt. The British had now advanced to within 800 yards of the city's line.[68]

Work on the "second parallel" works began immediately by the British after the first one was secure. It "intersected a swamp two hundred paces in front of No. 7 [battery] ... the center ... was 1,300 feet in front of the first, 500 feet from the enemy's abatis and wet ditch, and 880 feet from the central fortification." The British first occupied the parallel on April 14 with a little over 50 troops, and the next day with "fifty jagers, fifty grenadiers, and fifty light infantry." The second parallel was finished

on the evening of the 17th. Occasional firing continued throughout the days between the combatants. On the evening of the next day a patriot deserter arrived at the British lines with intelligence that the patriots intended to "attack the right wing of our works." But there was no attack.[69]

When the news of Huger's defeat at Monck's Corner arrived in the city, General Scott was sent across the Cooper River with a "body of light infantry" to Lempriere's Point to keep open communications and allow for fresh provisions from the country. The enemy continued to build their parallel works and batteries, and were within 250 yards by April 19. That same day the British appeared at Lempriere's post, but retired when they were fired upon. Although General Scott had no cavalry, he mounted a few men and began to reconnoiter the area. While on this mission, Scott was summoned to a Council of War at General Moultrie's headquarters. The meeting was first expected to be at General Lincoln's headquarters, but the environment was so chaotic with constant interruptions that no real business could be conducted there.

The council was attended by Major General Lincoln, brigadier generals Moultrie, McIntosh, Woodford, Scott, and Hogan and Colonel Laumoy, the engineer-in-charge, Colonel Beckman of the artillery and Colonel Maurice Simons of the Charles Town Militia. Discussion of evacuation was immediately rejected, although it had been constantly discussed since the last council session. Lincoln covered the strength of the garrison, the British condition, the status of reinforcements, along with the situation with "obstructions ... made in the river between the Exchange and Shute's Folly." Lincoln charged the council with maintaining the strict secrecy of the proceedings, and after concluding his report, asked for the opinions of the council as to the next actions. The officers discussed the possibility of evacuation, which General McIntosh favored. McIntosh proposed that the militia guard the garrison until the Continental troops left the city. Colonel Laumoy opposed McIntosh's idea and wanted to offer terms of capitulation immediately.

At this critical point in the council session, Lieutenant Governor Gadsden entered the room, as General Lincoln proposed that he be allowed to sit as a member of the Council. The weakness in Lincoln's character again showed as he allowed general discussion to influence the decisions, rather that act with military directness. Lincoln was now merely a "moderator." From the moment Lincoln allowed Gadsden to address the council, Gadsden was in control of it. Gadsden's dominant character took over. The question before the group was whether to evacuate or capitulate, but Gadsden at once expressed his surprise and displeasure that either idea was being considered.

He indicated that he would consult with his own council and if there were to be a capitulation, he would need a few hours to consider the terms for the citizens of Charles Town.

The military council adjourned until that evening. The next session began without Gadsden being present, as Colonel Laumoy covered the poor conditions of the defensive fortifications. Laumoy felt it was improbable that they could hold off many more days, and that it would be nearly impossible to conduct a successful evacuation because of the positioning from the British. At this point in the meeting, Gadsden stormed into the room with his entire council of Ferguson, Hutson, Cattell and Dr. Ramsay. The lieutenant governor tried to speak for the militia, even with Colonel Simons present. He expressed his opinion that the militia was willing to "live upon rice alone rather than give up the town upon any terms." Gadsden said that while he was for defending, if the military felt that they should give up, he had the terms of capitulation in his pocket. Then Mr. Ferguson declared that if the Continental troops took any action to collect boats, he would open the gates for the enemy and assist the British in attacking the Continentals before they could depart. Certainly this threat should have resulted in Ferguson's arrest and ejection from the proceedings, but Lincoln did nothing. The meeting would soon end with the decision to continue defending the city.

Lincoln had let the wrong individuals decide the fate of not only the citizens of Charles Town, but also that of the American Continental troops. While it may, indeed, have been too late to evacuate at this point on April 19, the conduct of these proceedings was a disgraceful example of Lincoln's weakness of character in relinquishing his responsibility. With the eventual fate of the city known for many days, if not for weeks, earlier, it was certainly a poor decision to lose the troops and the city. On Lincoln's shoulders would this sad mistake be placed for history to reflect upon.

On April 20, a cold and windy day in this Southern city of 1780, Lincoln again called together the Council of War. That day two magazines at Gibbes' Battery were blown up by British shelling. Colonel Laumoy again urged capitulation based on the current situation: a large body of British horsemen and troops had appeared on Wando Neck and enemy boats had been hauled across the Charles Town Neck from the Ashley to the Cooper rivers, which threatened to cut off all communications to the north side of the city. The council now reached a decision to open negotiations with Clinton for surrender. Lincoln then derived the written terms of the surrender with the only assistance coming from Colonel Ternant. There is no evidence that Gadsden's terms were considered, or available to Lincoln.

The next day, April 21, Colonel Tinning arrived with 200 North Carolina militia, having evaded the British and come to the city from Lempriere's Point. The shelling continued as the numbers of killed and wounded began to mount. With the British only 250 yards off the city's defensive walls and no real hope for success, General Lincoln sent out his flag to Clinton, with his terms and request for six hours of truce. Clinton replied that he should have addressed his request to both Clinton and Admiral Arbuthnot, but gave his approval. This time period was mutually extended by both parties during the negotiations. General Lincoln's twelve terms were as follows:

(1) That all acts of hostility and works should cease between the naval and land forces of Great Britain and America....

(2) That the Town, Forts, and Fortifications belonging to them [the Americans] should be surrendered to the Commander-in-chief of the British Forces....

(3) That the several troops garrisoning the Town and Forts including the French and American sailors, the French Invalids, the North Carolina and South Carolina militia, and such of the Charlestown militia ... should have thirty-six hours to withdraw to Lempriere's after the capitulation had been accepted and signed on both sides ... and that those troops should retire with the usual honors of war, and carry off during that time their arms, field artillery, ammunition, baggage, and such of their stores as they might be able to transport.

(4) That after the expiration of the thirty-six hours mentioned the British troops before the town should take possession of it and those now at Wappetaw should proceed to Fort Moultrie.

(5) That the American army thus collected at Lempriere's should have ten days from the expiration of the thirty-six hours before mentioned to march wherever General Lincoln might think proper to the eastward of Cooper River without any movement being made by the British Troops or part of them out of the Town or Fort Moultrie.

(6) That the sick and wounded of the American and French Hospitals with their medicines, stores, the Surgeons and Directors General should remain in the town and be supplied with the necessaries requisite until provision could be made for their removal.

(7) That no soldier should be encouraged to desert or permitted to enlist on either side.

(8) That the French Consul, his house, papers and moveable property should be protected and untouched, and a proper time granted him for retiring to any place that might afterwards be agreed upon.

(9) That the Continental ships of war, Boston, Providence and Ranger, then in the harbor [which had not

been sunk] with the French ship of war *Adventure*, should have liberty to proceed to sea with necessary stores on board and go unmolested, the three former to Philadelphia and the latter to Cape Francois with the French Invalids mentioned in article 3d.

(10) That citizens should be protected in their person and property.

(11) That twelve months should be allowed such as would not be choose to continue under the British government to dispose of their effects real and personal in the State without any molestations whatever, or to remove such part as they chose, as well as themselves and their families, and that during that time they might have it at their option to reside occasionally in town or country.

(12) That the same protection to their persons and properties, and the same time for the removal of their effects, should be given to the subjects of France and Spain residing in the town as are required for the citizens.

The British answer came at 8 P.M. The British required that the Americans surrender immediately and that responsible hostages of the rank of field officers should be sent as security according to the customs of war. Lincoln's council considered their situation and reconsidered the possibility of evacuation. Evacuation was considered "inadvisable because of the opposition made to it by the civil authority and the inhabitants, and because even if they could succeed in defeating a large body of the enemy posted in their way, they had not a sufficiency of boats to cross the Santee before they might be overtaken by the whole British army." While there was no way out of surrender, the council could not bring themselves to surrender with the terms offered by Clinton and Arbuthnot.[70]

The British and patriot forces were "now everywhere within point-blank shot" of each other. Saturday the 22nd was a day of heavy cannonading, as the work on the approaches from the British continued. On Sunday, Clinton finally gave Cornwallis what he wanted — a separate command. That night Clinton called the earl in for his instructions "to seize the Rebel Communication." The next day Cornwallis, with 1900 men, crossed the river and established his headquarters at St. Thomas Church. Cornwallis would not return to the city until all the central events of the siege were concluded. Cornwallis now took charge of Lieutenant Colonel James Webster's 1500 troops.

The key points of interest for Cornwallis north of the Cooper were Lempriere's Point and Mount Pleasant. Lempriere's Point, at the junction of the Cooper and Wando rivers, opposite the city, commanded the entrance to the river from Hog Island channel. Mount Pleasant on Haddrell's Point below Fort Moultrie was within easy artillery range of Arbuthnot's ships. The patriots had recently placed an 18-pounder on Mount Pleasant and had fired at the British fleet. Admiral Arbuthnot wanted Cornwallis to clear the patriot forces from Mount Pleasant.[71]

On April 25 at 2 P.M. Cornwallis advanced from Wappetaw Bridge and took Haddrell's Point on the mainland between Lempiere's Point and Fort Moultrie. The next day Cornwallis led his force against Mount Pleasant in the early morning and captured the 18-pounder without firing a shot. That Wednesday night, April 26, patriot Colonel Malmedy retreated in confusion with his detachment from Lempriere's Point after they spiked the 18-pounders they left behind. Cornwallis' men immediately took possession.[72] Hessian Captain Hinrichs reported that "In the afternoon [of April 27] Lord Cornwallis arrived at Hobcaw Ferry. The enemy deserted it, leaving behind four guns. And before evening our flag was hoisted on the fort. Three row-galleys, the *New Vigilant*, with eighteen 18-pounders, and one armed schooner went to Spencer's Inlet today and exchanged shots with the enemy's bridge battery on Mount Pleasant."[73]

The British reported that on April 30 "the enemy lost their best bombardier, a major of the artillery, who was killed by a rifle shot." The first six days of May went on with no special incidents on the line, except that the British had begun to taunt the patriot garrison by firing some shells loaded with rice and sugar. On May 4 the garrison's meal ration was reduced to six ounces, with some coffee and sugar still allowed.[74] Hessian Captain Ewald reported that work in the trenches on the parallels continued with a force that "consists of twelve hundred men." Ewald continued that "Last night [May 6] we finished our batteries in the second and third parallels, but did not open them. These mounted twenty-three pieces, two howitzers, and some twenty mortars...." Another Hessian officer revealed, "The enemy fired more briskly than ever [May 6]. At one o'clock there was a tumultuous noise in the city. It seemed as though the yelling would never end, as though a panicky fear had seized them all."

But things changed on Sunday, May 7, 1780, when Admiral Arbuthnot landed 200 marines and sailors under the command of Captain Hudson of the *Richmond* to the west of Fort Moultrie. The bridge battery, which was manned by Captain Williams and some 20 men, was taken first without a shot. When the patriot garrison commander of Fort Moultrie, Lieutenant Colonel Scott, with his 200 troops, saw the British force and the fleet, he knew there was no hope of resistance or escape. At 2 A.M. the British sent a summons to Scott noting that "the Admiral advised that they accept this arrangement, and that, in case the garrison should not surrender before daybreak, he would take position below the fort with six ships and play their guns upon it."[75] Scott accepted the terms of surrender, and received the honors of war. The officers were to be considered as prisoners of war at large on their parole, and were allowed to live in their homes with their families anywhere but Charles Town while it was under siege. The British flag was flying over the fort by day's end. A British journal would record the event, "Fort Moultrie the Great has fallen!"[76]

At Fort Moultrie the British "found respectable stores of livestock, bread, flour, and rum. There were several good wells, but no salt meat. Furthermore, we got possession of forty guns, 6- to 24-pounders, one 10-inch howitzer with 125 shells, and considerable ammunition."[77] The British celebrated the victory, as the patriots in Charles Town were dispirited. Another near disaster occurred the same day Fort Moultrie fell. In horror the citizens watched a 13-inch shell fall just ten yards from the main ammunition magazine near St. Philip's Church. General Moultrie had thankfully moved some 10,000 pounds of powder from the church to the northeast corner of the exchange behind a brick wall.

Unknown to the occupants in the city, there was another event going on that would serve to keep the patriot spirit down and out in the surrounding countryside. After the defeat at Monck's Corner, the remains of Brigadier General Huger's cavalry withdrew to the north of the Santee where they joined Colonel Anthony White's Moylan's Regiment. When Cornwallis' troops approached the Santee while foraging, Colonel White's men attacked the unit, captured most of the party and moved back to Lenud's Ferry on the Santee. White then reported his success to Lieutenant Colonel Buford who was commanding a 400 man regiment of the Virginia Line. Buford was located on the opposite shore near the ferry. White also asked for transportation to the opposite bank for his troops and the British prisoners.[78]

Unfortunately for the patriots, Lieutenant Colonel Tarleton was heading toward Lenud's on May 6 with his cavalry. Having gained intelligence of White's success, Tarleton pressed to attack White's group. The ruthless Tarleton cavalry attacked White's regiment as it was waiting on the shore, unprotected, for Buford's boats. It was another rout for the British, who killed or wounded between 30 and 40 patriot men. Some of White's force managed to escape into the swamps or across the river. Tarleton again captured more horses, having secured an additional 50 to 60 to allow the dragoons to continue the plundering of the area. Now Charles Town was indeed surrounded by the British with no means of escape. The British held all areas on the north of the Cooper River, the Santee River area, the Charles Town Neck, James Island, and the harbor.[79]

On Monday May 8, Clinton sent the following summons to the city:

> Circumstanced as I now am with respect to the place invested humanity only can induce me to lay within your reach the terms I had determined should not again be proffered. The fall of Fort Sullivan, the destruction (on the 6th instant) on what remained of your cavalry, the critical period to which our approaches against the town have brought us, mark this as the term of your hopes of succour (could you ever have framed any), and as an hour beyond which resistance is temerity. By this last summons, therefore, I throw to your charge whatever vindictive severity exasperated soldiers may inflict on the unhappy people whom you devote by preserving in a fruitless defence. I shall expect your answer until eight o'clock, when hostilities will commence again unless the town be surrendered....

Lincoln immediately called another Council of War, with officers numbering some 60 in all, including the officers from the militia, and the Continental frigates. Lincoln did not invite Lieutenant Governor Gadsden, but he did send a message to Colonel Simons asking him to submit "whatever propositions he desired for the citizens." Lincoln asked Clinton to delay commencement of hostilities until 12 noon to allow the various parties to consider the terms. Later Lincoln had to delay the negotiation time to 4 P.M., which Clinton granted. Clinton finally received Lincoln's reply to Clinton's summons at 5 P.M. Lincoln had proposed various revisions to his first 12 capitulation articles. Clinton asked Lincoln if he could review the articles until 8 A.M. the next day, which he agreed to.

The morning of May 9 saw the modifications from Clinton and Arbuthnot being presented to Lincoln. The issues centered on the treatment of the militia and citizens of the city. Lincoln responded that he could not agree to the present terms, and recommended that two or three officers be appointed to meet and confer on the terms, especially on the issues of (1) the militia should not be considered as prisoners, (2) that officers might be able to keep their horses, (3) that the garrison could march out of the city with drums beating a British march, (4) that the French consul should not be considered as a prisoner, (5) that the citizens should not be considered prisoners, (6) that they be given paroles, (7) that the article regarding the French and Spanish stand as proposed, (8) and finally, that the continental soldiers should have their property secure.[80]

When Clinton and Arbuthnot reviewed Lincoln's latest revisions, they were upset. They sent Lincoln notification that the latest proposals were unacceptable, and that hostilities would begin again at 8 P.M. When that time arrived, "The enemy rang all the bells in the city and after a threefold 'Hurray!' opened a cannonade more furious than any before...."[81] General Moultrie described the event as follows:

> After receiving the above letter, we remained near an hour silent, all calm and ready, each waiting for the other to begin. At length we fired the first gun and immediately followed a tremendous cannonade, and the mortars from both sides threw out an immense number of shells. It was a glorious sight to see them like meteors crossing each other and bursting in the air: it appeared as if stars were tumbling down. The fire was incessant almost the whole night; cannon-balls whizzing and shells hissing continually amongst us; ammunition chest and temporary magazines blowing up; great guns bursting, and wounded men groaning along the lines. It was a dreadful night! It was our last great effort, but it availed us nothing.[82]

During the next several nights the 200–cannon bombardment continued as "musket fire, grapeshot, bombs, and red-hot cannonballs" fell on the city. Twenty houses were hit and set afire. Fire bucket brigades manned by slaves tried to put out each blaze, with limited success. Even as the battle roared on, on May 9 Gadsden wrote a letter to Lincoln at 9:50 P.M. declaring, "What reason may have induced you to make proposals, and what they were, I know not; but my duty to my country obliges me to tell you that I had a right to be consulted on the occasion, and as I was not, I do solemnly protest against such treatment, and send you this to let you know I do so." The letter was never sent, as Gadsden's council persuaded him to wait until after the surrender.

On Wednesday, May 10, a petition was submitted to Lincoln from the citizens of Charles Town and the militia indicating that they "thought it their indispensable duty in the perilous situation of affairs to request Lincoln to send out a flag in the name of the people." The British continued to battle the patriot line, and Thursday, May 11, saw the British crossing the wet ditch within 25 yards of the lines.[83] Captain Hinrichs reported that the patriots continued firing until "about noon, when again a flag was sent out. But since our fire was so violent that we did not see them coming, they were compelled to withdraw. At two o'clock in the afternoon the enemy hoisted a large white flag on the hornwork and dispatched a second flag, offering the capitulation of the city...." The siege of Charles Town was over.

At 2 P.M. the British commanders "rode into the city accompanied by many staff officers and adjutants ... followed by two grenadier companies. Then followed the king's flag. At the gate the generals were received by Major General Lincoln on horseback and Major General Moultrie on foot, who surrendered the city. The moment the British grenadiers came under the gate the oboists played

'God Save the King.'"[84] As a Hessian officer observed when entering the city, "people looked greatly starved," with the houses "full of wounded." The homes of the well-to-do were "empty and locked."[85] About 30 homes in Charles Town had been burnt and many others damaged.[86]

At 11 A.M. on May 12, 1780, Lincoln's force of between 4000 and 5000 troops marched out of the city and piled their arms on the left of the hornwork. The American officers then marched the troops back to the barracks where a British guard was placed over them. One onlooker recorded that he saw "tears coursing down the cheeks of General Moultrie." Most of the militia remained in the city, but "the next day ... [they] were ordered to parade near Lynch's pasture and to bring all their arms with them, guns, swords, pistols, etc."[87]

It was a staggering defeat for the patriots and the American cause. The British loss was 76 killed, 189 wounded and they captured 5466 armed men, 391 artillery pieces, 5916 muskets, 33,000 rounds of small arms ammunition, 8000 round shot and 376 barrels of powder. Even with the 42 days of siege by the British, there were only 20 citizens killed.[88] The patriots lost 89 killed and 138 wounded.[89] The British took some 49 American ships, including the 36-gun *Boston*, 32-gun *Providence*, the 24-gun *Ranger*, the 24-gun *Adventure*, the 32-gun *Queen of France* frigate and others.[90] Clinton wrote that "By this very important acquisition there fell into our hands seven generals and a multitude of other officers, belonging to ten Continental regiments and three battalions of artillery, which, with the militia and sailors doing duty in the siege, amounted to about six thousand men in arms."[91]

On May 13, while the captured patriot officers shouted "Long Live Congress," Sir Henry Clinton issued the following proclamation:

> The commander in chief receives the highest pleasure in giving the Army, by whose Courage and Toil he has reduced this important place, the Tribute of Praise & of Gratitude they so well deserve.
> His Excellency presents his warmest thanks to Lieu. Gen. Earl Cornwallis, Major Gen. Leslie, Huyne, Kospoth, and Brigadier Gen. Paterson for their animated Services during the Siege:
> To the Officers and Soldiers of the Royal Artillery, of every Corps British and Hessian, of the Jagers, and to Capt. Elphinston & the Officers and Seamen of the Royal Navy, who have acted with us on shore, His Excellency also addresses the assurance that he holds himself under the most permanent obligations to them, for having so well seconded in their spirited efforts all his operations.
> His Excellency further expresses his great obligations to Lieu. Col. Webster, and the Corps with which he broke in upon the most essential of the Rebel Communications;

and particularly to Lieu. Col. Tarleton and the Corps of Cavalry & to the Infantry of the Legion, for the Soldierly conduct & Gallantry which gave them such Brilliant advantages over the Enemy.

To Major Ferguson the General declares himself much indebted, for his great activity and good Services, & particularly for the useful application made of his Talents in field Fortification.

But to Major Moncrieff who planned & Conducted this Seige, with such great Judgement, such unrelaxed assiduity, & so much intrepidity, & to the very Capable Officers under him, as well as to every other person in this department: His Excellency could wish to convey impressions of His Gratitude greater than he is able to express.

On May 15 at around 1 P.M. an incredible event occurred, as recorded by Hessian Captain Ewald:

When the artillery were engaged in putting the muskets of the prisoners away in a building which had been used as a powder magazine by the enemy, the building blew up, and the ensuing fire destroyed six houses, including a brothel and a poorhouse. Over two hundred persons lost their lives, among them Captain Collins and one subaltern of the Artillery, Lieutenant Maclow of the 42nd Regiment, seventeen English and two Hessian artillerymen, one Hessian grenadier, and several other English and Hessian rank and file not to mention the inhabitants and rebel soldiers who happened to be near by. During the years that I have been a soldier I have witnessed many sad spectacles of war, but never such a horrible one as this. Some twenty charred and maimed persons were dug out of the debris. Some had been blown against a neighboring church, and were so mutilated that one could not make out a human figure. A great many were half dead and, suffering from burns, writhed like worms on the ground. Here and there one found parts of human bodies scattered about.... A battlefield could not look sadder.[92]

This was a tragic end to the siege of the great Southern City of Charles Town. It was the greatest victory in the war for the British and there was great celebration in England over the fall of the city. The king was out riding when Clinton's aide, the Earl of Lincoln, told him of the good news. The returning troops were paraded before their cheering citizenry. In Dublin the city was greatly illuminated, as the friends of America were depressed.[93] Was this the end to the American Revolution in the South?

11

WAXHAW'S CREEK AND CAROLINA PARTISAN CONFLICT

From his new headquarters in Miles Brewton's house on lower King Street, Sir Henry Clinton ruled over the pride of the South, Charles Town. The defeated American officers, including General Lincoln, and Continental troops were secure under guard at their barracks in the city, nearby at Mount Pleasant or aboard British transports in the harbor.[1] On May 19 and 20 the South Carolina militia were paroled to their homes, while the officers were sent to "Haddrell's Point, where they are permitted to go about the country within a radius of six miles."[2]

Clinton sought to establish some type of civil administration. In this regard and to his displeasure, Germain sent instructions dated April 5, 1780, that both Clinton and Arbuthnot were to be "His Majesty's Commisioners [sic] for restoring Peace" in Charles Town and South Carolina. They were empowered to restore peace, but they were also required to report "all propositions which shall come under Your Consideration" while they were forbidden to agree to matters "that may be construed to preclude Our Royal Determination." Clinton complained to Germain that he was required to share his commissionership, and both men wrote of their displeasure with the restrictions placed on their actions.

Another serious problem with the issue of administration of South Carolina was that Arbuthnot and Clinton did not agree on how to accomplish it. Admiral Arbuthnot was most interested in turning control over to the royal officials, while making the colony an example for the other rebel colonies and an "asylum for neighboring loyalists." The Admiral thought the civil and military government "to be so wedded." Sir Henry Clinton saw it

differently. As the military commander he saw his role in "slowly" establishing civil government. In a letter to William Eden, dated May 30, Clinton declared that "It [self-government] would intoxicate." This situation was also amplified by Clinton's basic dislike for Arbuthnot.

On May 22 Clinton and Arbuthnot issued a proclamation revealing that all "faithful and peaceable Subjects" would receive the protection of the British Army and that people who were guilty of intimidating the loyalists, or preventing them from declaring their allegiance, would receive severe punishment and confiscation of their property. All were required to assist the army to restore peace, and additionally, the commissioners agreed to restore civil government "whenever the Situation of the Country will permit." Nine days later the commissioners issued another proclamation, which promised a full pardon to everyone who would pledge their allegiance. Also, upon taking an oath of allegiance they would be guaranteed all the rights and immunities they once had under the former royal government. An exemption from taxation except by their own legislature was also granted to oath takers, an old and original issue in the American Revolution.

On June 3, 1780, Clinton released a third proclamation indicating that on the 12th of June, all prisoners on parole, except those taken during the siege of Charles Town, would automatically be released from their paroles and restored to their full rights as citizens. The controversial element of this proclamation was the inclusion of the statement that any persons who afterward failed to take an oath of allegiance to his majesty's government would be considered in rebellion. With this measure Clinton had ensured the continuance of the Revolution in South Carolina, for now one could not be allowed to remain on parole and be neutral. Clinton later tried to defend his proclamation from criticism by attempting to prevent rebels from resisting, and explaining, "By thus obliging every man to declare and evince his principles I gave the loyalists an opportunity of detecting and chasing from among them such dangerous neighbors."

Now the chances that any citizens who actually became true loyalists after taking the oath were essentially invalidated by Clinton's action. The effects of the third proclamation were noted a month later when Lord Rawdon wrote to Cornwallis, "That unfortunate Proclamation of the 3d of June has had very unfavorable consequences. The majority of the Inhabitants in the Frontier Districts, tho' ill disposed to us, from the circumstances were not actually in arms against us; they were therefore freed from the Paroles imposed by Lt. Colonel Turnbull and myself; and nine out of ten of them are now embodied on the part of the Rebels...."[3]

And take the oath of allegiance, they did. On June 3, 1780, citizens of Charles Town, including the "principal and most respected inhabitants," pledged their loyalty with their "warmest congratulations on the Restoration of this Capital and Province to their political connection with the crown and Government of Great Britain." During the months to follow hundreds of citizens would take the oath. Well known among these oath-takers were Henry Middleton and Charles Pinckney, former presidents of the South Carolina Assembly; Rawlins Lowndes, the former governor of the state; Gabriel Manigault, the richest man in the city; and Daniel Huger, the aide to Governor John Rutledge. Many felt compelled to take the oath though their true feelings differed. One such man, Dr. George Carter, who took the oath in order to continue his medical practice, revealed his actual passions while standing to deliver a toast. While entertaining guests late one evening, Dr. Carter forgot that a loyalist was still present when he raised a toast to "the American Congress." From the dark corner of the room came the statement, "What is that you say? Do you mean to insult us with such a toast?" Recovering, Dr. Carter finished his toast with the shrewd remark to his British guest, "My dear friend, hear me out. I meant to add, 'May they all be hanged.'" Such were the ways of survival in 1780.

Now that Charles Town was under British control and Savannah, and Georgia, subdued, Sir Henry Clinton wanted to secure the remainder of South Carolina. With that direction, Lord Cornwallis departed his headquarters at Christ Church Parish on May 18 with 2500 men on a march to Lenud's Ferry, on his way across the Santee River toward Camden. Two other British divisions left the city and headed to Dorchester, and then separated into the

countryside. Lieutenant Colonel Browne moved his forces up the Savannah River to Augusta, while the second force under Lieutenant Colonel Balfour marched along the Congaree to Ninety Six. Soon the divisions were to be in possession of Camden, Augusta and Ninety Six, having encountered no patriot resistance at all.

Lord Cornwallis had taken off toward Camden after receiving information that it was the location of 350 men, the remnants of 3rd Virginia Continental forces in the South under command of Lieutenant Colonel Abraham Buford. Cornwallis had been delayed in crossing the Santee River because the patriots had either destroyed or concealed the local boats. But as had happened on other occasions, information was gained from blacks that led to some of these boats, allowing the British to cross. While the remaining troops under Cornwallis crossed the Santee, Colonel Tarleton's Legion and a detachment of dragoons were directed to Georgetown to put down any resistance, which he did forthwith and without opposition.

By May 22 Cornwallis was heading along the eastern banks of the Santee at Nelson's Ferry, the same path taken earlier by the retreating Buford. Buford had begun to retreat to North Carolina on hearing of the surrender of Charles Town while just 30 miles from the city. With tactical brilliance in realizing that the speed of the main body of his army would never overtake Buford's Continentals with over a week's lead, Cornwallis detached Lieutenant Colonel Banastre Tarleton on May 27 with 40 men of the 17th Dragoons, 130 legion troops and 100 mounted infantry to pursue the patriots. Tarleton's men, except for a few British officers, were primarily American loyalist militia forces from New York and Pennsylvania. Leaving his infantry to follow, Tarleton's force moved with incredible speed at the expense of a number of horses that were disabled from the heat and exertion. At daybreak the next day, Tarleton reached Clermont. He would have captured Governor Rutledge, and two of his council members, Daniel Huger and John L. Gervais, if it had not been for the warning given by their Englishman host. At midnight Colonel Rigeley, who had entertained the governor and his two councilmen, woke up his guests and advised them of Tarleton's approach.

Meanwhile, 700 North Carolina militia under General Caswell, with a regiment of 350 Continentals and a small unit of Washington's horsemen joined with Buford's force at Camden. At Camden the unfortunate decision was made to split the American commands, with Caswell heading to the Pee Dee River as Buford's forces continued on toward North Carolina in the hope of reaching a force under Lieutenant Colonel Potterfield. Potterfield's force had marched from Virginia in late April with 400 men including a horse corps and artillery toward the South Carolina border. Continuing to work his horses as he gathered replacements along the way, Tarleton pushed forward. The next day he reached Camden only to find that Buford had left Rugeley's Mill located some 15 miles up the road on May 26. Buford was marching to reach promised reinforcements in Salisbury, using the road through Charlotte, North Carolina.[4] After a rest, Tarleton's forces departed Camden at 2 A.M. and reached Rugeley's Mill at daybreak. Tarleton then learned that "the continentals were retreating above twenty miles in their front, towards the Catawba settlement, to meet their reinforcement."[5]

As a tactic to delay Buford, "Captain Kinlock, of the Legion, was employed to carry a summons to the American commander, which, by magnifying the number of the British, might intimidate him into submission, or at least delay him whilst he deliberated on an answer." Tarleton had only 270 men and Cornwallis with the main body was still marching between Nelson's Ferry and Clermont. Buford replied defiantly to Tarleton's summons, but did not slow his march as he considered his wording.[6] "I reject your proposals, and shall defend myself to the last extremity" were Buford's words to Tarleton.[7]

After having traveled 154 miles in 54 hours, Tarleton finally approached Buford's forces in the Waxhaws, located near the North Carolina border in what is today Lancaster County. While there are differing British and American accounts of the ensuing battle at Waxhaw Creek, the British met a "serjeant and four men of the American light dragoons" at 3 P.M. on May 29 near Waxhaw Presbyterian Church. The Americans were taken prisoners. According to American accounts, as soon as the truce flags were passed, Tarleton's cavalry bugles sounded an initial charge at the rear guard commanded by Lieutenant Pearson. Tarleton's men attacked fiercely, as Pearson was mangled "with his nose and lip ... bisected obliquely and the lower jaw completely divided." Tarleton's right wing force of 60 dragoons and a like number of mounted infantry under Major Cochrane attacked the American flank. "Captains Corbet and Kinlock were directed, with the 17th dragoons and part of the legion, to charge the center of the Americans; whilst Lieutenant-colonel Tarleton, with thirty chosen horse and some infantry, assaulted their right flank and reserve." Then, "within three hundred yards of their front, the cavalry advanced to the charge."[8]

The Americans' account recalls that at the moment Buford considered the situation hopeless for his men and the surrender flag was hoisted, Tarleton's men continued to assault Buford's men with inhuman savagery. The Americans tried to make the personal decision to either lay down their arms or continue to defend themselves. Ensign Cruit, who advanced with the flag of surrender, was cut down immediately, as the Americans asked for the usual quarter. But Tarleton and his men did not cease

their brutal attacks for some 15 minutes. A surgeon, Dr. Robert Brownfield, riding with Buford, wrote, "The demand for quarter, seldom refused to a vanquished foe, was at once found to be in vain."[9] A Captain John Stokes from Pittsylvania County, Virginia, recalled the massacre in a most personal way. He had been attacked with deadly blows at his head by one British dragoon, as another dragoon cut off his right hand in one stroke. As he tried to defend his head with his left hand, his attackers hacked eight to ten cuts from his wrist to his shoulder, and cut off his finger. Stokes' head was "laid open almost the whole length of the crown to the eyebrows, and after he fell he received several cuts on the face and shoulders." He then received two bayonet strikes to his body as he lay on the ground. The carnage was indescribable.[10]

Even though Captain Stokes actually lived to tell his story, Tarleton's force had killed outright 113 men, and another 150 badly wounded. The British also took 53 prisoners capable of moving. The wounded were cared for by the citizens at Waxhaw Church, but most of them died of their wounds. At the church trenches were dug to bury the mutilated bodies of the American wounded. Some 84 bodies were buried in one mass grave, and 25 more were likewise set to rest about 300 yards away.[11] Tarleton had lost only five killed and 14 wounded.[12] As news of the terrible massacre filtered out to the countryside, the infamous cry of "Tarleton's Quarter" would ring out to all who wished to reflect on whether they were prepared to take up the patriot cause in the South. This act of barbarous inhumanity would do much to settle the case against the British for those who had remained neutral.

The news of the British victory reached Cornwallis, as he was only 40 miles from Nelson's Ferry. The facts of the battle were given to Lord Cornwallis when Tarleton joined up with the main body in Camden a few days later with additional "American cannon, royals, waggons."[13] Tarleton explained that the savage attack had been caused when he had his horse shot out from under him, and the false word had gone out that he had been killed. By the time he had regained a mount, it was too late to stop the savagery. Cornwallis "found no fault" with Tarleton's conduct. Sir Henry Clinton "reported it with exultation."

On June 4, 1780, from his headquarters at Miles Brewton's mansion in Charles Town, Clinton wrote Lord George Germain, the British secretary of state, "I may venture to assert that there are few men in South Carolina who are not either our prisoners or in arms with us." Indeed, it was a sad time for the patriot cause in South Carolina on this day. The British held Charles Town, Augusta, Camden, Ninety Six, and Georgetown. The militia had been disbanded, there were no Continental troops in the field, and the Continental officers like Lieutenant Colonel Francis Marion, General Isaac Huger and Major

Thomas Pinckney had escaped into North Carolina, along with Governor Rutledge and his council. General Lincoln, General William Moultrie, Colonel C.C. Pinckney and Lieutenant Colonel John Laurens were prisoners at Haddrell's Point. Continental soldiers were on prison ships in Charles Town harbor. Gadsden and other prominent men were British prisoners of war in Charles Town. Rawlins Lowndes, Henry Middleton, and Gabriel Manigault had retired to their plantations and accepted British rule. Henry Laurens, the president of the Continental Congress from South Carolina, was preparing to sail to Holland as minister plenipotentiary, but would be soon captured at sea and placed in the Tower of London until the end of the war.[14] Could the patriot struggle continue in South Carolina?

As Clinton prepared to depart for New York, he detailed his instructions on June 1, the king's birthday, to appoint Lord Cornwallis to command the Southern District. Cornwallis was to use "the utmost plenitude of power, civil and military" and to maintain "the safety of Charleston and tranquility of South Carolina as the principal and indispensable objects of his attention." He continued, "I left His Lordship at liberty, if he judged proper, to make a solid move into North Carolina, upon condition it could at the time be made without risking the safety of the posts committed to his charge."[15] Clinton wrote that he had planned to go to Chesapeake Bay until he had received information of the forthcoming visit from a French fleet, which forced him to now head to New York. As soon as he and Admiral Arbuthnot could deal with the French fleet, they would "probably be taking posts at Norfolk or Suffolk or near Hampton Road, and then proceeding up the Chesapeake to Baltimore." There would later be significant controversy over these instructions, as Clinton maintained that Cornwallis' moves across North Carolina and into Virginia were dependent on the success in South Carolina, while Cornwallis felt he had been given no discretion but to advance northward according to the ministerial plan of the Southern strategy.[16]

Boarding on June 5, and passing the Charles Town Bar with 99 ships and all the troops Cornwallis could spare, on June 8, 1780, Sir Henry Clinton left Charles Town for New York aboard the *Romulus* believing that Britain "was well warranted in the flattering expectations she entertained of soon seeing the war brought to a favorable issue."[17] This was not to be. After Clinton left Charles Town for New York, both Clinton and Lord Cornwallis were glad to see each other part company. Clinton wrote in his journal, "I can never be cordial with such a man. He will play me false, I fear." "Whenever [Cornwallis] is with me, there are symptoms I do not like," continued Clinton. "I leave Cornwallis here with sufficient force to keep [Charles Town] against the world,

without a superior fleet shows itself, in which case I shall despair of ever seeing peace restored to this miserable country."[18] On June 17 Clinton, his army and Arbuthnot's fleet dropped anchor in the Narrows near New York. On the morning of June 19 the British and Hessian troops were disembarked on Staten Island.[19]

Now, after four long years of campaigns following the orders of others, the 43-year-old Lord Charles, Earl Cornwallis, had an independent command in charge of the British military in the South. His powers were wide. He represented all British military and most civil authority in the South, including Florida. He could issue money through the paymaster general, hold general courts martial and control all supplies and provisions.[20]

Clinton had sailed to New York taking 4500 troops back with him, including most of the cavalry. Cornwallis was left with around 3000 troops. By June 25 Cornwallis had returned to Charles Town to assume his administrative duties to stabilize the city and plan his strategy for the upcoming campaign into North Carolina. Francis Lord Rawdon was left in charge of Camden with the principal force. It consisted of the 23rd and 33rd regiments, the Volunteers of Ireland (a corps of Irish deserters raised by Rawdon while in Philadelphia), Tarleton's Legion infantry, Browne's and Colonel John Hamilton's corps of the Scottish Royal North Carolina Regiment, and a detachment of artillery. Major McArthur with two battalions of the 71st moved to Cheraw, "in the vicinity of the Pedee river," to cover the area between Camden and Georgetown on the coast. At Georgetown was a detachment of provincials. To the west of Camden "was connected with Ninety Six by Rocky mount, a strong post on the Wateree, and occupied by Lieutenant-colonel [George] Turnbull, with the New-York volunteers and some militia."[21]

Lieutenant Colonel Nesbit Balfour was at Ninety Six until he returned in July to Charles Town to take over from Brigadier General James Patterson, who had left for England with an illness. At Ninety Six with Lieutenant Colonel John Harris Cruger were "a battalion of De Lancey's [New York Volunteers] and Innes's and Allen's regiments of provincials, with the 16th and three other companies of light infantry." Furthering the chain of British control, "Major Ferguson's corps and a body of loyal militia transversed that part of the province situated between the Wateree and Saluda, and sometimes approached the borders of North Carolina." At Augusta was Lieutenant Colonel Thomas Browne with his Florida Rangers and detachments from other regiments. Savannah "was sufficiently garrisoned by a corps of Hessians and provincials under the orders of Colonel Alured Clarke." At Charles Town were "the 7th, 63d, and 64th regiments of infantry, two battalions of Hessians [Dittfurth's and Huyn's Regiments], a large detachment of royal artillery, and some corps of provincials...."[22]

With Clinton out of his way, Lord Cornwallis promptly set about establishing a proper administration and some kind of "British normalcy" to the colony. In Charles Town he expanded the powers of the Board of Police to maintain civilian protection and created a commandant of the city to serve as the chief bureaucrat. Of course, one important requirement was the re-establishment of taxation of private property. Cornwallis discovered that all the "records and other public papers" of South Carolina had been "thrown into casks and boxes" and it would therefore be necessary to protect and organize them. Even more important to Lord Cornwallis was the acquisition of food and clothing for his troops. His forces were able to capture some gear, but most of his clothing would have to come from New York. For food he would have to live off the land, and not depend on the rations from New York. His commissary agents purchased food from local loyalists at fairly high rates, but he had no other choice. To carry out a military campaign in the South, he would need to transport his food and equipment by wagon, and he had none of those either.

Clinton was most responsible for keeping Lord Cornwallis chronically short of hard currency, and he was thus forced to sign warrants of future payment and bills of exchange to pay his bills. Confiscation of rebel property and goods helped to keep the military in reasonable supply, especially when the British were not on the move. Although looting was forbidden, it was widespread for the usual motivation of greed and as a result of the circumstances of "living off the land." Cornwallis created two key positions to handle "the confiscation and distribution of supplies to the army." The commissary of captures and the commissioner of sequestered estates were posts held by Charles Stedman, a loyalist from Pennsylvania, and John Cruden, respectively. Stedman, a "conscientious and zealous man" who served Cornwallis with pride, was responsible for securing, recording and distributing confiscated goods. Cruden's duties were to seize "real and personal property of every kind" including land, structures, cattle, horses, household goods and even black slaves. Seizures were often auctioned off after a 21-day newspaper notice, and plantation owners were supposed to receive a fourth of the proceeds to support their families. While Cornwallis placed various checks on the actions of these two men, they had the power to determine whether a family would starve or not.

Cornwallis took other actions to improve the administration and well-being of the province. He "opened up" trade from the upper country to Charles Town for a variety of manufactured goods, and he permitted the citizens to "receive payment in the produce of the country."

He re-established the jurisdiction of regular courts over wills, estates and inheritance "in the manner heretofore accustomed." Certain former justices of the peace were reappointed.[23]

The plight of the numerous runaway black slaves who flocked to Charles Town eventually became "dangerous to the community" in the eyes of the British officials. These officials ordered the arrest of many blacks. They were confined to a "large Sugar House" which was located near the western end of Broad Street on the Ashley River at the property of a well-known slave trader, William Savage. The slaves were often used to repair fortifications around the city and to clean streets. Even though the British spent significant efforts and funds on the "Sugar House," it remained "exceedingly filthy and detrimental to the health of the Inhabitants." Many blacks died and were buried in various lots around the city. One such "Negro burying ground" on Church Street became so "extremely noxious" to the citizens they complained to the British authorities. The cemeteries throughout Charles Town were filled not only by blacks, but also by whites as the smallpox and dysentery spread through the prison ships.[24] It was a tragic situation.

Perhaps Lord Cornwallis' most distressing problem in Charles Town during this period was determining what to do with the large number of prisoners. In the city alone were some 1500 Continental Army prisoners who were mostly being held on prison ships in the harbor. Over time the conditions were "truly shocking," according to one who witnessed their circumstances. The "rebell prisoners die faster, even, than they used to desert." While the mortality rate was high among American prisoners, even the British troops suffered with much illness and death during the hot summer of 1780.

The best estimate was that some 800 Americans died during the first 18 months of captivity at the hands of the British. Cornwallis searched for an answer to the dilemma of the prisoners. He paroled some to the various islands along the coast, and was able to exchange some for captured British and loyalist men. Based on a suggestion from Germain, Cornwallis was able to convince some 500 prisoners to leave the harsh prison ship conditions and take up the British military cause by serving in the West Indies. In this way the Americans were able to live the normal soldier's life without having to fight their countrymen. The plight of these living examples of war's tragedy continued to confound Cornwallis.

By far the major problem Cornwallis faced was trying to determine who was friend or foe, as he attempted to establish normalcy. Some of the citizens were loyalists one day and patriots the next. As always, some that had a chief motivation to protect their health and property would profess their loyalty to whoever was in power at the time. Others who had lost everything at the hands of the British were certainly more inclined to fight for independence. The pure intellectual patriot was perhaps a rare individual in the American colonies, but there were enough of these persons to seed the Revolutionary spirit. Those who were caught supporting the American rebels or who showed an instance of patriot leanings were hauled off to confinement in a dungeon that had been constructed in the cellar of the old exchange building on the eastern seawall of the city.[25] For all his efforts at creating a successful civilian-run administration in South Carolina and the city of Charles Town in the summer of 1780, Cornwallis and his associates were not able to calm the winds of change and Revolutionary spirit in the South.

Cornwallis, like Clinton, understood that the most important ingredient to building a strong and sustainable control in the backcountry of the Carolinas was the establishment of a loyalist militia. To this end the able, intelligent and temperamental Major Ferguson was appointed inspector of militia and major commandant of the first battalion of militia. On his appointment he headed immediately to Ninety Six and began to organize the loyalist militia. While Ferguson met with some success in organizing such a militia, he was eventually criticized for not carrying out all the responsibilities of his station. Cornwallis said Ferguson's role was to be "more that of a Justice of Peace than a Soldier." Lieutenant Colonel Nisbet Balfour, who was the commander at Ninety Six, felt Ferguson could not really be trusted "out of sight." He told Cornwallis that Ferguson "seems to me to want to carry the war into N. Carolina himself at once." Even though Ferguson never inspected a single militia unit in North Carolina or Georgia, and limited his South Carolina duties to the districts of Orangeburgh and Ninety Six, he did put together eight battalions of loyalist militia by the middle of July 1780.[26]

In early June Colonel Lord Rawdon with the Volunteers of Ireland and a detachment of cavalry moved up from Camden to the Waxhaws. Rawdon found that "The sentiments of the inhabitants did not correspond with his lordship's expectations: He there learned what experience confirmed, that the Irish were the most averse of all other settlers to the British government in America." Disappointed in this lack of support for the British, Lord Rawdon returned to Camden awaiting the offensive being planned by Cornwallis.[27]

Cornwallis continued into the summer of 1780 with the monumental task of organizing and establishing a proper administration of the lower South from Charles Town. With no sizable American army in the field to threaten him, the work of furthering the patriot cause fell to various partisan bands of men throughout North and South Carolina. Such was the case when on May 26 a group of loyalists gathered at Mobley's Meeting House some six miles west of Winnsboro in present day Fairfield County. To counter this gathering, Captain John McClure of Chester and Colonel William Bratton of York assembled their patriot supporters, and attacked and dispersed the loyalist group. Another such encounter occurred at Beckham's Old Field near Fishing Creek in Chester County.[28] These would only be the beginning of significant partisan engagements in the months to come.

As it became clear that Cornwallis would surely strike into western North Carolina after the defeat of Buford at the Waxhaws, Brigadier General Griffin Rutherford of North Carolina called the militia to assemble to defend the state. On June 3 General Rutherford assembled some 900 militia at Reese's Plantation near Charlotte, accompanied by 65 horsemen under Major William Richardson Davie and 300 light infantry of the First North Carolina Continental Regiment under Lieutenant Colonel William L. Davidson. With the news that the British had moved back to Camden, the patriot militia forces were dismissed. But when Lord Rawdon advanced to the Waxhaws for his short visit, General Rutherford again called together his militia. By June 14 the force was organized and ready. Davie's cavalry was formed into two troops under captains Lemmonds and Martin. The infantry was under Davidson and the remaining militia commanded by General Rutherford. News arrived that a large body of loyalists had gathered at Ramsour's Mill, located some 20 miles northwest of Charlotte at the present day Lincolnton.[29]

After the capture of Charles Town, the loyalists in the Carolinas began to feel a sense of power they had not felt for some time. Lord Cornwallis, in correspondence with many such friends of the British in North Carolina, requested them to attend to their harvests and wait until the British forces entered that province before taking any action. But this request went unheeded for loyalist Lieutenant Colonel James Moore. On June 7, 1780, Moore arrived at his father's home located just six miles from Ramsour's Mill, and began to tell his family about his exploits with the British. Moore had joined the British in the previous winter, served at the siege of Charles Town and left for his father's home on Lord Cornwallis' march to Camden.[30]

On June 10, in the woods at Indian Creek, some seven miles from Ramsour's Mill, Moore assembled a group of 40 loyalist men, revealing to them the instructions from Lord Cornwallis. Just before the meeting ended, a messenger arrived with news that 20 patriot men under Major McDowell of Burke County were eight miles away looking for the "principal persons of their party." The group determined that they would attack McDowell. The next morning they headed to find him. As it turned out, Moore's men were unable to overtake McDowell, as the patriots had retired. Moore then asked his force to re-turn to their homes and re-gather at Ramsour's Mill on June 13.

On that day some 200 men joined Moore, and on the next day even greater numbers arrived, including Major Nicholas Welsh, a regimental commander under Colonel Hamilton. Welsh, who was also a local resident, told the gathered group of the events of the defeat of Buford at Waxhaw's Creek. Welsh, wearing his impressive regimental uniform, did much to encourage and inspire the men to support the British cause. Moore wore a "soiled red coat and carried a sword."[31] This group remained at Ramsour's Mill until June 20, and by that time numbered some 1300 men. Nearly one-fourth of the loyalist men had no weapons. While assembled, a detachment tried to capture Major Joseph McDowell and Colonel Hugh Brevard, but they were again unsuccessful.[32]

With word of the large loyalist gathering, General Rutherford departed his encampment located south of Charlotte on June 18, and marched toward Ramsour's Mill. As evening fell, Rutherford sent a dispatch to Colonel Francis Locke of Rowan County to join his force at Tuckaseegee Ford on the Catawba River on the evening of the 19th or the morning of the 20th. At Mountain Creek Colonel Locke had 400 men assembled from Rowan, Burke and Lincoln counties, supported by Major Robert Wilson of Mecklenburg County. Locke did not receive Rutherford's dispatch before he and his council of officers decided to attack the loyalists. Locke's force departed on their march late in the evening of Monday, June 19, toward Ramsour's Mill, 16 miles away.

Colonel Locke's force moved down the south side of the mountain, stopping at the west end to plan the attack. Patriot companies under captains Falls, McDowell and Brandon were to move on horseback with their men marching in front. The movement continued and at daybreak Locke's men were located just one mile from the loyalists' camp. The loyalists were encamped on the summit of a hill 300 yards east of Ramsour's Mill. They were positioned on the south side of a millpond, with the Tuskaseegee Ford road by the mill. Below the ridge was a gentle slope, which allowed the loyalists 200 yards of open area to fire across. When the patriot horsemen of Falls, McDowell and Brandon came into sight, Moore's 12 pickets, located in the road 600 yards from the loyalist position, fired and moved back to Moore's position. The battle had begun.

In some confusion, Locke's men were able to get "on the flank and rear of the enemy." The loyalists were driven over the ridge and down the ridge on the other side toward the millpond. Locke's men eventually held the entire ridge, as the loyalists formed across the creek beyond the mill. Locke tried to form another line to attack, but initially he could gather only 80 men. Eventually 110 men were gathered. Messengers carrying word of the action reached General Rutherford some six miles from Ramsour's Mill. At once Major Davie's cavalry advanced, as Colonel Davidson's infantry moved with all haste. Other messengers reached the patriots at two miles from the battle with word that the loyalists had fled. Finally, General Rutherford's forces reached the battle area two hours after the fight was over.

The loyalists, in retreating, sent out the white flag proposing that hostilities suspend to allow each side to care for the wounded and dead. Major Rutherford and another officer met the loyalists at a point away from the immediate area, to hide the fact that the main body had not arrived yet. Major Rutherford demanded that the loyalists surrender in ten minutes. Moore and Welsh gave orders to have as many men as possible to flee the area as fast as possible. By the time the flag was returned, there were only some 50 loyalists about, and they fled the area as best they could. Major Davie's cavalry pursued the loyalist men in retreat until they were fully scattered. He then took up position "below Charlotte to look for British."[33] Moore and Welsh with 30 men moved to join the British at Camden, where Moore was threatened to be brought up on charges for disobeying Lord Cornwallis' orders not to engage the patriots. But the matter was dropped.[34]

The battle had been a bloody one. Fifty men were lying dead on the side of the ridge, with many scattered on the flanks of the main action. It was believed that about 70 were killed on each side, with some 100 wounded on each side. Locke took 50 loyalist prisoners. The battle tallies were inaccurate because the action was so scattered and the men wore no distinguishing uniforms to differentiate which side they were on. The battle was more of a "savage brawl" than a disciplined engagement. It was really a fight between backwoods farmers, not professional soldiers. Without ammunition, both sides often used their muskets as clubs. A patriot who took part in the battle at Ramsour's Mill commented, "In this battle neighbors, near relations and personal friends fought against each other, and when the smoke would from time to time blow off, they would recognize each other."[35]

The patriot victory at Ramsour's Mill of Colonel Locke's force of 400 over Moore's 1300 loyalists so crushed the loyalist movement in the area that they never attempted to reorganize again during the remainder of the Revolution. Not surprisingly the loyalist defeat received little attention from the British. By late June Lord Cornwallis stated, "that with the force at present under my command ... I can leave South Carolina in security, & march about the beginning of September with a body of

Troops into the back part of North Carolina, with the greatest probability of reducing that Province to its duty...."[36] The optimism in late June of Cornwallis was interesting, as the patriots and loyalists continued to pursue each other with determined violence. As the summer continued, Cornwallis would soon paint a sadder picture of the partisan warfare in the Carolinas, and become disappointed with the loyalist militias. It was Moore's Creek Bridge all over again.

After the battle at Ramsour's Mill, General Rutherford headed off to the Yadkin River area to engage a force of loyalists gathering with Colonel Bryan. Meanwhile Major Davie, with his cavalry, was ordered to position to seek out British foraging parties along the border of North and South Carolina. Davie took up a position some 14 miles south of Clem's Creek on the north side of Waxhaw's Creek in South Carolina. Major Crawford, with some South Carolina volunteers, 34 Catawba Indian warriors under Chief New River and some militia from North Carolina, joined up with Major Davie.[37]

After Lord Rawdon's forces moved back to Camden from the Waxhaws, he established a post between the present Lancaster and Kershaw counties, some 24 miles from Camden at Hanging Rock. Major Davie's men, on a "rapid and long march in the night, having eluded the hostile patrols, gained the route of the convoy...."[38] On July 2 Major Davie intercepted a convoy of British supplies at Flat Rock located 4.5 miles from Hanging Rock. The escort of dragoons and loyalist volunteers was caught by surprise, and they were captured without incident. The wagons and supplies were destroyed as the mounted prisoners were led away in the dark. Retreating from the Flat Rock engagement, Davie's men were ambushed at Beaver Creek by British hoping to free their captured associates. Davie tried to avoid the center of the heavy fire by rushing through the area, but his men retreated back in the direction they came from. Davie lost Lieutenant Elliott who was killed, with two men and Captain Petit wounded.[39]

Major Davie was beginning to show his courage and ability in the Carolina partisan operations. He was a unique person with a wide sphere of interest and achievement. Of Scottish descent, Davie was born on June 20, 1756, in Egremont in Cumberland County in the north of England. At age 5 he moved to Landsford, South Carolina, on the Lancaster side of the Catawba River. He was adopted by his uncle who was the Reverend William Richardson of the Waxhaw Presbyterian Church. He grew up in the border region south of Charlotte, and was greatly familiar with the area during the Revolutionary actions. Davie attended Liberty Hall, an academy known as the "Queen Museum." He then attended Princeton College and was doing well when he decided to join Washington's Continental Army in the summer of 1776. After

serving in Washington's Long Island Campaign, he returned to college and graduated that fall. His college studies continued in Salisbury at law school for two quiet years.

When the war came to the South, he entered the action. Davie influenced a wealthy man, Barnett, in 1779 to establish a "troop of horse," and he served as lieutenant. Davie, who took over the cavalry, served as part of Pulaski's Legion at the siege of Charles Town, but was badly wounded at the battle at Stono in June of 1779. While recuperating from his wounds, he completed law school and was admitted to the bar. Returning to the war, Davie gained authority from the North Carolina General Assembly to raise a troop of cavalry and two companies of mounted infantry. With proceeds from his estate, left to him from his uncle, he outfitted the entire unit. Davie was well spoken of. A Dr. Caldwell said of Davie, "This distinguished leader although younger by several years, possessed talents of a higher order and was much more accomplished in education and manners" than any of the prominent Carolinian partisans of his time. Davie was "tall, graceful and strikingly handsome," and "His delight was to lead a charge...."[40] At this most critical point, after the defeat of Buford and the surrender of Charles Town, young Davie at age 24 was one of those brave, intelligent and inspired Southern men who raised the hope of the patriot cause.

A strange meeting occurred at Bullock's Creek Meeting House which had been called by colonels Bratton and Watson. At the meeting these two officers gave their opinion that there was no reason to continue opposition to the British. The news of the meeting had been communicated to Lord Rawdon, who was then at the Waxhaws. The meeting moved to Hill's Iron Works on Allison Creek, where a commission from Lord Rawdon was read to the citizens. The commission indicated that the American Congress had given up the two Southern states and that Washington's army was now a small force, which had fled to the mountains. At this point in the meeting, Colonel William Hill interrupted the commission and told the group that the information was false. He reminded them that they had taken a pledge to maintain the independence of the state "to the utmost of their power." The remarks of Hill changed the direction of the meeting, and the reaction was most positive to the patriot cause. The meeting turned into an organizational gathering, where Hill and Andrew Neel were elected the colonels to lead the militia force.

When Lieutenant Colonel Turnbull at Rocky Mount learned of the patriot action near Fishing Creek, he sent Captain Huck with 35 dragoons of the legion, 20 mounted infantry of the New York Volunteers, and some 60 loyalist militia to investigate. Captain Christian Huck, an

American, had already become notorious for his cruelties and violence with Tarleton. As a Philadelphia lawyer, he had joined the British in New York. On Sunday morning, June 11, Captain Huck and his force headed toward the church at Fishing Creek expecting to find the pastor John Simpson, who was a patriot and had led the group that dispersed the loyalists at Mobley's Meeting House and Beckham's Old Field. On the way the British killed William Strong, a pious young man who was assaulted while reading his Bible.

When Huck's force arrived, Mrs. Simpson, the wife of the pastor, was sitting at her breakfast table. She immediately fled with her four children into their orchard to hide. Captain Huck's men rifled through the Simpson home looking for valuables, destroyed the bedding, took their clothes and set the home on fire. The home burned to the ground, which destroyed a valuable library containing important manuscripts and books. Huck then moved to Hill's Iron Works, where his men destroyed everything they could not carry. They burned "the forge, furnace, grist and saw mills," all the buildings, the black huts, and carried away 90 black slaves. After this, Huck moved to White's Mills on Fishing Creek in present day Chester County about six miles from the York County line.

Meanwhile, Thomas Sumter had taken the wagons, horses, and supplies with authorization gained from the victory at Ramsour's Mill and proceeded to Clem's Creek in Lancaster County and established his camp there. He was joined by colonels Hill and Neel from York County, Richard Hampton from the Tyger River at Spartanburg, Captain Samual Hammon, Colonel Elijah Clarke of Georgia, and others who had evaded the British outposts in the Carolinas. Here they all learned of Huck's actions in destroying the valuable iron works used to forge patriot cannon and ordnance. Colonel Hill and Neel with 133 men were then sent to York County across the Catawba to reinforce their unit and gather provisions.

Huck was now ordered by Colonel Turnbull to take his cavalry to the frontier to gather loyalist militia and "to push the rebels." On his advance Huck stopped at Mrs. McClure's Plantation which they plundered and destroyed. There Mrs. McClure's son, James, and son-in-law, Edward Martin, were caught melting down her mother's pewter dishes and molding bullets. Huck made them prisoners and ordered them to be hanged the next day. Mrs. McClure was treated brutally, being struck by the flat of Huck's sword. Daughter Mary escaped the British and rode to see Sumter's camp. There she told her brothers, John and Hugh McClure, about the events at the McClure home. With 150 men, Colonel William Bratton and Captain John McClure set out that evening toward the McClure home some 30 miles away.

Meanwhile Captain Edward Lacey had gathered volunteers and joined the patriot group at Clem's Creek. The total force now had some 500 men to drive out Huck from the area. At sundown of July 11 the force learned that Huck's forces had moved toward White's Mills. Before reaching their destination, the patriots learned that Huck had reached Bratton's Plantation in York County, which was located some 12 miles from White's Mills. Due to some confusion in setting their offensive actions, 150 men mounted their horses and headed to Charlotte, 40 miles away. With the remaining force of 350 men, the patriots moved to attack Huck's force, which was believed to have some 1000 British troops with them. The patriot force, now reduced by 90 along the way, moved to Bratton's Plantation, dismounted and encamped there to wait. They then learned that Huck had moved to the home of James Williamson's Plantation located a quarter mile away on a creek.

While invading the privacy at Colonel Bratton's home, Huck ordered Mrs. Bratton to fix a meal for him and his troops. He also wanted to know where her husband was. She replied that he was "In Sumter's army," and that her husband would rather die in defense of their state than join with the loyalists. On that response, one of Huck's men tried to kill her with a reaping hook, but he was restrained by one of Huck's officers.

As night came the patriots moved to a thicket within sight of the British campfires around Williamson's plantation. Colonel Bratton reconnoitered the area including his own home. They then held a council to plan the attack of Huck's force. It was decided that colonels Bratton and Neel would lead half the force, with Colonel Lacey commanding the other group. Huck had sentinels in front of the home but no other pickets or patrols were sent out. On the morning of July 12 the patriot force had moved into position to attack.

At dawn the patriot teams attacked in silence, cut the pickets off their horses, and opened their fire some 75 paces from the British. From behind a fence on the road the patriots fired at the British, as the British fired back. Huck's troops tried three times to charge with bayonets, but each time the American rifle fire was deadly and accurate. At first Huck did not even leave his bed, thinking the action was insignificant, but finally he was "aroused to his danger." Without even his coat, Huck mounted his horse and as he tried to rally his men, he was shot and killed. As Huck was falling from his horse he was heard to say, "Boys, take the fence and every man his own commander." At that instant the Americans jumped over the fence and rushed the British, who immediately dropped their arms and fled in great confusion. Some of the patriot men pursued the British with a vengeance on horseback for 14 miles.[41]

The battle at Williamson's Plantation had lasted for

about an hour with only one American killed. The British lost "Huck and 35 of his officers and men," with some 50 wounded.[42] Of the wounded who fled, many were later found in the woods dead. After the action, Mrs. Bratton showed the greatest attention to her invaders by tending to their care and feeding. The officer that had saved her life was presented to her and treated with hospitality. This Southern woman showed her patriotic spirit in the face of death, as well as her mercy for the enemy when they had fallen. The prisoners James McClure and Edward Martin were released from their confinement the next morning.

This battle at Williamson's Plantation was unique relative to the other actions of partisan groups in the Carolinas up to this point in that the local patriots had engaged British regulars, led by the loyalist Huck. It was a turning point in the Southern American Revolution. Now patriot men with limited military organization were willing and able to attack and defeat professional British soldiers. Even with the defeats at Charles Town, Monck's Corner, Lenud's Ferry, and the Waxhaws, the American patriot movement was more alive and personal than it had ever been. For once in the Carolinas, whether one was a loyalist or a patriot could have dire results. The time for reflection was over. It was now a time of action. The victory at Williamson's Plantation helped the patriots, and now some 600 additional men joined with others at the Clem's Creek encampment.

About this time in the summer of 1780 Colonel Thomas Brandon, who was camped near the present town of Union, South Carolina, was in the process of gathering volunteers to support the patriot cause. During the recruiting activities they had managed to capture a loyalist, Adam Steedman, but unfortunately he escaped and informed the local loyalists. Brandon was attacked at his camp by a large group of loyalists and was completely routed. A Captain Young, who had lost his brother in the attack, joined what remained of Brandon's force, avowing to avenge his brother's death. The loyalists were known to camp at Stallions in York County. With some 50 men, separated into two parties, the patriots attacked. Captain Love with his 16 men attacked from the front, while Colonel Brandon engaged from the rear. Mrs. Stallions, the sister of Captain Love, ran out to plead with him not to fire on the house, but as she turned back toward the house she was shot dead by an unknown bullet from the open door of the house. A short action began, but the loyalists surrendered after seeing no way to escape the brutal fire. The loyalists lost two killed, and four wounded, with 28 taken prisoner. The prisoners were transported to Charlotte.

Meanwhile on the same day, July 12, Mrs. Thomas was visiting her husband, patriot Colonel John Thomas, and her two sons who were all confined at Ninety Six as prisoners of the British. Elder Thomas had been confined after the surrender of Charles Town for violating his parole. While there Mrs. Thomas overheard a conversation between two women who revealed that "On tomorrow the loyalists intend to surprise the Rebels at Cedar Spring." Since Cedar Spring was the camp where her son, Colonel John Thomas, Jr., was gathering men to join Sumter, she was determined to warn them. The next morning Mrs. Thomas traveled to Cedar Spring and delivered the news.

With knowledge of the British intentions, Colonel Thomas with his group of 60 men moved to the rear of their campfires and waited. Soon the British arrived with 150 men, and rushed the camp in the dark. To the surprise of the British, the patriots were not sleeping. Instead they fired a fierce volley that made a quick end to the British attack. The British were totally routed, with a number of British dead. The Cedar Spring engagement was over with another patriot victory.

The British detachment that attacked the patriots at Cedar Spring had come from the overall command of Colonel Ferguson. He had been detached from Lord Cornwallis' corps with 200 American Volunteers when he crossed the Santee River at Lenud's Ferry. On June 22, 1780, Ferguson's group arrived at Ninety Six to support Colonel Balfour's force there. It is believed that Colonel Ferguson had a special commission from Clinton which was independent from that of Colonel Balfour at Ninety Six. Ferguson was a Scotsman born to Lord Pitfour. At age 15 he entered the British Army as a cornet of dragoons, serving in Flanders and Germany. He served with the 70th Regiment of Foot in the Caribbean Islands during an insurrection on the island of St. Vincent. After hearing rumors of the skill of Americans with rifles as the conflict with the colonies surfaced, he invented a breech-loading rifle which received great attention with high ranking officers and King George III in June of 1776.

Ferguson joined with Clinton as the head of the corps of riflemen and participated in the operations at Philadelphia, Brandywine and Monmouth in 1777-78. He came to the South with Clinton to Charles Town in 1779 commanding the Loyalist American Volunteers unit of 300 men. His force joined with Major Hanger's corps of 200 Hessians, and for his service he was promoted to lieutenant colonel. In South Carolina he joined Clinton at Stono River on March 25, and supported Tarleton's attack on Huger at Monck's Corner on April 12. Ferguson was known as more of a humanitarian than Tarleton, as well as being dedicated and professional. After the Charles Town siege, he was now in the backcountry of South Carolina carrying out his work with his commission. His authority included exacting oaths of royal service, establishing militias and conducting various civil services like marriages.

After Ferguson arrived at Ninety Six he moved 16 miles forward and established works on the Little River, as his provincials set up camp at the plantation of James Williams in Laurens County. This had long been a loyalist camp from the times of General Cunningham. In the Little River area, Ferguson moved about the locals stating that "We come not to make war on women and children, but to relieve their distresses." He was quite effective at speaking with the citizens and influencing them to maintain their British loyalty. Over time many loyalist men joined him as he roamed from Rocky Mount to Ninety Six through the counties of Newberry, Union and Spartanburg. His forces "plundered the Whigs of their cattle, horses, beds, wearing apparel, guns and vegetables…." As the appointed inspector general of the militia, he was the man to gather some 4000 loyalists for the British cause in this country.

While the loyalists were being hit at Cedar Spring, Ferguson moved across the Enoree River at Kelly's Ford and camped at the plantation of Colonel James Lyles. Lyles was then supporting Sumter's patriot group on the Catawba River. Ferguson sent out units in all directions, marched into Union County, camping at the Tyger River just below Blackstock's Ford. He then moved into "The Quaker Meadow" known today as Meadow Woods, and on to Fair Forest. As the loyalists moved through this area, they continuing their plundering and foraging.

On June 11, some 140 men under Colonel Elijah Clarke, a Georgia partisan, gathered at Freeman's Fort in Georgia and then moved across the Savannah River, six miles below Petersburg which was ten miles west of present day Abbeville. When Clarke learned of the large British and loyalist forces located in front of him, he moved his volunteers back to Georgia fearing the danger to wait for a more favorable time. Colonel John Jones of Burke County objected to the retreat, and was able to influence some 35 men, along with Lieutenant John Freeman, to join him in a plan to move through the South Carolina backwoods and to somehow join up with the Continentals. To pass through the loyalist area, Jones' men pretended to be loyalists. When they came to the headwaters of the Tyger River, one of the guides helping them told them that rebels had attacked them the night before at Cedar Spring. The guide then escorted them to the loyalist camp at Gowen's Old Fort, where at 11 P.M. on the night of July 13, 22 men of Jones' group attacked the loyalists. He killed one, wounded three and took a total of 32 prisoners.

After taking horses and guns, the patriot force of Jones was guided to Earle's Ford on the Pacolet River in Spartanburg County, where they joined with Colonel McDowell's forces of 300 men. Both groups were quite fatigued, as McDowell's force had had a "tedious march" and Jones' unit had not stopped for rest for three days and nights. McDowell's camp was on high ground on the eastern side of the North Pacolet River near the borders of North and South Carolina in Polk County, North Carolina. Some 20 miles from McDowell's camp was the British and loyalist Prince's Fort, commanded by Colonel Innes. The camp was located on high ground at the head of one of the branches of the North Fork of the Tyger River and seven miles northwest of Spartanburg.

Unaware of McDowell's large force, yet having gained intelligence on the actions of Colonel Jones' unit, Colonel Innes on July 15 detached Major Dunlap with 70 British dragoons and some loyalists under Colonel Ambrose Mills to find and attack Colonel Jones. Dunlap's force reached the area of McDowell's camp late at night and attacked with their swords drawn. Dunlap's men were able to reach the Georgia men first before most of them were awake. Jones was cut on his head with eight wounds; Freeman was able to rally and joined a Major Singleton behind a fence some 100 yards away. Then McDowell "formed the main body on Singleton's right," and ordered a patriot counterattack. Dunlap's forces retreated across the river without loss except one man wounded, as the Americans suffered eight killed and 30 wounded.

As the sun rose the next morning, July 16, McDowell ordered Captain Edward Hampton and 51 other able patriots, including Freeman and 14 of the Georgia group, to mount the best horses and pursue the British. With a fierce chase of two hours, Dunlap's force was engaged some 15 miles away. Dunlap's force was routed, with eight killed initially. Captain Hampton's men continued to pursue Dunlap's men as they took more killed and wounded moving back to Prince's Fort, where some 300 British and loyalists were ready to assist. By 2 P.M. Captain Hampton returned to McDowell's camp with 35 horses with all dragoon equipment, and some of the enemy's baggage. Hampton had not lost a single man.

Colonel John Moore, a noted loyalist, was in command of Thicketty Fort which was located a quarter of a mile north of Goucher Creek, not too far from the Broad River. This post had been a fortress to fight off the Cherokees and was surrounded by an abatis. Sumter, who had heard of Ferguson's movement beyond the Broad River, directed Colonel Clarke and his Georgia men to head there. At Cherokee Ford they met up with a force of 600 patriot troops under colonels McDowell, Shelby, and Hampton, along with Major Charles Robertson, and gathered to take Thicketty Fort some 20 miles away.

At sunset on July 29, the Americans began the march and by daybreak they had arrived and surrounded the post. Colonel Shelby had sent ahead William Cooke to demand that the fort surrender. Colonel Moore answered that he would defend the fort, but when Shelby's force came within musket range, he agreed to surrender if the Americans would let his men be paroled while agreeing not to engage in the war. This was accepted, and 93 loyalists and one British sergeant major surrendered without a shot being fired. The loyalists lost 250 arms fully loaded. With Thicketty Fort captured on the Sunday morning of July 30, Colonel Shelby's force returned to McDowell's camp at Cherokee Ford in victory.[43]

On the same Sunday a patriot council was held at Landsford on the Catawba River with colonels Sumter, Lacey, Neel and Irwin, along with Major Davie, to determine their next moves. Colonel Irwin commanded 300 men from Mecklenburg, North Carolina, with the other three colonels directing various South Carolina volunteers. The council decided to attack the British posts at Hanging Rock and Rocky Mount. Sumter, with colonels Hill and Lacey, would handle the Rocky Mount attack, while Davie, heading his own corps along with some North Carolina volunteers, would follow Colonel Heaggins and move on to Hanging Rock.

On August 1, Sumter approached Rocky Mount, which was a post located on a summit with woods surrounding in all directions. The post was also surrounded by a small ditch with abatis, and three log buildings. Sumter tried three times to penetrate the defenses, but was driven back each time. Then he ordered an assault with Colonel Neel against the abatis, but Neel and five of his men fell in the exchange. Sumter then ordered a retreat. The British had lost 12 men killed and wounded.

At Hanging Rock on August 1, Major Davie, with 40 riflemen on horses and a similar number of dragoons, approached the area to be met by intelligence that three companies of mounted infantry from Bryan's North Carolina loyalists were encamped at a house near the post. Davie decided to attack this group immediately. His attack plan placed the enemy between two divisions at the house in full view of the post. The riflemen, who were dressed similarly to the loyalists, were able to move past the enemy sentinels without challenge. After they passed them, they dismounted and directed their rifle fire at the loyalists. Surprised, the loyalists fled down the road where they were met by the dragoons who had charged brazenly. Even attempts by the loyalists to run in new directions were met with Davie's men and cut to pieces. Only a few loyalists survived, as most were killed or wounded. Davie's group was able to capture 60 horses and 100 muskets, and to retire quickly without losing even one man. It was another grand patriot victory and tribute to Davie's leadership skills.

As events were taking place in upper South Carolina, the Lowcountry was beginning to see partisan action largely due to the brutality of the British and loyalists in that area. After the fall of Charles Town, a Major James Wemyss led his 63rd British Regiment as it marched from Georgetown to Cheraw on the west side of the Pee Dee River. His force proceeded to destroy local property and show considerable cruelty toward the citizens. After completion of his march of terror, he returned to Georgetown.

Since early June, Major McArthur with the 71st Regiment had been stationed at the Parish Church of St. David's in Cheraw to cover the area between Camden and Georgetown. Shortly after arriving, McArthur offered a reward for the capture of a patriot rebel, Thomas Ayer. Ayer was a leader of a company of mischievous men. When McArthur captured some of the company, he hanged them all. Prompted by the reward, a party of 16 loyalist neighbors were able to secure Thomas Ayer at night at the home of his family. They tied him up and proceeded to bring him to Major McArthur. On the way the group ran into a thunderstorm at Hunt's Bluff and decided to stop and leave Ayer at the home of Captain George Manderson, while several others proceeded to the nearby home of Jonathan Johns.

What the loyalists did not know was that some hours after they took Ayer away from his residence, his oldest brother, Hartwell Ayer, with five men set out to pursue them. Under the cover of night and the fierce storm Hartwell's men found where Ayer was being held and attacked those guarding him with complete surprise. All except one loyalist was killed either by bullet or saber. Hartwell then headed to Johns' home and shot Captain Manderson, but he escaped into the swamp and lived after having received only slight wounds. When news of the episode reached McArthur, they crossed the river with a considerable force and attempted to capture Ayer with no success. McArthur did burn down Ayer's home and killed his livestock.[44]

Another event occurred at Hunt's Bluff on August 1, 1780. Major McArthur had been ordered to move toward Camden. McArthur had moved his "two battalions of the 71st regiment" to camp at Lynch's Creek on the east branch. There he decided to send some 100 sick men who were "sufferers by the unhealthy climate of Carolina" by boat down the Pee Dee River to Georgetown under the command of Lord Nairne supported by a detachment of the royal militia under Colonel William Henry Mills. Colonel Mills, a physician, had been a patriot supporter until the British had found local success at Charles Town and he switched sides. Hearing of the British movement down the river, James Gillespie and a group of patriots gathered at Beding's Fields some three miles from Cheraw. They decided to move to Hunt's Bluff to surprise the boat expedition.

As they moved to Hunt's Bluff, which was 25 miles below Cheraw, their numbers grew, and they were assigned under Major Tristram Thomas' command. The patriots built a battery of wooden guns on a bend in the river. As McArthur moved to Black Creek the British flotilla departed. On August 1 the flotilla came around the bend in the river to partake of the sight of the fortifications and surprisingly surrendered unconditionally. Colonel Mills was able to escape to Georgetown, but the entire British and loyalist party was taken prisoner. The British called the event treason and described that "the militia mutinied, and securing their own officers and the sick, conducted them prisoners to General Gates, in North Carolina."[45] For the British and loyalists in the Lowcountry, nothing was going to be easy again.

Back upstate, another gathering of patriot leaders was held on August 5 at Landsford. The forces assembled included the North Carolina Militia commanded by Colonel Irwin, with Major Davie's corps, totaling some 500 men, and the South Carolina forces under colonels Sumter, Lacey and Hill consisting of another 300 men. The council agreed that they must attack Hanging Rock again and eliminate the post. The patriot forces marched toward Hanging Rock, stopping at midnight within two miles of the post. The enemy at Hanging Rock now consisted of around 500 men, made up of 160 infantry of Tarleton's Legion, the Prince of Wales American Regiment, part of Browne's Corps of Provincials and the remaining men from Colonel Bryan's North Carolina loyalists unit.

After some disagreement between Sumter and Davie, the attack plan was decided. With Sumter in overall command, Davie headed the right column with his corps, with companies of volunteers from North and South Carolina. Colonel Hill commanded the left column of South Carolinians, with Colonel Irwin in the center with his North Carolina Mecklenburg Militia. These three columns headed to the British encampment. By mistake, due to poor direction of guides, the columns all attacked Bryan's loyalist group. They were slaughtered. The British Legion forces along with companies from Browne's Regiment fired on the Americans with a deadly effect, but the patriot men pressed forward and captured the post. Even with a well-executed movement by part of Browne's force to get behind the patriots, it was to no avail. As Sumter's force routed the enemy, they became quite disordered, and only some 200 men and Davie's infantry maintained some degree of organization. Under Davie's battlefield leadership, an assembly of enemy forming at the opposite side of the camp was routed and dispersed by moving around undetected through the woods.

Realizing the situation he was in, Major Davie returned to the post where the Americans were beginning to plunder the area. The British and loyalist survivors remained at the woods taking no offensive action against the Americans. Since the patriots had expended most of their

ammunition, the decision was to retreat, which was begun at 12 noon in no great hurry. As they retired, Sumter's men noticed two companies of the British Legion approaching up the Camden road. Davie immediately charged this group with his dragoons and the enemy ran to the woods. The American losses were not recorded, but were believed to be less than the British. The British lost some 200 dead and wounded on the field.

Meanwhile, at McDowell's encampment at Cherokee Ford was a force of over 1000 patriot men ready to confront the British and loyalists. McDowell detached a combined force of 600 mounted men under colonels Shelby, Clarke and William Graham to watch the activities of Colonel Ferguson's forces. The Americans moved down the Broad River some 24 miles to Brown's Creek in present day Union County. Fearing being outnumbered by Ferguson's force, they moved on toward Fair Forest at the present day Spartanburg. On the evening of August 7, Colonel August Clarke and Colonel Shelby camped at Fair Forest Creek, two miles west of Cedar Spring. Keeping their eyes open, scouts arrived the next morning to tell that the enemy, under Major Dunlap, was within half a mile of their camp. After a shot was heard in the distance, the patriots hustled back and formed at the old Iron Works at Lawson's Ford on the Pacolet River, a mile from Cedar Spring.

The next morning Major Dunlap attacked the Americans in what became a short half-hour battle. Dunlap's mounted riflemen out front led the action, but they were repulsed. Dunlap led another charge with his dragoons as his mounted riflemen followed. The action turned to hand-to-hand combat, but the British were overtaken and fled the scene. The Americans pursued Dunlap and his retreating men, but some two miles below the battle, Dunlap met up with Colonel Ferguson's main force. Shelby and Clarke then retreated, leaving several wounded behind. Ferguson now pursued in the hope of retaking his prisoners, but the Americans formed frequently to fire back at the advancing enemy, which allowed the patriots to disperse successfully. The battle resulted in four Americans killed and 20 wounded, while the British lost between 20 and 30 killed or wounded.

About this time in the annals of Carolina history a Southern Revolutionary leader emerged who would eventually gain folklore status. This rather short man and true patriot was Francis Marion, who became known as the "Swamp Fox" for due cause. Francis was born in St. John's Berkeley, South Carolina, in 1732 to Huguenot parents. At age 27 he settled at Pond Bluff in St. John's Parish. That same year he volunteered to join his brother's troop in a local cavalry to fight in the Cherokee War. In 1761 Marion served as a lieutenant in Captain William Moultrie's unit where he was known as a "brave and hardy soldier" and an excellent officer. Marion served in the Provincial Congress of 1775, and became a captain, and later a major, in Moultrie's 2nd Regiment. Marion served with Moultrie during Prevost's invasion in 1779 and was present in the siege of Savannah.

When the siege of Charles Town began Marion joined Moultrie at Bacon's Bridge. While in the town Marion attended a party at the house of a friend and seriously dislocated his ankle trying to leave the party from the second floor bedroom. With his severe ankle problem, Marion was carried by litter to the seat of St. John's Parish and avoided the capture of his garrison by the British. After the patriot defeat at Monck's Corner, the British roamed freely throughout the area foraging and scanning for patriots. Marion was forced to move from house to house to hide from the British. He eventually met Major Peter Horry who was heading for North Carolina to join the patriot forces gathering in Hillsborough. While in North Carolina, Marion was introduced in Deep River to Baron De Kalb, who was then in command of a force sent by Washington to aid South Carolina. While Marion was recognized by De Kalb for his experience and even named his aide, he was not especially revered for his uncouth clothing and appearance. While on the advance towards South Carolina, Marion was sent out to the Santee to gain intelligence on the British and secure all the boats he could in the river areas. On August 10 Marion reached his post at Lynch's Creek and took command of a patriot unit and all the area from Camden to the coast, between the Pee Dee and the Santee rivers. From here the legend began for Francis Marion.

At dawn on August 12, Marion's force crossed the Pee Dee River at Port's Ferry and attacked a large force under Major Gainey at Britton's Neck. Marion carried out the surprise attack with Major John James at the head of a volunteer troop of horsemen. The target was Major Gainey himself. Major James pursued Gainey and when he was within sword range of him, some loyalists came out from behind a thicket to challenge James. He called out, "Come on, my boys! Here they are! Here they are!" The loyalists immediately fled into the swamp. Meanwhile, Marion led an attack against loyalists under a Captain Barfield, who was a former member of the South Carolina regiment. Marion faked a retreat and led Barfield's men into a successful ambush.

The partisan engagements were having a significant impact on the war in South Carolina. At Ramsour's Mill the British and loyalists had lost 170 men killed or wounded, with another 50 taken prisoner. During the 12 engagements from Williamson's Plantation on July 12 to Port's Ferry on August 12, they had lost 300 killed or wounded, and some 200 prisoners. The Americans' loss was not half that number.[46] These battles, and others that will go unrecorded in the history in this region, were fought by patriot volunteers who took up the cause without any professional plan or campaign strategy. The actions were the moves of determined patriots who wanted to send the British, and perhaps even more, the loyalists, a message that the battle for the South was not completed even after the defeats at Charles Town and the Waxhaws.

The contribution of Southern partisan leaders like Marion, Davie, Bratton, Sumter, McDowell, Rutherford and others was evidence of the fighting patriot spirit at work in the South in the face of their deepest hours of disappointment after the seizure of Charles Town and the defeat at the Waxhaws. The fighting in this period in the Carolinas was more like a civil war among the local citizenry than a battle with the British "occupiers." It was without strategic campaign planning, yet it was motivated by loyalty, respect and a spirit of teamwork in these most dangerous of unsponsored activities. These leaders, and the men who followed them, were among the many courageous, yet unheralded, heroes of the American Revolution in the South.

In his report to Clinton dated June 30, Lord Cornwallis had been optimistic that the loyalist militias would be successful and all of South Carolina would live under the "King's peace." But his optimism began to wane. Only two weeks later he reported that "the Aspect of Affairs is not so peaceable as when I wrote last." Cornwallis noted of the loyalist militia, "Their want of Subordination & Confidence in themselves, will make a considerable regular Force always necessary for the defense of the Province, until North Carolina is perfectly reduced." While Cornwallis had not abandoned his plan to move north with the problems in South Carolina, he did feel that the backcountry of both of the Carolinas would not be successful until the North Carolina Piedmont was under British control. On August 6, Cornwallis wrote Clinton, "The whole Country between Pedee & Santee has ever since been in an absolute State of Rebellion; every friend of the Government has been carried off, and his Plantation destroyed; & detachments of the enemy have appeared on the Santee, and threatened our Stores, & Convoys in that river."[47]

It was at this time that Cornwallis learned that a considerable American army was moving toward the South.

12

CAMDEN

During the siege of Charles Town and reacting to pleas from the city's military commander, General Benjamin Lincoln, Washington directed seven regiments from the Maryland Continental Line and the Delaware First Continental Regiment to head for the besieged city for relief. These two regiments had indeed served in every battle that General Washington had fought from Long Island to the battle at Monmouth Court House. At Long Island in 1776 a counterattack from the Maryland force had saved the army, and at Brandywine their courage had helped to avert a real disaster. The Delaware Regiment had also served with much distinction in every engagement, suffering severe losses including five of its commanders who were either killed or wounded in action, and the loss of all but two companies of 96 men each. This total force of only 1400 men was small, but was without question one of high quality.[1]

Leading this brave and courageous force was the "Baron," the 59-year-old General Johann De Kalb. De Kalb was a fearless, husky, six-foot, broad-faced "bull of a man." Born in 1721 in Huttendorf, Germany, as the son of a Bavarian farmer, he had spent years in the grain fields until he left home at age 16. In his early 20s he had become a lieutenant in a French infantry unit serving under the rather fraudulent aristocratic name Jean De Kalb. From 1740 to 1748 he fought with distinction in the War of Austrian Succession and was raised to the rank of major by the beginning of the Seven Years' War. In 1764 he married an heiress and in 1765 retired from military service. In 1768 De Kalb traveled widely in the American colonies as a secret agent for French Foreign Minister Etienne Francois Choiseul. De Kalb returned to military service in 1774 and became a brigadier general in November 1776.

In Paris De Kalb was recruited by Silas Deane and in April 1777 sailed to America along with Marquis de Lafayette to join the patriot cause. In September 1777 De Kalb was appointed major general in the Continental Army, joining Washington's army in November. He served at Valley Forge and at Monmouth without his own command. In April 1780 he would have his chance.[2]

On April 2, 1780, Washington gave the Maryland Line and Delaware Regiment marching orders for South Carolina, remarking, "Something should be hazarded here ... for the purpose of giving further succor to the Southern States." Even though Washington expected that Charles Town would be lost, he hoped that this force would "assist to check the progress of the enemy and save the Carolinas."

De Kalb headed first to Philadelphia to arrange for supplies and what little money he could obtain from the Board of War. While rumors of French assistance in the war was about to become news, De Kalb left Philadelphia on May 13 and arrived in Petersburg, Virginia, ten days later. His new command had been on the march through New Jersey and Pennsylvania. They were loaded aboard ships at the Head of Elk, Maryland, sailed down the Chesapeake Bay and marched into Petersburg several days after De Kalb arrived.[3]

Though he had been promised that elements of the Virginia and North Carolina militia would join him at Petersburg, "such is the dilatory manner in which all things are done here, that I cannot depend on them, much less wait for them." De Kalb had also been promised wagons and teams to drive them, but none came until the first week in June, arriving a few at a time. Governor Thomas Jefferson and his government had provided little but token support or provisions to De Kalb.[4] The last of his units left the town on June 8, frustrated by the lack of co-operation. De Kalb wrote, "I met with no support, no integrity and no virtue in the State of Virginia, and place my sole reliance on the French fleet and army which are coming to our relief." Before he left Petersburg he was informed of the British capture of Charles Town and that Lincoln and his entire force had been taken prisoner. As De Kalb passed into North Carolina on June 20, he learned of Buford's disastrous defeat at the Waxhaws on May 29. There was little optimism in De Kalb's force, but they continued southward anyway.[5]

On June 22, the "Baron" De Kalb and his tired and hungry troops arrived in the temporary capital of North Carolina, Hillsborough. De Kalb was even more upset with the lack of support for his troops in North Carolina than he had been in Virginia. The new state government, which had been under Governor Abner Nash since December 1779, gave him little comfort. With no support, De Kalb was forced to resort to sending out foragers to strip the countryside, which did little to endear the citizens to the patriot cause. After a week of rest, and finding no sympathy or support in the form of provisions from the North Carolina governor, his executive council or the local citizens, De Kalb moved his force out of Hillsborough. The situation that De Kalb's forces endured in North Carolina was recounted by one of his men, "We marched from Hillsborough about the first of July, without an ounce of provision being laid up at any point, often fasting for several days together, and subsisting frequently upon green apples and peaches; sometimes by detaching parties, we thought ourselves feasted, when by violence we seized a little fresh beef and cut and threshed out a little wheat; yet, under all these difficulties, we had to go forward." De Kalb's patriot force moved onward to Chatham Court House, and on to Buffalo Ford on the Deep River.

The North Carolina state government had named the former and first state governor, Richard Caswell, as major general of the North Carolina Militia. This force of 1500 consisted of two brigades commanded by brigadier generals Isaac Gregory and John Butler. Caswell's militia was preparing reluctantly to join up with De Kalb's force, along with a small force of Virginia Militia under Brigadier General Edward Stevens.[6] Caswell had gained a reputation "by the gallant stand he had made, in 1776, at Moore's Bridge," while Stevens, who had "fought under Washington in all the battles of those years [1777 and 1778], [was] very much respected as a brave, vigorous, and judicious officer."[7] These troops were expected to join De Kalb as soon as possible.

Meanwhile, the Congress was settling in on a replacement for the command of the Southern Department since the former commander, General Lincoln, was now in a British prison at Charles Town. The Congress, without seeking the advice from the commander-in-chief, selected General Horatio Gates by unanimous vote on June 13. Still living off his status as hero of the most significant American victory so far at Saratoga in 1777, Gates had done little since then to maintain this high opinion he had of himself. Gates' great ambition and vanity had involved him in activities to replace Washington as head of the army, known as the Conway Cabal. He had not repaired his relations with Washington and after continuing to complain about his assignments, he asked to be relieved of duty and went home to his plantation in Virginia.[8]

Horatio Gates was born in England in the county of Kent in 1728 to Robert Gates, a housekeeper for the Duke of Leeds. Joining the British Army at a young age, Gates served in the French and Indian War, which included action with General Braddock in the unsuccessful attempt to capture Fort Duquesne in 1755. After fighting in Martinique and a tour of duty in Ireland, Gates retired from the army in 1765 with half-pay at the rank of major. With the help of George Washington, Gates sailed to America in 1772 and settled down first on a farm called "Traveller's Rest" in Berkeley County, Virginia, in the Shenandoah Valley, and later to Jefferson County, West Virginia.[9] When the Revolution broke out, Gates' life as a Virginia squire was interrupted. Siding with the patriots, Gates was made Washington's adjutant general with the rank of brigadier general.[10]

Horatio Gates was a "flabby, bespectacled, grandfatherly looking" gentleman who gave the image of a man without a military bearing.[11] He had slanted eyes which gave him a "hangdog appearance" but his large, hooked nose and long skinny face presented the appearance of firm stateliness. Gates was a truly ambitious and scheming man. In May 1776 he was assigned to the Northern command under General Schuyler and promoted to major general. Attempting to unseat General Schuyler, Gates encouraged rumors reflecting on Schuyler's "character, competence and loyalty." Schuyler's New England friends in Congress supported his cause, but in August of 1777 they decided to replace Schuyler with Gates after the British took Fort Ticonderoga. Gates took command of the Northern Department on August 19, 1777, followed soon by the victory at Saratoga against Burgoyne. Though Benedict Arnold distinguished himself more than Gates, Gates received most of the laurels of victory. After the Conway Cabal affair passed, Gates resumed his command of the Northern Department, and later the Eastern Department in Boston, before this new appointment as the Southern Department commander.[12]

On July 13, 1780, De Kalb received a letter from Major General Gates announcing that he had been named as commander of the Southern forces. De Kalb immediately replied to Gates with the following report on the situation:

> I am happy by your arrival, for I have struggled with a good many difficulties for Provisions ever since I arrived in this State; and although I have put the troops on short allowance of bread, we cannot get even that; no stores laid in, and no disposition of any, but what I have done by military authority; no assistance from the legislature or Executive power, and the greatest unwillingness in the people to part with anything.... I am to move towards Coxe's mill higher up on Deep River, where I am to be joined by the North Carolina Militia under M.G. Caswell of about 1200; the Virginia militia are still at Hillsboro.... [To reach this army] your shortest road will be by Lindsay's mill, Colonel Thaxton, and Rocky river. Your waggons, if you have any, would go better by Chatham Court house.[13]

After receiving notification of his new assignment, Gates hastened from Traveller's Rest and headed to Hillsborough, North Carolina, to take command of what he termed the "Grand Army of the Southern Department."[14] From Fredericksburg, Gates wrote his old friend General Lincoln in a most wary mood:

> I feel for you. I feel for myself; who am I to succeed, to What? To the command of an Army without Strength — a Military Chest without Money, A Department apparently deficient in public spirit, and a Climate that encreases Despondency instead of animating the Soldiers Arm. I wish to save the Southern States. I wish to recover the Territories we have lost. I wish to restore you to your Command and to reinstate you to the Dignity, to which your Virtues, and your Perseverance, have so justly entitled you — with me you have experienced that the Battle is not to the Strong. Poor Burgoyne in the pride of Victory was overthrown. Could the Enemy's Triumph over you, meet with the like Disgrace, I should be content to die in Peace, so that America be free and independent: and its future happiness under God rest solely upon itself.[15]

While passing through Petersburg, Virginia, Gates visited with General Charles Lee, where Lee was said to have given Gates his advice on parting for his new position with the words, "Beware lest your Northern laurels should turn into Southern willows!"[16] When Gates reached Hillsborough he conferred with Governor Nash and the executive council. After reading the depressing letter from De Kalb on the state of his situation, he approached Nash, who attempted to explain the lack of support given to De Kalb from North Carolina:

> The army you are going to command unhappily has suffered greatly and been much distressed and impeded for want of provisions, spirits and other necessities. The Commissary says it is for want of money, and yet I have not only paid every Congress draft that has come to hand, but have advanced over and above £500,000 to the credit of the United States."[17]

From New Bern on July 29, Governor Nash was to write Gates presenting another view of the supply situation:

> It was not from ignorance of the state of the Army, or neglect in the Executive department, that they have been so badly supplied. The requisition of specific supplies came too late to be of any service. The provisions of the preceding year had been brought up and appropriated, and 'tis surprising to me that the Commissary did not get his share of them. Since April he had of me upwards of 2,700,000 dollars, to pay, as I understood, the contracts he had provisions, and the Quartermaster and Commercial Agent have drawn very large sums, the latter for the express purpose of purchasing Corn, Spirits, Sugar, &c for the army.... The resources of this Country are abundantly sufficient for the supply of the Army and the spirit of the People free to yield them on proper terms. P.S. We have a considerable quantity of Spirits, Coffee and other articles wanted and only wait till waggons can be had to transport them.[18]

Meanwhile in Charles Town, Cornwallis was now becoming more concerned with the situation in the Upcountry of South Carolina. Reports of the Carolina Upcountry continued to describe problems. Balfour sent word of rebel uprisings in his area. Ferguson wrote that "if we do not cover the Militia Regts on the frontier by a strong advanced force we will lose all credit and influence with our friends and every hesitating man will rise against us."[19] Cornwallis wrote, "I will not say much in praise of the militia of the Southern Colonies, but a list of British officers and soldiers killed and wounded by them since last June, proves but too fatally that they are not wholly contemptible."[20] Cornwallis began to consider making his move into North Carolina. His July 14 letter to Clinton revealed that he felt he had to take action, as "The effects of the exertions which the enemy are making will, I make no doubt, be exaggerated to us: But upon the whole there is every reason to believe that their plan is not only to defend North Carolina, but to commence offensive operations immediately; which reduces me to the necessity, if I wanted the inclination, of following the plan which I had the honor of transmitting to Your Excellency in my letter of the 30th June, as the most effectual means of keeping up the spirits of our friends and securing this Province."[21]

On July 25 Gates arrived at De Kalb's headquarters at Deep River, assumed command of the Southern Department, and immediately announced that he intended to march on to Camden on July 27. The event was recorded by Colonel Williams:

General Gates was received with respectful ceremony; the baron ordered a Continental salute from the little park of artillery — which was performed on the entrance into camp of his successor, who made his acknowledgments to the baron for his great politeness, approved his standing orders, and, as if actuated by a spirit of great activity and enterprise, ordered the troops to hold themselves in readiness to march at a moment's warning. The latter order was a matter of great astonishment to those who knew the real situation of the troops. But all difficulties were removed by the general's assurances that plentiful supplies of rum and rations were on the route, and would overtake them in a day or two....[22]

Gates' decision to move with haste to engage the British was not without its risks. If he had delayed and consolidated his forces, he might have received critical food and supplies, much needed at this juncture. But based on the information he had from partisan leader Thomas Sumter — that the British were scattered from Camden to Augusta with Cornwallis not in sight — it was a calculated risk he was willing to make. The real risk was the perilous condition of his forces, and the potential battlefield support he might expect from a force dominated by militia troops. If he could gain a victory at Camden against Lord Rawdon before he could bring up additional forces, he could see the British retreating back to Charles Town.[23] The patriots would again gain the offensive in the South, and Southern morale would be recovered. In Gates' mind, the gamble was worth taking.

At Deep River, besides the Maryland Line and Delaware Regiment, was "the command of Colonel Armand, being about sixty cavalry and as many infantry; and Lieutenant Colonel Carrington's detachment of three companies of artillery, which had joined in Virginia." Gates' "Grand Army" took to the road "early in the morning of the 27th of July," in the mid-summer Carolina heat.[24] Gates was forced to leave behind at General Parsons' Plantation ten of his 18 guns because of the shortage of horses.[25] He took his force on the most direct route to Camden "through the sparse pine barrens" by what was a rather loyalist region of little or no food and yielding "lean cattle, fruit and unripe Indian corn." Colonel Otto Holland Williams, who was the commander of the 6th Maryland and the assistant adjutant general to Gates, urged him to march west through Salisbury and Charlotte, which was an area more sympathetic to the patriot cause. Since the route through Charlotte would add a third more distance to be traveled, Gates chose the direct one toward Camden.[26]

The militia units endeavored to comply with Gates' directions to push toward South Carolina to meet the British. General Rutherford wrote on July 30 from his encampment near Cheraw, "I am bussey hear collecting A Quantity of provision, and would wish to Stay Until I re-

ceive your Orders." On August 1, 1780, General Edward Stevens of the Virginia Militia wrote from Coxe's Mill, "I have had a terrible time of it, and Militia will not be Satisfied with what Regular troops would think themselves well off with." Another letter from Stevens stated, "The Waggons I sent to Virginia for Grain is not yet come up. I am greatly distressed in moving for want of them." General Caswell wrote to Gates saying, "If you had been pleased to have allowed me to remain on P.D. [Pee Dee River] below the Cheraws I could have procured almost any quantity of Corn.... If Waggons can be had, as soon as the waters fall, the Whole Army may be supplied with Bread on both sides P.D. between the Cheraws and Long Bluff, distant about 15 miles." The grumbling was continuing.[27]

Gates' army could only make 10 to 15 miles per day in the heat, with occasional foraging excursions to search for food. Williams wrote, "The troops, notwithstanding their disappointments in not being overtaken by a supply of rum and provisions, were again amused with promises, and gave early proofs of that patient submission, inflexible fortitude, and undeviating integrity which they afterwards more eminently displayed." The commander's orders of the day told of supplies coming any day, but as Colonel Williams said, "assurances ... certainly were fallacious and were never verified." De Kalb wrote, "The land traversed was poor and desolate, hardly reclaimed from its natural condition and rather worse even than the gloomy descriptions which had been made of it. The first rude efforts at civilization and culture, which appeared here and there, had been either abandoned by their owners or plundered by their neighbors. All men had fled this wilderness.... In consequence, the distress and misery of the troops increased from day to day."[28] Major William Seymour of the Delaware Line wrote in his journal that on a 14-day march the troops drew rations of only a half a pound of flour.[29]

On August 3, Gates' force reached the Pee Dee River at Mask's Ferry in North Carolina. Lieutenant Colonel William Porterfield, "an officer of merit," and his 400 Virginia Continentals joined him on the southern bank. Porterfield's force had been in South Carolina for some time "after the disaster at Charleston, retired with a small detachment and found means of subsisting himself and his men in Carolina."[30] Gates' men had been told that the area would be fertile, "but the preceding crop of corn ... was exhausted and the new grain, although luxuriant and fine, was unfit for use." The men boiled the grain anyway and green peaches "were substituted for bread" which caused significant gastric problems. Some officers created soup of extremely lean beef enhanced with hair powder.[31] Covered in ticks, in the heat of the Southern day and advancing along sandy roads were the men of Gates' army, struggling to continue, with many suffering from diarrhea and scurvy.[32] It was a sad affair.

At this time Gates made another mistake in judgment when he paid no attention to the requests from colonels White and Washington to join up with him against the British. Both White and Washington had retreated into North Carolina, after the fall of Charles Town and the defeats at Monck's Corner and Lenud's Ferry, to recruit new regiments of cavalry. Gates now chose to ignore some of the most active corps in this Southern region.[33] This was nothing new for Gates. By not traveling through the patriot stronghold of the Piedmont from Salisbury through Charlotte and Mecklenburg County, Gates would not have the support of some of the most courageous and brave Southern leaders like colonels Davidson, Polk or Davie. Certainly Gates was making a severe error. Henry Lee wrote, "To the neglect of this salutary proposition, may with reason be attributed the heavy disaster soon after experienced. In no country in the world are the services of cavalry more to be desired than in that which was then committed to the care of Major-General Gates; and how it was possible for an officer of his experience to be regardless of this powerful auxiliary, remains inexplicable."[34]

The difficult march by Gates' army through the sand hills to Camden was most notably recorded by Colonel Otto Holland Williams. Williams, an able 31-year-old officer from Prince Georges County in Maryland, revealed that Gates understood the problems of his men and took responsibility for his actions. Gates also complained of the near insubordination of General Caswell in not joining up with De Kalb or his own force. Gates said, "I should not be sorry to see checked by a rap on the knuckles, if it were not that the militia would disperse and leave their handful of brave men without even nominal assistance." Finally, to the delight of everyone in Gates' army, at May's Mill a small amount of quality Indian corn was found, milled and served as meals to all the men present in just a few hours.[35]

On the march to Camden, Gates' force encountered a curious band of men led by "Colonel Marion, a gentleman of South Carolina." Colonel Williams' account of these men revealed, "their number did not exceed twenty men and boys, some white, some black, and all mounted, but most of them miserably equipped; their appearance was in fact so burlesque that it was with much difficulty the diversion of the regular soldiery was restrained by the officers; and the general himself was glad of an opportunity of detaching Colonel Marion, at his own instance, towards the interior of South Carolina, with orders to watch the motions of the enemy and furnish intelligence." Williams continued, "These trifling circumstances are remembered in these notes to show from

what contemptible beginnings a good capacity will rise to distinction."[36]

On July 30 from Island Creek, located some five miles below Anson Court House, and on his way to Ancrum's Plantation to join up with Harrington and Rutherford, General Caswell wrote Gates that "I am inclined to think he [Cornwallis] will collect his utmost strength to Camden, where he either intends making a stand or to retreat to Charles Town. I have prevailed on Brigadier General Harrington, a very intelligent Gentleman, who is well acquainted with this part of the country … to wait on you. The information he can give you of these matters and regarding provisions may be of essential service."[37]

On August 3 the American army had marched to Thompson's Creek and the next day Gates crossed the border into South Carolina. He immediately issued a proclamation inviting the patriot citizens to assemble to "vindicate the rights of America," and gave amnesty to all those who had been forced to sign paroles at the hand of the British. When Gates entered South Carolina, the British post at Hanging Rock was abandoned and Lord Rawdon took up his position on the west branch of Lynch's Creek located 14 miles from Camden. With Lord Rawdon were the British 23rd, 33rd and 71st regiments of infantry, the Volunteers of Ireland, Lieutenant Colonel Hamilton's Provisional corps, and 40 dragoons from the Legion.[38] That same day General Caswell wrote Gates from Jennings' Branch, South Carolina, that he had found 700 encamped and venerable British troops at Lynch's Creek. The next day at 1:00 A.M. Caswell hurriedly wrote to Gates with the news that the British had 2900 men that were ready to attack.[39]

On August 6, 1780, Cornwallis wrote to Clinton that "The reports industriously propagated in this Province of a large army coming from the Northward [have] very much intimidated our Friends, encouraged our Enemies, and determined the wavering against us, to which our not advancing and acting offensively likewise contributes…. This unfortunate business, if it should have no worse consequences, will shake the confidence of our Friends in the Province, and make our situation very uneasy until we can advance…. It may be doubted by some whether the Invasion of North Carolina may be a prudent measure, but I am convinced it is a necessary one, and that if we do not attack that Province, we must give up both South Carolina and Georgia, and retire within the walls of Charleston."[40]

On August 7 Caswell's militia force of 2100 men finally joined with Gates' Continental Army at Cross Roads, east of the east branch of Lynch's Creek, placing them some 15 miles from Lord Rawdon. Gates organized the force into two divisions, with De Kalb commanding the Continentals and Caswell directing the militia.[41] The

American army marched and arrived on August 11 at Little Lynch's Creek, where Lord Rawdon had retreated. Little Lynch's Creek was above Camden. Gates was later criticized for not being more aggressive at attacking Lord Rawdon before he joined up with Cornwallis. Gates had marched his forces on a detour of six miles at night and by the 13th he had moved the 16 miles to Rugeley's Mill. There he was joined by General Stevens and his 700 Virginia Militia. Just a few miles away, Gates' engineer, Colonel Kosciusko, had discovered a place where a stand could successfully be made against the British if required. The location was in the middle of a swamp surrounding Saunders' Creek above Camden.[42] Tarleton recounted the actions of Lord Rawdon during this period of four days during which the opposing forces faced each other across a creek:

> While the two armies remained facing each other at Lynche's creek, Lord Rawdon sent an order to Lieutenant-colonel Cruger, to forward to Camden, without lots of time, the four companies of light infantry, under Captain Charles Campbell: He likewise directed the troops at Rugeley's mills to quit their position: Major Carden, with the detachment of Browne's, was ordered to Camden; and the legion infantry, under Captain Stewart, were desired to find the most direct road from their present situation to the camp at Lynche's creek.... Lord Rawdon withdrew the corps from Rugeley's mills, on account of its exposed situation; and suspecting yet that the enemy meant to detach against some of his outposts, he desired Lieutenant-colonel Turnbull to evacuate Rocky mount, and to join Major Ferguson at his position on Little river, where he had erected some field works, with his corps of provincials and loyal militia.[43]

Back in Charles Town on August 9, Cornwallis received two dispatches from Lord Rawdon with news that Gates' army was approaching Lynch's Creek and advancing with some 5000 men exclusive of the militia. For Cornwallis, it was good news. After concluding his immediate business, Cornwallis departed the city on the evening of the 10th. Leaving the swampy, flat land of the Lowcountry, he was now back in more European-like territory of rolling hills in the tall pines of Upcountry South Carolina. He arrived at Camden on the night of August 13 and made his headquarters at the three-story home of the town's leading merchant, Joseph Kershaw. This patriot had been sent off to Bermuda, while his wife and children were forced to live in a room in their attic.[44] Kershaw had been characterized as "a very violent man ... said to have persecuted the loyalists."[45]

Lord Rawdon had retired from Lynch's Creek and fell back 15 miles to Logtown just outside Camden to welcome Cornwallis. On August 13 Gates advanced to Colonel Rugeley's place, Clermont. Gates had kept his route to himself and when his army arrived at Rugeley's, the patriots were surprised to see them.[46] The town of Pine Tree Hill, South Carolina, had been renamed Camden in 1768 in honor of a leading British opponent of the Stamp Act. The town, originally settled by Scots-Irish Presbyterians and Irish Quakers, was a quaint place, with streets neatly laid out around a town square. On the square was the courthouse, built only nine years earlier, and now serving as a symbol of legal and administrative substance for the district. Products brought to market at Camden included flour, indigo, tea, corn, rum, hams, butter, tobacco, cattle, sheep, axes and cloth. There were numerous grain and log mills in and around the town, as well as breweries and even a pottery. Joseph Kershaw owned several of these mills. This was a key place to show British authority to the entire region.[47]

The next day saw Cornwallis walking among the poplar-covered grounds of Kershaw's estate, in addition to inspecting his troops. Reflecting on his present condition, Cornwallis had to decide whether he should retreat or engage the large patriot force gathering before him. The British had some 2239 men while the patriot forces were believed to have nearly 6000 men.[48] He later wrote to Germain on the matter, "I must have not only left near 800 sick and a great quantity of stores at this place, but I clearly saw the loss of the whole province except Charlestown, and of all Georgia except Savannah, as immediate consequences, besides forfeiting all pretentions to future confidence from our friends in this part of America." Even with the opposing force odds against him, for Cornwallis it was not a difficult decision. Cornwallis wrote, "Seeing little to lose by defeat, and much to gain by victory, I resolved to take the first good opportunity to attack the rebel army."[49]

On the same day, August 14, as Cornwallis was walking among the poplar trees at Kershaw's estate, a Camden citizen arrived at Gates' American camp. He gave pretentions that he was not aware of the American approach, claimed friendship with some Marylanders and indicated that he would be out in a few days to provide intelligence to Gates of the situation in Camden. The "friend" gave Gates some information about the Camden situation, but not all the truth. Some of the other officers were suspicious, but Gates' feeling about him allowed the man to roam about at will. When this person left the American camp, he returned to Camden and gave Cornwallis valuable intelligence concerning Gates, including the estimated American troop strength.

At this point Gates received a request from Brigadier General Thomas Sumter via dispatch rider for additional troops to intercept a British supply convoy moving from Charles Town. When the British had learned that Francis Marion was roaming the countryside around the Pee Dee, they diverted from the road over Nelson's Ferry over the

Santee to a higher route through McCord's Ferry over the Congaree. The convoy with escort contained clothing, arms and store for the troops at Camden. Gates supported Sumter's request with much enthusiasm providing 100 Maryland Continentals and 300 North Carolina Militia, with two brass field guns under Lieutenant Colonel Woodford. At that moment the reinforcements arrived, Sumter immediately began to march toward Camden Ferry.

At the break of day on August 15, Sumter had advanced to Carey's Fort. Colonel Thomas Taylor with a strong detachment raced to the rear of the fort to cut off the retreat of Carey's British troops in order to prevent them from supporting the convoy. Taylor approached with such caution that the British were taken by surprise. The British lost seven men killed and 30 taken as prisoners. Taylor learned from the British that the convoy was not too far off to the rear, and he advanced immediately. Taylor surrounded the convoy by surprise and took 70 prisoners. Sumter and his forces moved to the western side of the Catawba River.

Gates was under the impression that Sumter's movements on Fort Carey would take place on August 16. He had planned to attract the attention of the British in Camden by the presence of his army from the front. Thus on the 15th Gates ordered that the army march that evening at 10 o'clock. Aware of the closeness of his forces to the British, Gates ordered that a strict silence from gunfire be observed, under the penalty of instant death for violation. The march would proceed with Armand's Legion in front. To Armand's right was to march Colonel Porterfield's light infantry in single file order. Major Armstrong's light infantry would do the same on Armand's left flank. Gates ordered, "In case of an attack by the enemy's cavalry in front, the light infantry upon each flank will instantly move up and give and continue the most galling fire upon the enemy's horse. This will enable Colonel Armand not only to support the shock of the enemy's charge, but finally to rout them; the Colonel will therefore consider the order to stand the attacks of the enemy's cavalry, be their number what they may, as positive." Gates also directed that "When the ground will admit of it, and the near approach of the enemy renders it necessary, the army will (when ordered) march in columns."

After Gates prepared the orders, he showed Colonel Williams, his adjutant general, the rough estimate of the forces under his command, placed at around 7000 men. Colonel Williams was most doubtful of this estimate, and called a meeting with the general officers of all the units at Rugeley's barn to discuss the matter. Just as the meeting was breaking up, Gates came through the door. Williams gave Gates the tally he had collected of the command strength, which totaled 3052 men fit for duty. Gates,

in front of 13 general officers, eyed the tally with special shock as Williams covered the marked difference between Gates' estimates and the actual tally. Gates then remarked in defiance and embarrassment, "There are enough for our purpose." He then barked, "There was no dissenting voice in the council where the orders have just been read." The marching orders were then directed to be published.

Although there had been no discussion on the orders in council, afterwards the tune had changed. Most could not believe that an army made up of two-thirds militia could perform coordinated military movements in the dark of night. Colonel Armand was the most vocal. He objected to the wording of the orders which gave cavalry instructions to stand the attack and to be placed out in front where it had never been located before. Armand even charged that Gates put his men there because of an earlier altercation between he and Gates while in transit. After much discussion, according to Williams' account, the meeting broke off with all believing that they would not meet any sizable British force on the road to Camden.[50]

It was a significant error in fundamental military operations not to know the size of one's forces under his command. How Gates had come up with the faulty strength estimates is unknown, but the fact was that this was just another in a series of errors of judgment on Gates' part. Gates' army consisted of some 900 Continentals, reduced in numbers from sickness, desertion and detaching 100 troops to support Sumter. Armand had 60 mounted cavalry and 60 foot infantrymen. Edward Stevens and Richard Caswell had 2800 Virginia and North Carolina militiamen. The South Carolina Militia consisted of 70 mounted volunteers and 100 men supporting the seven-gun artillery group. Of these roughly 4100 troops, only 3052 were ready for action.

With night coming on, the patriot troops gathered firewood and prepared a "hearty" ration of corn meal mush mixed with molasses, served with baked bread and freshly-killed beef. The idea was to give these men a good meal before heading out to Camden. Molasses had been the substitute for rum, which was not available. These men, who were already half sick on a diet of green corn and apples, with bad water, were now to have this added heavy meal. Almost the entire army fell into a groggy sleep, interrupted by frequent trips to the latrine due to much intestinal disorder. The American Army going into battle the next day was extremely tired, and ailing from their diet. It was another error for the self-confident Gates.[51]

On this important day for planning, August 15, Tarleton recounts the following regarding the British moves:

> On the 15th the principal part of the King's troops had orders to be in readiness to march: In the afternoon Earl Cornwallis desired Lieutenant-colonel Tarleton to gain circumstantial intelligence, by intercepting a patrol, or

carrying off some prisoners, from an American picket: About ten miles from Camden, on the road to Rugeley's mills, the advanced guard of the legion, in the evening, secured three American soldiers: The prisoners reported, that they came from Lynche's creek, where they had been left in a convalescent state, and that they were directed to join the American army, on the high road, that night, as General Gates had given orders for his troops to move from Rugeley's mills to attack the British camp next morning near Camden. The information received from these men induced Tarleton to countermarch before he was discovered by any patrol from the enemy's outpost: The three prisoners were mounted behind dragoons, and conveyed with speed to the British army: When examined by Earl Cornwallis, their story appeared credible, and confirmed all the other intelligence of the day. Orders were immediately circulated for the regiments and corps, designed for a forward move, to stand to their arms. The town, the magazine, the hospital, and the prisoners, were committed to the care of Major M'Arthur with a small body of provincials and militia, and the weakest convalescents of the army.[52]

At 10 P.M. Armand's Legion of soldiers of fortune and British deserters headed out into the darkness and summer heat with the rest of Gates' Southern American Army following along. With Colonel Charles Porterfield's and Major John Armstrong's light infantry 200 yards on the right and left of Armand's force came the advanced guard of infantry, with what was remaining of the artillery. The Delaware and Maryland Continental brigades were next, followed by Caswell and his North Carolina Militia. In the rear guard spot was General Edward Stevens' Virginia Militia and the South Carolina Militia with the baggage wagons.[53]

Meanwhile, Cornwallis' forces moved from Camden "At ten o'clock ... and formed their order of march on the road to Rugeley's mills...." The British positioned Lieutenant Colonel Webster's division in front, made up of "his advanced guard of twenty legion cavalry, and as many mounted infantry, supported by four companies of light infantry, and followed by the 23rd and 33rd regiments of foot. The center of the line of march was formed of Lord Rawdon's division, which consisted of the volunteers of Ireland, the legion infantry, Hamilton's corps, and Colonel Bryan's refugees: The two battalions of the 71st regiment, which composed the reserve, followed the second division. Four pieces of cannon marched with the divisions, and two with the reserve: A few waggons preceded the dragoons of the legion, who composed the rear guard."[54] Both armies were now on the same road heading towards each other in the dark.

Cornwallis' force moved over a flat road from Camden for five miles until the road dipped down toward Saunders Creek, where they crossed to climb upward. Just then, at around 2 A.M. on August 16, Tarleton's advance British cavalry unit with 20 Legion and 20 mounted infantry ran into elements of Armand's head guard at Parker's Old Field, a flat area of a few tall pine trees along the road with a swamp on both sides of the road. Both advance units fired haphazardly at each other. The British officer in the lead was wounded and his detachment retreated. A few of Armand's cavalry were wounded and their retreat caused much disorder in the American ranks, especially the first Maryland brigades. Charles Porterfield's and John Armstrong's flanking light infantry came out of the woods and fought off Tarleton's dragoons who had advanced with a saber charge toward the retreating Armand's cavalry in the dark.[55] Porterfield was hit by a stray bullet and killed. The British recoil of the Legion was re-established by the support of the 23rd and 33rd infantry regiments of Lieutenant Colonel Webster. The American infantry units fired toward the British for nearly a quarter of an hour, when both sides ceased action and moved back to reform. [56]

Prisoners were taken on both sides and their intelligence was quickly uncovered. Colonel Williams learned from one prisoner that Lord Cornwallis was the commander in charge of the British force and that there were some 3000 troops in front of them. Williams informed Gates, who was astonished to find he had run into not only a large British force at this point, but also he now faced an army led by Cornwallis. Gates was shocked and upset. He immediately called a war council with his senior general officers in the rear of the line. Gates, wearing his light blue coat with big gold epaulettes, remarked, "Gentlemen, what is best to be done?"[57] After a long silence, General Stevens responded, "Gentlemen, is it not too late now to do anything but fight?" No one commented on Stevens' question, and Gates finally ordered his officers to move to their commands and prepare for battle. Baron De Kalb apparently assumed that Gates would have retreated, but Stevens' comment had influenced the decision of the moment.[58]

From questioning several of the prisoners, Cornwallis was now quite confident that he had indeed run into Gates' army. Tarleton's journal recorded that based on the guides and information of the prisoners, "Earl Cornwallis discovered that the ground the British army now occupied was remarkably favorable to abide the event of a general action against the superior numbers of the enemy: The fortunate situation of two swamps, which narrowed the position, so that the English army could not be outflanked, instantly determined the British general to halt the troops upon this ground, and order them to lie down to wait the approach of day." For the rest of the pre-dawn morning, "Except a few occasional shots from the advanced sentries of each army, a silent expectation ushered in the morning."[59]

In the early morning just before dawn, Colonel Otto Williams who was riding along the American line saw the British advancing up the road. He immediately summoned Captain Singleton of the artillery, who remarked that the British were only some 200 yards away since he could begin to make out the uniforms. Williams ordered Singleton to open fire and he did so. The British then responded by moving into battle lines on either side of the road. Williams rode back to Gates with the news.[60]

Colonel Williams suggested to Gates that if the British were caught in the act of deploying onto the field of battle by an attack from General Stevens' brigade, the effect might be fortunate. Gates only remarked, "Thats right — let it be done." General Horatio Gates, the "hero of Saratoga" and the delight of Congress, showed no "heroic" or even basic military leadership traits in preparation for the ensuing battle. He developed no plan and gave no orders. Williams hastened to Stevens, who had his force already formed in a line, and Stevens advanced his brigade in good spirit. Unfortunately, the British right wing of the enemy was found to already be in line and prepared for action.[61]

Cornwallis had formed up his army. On his right of the road, and commanded by Lieutenant Colonel James Webster, was the small corps of light infantry on the edge of the swamp, followed by the three companies of the 23rd Regiment and 33rd Regiment in the center. The division on the left, from right to left, consisted of the Volunteers of Ireland, followed by the Legion infantry, and part of Hamilton's Royal North Carolina Regiment, and just behind on the far left flank was Samuel Bryan's North Carolina Volunteers. All the British forces on Cornwallis' left were under command of Francis Lord Rawdon. The Highlanders' five companies of the 71st Regiment was in reserve with two six-pounders, split between the right and left sides of the road in the rear. The Legion Cavalry was behind the 71st regiment on the right under Tarleton.[62]

Gates' force had formed up before dawn on the American right. On the American right were De Kalb's forces with General Mordecai Gists' Delaware Regiment and the three regiments of the 2nd Maryland Brigade next to the road. On the American left was General Richard Caswell's North Carolina Militia, then the Virginia Militia under General Edward Stevens. Charles Armand's small cavalry unit was next to the Virginia Militia. General Gates with his staff was located 600 yards behind the first line of American forces, and in front of General Smallwood's 1st Maryland Brigade in the rear being held in reserve. "The principal part of the American artillery was posted to the left of their right wing of continentals: The remainder was placed in the road, under the protection of their reserve."[63] The two armies' front lines now faced each other, separated by only 250 yards.[64]

General Gates made his last and, perhaps, his most fatal error in lining up his forces in an inappropriate manner. Opposite the inexperienced Virginia and North Carolina militias were the finest and most veteran British forces — Cornwallis' own 23rd and 33rd Regiments of Foot. Lined up in front of the seasoned American Continentals under De Kalb were Lord Rawdon's Volunteers of Ireland, Tarleton's infantry and Hamilton's Royal North Carolinians. It was an incredible mistake for Gates and would be tragedy for the "Grand Army" of the Southern Department.[65]

"At the dawn," wrote Cornwallis, "I made my last disposition when I perceived that the enemy, having persisted in their resolution to fight, were formed in two lines opposite and near to us. And observing a movement on their left, I directed Lieutenant Colonel Webster to begin the attack, which was done with great vigor, and in a few minutes the action was general along the whole front."[66] Cornwallis had noticed the movement of Stevens' Virginia Militia, and thinking it was a move by Gates to reposition his left flank, rode over to Webster to alert him to engage the militia with haste. Webster advanced his 33rd Regiment as General Stevens on the American left flank continued moving the Virginia Militia forward in somewhat less than perfect military precision. When the two forces were within 50 yards of each other Stevens shouted out to his men, "My brave fellows, you have bayonets as well as they, we'll charge them." Cornwallis then sent an *aide-de-camp* racing across the road and along the battle line to Lord Rawdon's forces with orders to open fire immediately on the American Continentals in their front.[67]

On the American left, Williams had dismounted and was leading a group of 90 volunteers to within 40 yards of the British. The Americans took cover behind trees and began to fire at close range. The remaining Virginia Militia was advancing rather slowly as Webster's 23rd Fusiliers and 33rd Foot Regiments formed closer ranks shoulder-to-shoulder, fixed bayonets and moved forward. A few militiamen fired at the British with some effect, but the awesome sight of British precision marching towards them was too frightening.[68] Websters' redcoats advancing ahead "firing and huzzahing threw the whole body of the militia into such a panic that they threw down their loaded arms and fled, in the utmost consternation."[69]

One militiaman confessed that "I was amongst the first that fled." He continued:

> The cause of that I cannot tell, except that everyone I saw was about to do the same. It was instantaneous. There was no effort to rally, no encouragement to fight. Officers and men joined in the flight. I threw away my gun, and, reflecting I might be punished for being found without arms, I picked up a drum, which gave forth such sounds

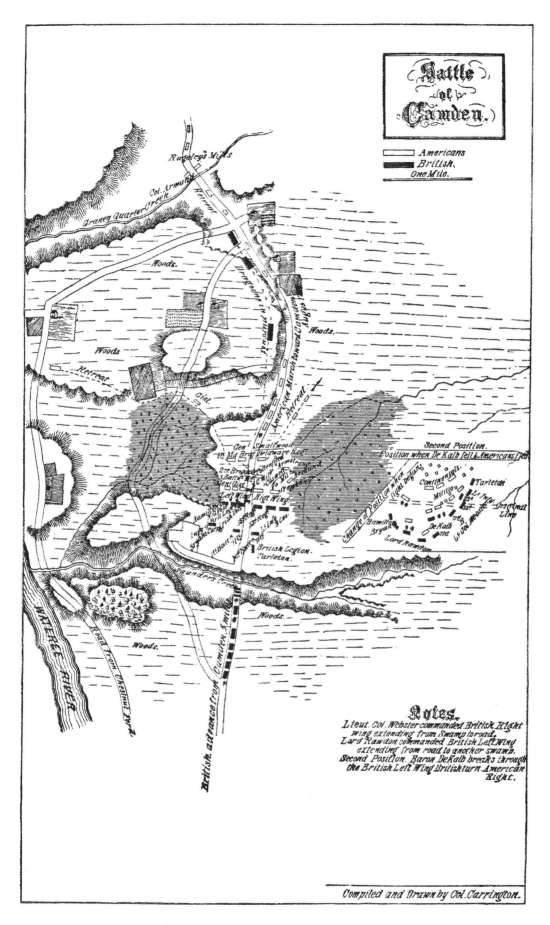

Battle of Camden. (*Battles of the American Revolution.*)

when touched by the twigs I cast it away. When we had gone, we heard the roar of guns still.[70]

A soldier, Sergeant Roger Lamb of the British 23rd, who was carrying the colors on Webster's middle of the right wing, noticed that Webster was "cool, determined, vigilant, and active," as they advanced toward the American militia. Lamb remembered that he lost sight of Webster, the Americans and even of his own comrades as smoke from the musket firing "occasioned such thick darkness, that it was difficult to see the effect of fire on either side."[71]

The retreat of the Virginians and the British line of redcoat advance was too much for Caswell's North Carolina Militia. They also immediately broke ranks, threw down their muskets, and fled. Williams wrote, "only a small part of the brigade commanded by Brigadier General Gregory made a short pause. A part of Dixon's regiment of that brigade, next in the line to the Second Maryland Brigade, fired two or three rounds of cartridge. But a great majority of the militia (at least two-thirds of the army) fled without firing a shot." Williams continued, "He who has never seen the effect of a panic upon a multitude can have but an imperfect idea of such a thing. The best disciplined troops have been enervated and made cowards by it…. Like electricity, it operates instantaneously — like sympathy, it is irresistible where it touches."[72] Over 2500 startled militiamen ran through the formation of the 1st Maryland Brigade in the rear, throwing them into confusion. General Horatio Gates saw the fleeing militia, and assuming all was lost, mounted his celebrated racehorse, the progeny of a sire called Fearnaught, and hurried away from the battle.[73] Williams wrote of the events, "The militia, the general saw were in the air; and the regulars, he feared, were no more." Gates fled to Charlotte, some 65 miles away, without stopping, in full gallop.[74]

On the other side of the road the battle story was different. It had started when Lord Rawdon's force fired its first major volley. De Kalb's men fired back in response, and the firing became more general. The events were again recorded by Colonel Williams:

> The regular troops, who had the keen edge of sensibility rubbed off by strict discipline and hard service, saw the confusion with but little emotion. They engaged seriously in the affair; and notwithstanding some irregularity, which was created by the militia breaking pell-mell through the second line, order was restored there — time enough to give the enemy a severe check, which abated the fury of their assault and obliged them to assume a more deliberate manner of acting. The Second Maryland Brigade, including the battalion of Delawares, on the right, was engaged with the enemy's left, which was opposed with very great firmness. They even advanced upon

them and had taken a number of prisoners when their companions of the First Brigade (which formed the second line), being greatly outflanked and charged by superior numbers, were obliged to give ground.

> At this critical moment the regimental officers of the latter brigade, reluctant to leave the field without orders, inquired for their commanding officer (Brigadier General Smallwood) who, however, was not to be found. Notwithstanding, Colonel Gunby, Major Anderson and a number of other brave officers, assisted by the deputy adjutant general and Major Jones, one of Smallwood's aids, rallied the brigade and renewed the contest. Again they were obliged to give way, and were again rallied. The Second Brigade was still warmly engaged. The distance between the two brigades did not exceed two hundred yards….

> At this eventful juncture, the deputy adjutant general, anxious that the communications between them be perserved … hastened from the First to the Second Brigade, which he found precisely in the same circumstances. He called upon his own regiment (the 6th Maryland) not to fly, and was answered by the Lieutenant Colonel Ford, who said, "They have done all that can be expected of them. We are outnumbered and outflanked. See the enemy charge with bayonets!"

> The enemy having collected their corps and directing their whole force against these two devoted brigades, a tremendous fire of musketry was for some time kept up on both sides with equal perseverance and obstinacy, until Lord Cornwallis, perceiving there was no cavalry opposed to him, pushed forward his dragoons, and his infantry charging at the same moment with fixed bayonets put an end to the contest…. His victory was complete.[75]

Major General De Kalb's Continentals had fought for nearly an hour until the battle ended. Webster had moved his 23rd and 33rd Regiments around to push against the Continentals' left flank after the militia had fled. De Kalb had lost his horse earlier in the engagement and on foot, with sword in hand, he continued to lead his men against the British. He killed one British soldier that opposed him at one point. He and his men repulsed attack after attack without surrender. De Kalb led the last countercharge with his head laid open by a saber cut. He was finally cut down, mortally injured with no less than 11 saber, bayonet and bullet wounds. When the British soldiers ran up to finish off De Kalb, one of his aides, Chevalier De Buysson, put himself in front of the general, calling out De Kalb's name and title. As the wounded and dying general was propped up against a wagon wheel by the British, Lord Cornwallis rode up and ordered him carried by litter for medical treatment. De Kalb died three days later, and was buried with full military and Masonic honors. According to legend, both Lord Cornwallis and De Kalb were Masons.

The remaining Continentals scattered as the battle ended. Three officers, John Eager Howard, John Gunby and Robert Kirkwood, were able to escape with 60 Marylanders and Delawares through the woods as a fighting unit.[76] General Gist and about 100 Continentals escaped by wading through the swamp on the right of the American position. The Delaware Regiment was annihilated. The Virginia Militia that had started the infamous retreat in chaos had escaped in total. As the unarmed American militia had retreated on the road towards Charlotte, they were met by Tarleton's Legion. He recorded the events:

> As soon as the rout of the Americans became general, the legion dragoons advanced with great rapidity towards Rugeley's mills: On the road, General Rutherford, with many other officers and men were made prisoners. The charge and pursuit having greatly dispersed the British, a halt was ordered on the south side of the creek, in order to collect a sufficient body to dislodge Colonel Armand and his corps, who, together with several officers, were employed in rallying the militia at that pass, and sending off American baggage. The quick junction of the scattered cavalry counteracted the designs of the enemy: Colonel Armand's dragoons and the militia displayed a good countenance, but were soon borne down by the rapid charge of the legion: The chase again commenced, and did not terminate till the Americans were dispersed, and fatigue overpowered the exertions of the British. In a pursuit of twenty-two miles, many prisoners of all ranks, twenty ammunition waggons, one hundred and fifty carriages, containing the baggage, stores, and camp equipage of the American army, fell into the hands of the victors.[77]

South of the battlefield a young 7-year-old daughter of an exiled patriot, Mary Kershaw, watched the events of that day and night of August 16, 1780. From her father's house, she saw the exhausted American prisoners driven like sheep into the backyard of her home and this temporary British headquarters.[78] In addition to the British pursuit, the fleeing Americans ran into "many of their insidious friends, armed, and advancing to join the American army; but, learning its fate from the refugees, they acted decidedly in concert with the victors; and captivating some, plundering others and maltreating all the fugitives they met, returned exultantly home...." So much for loyalty in the backcountry.

The Battle of Camden had cost the American cause a grave price. While the exact toll will never be known, Cornwallis reported that some 800 to 900 Americans were killed or wounded and some 1000 prisoners were taken. The Maryland and Delaware regiments lost 162 known dead, and 63 more were reported dead in the North Carolina Militia. The British had lost 68 killed, 245 wounded and 11 missing in action, for a total of 324. While the numbers of British loss was lighter than the American loss, Cornwallis had lost some 20 percent of his redcoat regulars, with 36 percent of the 33rd Regiment's men and half its officers out of action. Lord Rawdon's Irish Volunteers had lost more than 20 percent of their men. Remembering that Cornwallis had some 800 men hospitalized in Camden before the battle, the effects of attrition would now begin to take on some importance since there was little hope of getting replacements from Clinton in New York.[79]

By the time the battle actually ended for the Continentals, General Horatio Gates was already five miles away at Rugeley's Mills having decided to depart the battle. He later explained that "By this Time the Militia had taken to the Woods in all directions, and I concluded with General Caswell to retire towards Charlotte."[80] Gates had fled away from the Camden rout followed by bands of militia and later the Continentals. He had entertained some hope of producing a rally at Clermont to cover the retreat of the regulars, but he did not stay to make it happen. Rather, he rode to Charlotte, some 70 miles away, with all due speed on his racehorse, ahead of the others in his party. On the trip Lieutenant Colonel Senf, who had been with Sumter, informed Gates that Sumter's expedition had been successful, and that Sumter was on the other side of the Catawba River with 100 prisoners and 40 captured British. But Gates revealed no interest on the matter, and he gave no orders to warn Sumter of Cornwallis' presence.

Further along his trip, Gates ran into Major Davie and his cavalry unit returning from Charlotte and their escort duty for the wounded at Hanging Rock going to a hospital on the 6th. Davie's force was now moving to overtake the army at Rugeley's Mills. Shortly before meeting Gates on the road, he had captured an American deserter who revealed details of the Camden defeat. Gates confirmed the bad news and called for Davie to move back to Charlotte to face the British dragoons of Tarleton's unit. Davie responded to Gates that his men were accustomed to Tarleton and did not fear him. Then General Isaac Huger rode up and Davie inquired if he should obey Gates' directions to move back to Charlotte or not. Huger replied that Davie could follow him or not, "Just as far as you please, for you will never see him again." Davie sent an agent to Gates to say that if Gates desired, he would go to the scene of the battle and bury the dead. Gates replied to his agent, "I say retreat! Let the dead bury their dead."

Davie did not follow Gates' directions and he continued on to see if he could be useful in saving any soldiers, baggage or stores. Having learned from Huger that it was likely that Sumter had not been warned of the Gates' defeat, he immediately sent Captain Martin with two dragoons to inform Sumter. Sumter was then moving up the western bank of the Catawba River. Davie said that Sumter must be encouraged to move with haste to Charlotte with all the forces he could muster. Captain Martin reached Sumter on the night of August 16. Sumter then moved his forces and loot toward Rocky Mount, some 30 miles from Camden.

Meanwhile, after the battle, Cornwallis recalled the issue of Sumter's forces in his area and on the morning of the 17th ordered Lieutenant Colonel Tarleton with his 300-man Legion Cavalry and infantry force to find and attack Sumter. Cornwallis also directed Lieutenant Colonel Turnbull and Colonel Ferguson, who were on the Little River, to likewise attack Sumter. Rather than resting for only a short while, Sumter encamped on the night of the 17th at Rocky Mount, and departed the site the next morning. Passing Fishing Creek at eight miles from Rocky Mount, Sumter again halted. He placed his troops at a bridge adjacent to the north side of the creek with rearguard and two vedettes posted at a little distance out front. Sumter seemed to be only mildly concerned for the possibility of an attack, even though he had been warned. His troops' arms were stacked and his men were generally relaxing.

As ordered, Tarleton had set out the morning of the 17th and marched up the eastern side of the Wateree (Catawba), planning to cross the river at or near Rocky Mount. On the way Tarleton captured some Continentals and discovered that Sumter was moving along the western bank. He arrived at the ferry opposite Rocky Mount at dusk and noted Sumter's campfires off the river some miles away. Tarleton, undiscovered, crossed the river and at daybreak found that Sumter had broken camp. Tarleton's men proceeded to Fishing Creek by noon, but they were forced to halt due to fatigue. Even so, Tarleton then selected 100 hearty dragoons of the Legion and another 50 light infantry on foot to continue to pursue the enemy, leaving the remaining force to cover his retreat if necessary.

Following the tracks of Sumter's force on August 18, Tarleton's force came upon the two American vedettes posted as the rear guard as they received fire. The patriots first killed one Legion dragoon in the first volley, but the two vedettes were killed in response. A Legion sergeant and four men approached the patriots on a summit where they immediately crouched on their horses and made signals to Tarleton. Tarleton rode forward and saw the American camp, not the least bit alarmed by the previous firing of the rear guards. Tarleton formed up his cavalry in one line and with a shout ordered the charge. Sumter's arms were taken before Woodford's men could be assembled. The men ran in chaos, as a few Americans fired from behind wagons. Quickly, the engagement was over at the camp, as the Americans were in general flight from the scene. Sumter was under a wagon asleep, and was barely able to escape with his life. He fled on horseback without his saddle,

hat, or coat and arrived at Major Davie's camp at Charlotte by himself two days later.

At Fishing Creek, Sumter had lost 150 officers and men killed or wounded, 10 Continentals, 100 militia, many militia officers and some 200 privates were made prisoners. The British had recaptured Sumter's booty including two three-pounders, two ammunition wagons, 1000 stand of arms, 44 wagons loaded with baggage, rum and other stores. The British had lost only Captain Charles Campbell, who was killed, along with 15 noncommissioned officers and men killed or wounded.[81]

Gates spent only one night in Charlotte, reflecting that "there was neither Arms … nor any prospect of collecting any Force at that place…. I proceeded with all possible Despatch hither."[82] He left Charlotte and moved on to Salisbury, then on to Hillsborough. He had fled the battle before it was completed, having covered some 200 miles in three and one-half days. He had left no orders at any location for his retreating Americans. Soon about 700 survivors had reached Charlotte, arriving without food, clothing or arms. These men were sent on towards Salisbury, where General Smallwood took command and marched them to Hillsborough.

The defeat of Gates' army at Camden was the second major American defeat in the South during the Revolution. General Gates was widely criticized for his handling of the Southern Army and the defeat. Twenty-five years later, by then a general, Davie would write the following blunt narrative concerning Gates' performance in the South:

> General Gates had joined the army but a few days which time was employed in continual marches, he was entirely unacquainted with the character of the officers or the merits of the different corps which composed his army, and was ignorant of their numbers, having never received a return until after the orders of the 15th were issued, the whole of the militia wanted arrangement and the ordinary preparation for a battle was entirely neglected among them, in Rutherfords Brigade there was scarcely a cartridge made up, and their arms were generally in bad order; the consequence of continual marching and exposure. A man must have had more than ordinary good fortune to avoid a defeat under so many circumstances.[83]

The news of the Camden defeat reached Washington's headquarters on September 6 and it evoked much discouragement and anger. Alexander Hamilton took the news poorly and wrote to James Duane exclaiming, "Was there ever such an instance of a general running away … from his whole army? And was there ever so precipitous a flight? One hundred and eighty miles in three days and a half! It does admirable credit to the activity of a man at his time of life…. But what will be done by Congress? Will he be changed or not? If he is changed, for God's sake overcome prejudice, and send Greene.... I stake my reputation on the events give him but fair play."[84] It was indeed a crushing defeat for the American patriots and the South. Within 13 weeks the British had eliminated the armies of Benjamin Lincoln and Horatio Gates. North Carolina Governor Nash wrote to Washington expressing how much his state had given:

> Sir, The loss of these brave men was not our greatest loss. We had expended upwards of twenty-five million dollars on this army. We had drained every source and exhausted every fund in purchasing tents, wagons, horses, arms, ammunition, provisions, spirits, sugar, coffee, camp equipage of every kind, in short, everything appertaining to any army; and in a single half hour all is completely lost, and the army in a manner annihilated.[85]

Cornwallis was encouraged by the victory over the Southern Army. Of Tarleton's defeat of Sumter, he remarked, "This action was too brilliant to need any comment of mine." To George Germain he wrote on August 21:

> A number of prisoners, near 150 wagons, a considerable quantity of military stores, and all the baggage and camp equipment of the rebel army fell into our hands. The loss of the enemy was very considerable. A number of colors and seven pieces of brass cannon, with all their ammunition wagons, were taken.[86]

The British celebrated their victory. Lord Rawdon, who was quite pleased with his Irish Volunteers, ordered a silver medal struck off. He then awarded the medals to several of the men who had distinguished themselves. Captain Alexander Ross, the *aide-de-camp* to Cornwallis, hastened to Charles Town, where he soon sailed for England on August 30. He arrived in England on October 9 where he took the news to the capital, and soon became "Major Ross." The next two weeks saw London citizenry talking of nothing but the Camden victory and the military virtues of their national son, Lord Cornwallis.[87]

At Hillsborough, Gates was still at least technically in command of the remnants of the Southern Army as he tried to cover his past and disgrace. To General Washington he wrote his depressing comments:

> Anxious for the Public Good, I shall continue my unwearied Endeavours to stop the Progress of the Enemy ... and recover all our Losses in the Southern States.—But if being unfortunate is solely a reason for removing me from command, I shall most cheerfully submit to the Orders of Congress, and resign an Office few Generals would be anxious to possess.... That Your Excellency may meet with no such Difficulties ... that your Road to Fame, may be smooth and easy is the Sincere Wish (of etc.).

It would take two months for Congress to remove General Horatio Gates from the leadership of the Southern Department and his failed command.[88]

13

KING'S MOUNTAIN

After the great British victory over Gates outside Camden, Lord Cornwallis moved his forces back to the town for "rest and refreshment" while he waited for reinforcements from Charles Town. Gates was in Hillsborough, North Carolina, licking his "wounds" while trying to defend his previous actions and obtain more troops and supplies.

Meanwhile, Colonel Francis Marion was still roaming the Pee Dee area looking for opportunities to hit the British and the loyalists as best he could. The day after the Camden battle, August 17, Colonel Marion detached Major Peter Horry with four companies to destroy all boats and canoes located on the Santee River from the Lower Ferry to Lenud's; to post guards to stop all British communications with Charles Town; and to obtain 25 weight of gunpowder, ball or buckshot and flints. Then Marion headed to the upper Santee to execute the same actions as he had directed Major Horry.

On the way Marion learned of the Camden defeat. He kept the bad news to himself as he continued to proceed toward Nelson's Ferry, where all communications between Camden and Charles Town had to pass. Marion approached the ferry on the evening of August 20 and was informed by his scouts that a group of prisoners under British guard was stopped at a house at the Great Savannah, a swamp on the main road east of the river and near the line between the present-day counties of Berkeley and Orangeburg.

Just before daybreak on the next morning Marion gave orders to Colonel Hugh Horry to take 16 men to gain possession of the road at the pass at Horse Creek, which runs through the swamp "two mile from and parallel with the Santee." He then led the main body to attack the guards from the rear. As Colonel Horry moved to his po-

sition, he unfortunately alerted a sentinel who fired on him. Understanding his situation and the need to work fast, Colonel Horry rushed the house, took the British arms stacked before the door, seized 22 British regulars of the 63rd Regiment, two loyalists, one captain and a subaltern, and freed 150 Maryland Continentals. Only one loyalist was killed and Major Benison was wounded. Josiah Cockfield was shot through the chest, but lived to fight another day.

After the action Colonel Marion began to march back to his camp at Port's Ferry. Surprisingly, all except three of the Continental troops he had just rescued refused to join his unit in support of patriot work. Although morale dipped somewhat, Marion's band quickly revitalized and set out for another attack. Around August 27, having gained intelligence, Marion's group crossed Lynch's Creek to engage Major Wemyss' command, the 63rd Regiment, in company with Major Harrison leading some loyalists.

Major John James was sent ahead with the patriot volunteers to reconnoiter the British. That night, Major James hid in a thicket near the present-day town of Kingston in Williamsburg County to wait for Major Wemyss and his force to march by. As the British marched by in bright moonlight, Major James' unit ran out from the hiding place just as the rear guard came by. The patriots were able to kill or capture 30 of the group of 49 enemies.

Later that morning, just before light, Marion met with Major James and the decision was reached to retreat back to Lynch's Creek. It was learned that the British force twice the size of Marion's had been located and that a unit under Gainey was estimated to have some 500 men. In retreat Marion re-crossed the Pee Dee River at Port's Ferry, and on August 28 began the retreat into North Carolina. Half of Marion's men left him to take care of their families and property. With the remaining force of 67 men, Marion marched to Avery's Mill on Downing Creek on the eastern branch of the Little Pee Dee River. There he detached Major James with a small unit to return to South Carolina and recruit volunteers. He then proceeded to encamp at the eastern side of White Marsh located near the head of the Waccamaw River in North Carolina.[1]

While Marion was active around the Pee Dee after Camden, Colonels Isaac Shelby, Elijah Clarke and James Williams with some 200 patriot frontiersmen under orders from Colonel Charles McDowell departed on August 17 from Smith's Ford, on the east bank of the Broad River in York County, to attack a loyalist group believed to be at Musgrove's Mills. Musgrove's Mills, located on the south side of the Enoree River in present day Laurens County, was the place Colonel Ferguson had sent his wounded after the battle of the Old Iron Works at Cedar Springs on August 8. With Colonel James Williams and acting as guides were Colonel Thomas Brandon, Colonel James Stein and Major Joseph McJunkin of the 96th Brigade of Militia. Since Williams and Brandon knew the country quite well, they moved 26 miles from Smith's Ford to Brandon's settlement in Fair Forest by riding all night. At dawn the patriots reached an old Indian field 14 miles beyond Fair Forest, only one mile north of Musgrove's Ford, where they sent out an advance party of scouts to reconnoiter. The scouts crossed the Cedar Shoal Creek, a short distance below Musgrove's Mill, and were able to sneak up to the loyalist camp covertly.

The scouts, with two wounded, returned to report their findings after encountering a loyalist patrol at the west of Cedar Shoal Creek. They killed one and wounded two, while two enemy men escaped back to the loyalist camp. Shelby and Clarke moved the unit up to the timber ridge just to the east of Cedar Shoal Creek, within a half mile of Musgrove's Ford and Mills. The commanders were then informed by a local countryman that the British had just been reinforced by some 200 Provincials and loyalists from Ninety Six under Colonel Alexander Innes. The enemy force, now 500 strong, was deemed a worthy force, but the decision was reached to attack anyway.

A makeshift breastwork of old logs, trees and brush was prepared, forming a 300-foot line along the ridge in a semi-circle. Mounted troops were placed at the flanks of the battle line. Having been alerted by the loyalist scouts of the earlier firings, the loyalist camp was wild with activity. Colonel Innes preferred to march immediately over the river to attack the rebels, but his advisors convinced him to delay until at least the return of the 100-man scouting party arrived from Jones' Ford. With the 100 men in camp, Innes prepared to attack. Mean-

while, Captain Shadrach Inman and 25 mounted men were sent out to draw the loyalists to cross the river and approach Shelby and Clarke's battle line.

The approach by Inman and party did as expected and drew the loyalists and British out to within 200 yards of the American battle line. The enemy formed in a line and moved forward some 50 yards before they fired. The heavy firing was countered by frontiersmen firing from behind trees, a fence and breastwork. The Provincials under Innes and Fraser drove the Americans from the right wing of the breastwork at bayonet point. While Shelby's right wing was beginning to give way under fierce fighting, the left wing fighting the loyalists was holding their own. Seeing the plight of the right wing, Clarke sent Shelby a small reserve unit to help. Just at this moment Innes was badly wounded by a Watauga volunteer. Innes fell from his horse and the volunteer shouted, "I've killed their commander!" With this Shelby rallied his men who with a frontier Indian yell rushed the enemy and forced them back.

At this point the battle turned in favor of the Americans. Within short order the loyalists and British were in full retreat, pursued by the mountaineers. The enemy fled through the woods to the river, crossed, and continued to attempt their escape. Meanwhile, the reserve force that had been patrolling along Jones' Ford heard the shots and hurried to the scene of the action to no avail. By the time they arrived and inquired of the situation, the battle was over. The Americans were off with their prisoners and the surviving men were carrying their wounded toward the hospital at Musgrove's. The defeated encamped a few miles off for the night, and the next morning they headed back toward Ninety Six under Captain Kerr.

Shelby, Clarke and Williams decided to take the offensive at the hands of their successful action the previous day, and to pursue the enemy as they moved toward Ninety Six. Just as the men were about to mount their horses to depart, Francis Jones, an express rider from Colonel McDowell, rode up in haste with a letter from General Caswell. Caswell's letter told of the defeat at Camden and apprised McDowell to get out of the way of the British. McDowell sent the rider instructions to move their forces to Gilbert Town. The commanders on horseback agreed to move as directed using a route through the backwoods to avoid any opportunity to engage the British and especially Ferguson. Indeed a detachment of Ferguson's men was in pursuit of the Americans, but late in the evening of August 18 they abandoned the effort. The fatigued, but victorious, patriots had left the same spot where Ferguson's party rested only 30 minutes earlier in the process of their retreat. The full episode was finally concluded.

The incredible events of the victory and rushed retreat

yielded 63 British dead, some 90 wounded and 70 taken prisoner. The wounded enemy included Colonel Innes, Major Fraser and other officers. The skilled American frontiersmen lost only four killed, including Captain Inman, and nine wounded. Shelby was quoted as saying that the battle was the "hardest and best fought action he was ever in." It was certainly one of the most important small arms battles of the Southern Revolution. In less than three days, these 200 Americans had moved 100 miles, fought a spectacularly victorious battle, and retreated some 60 miles with prisoners in company. The force never stopped to eat, making use of peaches and green corn as they moved. The fatigue was quite extreme when it was all over. It was said that the faces and eyes of the patriot officers were so bloated that they were barely able to see. While the British and loyalists fought bravely, they could not overcome the courageous Southern fighters.

As September 1780 arrived, there was no organized loyalist force in South Carolina. Marion was at White Marsh, North Carolina, soon to return. Colonel Davie was at Charlotte with his cavalry. Sumter was gathering refugees and recruiting. To the west were Shelby, Clarke and Williams just inside North Carolina considering the next place to attack the British. And Gates was in Hillsborough. By this time the glow of the great victory against the Americans at Camden was fading rapidly for Cornwallis. In his letter to Clinton on August 29 Lord Cornwallis expressed his concern: "We receive the strongest professionals of Friendship from North Carolina; our Friends, however do not seem inclined to rise until they see our Army in motion. The severity of the Rebel Government has so terrified and totally subdued the minds of the People, that it is very difficult to rouse them to any exertion."[2]

Cornwallis was now convinced that he needed Clinton to invade the Chesapeake as a diversion in support of any move he would make into North Carolina. He knew it would be the decisive strategic move of the campaign in the South, and he wanted it to proceed with the best chance for success. As Clinton departed Charles Town, leaving the reins to Cornwallis in the South, he had directed that "Should your Lordship so far succeed in both provinces [of the Carolinas], as to be satisfied they are safe from any attack during the approaching season, after leaving a sufficient force in garrison … I should wish you to assist in operations which will certainly be carried on in the Chesapeak."

Cornwallis' letter to Clinton of August 23 remarked that his actions in North Carolina "will depend on the operations which your Excellency may think proper to pursue in the Chesapeak, which appears to me, next to the Security of New York, to be one of the most important objects of the War." Eight days later Cornwallis wrote, "I most sincerely hope that Nothing can happen to prevent your Excellency's intended Diversion in the Chesapeak. If unfortunately any unforeseen Cause should make it impossible, I should hope that you can see the absolute Necessity of adding some Force to the Carolinas."

A change in strategic view of the Chesapeake operation had now occurred between Clinton and Cornwallis. Clinton's instructions had shown that he expected that Cornwallis must secure the Carolinas as a pre-condition to supporting his Chesapeake operations. Now in late August Cornwallis looked upon the operation as a necessary diversion in order to assist him in subduing North Carolina, thereby solidifying his position in South Carolina. Regardless, Clinton informed Germain that "By letters I have lately received from Lord Cornwallis I hold myself powerfully called upon to make a diversion in his favor in Chesapeake Bay. I have prepared for it…." In six weeks Clinton ordered General Alexander Leslie back to Virginia with a force of 2500 men.[3]

After the failure at Camden, the North Carolina General Assembly at Hillsborough issued a call for the militia to assemble at Charlotte, Salisbury, Hillsborough and Ramsey's Mill on the Deep River in Chatham County. Some 800 men formed at Ramsey's Mill under Brigadier General Jethro Sumner. Eventually joined by Major General Richard Caswell, they moved this group to join Davidson's force of 400 militia from Mecklenburg and Rowan counties at his encampment, McAlpin's Creek, located eight miles south of Charlotte. William L. Davidson reported that, "Our troops are in high spirits, and seem determined to stand out to the last extremity rather than to submit to the fate of South Carolina."[4]

At Gates' headquarters in Hillsborough, the mood was not upbeat. Even with polite expressions of regret and understanding, Gates' situation was not a good one. There were many critics of Gates now in evidence, including Governor Abner Nash of North Carolina, who was asking Congress to remove him. In defiance of Gates' position, Nash created a state Board of War, which began to issue orders to the militia. Major Davie criticized the makeup of the board when he wrote, "Nothing could be more ridiculous than the manner this Board was filled. Alexander the Little, being a Warrior of great fame, was placed at the head of the Board — Penn who was only fit to amuse children, and O. Davis who knew nothing but the game of Whilst composed the rest of the Board." General Gates was angered by Nash's actions and declared that he would indeed arrest any officer "who in contempt or opposition to His orders shall dare obey an order from the Board of War." It was an interesting situation for the officers in North Carolina.[5]

On August 31 a meeting of officers was held at Salisbury to petition the North Carolina legislature to appoint

William L. Davidson to command the western militia with the rank of brigadier general, to replace Rutherford, who had been taken at Camden. The 34-year-old Colonel Davidson held a Continental commission and had been a veteran of Washington's army, as well as serving in the backcountry of the Carolinas. The petition, which was supported by William Davie, was approved and Davidson ordered out the militia. One of Nash's first actions was to give the state militia over to a Marylander, Major General William Smallwood. Nash had explained his action in that Smallwood was "the only general officer who survived the rout at Camden with an increased reputation for courage and military talent."

Even though Gates knew he might be replaced, he continued to attempt to reorganize some resistance for the British. He continued to press for supplies and men under difficult circumstances. Gates' force consisted of the 800 Continentals that had made their way back from Camden. Gates put these returning Continentals in one regiment under Otto Holland Williams, the 31-year-old colonel who had served with the Maryland Line since 1775. Eventually Gates would gather in a number of valuable patriot forces. Joining him was 28-year-old Lieutenant Colonel William Washington, the cousin of the commander-in-chief and an expert with the dragoons. Washington commanded some 70 cavalry.

Gates also added a company of Delaware Continentals and 60 Virginia riflemen, which he placed under another young officer from Maryland, Colonel John Eager Howard. Gates was delighted when his former comrade in arms, Daniel Morgan, joined his force. Morgan, who had served in Canada with Arnold in 1775-76 and fought with distinction at Saratoga, had been out of the war since 1779 after being passed over for promotion to general and having failing health. Morgan, known as the "Old Waggoner," decided to rejoin the patriot cause because of the desperate situation in the South and a belated promotion from Congress. To brighten up Gates' mood even more, word soon arrived that Sumter had recruited a force of some 1000 men.[6]

On September 8, 1780, British reinforcements to Cornwallis' army finally arrived in Camden from Charles Town. The forces included the 7th Regiment and recruits for the Provincial regiments. With these forces and his main army, "composed of the 7th, 23rd, 33rd and 71st regiments of infantry, the volunteers of Ireland, Hamilton's corps, Bryan's refugees, four pieces of cannon, about fifty waggons, and a detachment of cavalry," Lord Cornwallis began his move toward North Carolina and marched by Hanging Rock to the Waxhaw settlement, located 40 miles from Charlotte. Lieutenant Colonel Tarleton's forces, consisting of "the body of the British dragoons, and the light and legion infantry, with a three pounder, crossed the Wateree [Catawba River], and moved up the east side of the river." Tarleton wrote that the "scarcity of forage in the district of the Wacsaws was the principal reason for this temporary separation. Flour, cattle, and forage were collected with difficulty by the main army, to supply the men and horses upon the march, the depredations of both parties having made desert of the country."[7]

Meanwhile, the victors of Musgrove's Mill had fled into the backwoods of North Carolina. They had joined up with Colonel McDowell near Gilbert Town after a 48-hour march with their eyes and faces bloated from hunger and fatigue. Before leaving for a short visit to his home, Shelby proposed that an army be raised on both sides of the mountains to deal eventually with Ferguson. The word was, "Tell it in Gath, publish it in the streets of Askelon."[8]

The sad situation was that the term of enlistment had expired for nearly all of McDowell's forces. It was agreed that the Musgrove prisoners should be sent to a secure place, while the officers returned to their homes to recruit for the next engagement. The men now retired to their homes in Washington and Sullivan counties, in present day East Tennessee. It was agreed that McDowell would remain to keep the other patriots informed of the enemy's positions and to preserve the beef and stock in the valleys and caves of the Upper Catawba region. McDowell sent express riders to colonels Cleveland and Herndon and Major Winston urging them to recruit volunteers and join up with the American forces.[9]

The Musgrove prisoners were entrusted to Colonel Clarke, who traveled with them for some distance before deciding to return to Georgia via the mountain trails for an expedition of his own. He left the prisoners in the care of Colonel Williams and his associate Captain Hammond, who conducted them to Hillsborough. Colonel James Williams was a farmer, miller, merchant and delegate to the South Carolina Provincial Congress.[10]

Colonel Williams was met by Governor Rutledge of South Carolina and made it known that he should be given the credit for the victory at Musgrove's Mill.[11] The governor was so impressed that he promoted Williams to brigadier general in the South Carolina Militia as a reward for his supposed gallantry. The news traveled fast. Only 17 days later a prominent public figure wrote the following from Halifax: "Colonel Williams of South Carolina, three days after the Gates' defeat, fell in with a party of the enemy near Ninety-Six and gave them a complete drubb, killing seventy on the spot; and taking between sixty and seventy prisoners, mostly British, with the loss of four men only." The circumstances of Williams' promotion without mention of the efforts of his peers, Shelby and Clarke, were to create a significant point of contention for years to come.[12]

When the battle at Camden had ended, Cornwallis had sent orders to Lieutenant Colonel Thomas Browne, who was then in charge of Augusta, with wording as follows:

> I have given orders that all the inhabitants of this province, who had not submitted and who had taken part in the revolt, should be punished with the greatest rigor; that they should be imprisoned and their whole property taken from them and destroyed. I have likewise directed that compensation should be made out of their effects to the persons who have been plundered and oppressed by them. I have ordered in the most positive manner, that every militia man who had borne arms with us and had afterwards joined the enemy, should be immediately hanged. I have now, sir, only to desire that you take the most vigorous measures to extinguish the rebellion in the district in which you command, that you will obey in the strictest manner, the directions I have given in this letter, relative to the treatment of the country.[13]

The next morning five men were taken from the jail by orders of Colonel Browne and hanged without trial. Earlier in the war, Browne had been tarred and feathered for his loyalist opinions. He now had a passion for cruelty toward the patriot movement and its supporters. Around Augusta he already had a reputation for plundering and burning the property of patriots.[14] Both Browne and his colleague Major James Wright, Jr., the son of the former royal governor of Georgia, were to give Cornwallis more trouble than help. The two men had volunteered to raise the local loyalist militia along the frontier border of Georgia and South Carolina. They never met their recruiting goals as they resorted to unorthodox methods in their attempts to reach the set goals. They even raided the prison ships in Savannah and at the barracks of the American prisoners in Charles Town. As Cornwallis was to learn of "all the tricks of recruiting to the great terror & disgust of the inhabitants," he ordered Browne and Wright out of South Carolina.[15]

To right the wrongs of Browne's actions, and to recover some portion of his state, Colonel Clarke had turned over the prisoners to Williams and headed to the western part of the Ninety Six district to raise a force against the loyalists. Accompanying him was Lieutenant Colonel James McCall of South Carolina. Since that area was a loyalist haven, it would not be an easy recruiting effort. McCall had called on Colonel Pickens, the most influential former officer of the regiment, but with no success. Pickens was not open to violating the condition of his parole unless conditions changed as a matter of honor. Though McCall had planned for recruiting some 500 men, he could only round up 80. With these men he marched to Soap Creek, Georgia, located some 40 miles northwest from Augusta. Colonel Clarke had been more successful, having gained 350 followers.

When Colonel Clarke's forces reached their destination near Augusta on the morning of September 14, the British or loyalists had not detected them. The American forces were divided into three groups: the right command given to McCall, the left command to Major Samuel Taylor and in the center Colonel Clarke took command. By accident Taylor moved into an Indian camp near Hawk's Creek in the west and with some firing the Indians retreated to Augusta and their allies. Taylor continued to move forward and took possession of McKay's Trading House, known as the White House, located just a mile and a half from the town. At the house the retreating Indians had joined up with a unit of the King's Rangers under Captain Johnston.

Taylor's attack at the house served as the first alert to Browne of the presence of patriot forces. Browne immediately moved at the head of his main force to reinforce Johnston. The groups from Clarke and McCall completely surprised the remaining garrison and fort and they took control without much resistance. Clarke took 70 loyalist prisoners and all the Indian men present under a guard unit and headed to assist Taylor. As Clarke's forces arrived, Browne and his men took shelter at the White House and planned to defend it. The firing continued from 11 A.M. until night, but the loyalists were not dislodged. The house was located some 80 yards from the river. The Indian force took retreat behind the banks at the river. As the day ended, the firing finally stopped. Guards were posted to keep the enemy in place. Under the cover of night Browne added some strength to the house by filling earth between the spaces in the weatherboards and closing up the windows with the boards from the floor.

The next morning the Americans had brought up two artillery pieces from the British works to bear upon the house. Unfortunately the guns were not field worthy with proper carriages, and they proved to be of little use. The firing did continue throughout the day with small arms, but the loyalists did not budge. The morning of the 15th, Americans fought off the Indians from the riverbank and cut off their water supply. Unknown to Clarke, Browne had been shot through both thighs early in the engagement and was enduring much suffering along with other wounded men. That night 50 Cherokee Indians were able to reinforce the loyalists by crossing the river by canoe. Though the suffering of the loyalist wounded was extreme and the smells were nauseous, they would not surrender. On September 17 Clarke sent a summons to Browne to surrender, warning of the destruction his decision would bring on the people of Georgia. The warning was rejected. In the afternoon another summons was sent in, with the additional provision that Browne would be held personally responsible for the consequences of his failure to submit. This too was rejected. Browne was determined to hold out to the end.

When Browne first was alerted of the presence of the Americans, he sent dispatch riders by two routes to Colonel Cruger at Ninety Six telling of the situation at Augusta. Early the next day, September 15, one of the riders, Sir Patrick Houston, arrived at Cruger's headquarters. On the evening of the 17th scouts alerted Clarke of the presence of Colonel Cruger in company with 500 British regulars and loyalist militia. At 8 A.M. on the 18th, the British troops appeared on the opposite side of the river. Since many of Clarke's men had availed themselves of the opportunity to visit friends and families around Augusta, or left outright, Clarke was quite reduced in force strength.

With the British now on the scene, Clarke decided to retreat, but without sustaining some 60 killed and wounded. Clarke's men dispersed to meet around the end of September at a place of planned rendezvous. When this event occurred, Clarke found he had some 300 men, with around 400 women and children in train behind them. With this sad group Colonel Clarke began a march of almost 200 miles through the mountains to avoid the enemy. They reached the Watauga and Nolichucky rivers on October 11 in a starved and forlorn condition. The only comfort was the great hospitality of the fellow patriots there who gave them all they needed. Colonel Cruger had first attempted to pursue Clarke's retreating force, but as the patriot force headed too far from Ninety Six, he gave up the effort.[16]

The results of the battle at Augusta were profound and sad for the American cause. Clarke had begun the attack on Browne with some 430 men, but saw his force diminish as the days progressed. Browne had about 350 to 450 Provincials and 200 Cherokee Indians — with another 50 Cherokees added on the 15th. When Clarke had retreated, he had paroled two officers and 41 men from the King's Rangers and one officer and 11 men from Delancey's Corps and one surgeon. Tarleton reported that other than Browne who was wounded, the loss was only "Captain Johnson, a very promising officer of the same corps..." and that the loss "otherwise, was not considerable, and fell principally upon the Indians."[17]

The Americans were to see cruel treatment. A Captain Ashby with 12 other of the wounded prisoners were hanged by the British on the staircase of the White House. Their bodies were scalped by the Indians and their corpses were mangled and thrown into the river. The other American prisoners were delivered to the Indians, who formed a circle around them and scalped and burned them alive in fires. The details of these gruesome events were proudly communicated by British officers in various writings to their friends in Savannah, Charles Town and London. On September 23, Cornwallis wrote to Ferguson that he "had the satisfaction to hear from Lieutenant Colonel Cruger,

that he had arrived in time to save Browne, and retake the guns, and totally routed the enemy, who had retired with great precipitation; that the Indians had pursued and scalped many of them."[18]

On September 22 Cornwallis began his move to Charlotte. His real goal was the North Carolina capital, Hillsborough, where he planned to "there assemble, and try to arrange the friends who are inclined to favour; and endeavor to form a very large Magazine for the Winter of flour and meal from the country, and of rum, salt, &c. from Cross Creek, which I understand to be about eighty miles carriage."[19] He ordered the Legion with Tarleton "to cross the Catawba at Blair's ford, in order to form the advanced guard, for the immediate possession of Charlotte town."

The movement was delayed a few days due to the sickness of Tarleton, who was laid up with fever. In his letter to Clinton dated August 29, Cornwallis revealed his feeling that "The post at Charlotte-town will be a great security to all this frontier of South Carolina, which even if we were possessed of the greatest part of North Carolina, would be liable to be infested by parties, who have retired with their effects over the mountains, and mean to take every opportunity of carrying on a predatory war, and it will, I hope, prevent insurrections in this country, which is very disaffected."[20] Maybe Cornwallis could fare better in Charlotte in controlling the countryside than the past had seen.

Seeing that the British were continually foraging around the Waxhaw area, Colonel Davie saw the opportunity to attack. While the main body of the British were camped on the north bank of the Catawba River, some of the light infantry and loyalists were camped on the southern bank at some distance away from the main British forces. On the evening of September 20, Davie's forces came around the left of Cornwallis main body and came close to the light infantry troops at Wahub's Plantation. Captain Wahub was currently with Davie as a volunteer, along with other men who knew the settlement and had friends, property, wives and children there too.

Early on the next morning, September 21, Major Davie's cavalry came within sight of Wahub's house, where they found the loyalist and British cavalry mounted near the home. Davie detached Major Davidson with the majority of the riflemen to move through a cornfield to seize the house, while he moved in via the lane leading to the home. Davie ordered "to take no prisoners." The Americans totally surprised the loyalists and British, who most quickly hurried off in desperation. The Americans killed 20 and 40 others were wounded. Only one American was wounded. Davie collected 96 horses with equipment and 120 stands of arms. Captain Wahub's wife and family ran out of the house as the firing ceased to embrace the owner of the plantation. Unfortunately for the Wahub family, some British troops returned to the house and set it afire. They watched in despair as their property disappeared in flames. Davie's force returned to his camp at Providence, after having moved 60 miles in 24 hours. As he had shown earlier on August 1 at Hanging Rock, where he cut the British to pieces while acquiring 60 horses and 100 muskets, and now repeated at Wahub's Plantation, Colonel Davie was indeed one of the most brilliant and brave officers of the Revolution in the South.[21]

On the very day Colonel Davie returned to his camp, he was met by generals Sumner and Davidson with their North Carolina Militia brigades who had just arrived. With Cornwallis' forces heading toward Charlotte, the decision was made to take the militia to Salisbury, leaving Davie and 150 men with some volunteers under Major Joseph Graham to continue to annoy the British. On the night of September 25, Colonel Davie and his forces entered Charlotte with the British only a few miles behind. At that time Charlotte was a town of some 40 houses on a slightly elevated terrain along two intersecting streets (subsequently Tryon and Trade streets) "which cross each other at right angles in the intersection of which stands the Court House" according to Davie.[22] The courthouse was a frame building set on eight brick pillars ten feet high. A three and one-half foot high wall extended between the pillars and served as the town market. Davie had three lines of militia to the north straddling the north-south road and another troop of cavalry on each side of the courthouse. The troops to the west were placed behind and inside a log house, and the ones on the east used a brick house. Davie and 20 men were located in the path of the approaching British behind McComb's house just south of the courthouse.[23]

In place of Tarleton, who was still sick, Cornwallis ordered Major George Hanger, the third son of Gabriel, Lord Coleraine, to advance into Charlotte with the Legion. Hanger was an interesting soul, more known for his interest in women than his career. During the siege of Charles Town, Hanger had been promoted by Tarleton to major. At an early age his father had sent him away to a number of schools, eventually enrolling him at Eton, where he apparently spent more time chasing women than studying. Being rather bored with studies, Hanger was sent off to Europe to the University of Gottingen, which he deserted to join the cavalry unit of Frederick the Great's army. When Hanger returned to England, his father bought him a commission in the First Foot Guards. As a young ensign in England, he proceeded to spend a fortune on clothes, fencing lessons, gambling and every type of pleasure he could. In 1776 Hanger resigned from the army, saying he had not been treated fairly in promotion, and secured a commission in the Hessian Jagers.

He mortgaged his estate for £13,000, left his estate with an agent and sailed to America. Unfortunately, his agent died and his estate was auctioned off for half its value, leaving him penniless.[24]

This curious and rather reckless man now led the famous Legion into this small Southern town to meet Colonel Davie and company. When the Legion cavalry reached within 60 yards of the courthouse, Davie opened fire and cut down some of the Legion. Concerned that the Legion was too hesitant, Lord Cornwallis rode up in person and addressed the group, appealing to their pride with, "Legion! Remember you have everything to lose, but nothing to gain." Major Hanger then ordered a charge, but the Legion cavalry uncharacteristically hesitated at approaching Davie's small company of men. The Legion cavalry did not advance, but it retreated. In frustration Cornwallis ordered the light infantry and the infantry of the Legion to advance, which they did immediately. Davie then ordered a retreat, as the British pursued.

During the pursuit for several miles, the Americans lost 30 killed, wounded or taken prisoner plus Colonel Locke, who was killed, and Major Graham, who was severely wounded. The British had lost Major Hanger, Captain Campbell, and Captain McDonald, who were wounded, along with another 12 non-commissioned officers and men who were killed and wounded.[25] Charlotte was now in Cornwallis' hands, but to Colonel Davie's credit, his company of 20 men had held the pride of the British cavalry, the Legion, backed up by the whole of Cornwallis' army, for some minutes before being forced to depart. Though Major Hanger called the whole affair "a trifling insignificant skirmish," Davie and his men had again revealed their courage in the face of overwhelming odds.[26]

Brigadier General Davidson wrote at Phifer's Mill in Mecklenburg County of the arrival of the British at Charlotte in a letter to General Gates:

> Sir, This day at 11 o'clock the Enemy march'd into Charlotte in force. According to the best information, Col. Davie skirmished with them at that place, and for several hours since, retreating as per Express. At 2 he was reinforced by about 300 cavalry and infantry, but no intelligence since they joined him. He is directed to continue skirmishing with them to cover our retreat. The Inhabitants are flying before us in consternation, and except we are soon reinforced the west side of the Yadkin must inevitably fall a prey to the enemy. Rowan is able to give us very little assistance on account of Col. Ferguson's movement to the West Ward.[27]

While Cornwallis planned to move on to attack Hillsborough, he decided to stay in Charlotte for a while. Tarleton here described that Charlotte:

> afforded some conveniences, blended with great disadvantages. The mills in its neighborhood were supposed of

sufficient consequence to render it for the present an eligible position, and, in future, a necessary post, when the army advanced: But the aptness of its intermediate situation between Camden and Salisbury, and the quality of its mills, did not counterbalance its defects. The town and environs abounded with inveterate enemies; the plantations in the neighborhood were small and uncultivated; the roads narrow and crossed in every direction; and the whole face of the country covered with close and thick woods.

He continued to describe the situation in and around Charlotte:

> In addition to these disadvantages, no estimation could be made of the sentiments of half the inhabitants of North Carolina, whilst the royal army remained at Charlotte town. It was evident, and it had been frequently mentioned to the King's officers, that the counties of Mecklenburg and Rowan were more hostile to England than any others in America. The vigilance and animosity of their surrounding districts checked the exertions of the well affected, and totally destroyed all communication between the King's troops and the loyalists in the other parts of the province. No British commander could obtain any information in that position, which would facilitate his designs, or guide his future conduct. Every report concerning the measures of the governor and assembly would undoubtedly be ambiguous; accounts of the preparation of the militia could only be vague and uncertain; and all intelligence of the real force and movements of the continentals must be totally unattainable.[28]

The stay in Charlotte for Cornwallis was not cordial in the least. As Tarleton describes, "Foraging parties were every day harassed by the inhabitants, who did not remain at home, to receive payment for the produce of their plantations, but generally fired from covert places, to annoy the British detachments."[29] Davie wrote that the British in Charlotte spent their time working their propaganda with reluctant patriots "bringing large quantities of liquors with them and provision." A leader in this effort and one of the loudest was the former royal governor, Joseph Martin, who was accompanying Lord Cornwallis into North Carolina. From his quarters outside Charlotte at the home of Colonel Thomas Polk, Cornwallis now rested his troops in preparation to begin the further exploitation of North Carolina.

On September 27 Colonel Davie received reinforcements from General Sumner consisting of 200 infantry and 60 mounted horsemen under the command of Colonel John Taylor of Granville County. Meanwhile, Sumner joined with his friend Davidson against Gates' direction after having pushed westerly beyond the Yadkin. He had been forced by high water to cross the Yadkin River above Salisbury. General Gates wrote Sumner with orders, "If you should have been obliged to cross the Yad-

kin — you must under no Account abandon the Defence of that Ford, nor withdraw your Guard from the West Side of that River, until you are by the near Approach of a superior Number of the Enemy obliged to do it." Gates wrote, "I will not risque a Second Defeat, by marching through Famine, and encountering every distress." Morgan with some light infantry was also sent to aid Sumner.[30]

From the beginning of the operation into North Carolina, Cornwallis had planned to coordinate his movements toward Charlotte with those of Lieutenant Colonel Patrick Ferguson out in the west. In his report to Clinton back on August 23, Cornwallis stated that "Ferguson was to move into Tryon County."[31] Ferguson, the self-confident Scotsman with a "commanding appearance," would now take center stage in the next major Southern battle. He was perhaps one of the most interesting and colorful men in the British Army. One might have called him a colonial renaissance man in his time. He was soon to gain significant reputation. Here was a man born to royalty, yet of such a practical mind to invent the most superior rifle of the day, a "rapid-firing, breech-loading rifle that was demonstrated even to the King George III." He was regarded as the "best rifle shot in the British army, if not the best marksman living...."[32]

Incredibly, in 1777 Ferguson had a profound opportunity to change the course of the American Revolution. While lying in ambush with his riflemen in the battlefield at Brandywine, Ferguson noticed an American officer who was "dressed in dark green or blue, mounted on a bay horse, with a remarkably large cocked hat" had moved to within 100 yards of his units' right flank. In company with the American was a Hessian officer. Immediately Ferguson ordered three of his best shots to fire at the two men. Then he quickly retracted his order indicating that firing on two unsuspecting gentlemen "disgusted" him.

The two officers rode out of sight, but soon returned. This time the Hessian officer stayed back out of rifle range, but the American officer came to within less than 100 yards of Ferguson's position. So confounded, Ferguson came out from cover and addressed the American officer asking him to stop. But the American slowly moved off while surveying his British onlooker. Later Ferguson was to explain that he could have "lodged a half dozen balls in or about him before he was out of my reach." Soon after this encounter with the mystery American officer, Ferguson was severely wounded with a shattered right arm and retired to convalesce away from the front. It was then he was to learn that the officer on the field at Brandywine was none other than General George Washington. Ferguson later wrote, "It was not pleasant to fire at the back of an unoffending individual, who was acquitting himself very coolly of his duty, so I let him alone." This was the measure of his character and chivalry.

Other stories eventually surfaced about this most unique adversary. Ferguson was said to have punished a soldier who killed a chicken on the plantation where he was camped. Soon after the fight at Monck's Corner, some of his fellow Tarleton dragoons broke into the home of Lady Colleton, wife of Sir John Colleton. One of the dragoons wounded the mistress of the house with his sword and attempted to rape her, but she was able to fight off his advances. Two other ladies were attacked by the British at the plantation. When Ferguson learned of the incident, he demanded that the men be put to death immediately, regardless of the military law or custom. Only Lieutenant Colonel Webster was able to prevent Ferguson from carrying out his requests, by enforcing the court-martial procedures.[33]

Ferguson had gained a unique command under appointment of Sir Henry Clinton as inspector of the militia. In this role in the summer of 1780, he focused not on inspection, but on building a loyalist army to support Cornwallis in the South. With a sincere personal involvement and countless hours in drill, he had put together seven battalions of loyalist militia approaching 1000 men. He tended to treat the American loyalists with less haughtiness than the usual British officer who considered the locals as inferior. Nathanael Greene agreed that Ferguson had a pleasant disposition, and that he was "a fit associate of Tarleton in hardy, scrambling, a partisan enterprise; equally intrepid and determined, but cooler and more open to impulses of humanity." Gates wrote of him, "It was his peculiar characteristic to gain the affections of the men under his command."[34]

While Lord Cornwallis was certainly aware of Ferguson's brilliance and energy, he felt that there was some justification for worry. In a letter to Balfour at Ninety Six on July 3, his lordship wrote, "Entre nous I am afraid of he getting to the frontier of N. Carolina & playing some cussed trick." Ferguson's rather semi-independent view of his command was another point of concern for Cornwallis. Ferguson, being only six years younger than his commander and having endured sickness and wounding, was impatient and interested in proving to his superiors that he was a warrior leader. Ferguson looked at the North Carolina operation as an opportunity to show his worth and to increase his fame. Regardless of his apprehensions regarding this unique officer, Cornwallis wrote to Clinton of Ferguson before leaving Camden, "he is sure he can depend upon for doing their duty and fighting well."[35]

After Ferguson had failed to intercept Shelby, Clarke and Williams retreating from the battle at Musgrove's Mill, he camped for a period at Fair Forest in the Brandon settlement. Then they sent out detachments to seek out the rebels. Ferguson then "marched into Union District on the Tyger river, and thence northward through Spartanburg district to the 'Quaker's Meadows' in Burke county North Carolina, the home of Col. Charles McDowell. The Tories as they went, plundered the citizens of cattle, horses, beds, wearing apparel; even wresting rings from the fingers of ladies, until they were heartily despised by the British officers as well as their own countrymen who were contending for liberty."[36]

Trying to catch the patriot leaders, Ferguson moved toward Gilbert Town, some three miles north of the present town of Rutherfordton. In an attempt to hurt Ferguson, yet without the total force necessary to be successful, Colonel Charles McDowell with 160 followers planned an ambush at Cowan's Ford on Cane Creek, some 15 miles from Gilbert Town. As the loyalist force crossed the ford, they were fired upon by McDowell's men, severely wounding Major Dunlap, a favorite officer of Ferguson. Several others were killed or wounded. Ferguson retreated to Gilbert Town, while McDowell's force moved off up the Catawba Valley.[37]

At Gilbert Town Ferguson was to carry out a relatively small event that would eventually lead to a most faithful battle. Ferguson paroled a wounded prisoner from a previous engagement, Samuel Philips, a distant relative of Colonel Shelby. With Philips, Ferguson sent a verbal message to the leaders of the western waters around Watauga and Nolichucky, and Holston warning them that if they did not refrain from operating against the British and loyalists, he would march over the mountains, hang the leaders and lay waste to the country with fire and sword. Philips, who lived close to Colonel Shelby, went directly to Shelby's residence and gave Shelby the threat message, along with intelligence regarding the enemy's strength, location and intentions. Shelby, who wrote of himself in third person, explained, "It required no further taunt to rouse the patriot indignation of Col. Shelby. He determined to make an effort to raise a force, in connection with other officers which should surprise and defeat Ferguson."[38] Colonel Shelby immediately rode 50 miles to meet with Lieutenant Colonel John Sevier, who commanded the militia at Washington County, North Carolina. The discussion led to their decision that the time was right to take the promised action made by an agreement set the previous month by Shelby, Clarke and Williams and engage in a surprise attack on Ferguson. It was agreed that all forces possible would be raised and were to gather on September 25 at Sycamore Shoals on the Watauga with necessary supplies.[39]

An express rider was sent to Colonel Cleveland of Wilkes County, North Carolina, to alert him of the situation and to gather on the eastern side of the mountain at Quaker Meadows in Burke County. The place was two miles north of Morganton and the home of the McDowells. Meanwhile, Colonel Shelby knew the actions required expense money but the people had none. Therefore he applied to the entry taker of Sullivan County (now East Tennessee) for the sale of North Carolina lands for a loan. John Adair, the agent, indicated that "I have no authority by law to make that disposition of this money; it belongs to the impoverished treasury of North Carolina, and I dare not appropriate a cent of it to any purpose; but if our country is over-run by the British, our liberties are gone. Let the money go too. Take it. If the enemy, by its use, is driven from the country, I can trust that country to justify and vindicate my conduct. So take it." The patriots received $12,000, which was later legalized by the North Carolina Legislature.[40]

Shelby rushed home and wrote a letter to William Campbell, the colonel commandant of Washington County, Virginia. Shelby had his brother, Captain Moses Shelby, ride to deliver the letter to Campbell, some 40 miles away. Shelby had urged Campbell to join the Ferguson expedition. Campbell initially hesitated because he felt his first duty was to Virginia and that meant he had to maintain his regiment for action to repel the invading Cornwallis. But in a second letter, Campbell agreed to cooperate with the engagement.[41]

On the appointed day of rendezvous, September 25, 1780, the frontiersmen's militia formed as requested. Colonel William Campbell arrived with 450 men from Virginia. Lieutenant Colonel Sevier came with 240 men, while Shelby commanded another 240. Colonel Charles McDowell was at the head of his refugee force of 160 volunteers. This force of over 1000 men was without even one Continental Army soldier or officer, and it was not directed to form by any act of the Continental Army or Congress. Most of the men came mounted and were armed with their Deckard rifles and no bayonets. This rifle was to play a significant part in the upcoming battle with Ferguson. This rifle of .43- to .53-caliber was a long rifle not intended for close-range combat, but for accurate hunting. It had a range of 300 yards, which was over three times the range of the typical smoothbore Brown Bess flintlock musket rated at only 90 yards. The error of the musket at 200 yards was around nine feet. The deadly accuracy of the skilled frontiersmen using their Deckard rifles was about to be proven in stark terms.

This gathered army of frontiersmen was quite a sight on that day. Along with their rifles they carried no baggage wagons or quartermaster stores, but were self-sustaining with their horse, wallet of parched meal, other rations, their blanket, tin cup, tomahawk and knife. Clothed in their homemade linen hunting shirts, buckskin leggings, moccasins and fur caps, they were indeed an informal bunch.[42] At the site were the women, the wives or mothers of these men who would soon head for action against Ferguson. Left behind to guard the frontier against Indian attacks at assigned posts and, thus, not in company, were the old and less active men of the militia.[43]

On the morning of September 26, the Reverend Samuel Doak, a missionary to the Watauga settlement, led a prayer for the occasion. He offered a prayer for the protection of the people from danger, and preached from the Old Testament on Gideon's people rising against the Midianites. He asked them to take the battle cry, "The Sword of Gideon and the Lord." It was an emotional display for these deeply religious frontiersmen and many a tear was shed. This deadly force, made up of men without uniforms, then mounted their horses and rode away up Gap Creek toward the mountains with their officers in the lead to find Ferguson.[44]

The men who led this force of volunteers against Ferguson were notable men. Although they were generally not backwoodsmen themselves, they had strength of character and tough demeanor to lead these frontiersmen in battle. One such man, the "portly, balding, droopy-eyed, yet determined-looking" Isaac Shelby, the son of Evan Shelby from Wales, was born near North Mountain, Maryland, in present day Washington County, Maryland, on December 11, 1750.[45] At age 21 Shelby went into the cattle business in the western Allegheny Mountains and with his family moved to Holston County, Virginia. Indian trouble led him to join the local militia in 1774 and at Point Pleasant in October of that year, as second in command of his father's company, Lieutenant Shelby was distinguished for his gallantry. Having defeated the Indians, the company was turned into a garrison until July of 1775 when it was disbanded by Lord Dunmore to avoid any patriot leanings.

In 1776 Shelby was involved in exploring the wilds of Kentucky, commercial surveying and purchasing tracts of land from the Cherokees. He was commissioned a captain in 1777 and Governor Patrick Henry appointed him commissary of supplies for the various frontier garrisons. He supported the Continental Army, joined the Virginia Legislature in 1779, and was commissioned a major by Governor Thomas Jefferson to escort the commissioners extending the boundary line between Virginia and North Carolina. The new boundary put Shelby's home in North Carolina, and he was then appointed colonel and magistrate of Sullivan County. When 1780 rolled around, Shelby entered service after the fall of Charles Town, and with the pleading of Colonel Charles McDowell, Shelby raised some 200 mounted riflemen for the patriot cause. Shelby fought with McDowell's forces at Fort Thicketty, at the second battle of Cedar Springs, and at Musgrove's Mill.[46]

The prominent family of William Campbell goes

back to near the end of the reign of Queen Elizabeth, about 1600, when this branch of the Campbell family immigrated to Ireland from Scotland. After generations, in 1726 John Campbell came with his family of 12 children to Lancaster County, Pennsylvania. Three years later John moved to Augusta County, a rich valley of Virginia with three of his sons. One of the sons, Patrick, later was to father Charles Campbell who was to become a prominent pioneer farmer in the Augusta Valley. He eventually married Miss Buchanan and from this union came William Campbell, born in 1745. When his father died, William at age 22 decided to move his mother and four young sisters to the frontiers of Holston and settled on the fine plantation called Alpenvale, at the present day town of Abingdon, Virginia. In 1773 William Campbell was appointed a justice of Fincastle County and the next year a captain in the militia. William raised a company and joined with Colonel Christian's regiment and supported operations against the Indians into Ohio.

Campbell joined with his fellow frontiersmen in the patriot movement in 1774. On January 20, 1775, William Campbell joined with other leaders at Holston settlement in sending a pronouncement to the Continental Congress declaring that

> If no pacific measures shall be proposed or adopted by Great Britain, and our enemies attempt to dragoon us out of those inestimable privileges which we are entitled to as subjects, and reduce us to slavery, we declare that we are deliberately and resolutely determined never to surrender them to any power upon earth at the expense of our lives. These are our real, though unpolished, sentiments of liberty and loyalty, and in them we are resolved to live and die.

This event was three months before Lexington. In September 1775, he and his hunting-shirt riflemen marched to Williamsburg to join the First Regiment commanded by Patrick Henry. When Henry later resigned his command, Lieutenant Colonel Christian succeeded him. Campbell took part in the dislodging effort against Lord Dunmore at Gwynn's Island on July 9, 1776. In April 1780 Campbell was promoted to colonel and later served in the House of Delegates. In August 1780 Campbell and Colonel Preston took to the field commanding 150 men operating against loyalists around Wytheville and Round Meadows.[47] Campbell was a six-foot-tall redheaded Scotsman who brandished a broadsword.[48]

John Sevier, a descendent of an ancient French family, Xavier, was born on September 23, 1745, in Rockingham County in the Shenandoah Valley of Virginia. When the French and Indian War broke out in 1755, the Sevier family moved to Fredericksburg for safety reasons. Young John attended the Fredericksburg Academy there until the family returned to their burned-out home in the mountains. Then John was sent to school in Staunton, Virginia. Now considered a well-educated man for his day, John Sevier returned to the trading business with his father. At age 16 he married Miss Sara Hawkins, settled on a farm and engaged in expeditions against the Indians.

Sevier became known as a celebrated Indian fighter. He founded a village called New Market located six miles from his father's home, where he was engaged as a merchant, innkeeper and farmer. In 1772 Sevier was appointed a captain in the Virginia Militia by Governor Dunmore. The next year he moved his family to Holston County on the western slope of the Alleghany Mountains. In 1773 Dunmore began a war with the Shawnee and other tribes, with Sevier in support. Sevier took part in the great battle at Point Pleasant in October 1774 with some 1100 Virginia Militia against the Shawnees under Chief Cornstalk.[49]

Captain Sevier served in various roles as the Revolution evolved. As a representative for the united settlements to the North Carolina Convention at Halifax in 1776, he drew up the petition that was granted to annex to the colony of North Carolina the Watauga area. The area became known as the Washington District, or as known today, Tennessee. Sevier took part in various Indian engagements against the Cherokees, became county clerk and district judge and representative for Watauga in the North Carolina Legislature. In 1777 he became lieutenant colonel for Washington County and began recruiting his own militia. His principal duties were to guard against Indians, loyalists and horse thieves. In 1779 Sevier and his men moved to the center of the savage territory and managed to burn their villages and lay waste to the countryside.[50]

These proud frontier warriors headed out to defeat Ferguson almost due south to the head of Gap Creek, between Greer and Jenkins mountains, then turned eastward around the shoulder of Stone Mountain to Tiger Valley. They crossed between Fork Mountain and Ripshin Ridge, and up the narrow yet swift Doe River. The Doe River had its source at the top of Roan Mountain. They made 20 miles the first day and made camp in native grass at a large rock jutting out of a hill. On the next day, Wednesday, September 27, they marched up the Doe to the actual foot of the mountain. At the bottom of Round and Yellow mountains, they decided that it would be impossible to drive cattle to the peaks ahead, so they halted after only four miles and slaughtered the cattle immediately. Now unencumbered, they took an old hunting trail known as "Bright's Trace" up the Carver Gap.

Their march up the rugged slope to the summit of Roan Mountain was resumed on Thursday, the 28th. Near the top they ran into colder air, with dark clouds hiding the mountain tops. Here they found some new-fallen snow up to their ankles. At the "Bald of the Roan" the militia found a broad, level plain of hundreds of acres of beautiful land. As the men looked out through the clouds, they saw a beautiful high plateau of the Blue Ridge stretched out for 40 miles wide at this point, with valleys no lower than 3000 feet above sea level. The frontiersmen called the range the "Yellow Mountains." They camped there for the night as they fired off their guns, cleaned and reloaded them. Colonel Shelby even held a full-dress parade of his men. Unfortunately for the patriots, two men, James Crawford and Samuel Chambers, deserted the patriot force and eventually made their way to Ferguson's camp at Gilbert Town.

Alerted to the desertions, the patriot officers decided to take a different route from the chosen one. Colonel Charles McDowell with a small number of men took the easy route by way of Carter Creek and Roan Valley, with orders to return with any word of Ferguson's movements. The main body headed eastward along the side of Round Bald. After only two miles they camped at a spring at Elk Hollow at 5200 feet elevation in the still-cold air. The day dawned as the men rode down Elk Hollow Branch to Roaring Creek, following it to North Toe River, a drop of 1000 feet. Now the temperatures moderated. They slowly descended down the west bank of the Toe River, stopping for lunch at a spring. By night they camped at the mouth of Grassey Creek, having achieved a distance of 20 miles. The next morning, Friday, September 29, they moved up the valley of Grassey Creek to the southeast, where the creek leaves the Toe and meanders to a junction with the South Toe River and back to the west to become the Nolichucky River. The force emerged from the mountains near Jonesborough, the place where Sevier and Shelby had previously met to plan the expedition.

Marching uphill for 10 miles, they reached the eastern crest of the Blue Ridge, overlooking Hawksbill Mountain, with rugged Grandfather Mountain rising to the left. As another precaution, the army now divided. Colonel Campbell and his Virginians headed south into Turkey Cove, using a trail six miles south of Wofford's Fort. The others moved east to North Cove where they camped for the night. Colonel McDowell then rejoined the main body. On the morning of Saturday the 30th, the patriot main army climbed over Linville Mountain and moved south to the head of Paddy Creek. There Campbell, deciding that no trap was in place, rejoined with the main force. Together they moved down the creek to the Catawba. Then they headed eastward past the mouth of the Linville River to the fields of Quaker Meadows, the home of Charles and Joseph McDowell. The frontier army was now some 4500 feet below the Bald of the Roan, as "summer had returned."[51]

Meanwhile, back on September 27, Ferguson had left Gilbert Town with intentions to catch Clarke's refugees from Augusta. He moved to Green River in present day Polk County to set up camp at James Step's House. On Saturday, September 30, the two patriot deserters, Crawford and Chambers, reached Ferguson and informed him that the frontier militias were heading his way. Ferguson was concerned, for he had allowed many of his loyalist ranks to go on furlough to the surrounding areas. Realizing his predicament, Ferguson immediately sent riders to hurry the men back to him, and to Lord Cornwallis in Charlotte and to Lieutenant Colonel Cruger in Ninety Six with messages discussing his situation and asking for reinforcements. On Sunday, October 1, he visited Baylis Earle's Plantation on the North Pacolet, which his men plundered. Then he marched north to Denard's Ford on the Broad River, where he camped for the night. At this place Ferguson issued the following strange proclamation to the local patriots:

> Denard's Ford, Broad River.
> Tryon County, October 1, 1780.
>
> Gentlemen: Unless you wish to be eaten up by an inundation of barbarians, who have begun by murdering an unarmed son before the aged father, and afterwards lopped off arms, and who, by these shocking cruelties and irregularities, give the best proof of their cowardice and want of discipline—I say, if you wish to be pinioned, robbed, and murdered, and see your wives and daughters in four days abused by the dregs of mankind—in short, if you wish or deserve to live and bear the name of men, grasp your arms in a moment and run to camp.
>
> The Back-water men have crossed the mountains. McDowell, Hampton, Shelby, and Cleveland are at their heads, so that you know what you have to depend upon. If you choose to be degraded forever and ever by a set of mongrels, say so at once, and let your women turn their backs upon you and look out for the real men to protect them.
>
> Patrick Ferguson, Major 71st Regiment.[52]

The next day, anticipating an attack at any moment, Ferguson marched only four miles before settling down his forces for the evening with arms in hand. At four o'clock the following morning of Tuesday, October 3, the march continued for 20 miles on a route north of the Broad River. They crossed at Second Broad River at Camp's Ford, and Sandy Run Creek at Armstrong's House, stopping near Tate's Plantation on Buffalo Creek.[53] That night Ferguson made the fateful decision to fight the patriots even with no reinforcements, as it was explained in a letter to Cornwallis. He said if the enemy had numbers "within bounds," he would take strong ground and meet his attackers head on.[54]

After reaching the eastern foothills at the Catawba River and at Quaker Meadows on Saturday, September

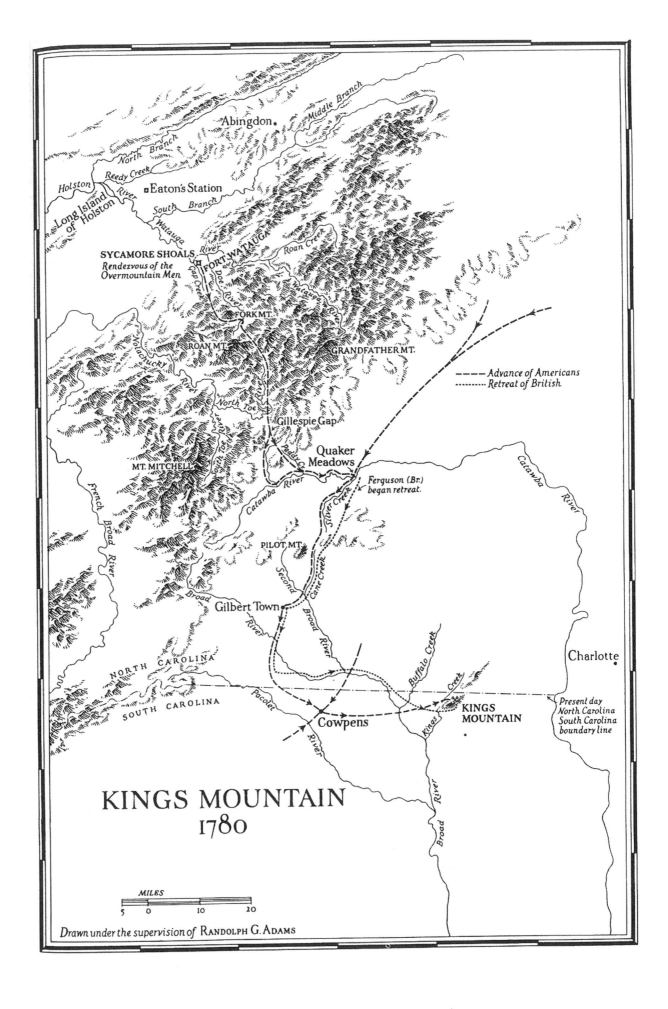

Abingdon

Middle Branch

North Branch

Reedy Creek

Holston

Long Island of Holston

□ Eaton's Station

Holston River

South Branch

Watauga

Roan Creek

SYCAMORE SHOALS
Rendezvous of the Overmountain Men

FORT WATAUGA

Gap Creek

Doe River

Watauga River

FORK MT.

ROAN MT.

GRANDFATHER MT.

Nolachucky River

North Toe

− − − *Advance of Americans*
· · · · · *Retreat of British*

Gillespie Gap

MT. MITCHELL

South Toe

Paddis Cr.

Quaker Meadows

Catawba River

Ferguson (Br.) began retreat.

Silver Creek

Catawba River

French Broad River

PILOT MT.

Second Creek

Charlotte

Broad River

Cane Creek

Buffalo Creek

Broad River

Gilbert Town

NORTH CAROLINA

Pacolet

SOUTH CAROLINA

Kings Creek

Present day North Carolina South Carolina boundary line

Cowpens

KINGS MOUNTAIN

River

Broad River

KINGS MOUNTAIN
1780

MILES

5   0   10   20

Drawn under the supervision of RANDOLPH G. ADAMS

30, the frontier militia was joined by some 350 men from Wilkes and Surry counties in North Carolina under the command of Major Joseph Winston and Colonel Benjamin Cleveland.[55] The force set out on their march on a bright and fair Sunday morning, October 1. By noon they had passed Brindletown. After they had traveled 18 miles, they set up camp in a gap at South Mountain. That evening the rain started and continued throughout the next day, causing the troops to remain in camp all day. They were now only 16 miles from Gilbert Town.[56]

Colonel Benjamin Cleveland, who was born in Bull Run, Virginia, in Prince William County in May of 1738, was reputed to have been a better hunter and Indian fighter than Daniel Boone. He was also well known to be a ruthless man. The Cleveland family goes back to an ancient group who took their names from the tract of land by the same name in North Riding of Yorkshire, England. At a young age Ben showed his drive for action and his bravery. At age 12 he ran off some drunken rowdies who had come to his home while his parents were away. Ben became more of a hunter than a farmer, and eventually joined in the French and Indian War. He married and in 1769 his family moved to North Carolina at the foot of the Blue Ridge Mountains at Roaring Creek of the Yadkin River.

After much exposure in dealing with Indians on various hunting expeditions and other backwoods activities, Ben took up the cause of the patriot movement in 1775 when he joined with Colonel James Moore in countering loyalist activities in North Carolina as a captain. In 1776 he was engaged in operations against the Indians in the western frontier, and in 1778 he was made a colonel of the militia and representative in the House of Commons. Cleveland had taken part in the battle for Georgia in 1778-1779 under General Rutherford. Back in North Carolina he worked against loyalists, and was involved in capturing and hanging notorious enemy leaders and outlaws in the New River region.[57]

Accompanying Cleveland was the 34-year-old Joseph Winston. The Winston family, originally from Yorkshire, England, had migrated to Virginia from Wales. On June 17, 1746, Joseph Winston was born in Louisa Country, Virginia. At age 17 Winston joined a company of Rangers to fight Indians and soon gained a name for himself as a gallant and courageous fighter under fire. Around 1769 he moved to Town Fork of the Dan River in North Carolina. By 1775 he had become a member of the Hillsborough Convention and in the next year fought against the Scots loyalists at Cross Creek. That same year he became a Ranger—warden for the forests of Surry County—and a major in the militia. In 1777 he was elected to the House of Commons and became the commissioner assigned to deal with the Cherokee Indians. Before serving with Colonel Cleveland, Winston had worked with Colonel Davidson's expedition against loyalist Colonel Bryan.[58]

While encamped, the issue of overall command leadership came up during a meeting of the officers. With Colonel Charles McDowell presiding as the senior officer by date of commission, it was suggested that since there were leaders from several states, there was no obvious commander with leadership rights. While numerous reasons were given, the simple fact was that Colonel McDowell was not considered to be much of a battlefield commander. Shelby considered him too cautious, while Cleveland and Winston considered his reputation as an "armchair general" to be true. As a face-saving move, and to clear up the issue, it was suggested that a messenger be sent to General Gates in Hillsborough to request that a general officer be assigned to lead them into battle. The Gates letter dated from "Rutherford County, Camp near Gilbert Town, October 4, 1780" was signed by Cleveland, Shelby, Sevier, Hampton, Campbell and Winston with the closing words, "Your most obedient and very able servants."[59] McDowell agreed to personally take the letter to Gates, leaving his brother, Major Joseph McDowell, in charge of his men. The hope was that Gates would name General Morgan to lead the patriots.

In the meantime, as soon as Charles McDowell was out of camp on his 200-mile trek to Gates, another council meeting was called. Command representatives proposed that they would hold daily council meetings to resolve decisions required. Colonel Shelby was not at all satisfied with this arrangement since the force was only 18 miles from Gilbert Town where Ferguson was supposedly located. He recommended a prompt decision, and thus presented that Colonel Campbell should be named the overall commander since he had supplied the greatest number of men in their party, 450, and was "known to be a man of common sense and devoted to the cause." The officers agreed to Campbell, but they retained their right to set policy at daily council meetings.[60]

On the Tuesday morning of October 3, while still at South Mountain, the officers formed the men in a circle and Colonel Cleveland gave them a stirring speech intended to raise their spirits:

> Now, my brave fellows, I have come to tell you the news. The enemy is at hand, and we must stand up at them. Now is the time for every man of you to do his country a priceless service—such as shall lead your children to exult in the fact that their fathers were the conquerors of

Opposite page: King's (Kings) Mountain, 1780. (*Atlas of American History.*)

Ferguson. When the pinch comes, I shall be with you. But if any of you shrink from sharing in the battle and glory, you can now have the opportunity of backing out and leaving, and you shall have a few minutes for considering the matter.

Colonels McDowell and Shelby made similar addresses, with the message made clear that "those who desired to back out should step three paces in the rear." Not one man accepted the offer to back off. Shelby then gave instructions to the men:

> When we encounter the enemy, don't wait for the word of command. Let each one of you be your own officer and do the best you can. If in the woods, shelter yourself and give them Indian play. The moment the enemy gives way, be on the alert and strictly obey orders.[61]

This event served to instill great confidence in the mission and that they could trust their fellow men who would be standing next to them in the coming engagement. The men were dismissed and told to prepare rations and be ready to march in three hours.[62]

On the morning of October 3 the patriot force pushed eastward, and according to 16-year-old James Collins, "We traveled all that night and the next day through heavy rains."[63] The following day they reached a location near the mouth of Cane Creek and outside Gilbert Town. It was then that they were joined by club-footed Jonathan Hampton, who presented the news that Ferguson had retreated from the town.[64] Soon a party of 30 Georgians rode up with Major William Candler and Captain Johnston, both refugees from serving under partisan fighter Colonel Elijah Clarke at Augusta. Word was that Ferguson had gone some 60 miles southward toward Ninety Six, which was some 100 miles away. A council of officers was held and it was decided that they would follow Ferguson's retreat to the British post at Ninety Six in an attempt to attack him before he got there. The patriots continued their march following the enemy track to Denard's Ford on the Broad River. At this point they lost track of Ferguson's trail, but continued on to Alexander's Ford on the Green River.[65]

Another body of patriot militia had also been forming in the Carolinas over the same period as the current frontiersmen's expedition. When Colonel James Williams had been commissioned "brigadier general" by Governor Nash as a result of carrying Musgrove's Mills prisoners to Hillsborough, he asked for permission to recruit 100 men to form his command. Williams made his call for men on September 23 with the place of rendezvous being Higgins' Plantation in Rowan County. With him were two well-known officers, Colonel Brandon and Major Samuel Hammond, and the 70 men who gathered there.

Camped at the South Fork of the Catawba River on October 2, near Williams' new command, was a detachment under colonels Edward Lacey and Hill. Colonel Edward Lacey from Pennsylvania had run away from home at age 13 and joined the pack horse unit for Braddock's army. When his father finally found him and returned him home, he ran away again and this time came to South Carolina. Lacey had served with Sumter at Rocky Mount, Hanging Rock and Fishing Creek.[66] This detachment was originally part of Sumter's force when Sumter had returned to the field after the defeat at Fishing Creek.

At that time Colonel Lacey had been sent into the country to recruit in what is now Chester and York counties. Lacey and Hill were presently intending to join up with Davidson and the North Carolina Militia having crossed the Tuckaseegee Ford a few miles north of Charlotte. When they were confronted by "General Williams" and ordered to place themselves under him, they flatly refused. After some heated discussion, Williams departed. An express to Davidson was sent which yielded a reply through Colonel Charles McDowell indicating that the frontiersmen were heading to attack Ferguson. Lacey and Hill immediately decided to abandon their plans to join Davidson, and planned to join with the frontiersmen against Ferguson. They crossed the Catawba River at Beattie's Ford in route to the west.[67]

That same day, October 2, a party of some 60 men from the Gilbert Town area under the command of colonels Graham and Hambright joined the South Carolinians, Lacey and Hill. On advice from Colonel Hill that evening Lacey agreed that it might be better to join with Williams in the coming engagement. Lacey then proposed that the troops be set up into three divisions — Lacey and Hill with the South Carolinians, Graham and Hambright with the North Carolinians, and Williams with his own militia now joined by a company led by Captain Roebuck. The next morning the proposal was rejected by Williams, who believed only he had the right of full command. Williams was warned not to try to join with the other forces. From this point forward, the situation of troop movement between Lacey and Williams would not improve until the frontiersmen patriots soon joined all. News soon arrived that the frontiersmen were advancing and on the next day, October 5, it was learned that Ferguson had sent a dispatch to Cornwallis asking for reinforcements and indicating that he had pitched his tents at a strong position.

During that day Colonel Hill was informed that Williams and Brandon had disappeared toward the mountains. Strangely the two men returned after sunset when they were immediately questioned by Hill where they had been. Williams first resisted, but soon gave in and explained that they had visited the frontiersmen on their march from Gilbert Town. Williams indicated that the men expected them to join them at the Old Iron Works at Lawson's Fork in what is today Spartanburg County, South Carolina. Hill remarked that such a march would be out of the way of Ferguson's advance. Looking rather embarrassed ,Williams soon admitted that he had made a deception in order to direct the frontiersmen toward Ninety Six rather than to Ferguson. Colonel Hill remarked, "I then used the freedom to tell him that I plainly saw through his design, which was to get some of his property, and plunder the Tories." Hill informed Colonel Lacey of Williams' admission and that someone must warn the frontiersmen of Williams' deception. Since Hill was still suffering from the wound he received at Hanging Rock — still carrying his arm in a sling — Lacey agreed to ride to the patriots.[68]

Meanwhile, Ferguson waited for intelligence of the frontiersmen at Tate's Plantation for two days. While there, "an old gentlemen called on him, who disguised the object of his visit." Ferguson was soon convinced that the man was a real loyalist and, unknowingly, he gave the "spy" information that he intended to fight the rebels at King's Mountain. The next day, the spy rode northeast 20 miles to the camp of colonels Hill and Lacey and General Williams on Cherry Mountain. Armed with this new intelligence and the knowledge gained from General Williams' attempt to divert the frontiersmen to Ninety Six, that night Colonel Lacey made his way to the frontiersmen and communicated his news to Colonel Campbell and others. At first Lacey had doubted the gentleman too, but eventually he came to believe the truthfulness of his statements, and thus gave convincing word to Campbell. By agreement, it was decided that they would join their forces without delay at Cowpens, to march against Ferguson.[69]

On Friday morning, October 6 at four o'clock, Ferguson renewed his march. He proceeded up the "Old Cherokee Ferry road between the waters of Buffalo and King's Creek until he came to the forks near where now is Whitaker's Station" on the railroad. There he took the right fork across King's Creek, through the mountain pass and on to the direction of Yorkville. After crossing a creek on the right of the road, he came to King's Mountain, some 16 miles from Tate's Plantation.[70] There he pitched his camp and exclaimed that he "had selected his ground and that he defied God Almighty and all the rebels out of hell to overcome him."[71]

During this last day of travel, Ferguson issued the following letter to Cornwallis:

> My Lord: A doubt does not remain with regard to the intelligence I sent your lordship. They are since joined by Clarke and Sumter, [and have] become an object of some consequence. Happily their leaders are obliged to feed their followers with such hopes, and so to flatter them with accounts of our weakness and fear that if necessary I should hope for success against them myself; but numbers compared, that must be doubtful.
>
> I am on my march toward you by a road leading from Cherokee Ford, north of King's Mountain. Three or four hundred good soldiers, part dragoons, would finish the business. Something must be done soon. This is their last push in this quarter, etc.
>
> Patrick Ferguson

Unfortunately for Ferguson, these last two dispatches, of September 30 and October 6, would not reach Lord Cornwallis in time to affect the events to come. The September 30th letter was sent via Abraham Collins and Peter Quinn. On their way toward Charlotte these two riders, disguising their intentions, happened to stop at the home of a patriot, Alexander Henry, for refreshments. By renewing their journey with haste, the Henry family became suspicious and Mr. Henry's son immediately took off after the two couriers. In order to avoid the pursuing Henry sons, Collins and Quinn took a more circuitous route and did not arrive at Cornwallis' headquarters until the morning of October 7. Ferguson's letter of October 6 fell into patriot hands and never reached Cornwallis at all.[72]

That same day at sunset, after marching 20 miles, colonels Lacey, Hill and Graham and General Williams, with their force of 400 men, arrived at Cowpens, South Carolina. Cowpens was located at a midpoint between the Broad and Pacolet rivers in what is now Spartanburg County, some four miles below the North Carolina line. Soon the frontiersmen arrived at the Cowpens bivouac to join the South Carolinians. The combined patriot force was now some 1100 men, and nearly all were armed with rifles. A wealthy English loyalist, Hiram Saunders, who raised cattle there, owned the cowpens or ranches. Saunders was at home that day and was in bed with a sickness, from which he was pulled and treated roughly. Saunders was interrogated as to what time Ferguson had passed that place. He responded by saying that Ferguson had not passed that way, and if they could find evidence of the contrary, they could hang him or what ever they wanted. The search turned up nothing. Several of Saunders' cattle were immediately shot and slaughtered to feed the hungry troops after cooking. Also, 50 acres of corn nearby was harvested in 10 minutes and fed to the horses.[73]

Resting at Cowpens, the militia was joined by Joseph Kerr, who was a master spy in the service of Colonel McDowell. Having been crippled since birth and therefore unable to serve in the usual manner, Kerr had offered his services to McDowell in the role of spy earlier in the year. Posing as a beggar, his usual masquerade, Kerr had visited Ferguson at Peter Quinn's Plantation, where he had stopped to eat at noon that day, only six hours earlier. Kerr revealed that Ferguson had some 1500 men and was at that time only six miles from King's Mountain. Orders were given to break camp immediately. Campbell sent out scouts to pinpoint the exact location of the enemy. Kerr had also indicated that a large body of loyalists was encamped only four miles from their location. Though he was most interested in Ferguson's force, Campbell detached Ensign Robert Campbell with 80 men to investigate. The ensign's unit later returned after finding the enemy camp deserted.[74]

A council meeting was called and it was decided that the most select men, with the best horses and best shots, were to press Ferguson in this pursuit since they were so close. Many of the men had been rather worn out by the trip from the Blue Ridge, and had sore feet and other maladies. The select group of mounted riflemen was around 910 men. At 8 P.M. the mounted column finally departed Cowpens, moving east toward the Broad River and to King's Mountain. Enoch Gilmer, the designated scout, was sent ahead to see if the river crossing was safe. Campbell's Virginians became lost and it was necessary to send out men the next morning to round them up. That night was dark, with no moon. Soon it began to rain. Based on their orders to keep the powder dry, the men wrapped their rifles with blankets and even their shirts to keep them dry. Gilmer returned to give the all clear for the crossing. Eventually, around sunrise, the frontiersmen reached the Broad River, where they crossed the high river in the rain. They had come some 18 miles from Cowpens and were still nearly 15 miles from King's Mountain. Scout Gilmer was sent ahead of the column again to find the enemy.[75]

Riding at a slow pace ahead of their men, the American officers reached the former encampment of Ferguson some three miles above their crossing location at Cherokee Ford. The men were allowed to stop for a snack from their saddlebags or wallets. The rain started to fall so heavily that Campbell, Sevier and Cleveland decided that the men and horses were in no condition to continue until they were refreshed. Shelby protested, exclaiming, "By God, I will not stop until night, if I follow Ferguson into Cornwallis' lines." The militia continued the march and after a mile was traversed, a local revealed that Ferguson was only seven miles ahead of them and motionless. With the positive news the men stopped grumbling. Suddenly the rain stopped and the sun broke through as a cool breeze started.

After another two miles, several of Sevier's men came upon a house where they sought information. A young girl pointed to the wooded ridge and said that Ferguson was there some three miles away. Out the back behind the house Sevier's men spotted Gilmer's horse tied up to a gate. It happened that Gilmer was inside having a hearty meal. Soon Colonel Hambright, Major Chronicle

and Campbell gained intelligence from the 14-year-old John Ponder, the brother of a reported loyalist, that Ferguson was wearing a checkered shirt as a duster over his glittering uniform. Hambright, a German native and long-time resident of Pennsylvania and later North Carolina, remarked, "Well boys, when you see dot man mit a pig shirt on over his clothes, you may know who him is and mark him mit your rifle." It was mid-afternoon as the sun shone brightly on the oaks and maples. The word was passed among the patriots, "Fresh prime your guns," and the countersign is "Buford."[76]

Within one mile of the mountain, the militia came upon a patriot, George Watkins, who had been released as a prisoner by Ferguson. Watkins revealed the very latest intelligence on the position of Ferguson on the mountain. The officers, who made sure the details were communicated to the volunteers, made a brief halt. The American forces were to surround Ferguson on King's Mountain and shoot them up the mountain. Just after 3 P.M. the patriot attackers arrived at the base of the mountain. They "tied all their loose baggage to their saddles, fastened their horses, and left them under charge of a few men, and then prepared for an immediate attack," according to Shelby. The men were instructed by one officer on how to proceed:

> I will show you by my example how to fight.... Fire as quick as you can, and stand your ground as long as you can. When you can do no better, get behind trees, or retreat; but I beg you not to run quite off. If we are repulsed, let us make a point of returning and renewing the fight. Perhaps we may have better luck in the second attempt than the first.

With queasy stomachs, yet feeling a strange joy, the attackers scurried to the base of the mountain in four columns. Young James Collins recalled that "Here I confess I would willingly have been excused … but I could not swallow the appellation of coward." Shelby and Campbell took their force to the narrow end of the mountain on the southwestern end. Cleveland and Sevier surrounded the broadest end of the mountain on the northeast.[77] In the first column was the Campbell regiment in the right center with his 200 Virginians. The second column of 120 men commanded by Shelby was on the left center. Colonel Sevier's regiment, the third column on the right flank, consisted of 120 with Sevier, 90 men under McDowell and 60 men under Winston. The fourth column on the left flank was commanded by Colonel Cleveland and included 120 of Cleveland's troops, 60 from Williams' unit, 10 Georgia patriots, Graham's and Hambright's 50 troops and Lacey's and Hill's 100 South Carolinians. The largest contingent of the patriot force at King's Mountain was the 510 men from North Carolina.[78]

Ferguson's force consisted of about 1100 men, made up mostly of 1000 loyalist militia from North and South Carolina. He also had some 100 Provincials dressed in scarlet coats and white breeches from the King's American Regiment from the New York area, and the Queen's Rangers and the New Jersey Volunteers. With Ferguson were his two most dependable officers, Captain Abraham de Peyster of the New Jersey Volunteers and Captain Alexander Chesney of the South Carolina Loyalists. The North Carolina Loyalists were commanded by Colonel Ambrose Mills. Ferguson, the only British officer present at the battle, had his own cook and two mistresses with him at King's Mountain. One mistress, "Virginia Sal," had red hair and would be killed. The other mistress was "Virginia Paul."[79]

The King's Mountain battlefield was situated one and one-half miles below the North Carolina border in York County on a hill along a 16-mile mountain range. It rises some 60 feet above the surrounding country plateau, with a rather flat top measuring 600 yards long and from 60 to 100 yards wide and tapering to the southwest. Ferguson, who sat atop the mountain on this rainy October 7th day waiting for the Americans to arrive, chose this place for the upcoming battle. Pickets had been deployed at the bottom of the hill to keep watch for the frontiersmen. Ferguson's troops confidently "lounged about in their tents, hauled supplies from their wagons, or cleaned their weapons." Just before the Americans had surrounded the mountain in mid-afternoon Captain Alexander Chesney rode to all the pickets and returned to the mountain summit to report to Ferguson that all was well.[80]

The battle began from the north side of the mountain when Shelby's column began firing. Shelby cried, "Press on to your places and your fire will not be lost," as his men struggled to get in position. Colonel Campbell's men reached their assigned positions before Shelby's group as Campbell tore off his coat, waved his sword, and yelled, "Here they are my boys; Shout like hell and fight like devils." The patriots started a fierce frontier Indian yell as a war cry. Ferguson's men were totally surprised. Some of the pickets had been eliminated without an opportunity to alert the other loyalists. Hearing the familiar shouts, de Peyster turned to Ferguson and commented, "Things are ominous. Those are the same yelling devils I fought at Musgrove's Mill." At the top of the hill Ferguson's men scrambled to form a line around the crest to the roll of drums and blast of Ferguson's silver whistle.[81]

It took some five minutes to get the remaining patriot troops into position at the base of the mountain and firing, while Shelby's and Campbell's columns were already fighting. The mountainsides were thick with foliage and trees all the way up to the top in all directions.

The rain-drenched low-lying ground in their path slowed Colonel Cleveland's men. Lacey's and Hill's force of 400 South Carolinians approached on the most level side of the mountain, while Campbell's side was the roughest. Campbell's Virginians reached the summit of the mountain first, as they rode on horseback or climbed by foot between the trees and rocks. Ferguson ordered the first bayonet charge against Campbell's men, carried out by the Rangers and some loyalists. Those Virginians who held their ground were immediately thrusted through by the bayonets, as their comrades fled down the slopes. But as soon as they reached cover near the bottom, the patriots rallied with fierce rifle fire to stop the advancing enemy. This forced Ferguson's men back up the slope.

As the Rangers were forcing Campbell's men downward, Shelby's men were pressing them from the opposite side, the southwestern end of the mountain. This caused the Rangers and loyalists to cover both columns, which proved to be quite difficult. Soon Ferguson began to wonder if the advantage of their position on the mountain's summit was really an advantage at all. The top of the mountain was clear of trees and offered the perfect opening for accurate rifle fire. The patriots who reached the summit were firing from the edge of the clearing behind trees at the exposed loyalists.

Lacey's and Hill's men pressed forward. In the first wave of firing, Lacey's horse was shot from under him. Majors Chronicle and Hambright were also beginning to ascend on the northeast end. Right at the base of the mountain Major Chronicle was killed, but the men continued to advance. At the summit de Peyster charged with bayonets. Colonel Sevier's column reached the summit and attacked the enemy's left flank without a corresponding bayonet charge. Now his men were intermingled with the loyalists. Williams, who had been quite offended by the treatment he had received after earlier attempting to divert the entire patriot force to Ninety Six, had decided that he would not take part in the engagement. But as the events unfolded, he felt a sense of loyalty toward the cause and joined in with his unit.

Colonel Shelby continued to drive his men in the attack, and was heard to call out, "Come on, my boys — the old wagoner never yet backed out." Though he had only his small band of 120 North Carolinians, he had some experienced partisan officers like Roebuck, Brandon, Hammond, Hayes and Dillard. Major Samuel Hammond broke through the loyalist lines and caused havoc. Shelby's and Campbell's men had been driven down the mountain three times during their battle. The third time was almost a rout, as some of the men were bayoneted and some fell off the cliffs. During the last time a rumor began to carry throughout the force that Tarleton's Legion of Cavalry had arrived, which created much concern with the men. This false information was countered by the officers who rode among the troops and calmed them. Again, as soon as the enemy turned their backs at the bottom of the mountain, the patriot men began their ascent fighting back.

As time progressed, the Provincial Rangers and loyalists under de Peyster became weary and discouraged. It seemed nothing was at all permanent for them, as the patriot attackers seemed to always rebound. The ranks of the loyalist troops were beginning to thin out. On the southwestern end of the mountain they began to give way as Campbell's, Shelby's and Sevier's men advanced. By this point in the battle, Ferguson had been wounded in the left hand, but he continued to coolly call out orders and ride to and from the various fronts. Then he ordered de Peyster to reinforce a position some 100 yards ahead, but before they reached the position, the force was too thin to do much. Ferguson then ordered the cavalry to mount for an attack to support de Peyster. But as soon as the men mounted, they were shot down from deadly accurate rifle fire.

Ferguson, in vain, rode from end to end blowing his silver whistle trying to encourage his men to continue the brave fight. Slowly the patriots were overwhelming the loyalists. At this point a token white flag appeared in the open, but Ferguson rode over and cut it down. Then a second flag appeared, and the same thing happened. Realizing the futility of continuing the engagement, de Peyster, the second in command, urged Ferguson to surrender. But Ferguson indicated that he would never give up in the face of such a damned set of banditti. As Ferguson became satisfied that all was lost, and resolving that he did not want to fall into the hands of the rebels, he made a desperate attempt to break through the line and escape. In company with Colonel Vesey Husbands of the North Carolina Loyalists and Major Plummer of South Carolina, Ferguson charged the line. With sword in hand, as he slashed and cut, Ferguson was killed along with the others by the frontiersmen along the line.[82]

On Ferguson's death, James Collins wrote, "On examining the body of their great chief, it appeared that almost fifty rifles must have been leveled at him at the same time. Seven rifle balls passed through his body, both his arms were broken, and his hat and clothing were literally shot to pieces." One bullet had ripped into Ferguson's thigh and another shattered his crippled right arm. One shot penetrated his skull, sending blood down his face. With one foot still in the stirrup of his great white horse, the brave British warrior was dragged into the trees at the northeastern end of King's Mountain as he died. Tragically, soon Ferguson's dead body would be stripped naked as some frontiersmen, with joyous cheering, urinated on his corpse.

Now Captain de Peyster was in command. The patriots were firing at near point-blank range, and as young James Collins reported, "The dead lay in heaps on all sides, while the groans of the wounded were heard in every direction. I could not help turning away from the scene before me, with horror, and thought exulting in victory, could not keep from shedding tears."[83] With no hope of turning the tide of the battle, de Peyster raised the white flag and asked for quarter. There was general cessation of firing, but it was not total. Some of the men did not recognize the signal and continued firing. Others wished to avenge the likes of Tarleton's actions at the Waxhaws. Shelby attempted to stop the action by calling out for the loyalists to throw down their weapons. The loyalists continued to call out "Quarter! Quarter!" In frustration Shelby cried, "Damn you, if you want quarter, throw down your arms." Riding to within 15 paces of the enemy line, Shelby continued his demand. Now the loyalists were surrounded into a pocket 60 yards by less than 40 yards wide. They finally surrendered. Colonel Campbell called out for three huzzahs for liberty, which was immediately shouted out in joy. The battle had lasted 50 minutes.[84]

Sadly, more blood was to be shed this day. Just as the firing stopped, a loyalist party arrived from foraging and began firing at the patriots. General Williams was hit immediately and was severely wounded as he exclaimed, while still in his saddle swaying, to William Moore of Campbell's company, "I'm a gone man." Colonel Campbell was close at hand and ordered Williams' and Brandon's commands to fire. The order was obeyed as some 100 more loyalists were killed. Apparently Campbell had feared that perhaps Tarleton's men were near and that the prisoners might make their escape. It was a tragic event, and one that Campbell deeply regretted later. In a private conversation later to Shelby, Campbell responded in a low tone that "Sir, I cannot account for my conduct in the latter part of the action."[85]

The battle at King's Mountain was ended. The arms were then taken from the enemy and a strong guard placed around them. The surviving officers turned over their swords. Some 664 loyalists were prisoners, with 119 killed and around 123 wounded. The patriots simply left the wounded to die, as New York loyalist Anthony Allaire recorded, "They thought it necessary to move us sixteen miles."[86] The rest of Ferguson's force of around 190 were believed to have been out foraging and missed the battle. The patriot militia loss was officially set at 28 killed and 62 wounded. Seventeen baggage wagons were captured, but since the men wanted nothing to encumber them, they were drawn across the campfires and burned.

The next morning, a bright, brisk October 8, 1780, rumors still persisted that Tarleton's Legion was coming to rescue the loyalists. With frost still on the dead men and dead horses, preparations to depart continued that morning, and at 10 A.M. the march was started. Campbell, Shelby, Cleveland, Sevier, Hammond and Brandon, with the Virginians and North Carolinians guarding the prisoners, departed for the mountains of North Carolina. Among the prisoners was the surviving mistress of Ferguson, Virginia Paul, who stayed with the party until they reached Quaker Meadows where she disappeared into history. The captured loyalist arms, numbering between 1200 and 1500, were a problem to transport. It was decided that the strong prisoners would carry them.

Campbell took charge of a burial detail left behind to dispose of the dead. Two large pits were dug—one for patriots and another for loyalists. The bodies were sadly tumbled into the pits without ceremony. The work was accomplished in great haste, as the fear of Tarleton was in evidence. Some were not even buried below ground, as James Collins wrote:

> They were thrown into convenient piles and covered with old logs, the bark of old trees, and rocks; yet not so as to secure them from becoming a prey to the beasts of the forest or the vultures of the air; and the wolves became so plenty that it was dangerous for any one to be out at night, for several miles around; also, the hogs in the neighborhood gathered in to the place to devour the flesh of men, so much that numbers chose to live on little meat rather than eat their hogs, though they were fat. Half the dogs in the country were said to be mad and were put to death. I saw, myself, in passing the place a few weeks after, all parts of the human frame lying scattered in every direction."

The wounded were not cared for and in fact were left behind. Captain de Peyster recorded in his official report to Cornwallis:

> Our wounded are left at one Wilsons, four miles this side of the place of action. They are without body cloths or blankets, and I fear the man who attends them [is] without medicine and is not sufficiently capable.

The actions of the frontiersmen after the battle were no doubt disgraceful, but in the condition that war creates, it was not all that unusual. As a Scottish proverb proclaims, "War begins when hell opens." This battle was a civil action between loyalist and patriot American colonials, with Ferguson being the only British soldier present. These frontiersmen were volunteers, not truly trained and educated in the traditions of military "morality" or code of conduct. The victors had no practical way to transport the wounded except by wagon, which was deemed too slow to avoid the likes of "Bloody Tarleton" who was rumored to be on their heels.

Lord Cornwallis, a product of the cream of the British military system, was never particularly concerned about his wounded either. The frustrations of defeats at Charles Town and Camden had fired the spirits of these men. The indignities were opened for all to see. With the victory came the spoils of war. Samuel Talbot turned over Ferguson's mangled body and took his pocket pistol. The young loyalist and Ferguson's personal orderly, Elias Powell, took his silver whistle from his pocket. Sevier took home Ferguson's silken sash, while Cleveland was given his white stallion. Ferguson's valuable inscribed sword, with a hilt of silver, was the new property of William Lenior. Lenior later wrote that because of the victory at King's Mountain, "many militia officers procured swords who could not possibly get any before."[87]

Lacey and Hill, who still commanded Sumter's force, remained in the area at Bullock's Creek within six miles of King's Mountain waiting for Tarleton to arrive.[88] The main army marched 12 miles the first day and encamped near the eastern bank of the Broad River, north of Buffalo Creek. There on the deserted plantation of a loyalist named Walden, the patriots found sweet potatoes, which were fed to all the hungry warriors. Campbell's men joined the group that evening. By Wednesday, October 11, the army had moved some 32 miles and reached the neighborhood of Gilbert Town, at Colonel John Walker's place. Since no provisions were found in the area, the Virginians and North Carolinians moved on the 13th to camp at Bickerstaff's Plantation, located nine miles northeast from the present day Rutherfordton in North Carolina. There a complaint was made by Colonel Campbell that some of the prisoners were robbers, house burners, parole breakers and assassins. A court was quickly organized and with little real law prevailing in the trial, 12 prisoners were condemned to death. On October 14, nine prisoners were executed, one escaped and two were pardoned reportedly by Shelby. Among the hanged was Colonel Ambrose Mills, the commander of the North Carolina Loyalists.[89]

Then they marched to the Catawba River at Island Ford, and camped at Quaker Meadows. While camped the next day, word arrived that the Cherokees were about to attack. Sevier was designated to take most of the main force toward the mountains to counter the Cherokees. On October 16 the remains of the main army that did not go with Sevier reached the head of the Yadkin River, known as the Happy Valley. Down the Yadkin they moved past Fort Defiance to the Moravian settlements. On October 26 the army reached Bethabara near Salem, North Carolina. Colonels Campbell and Shelby moved to Gates' headquarters at Hillsborough to discuss the prisoner disposition, as Colonel Cleveland stayed back with the prisoners and men. The ranks of the prisoners had now thinned as many of them managed to escape on the march. By November only 130 of the original 664 prisoners were in custody. They were marched to Hillsborough and confined. The events of the battle were now concluded.[90]

The battle of King's Mountain was the turning point in the American Revolutionary War in the South. General Washington proclaimed in a general order that the battle was an important victory and "a proof of the spirit and resources of the country." Gates said the victory was "great and glorious" and continued with a more personal note that, "We are now more than even with the enemy." Congress resolved that it was a "high sense of the spirited and military conduct of Colonel Campbell, and the officers and privates of the militia under his command, displayed in the action of October the 7th, in which a complete victory was obtained."[91] On the battle, General Davidson wrote to General Sumner, "Ferguson, the great partisan, has miscarried."[92] Thomas Jefferson wrote, "That memorable victory was the joyful annunciation of that turn of the tide of success which terminated the Revolutionary War with the seal of independence."[93]

The defeat of the Scotsman, Lieutenant Colonel Patrick Ferguson, and his provincial and loyalist men at King's Mountain was largely due to the poor geography of the battle site. With the top naturally clear of trees and the approaches up the mountainsides providing protection of rocks and trees for the patriots as they ascended, it was almost impossible to maintain a permanent advantage. The accuracy and range of the frontiersmen's long rifles over the loyalists' muskets was another unique advantage. As the 16-year-old patriot James Collins recorded, "Their great elevation above us had proved to be their ruin; they overshot us altogether, scarce touching a man except those on horseback." Aside from the disadvantages of the terrain, the spirit and bravery of these Southern frontiersmen and their determined officers were surely the best advantage. It was Sir Henry Clinton who later wrote that the defeat at King's Mountain had "unhappily proved the first link in a chain of evils that followed each other in regular succession until they at last ended in the total loss of America."[94] For Lord Cornwallis, the British in the South and the loyalists, things would never be the same.

14

COWPENS

While Ferguson was being pursued and defeated at King's Mountain, Cornwallis was being harassed around the Charlotte area by Colonel William Davie, under orders from General Sumner "to remain always with the principal body in the direction between Salisbury & Charlotte, and by no means to risque being generally engaged." As Davie himself recorded, "no party of the enemy ventured out without being attacked, and often retired with considerable loss." Davie was correct in writing that "His Lordship began to feel the greatest distress, under this species of blockade, for provisions forage and all the necessary supplies of the army."[1] So tight was the blockade around Charlotte that Lord Rawdon wrote to Clinton, "By the enemy having secured all the passes on the Catawba, Lord Cornwallis ... received but confused accounts of the affair for some time: but at length the truth reached him...."[2]

Collins and Quinn, the men who had been sent by Ferguson from Tate's Plantation on September 30 to inform Cornwallis of the coming of the frontiersmen, had been delayed and did not reach Cornwallis until the very day of the battle at King's Mountain, October 7. Previously Cornwallis had become concerned regarding Ferguson's situation and he had urged Tarleton to look for Ferguson. Tarleton had pleaded his case not to move toward Ferguson because he was sick with fever. Even with the news from Collins and Quinn, Tarleton did not head out to find Ferguson until October 10 with light infantry, the British Legion of cavalry, and a three-pounder. Tarleton had marched some 15 to 20 miles to the ford just below the forks of the Catawba River when the sad news of Ferguson's defeat arrived. As Tarleton crossed the Catawba, he learned that the patriots had left the area near King's Mountain, except for Lacey and Hill who were believed to still be in the neighborhood. Surprisingly, Tarleton decided to stay in camp for the next three days without attacking.[3]

Shortly after Tarleton had left to look for Ferguson, news arrived at Cornwallis' headquarters that Ferguson's army was destroyed. Cornwallis was quite alarmed. The words of Tarleton best express the situation and thinking of Lord Cornwallis:

> The destruction of Ferguson and his corps marked the period and the extent of the first expedition into North Carolina. Added to the depression and fear it communicated to the loyalists upon the borders, and to the southward, the effect of such an important event was sensibly felt by Earl Cornwallis at Charlotte town. The weakness of his army, the extent and poverty of North Carolina, the want of knowledge of his enemy's designs, and the total ruin of his militia, presented a gloomy prospect at the commencement of the campaign. A farther progress by the route which he had undertaken could not possibly remove, but would undoubtedly increase his difficulties; he therefore formed a sudden determination to quit Charlotte town, and pass the Catawba river. The army was ordered to move, and expresses were dispatched to recall Lieutenant-colonel Tarleton.[4]

Thus, on the night of October 12, 1780, Cornwallis' forces marched out of Charlotte. Before 7 A.M. on the 13th, General Davidson dispatched a messenger to General Sumner that he had the day before "received Intelligence of a party of the Enemy's marching out of Charlotte towards Beger's Ferry on the Catawba River consisting of 800 with [one] Field piece." Davidson also reported that he had "a Report by a Man of Veracity just arrived from within 6 Miles that the Enemy have evacuated

Charlotte, and that last Night at 10 o' Clock the Rear of the Army passed Barnett's Creek, five miles beyond Charlotte on the road to Beggar's Ferry."

One informer of the news from Charlotte was a patriot Irish merchant, William McCafferty, who had stayed in Charlotte to save his property. He had led the British to "Barnetts Creek 5 Miles below Town, on the Road to Armours Ford." On the way he indicated to Major Graham that they were on the wrong road and it would be necessary for him to ride out to the left to find the correct road. When McCafferty was out of sight of the British, he turned around and headed to alert Davidson. Thanks to McCafferty the British army spent a terrible night in the dark and rain completely lost, stumbling about the "thick woods, briars, deep ravines, marshes, and creeks scarcely fordable." It was not until noon the next day that the British army reformed some seven miles below the town, having lost the "twenty waggons containing a large part of the baggage of the 71st regiment & legion Infantry."[5]

The British moved across the Catawba from Lancaster to Chester County at Landsford, westward across Fishing Creek, and then at a point some two or three miles from the present town of Chester crossing the Rocky Creek. Then the army turned south on the road to Winnsboro, South Carolina.[6] As the march continued, the rains, continuing for several days, turned the red-clay roads into sloppy quagmires as the men trudged as best they could. The miserable march, ending October 29, 1780, took 16 days, during which Cornwallis became sick with "bilious fever."

Two days before the Battle of King's Mountain, the Continental Congress passed a resolution declaring "that the Commander-in-Chief be and is hereby directed to appoint an officer to command the southern army, in the room of Major General Gates."[7] The resolution from the Continental Congress reached Washington's headquarters near Passaic Falls, New York, on October 13. He immediately wrote Nathanael Greene that "It is my wish to appoint You" and further explained that his desires concurred with those of the delegates from Georgia, North and South Carolina who had informed him of such on October 6. On October 15 General Washington wrote Congress, "Major General Greene is the Officer I shall nominate." Washington first added in his letter to Congress the remark, "I very sensibly feel this fresh mark of the confidence of Congress in leaving to me the appointment of a General Officer to so important a command," but, after reflection, he directed his military secretary to strike that last sentence. On October 31, the president of the Continental Congress, Samuel Huntington, wrote the following letter to Major General Nathanael Greene:

Sir:

You will receive herewith enclosed a copy of an act of Congress of the 30 inst. by which you will be informed that your appointment to the command of the Southern Army meets with their approbation; and that Major General the Baron de Steuben [sic] is directed to repair to that department under your command.

That the army for that department will consist of the entire regular regiments and corps raised or to be raised from the States of Delaware to Georgia inclusive until the further Orders of Congress or the Commander-in-Chief.

That all the powers given to General Gates while in that command are now vested in you, and acts of Congress during that period be considered as instructions to you in that department.

You, sir, are authorized to organize and employ the army under your command in the manner you shall judge most proper, subject to the control of the Commander-in-Chief; and it is earnestly recommended to the legislatures and executives respectively in that department to afford you every necessary assistance and support and you are authorized to call for the same....

The necessary information on this subject will be forthwith communicated to the supreme executive in the respective States in the Southern Department.

Be assured, sir, that my best wishes accompany you, that your command may be attended with desired success to the satisfaction of your country and your personal honor.

I am with sincere Esteem and Respect you most obedient and most humble servant.

Sam. Huntington, President[8]

The new commander of the Southern Department was born in a Quaker family on July 27, 1742, in the village of Potowomut, Rhode Island. Young Nathanael Greene was reared in a stern, yet caring, environment. His father, the preacher and spiritual leader of the surrounding Quaker community of East Greenwich, served to influence his offspring to live a life that would "glorify God by living upright, sober, and above all else, useful lives." Naturally Greene developed to be known as a true man of character. In 1770 Greene moved to Coventry, Rhode Island, where he took charge of the family's ironworks. This significant enterprise manufactured such items as anchors, chains, and other primarily maritime articles. Out of his experiences as a Quaker and business leader, Greene was now skillful in administration while presenting his most social manner as a born leader.

In 1774 he volunteered to serve with the Rhode Island Militia as a private. In the next year Greene was promoted from private to brigadier general and selected to lead his state's militia to assist the citizens of Boston during the unrest that followed the events at Lexington and Concord. In July of 1775 he met General Washington. Washington and Greene were to develop a special trust and respect for each other that would continue throughout the war. Greene's reputation around Boston was as a strict disciplinarian and focused leader with an appreciation for details. Greene required his men to always be properly dressed and required that "during the march no soldier be permitted to talk." An aide to Washington spoke of Greene that "He is beyond doubt a first-rate military genius, and one in whose opinions the General places the utmost confidence."

After the British evacuated Boston in March of 1776, Greene marched with Washington to New York. Arriving there on April 17, Washington placed the defenses of Long Island in Greene's hands. In the August battle at Long Island, Greene was too sick to take part, but after returning to health in September he was to serve with Washington in every engagement for the next three years. After New York fell, Greene retreated into Pennsylvania, later crossed the Delaware with Washington to attack the Hessian forces at Trenton, New Jersey, on Christmas Day 1776, spent the second winter of the war at Morristown, and then lived through the infamous third winter at Valley Forge with the Continental Army. Greene fought against Cornwallis at Brandywine in September 1777, Germantown in October of the same year and at Monmouth Court House in June 1778.

In 1778 Washington appointed Greene to be quartermaster general of the Continental Army. Though Greene carried out this role with superior skill, he was not particularly happy with the assignment. He remarked to Washington that "There is a great difference between being raised to an office and descending to one which is my case." In a letter to his brother he noted that "No one ever heard of a quartermaster in history." In spite of his reluctance in taking on his new role, he would turn out to be invaluable to the operations in the South. He managed some 3000 men including wagonmasters, clerks, foragemasters, and deputy quartermasters all engaged in transporting and providing the supplies that fed, clothed and even housed the army. William Moultrie wrote of Greene that "His military abilities, his active spirit, his great resources when reduced to difficulties in the field, his having been quarter-master general ... all these qualities combined together rendered him a proper officer to collect and organize an army that was broken up and dispersed."[9]

After serving for two and one half years in this thankless position as quartermaster general, Greene became so distressed when some in Congress accused him of lining his own pockets through his purchasing activities, that he wrote a "less than diplomatic" letter of resignation to the Continental Congress. Greene wrote:

> Administration seem to think it far less important to the public interest to have this department well filled and

arranged for than it really is, and as they will find it by future experience. My best endeavors have not been wanting to give success to the business committed to my care, and I leave the merit of my services to be determined hereafter by the future management of it under the direction of another hand.... The sacrifices I have made on this account, together with the fatigue and anxiety I have undergone, far over-balance all the emolument.... Nor would double the consideration induce me to tread the same path over again, unless I saw it necessary to preserve my country from utter ruin and disgraceful servitude.

Some members of the Continental Congress were outraged at Greene's use of the word "administration" and deemed it a "gross insult" by reference to the days when Britain "administration" attempted to further subjugate the American colonists. A motion to remove Greene from the army by Congress on August 5, 1780, did not carry, but he was replaced by a Colonel Pickering while a committee of five was set up to consider the next moves against Greene. Washington wrote to the Congress on this matter:

> Let me beseech you to consider well what you are about before you resolve, I shall neither condemn nor acquit General Greene's conduct.... My sole aim at present is to advise you of what I think would be the consequences of suspending him from his command in the line without a proper trial. A procedure of this kind must touch the feelings of every officer. It will show ... the uncertain tenure by which they hold their commissions.... It does not with you, I am sure ... arguments to prove that there is no set of men in the United States, considering as a body, that have made the same sacrifices of their interest in support of the common cause, as the officers of the American army....

The Congressional Committee did not act, and Greene was not suspended from the Continental Army. Greene was serving as the commander of West Point at his own request at the time of his appointment as the commander of the Southern Department.[10]

Meanwhile, after learning from General Davidson that the British had evacuated Charlotte, Sumner, who was camped at the forks of the Yadkin, wrote Gates that he would "recross the River Tomorrow, or early next Monday, with all the Troops at the place ... and march after the Enemy, so as to annoy as much as possible, preventing General Action." On the night of October 13 Davidson had marched to Charlotte. There he found that the British had apparently departed the town in great alarm, "from what circumstances uncertain." Some deserters told Davidson that Clinton had been defeated at West Point, while others talked of the rumor that the patriots had some 5000 men coming their way. The locals in Charlotte revealed that the British "left their Kettles on the fire; & twenty Waggons which they left 5 miles from town, with a quantity of Valuable loading [have] fallen into our hands."

As soon as Colonel Davie heard of the retreat, he immediately marched through Charlotte, and sent scouts ahead to find the British. Davie's men found the rear guard that "was composed of nearly half their Cavalry and marched in close order." The word was that the march was "so condensed and in such perfect order, that, though Davie marched parallel to them, at a distance of three quarters of a mile, it was impossible to attack them without encountering at the same time, their whole army." Unable to attack, Davie returned to Sugar Creek to gather provisions. On October 16 Davie reported to Sumner that Cornwallis' baggage had reached Old Nation's Ford at 3 P.M. the previous day as Davie was retreating. Tarleton, with 200 dragoons and 400 infantry, had crossed the river some two days before Cornwallis arrived at the ford. The river was high, and Davie, like Sumner, knew that they would be putting the pressure on Cornwallis. But Cornwallis did reach Winnsboro in retreat.

With Cornwallis now in Winnsboro, the North Carolina forces and the government could feel a short sigh of relief. In that state were now some 1000 militia under brigadier generals Davidson and Sumner, 900 men under Allen Jones, 300 commanded by Colonel Davie, with an additional 1400 troops under the frontier colonels William Campbell, Isaac Shelby, John Sevier, Charles McDowell and Benjamin Cleveland. General Gates commanded the remnants of the Maryland Line and the Delaware Continentals consolidated in a single regiment under Colonel Otto Williams of Maryland. Daniel Morgan of Virginia, who had been promoted to brigadier general, was given the Virginia Line, which had just arrived. Colonel William Washington commanded a reorganized cavalry from Virginia. In total, Gates had some 1400 Continentals under his control.[11]

General Greene conferred with Washington at Preakness, New York, just before he departed for his new assignment on October 23, 1780. In his discussions with the commander-in-chief, Greene had learned that Baron Von Steuben, the Prussian officer revered for his outstanding military training effort for the Continental Army, was to be assigned to Greene's command. In addition, he would gain the command of Lieutenant Colonel "Light Horse Harry" Lee with his dragoons and mounted infantry. Greene gained Washington's approval for a campaign to employ "hit-and-run" tactics similar to those being conducted by Sumner, Davie and Marion. The strategy was to force Cornwallis to continually defend his positions, rather than conquering new territory. Washington warned Greene that the region he was about to enter was crisscrossed by numerous formidable rivers and creeks, and that he should "direct particular attention to the boats." Greene was indeed to take his leader's advice in the coming campaign.[12]

Greene's first stop was at Philadelphia, where he gave the Congress a letter from Washington naming him as successor of Gates. The Congress was unable to provide any supplies for his struggling army since the public treasury was bare, and all they could do was to encourage him to seek assistance from the states. Greene sought assistance from Pennsylvania Governor Joseph Reed, but all he could provide was 1500 stand of arms. Greene tried to encourage the merchants of Philadelphia to furnish him 5000 suits of clothes for his army in payment for bills on France, but they declined.

In Annapolis Greene pleaded his case for support to the legislature that was conveniently in session at the time, but he was told they had neither money nor credit. News of the King's Mountain victory seemed to give the Marylanders a false hope of quick defeat over Cornwallis, which tended to complicate matters more. To continue to seek assistance, Greene left General Mordecai Gist behind in Annapolis to serve as his agent to forward any supplies he could gather. He directed Gist to "Make all your applications in writing, that it may appear hereafter for our justification that we left nothing unessayed to promote the public service."

After a short visit at Mount Vernon, Greene, with Baron Von Steuben, hurried south to Richmond where Greene had a personal meeting with the legendary red-headed Virginia governor, Thomas Jefferson. Jefferson told Greene that he had been trying to collect 100 wagons for his army for three weeks, but at present he had acquired only 18. While Greene was in Richmond from November 16 to 21, he acquired a healthy distrust of Jefferson's understanding of military matters. Even the citizens were a "lifeless and inanimate mass, without direction, or spirit to employ … for their own security."

At least one positive idea did emerge at Richmond. Greene and Jefferson came up with a scheme that would profoundly impact the future operations against Cornwallis in the Carolinas. It involved fitting out light boats with wheels for easier transport as they moved with the army from river to river. To use this new innovation, and to heed the warning from Washington regarding the number of rivers in the South, Greene engaged the young artillery officer from the Virginia line, Lieutenant Colonel Edward Carrington. He was to explore the Dan River for its uses for travel and retreat. Carrington had already conducted such work for Gates on the Roanoke River. Soon another unit under General Edward Stevens of the Virginia Militia was sent to explore the Yadkin and Catawba rivers, with similar instructions to determine distances between towns, the conditions of the roads, and determine the practicality of using flat-bottomed boats. The results of these excursions served Greene well. Weeks later General William Davidson would observe that Greene, who had never seen the Catawba River, knew more about it than men who had been raised on its banks. The genius of Greene's attention to details was already in evidence and it would soon serve him well when confronting Cornwallis.[13]

While Greene was still in Richmond, alarming news arrived that British Major General Alexander Leslie had landed with 2500 troops at Portsmouth. Actually Leslie and his army had arrived in the Chesapeake on October 20 under orders from Clinton "to proceed up the James River as high as possible in order to seize and destroy any magazines the Enemy may have at Petersburg, Richmond, or any of the places adjacent, and finally to establish a post on the Elizabeth river." Leslie was ordered to correspond with Cornwallis and to put himself under his command since the real purpose of the expedition was to support Cornwallis as a diversionary tactic to engage American troops away from operations in the Carolinas. Leslie's force had sailed from Sandy Hook on October 17 in transports, under the command of Captain George Gayton, along with the warships *Romulus, Blonde, Delight, Otter, Halifax* (the ex–*Ranger* of the Continental Navy), and the *Beaumont.*

Leslie described his situation in his letter to Clinton on November 4:

> We anchored in Chesapeake, after a most favorable passage, and the next day proceeded up as high as Lynnhaven. The day following [October 22] the shipping proceeded to Sewell's Point. The parties that landed found the inhabitants either unwilling or unable to give any satisfactory intelligence relative to Lord Cornwallis' army. The principal [information] that could be collected was that the country was acquainted with our destination some weeks before arrival, which had given them time to take measures to oppose us by erecting batteries on the banks of the narrow parts of James river, fortifying Richmond, and collecting a formidable militia...."

The same day Leslie wrote the above letter to Clinton, he also dispatched a messenger with an urgent note to Cornwallis. The messenger was captured on his way from Portsmouth to the Carolinas, and the note was promptly delivered to Jefferson. The note read: "My Lord, I have been here near a Week Establishing a Post. I wrote to you to Charles Town. And by another Messenger by Land. I cant hear for a certainty where you are. I await your orders...." Back on October 24, Lord Rawdon, acting as Cornwallis' agent while his commander was sick with a fever, wrote Leslie from "a camp near the Indian Lands, West of the Catawba River, South Carolina." Rawdon's letter included rather ambiguous instructions, but asked him to relay what his intentions were.

Jefferson was having his share of problems reacting to the threat of Leslie's invasion. While his actions during the war were heavily criticized by many, he attempted to deal with the situation. As he called up more militia, which increased the need for everything from clothing and arms to tents, he maintained an orderly approach to the situation. He kept Washington, Congress and Governor Lee of Maryland informed of the events and his defensive plans. In his letter of November 2 to Governor Lee, which discussed the rumor that a deserter indicated the British planned to eat Christmas dinner in Baltimore, Jefferson showed his knowledge of Leslie's movements with considerable insight:

> I rather believe that Ld Cornwallis had expected to have been in this state at this time, that they were intended to join him here; that his precipitate flight had left them without an object, and that they wait for further orders. But we have not enough data to confide in any opinion....

Political attacks on Jefferson for his supposed "negligence and incompetence" were controversial at the time. While there was some basis for complaint, many agreed that Jefferson did his best to handle the monumental problems in Virginia. The defending view of Jefferson's actions was expressed by the editor of a paper, who wrote: "The larger record shows that no war governor worked more devoutly than he against odds more completely insuperable. None administered a larger or more vulnerable territory."[14]

Leslie was in desperate want of information from Cornwallis. While he waited for his commander's orders, he disembarked only enough troops to take Hampton, Suffolk and then Portsmouth. Since numerous refugees had returned to Virginia with his force, he was careful about disturbing personal property in the region. Leslie's actions, and those of Commodore Gayton, were focused against public stores and property only. Later, on November 26, Jefferson acknowledged the British record in the Tidewater region:

> I must do their General and Commodore the justice to say that in every case to which their influence or attention could reach as far as I have been informed, their conduct was such as does them the greatest honor. In the few instances of unnecessary and wanton devastation, which took place, they punished the aggressors.

Meanwhile, Cornwallis at Winnsboro considered his situation and what to do with Leslie. Since he was in need of more troops to again attempt to invade North Carolina, Cornwallis ordered Leslie to join him. Dispatches from Cornwallis were sent via H.M.S. *Iris* to Leslie and Gayton with orders to move south, first to Wilmington,

North Carolina, and ultimately, to Charles Town. On November 22, 1780, Leslie and his troops, aboard Gayton's fleet, abruptly departed the Chesapeake area bound for operations in the Carolinas. Clinton was distressed when he heard the news of Leslie's departure, writing that he felt it was "an end of all golden dreams in Chesapeake." In the letter to Clinton dated January 3, 1781, Germain likewise expressed his concern for the striking event:

> You will have seen by several of my former letters what high expectations were entertained here of the important effects which the Expedition into the Chesapeak would have, not only as a cooperation with Lord Cornwallis, by facilitating his Progress through North Carolina, but in reducing the Rebel Force, by destroying their stores and cutting off their Resources and at the same time encouraging the King's troops doing their utmost to deliver themselves from the tyranny of the rebel dominion and to recover the country to His Majesty, you will therefore readily conceive how great must have been the concern and disappointment at finding Col. Ferguson's misfortune [King's Mountain] was of such fatal consequence as to make it necessary for Lord Cornwallis to require Gen. Leslie to quit the Chesapeake and proceed to Cape Fear….

Concerned over the situation with Leslie's departure, Clinton immediately conferred with Admiral Arbuthnot about the possibility of sending a new force to the Chesapeake. On December 30, just over a month after Leslie abandoned Portsmouth, a new force of 1600 British troops under the command of British General Benedict Arnold arrived in Hampton Roads aboard Captain Symonds' fleet.[15]

Greene, who departed Richmond on November 21, appointed Von Steuben to the post of military commander of Virginia and directed him to stay behind to forward all the supplies he could find southward. On November 27, General Greene, a man who had never traveled farther south than Maryland, arrived in Hillsborough expecting to find his army. There he learned that Gates had moved to Salisbury in hopes of finding better food supplies. After pausing to write several letters to Governor Abner Nash of North Carolina, Greene left Hillsborough to find Gates and the army. Soon Greene learned that Gates was in Charlotte.

On December 2 Greene finally caught up with Gates in the army's camp just outside the town. As Greene arrived, the men viewed him with much curiosity. Since past relations between Gates and Greene had not been friendly, it was expected that the encounter between the two would not be cordial. But Otto Williams wrote that Greene met Gates "with respectful sympathy and Gates, whose manners were those of a man of the world, returned his greetings with dignified politeness." It was noted that "Their conduct was an elegant lesson of propriety exhibited on a most delicate and interesting occasion."[16]

The following day, after a short change-of-command ceremony, Gates departed for Richmond, where the Virginia Assembly surprisingly voted him a resolution of gratitude for his past services. Fortunately for Greene, he did not have enough senior officers in Charlotte to convene a court of inquiry, which the Continental Congress had ordered for Gates' conduct at Camden. Gates was not only sad at losing his command, but he was mourning the loss of his only son at the time. Gates' command was ended.

Greene's new command was a sad one. In a letter to Joseph Reed of Pennsylvania, he describes the fate of the Continental and militia forces in the South:

> I overtook the army at Charlotte, to which place General Gates had advanced. The appearance of the troops was wretched beyond description, and their distress, on account of provisions, was little less than their suffering for want of clothing and other necessities."

To Washington he reported that many of his men were "literally, naked; and a great part totally unfit for any kind of duty, and must remain so until clothing can be had from the northward." Greene also indicated that there was a serious lack of control over the troops at Charlotte, as "General Gates had lost the confidence of the officers, and the loss of all their discipline, and they have been so addicted to plundering that they were a terror to the inhabitants."[17] Greene's report to Washington continued, "The soldiers have no spirit, and it is impossible they should in their present situation…. However, I don't intend to be drove out of North Carolina if I can possibly avoid it." His views of the civilians were revealed in his remarks, "I believe the views and wishes of the great body of the people are entirely with us. But remove the personal influence of a few, and they are a lifeless and immature mass, without direction or spirit." It was difficult to believe Greene was talking about the same people who had defeated Ferguson at King's Mountain without any support from the Continental Army.[18]

One of Greene's first actions was to determine the true strength of his force. On paper he had 2307 infantry troops, 90 cavalrymen, and 60 artillerymen. Of these only 1482 were present and fit for any duty. Only 949 men were Continental troops, and a mere 800 were properly clothed and equipped. Even as small as the army was, it was too large for the exhausted area around Charlotte. When Greene arrived, there were only three days' rations for the army. During the first night in camp Greene met with Colonel Polk, who had acted as Gates' commissariat. The next day Polk remarked that Greene had gained a better understanding of the resource situation than Gates had the whole time of his command. The situation of the quartermaster department was just as bad as the commissariat. All the wagons and horses had been lost at Camden. Without hard currency, it was nearly impossible to remedy the situation.

Greene took immediate action in establishing his staff organization. By letter, dated December 4, he appointed the young artillery officer, Lieutenant Colonel Edward Carrington, who was then exploring the Dan River area, to be quartermaster general. Greene followed up with letters to the Southern governors informing them of his appointment of Carrington and requesting them to provide him with every assistance. Davie described Carrington as "a man of considerable talents and the most persevering energy." Carrington did not join Greene until February 7, 1781, at Guilford Court House.

Next Greene considered the post of commissariat general. Colonel Polk begged to be allowed to resign his post due to his family circumstances, his advanced age and fatigue. Greene found that the best candidate for this position was in General Daniel Morgan's unit, the 24-year-old cavalryman officer, Colonel William R. Davie. Since Davie's partisan cavalry unit had been disbanded at the end of November, his focus was in re-establishing his unit and serving under Morgan. Davie told Greene that he had no interest in being the commissariat general. Greene explained to Davie that he wanted him to apply the same method he had used to feed his cavalry to feed the army. Davie was talked into assuming this most critical post for the Southern Army.[19] Evidence of just how critical feeding the men had become was recorded in a letter written by Greene to LaFayette some two weeks after arriving with the Southern Army:

> Were you to arrive, you would find a few ragged, half-starved troops in the wilderness, destitute of every thing necessary for either the comfort or convenience of soldiers. Indeed ... the departments in most deplorable condition, nor have I a prospect of its mending. The country is almost laid waste, and the inhabitants plunder one another with little less than savage fury. We live from hand to mouth, and have nothing to subsist on but what we collect with armed parties.

The scarcity of any public money, especially specie, was a major culprit to improving the conditions of the army. Paper money was nearly worthless as depreciation of the Continental currency had reached 100 to one. The North Carolina paper currency was considered contemptible by the citizens because of "the public and careless manner in which it was given away at the printing office." On Christmas Day, 1780, John Bradley, an assistant issuing commissary, reported from Wilmington that if he had specie he "could purchase rice, flour, and liquor to a considerable amount." Major Burnet wrote Colonel

Davie that "If it is in your power to advance the expresses money sufficient for their journey, I beg you to do it, as it will be out of General Greene's power to supply them; but if not, we must do the best in our power."[20]

The most famous officer under Greene was the "boisterous, coarse, irreverent, and rowdy" Brigadier General Daniel Morgan from the Virginia frontier. Morgan had joined Gates' army just after the defeat at Camden. Known as a fierce warrior, Morgan had settled as a young man in Winchester, Virginia, in 1753 and soon became a teamster. Many found Morgan to be "a dangerous man to cross" as exemplified by one "mass brawl" during which Morgan and friends were "resorting to kicking, biting, and gouging" their way out of trouble. As the Revolution approached, Morgan, better known as the "Old Waggoner," was selected to lead a company of expert riflemen, where he served with distinction. In 1775 Morgan marched north to Massachusetts and joined Washington's Continental Army outside Boston. Taking part in the invasion of Canada, Morgan was captured by the British at Quebec. The following spring, Morgan was exchanged for British prisoners and rejoined Washington. Except for a brief period in 1777 when he was sent to support Gates on the upper Hudson, Morgan served with Washington continuously until 1779. Serving with distinction at Freeman's Farm in September and Nemis Heights in October of that year, he was to resign and return home to Winchester over not being selected to command a new unit of light infantry. But when asked to return to service by Gates, Morgan accepted.

On December 4, Greene wrote to another officer of great reputation, Colonel Francis Marion, known as the "Swamp Fox." Greene recorded that "I have not the honor of your acquaintance, but I am no stranger to your character and merit." Marion had been busy disrupting British supply lines between Camden and Charles Town and attacking enemy posts between the Santee and the Pee Dee rivers. Greene told Marion to stay where he was and provide him intelligence of British movements, and to continue "awing the Tories and preventing the enemy from extending their limits."[21]

Previously, having retreated in late August into North Carolina at White Marsh to hide from the British, Marion was to remain there only a few days. News from Major James concerning the degree of patriot desolation and suffering around the Pee Dee caused Marion to quickly return to South Carolina with a renewed purpose. On the second day of his forced march, his group of partisans had traveled some 60 miles and arrived at Lynch's Creek. There they were joined by a considerable force under John James and Henry Mouzon. On September 14, while encamped at Lynch's Creek, Marion was informed that a party of loyalists had formed at Black

Mingo, some 15 miles south of them, under Captain John Coming Ball. Although he could have waited only a short while for reinforcements, Marion's men encouraged him to head for the fight.

Since the loyalists had command of the passage of the deep navigable creek at Shepherd's Ferry on the south side of Black Mingo, Marion decided to approach them by crossing the creek one mile above using a causeway and bridge of planks. At midnight while approaching the bridge, the loyalists were alerted by gunfire. Marion immediately ordered his men to follow him at full gallop as they raced to the main road. After only a few minutes, Marion's force reached the main road, which led to the ferry located only some 300 yards in front of it. He dismounted his troops except for a small number. Also he sent a corps of officers under Captain Thomas Waties to head down the road and attack a house supposedly containing loyalists.

Marion dispatched two companies to the right under Colonel Hugh Horry, and the cavalry to the left to support the battle. The troops on the right encountered the enemy before the officers reached the house, and the enemy had left the house and was moving into the field opposite it. The advance was momentarily retarded by the first loyalist volley, which caused Horry's troops to fall back in some confusion. Soon they rallied under Captain John James. As the officers under Waties fired at the loyalists, who were receiving fire on their other flank by Horry's men, the loyalists found themselves in a crossfire. They retreated after only a few rounds into the Black Mingo swamp in their rear. The affair was over.

The exact count of the forces on either side or those wounded was not recorded, but Marion was believed to have around 150 men, with the loyalists numbering around 46 men. Captain Henry Mouzon and his lieutenant Joseph Scott were wounded. After hearing that Marion was marching for South Carolina, Captain George Logan of Charles Town, although sick in bed in North Carolina, rose from the bed and rode 80 miles to join up with Marion the day before the battle. Logan was killed during the battle the next day. Having defeated the loyalists, Marion allowed many of his followers to visit their families, as he moved to Waccamaw to await their return. After the men returned, Marion and now happily some 400 of his followers marched into Williamsburg.[22] On October 6, 1780, the governor of South Carolina, John Rutledge, issued in writing a commission of brigadier general in the South Carolina Militia to Francis Marion from his temporary headquarters at Hillsborough.[23]

On his march Marion learned that British Lieutenant Colonel Samuel Tynes was gathering a large group of loyalists at a fork in the upper Black River some 30 miles away. Colonel Tynes had summoned out the people of Salem to join the loyalist cause and was encamped at Tarcote Swamp in the fork. On October 25 in the late evening, Marion marched against Tynes by crossing the north branch of the Black River at Nelson's Plantation. Using the technique of surrounding the enemy on three sides, Marion again defeated a loyalist band. The enemy lost three killed, 14 wounded and 23 captured. Tynes escaped capture. Soon most of Tynes' men joined up with Marion and served him well for the remainder of the war. Now Marion and his force retired to Snow Island, which was located at the conflux of the Pee Dee River, Lynch's Creek and Clarke's Creek. Marion was in command of the area, which was protected in all directions by water. The loyalist elements were becoming quite intimidated in this region of South Carolina.[24]

Another partisan leader that Greene wanted to work with was Brigadier General Thomas Sumter, the Gamecock, of the South Carolina Militia. Though Greene wished to gain Sumter's cooperation in conducting joint operations, which by reputation had never been easy with Sumter, he was still convinced that the responsibility of defeating the enemy was the duty of the Continental Army and not the partisan and militia forces no matter how well intentioned. Greene wrote, "It requires more than double the number of militia to be kept in the field, attended with infinitely more waste and expense than should be necessary to give full security to the country with a regular and permanent army."[25] Regardless of Greene's observations about the value of militia forces, Sumter had been quite active and successful in recent months.

When Lord Cornwallis had vacated Charlotte and fell back to Winnsboro, General Smallwood managed to collect the force of several thousand militia under generals Jethro Sumner, William L. Davidson and Allen Jones, and established their post at Providence, located six miles south of Charlotte. Smallwood had commanded a brigade with Gates at Camden, but now he had assumed a North Carolina commission to raise this militia force. In South Carolina, as Colonel Davie moved with 300 cavalry to the British right at Landsford on the Catawba River, Sumter, who now commanded 425 men, moved to Fishdam Ford on the Broad River located 28 miles from Winnsboro toward the British left. After taking these positions around Winnsboro, Smallwood and Sumter devised a plan to draw Cornwallis out with at least a sizable detachment as Smallwood attacked the main British force at Winnsboro. Unknown to Sumter, Smallwood decided not to cooperate with Sumter, having learned that Greene was soon to take command of the Southern Department.

On November 7, Sumter crossed the Broad River at Fishdam Ford in Union County, entered Chester County, and set up camp on the left of the road to Charlotte.

Colonel Richard Winn's 125 men were located along the river on Sumter's left, with colonels Lacey, Bratton and Hill commanding some 300 men camped on high ground in the thick woods some 350 yards in front. Colonel Thomas Taylor's force was located along a gully on Winn's left. During the morning of the 8th, some 100 men from Georgia under majors Candler and Jackson came in and encamped between Winn's and Taylor's camp. Sumter had sent Colonel Taylor with 50 of his men to reconnoiter the country for intelligence on Cornwallis. That evening another force of 50 men commanded by Colonel McCall from Long Cane in the Ninety Six district came in also. That evening Taylor returned with no news.

Meanwhile, Cornwallis had gained fresh and detailed information of Sumter's exact location from loyalists in the settlement of Mobley. Cornwallis decided to attack Sumter by surprise. Major Wemyss with his 63rd Regiment would be the attacking force. With such detailed intelligence, the British plan called for five selected men to penetrate the patriot defenses and specifically attack Sumter in his tent. On the evening of November 8, Wemyss' force, led by guides, moved toward Fishdam Ford. On alert for the potential of just such a British undertaking, the patriots had set up large fires, posted pickets and required that all men sleep with their arms. At 1 A.M. on the 9th, Major Wemyss at the lead of his men attacked the patriot pickets head on. Of the first five patriot pickets' shots in return fire, two hit the arm and knee of Major Wemyss. Sumter was sound asleep and did not awaken until some moments into the engagement. It was not until the selected British were at his tent, as he was putting his coat on, that he reacted to the commotion. Sumter had to run out of his tent, leap over a fence and escape by the river bank.

As soon as the British heard the American pickets return fire, the British attacked the camp in full charge. When the dragoons reached the fires, which to some extent blinded them, they paused and dismounted along with the infantry forming a line of attack. The Americans fell back behind the fence and returned fire. Soon the enemy charged with bayonets, but they were repelled by the fierce firing in their direction. Taylor's men who formed on the British flank produced heavy fire on the British. After an engagement of some 20 minutes, the British infantry remounted and fled the area. Though Lacey's, Bratton's and Hill's men were not able to fire a single round in fear they would hit their comrades, the British sustained considerable loss. Major Wemyss was badly wounded, with some 20 British killed, and the many wounded scattered about the battleground. One British surgeon, who under flag of truce came in to take care of the wounded, returned to explain that he had never seen so many badly wounded men considering the relative few American troops engaged.

Hearing of the battle, Cornwallis sent out an urgent message to Tarleton saying, "Major Wemyss attacked Sumter at Fishdam at one o' clock this morning, contrary to his plan, which was to wait until daylight; the consequence is that Wemyss is wounded and left, and about twenty men. Lieutenant Hoveden is wounded, but I believe the Legion has not lost much. Must beg you to return immediately, leaving some horses for mounting men at Camden. I am under the greatest anxiety for Ninety Six, and trust that you will lose no time in returning to me." Now Tarleton had to abandon the pursuit of Marion. Sumter re-crossed the Broad River the day after the battle at Fishdam with prisoner Wemyss in company, and moved down the Union County to Niam's Plantation on the Enoree. Then he moved further south through Laurens County to Williams' Plantation on Little River.

Tarleton returned by the Wateree when he received orders from Cornwallis to lead his light troops to Brierley's Ferry to join up with the First Battalion of the 71st and a detachment of the 63rd Regiment, returning from the Fishdam affair. En route to the ferry, Tarleton received further instructions to cut off Sumter, who was heading toward Ninety Six. On the evening of November 18, Tarleton received word that Sumter was located at Williams' Plantation with about 1000 men. The next morning Tarleton set about with his light troops through Indian Creek on the Enoree, and marched with haste through Newberry County, stopping that night along the river to camp. If Tarleton could keep the surprise, he would reach Sumter's camp after another day's travel. Fortunately for Sumter, a British deserter from the 63rd Regiment told of Tarleton's approach. Sumter immediately moved upcountry to Blackstock, located on the south side of the Tyger River in Union County, 60 miles from Winnsboro and 35 miles from Fishdam Ford.

Sumter encamped his troops on an elevated level in the rear of the Blackstock house, which was actually a long, narrow tobacco log building made up of two 18 by 18 foot square apartments. As Tarleton continued his pursuit, he discovered before 10 A.M. on the 20th that Sumter had retreated. When he reached the Enoree River at a ford, he found out that Sumter's troops had passed there only two hours before. Just before 5 P.M. Tarleton's force caught up with Sumter at Blackstock. On receiving the American picket fire, the British infantry dismounted and with the cavalry, attacked the field against the Georgia troops under Colonel Twiggs. Sumter, with Bratton's, Taylor's, Hill's and McCall's men, attacked the British flank with some success. Colonel Lacey's mounted infantry advanced from the west side through a woods and saw 20 of Tarleton's Legion fall from their horses. From the house Colonel Henry Hampton's men fired at the British with total security. Tarleton fell back, reformed and advanced again toward the American left flank. He almost succeeded until Colonel Winn's men moved in to support the Georgians.

During the engagement, Sumter had received a shot to the right shoulder. After directing his aide to place his sword in its scabbard and to "Say nothing about it," Sumter instructed "Colonel Twiggs to take command." The battle soon ended with the Americans in charge of the field. Twiggs ordered the enemy's wounded to be collected and sheltered in the house. Fearing further attack from the Legion or regular British infantry of Tarleton's, Twiggs ordered the troops to cross the Tyger River, leaving Colonel Winn in command of the battlefield until nightfall. Winn set large fires and moved his men across the river to safety. While there were differing American and British reports of the casualties at Blackstock, the British lost 92 killed and some 100 wounded, while the American loss was reported at one killed and three wounded, including Sumter. Tarleton claimed to Cornwallis that it was a British victory, but most evidence leans more toward a real American victory. Cornwallis wrote Tarleton the following on November 23, 1780:

> I have no doubt but your victory will be attended with as good consequences to our affairs as it is with honor and credit to yourself; I shall be very glad to hear that Sumter is in a condition to give us no further trouble; he certainly has been our greatest plague in this country.

After the battle at Blackstock, Tarleton returned to Winnsboro with some prisoners, mostly boys and some old men he had captured on his return trip, and showed them off as trophies of the past battle. Some were "converted" to the loyalist side, some were jailed, and a respectable man and father in his community, Mr. Johnson, was hanged as a symbol to the American cause. Later, on January 13, 1781, the Continental Congress adopted the following resolution:

> Congress taking into consideration the eminent services rendered to the United States by Brigadier General Sumter of South Carolina at the head of a number of volunteer militia from that and the neighboring State, particularly in the victory obtained over the enemy at Hanging Rock on the 6th of August, in the defeat of Major Wemyss and the corps of British Infantry and dragoons under his command at Broad River on the 9th day of November, in which the said Major Wemyss was made prisoner, and on the repulse of Lieutenant Colonel Tarleton and the British cavalry and infantry under his command at Blackstock on Tyger River on the 20th of November last, in each of which actions the gallantry and military conduct of General Sumter and the courage and perseverance of his troops were highly conspicuous.
>
> Resolved, therefore, that the thanks of Congress be presented to Brigadier General Sumter and the militia aforesaid for such reiterated proofs of their patriotism, bravery, and military conduct which entitles them to the highest esteem and confidence of their country and that the commanding officer of the Southern department do forthwith cause the same to be issued in general orders and transmitted to General Sumter.[26]

On December 8, Greene set out from Charlotte to visit Sumter, who was convalescing at his rock home on the Catawba River near the Tuckaseegee Ford. Sumter told Greene of the forces on their way to Cornwallis in Winnsboro, and urged him to move boldly against Cornwallis. Greene agreed that he would give the matter consideration, and directed Sumter "to keep up a communication of intelligence, and of any changes of their disposition that may take place." Greene also told Sumter of his views on partisan activities in the following:

> The salvation of this army does not depend upon little strokes, nor should the great business of establishing a permanent army be neglected to pursue them. Partisan strokes in war are like garnishings on a table, they give splendor to the army and reputation to the officers; but they afford no substantial national security. They are matters which should not be neglected, and yet, they should not be pursued to the prejudice of more important concerns. You may strike a hundred strokes, and reap little benefit from them, unless you have a good army to take advantage of them.[27]

After returning from the Sumter visit, Greene sat down with his new officer staff to discuss his plans for the upcoming operations. The one thing he knew was that he would not be able to stay where he was in Charlotte. Greene knew his army was not ready to engage Cornwallis yet. In addition, troops from both sides had stripped the area of Rowan and Mecklenburg counties bare. Food shortage was a present danger with severe ramifications. What Greene needed was a place to repair his army's wagons, gather new horses, discipline the troops, and more than anything else, to find a more plentiful supply of food for his suffering army. After returning from an exploration assignment, Thaddeus Kosciuszko, the Polish officer, reported that Hicks' Creek on the east bank of the Pee Dee River, near the Cheraws in South Carolina, was just such a worthy site to satisfy Greene's requirements.[28]

Not ready to face Cornwallis, Greene made a monumental decision to split his army into two groups for the purpose of "desultory incursions in different, and nearly opposite quarters." Taking full responsibility for his action and against all classical military judgment, Greene explained in his orders which he issued without council of war: "In this command I am obliged to put everything to the hazard ... to make detachments that nothing but absolute necessity could authorize...." Greene sent his light troops to the western frontiers of South Carolina under Brigadier General Morgan to threaten Ninety Six and the other British outposts. Greene would take the remainder of the army to the Pee Dee region to alarm the area around Camden. Greene presented the reason for his actions against Cornwallis as follows:

> It makes the most of my inferior force, for it compels my adversary to divide his, and hold him in doubt as to his line of conduct. He cannot leave Morgan behind him to come at me, or his posts at Ninety Six and Augusta would be exposed. And he cannot chase Morgan far, or prosecute his views upon Virginia while I can have the whole country open before me. I am as near to Charleston as he is, and as near Hillsborough as I was at Charlotte; as I am in no danger of being cut off from my reinforcements.[29]

On December 16, both sections of the Southern army were put under marching orders, but several days of rain caused both groups to be delayed in departing Charlotte. Greene finally marched out of Charlotte for Hicks' Creek on December 20 with the Continental Brigade under Colonel Otto Williams, the Virginia Militia under General Stevens and the artillery unit. General Isaac Huger was given the overall command of both the militia and the Continentals. The next day Morgan detached to cross the western side of the Catawba River and operate between the Broad and Pacolet rivers with 320 Maryland and Delaware Continentals under Lieutenant Colonel John Eager Howard, 200 Virginia riflemen under Major Francis Triplett, and 80 light dragoons commanded by Lieutenant Colonel William Washington. The newly split Southern Army was now in the field.[30]

Meanwhile, Cornwallis was trying to rebuild his army in Winnsboro, in the hopes of again taking the initiative to restart his campaign in North Carolina. Although Cornwallis' intelligence had been faltering of late, he was well aware that Greene had relieved Gates as Southern Commander of the American forces. He was also generally aware of the strength of Greene's forces. The latest intelligence that Greene had split his forces was a curious move in the eyes of the Lord Cornwallis. Yet Cornwallis understood the situation it put him in. If he moved toward Morgan, Greene would have an open route to Charles Town. If he moved at Greene, Morgan would probably attack Ninety Six. He had to take appropriate action. Cornwallis also knew he could not just sit still in Winnsboro, as the experiences of constantly being harassed on his flanks by partisans Marion and Sumter were fresh reminders.

Although Cornwallis was still without his expected reinforcements of 1530 experienced troops with Major General Alexander Leslie, who were then struggling through swamps and swollen streams between Charles Town and Winnsboro to reach him, he decided to split his army like Greene had done. On December 28, Cornwallis conferred in his tent with Tarleton about sending a force of around 1100 men with him to protect Ninety Six against Morgan. On New Year's Day Tarleton was ordered to move westward with 300 dragoons and 250 infantry of the British Legion, 200 men of the First Battalion of the 71st Highlander Regiment, 200 men from the Seventh Regiment, 50 troops of the 17th Light Dragoons, a detachment of the Royal Artillery with two field guns, and a small party of loyalist militia. Cornwallis left him with the instruction that "If Morgan is still at Williams', or any where within your reach, I should wish you push him to the utmost."[31]

Cornwallis' plan called for Lord Rawdon to continue to command his garrisons, totaling some 5000 men spread from Savannah to his headquarters at Camden, which would head off most attacks, while he headed to intercept Greene. With him, once Leslie arrived, he would have some 3200 men — 450 Germans including 347 from the Bose Regiment with 103 Jagers, Provincials numbering 451 from the British Legion, 256 of the North Carolina Volunteers, and 2050 British redcoats. Cornwallis also knew that Clinton had sent American loyalist Brigadier General Benedict Arnold into Virginia with the hopes of assisting him in coordinated operations later. In the meantime Arnold could destroy stores in Virginia and help to divert troops away from him as he entered North Carolina. While one could not be over-confident, Cornwallis was certainly in a fine condition to take on Greene and his Southern Army. Later on January 21, as an insurance policy, Cornwallis sent Major James Craig with 300 men to the Cape Fear River at Wilmington, North Carolina, to establish a base of operations at this port for supplies and potential escape if retreat were necessary. As the earl remarked, it would be "a serious business to go into the heart of N. Carolina."[32]

After traveling 58 miles, Morgan camped on the Pacolet River near Grindall's Shoals on Christmas Day, 1780. Though the march was difficult in the miserable weather, Morgan was delighted when Major Joseph McDowell, of King's Mountain fame, arrived with his 190 North Carolina riflemen. With his strength near 800, Morgan was inspired. On December 27, he detached William Washington with his 80 dragoons and 200 mounted militia to attack a loyalist raiding party of 250 men who had been harassing the settlements near Fair Forest Creek.

During the second day of hard riding of another 40 miles, Washington's force engaged the loyalists at Hammond's Store located some 30 miles northeast of Ninety Six. With a furious vengeance, Washington struck the enemy, killing or wounding 150 and capturing another 40. Having been so successful, before leaving he sent Colonel Joseph Hayes 15 miles closer to Ninety Six with 40 dragoons and took the small Fort William. Though the patriots withdrew, Cornwallis received an urgent message on New Year's Day that the rebels were mounting a massive raid near Ninety Six. Morgan was already having the effect Greene wanted.

On hearing of Colonel Washington's successful penetration into dangerous territory, Morgan was somewhat concerned for his army's safety. Thus, he moved his entire force a number of miles to cover the return of Washington's force. Morgan's force, with Washington's unit recovered, was again in the area of Grindell's Shoals in Union County, changing camp sites every night to guard against a surprise. In spite of his accomplishments so far, Morgan wrote a rather gloomy letter to Greene dated January 4 in which he revealed his list of problems and concerns. Greene replied on the 13th with an upbeat message which recounted the enemy's woes and gave Morgan a key thought which Morgan would soon take action on. Greene wrote, "It is my wish also that you should hold your ground if possible, for I foresee the disagreeable consequences that will result from a retreat...."[33]

On January 4, Lord Cornwallis learned from Tarleton that "Morgan had retired," turning north and that he had "got too far to give any hopes of overtaking him." Tarleton was ordered to move northward on the east side of the Broad River in York County, as far as King's Mountain, to cut off the retreat of Morgan. On January 8, Tarleton reached the south side of the Enoree River, which was the southernmost of three parallel tributaries of the Broad River. Morgan was still on the Pacolet, the northernmost tributary. Heavy rains forced Tarleton to stop since he could not pass the swollen Enoree and Tyger rivers to get at Morgan.[34]

Meanwhile, on January 6, 1781, Greene's ragtag band at Hicks' Creek on the Pee Dee was treated to the arrival of a magnificent sight — the handpicked Legion of 140 horsemen and 140 mounted infantry of Lieutenant Colonel Henry "Light Horse Harry" Lee, Jr. Being fully equipped, wearing their white leather breeches, black boots, smart green jackets and shining brass helmets fixed with horsehair plumes, these troops were an incredible contrast to Greene's men. As a reflection of the regard he had for Nathanael Greene, General George Washington had sent his premiere light cavalry unit to support the operations in the South. Lee's unit had been distinguished in numerous engagements against the British, as Washington used the force for intelligence gathering, acting as his eyes.

Henry Lee, Jr., now 26 years old, had been born to the famous Lee family of Virginia. Raised in a cultured and socially aristocratic environment, Lee had every advantage of wealth and station. He had studied law at Princeton, and was known as a keen horseman. With his confident nature, handsome physical looks, gentle manners, intelligence and a genuine presence, Lee was a man who stood out in any group. Lee had performed well at Paulus Hook, Stony Point and Springfield under Greene's command. Washington was so impressed that all intelligence from Lee was marked "private" and was sent for Washington's eyes only. This most impressive young man was now to serve the Southern cause. Unknown to him at this time, Lee would, in middle age, father a son who would fight to defeat the Union he was now trying to create. Lee's son would become the most famous Southern general ever — Robert E. Lee.

Greene soon put Lee to work by issuing him orders to join Marion in the Santee region to aid in harassing Cornwallis' right flank. On January 13, Lee left to find Marion, and on January 23, their forces joined. With these two dynamic, independent, and resourceful leaders in joint operations, one might have expected a degree of conflict. But they were instant friends and allies. Marion wrote Greene that "Colonel Lee's Interprising Genius promises much," and that "Marion and Lee were singularly tender of the lives of their soldiers; and preferred moderate success with little loss, to the most brilliant enterprise, with the destruction of many troops." On January 24, Marion and Lee attacked the British garrison at the coastal town of Georgetown, South Carolina. They were able to capture the commandant in the sneak attack, but were unable to retake the town without the necessary artillery. The British were spread among the town's buildings and the patriots had no way to force them out. The new union was nevertheless forged.[35]

After sending Tarleton off to attack Morgan, Cornwallis broke camp at Winnsboro on January 8 and moved northward for Bullock's Creek. On the 9th Cornwallis was at McAlister's Plantation and behind schedule due to the rains.[36] He expected Major General Leslie's force to reach him during the next several days. Leslie's force had been reduced to short rations as they struggled through the swamps and muddy roads. Cornwallis sent Leslie 4000 pounds of meat and salt to Rocky Mount, located just northeast of Winnsboro. When Leslie reached Rocky Mount and the food, it was January 14. Cornwallis had left word for Leslie to join up with his force at Stewart's New Cross Roads. On January 16 Lord Cornwallis was at Hillhouse's Plantation between Turkey Creek and Bullock Creek. It had taken Cornwallis eight days to move 40 miles because of the rain. There he decided to wait for Leslie to join him.

Both Cornwallis and Leslie understood the necessity for their two forces to unite. With both forces divided, neither force could give Tarleton any assistance.

Meanwhile, on January 12, as the rivers fell, Tarleton again continued his march against Morgan. The Legion and others in Tarleton's force moved across the Enoree and Tyger rivers by the 14th, and two days later they crossed the Pacolet. Now Tarleton was indeed close to Morgan. Knowing that Tarleton had already crossed the Enoree River at Musgrove's Mill, Morgan fell back to Burr's Mills on Thicketty Creek and wrote a letter to Greene, dated January 15, indicating that he had "received certain intelligence that Lord Cornwallis and Lt. Col. Tarleton were both in motion, and that their movements clearly indicated their intentions of dislodging me...." Morgan learned that Tarleton was crossing the Pacolet at Easterwood Shoals about 6 A.M. on January 16.[37] In the letter to Greene, Morgan revealed that, "We have just heard that Tarleton's force is eleven or twelve hundred British." Tarleton was at that instant only six miles away. The Americans had broken camp so quickly to avoid the British that their breakfast was sitting only half-cooked.[38]

Morgan's militia, which had been previously sent out to forage, had orders to return to gather at Hannah's Cowpens on January 16. With Tarleton so close, and the only real escape toward the Broad River at Cherokee Ford being seven miles away, Morgan decided to engage Tarleton at Hannah's Cowpens. He had no desire to be overtaken by Tarleton while on the move. Hannah's Cowpens and the surrounding countryside was generally flat with some rolling hills. Major Joseph McDowell described to him the land around Cowpens—flat and rolling hills with stands of red oak, hickory and pine trees, and with no underbrush. The center of the area was marked by Green River Road which was about five miles from the Broad River. It was ideal for Morgan.[39] There was no real shield for anyone, but it was a "proper place for action," according to Tarleton too. In fact, Tarleton later wrote, "America does not produce many [places] more suitable to the nature of the troops under his command." It was perfect "cavalry" land. Morgan and his men were ready to take on the hated young leader and his British Legion. At 8 A.M. on the morning of the 16th Tarleton had written Cornwallis:

> My Lord,
>
> I have been most cruelly retarded by waters. Morgan is in force and gone for Cherokee Ford. I am now on my march. I wish he could be stopped.
> I have the Honor to be Your most Devoted Serv't
>
> Ban. Tarleton.[40]

In discussions with several of his officers, Morgan learned of Tarleton's usual aggressive battle tactics. Colonel Winn, who had commanded Sumter's reserve at Blackstock's Plantation, told Morgan that "His mode of fighting is surprise. By doing this he sends two or three troops of horse and if he can throw the party in confusion, with the reserve he falls on and cuts them to pieces." Around mid-afternoon a messenger rode in revealing that Andrew Pickens, with his 150 mounted militia force, was crossing the Broad River and coming in. Other groups of militia troops were also heading to Cowpens to fight the dreaded Tarleton.

Colonel Andrew Pickens, a Presbyterian elder, had broken his oath to the British to stay out of the remainder of the war when the loyalists had destroyed his property, feeling it was a violation of the British promise of protection. Pickens, who had been born in Bucks County, Pennsylvania, in 1737, had moved with his Huguenot family to the Waxhaw settlement in Lancaster County, South Carolina, in 1752. At the beginning of the Revolution, he had become a captain in the militia and soon rose in rank. His leadership during the defeat of 700 loyalists at Kettle Creek in February 1779 had increased his reputation as a brave patriot. Pickens was to be an important officer for Morgan in the upcoming engagement.[41]

Morgan surveyed the Cowpens terrain with Lieutenant Colonel John Eager Howard and his senior officers. Coming from the direction that Tarleton would cover, Morgan saw that the ground sloped gradually upward to a low crest at about 400 yards ahead. Beyond that crest was a ridge "formed by two small hills." With no swamps or underbrush as obstacles, Morgan did not have to fear flanking actions as much. Morgan wrote, "I would not have had a swamp in view of my militia on any consideration; they would have made for it.... And, as to covering my wings, I knew my adversary, and was perfectly sure I should have nothing but downright fighting. As to retreat, it was the very thing I wished to cut off all hope of.... Had I crossed the river [on January 16], one half of my militia would immediately have abandoned me."

The night before the battle was a nervous one for Morgan, who moved widely about the encampments at the Cowpens. Pickens' force entered camp, along with other groups of militia, arriving at random. Morgan had made sure the rations were issued for supper and that corn cakes would be cooked for breakfast. Each man got his allotment of 24 rounds of ammunition, his blanket roll from the baggage wagons, and detailed instructions, in some cases from Morgan himself. Youthful Thomas Young from Major Jolly's company of the South Carolina Militia wrote of this night with Morgan:

> It was upon this occasion that I was more perfectly convinced of General Morgan's qualifications to command militia than I had ever before been.... Long after I had laid down, he was going among the soldiers, encouraging them and telling them that the "Old Wagoner" would crack his whip over Ben (Tarleton) in the morning, as sure as he lived. "Just hold up your heads boys," he would say, "three fires, and you are free! And then, when you return to your homes, how the old folks will bless you, and the girls kiss you, for your gallant conduct." I don't think that he slept a wink that night.

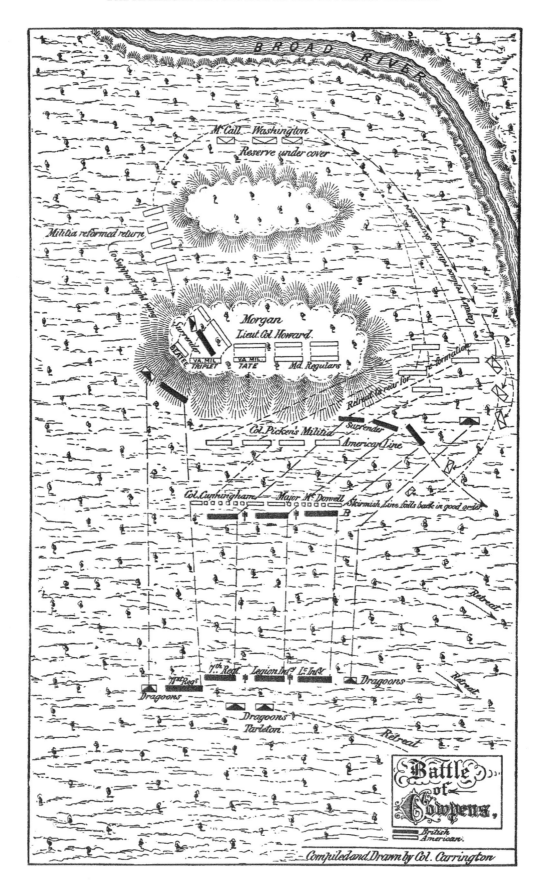

Battle of Cowpens. (*Battles of the American Revolution.*)

The next morning, in the cold of January 17, 1781, between 6 A.M. and 6:30 A.M., Morgan's vedettes were driven into camp by Tarleton's advancing troops. The commander of the vedettes, Captain Inman of the Georgia Militia, reported that the British were some five miles away, and marching light and fast. Morgan directed that the men be wakened, blankets loaded in the baggage wagons, and that a hot breakfast be served. Word had it that Morgan rode about the camp yelling, "Boys get up! Benny is coming…."

Morgan then organized his troops into their planned defensive positions in three battle lines. In the first line, using the Green River Road as the center, Morgan placed 150 handpicked riflemen made up of North Carolinians under Major Joseph McDowell and Georgians under Major John Cunningham. Their instructions were to take cover until the British were within 50 yards, then to fire at least two volleys at "the men with the epaulets," followed by falling back to the second line of militia.

The second line of militia with about 300 men was commanded by Colonel Pickens and was posted astride the road 150 yards to the rear of the first line. Morgan directed the second line to fire off at least two volleys at the killing distance of 50 yards or less, and then withdraw. Their withdrawal was to be in file off to the left flank, then passing around behind the third line to reassemble at the rear.

The third, and main, battle line was located just below the crest of the first ridge at 150 yards behind the second line. This line was manned by the Maryland and Delaware Continentals in the center astride the road, flanked on the right by Tate's Virginians and a company of Georgians. The left flank consisted of Triplett's Virginians. The entire third line force was in command of Lieutenant Colonel John Eager Howard. This battle-hardened line was made up of some of the most veteran infantry troops to be found in the Continental Army. Howard, of Maryland, had already served with distinction at White Plains, Germantown, Monmouth and Camden. Greene would later describe Howard to be "as good an officer as the world affords…. He deserves a statue of gold no less than Roman and Grecian heroes."

The reserve force was under the command of Colonel William Washington's 80 dragoons, supported by a provisional battalion of 45 mounted militiamen from North Carolina and Georgia under Lieutenant Colonel James McCall. The cavalry was stationed in the rear of the second ridge, which was about a half mile behind Howard's main line. Morgan's plan for them was to have them come around to attack Tarleton's force at the critical moment and cut the British down. The Americans were ready for action.

At 2 o'clock that same morning the British buglers had sounded reveille in Tarleton's camp, and within an hour the British were marching toward Cowpens. During the night, loyalists had captured a rebel militia colonel who had apparently lost his unit. Tarleton had questioned the colonel and learned that indeed Morgan was within striking distance, and not yet at the Broad River. Tarleton had left behind the wagons and baggage to follow at daybreak, and sent out the first three companies of light infantry supported by the Legion infantry. The Seventh Regiment and the First Battalion of the 71st made up the British Army's center, with the cavalry and mounted infantry bringing up the rear. The advance in the dark was through broken terrain which was intersected by ravines and creeks. Before dawn, the British passed Thicketty Creek and there moved the cavalry in front of the advance units.[42]

When Tarleton's advance guard ran into Captain Inman's vedettes, the British were able to capture two patriot troops, while the rest of them escaped to warn Morgan. The prisoners revealed to Tarleton that the Americans were encamped at Cowpens. Tarleton at once sent out Captain Ogilvie with two companies of the Legion dragoons. At about 6:45 A.M., some 15 minutes before sunrise, Ogilvie rode up the Green River Road and came out of the woods into Cowpens. The Legion captain then saw that Morgan had not just halted there, but that the Americans were formed for battle. He sent off a messenger immediately, who galloped off to tell Tarleton of the situation. The small British unit received a few shots from overeager riflemen, and they withdrew back into the woods for cover. Back with the main force, Tarleton was thrilled to hear the news that Morgan was close by. Even though his force had been marching in the dark for four hours in rugged terrain, Tarleton gave it no thought and issued orders to advance for immediate battle.[43] As Tarleton described, "on account of the vulnerable situation of the enemy, and the supposed vicinity of the two British corps on the east and west of Broad river, I did not hesitate to undertake those measures which the instructions of his commanding officer imposed, and his own judgment, under the present appearances, equally recommended."[44]

At about 7 A.M. the British Dragoons, dressed in their green jackets, began to appear from the woods at the far end of the meadow. Soon scarlet and white infantry appeared, along with kilts of the Highlanders, with more horsemen — some in green and others all scarlet. While the British lines were forming, Tarleton sent out a detachment of 50 cavalry to test Morgan's troops. As the detachment charged, the sharpshooters fired an impressive volley, and suddenly 15 saddles were emptied, as the British horsemen retreated. It was to be an omen of things to come.[45]

Morgan reported that "The enemy drew up in a

single line of battle, four hundred yards in front of our advanced corps." Thomas Young wrote "About sunrise, the British line advanced at a sort of trot with a loud halloo…" and "It was the most beautiful line I ever saw." Tarleton placed his light infantry on the right, the Legion infantry and the two grasshoppers in the middle, the Seventh Regiment on the left, and 50 dragoons on each flank. At some 180 yards behind the first line, he placed the 71st Regiment and the bulk of the cavalry as a reserve. The British were moving to form up for battle smartly.[46]

Without the advice of his two regimental commandants, majors McArthur and Newmarsh, Tarleton did not wait until the entire British lines were formed. He issued orders to attack, and directed the grasshopper cannon on the right to open fire at the Americans. As the light and the Legion infantry, loudly yelling their halloos, advanced to within 40 yards of the first line, the American riflemen fell back after firing their two fierce volleys. The first line of militia came back to Pickens' line and found places there. The second line was soon engaged. The British continued to advance, unrestrained by the efforts of the first American line, though casualties were taking a toll. The second line waited until the British advance was less than 100 yards in front and let go their first volley. It tore into the British line with devastating effect. That shock was quickly followed by another American volley. The British were stunned and hurt, and the advance halted. More than 40 percent of the British victims were officers, as Morgan had planned.

Even with the death all around, the British reformed, and with bayonets readied, they again advanced. Pickens' force executed Morgan's "filing off to the left" maneuver, as a river of men raced around Howard's left to the rear. Instead of immediately reforming in the rear, many of Pickens' men were heading briskly toward their horses which were tied up to trees. Lieutenant Joseph Hughes of the militia company on the right was so upset with the retreating men that he outran many of the them, and attempted to stop their exit with the flat of his sword, crying out, "You damned cowards, halt and fight!"[47] Eventually with the help of other officers like Hughes, the flood of fleeing men was stopped, and the group reformed into their companies. As Pickens' men fled, Tarleton ordered Captain Ogilvie to take 50 Legion dragoons and charge with sabers drawn into Pickens' men. To their surprise, Ogilvie's dragoons were being hit by strong fire from Triplett's Virginia riflemen. Then, as a counterattack, Washington and his dragoons, supported by McCall's mounted militia, arrived on Ogilvie's right flank, which sent the British dragoons retreating off to the rear. The battle was now just 20 minutes old.

At 7:15 A.M. Tarleton, with the American militia out of the way, it was time to focus on engaging the main force. The British infantry advanced cheering up the gentle slope to within 50 yards of Howard's third line of Continental soldiers. Howard's troops let go the first deadly volley at the British. They staggered momentarily, but continued to fire. The British returned a volley in reply to the Americans' fire. For the next 15 minutes these two opposing forces fired volley after volley at each other. Realizing that the forces were too balanced, at 7:30 A.M. Tarleton ordered his infantry reserve, McArthur's 71st Highlanders, to attack on Howard's right flank.

With the Highlanders' bagpipes playing loudly, Howard countered with Wallace's company of Virginia Militia. In order to meet the Highlanders properly, Howard had to reposition the Virginians. The maneuver required the troops to turn about, with their backs to the British who were firing at them, and execute a quarter circle to end up at right angles to the main line of Howard's force. There was much confusion in the Virginia ranks, and most of the men came to believe that they had been ordered to retreat. Howard and the other officers also came to sense this, but they were at least able to maintain a rather orderly "retreat." Morgan, seeing this unusual movement, was concerned and felt there must be some breakdown in discipline. He rode up to Howard and asked "Why are your men retreating?" Howard explained, "I am trying to save my right flank." Morgan responded, "Are you beaten?" Howard replied in defiance, "Do men who march like that look as though they are beaten?" Morgan then said, "I'll choose you a second position…. When you reach it, face about and fire!"

Morgan then rode out to a location where he wanted Howard's men to stop and turn toward the advancing Highlanders. The Highlanders came over the rise with much excitement and a little disorganized, but expecting to see the retreating Americans in chaos. Instead, the Highlanders were met with a devastating volley at near point-blank range, which left the survivors in shock and in complete confusion. At the same time Pickens' militia came into the British left to support the Virginians. Meanwhile on the British right at the same time, Washington, returning from pursuing the Legion's cavalry, came in on Tarleton's right flank with his cavalry. He had sent a messenger to Morgan saying, "They're coming on like a mob. Give them one fire, and I'll charge them." The charge from Washington's and McCall's cavalry at Ogilvie's dragoons smashed them quickly. With sabers drawn, the American cavalry continued through the dragoons and came into the rear of the shaken British infantry with deadly results. The end was near.[48]

The first British surrender was initiated by Major Newmarsh's troops of the Seventh Regiment, who threw down their arms and yelled for quarter. In the panic some 250 British horsemen, who had not yet joined in the battle, fled into the woods, while riding down their officers who got in their way.[49] Other troops tried to escape to the right rear, but McCall and his cavalry pursued and rounded up some 200 fugitives. The Highlanders were still engaged on the right with Howard's men, but Pickens' militia by then moved to their left rear and were firing at the Scots with effect. Tarleton sent in a company of Legion cavalry to support McArthur's men, but Pickens' and Howard's riflemen drove them off. McArthur attempted to break out, but with 16 of his officers down, and his men reduced to fighting hand-to-hand, he was forced to surrender his battalion.[50]

Tarleton tried to save the field guns, but his dash toward the blue-coated Royal Artillery gun crews was too late. Captain Anderson and Kirkwood had taken the field guns with a charge. The British gun crews tried to defend them to the last man, but they were unsuccessful. Seeing that the battle could not be won, Tarleton began to leave the field of battle with 14 officers and 40 other horsemen, "not unmindful of their own reputation, or the situation of their commanding officer." Washington followed in hot pursuit, hoping to make Tarleton his captured trophy. Tarleton turned and Washington slashed out at the officer on Tarleton's right. Washington's saber broke near the hilt, and before the officer could saber him back, he was shot through the shoulder on his saber arm by Washington's orderly, a 14-year-old named Collin.[51] The officer on the left then slashed at Washington, but patriot Sergeant Major Perry deflected the blow. Next Tarleton raised his sword and charged toward Washington. Washington raised his broken saber in defiance. Tarleton took out his pistol and fired toward Washington, only to wound the American's horse. Having failed to hit Washington, Tarleton fled toward the woods with his comrades heading toward the Pacolet.[52]

While Morgan reported of Tarleton to Greene that "He was pursued twenty-four miles, but, owing you our having taken a wrong trail at first, we never could overtake him," the battle of Cowpens was ended. The battle had taken only 50 minutes to complete. Morgan wrote in victory, "The troops I have the honor to command have

been so fortunate as to obtain a complete victory over a detachment from the British army, commanded by Lieut. Col. Tarleton."[53] The British had been dealt a major blow; suffering 110 killed, 830 captured, including some 200 wounded. Morgan wrote, "Not a man was killed, wounded, or even insulted, after he surrendered. Had not the Britons during this contest received so many lessons in humanity, I should flatter myself that this might teach them a little, but I fear they are incorrigible."[54] It was a far cry from the brutality of "Tarleton's Quarter." In addition the British lost two grasshoppers, 800 muskets, 35 baggage wagons, 60 black slaves, 100 cavalry horses, and large stores of ammunition. Morgan's American forces lost only 12 killed and 61 wounded. It was another stunning victory for the Southern Army.

Then prisoner William Moultrie wrote of the grim British reaction to Cowpens:

> This defeat of Colonel Tarleton's ... chagrined and disappointed the British officers and Tories in Charlestown exceedingly.... I saw them standing on the streets in small circles talking over the affair with very grave faces.... This great victory ... changed the face of American affairs.... In two actions, soon after each other, the British lost about two thousand men....

With King's Mountain, and now Cowpens, the British were getting hammered with each engagement. This had not been a victory over loyalist militia like King's Mountain, for Morgan had defeated British Regulars led by their fierce and bloody leader, Tarleton. Lieutenant Colonel Howard reported that Major McArthur said, "he was an officer before Tarleton was born, [and] that the best troops in the service had been put under 'that boy' to be sacrificed...." For their part in the victory at Cowpens, Brigadier General Morgan received a gold medal from the Continental Congress, lieutenant colonels William Washington and John Eager Howard received silver medals, while Colonel Pickens was granted a sword with a silver hilt and well ornamented.[55] News of the Southern Army victory spread north and south, and patriot spirits were raised to new heights.

15

THE NORTH CAROLINA CAMPAIGN AND GUILFORD COURT HOUSE

Morgan had won a great victory at Cowpens, but he knew well the tenuous situation he was in. Cornwallis was only some 25 miles away at his camp at Turkey Creek in York County. Since Tarleton had escaped from Cowpens, Morgan understood that he could potentially reach Cornwallis in as little as six hours. If Morgan stayed around the battlefield too long, soon he could be hearing the pounding of British cavalry in his vicinity. Morgan made a quick decision to head for the Catawba fords, and away from Cornwallis. Actually Cornwallis was closer to the fords than he was, but until Tarleton reached his camp, Morgan's location was unknown.

Morgan gave Pickens orders to remain in the field to bury the dead and comfort the wounded on both sides. The patriots used the captured British baggage to put up tents and beds. The wagons were loaded with the captured arms and other supplies of the British. The prisoners gathered, and by noon Morgan's force was underway. They crossed the Cherokee Ford and camped on the north bank of the Broad River by evening.

That night Cornwallis learned of the defeat from a few stragglers from Cowpens. He could only wait to confront Tarleton. Tarleton had spent the night of the 17th with his remaining dragoons after crossing Hamilton's Ford. Finally the next morning the remnants of Tarleton's force, some 200 dragoons, came into camp at Turkey Creek. The day was soon to be taken with many explanations from Tarleton.[1] Lord Cornwallis was angry as he learned that the reports he heard had been quite true. With his dress sword thrust into the ground, he rested his hands and weight on the sword until it snapped.

Cornwallis swore that he would retake Morgan's prisoners at any cost. Tarleton was so humiliated that a few days later he asked Cornwallis to give his "approbation of his proceedings [in the battle], or his leave to retire till an inquiry could be instituted, to investigate his conduct." Cornwallis had no other choice but to support Tarleton, and he wrote:

> You have forfeited no part of my esteem as an officer by the unfortunate event of the action of the 17th: The means you used to bring the enemy to action were able and masterly, and must ever do you honor. Your disposition was unexceptionable; the total misbehavior of the troops could alone have deprived you of the glory which is so justly your due.

Tarleton was ordered to begin to rebuild his Legion.[2]

Before daybreak that same morning, January 18, 1781, Morgan continued his march northward toward Gilbert Town in heavy rains, using the same line of retreat that the King's Mountain patriots had used after their victory. Morgan sent out scouts in the direction that Cornwallis was most expected. Morgan was soon delighted to learn that Cornwallis had not yet moved out to attack him. Soon Colonel Washington's cavalry joined with Morgan. Colonel Pickens had previously placed a yellow flag over the wounded at Cowpens, and placed the American surgeon, Dr. Pindell, in charge of the makeshift hospital supported by Robert Jackson, a surgeon's mate from the 71st Regiment. Colonel Pickens' mounted militia left on the 18th to return to Morgan's command.

Morgan crossed the Little Catawba at Ramsour's Mill

on January 21. When Morgan's force reached Gilbert Town, he detached most of his militia and some of Colonel Washington's cavalry to guard the prisoners. Determined not to let the British regain their prisoners, Morgan split off the prisoners and sent the detachment up the Cane Creek Road towards Morganton, crossing the Catawba River at Island Ford. With Pickens and company now back from Cowpens, Washington's cavalry turned over guarding of the prisoners to him. Soon Colonel Pickens turned his 600 British prisoners over to the commissary of prisoners, Major Hyrne, for the trip towards Charlottesville, Virginia, where prisoners were kept during this period of the Southern war. Washington's and Pickens' horsemen then rejoined General Morgan's troops on the east bank of the Catawba on January 23 at Sherrill's Ford. Morgan had brought his army some 60 miles since the 18th. Morgan hoped to remain at Sherrill's Ford until he received word from Greene on his next move.[3]

Cornwallis had indeed decided not to move to pursue Morgan until Leslie's force from Charles Town joined up with his. Later on the 18th the joining finally occurred, but the majority of the day was spent. As the weary day ended, Cornwallis wrote the following explanation to Clinton, putting a more positive face on the true nature of the defeat:

> Everything now bore the most promising Aspect; the Enemy were drawn up in an open Wood ... no room to doubt of the most Brilliant Success.... Tarleton ... charged and repulsed Washington's Horse, retook the Baggage of the Corps, and cut to pieces the Detachment of the Enemy who had taken Possession of it.... The loss of our cavalry is inconsiderable.... Your Excellency may be assured that Nothing ... shall induce me to give up ... the Winter's Campaign.

As it turned out, this letter with rosy images of the Cowpens disaster from Cornwallis arrived in New York aboard the *Halifax* on February 16, along with Clinton's first news of Ferguson's defeat at King's Mountain. It was a quite difficult day for Sir Henry.

According to Cornwallis' order book, his British troops departed from his Turkey Creek encampment at 2 A.M. on January 19. The wagons were directed to wait for daylight "when they will move under the escort of the Royal North Carolina Volunteer" commanded by Colonel John Hamilton. The army of some 3000 now headed up the east bank of the Broad River, toward King's Creek in the general direction of Cowpens. Cornwallis, having no real intelligence of Morgan's position, believed that Morgan would withdraw westward toward the mountains with his force estimated to be near 2000 men. On January 20 Cornwallis sent Tarleton with dragoons from the Hessian Jagers ahead to cross the Broad River and reconnoiter. He returned that evening to report that Morgan had passed the Broad River at Cherokee Ford, after leaving the wounded in the field under a flag of protection.[4]

Cornwallis now believed that his expectations of Morgan were correct, and that Morgan intended to hold the area near Broad River. Cornwallis moved across the Buffalo and King's creeks, to cross the Little Broad River by the 21st. That day he learned that Morgan had other plans. Morgan had turned to the east and was at Gilbert Town, north of Ramsour's Mill. He wrote to Rawdon, "I shall march tomorrow with 1200 Infantry & the Cavalry to attack or follow him to the banks of the Catawba." Cornwallis then turned to the northeast until he arrived at the Flint Hill Road. Down this road Cornwallis traveled with a determined pace until the evening of January 24 when he reached Ramsour's Mill on the Little Catawba, a branch of the Catawba that runs parallel and west of the main river. Even though Cornwallis had left behind his wagons and carts, he was not gaining on Morgan's forces. Morgan had already crossed the Catawba at Sherrill's Ford on January 23, some 36 hours before Cornwallis arrived at Ramsour's Mill. The next day Cornwallis wrote to Lord Rawdon, "My situation is most critical. I see infinite danger in proceeding, but certain ruin in retreating. I am therefore determined to go on, unless some misfortune should happen to you, which God forbid."[5]

On January 23 Morgan's aide, Major Edward Giles, trodded in heavy mud into General Greene's camp on the Pee Dee River with the news of the Cowpens victory. The camp suddenly broke out in celebration. Colonel Otto Williams wrote back to Morgan of the event:

> Next to the happiness which a man feels at his own good fortune is that which attends his friend. I am much better pleased that you have plucked the laurels from the brow of the hitherto fortunate Tarleton, than if they had fallen by the hands of Lucifer.
>
> We have had a feu-de-joie, drunk all your healths, swore you were the finest fellows on earth, and love you, if possible, more than ever. The General has, I think, made his compliments in very handsome terms. Enclosed is a copy of his orders. It was written immediately after we received the news, and during the operations of some cherry bounce.... Compliments to Howard and all friends. Adieu.
>
> Yrs. sincerely, O.H. Williams

The following morning Greene sent Major Giles on a fresh horse off to inform Congress and General Washington of the victory. Though the army was still not properly clothed or fitted out, Greene put them on marching orders. He then wrote Marion indicating that Lee was to continue to operate in the enemy's rear, with all other detachments recalled immediately. Greene could decide to attack the British rear, or join Morgan and bring the army together again. As Greene's forces prepared to move, three letters were received in rapid succession from Morgan. The first and shocking letter written on January 24 read:

> Dear Sir: After my late success and my sanguine expectations to do something clever this campaign, I must inform you that I shall be obliged to give over the pursuit by reason of an old pain returning upon me.... If I can procure a chaise, I will endeavor to get home. Gen. Davidson [and] Col. Pickens ... can manage the militia better than I can, and will well supply my place."

Indeed Greene could not be without his victorious officer. But Morgan was suffering from his periodic and serious bouts of sciatica and rheumatism, which had always plagued him. Would these infirmities finally put him out of service? The next day Morgan wrote the next second and third letters with increasing situations:

> Sir: I am this minute informed by express, that Lord Cornwallis is at Ramsey's [Ramsour's Mill] on their march this way, destroying all before them....

The last letter revealed:

> Dear General: I receive intelligence every hour of the enemy's rapid approach, in consequence of which I am sending off my wagons. My numbers at this time are too weak to fight them. I intend to move towards Salisbury, in order to get near the main army.... I expect you will move somewhere on the Yadkin to oppose their crossing, I think it would be advisable to join our forces and fight them before they join Phillips [in Virginia], which they most certainly will do if they are not stopped.... I sent to Davidson to join me, which I expect he will do tomorrow. His strength I do not know, as his men were collecting yesterday.

With this news, Greene's mind was made up. He was off to join with Morgan. He had already sent out to the commissaries at Salisbury and Hillsborough to be prepared to move their wagons and supplies to Virginia, and his quartermaster general, Carrington, was already preparing the flatboats on the Dan River for the potential of retreat into Virginia.

Meanwhile, Cornwallis contemplated his situation while encamped at Ramsour's Mill, looking at the rain-swollen Little Catawba River. From January the 19th to the 22nd, his force marched only 36 miles. After lightening his forward troops by ordering his heavy baggage train and the women to be left behind under command of General Howard, to move slowly forward in the rear, during the period of the 22nd to the 25th, they had still only covered 36 miles.[6] That was indeed too slow. Cornwallis was now deprived of most of his light troops due to the Cowpens defeat, and at the pace he was pursuing

Morgan's forces, he might not ever engage Morgan's troops before Greene joined up with him.

After reflection on the situation, Cornwallis made a significant decision to turn his force into light troops, and to rid them of any possessions that served to slow down the army. By example he threw out all of his personnel baggage, an action "which was followed by every officer of the army without a single murmur." Most of the wagons, along with the baggage, were burned. Only a few wagons remained, including four empty ones to be used for any wounded. Ammunition, salt and some hospital supplies were not fired. The rum kegs had been opened up and poured on the ground, to the dismay of all. Whether his actions were ultimately successful or not, one could debate, but Cornwallis' 41-year-old officer, Brigadier General Charles O'Hara, said that the event "must ever do the greatest honor to Lord Cornwallis' military reputation, and to the gallant persevering spirit of his little army."[7]

As it turned out, Cornwallis had another problem. His troops needed shoes. Fortunately enough leather was found at Ramsour's Mill to supply each man with a new pair. Cornwallis also directed that the men carry with them extra soles "as the like opportunity may not happen for some time." Although Cornwallis was delighted with his decision to relieve themselves of all comforts, like "tents, beds, wine, clothing, etc.," finding that the army responded with "the most general and cheerful acquiescence," some men did desert during the three days camped at Ramsour's Mill. Reports back to England showed a reduction of headcount of 227 men, with no battle being fought.[8] Perhaps these troops preferred frontier hardships more than the forced marches without the daily rum ration. O'Hara reported their plight: "In this situation, without baggage, necessaries, or provisions of any sort for officer or soldier, in the most barren inhospitable, unhealthy part of North America, opposed to the most savage, inveterate, perfidious, cruel enemy, with zeal and with bayonets only, it was resolved to follow Greene's army to the end of the world."[9]

On January 28, 1781, Cornwallis left Ramsour's Mill and marched to within sight of the Catawba River at Beattie's Ford, spending his night at Jacob Forney's home some four miles away. Morgan, while camped at Sherrill's Ford, also kept detachments at Beattie's, McCowan's and Island fords to watch Cornwallis' movements in his direction. Morgan knew Cornwallis would cross at one or more of these fords, and he was determined to resist any crossings to the extent his forces could. Having marched through the now muddy, red Carolina clay to reach the Catawba, Cornwallis was disappointed to find the river too high to cross. So he waited with his troops as they dried out the ammunition and cleaned their weapons.

While at Forney's Plantation, Cornwallis issued a notice in reaction to the complaints of the men regarding the loss of their rum ration:

> The supply of rum for a time will be absolutely impossible, and that of meal very uncertain. To remedy the latter, it is recommended either to bruise the Indian corn, or to rasp it after it has been soaked…. As the object of our march is to assist and support those loyalists in North Carolina, who have ever been distinguished by their fidelity to their King and their attachment to Great Britain, it is needless to point out to the officers the necessity of preserving the strictest discipline.

The same day Cornwallis left Ramsour's Mill, General Greene departed from his Pee Dee camp. Greene ordered General Isaac Huger to take the Pee Dee army to Salisbury while he proceeded with his aide and a few dragoons to join with Morgan at Sherrill's Ford. Greene traveled through heavy loyalist country for a distance of some 125 miles from Hicks' Ford on the Pee Dee to Beattie's Ford on the Catawba in only two days. Arriving at Morgan's camp on January 30, he called for a conference with Morgan, Davidson and William Washington. While no minutes were kept of the meeting, it leaked out that Morgan wanted to either retreat to the mountains or move behind Cornwallis to Ninety Six. Greene's strategy was to keep just out of reach of Cornwallis' forces by moving northward toward Virginia. Greene closed the conference with the words, "I shall take the measure upon myself." Greene decided to move the forces toward Salisbury to join with Huger, leaving behind General Davidson to oppose the British crossing of the Catawba as best he could.[10]

Before leaving camp on the Catawba, Greene wrote several letters. He directed Huger to continue to Salisbury, but to send the bulk of his stores to Guilford Court House. Colonel Lee was directed to break off with Marion and make a forced march to join the army where it was a "fine field and great glory ahead." Hoping to gain more militia, Greene wrote to William Campbell, the hero of King's Mountain, to join with him with 1000 mountain men because "Such a force will add our splendor to your own glory and give the World another proof of the bravery of the Mountain Militia." Greene also gained intelligence that a British force was en route to Wilmington. Greene thought it must be the rumored General Benedict Arnold at Wilmington. Actually, Lieutenant Colonel James H. Craig with some 400 regular troops from the 82nd Regiment from Charles Town was to occupy Wilmington.[11]

Back a month earlier, on December 30, 1780, and just over a month after Leslie had abandoned Portsmouth to sail to Charles Town, a new force of 1600 British troops under the command of the now British General Benedict Arnold had indeed arrived, not at Wilmington, but at Hampton Roads up the Chesapeake aboard Captain Symonds' fleet.[12] This new invasion took the Virginia authorities again by surprise, and as many felt, it "disgraced our Country." Intelligence had somehow failed the patriot officials. General Washington had warned Governor Jefferson back on December 23 that British ships had dropped anchor at Sandy Hook in New York harbor some three days before. The news of a sailing led Virginia officials to believe that the fleet was heading to South Carolina in view of the season. Some confusion arose about whether the fleet had been delayed and it was not until January 2 that Washington confirmed that the British ships had actually sailed back on the 21st. The message of confirmation did not reach Virginia until Arnold's fleet was already discovered in Hampton Roads.

Governor Jefferson received the news of Arnold's presence from General Nelson on Sunday, December 31, but he was reluctant to call out the militia until he was certain of the hostile intent. It was not until 10 A.M. on Tuesday, January 2, 1781, that Jefferson received confirmation of hostile events. Jefferson even admitted, "The first Intelligence had become totally disbelieved." During these two critical days, Arnold had already moved to Jamestown. Even though three of his troop transport ships had not arrived with 600 of the men, he had sailed his fleet — the 44-gun *Charon*, four frigates, the *Fowey*, three sloops, two brigs, and 16 lesser vessels — directly up the James River without stopping at Portsmouth as expected. With favorable winds upriver, Arnold wanted to surprise the Virginians. Chaos reigned with the citizens in Richmond and Petersburg. A witness wrote of the lack of warning, "The alarm was so great and sudden, that almost every person in the neighbourhood was endeavouring to put some of his Property in a state of safety by removing it."[13]

On Thursday, January 4, Arnold landed at the Byrd Plantation at Westover, and marched toward Richmond. Unopposed, he promptly took Richmond the next day after noon. In Richmond the locals had been rather successful at removing much of their treasured property. Jefferson boasted that the British "were most visibly disappointed in finding we had removed almost everything out of their reach, which had been effected in 19 hours." Arnold did proceed to dump five field cannons and five tons of gunpowder into the river at the local foundry, destroyed some tobacco warehouses, and took 300 arms, 120 sides of leather, some tools and clothing. The British burned two public storehouses, a craft shop and four private buildings. Most of the public records survived, although they were "totally deranged and dissorted." Jefferson characterized the events at Richmond by saying, "In truth we have escaped to a miracle."

Arnold stayed in Richmond for only 24 hours, and moved back to Westover and Berkeley, the home of patriot Benjamin Harrison. The British damaged his home and freed his slaves. One detachment moved up the Appomattox River, and was met by militia leader, General William Smallwood, who prevented them from capturing any tobacco ships. Another unit under Lieutenant Colonel John Simcoe with his Queen's Rangers had been sent to Westham, above the falls of the James River, to destroy a small arsenal there.[14]

On January 10 the British left Westover and moved down the James River, raiding as they went. At Hood's Landing they encountered patriot militia commanded by George Rogers Clarke and lost 17 killed and 13 wounded before driving the Americans off with a bayonet advance. At Cobham, Arnold captured 60 hogsheads of tobacco. Similar work was made of plundering at Smithfield too. By January 9, Arnold had moved back to Portsmouth and was settling in for the winter there.[15] Otto Williams wrote of the Virginia events, "A perfidious Villain laid her [Virginia] rich inhabitants under contribution, and her Honors in the dust.... The governor is said to boast he is no military man."[16]

The response of the Virginia militia had been poor. The militia that arrived at the gathering sites dismayed Baron Von Steuben, who was in command of the troops. He wrote Washington: "It is impossible to describe the situation I am in; nothing can be got from the state."[17] By the time Arnold was at Richmond, only some 200 militia had appeared. On January 10 Jefferson had complained of the slowness, but by the 12th it was reported that "large Numbers of men are hourly Crowding" into Petersburg. By the time Arnold was back at Portsmouth, some 3700 militia had reported to three designated sites: Fredericksburg, Williamsburg and Cabin Point on the south side of the James River. There were many critics of Jefferson's actions and that of the Virginia government on Arnold's easy taking of the state's capital. Jefferson worked hard to provide evidence to the Congress that the Virginia geography served well the enemy, but Madison remarked with sarcasm, "I am glad to hear that Arnold has been at last fired at." Only the news of the Cowpens victory in South Carolina served to lift the spirits of the Virginia citizens over their plight with Arnold.[18]

Another unfortunate event occurred for the patriot cause around the time of Arnold's invasion of Virginia. Congress was sad to learn that Henry Laurens from South Carolina, traveling as the minister-designate to Holland, had been captured at sea and placed in the prison in the Tower of London. While Laurens attempted to destroy important papers overboard, a quick thinking sailor retrieved a bag containing Laurens' instructions from Congress proposing a treaty with Holland. With relations between the British and Holland at a low ebb, the proposal caused a breaking point.

Although an official state of war was not created, the English Court of St. James issued letters of marque and reprisal against the United Provinces of Holland. Numerous Dutch ships were seized in British ports, as the Dutch did the same to the British. Because of the coalition that Holland had with other maritime powers, including Russia, Lord Sandwich with alarm warned the king of England that they were "on the point of being at war with the whole world." The king called a meeting at the Queen's House with his ministers on January 19, 1781, to discuss the serious situation. After much discussion, it was decided that a negotiated treaty with Russia must be accomplished to prevent a disaster. At the same time the ministers agreed to punish the Dutch in the Caribbean by attacking St. Eustatius and all Dutch shipping in those waters. All these events were caused by the capture of a single Southern patriot leader.[19]

Back in North Carolina, the British invasion was creating heightened activity. The North Carolina General Assembly was busy authorizing four more regiments of Continental troops, and approving a bounty of £200 and "one prime slave and 640 acres of land" for one year's service. The New Bern Council of State received and granted South Carolina Governor Rutledge's request for credit of £100,000, purchased 892 gallons of rum to be sent to the North Carolina prisoners at Charles Town and gave Virginia authorities permission to buy pork in the state. What would this third invasion by Cornwallis of North Carolina hold for the state?

Meanwhile, the Catawba River was out of her banks all during January 30 and early the next day. By the afternoon of January 31, the waters began to rapidly fall. General Davidson was now in charge of slowing down Cornwallis at the fords. He had posted some 300 militia at McCowan's Ford from Mecklenburg and Rowan counties under Major William , plus Captain Joseph Graham's horsemen. At Beattie's Ford, located four miles above McCowan's Ford, he posted Colonel Thomas Ford with the Orange County militia. With Greene's advice, he kept his mounted militia ready as a mobile force to move to any of the several fords the British might cross. The plan worked out with Greene was that after the planned crossing engagement with Cornwallis was completed, Davidson's forces were to join him at the home of David Carr, which was located some 16 miles down the road toward Salisbury. General Greene with a small escort moved off to the designated spot to await events.[20]

While the British waited for the waters to subside, Cornwallis had ordered a number of marches towards the various fords "so as to give the enemy equal apprehension for several fords." With the waters falling, Cornwallis had made his decision. He would make the crossing the next day with his main force at McCowan's Ford, while creating a diversion by sending Lieutenant Colonel Webster to Beattie's Ford. Webster, with the Highlanders, the Hessian Jagers and Cornwallis' own 33rd Regiment, was directed to make a noisy cannonade to attract the attention of Davidson's men away from McCowan's Ford.

At 2:30 A.M. Cornwallis set off from Forney's Plantation with the Brigade of Guards under Brigadier General O'Hara, the 23rd Regiment of the Welsh Fusiliers, the Hessian Regiment under de Bose, 200 cavalry under Tarleton and two three-pounders toward McCowan's. Along with Cornwallis were two former North Carolinians, the ex-governor, Josiah Martin, and Halifax native Lieutenant Colonel John Hamilton. The ford Cornwallis picked was really two fords, a wagon ford which was deeper yet led directly to the opposite bank, and a horse ford, which was more shallow, that angled for a longer distance upstream.[21]

In manning his fords, General Davidson had run into problems recruiting the militia, and more especially during this growing season. The group that did respond was not of the highest caliber, but the Patriot cause was needy. One such volunteer of 16 years age was young Robert Henry. He had received a bayonet wound at King's Mountain, and recovered. While he was attending school he received an urgent appeal from Davidson. His schoolmaster, Mr. Beatty, attempted to delay them, but Robert and his brother Joseph left with their squirrel rifles for McCowan's Ford when the Catawba had fallen. On the way they stopped to buy a half-pint of whiskey and a bushel of potatoes for $200 in Continental paper money. After finishing off the whiskey, they arrived at the ford where they found some 30 other men including the schoolmaster and a Joel Jetton. The officer of the guard led the newcomers to their assigned position at the wagon ford, where they waited for the action to commence.

While the patriot militia rested on their rifles at the shore, Davidson had posted Major Joseph Graham's cavalry force of some 300 men on draft horses to occupy a small knoll several hundred yards back from the river to protect the militia. At daybreak Jetton awoke to the sound of horses moving in the deep water. The loyalist guide, Dick Beal, had been leading the British to McCowan's Ford through woods and swamp. Out of confusion and concern for the patriot campfires, Beal had headed the horses into the wagon ford section, not the horse ford with lower water depths. As Jetton surveyed the river in the fog he was shocked to see the outline of three officers dressed in scarlet and white coming towards him. The three officers were Cornwallis, Leslie and O'Hara, in company with scores of troops. In stark terror he sounded the alarm, shouting, "The British, The British!" The British were already in midstream by this point. Robert Henry and his other companions woke, and as he wrote, "By the time I was ready to fire, the rest of the guard had fired. I then heard the British splashing and making noise as if drowning." Henry dashed some water into his eyes, and fired his rifle into the British in the river. The battle had begun.[22]

As some of the British fell to the river, bloody, they continued in high water to cross the ford. As Henry retreated to locate a tree to hide him as he reloaded, General Davidson and his cavalry came up to meet them. Henry, who had seen Schoolmaster Beatty as he retreated, remarked, "I thought I could stand it as long as he could." The firing continued at the British as they continued toward the riverbank. The British had fared as well as could be expected. Some men and horses had been swept away by the river current, and some had been killed or wounded by the first volleys. The infantry was "up to their breasts in a rapid stream, their knapsacks on their backs and sixty of seventy rounds of powder and ball in each pouch tied at the pole of their necks, their firelocks with bayonets, fixed on their shoulders." The Brigade of Guards led the way with the three senior officers mounted at the head. Leslie's horse was carried downstream and O'Hara's was turned over by the heavy current.[23]

Cornwallis' horse was shot as he crossed the ford, though the horse continued until it reached the other bank where it fell dead. Cornwallis wrote of the situation as they arrived on the opposite bank, "The light infantry landing first immediately formed, and in a few minutes killed or dispersed every thing that appeared before them, the rest of the troops forming and advancing in succession…. Their general [Davidson] and two or three other officers were among the killed … a few were taken prisoner."[24] Indeed, General Davidson had led his cavalry back from the river's edge and into the undergrowth. Unfortunately, the camp fires tended to silhouette them against the light and the British fire struck home. Davidson was hit by a musketball in the chest, and he died instantly. Without their leader the patriots ran. The British later reported that they had lost three killed and 36 wounded, but Robert Henry wrote, "A great number of the British dead were found on Thompson's fish dam, and in his trap…. The river stunk with dead carcasses, the British could not have lost less than one hundred men."[25]

As the Americans retreated, Cornwallis turned his troops upstream toward the force that opposed Webster's crossing at Beattie's Ford. Webster crossed unopposed as the patriots dispersed. The road to Salisbury was clogged with baggage and supply wagons of civilians who had been terrified by Webster's loud cannonade at Beattie's Ford. The militia joined with this retreating herd of people and fled. At Tarrant's Tavern, located some 10 miles from Beattie's Ford along the Salisbury Road, many of the retreating militia paused for refreshments. Mingled with civilians at Tarrant's, as the pails of whiskey were carried out of the tavern to the waiting militia, the word went out that "Tarleton was coming!"

In confusion and chaos the militiamen dispersed as best they could. Captain Nathaniel Martin led some men to cross a fence to prepare to stand against Tarleton. Others left in a hurry with their pails. Suddenly the green dressed dragoons burst on the scene. With a shout from Tarleton, "Remember, the Cowpens!" the dragoons immediately cut down with their sabers 50 men, according to Tarleton's report. A later survey of the spot by another British officer stated that "he did not see ten dead bodies of the provincials in the whole." Several of the ten were unarmed old men who had come to the tavern when the alarm went out.[26] Tarleton wrote of the events, "This exertion of the cavalry succeeding the gallant action of the guards in the morning, diffused such a terror among the inhabitants, that the King's troops passed through the most hostile part of North Carolina without a shot from the militia."

Greene had been waiting for Davidson at the appointed place at David Carr's house six miles from Tarrant's Tavern. At midnight a tired messenger arrived to tell Greene of the Davidson death and the dispersed militia. Immediately Greene departed to Salisbury to join with Morgan and his force. At Salisbury, Greene had breakfast at Steele's Tavern, where the landlady gave him two bags of hard money as a contribution to the war effort, with the words, "You need them more than I do."[27] While at Steele's Tavern, Greene wrote a letter to Huger directing him to change direction and head toward the northwest to meet with Morgan at Guilford Court House. Here Greene learned another bit of news; the long awaited arms promised by the North Carolina government turned out to be 1700 rusted muskets which were useless from poor storage. Greene moved on to join with Morgan.

Morgan and Greene joined up to cross the Yadkin River at Trading Ford, some seven miles northwest of Salisbury. The rains had continued all the day and night of February 1, and most of the 2nd. Due to Greene's incredible preplanning, there were boats at Trading Ford ordered up from Colonel Kosciuszko. Some were collected at the river and others were hauled to Trading Ford by wagon. On the night of February 3 Greene's force was on the opposite and eastern shore, encamped. Morgan was not in good shape physically. He was in much pain, suffering from a bad case of piles along with his rheumatism. He remarked, "This is the first time that I have ever experienced this disorder and from the idea I had of it, sincerely, prayed that I might never know what it was."[28] Morgan was sure he could not prolong this action in the field.

Meanwhile, Cornwallis had been slow in gaining on Morgan and Greene. After the action at Tarrant's Tavern, Cornwallis reunited his army on the Salisbury Road. Knowing that the rains his troops had encountered during the period would cause the Yadkin to rise, he wanted to catch up with Morgan and Greene before they were able to cross. Cornwallis was unaware that Greene had boats, and, thus, he expected that the Americans would be trapped. He ordered General O'Hara to take the cavalry and the mounted infantry and advance to find Morgan and Greene. His experience with the remaining wagons in the muddy red clay caused him to order another baggage wagon burning event. O'Hara's men reached Trading Ford at midnight on February 3 to encounter a small rear guard holding some baggage wagons. The British recorded that "after giving a few shots, in the language of this country, [the guard] split and squandered, that is run away." The militia dispersed in the dark.[29]

As the British marched after Greene toward Salisbury, they took part in considerable plundering of civilians. Being alarmed at creating more problems for his maintaining at least the guise of supporting the loyalist movement, Cornwallis issued this order from Canthard's Plantation on February 2nd:

> Lord Cornwallis is highly displeased that several houses were set on fire during the march this day, a disgrace to the army, and he will punish with the utmost severity any person or persons who shall be found guilty of committing so disgraceful an outrage. His Lordship requests that the commanding officers of corps will endeavor to find out who set fire to the houses this day.

Cornwallis also issued another posting to his army on a different issue:

> Lord Cornwallis desires the Brigade of Guards will accept his warmest acknowledgments for the cool and determined bravery which they showed at the passage of the Catawba when rushing through that long and difficult ford under a galling fire without returning a shot, it gives him a most pleasant prospect of what may be expected from that distinguished corps.[30]

After marching through the miserable rain along a muddy road, Cornwallis, with the main army, entered Salisbury at mid-afternoon on February 3. At O'Hara's request, Cornwallis sent ahead the artillery to fire at the Americans. The next day Cornwallis arrived at Trading Ford to discover that indeed the patriots had escaped across the Yadkin. The British were left to wait until the river subsided to attack the rebels. The British artillery volleys fired at the only target they had across the river, the tin roof of the cabin where General Greene sat as he wrote his letters. Dr. William Read watched Greene as he wrote his letters, "His pen never rested, but when a new visitor arrived … answer was given with calmness and precision, and the pen immediately resumed."[31] Unfortunately for the British, the American camp was located behind a rocky ridge, which paralleled the Yadkin River. Here Greene wrote of the battle at Cowpens, Morgan's retreat across the Catawba, the death of Davidson, Cornwallis' advance, the dispersal of the militia, and the crossing of the Yadkin. Greene ordered Lee to move up to Guilford too. The time had come for another critical decision for Greene. Where should he go to avoid Cornwallis and his stronger army?

Morgan and Greene seemed to be content to remain on the eastern side of the Yadkin while the rains swelled the river. But as the river quickly began to fall on the evening of February 4, the patriot leaders decided that they must leave, or risk having the British army on their side of the river the next morning. So that night Greene's forces marched from Trading Ford northward toward the Upper Dan River area and the Virginia border.

At Abbott's Creek, not far from Salem, Greene's army stopped and received intelligence of Cornwallis' movements. Morgan, with a detachment and the wagons, turned in a new direction to the northeast and headed to Guilford Court House. From Abbott's Creek, Greene wrote Huger a letter telling him to locate a worthy site for an engagement with Cornwallis. His intentions were thus revealed as he wrote, "From Lord Cornwallis pushing disposition, and the contempt he has for our army, we may precipitate him into some capital misfortune. If Cornwallis knows his true interest he will pursue our army. If he can disperse that, he will complete the destruction of the state; and without it he will do nothing to effect."[32]

As he waited Cornwallis set up his weekend headquarters in Salisbury at the home of Maxwell Chambers, a loyalist merchant. From there he wrote Lord Rawdon in South Carolina the following: "I am distressed by the rivers and creeks being swelled, but shall try to pass the Yadkin at the shallow ford as soon as possible…. I long to hear from you." Cornwallis learned from locals that Greene had broken camp and was heading northward. Cornwallis was now convinced that he was going to Virginia. Being assured that the lower fords of the Dan could not be passed without ferry capability, Cornwallis decided that he would catch Greene's army as they retreated to the Upper Dan region.

On February 6, Cornwallis' main army moved toward Shallow Ford on the Yadkin, some 25 miles above Trading Ford. After only a short time, Tarleton's men ran into a small militia unit under Colonel Francis Locke at a bridge over Grant's Creek. Surprisingly, the patriots put up such a fierce action, that the army's movement was delayed some three hours until they were dispersed. Locke and his men destroyed the bridge, which caused a British

delay while they rebuilt it. On the night of the 6th, Cornwallis' army rested at Rencher's Ford on the South Fork of the Yadkin River.

On that same day Morgan reached Guilford Court House, having marched his army 47 miles in 48 hours in spite of rain, poor roads and hungry men on short rations. From that location Morgan wrote Greene a sad letter relating his situation, "I arrived here last evening, and sent a number of prisoners that were here, to join the main body. About 4000 pounds of salted meat, corn meal and forage equipment is promised me. I am much indisposed with pain. When I get everything in as good a trim as possible respecting provisions, etc., I shall move on slowly to some safe retreat and try to recover."[33] Greene had stayed behind at Abbott's Creek until the morning of February 8, when he was sure that Cornwallis had taken his bait. Discovering Cornwallis was on the way to Shallow Ford, he departed for Guilford Court House, where he arrived that same day.[34]

Meanwhile, Cornwallis crossed at Shallow Ford on February 8, camped at Lindsay's Plantation that night, and by noon the next day entered Bethania, a Moravian settlement. The British passed into the settlement, according to Cornwallis' order book: "Jagers, Cavalry, Half the Pioneers, 2 three-pounders, Lt. Col. Webster's Brigade, 2 six-pounders, Regiment of Bose, North Carolinians [Hamilton's], 2 six-pounders, Brigade of Guards, Bat horses, Half the Pioneers, Wagons, an officer and twelve Dragoons [who] will march with the rear guard." The British army, who filled all the houses and took over the area, overwhelmed the village of 90 persons. Soon they had their hands on 300 pounds of bread, 100 gallons of whiskey, 60 head of cattle, many sheep and poultry, and all the available flour they could find. They also took 17 horses. The sight of serious drinking caused Cornwallis to remark, "He begs it may be told to the men that if they commit such irregularities, he shall not think it necessary to trouble the Commissaries in providing any more rum for them." But Cornwallis allowed them to receive their 6 A.M. ration of rum before the day's march started at 7 A.M.

By 10 A.M. the British had entered Salem, another small Moravian village of some 160 citizens. The lord remained at the house of Traugott Bagge, a local loyalist merchant, for about an hour with his staff. Resting at Salem only long enough to eat, the British then moved to their next camp at Miller's Plantation, as they continued to move toward Greene and Guilford Court House.[35] The British had found the Moravians to be "mild and inoffensive folk," but as the army moved on, the camp followers looted the village, followed soon by overeager patriot guerrillas who stripped the Salem citizens clean, leaving little behind. Lord Cornwallis again issued another order to the officers that "If their duty to their King and their country and their feelings of humanity were not sufficient to enforce obedience [to orders against plundering] ... he must make use of such power as military law placed in his hands."[36]

At Guilford Court House, Greene was considering his next move. Cornwallis was now outside Salem, less than 25 miles away. On February 9, General Huger arrived to finally reunite the Southern American Army for the first time in several months. Huger had traveled up from the Pee Dee and entered the camp with Light Horse Harry Lee and his cavalry. Present in the patriot camp were some 2036 soldiers, made up of 1426 seasoned Continental troops and the remaining consisting of militia and recruits.[37] Greene was dismayed by the poor turnout of the North Carolina Militia. In a letter to John Butler, the brigadier general from the Orange County militia, Greene wrote in disgust, "Not more than 120 men are left with this army to render the regulars the least assistance." The next day he reported to Butler, "All the militia of your state have deserted me except about 80 men."[38]

While camped, Greene had conducted a thorough review of the surrounding terrain, and considered the condition of his troops. The men were in poor condition with their clothing worn out, their shoes in either poor condition or missing, having few blankets among them and suffering from hunger. The only American unit with any semblance of military bearing was Lee's Legion of cavalry. Their white breeches were now muddy red, and the men were extremely tired after having completed their forced movement to catch up with Huger. The area around Guilford Court House was ideal for a battle, in Greene's opinion.

Greene called a rare Council of War with his key officers to consider the prospect of engaging action with Cornwallis at Guilford Court House. Present at the council with Greene were Morgan and Huger, and Light Horse Harry Lee, William Washington, Otto Williams, and John Eager Howard. Greene proceeded to present his case for a battle. He believed that the British were now low on supplies, reduced in strength, and far away from their base of operations. In addition, Greene felt that the grounds were well suited for defensive operations. If they retreated into Virginia, they were abandoning the patriots in North Carolina to the British and the loyalists. But the officers were emphatic in their opposition to making a stand against Cornwallis. They argued that the army was indeed in sad condition, lacking clothing, and that the men had just completed grueling marches under difficult conditions. They believed that they were no match for Cornwallis under their weakened condition. Greene backed down and agreed to continue the strategy of evading Cornwallis.[39]

With spies nearly moving freely between the close British and American positions, keeping each informed of the other's movements, it was important to Greene to organize a successful movement away from his current environment. Greene took immediate steps to organize his army. To screen the true movements of his main army, Greene entrusted the effort to his most experienced officers: William Washington's 250 cavalry, 280 of John Eager Howard's Maryland and Delaware Continentals, 60 riflemen from Colonel William Campbell, and some 100 cavalry of Lee's Legion.

To command this critical screening force, he asked the Old Waggoner, General Daniel Morgan. Morgan would not accept the command. He pleaded his case that he was suffering from hemorrhoids, in addition to bouts of rheumatism and sciatica. Lee tried to persuade Morgan to accept the assignment, even to the point of calling to question his retirement which would present a poor light on his patriotism. Lee later wrote, "These observations appeared to touch the feelings of Morgan; for a moment he paused; then discovered a faint inclination to go through with the impending conflict; but finally returned to his original decision."

On February 10, 1781, Morgan left the army at Guilford Court House in a carriage to return to his farm in Winchester, Virginia. Greene remarked sadly, "Great generals are scarce. There are few Morgans to be found."[40] Greene followed that with the record, "Camp at Guilford C.H. Feb. 10th, 1781. Gen. Morgan, of the Virginia line, has leave of absence until he recovers his health, so as to be able to take the field again."[41] It was Morgan's last campaign with the regular forces of the Southern American Army. The screening command was given to Colonel Otto Holland Williams of Maryland.

It was February 10 when Colonel Otto Williams left camp and headed westward, straight for the British. At Reedy Fork his cavalry and infantry force of 700 found the lead elements of Tarleton's Legion with a contingent of Jagers. Several shots were fired between the parties, and Tarleton stopped to wait for the main army to come forward. Cornwallis understood that this was probably a scouting party, or perhaps a rear guard unit of the main army. Cornwallis was cautious enough to close his columns, which had been stretched out for four miles. Occasional firing continued as the Americans destroyed the bridge across Reedy Fork. After several hours of delay, the British army was underway again. Both forces pushed hard and only the constant attention of Williams and his men would keep them ahead of the British. The screening unit was leading Cornwallis north, keeping the British away from Greene's main army moving ahead to the east and on a parallel track.

Williams finally halted at nine o'clock that evening,

allowing only half of his men to sleep, with the other half serving as pickets. At 3 A.M. the camp was broken, and the men took to the road again for several hours. This maneuver allowed the force to stop for breakfast, the only meal of the day, and still remain ahead of Cornwallis. It was a hard way to live, with only six hours sleep in every 48 hours. The march was so brutal that when the unit made camp, the men literally dropped in their tracks to sleep, not having the energy to eat even if they could. Light Horse Lee was proud of the men and of being part of the screening command, and wrote, "Notwithstanding this privation, the troops were in fine spirits, and good health, delighted with their task and determined to prove themselves worthy of the distinction with which they had been honored."[42] Cornwallis' men were better clothed than the Americans were, but they were also tired and hungry. Cornwallis wrote that "Nothing could exceed the patience and alacrity of the officers and soldiers under every species of hardship and fatigue."[43]

Meanwhile, Greene and the main army also broke camp at Guilford Court House on February 10 and headed directly for the Lower Dan River, moving toward Irwin's Ferry located 70 miles away. Before he departed, Greene had worked out a plan for crossing the Dan at Irwin's Ferry as proposed by Lieutenant Colonel Carrington. Colonel Kosciuszko had been sent ahead to Irwin's to prepare for defending the crossing site. Carrington and Kosciuszko had been gathering flatboats on the Lower Dan River for some time. Greene's army marched in the poor weather, with the troops trudging through the slushy red clay mud from the days of rain and occasional snow. The going was slow even with determined parties in both armies.

General O'Hara led the British advance guard of light infantry. Like the Americans, the British were able to make some 30 miles per day, in spite of the difficult ground and weather. Lee and Washington's cavalry units had brief clashes with O'Hara's forward guard as the days progressed. Williams' screening command was indeed taking the British toward Dix's Ferry, which was some six miles downstream and to the east of Irwin's Ferry. The deception continued until the evening of February 12 when Tarleton reported to Cornwallis that Greene's main army was heading toward the Lower Dan to the east. Cornwallis broke camp after midnight and scouts came upon the road being used by Williams' force.

Early that same morning, Williams received word from Greene that his army was approaching Irwin's Ferry and that he must now head straight for that crossing. Williams forwarded the message to Lee's men serving as the screen's rear guard. Lee was having a leisurely breakfast that morning of February 13 when a local farmer came hurrying into the Lee's camp with word that the British

were only four miles away. Lee's quickly rose and took off with his cavalry in the direction of the enemy. Lee came into contact with Tarleton's dragoons. Lee pulled his men off the road and allowed some of Tarleton's troops to pass. Then Lee attacked Tarleton's men from the rear. Soon Tarleton came up the road to discover 18 bodies dead on the road. Lee resumed his rear guard station for Williams' force. Throughout the 13th, and into the night, the British pursued Lee's unit and as Lee wrote, "More than once the Legion of Lee and the van of O'Hara were within musket shot...." Both the British and Americans were fatigued, and Lee recorded that "The demeanor of the hostile troops became so pacific in appearance that a spectator would have been led to consider them members of the same army."[44]

At 8 P.M. on the evening of the 13th Lee and Williams saw the campfires burning ahead in the direction they were heading. Both men were concerned if this was indeed Greene's army just ahead, for they might be forced to engage the British and meet with a disaster. But as it turned out, the fires had been kept burning by local patriots after Greene's men had departed two days before. Williams and Lee could not rest, and they continued into the night toward Irwin's Ferry. When word came that the British had halted to rest, the Americans stopped and slept for several hours. The march continued, and around noon on February 14, a message arrived by courier from Greene that "All our troops are over and the stage is clear.... I am ready to receive you and give you a hearty welcome." The word was passed and the Americans cheered so loud that the advanced troops with O'Hara could hear them. There was still 14 miles to cover before Irwin's Ferry.

Both armies now raced for the Dan. In mid-afternoon Williams sent Lee back with cavalry to protect the infantry's rear. The British had marched four miles in 25 hours, but the Americans had accomplished the same distance in 16 hours. Finally, at dusk Williams reached the ferry, and began to cross the Dan in the waiting boats. Around 8 P.M. Lee's horsemen arrived and were soon ferried across, under the direction of Carrington himself. Carrington had Lee's horses "unsaddled and driven into the water to swim across, while their weary riders clutching their saddles and bridles, crowded into the boats." Lee wrote that "in the last boat the quartermaster-general attended by Lt. Colonel Lee and the rear troops, reached the friendly shore."[45]

Less than an hour later, O'Hara arrived at Irwin's Ferry only to see that the Americans had escaped across the Dan. The British had lost the "race to the Dan." The success of the American escape was due to the brilliance of Greene's planning, the tireless effort of Carrington and Kosciuszko to position the boats at the correct sites, the sacrifice of the Continental and militia troops, and the dedication and bravery of the screening units of Williams and Lee. Cornwallis wrote, "All our exertions were in vain. For upon our arrival at Boyd's Ferry on February 15 we learned that his rear guard had got over the night before…. More flats had been collected than had been represented to me as possible." Tarleton gave honor by recording, "Every measure of the Americans, during the march from the Catawba to Virginia, was judiciously designed and vigorously executed…."[46] Clinton likewise told of the events just concluded:

> Lord Cornwallis pushed on his troops twenty-three miles the next day, in full expectation of still catching the chief part of the enemy on the south side of the river, as his intelligence had assured him that it was impossible to procure flats anywhere on its banks sufficient for their transportation…. The enemy had secured all the craft on the opposite side of the river.[47]

So, on the evening of February 14, 1781, the Southern Army was in a sound slumber on the shores of the Dan River in Virginia. These fatigued warriors, many of whom traveled through the terrain shoeless and bloody, had been chased some 230 miles while averaging some 27 miles per day through the Piedmont of North Carolina, with Cornwallis at their heels. Greene, who wrote dispatches that night to Washington, Steuben and Jefferson from his tent, had outfoxed Lord Cornwallis. "Happily for these States, a soldier of consummate talents guided the destinies of the South," Light Horse Harry Lee scribed of Major General Nathanael Greene.[48]

This was an unfortunate dilemma for Cornwallis. He and his army now sat on the Dan River with no boats to cross over to attack Greene. He considered moving to the upper fords of the Dan to attempt a crossing, but realized that Greene would be effective at preventing any such endeavor. Cornwallis wrote, "My force being ill-suited to enter by that quarter so powerful a province as Virginia; and North Carolina being in the utmost confusion; after giving the troops a halt of a day, I proceeded by easy marches to Hillsborough."

The British were tired and they were some 230 miles from their original home base, 200 miles from Lord Rawdon's garrison at Camden, and 150 miles from their nearest supply base at Wilmington. Cornwallis moved to Hillsborough, some 62 miles from the British location. He arrived at Hillsborough on February 20, after having crossed two branches of the Hycotee in addition to three creeks on his journey. At Hillsborough, the North Carolina capital and home of the headquarters of the North Carolina Board of War, Cornwallis hoped to take advantage of his situation. With no organized American Army from Virginia to Georgia to oppose him and Greene's army resting across the Dan to the north, he would gath-

er loyalist support around the British banner in North Carolina.[49] The rich language in Cornwallis' proclamation of February 22 (the 49th birthday of General George Washington) is in evidence:

> Whereas it has pleased the Divine Providence to prosper the operations of His Majesty's arms, in driving the rebel army out of this province; and whereas it is His Majesty's most gracious wish to rescue his faithful and loyal subjects from the cruel tyranny under which they have groaned for many years … [all were invited to repair] with their arms and ten days provisions to the royal standard.[50]

The success of the effort to breed loyalist support through this Hillsborough proclamation and previous actions was marginal at best. The commander of the guards, General O'Hara, wrote of his view:

> The novelty of a camp in the backwoods of America more than any other cause brought several people to stare at us. Their curiosity once satisfied, they returned to their homes. I am certain that in our march of near a thousand miles, almost in as many directions, thro' every part of North Carolina, tho every means possible was taken to persuade our friends as they are called and indeed as they call themselves to join us, we never had with us at any one time one hundred men in arms. Without the experiment had been made, it would have been impossible to conceive that government could in so important a matter have been so grossly deceived. Fatal infatuation! When will government see these people thro' the proper medium? I am persuaded never.[51]

Cornwallis rested for six days in Hillsborough. His lordship first stayed at W.A. Graham's house, but soon moved to the home of John L. Bailey, which eventually became known as Morris' Hillsborough House. His office was at "a large frame building situated in the rear of Morris's Hillsborough House on King street," and across the street from the Union Hotel. The town guard of 40 men was set up from Lieutenant Colonel Webster's brigade. A 12-man unit from Bose's Regiment of Hessians and Colonel Hamilton's North Carolina Volunteers guarded Cornwallis.

The British spent time making needed repairs to clothing and wagons as they rested. They had some difficulties in moving the artillery through the red clay mud through the town. Soon the engineers directed work on putting down stone pavement from the camp to 150 yards distance in each of the four compass directions to ease transporting the cannons. The men were restless as they filled their stomachs and continued to seek out spirits. Two days after arriving at Hillsborough, Major Ross issued the following notice:

> It is of great concern that Lord Cornwallis hears every day reports of the soldiers being taken by the enemy, in

consequence of their straggling out of camp in search of whiskey. He strictly enjoins all officers and non-commissioned officers commanding the outposts and pickets of the army to do their utmost to prevent any soldier from passing them.[52]

Meanwhile, Greene was satisfied that his troops could finally refresh themselves, building their strength, and be resupplied. Greene was still waiting for supplies from General Steuben while his army foraged as best they could. Greene found some supplies in the region, including clothing for his ragged troops. While in camp at his temporary headquarters at the Halifax Court House, Greene was encouraged to see new militia forces arrive, including 400 riflemen from Colonel William Campbell. His army in Virginia now totaled some 2000 men, including 1000 Continentals, and Washington's and Lee's cavalry.[53]

Although Greene was thankful for all the reinforcements he could get, he had continued to be upset with the poor support from the North Carolina government and her militia. In this hour of need, Greene was to eventually discover that the North Carolina Legislature had countermanded his orders and diverted militia to Wilmington. Some of the Virginia Militia from the counties that bordered the Dan River had rushed to form up as Cornwallis was near, but were told by their county militia officers that the call was not lawful. General Steuben had raised some 2600 militia and 400 new Continentals in Virginia, but as rumors developed that Cornwallis was retreating toward Wilmington, he stopped the forces and sent only the Continentals forward under Colonel Richard Campbell.[54] In frustration Greene wrote to Joseph Reed of Pennsylvania a disparaging treatise:

> Our force is so small and Lord Cornwallis' movements so rapid that we got no reinforcements of militia, and therefore were obliged to retire out of State, upon which the spirits of the people sunk, and almost all classes of the inhabitants gave themselves up for lost. They would not believe themselves in danger until they found ruin at their doors. The foolish prejudice of the formidableness of the militia being a sufficient barrier against any attempts of the enemy prevented the Legislature from making any exertions equal to their critical and dangerous situation. Experience has convinced them of their false security.
>
> It is astonishing to me how these people could place such a confidence in a militia scattered over the face of the whole earth, and generally destitute of everything necessary for their defense. The militia in the backcountry are formidable, the others are not, and all are ungovernable and difficult to keep together. As they generally come out, twenty thousand might be in motion, and not five hundred in the field.[55]

Though Greene was safe in Virginia, he was most interested in resuming his movements against Cornwallis. Being chased out of the Carolinas was indeed rough on this Quaker's ego. He had gone to Virginia only to rest and resupply, not to give up on the South. Understanding the importance of having remounts for his cavalry, Greene asked Governor Thomas Jefferson to allow his army to requisition horses from the surrounding farms and plantations in the Halifax County area. Jefferson approved the plan, and Greene directed William Washington to round up fresh horses. Although he had approved the action, Jefferson complained to Greene that "the harsh act of taking their valuable Horses by Force ... has been frequently accompanied by defenses of civil Power ... free People think they have a right to an Explanation of the Circumstances which give rise to the necessity under which they suffer." Greene responded with the words, "Superior Cavalry is of the greatest importance to the salvation of this Country and without them you would soon hear of detachments being cut to pieces in every quarter."[56]

On February 18 Greene ordered Lee's Legion of mounted infantry and cavalry, along with two companies of the Maryland Continentals, to cross the Dan and to join up with Colonel Andrew Pickens. Pickens was still south of the Dan, working to harass and monitor British movements and to suppress loyalist uprisings with his South Carolina Militia. By the end of the next day, Lee had crossed the Dan and was 25 miles from Hillsborough beginning to observe the "flocking" of loyalists to Cornwallis' flag. Lee sent word back to Greene, writing, "I think you had better get in motion."[57]

As February 20 arrived, Greene, ready to send out the main army, was to take advantage of the screening command by sending out Colonel Otto Williams across the Dan with the Legion and light infantry, the cavalry of William Washington's and Pickens' riflemen. Pickens, who had been operating in the vicinity of Guilford Court House, moved to join with Lee, which occurred on the morning of the 23rd. Pickens was only 10 miles from Cornwallis' camp at Hillsborough by the evening of the 21st. Several actions occurred around Hillsborough about this time. The British detachment, on their way to Hart's Mill some four miles west of Hillsborough across the Eno River, was attacked by ambush by Captain Graham's unit with all killed.[58] On the night of the 21st, a similar attack on pickets by 40 volunteers under Colonel McCall resulted in eight killed or wounded, with nine British taken prisoner along with some horses. Pickens wrote Greene, "We had not a man hurt."[59]

On February 23 some 600 Virginians under General Edward Stevens arrived, bringing Greene's total and extended force to around 2600 men. Feeling this was the time to begin the effort southward, Greene and Huger crossed the Dan River. Writing to Jefferson, he exclaimed, "I have been obliged to effect that by finesse which I dare not attempt by force." They marched down to the Haw above Buffalo Creek, crossed the river and encamped at High Rock Mill in southeastern Rockingham County to replenish their food. Then Greene moved to Troublesome Creek and then to McCuiston's Farm.

With rebel action so close to Hillsborough, and with new intelligence that loyalist Dr. John Pyle, who held a royalist militia commission of colonel, had raised a force of 300 to 400 men east of the Haw River, Cornwallis was prompted to send out Tarleton to the country between the Haw and Deep rivers some 15 miles from Hillsborough. Thus, on February 23, Tarleton departed Hillsborough with "200 cavalry, 150 of Webster's brigade, and 100 Hessian sharpshooters...."[60] His lordship was unaware of the location of Greene at this point, but he felt confident that Tarleton could escort the loyalists into camp. Meanwhile Lee and Pickens were also heading to the Haw with an understanding that supplies were being gathered from that area for delivery to the British. While picking up guides and sending out foraging parties, Lee and Pickens moved ever closer to the Haw. By mid-afternoon on February 24 Lee and Pickens arrived at General Butler's Farm. Here they learned of the existence of the loyalist force and the presence of British that were deemed "considerable, their objects extensive and their commander Lt. Col. Tarleton."

Friends at Butler's Farm told Lee that Tarleton had crossed the Haw and was camped at Mr. Hall's located some four miles westward of the river. It was expected that Tarleton would join with Dr. Pyle's North Carolina Loyalist Militia and a unit of Colonel Hamilton's regiment. While a combined British and loyalist force outnumbered them, Lee and Pickens decided to head to Mr. Hall's home. They reached there at 5 P.M. on February 24, but Tarleton was then some four miles away at Major O'Neal's. With Lee's cavalry in the front and Pickens' mounted militia in the rear, they took off for O'Neal's.[61]

On the road to O'Neal's in the afternoon light of the wooded country, Lee's Legion came upon two young mounted loyalists wearing red cloth on their hats who mistakenly thought Lee was Tarleton. Since Lee's Legion was dressed in green coats with a similar shade as Tarleton's, who they were in search of, and Light Horse Harry Lee had the air of a Tarleton, they agreed to go back to Pyle's unit and have them move aside to the edge of the road so they could pass. As the Americans came up in their short green coats, the loyalists cheered with shouts of "God save the king." Not having time or opportunity to warn Pickens, Lee continued to pass by the loyalists on his right. As soon as some of the loyalists saw Pickens' militia from the rear come into view, they began firing at

them. The firing immediately turned into a general engagement. Captain Eggleston of the Legion in its rear ordered a charge. Lee's men already had their swords out as if to salute. Now they thrust their swords at Pyle's men before they could aim their weapons, as Pickens' men fired their rifles. The slashing and hacking continued, and it was over quickly.[62]

"In ten minutes the whole body of the enemy was routed; the greater part was left on the ground dead and wounded.... The night came on and we necessarily deferred further operation."[63] The engagement was over "and bloody on one side only. Ninety of the royalists were killed and most of the survivors wounded ... in some parts of the line the cry for mercy was heard ... but no expostulation could be admitted in a conjuncture so critical." The Americans did not lose even one man in the fight. While later criticized, Lee defended his actions on the rule of war that says, "...to take care of your own safety, and our safety was not compatible with that of the supplicants, until disabled to offend." The action was to be forever known as "Pyle's Hacking Match." Greene wrote to Lee that the victory over Pyle was "so happily timed, and in all probabily will be productive of such happy consequences, that I cannot help congratulating you on your success."[64]

The day after the Pyle action, Pickens sent out patrols led by two officers. Commanded by Captain Jesse Franklin (who would one day be a governor of North Carolina), and Major Micajah Lewis of Surry County (a Continental army officer of the Fourth Regiment), the detachment ran into a unit of British troops at Dickey's Farm as darkness fell. Lewis was deceived in the darkness that he had come upon other Americans and found the British firing at him. Lewis struggled to the nearest farmhouse only to die from several bleeding wounds.

Meanwhile, Cornwallis learned of Greene's crossing at the Dan on the evening of Pyle's engagement, and was to send out three dispatches in rapid order to Tarleton directing his immediate recall. The first message read:

> Dear Tarleton — I have received intelligence from two persons, that Greene passed the Dan on the 22nd, and was advancing to Dobbyn's. They mention so many particulars that I cannot help giving some credit, I therefore wish you to join me as soon as possible....

Cornwallis marched out of Hillsborough on February 26, as reported in Tarleton's memoirs, "The royal army marched by the left, passed through Hillsboro and pointed their course toward the Haw." Tarleton's Legion led the force, with the light infantry Guards and the Hessian Jagers forming the advance guard. A local recorded Tarleton's appearance:

His dress was a jacket and breeches of white linen, fitted to his form with the utmost exactness. Boots of russet leather were half way up the leg. The road tops of which were turned down, the heels garnished with spurs of an immense size and length of rowel. On his head was a low crowned hat, curiously formed from the snow-white feathers of swan, and in his hand he carried a heavy scourge, with shot well twisted into a knotted lash.[65]

Cornwallis crossed the Haw River and camped near one of its tributaries, Alamance Creek, at a place known as "Stinking Quarter." General O'Hara wrote that from the time of this event to March 15, 1781, "The two armys were never above twenty miles asunder, they constantly avoiding a general action and we as industriously seeking it. These operations obliged the two armys to make numberless moves which it is impossible to detail."[66] This encampment placed Cornwallis near the junction of roads that could lead him either west to Guilford Court House, or downriver to Cross Creek and Wilmington. That same day General Otto Williams left Hillsborough, crossed the Haw and set up camp on the north side of the Alamance Creek, only a few miles from Cornwallis on the south side. With Williams were Pickens' mounted militia, the 300 Virginia riflemen under Colonel William Preston, Colonel William Campbell's Virginia Militia, Lee's Legion, and Washington's cavalry.[67]

On February 28 General Williams reported to Greene that Cornwallis was possibly backtracking and might be on the west side of the Haw. But actually he was not moved at all. He wrote Greene, "Our present situation Appears to me not to be a bad one tho' not so agreeable as I could wish." With his forces circled around Cornwallis on Alamance Creek, Williams reported to Greene, "While Lord Cornwallis keeps his position like a Bear with his Stern in a corner, I cannot attack him but at tooth and nail." By this time Greene's main army was located 15 miles above the British camp, and hoping for more patriot reinforcements, while Williams' force screened him nearer Cornwallis.

Operations during this period between the British and the Americans took place between Speedwell's Iron Works, located on Reedy Fork, and Boyd's Mill on Troublesome Creek. Troublesome Creek was one of the three tributaries of the Haw River, which was located 20 miles north of Cornwallis on the Alamance Creek, the southernmost tributary. Reedy Fork was a stream that empties into the Haw almost midway between Troublesome and Alamance creeks. Greene shifted his camp position every two nights to avoid a British surprise. Williams' force also was in continual motion, harassing the enemy at any quarter. Cornwallis had Tarleton doing the same thing as the Americans.

On the night of March 3, Williams sent Captain Kirkwood with his company and 30 riflemen directed by Captain Baker to harass Tarleton at Clapp's Mill on Alamance Creek. Kirkwood and Baker were successful at killing several British pickets and took two prisoners. The tactic did little except to provide some "inducement to Lt. Col. Tarleton to leave his Camp with seeming haste this morning early. A considerable quantity of Flour was left in hogsheads and in small parsalls, kittles left over the fire, plates and other furniture, with a few cast Horses...."[68]

On March 6 Cornwallis struck back across the Alamance in response to the harassing event of the 3rd. In a heavy fog of the morning the British advanced to surprise the Americans at Wetzell's Mill on Reedy Creek. Williams had learned of Cornwallis' movements to the left of his position and quickly moved his troops to Wetzell's Mill ahead of Cornwallis. Placing his troops on the north side of Reedy Creek, Williams was able to hold off a storming party led by Colonel James Webster and troops of the 23rd Regiment until the valuable wagons of meal escaped. When Webster crossed the creek, Lee ordered his riflemen to hide in a nearby cabin to shoot the British commander. The men "discharged their rifles at him, one by one, each man sure of knocking him over ... eight or nine of them emptied their guns a second time. Strange to tell ... himself and horse were untouched." Webster drove Williams back for several miles, but they were unable to catch Williams, since Lee and Washington harassed the flanks of the British force as they advanced. Losses on both sides were between 25 to 30 men killed and wounded.[69]

Greene now camped at Troublesome Creek ironworks while Cornwallis returned to his former camp on the Alamance. His lordship moved from Alamance to Bell's Mills on Deep River; followed by movements to Alton's, Duffield's, Gorrell's and then on March 12 arriving at McCuiston's Farm where he quartered his troops with the locals. At McCuiston's Cornwallis released orders as follows: "The officers of pickets are desired to be very alert and particularly attentive to people that pass their party; no one must be suffered to pass but by authority from head-quarters. Women particularly are to be attended to." The next day passing Mendenhall's Mill, Cornwallis placed some 50 soldiers to guard the flour in the process of being ground.[70]

Greene had been anticipating reinforcements for weeks and on March 10 he finally got them. That day Brigadier General John Butler and Colonel Pinketham Eaton arrived with two brigades of the North Carolina Militia totaling some 1060 men. Another 1000 men from Virginia under General Robert Lawson joined Stevens' command, swelling his totals under arms to 1700. The next day some 550 Virginia Continentals came in from

Steuben's command in Southside, Virginia.[71] Now Greene had an army of some 4000 men, including 1600 Continentals.

Cornwallis' overall strength in arms had actually been reduced to about 2200 men. He had experienced the loss of 227 men due to sickness or combat in February alone. Cornwallis also knew his men were tired, their renowned endurance suffering. The truth was that British troops were not trained to live in such harsh conditions as they had encountered. Sleeping outdoors in the cold, marching 20 miles or more per day, receiving less than adequate quantities of food and drink, and finding themselves harassed by periodic patriot skirmishes was almost too much to endure. One British soldier, Sergeant Lamb, described what it was like to live through these times:

> Sometimes we had turnips served out for food when we came to a turnip field; or arriving at a field of corn, we converted our canteens into rasps and ground our Indian corn for bread; when we could get no Indian corn, we were compelled to eat liver as a substitute for bread, with our lean beef. In all this his lordship participated, nor did he indulge himself even in the distinction of a tent; but in all things partook our sufferings, and seemed much more to feel for us than for himself.

Cornwallis knew that he would soon have to move to a safer and more plentiful area to rest his troops.[72]

Now that Greene had enough troops to engage the British the game of cat and mouse was soon to be over. On March 13 Cornwallis moved his troops to Quaker Meeting House at New Garden. Greene was aware of his location. That same day Major St. George Tucker in Greene's army wrote his wife, "We marched yesterday to look for Lord Cornwallis.... We are now strong enough, I hope, to cope with him to advantage."[73] Greene was near Speedwell Iron Works, just a one-hour ride from Guilford Court House. His light troops and militia were positioned between the branches of Reedy Fork. Both armies knew that a major engagement was about to happen. Greene moved to Martinsville, closer to Guilford Court House. Cornwallis then recognized that the battle was in the air. He sent the invalids under guard with Colonel Hamilton's North Carolina Loyalist Regiment to Bell's Mill. The next day Cornwallis reacted with haste and he marched up the New Garden Road toward Guilford Court House. Greene had moved that afternoon, February 14, to a position just south of the courthouse. The battle was impending.[74]

Without any breakfast, for want of supplies, Cornwallis marched with his army toward Guilford Court House to attack Greene on the frost-dampened morning of March 15, 1781. Along the New Garden Road, the main road linking Salisbury with Hillsborough, Tarleton led the forces in two columns. The left column was made up of the main army with artillery, with Hamilton's Carolinians and some dragoons in the right column. While the army had passed through this area six weeks earlier, Cornwallis had no particular notes on the terrain. Also, he had no fresh intelligence, as the prisoners taken could provide no information of the positions or order of the Americans.[75]

The territory around Guilford Court House was well suited for defensive operations. From the New Garden Road some one and one-half miles away at a small stream named Little Horsepen Creek, the ground rose "in a gradual slope as it bisected the battlefield." The surrounding countryside on gently rolling hills was filled with thick woods, which served to protect the American flanks. From east of the creek for some 800 yards were various open cornfields, coming up to the open area around the courthouse itself.

Just before the battle, Greene received a letter from Daniel Morgan, who presented battle tactics to him. Morgan wrote, "You will beat Cornwallis; if not he will beat you and perhaps cut your regulars to pieces...." Along with these words, he advised Greene to use a three-line strategy, which had been so effective at Cowpens.[76] Greene took his advice. He had also taken time on his first passing to Guilford, and now, just before the engagement, had surveyed the area with considerable attention. He deployed his troops with much care. In front he positioned his greenest troops, the 1000 North Carolina Militia under Butler and Eaton. They occupied a fence line 400 yards uphill from the woods east of Little Horsepen Creek, and about a half mile from the courthouse.[77]

On both sides of the militia, protecting their flanks, were William Washington's cavalry and Kirkwood's Delaware veterans on the right, and on the left Lee's Legion of 150 cavalry and infantry and 200 of William Campbell's riflemen. Some 300 yards east of the first militia, in the dense woods, was the second line of defense, consisting of some 1200 men from the two brigades of the Virginia Militia. General Robert Lawson's men were located south of the New Garden Road. On the north side of the road were positioned the Virginia Militia of General Edward Stevens, with marksmen placed behind them to dissuade any men from running off. Over 500 yards east of the second line, on the hillside just west of the courthouse and north of the New Garden Road, were General Huger's 1400 experienced Continentals from Maryland, Delaware and Virginia. Their formation consisted of Colonel Benjamin Ford's Second Maryland Regiment on the American left, Colonel John Gunby's First Maryland Regiment in the center, and Colonel John Green's and Lieutenant Colonel Samuel Hawes' Virginia Regiment on the right.[78]

The night before the battle, Lee had sent out Lieutenant Heard with a small unit of dragoons to stay near

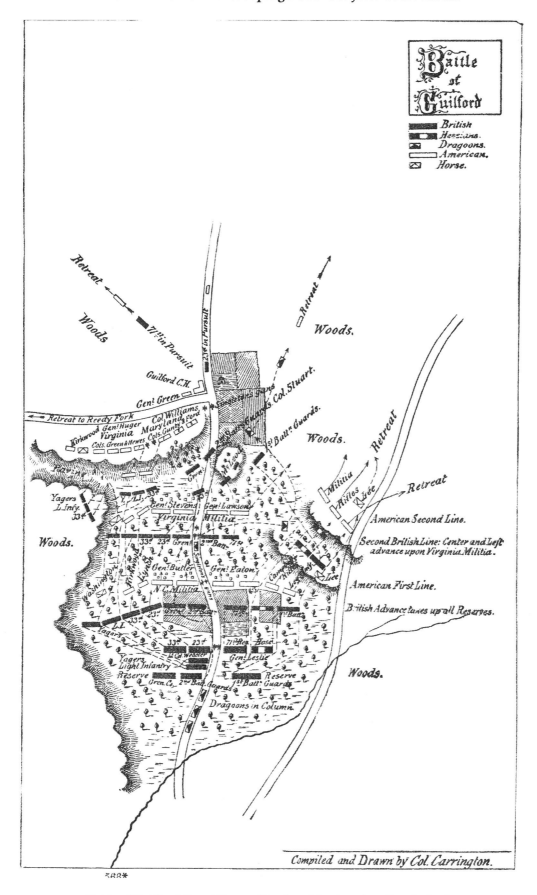

Battle of Guilford Court House. (*Battles of the American Revolution.*)

the British and provide periodic movement reports. Early on the predawn of the morning, Heard reported back that he was having difficulty approaching Cornwallis' camp at New Garden, some 12 miles away to the southwest, because of the constant British patrols. Later Heard passed the message on that he could hear the sound of rumbling wagons along the road. Greene immediately ordered Lee and the balance of his reconnaissance force forward.

With the British march starting at dawn, Tarleton and his lead units reached a point some four miles from Guilford Court House by mid-morning. There they ran into Lee's patrol and a brief skirmish ensued. Both sides declared the short encounter a victory. Greene claimed that Captain Armstrong from Lee's Legion "cut down near 30 dragoons." Tarleton wrote that he drove Lee back and took prisoners. Lee explained that he took prisoners and saw "Not a single American soldier or horse injured." In the conflict, Tarleton had been struck in the right hand, which maimed his first and middle fingers. For the rest of the day, Tarleton had his right hand in a sling and guided his horse reins with his left hand.[79]

By noon the first line of North Carolina Militia began to hear the beat of drums down New Garden Road. Greene shouted, "Three rounds, my boys, and then you fall back." Light Horse Harry Lee "rode along the front line from one end to the other, exhorting them to stand firm and not be afraid of the British." The young American troops were scared as they awaited the seasoned British adversaries. Major Richard Harrison wrote to his wife, "It is scarcely possible to paint the agitations of my mind." At around noon the leading elements of Cornwallis' army were at the edge of the woods and were able to look across the cornfield at the patriot force of Butler's and Eaton's squatting behind the fence.[80]

As soon as the British began to deploy into battle formations, Captain Anthony Singleton's artillery unit started firing their two six-pounders at the British from the center of the militia line. Captain Alexander McLeod's Royal Artillery responded with their three-pounders. The artillery duel lasted for 30 minutes with little effect as the British formed their battle line. The British formed up in two "wings." The right wing under Major General Leslie deployed the blue-coated Hessian Regiment under Von Bose, with Fraser's 71st Highlanders on the left. The left wing, commanded by Lieutenant Colonel James Webster, lined up on its right the 71st Highlanders in tartan kilts, in the center the 23rd Regiment of Royal Welsh Fusiliers and to the left the 33rd Regiment of Foot. In reserve, Cornwallis placed the First Guards Battalion behind Leslie's wing and put the Jagers, the Second Guards Battalion and the companies of the grenadier and light infantry behind Webster. General Charles O'Hara commanded the reserve. Back with the reserves were Tarleton's

dragoons in their green coats. The Americans looked out at a magnificent scene — with the British red-coated regular troops, mixed with the green coats of the Jagers and Tarleton dragoons, the kilts of the Highlanders and the blue coats of the Hessian and Regiment Bose Germans. The British were ready as their musket barrels and bayonets shined in the midday sun, while the drums and fifes played.[81]

At around 1:30 P.M. the British advanced from the edge of the woods at 400 yards downhill from the front line of the Americans. They proceeded to march toward the patriots with mechanical precision. The 27-year-old Captain Roger Lamb of the Royal Welsh Fusiliers recalled the advance:

> The colonel rode on to the front and gave the word "Charge!" Instantly the movement was made in excellent order in a smart run.... When [we] arrived within forty yards of the enemy's line, it was perceived that their whole force had their arms ... resting on a rail fence.... They were taking aim with the nicest kind of precision.... At this awful period a general pause took place. Both parties surveyed each other for the moment with the most anxious suspense.... Colonel Webster ... said ... "Come on my brave Fusiliers!" This acted like an inspiring voice. They rushed forward amidst the enemy fire. Dreadful was the havoc on both sides.

The Americans fired first, as the British responded in kind. As the black smoke rose, men fell on both sides. From the second patriot volley, the British army reeled. Captain Dugald Stuart of the 71st Regiment wrote, "One half of the Highlanders dropped on that spot." Patriot William Montgomery, who looked on from behind the American position at the cornfield, wrote that the British dead and wounded looked like "the scattering stalks in a wheat field, when the harvest man has passed over it with his cradle." The North Carolina Militia had fired three volleys, and seeing the British and Hessian approach the fence line, they scattered into the woods toward the Virginians.[82]

As the North Carolinians broke, their officers, Eaton and Butler, aided by others including Colonel Davie and Major Harrison, tried desperately to stop them. Lee wrote as he left his post and attempted to spur them on not to retreat, "All was vain; so thoroughly confounded were these unhappy men, that, throwing away arms, knapsacks, and even canteens, they rushed like a torrent headlong through the woods." Only a few North Carolinians under Pinketham Eaton's brigade joined up with William Campbell's Militia and the Legion infantry to hold their ground bravely. The rest of the men tore through the second Virginia line. The Virginians opened their line to let the Carolinians pass, but not without jeers. The retreat of the center militia of the first line had not affected the flanking forces on the right and left.

The British and Hessians advancing toward the second line were confronted with steady fire from Kirkwood's Delawares and Lynch on the American right and the Legion infantry and the riflemen of William Campbell's force on the left. To counter the fierce fire, the Jagers and 33rd Regiment turned to the left toward Kirkwood and Lynch, while the Von Bose Regiment and Highlanders wheeled around on to the left on Lee and Campbell. The gap in the British line, which then appeared in the center, was quickly filled with Grenadiers and the Second Battalion of the Guards under Leslie's orders.[83]

The fighting had now entered the woods and the cavalry was of no use. The British met stiff resistance in this unfamiliar battlefield. Both Stevens' and Lawson's men took a heavy toll on the British redcoats, until finally the Virginians were pushed back. The heaviest fighting in the woods under the weight of Webster's and O'Hara's troops was against Stevens' brigade on the American right, where the Grenadiers, the 33rd and Guards Second Battalion and Jagers and the light infantry directed all their focus. The brigade was forced to move back on its right.

The left side of the brigade held as the right side was forced to wheel around. Colonel Webster had considered his situation with his 23rd and 71st forces having been held up on the American line, and decided to break off the 33rd Regiment, the light infantry and the Jagers to head toward the third American line near the courthouse. They emerged from the woods to confront the best troops Greene had — the Continentals of the First Maryland and the Fifth Virginia. Waiting on the forward slope of the high ground just south of the Reedy Fork Road, the Continentals had begun to see little groups of Virginia Militia come out of the woods and head toward the rear. Later, when the groups became a steady stream of men, the Continentals knew that the second line had broken. Soon Kirkwood's Delaware Continentals and Lynch's Virginia riflemen came out of the woods and formed up on the right of Colonel Green's Fourth Virginia Continentals.[84]

Most of the fighting was now occurring between two clearings, as Stevens and the militia resisted the center. Soon Webster found his force out of the woods and ahead of the other British lines. Without delay, Webster straightened his line and charged the Continentals. The American fire was fierce and the resistance stunned the British. The patriots had waited until the British were within 40 yards of Webster's men before firing their deadly volley. Webster and his force fell back across a ravine and waited for the rest of the British line. This was the point when the Americans might have won the battle, if Greene had immediately attacked Webster while the rest of the British force was still engaged in the woods with the Virginia Militia. Greene was not willing to commit every reserve to win this battle, continuing to use the strategy of hurt-

ing the British as he ensured the continued existence of the Southern American Army.

The battle had now lasted for an hour, as Stevens' force gave way in the center. The entire Virginia force broke after fighting off three bayonet attacks and holding out against the 23rd, the Royal Welsh Fusiliers and the 71st Regiment. Stevens was hit in the thigh and carried from the field of battle. At this point the entire strength of the British came to bear on the third line of the Continentals. The British under Colonel Duncan Stuart with his Second Guards were at the lead, as they engaged the Second Maryland made up of green recruits with few veterans. Without firing a shot, the British saw the Second Maryland turn and run. Stuart and force continued to move forward and were able to emerge from the woods through the gap in the American line.

Colonel John Gunby, who had led Continental charge against Webster, was fortunate to find himself moving to his original position on a hill on the flank of the advancing British. Seeing the opportunity, he swung around into position to attack as his horse was shot from under him. He was pinned under his own horse, yielding to Colonel Howard to take command of his units. At about the same time, William Washington came up and proceeded to send in his dragoons, who wheeled their sabers in the air as they advanced against the British. The Grenadiers and Guards were also engaged by the First Maryland under Howard to give a destructive blow. The British right was fully engaged as the Maryland and Virginia Continentals pushed them back. Colonel Stuart was cut down and his redcoats halted.

Cornwallis saw the action from a position near Lieutenant McLeod's artillery unit, which was now firing grapeshot. McLeod was firing into his own men along with the Americans. Cornwallis looked on with cold passion. General O'Hara was wounded nearby as the grapeshot tore into the Guards and the First Maryland. The Americans were finally broken as the Highlanders were up and moving with the other British units. Greene ordered a retreat. On the left the American line of Campbell and Lee's Legion had continued to fight the British. As the First Battalion of the Guards broke off to rejoin with the main British line, Lee pulled his force since he now had no Americans on his right. Campbell was now alone with the Germans. Lee recalled, "Every obstacle now removed, Lee pressed forward, followed by Campbell, and joined his force close to Guilford Court House."

Campbell was furious with Lee's action to pull out so soon. Tarleton recounted the events, "The enemy gave way on all sides, and were routed with confusion and loss." Actually Tarleton failed to reflect the fact that Greene had already called for the retreat by that point in the battle. But Colonel Campbell was so upset with Lee that he left the army several days later. Cornwallis ordered a pursuit of the Americans as Greene's forces retired with order. The Americans, as Cornwallis recalled, "went off by the Reedy Fork beyond which it was not in my power to follow them." The British forces were exhausted. This allowed Greene to stop only three miles from the battlefield to rest his men and collect stragglers.[85] Concerned that Cornwallis might catch up with him, Greene moved forward 10 miles to his old camp at the iron works on Troublesome Creek. As Greene finally sat to rest, with his army now safely away, he fainted.

Cornwallis had technically won the battle since he held the field at the end. But his losses were extreme—one-fourth of his force. The British had 93 dead and 439 wounded, including four officers killed and 24 wounded. The Guards took the greatest casualties. Greene's losses were much lighter, with 78 killed and 156 wounded. The list of missing Americans included 161 Continentals and 885 militia. Among this honorless group were 563 from North Carolina.

The Guilford battlefield was a sad place on the night of the 15th. The day had seen the sun shining until around 3 P.M. When Greene's force retreated, the rains began to come down in torrents as darkness fell. It rained all night. The men were tired, wet and hungry. The wounded suffered too, as there were no tents, surgical supplies or food. The morning at Cornwallis' camp on March 16, came with 50 more dead from exposure during the night.

By the time the foragers were able to find cattle and flour, the British had gone 48 hours without food.[86]

The Guilford Court House battle was the bloodiest battle of the American Revolution in North Carolina. Some 6000 men had been engaged in this brutal affair. Commissary Stedman described the scene at the battlefield as being one of "horror and distress ... [and] the cries of the wounded and dying who remained on the field of action during the night exceed all description." A wounded British man recalled his view of the situation:

> I never did and I hope I never shall experience two days and nights as those immediately after the battle. We remained on the very ground on which it had been fought, covered with dead, with dying and with hundreds of wounded, rebels as well as our own. A violent and constant rain that lasted above forty hours made it equally impracticable to remove or administer the smallest comfort to many of the wounded. In this situation we expected every moment to be attacked. There could be no doubt that the enemy must be very well informed of our loss, and whatever their loss might be their numbers were still so great as to make them very formidable. And they had only retired eighteen miles from us. Fortunately for us they did not, or even followed us when we marched but at a very respectable distance, or have ever fired a single shot since the affair of the 15th.[87]

The British had won the battle, but Cornwallis had lost the North Carolina Campaign with his terrible losses.

16

BACK TO SOUTH CAROLINA

The day after the battle of Guilford Court House found the two armies located only ten miles apart. Knowing of the carnage at the battlefield, Greene sent his surgeon, Dr. Wallace, to Cornwallis to care for the American casualties, along with some supplies and provisions.[1] From his camp Greene wrote to Colonel Lee:

> I mean to fight the enemy again, and wish you to have your Legion and riflemen ready at the shortest notice. Lord Cornwallis must be soundly beaten before he will release his stronghold.[2]

Both the British and American surgeons worked hard to aid the wounded who lay in the woods, in the surrounding farm houses, and filled the Quaker Meeting House at New Garden. Cornwallis wrote Greene on that day the following:

> I have given orders to collect the wounded of your Army at Guilford Court House, where every possible Attention shall be paid to them, but as it is not in my power to give them sufficient Assistance I must recommend it to You to send immediately Surgeons to take care of them, & a Supply of necessaries & Provisions.

Greene had already sent his surgeon before he received Cornwallis' letter, but the next day he replied to Cornwallis his thanks and indicated that supplies would be forthcoming.[3]

Later in the month Major General Greene wrote to his fellow Quakers asking for their support in helping the wounded:

> Friends and Countrymen: I address myself to your humanity for the relief of the suffering wounded at Guilford Court House. As a people I am persuaded you disclaim any connection with measures calculated to promote military operations; but I know of no order of men more remarkable for the exercise of humanity and benevolence; and perhaps no instance ever had a higher claim upon you than the unfortunate wounded now in your neighborhood.
>
> I was born and educated in the profession and principles of your Society; and am perfectly acquainted with your religious sentiments and general good conduct as citizens. I am also sensible from the prejudices of many belonging to other religious societies, and the misconduct of a few of your own, that you are generally as enemies to the independence of America. I entertain other sentiments, both of your principles and wishes. I respect you as a people, and shall always be ready to protect you from every violence and oppression which the confusion of the times afford but too many instances of. Do not be deceived. This is no religious dispute. The contest is for political liberty, without which cannot be enjoyed the free exercise of your religion.
>
> The British are flattering you with conquest and exciting your apprehensions respecting religious liberty. They deceive you in both. They can neither conquer this country, nor will you be molested in the exercise of your sentiments. It is true, they may spread desolation and distress over many parts of the country, but When the inhabitants exert their force, the enemy must flee before them.... Having given you this information, I have only to remark that I shall be exceedingly obliged to you to contribute all in your power to relieve the unfortunates at Guilford, and Dr. Wallace is directed to point out the things most wanted, and to receive and apply donations, and from the liberality of your order upon the occasion I shall be able to judge of your feelings as men ... and principles as a Society.
>
> Given at Headquarters, North Carolina, March 26, 1781, and the fifth year of American Independence.

Nathanael Greene
Major General Continental Army.

The Quaker response was as follows:

"Friend Greene: We received thine.... Agreeable to thy request we shall do all that lies in our power, although this may inform that from our present situation we are ill able to assist as much as we would be glad to do, as the Americans have lain much upon us, and of late the British have plundered and entirely broken up many among us, which renders it hard, and there is at our meetinghouse in New Garden upward of one hundred now living, that have no means of provision, except what hospitality the neighborhood affords them, which we look upon as a hardship upon us, of not an imposition; but notwithstanding all this, we are determined, by the assistance of Providence, while we have anything among us, that the distressed both at the Court House and here shall have part of it with us. As we have as yet made no distinction as to party and their cause — and as we have none to commit our cause to but God alone, but hold it the duty of true Christians, at all times to assist the distressed.

Guilford Court House, N.C. Third mo. 30, 1781.

Lord Cornwallis sent his walking wounded and 17 wagons of those wounded able to travel on March 17 to Bell's Mill with Colonel Hamilton's North Carolina Royal Volunteers. Cornwallis also ordered, "All the women of the army except one a company, to be immediately sent after the wounded men of the army."[4] He had indicated to his army that he was "thoroughly sensible of the distress they suffer for the want of flour or meal," but it was necessary to stay at Guilford a little longer since "their Continuing here at Present is Necessary for the Safety of their Wounded Companions." At Guilford Cornwallis wrote of his valiant officers and men and sent his dispatches with his *aide-de-camp*, Captain Brodrick, to England. Brodrick arrived in London on June 5, with the news of the dubious "victory."[5] But that day, March 17, Cornwallis wrote Lord George Germain of his "signal victory." Cornwallis also recorded the following: "Our troops were excessively fatigued by an action which lasted an hour and a half, and our wounded, dispersed over an extensive space of country, required immediate attention. The care of our wounded and the total want of provisions in an exhausted country, made it equally impossible for me to follow the blow the next day."

Another witness to the events, Stedman, wrote: "In this battle the British troops obtained a victory most honourable and glorious to themselves, but in its consequences of no real advantage to the cause in which they were engaged.... A victory achieved under such disadvantages of numbers and ground ... placed the bravery and the discipline of the troops beyond all praise, but the expense at which it was obtained rendered it of no utility."[6]

Greene, who knew Cornwallis was now significantly crippled in offensive potential, wrote the following:

I have never felt an easy moment since the enemy crossed the Catawba until since the defeat of the 15th, but now I am perfectly easy, being persuaded it is out of the enemy's power to do us any great injury. Indeed, I think they will retire as soon as they can get off their wounded.[7]

Greene wrote to the president of the Congress later on March 23:

On the 16th I wrote Your Excellency giving an account of an action which happened at Guilford Court House the day before. I was then persuaded that, notwithstanding we were obliged to give up the ground, we had reaped the advantage of the action. Circumstances since confirm me in opinion that the enemy were too much galled to improve their success.[8]

On March 18 Cornwallis departed from the battlefield, leaving 64 of "the bad cases" behind at New Garden at the Quaker Meeting House with surgeon Hill and two medical associates. Hill's surgical instruments were mainly a knife and saw, yet he had lost only 18 men, or one-quarter of the wounded under his care. For these men who died, the suffering was finally over. Now the rest of the wounded were prisoners of Major General Greene. With his remaining force and wounded configured in horse litters, Cornwallis sent off for Cross Creek where he believed he would find a store of supplies from Wilmington provided by Colonel Balfour, the commandant of Charles Town.

The day the British left Guilford, Cornwallis issued a proclamation calling for "all loyal subjects to stand forth & take an active part in restoring order & government." In addition, the proclamation promised amnesty to all rebels, "murderers excepted," who would "surrender themselves with their arms & ammunition at headquarters or to their places of residence on or before the 20th day of April next...." The proclamation yielded few results. One Quaker loyalist wrote of his disappointment with the British, saying, "They had been so often deceived in promises of support, and the British had so often relinquished posts, that the people were now afraid to join the British army, lest they should leave the province, in which case the resentment of the revolutioners would be exercised with more cruelty; that although the men might escape, or go with the army, yet, such was the diabolical conduct of these people, that they would inflict the severest punishment upon their families."[9]

On March 20 Greene broke camp at Troublesome Creek and took off after Cornwallis. Greene was not sure if Cornwallis was heading for Cross Creek and Wilmington, or to the Pee Dee and on to South Carolina. Regardless,

Greene wanted to slow down the enemy's progress if possible. Lee with his Legion continued to stay on the flanks and rear of Cornwallis' army, having been directed in that mission by Greene soon after the battle. Colonel Malmedy was ordered to join General Lillington, the Commander of the Wilmington District, in the area between Cross Creek and Wilmington. Lillington's orders were to prevent Major Craig's force in Wilmington from merging with Cornwallis, while discouraging the local loyalists.

Greene's army pursued Cornwallis through heavy rains and along muddy roads, reaching Buffalo Creek on March 22, and Rigdon's Ford on the Deep River by the 26th. The patriots were traveling though country full of loyalists and food was scarce. On the 27th Greene was informed that the Virginia and North Carolina militias had agreed to their enlistment for six weeks, which unfortunately had started from the day of their initial gathering, not the day they joined the American cause officially. This meant that Greene had only four days left with most of his militia. Greene pleaded with them to stay, but most were determined to go home. Those who did stay indicated they would stay at their own pleasure, and could leave at any point. Greene recounted these events to Jefferson remarking that, "Upon such a precarious footing … no measure can be taken with certainty."

Important news arrived that the British were at Ramsey's Mill on Deep River, only 12 miles away from their location at Rigdon's Ford, and on the same side of the river. Greene reached Ramsey's Mill on the 28th, only to find that the British had bridged the river and were miles away to the south. Greene wrote that Cornwallis had "left with the greatest precipitation so much as to leave their dead unburied on the ground. I wish we had provisions to enable us to continue our pursuit." Only the quick action of Lee had prevented the British from destroying the bridge as Cornwallis had wished. Greene's army had a bridge to pursue the British, but his men were so hungry that they devoured half-cooked the lean beef they found.

Greene decided to allow his army to rest and recuperate at Ramsey's Mill. While halted on March 29, Greene wrote General Washington:

> In this critical and distressing situation, I am determined to carry the war immediately into South Carolina. The enemy will be obliged to follow us, or give up his posts in that state. If the former takes place, it will draw the war out of this state…. If they leave their posts [in South Carolina] to fall, they must lose more than they can gain here. If we continue in this state the enemy will hold their possessions in both.[10]

Greene continued his letter:

> I expect to be ready to march in about five days, and have written to General Sumter to collect the militia to aid the operations. I am persuaded the movement will be unexpected to the enemy, and I intend it shall be little known as possible. Our baggage and stores not with the army, I shall order by route of the Saura Towns and Shallow Ford to Charlotte: By having them in the upper country we shall always have a safe retreat, and from those inhabitants we may expect the greatest support.[11]

On April 1, Cornwallis arrived at Cross Creek, at the head of the Cape Fear River. His movement was with continued fear that the Americans were still following him. The actions of Greene, with Lee's Legion at his heels, "kept His Lordship for some time in ignorance of the course he proposed to take and made him apprehend that he was still inclined to follow him, which induced His Lordship to force his troops on at the rate of sixteen, seventeen, and eighteen miles a day — a pace but very ill suited to their then crippled state and naked condition, being encumbered with above six hundred sick and wounded and almost without a shoe to the soldier's feet."

Cornwallis was disappointed "to find that no supplies had been sent up for his army from Wilmington on account of the distance and impracticability of the Cape Fear River, and that the inhabitants of that friendly district, though ready to afford every assistance in their power, were not much inclined to join him."[12] Cornwallis wrote, "Provisions were scarce — not four days' forage within twenty miles — and to us the navigation of the Cape Fear River to Wilmington impracticable, for the distance by water is upwards of a hundred miles, the breadth seldom above one hundred yards, the banks high, and the inhabitants on each side generally hostile."[13] So Cornwallis had to move down to Wilmington on the coast using the King's Highway.

It took six days for the British to travel from Cross Creek to "cover at McLeane's Bluff, opposite Wilmington, on the 7th of April."[14] The movement of the British army down the west side of the Cape Fear was accompanied by devastation and plundering of the houses and inhabitants for food and valuables by camp followers. Soldiers took horses, cattle and even the clothes of the inhabitants. The women camp followers gathered with the troops like "a swarm of beings … who followed … in the character of officers' and soldiers wives …. They were generally mounted on the best horses and side saddles, dressed in the finest and best clothes that could be taken from the inhabitants."[15]

Those wounded that did not survive the rough trip were left along the road. In route some five British officers died, including the much beloved Lieutenant Colonel Webster of the 33rd. Webster had come some 160 miles by horse litter with wounds on his arm and leg. So upset by Webster's death, Cornwallis "was struck with such sorrow" that he turned to look at his sword and remarked,

"I have lost my scabbard." Tarleton wrote of Webster, "He united all the virtues of civil life to the gallantry and professional knowledge of a soldier."[16] Webster was buried in Elizabethtown, located 40 miles upriver from Wilmington. When Cornwallis reached Wilmington, he wrote the painful words, "You have for your satisfaction, that your son fell nobly in the cause of his country, honored and lamented by his fellow soldier...." to Webster's father, Reverend Dr. Webster.

At Wilmington Cornwallis took up residence at an impressive white frame house belonging to Judge Joshua Wright. The house had belonged to loyalist John Burgwin, the former treasurer of North Carolina, who had seen the writing on the wall several years before and departed to London as many other loyalists had done. The Wright family was allowed to stay in their home with Cornwallis, as the daughters served the British officers tea in the afternoon and generally took charge of their comforts. Cornwallis was now to rest his force of 1400, with his 397 wounded and 436 sick, and determine his next move.[17]

On April 10 Cornwallis wrote his good friend General Phillips a letter reflecting his mood:

> I have had a most difficult and dangerous campaign and was obliged to fight a battle 200 miles from any communication against an enemy seven times my number. The fate was long doubtful.... The idea of our friends rising in any number and to any purpose totally failed, as I expected, and here I am, getting rid of my wounded and refitting my troops at Wilmington....[18]

Meanwhile, General Greene was preparing his force to travel. Monday, April 2, saw the last of his militia departing. The next day he directed his men to "clean themselves, to get their arms in good order, and be prepared to march at a short warning." Greene with some 2600 men, including 1600 Continentals, moved from his camp at Colonel Ambrose Ramsey's Mill on April 6 southward. He crossed at Mark's Ferry on the Yadkin River, then south toward Camden, down the Pee Dee and across the Rocky River and Lynch's Creek.[19] Greene, in a letter to Joseph Reed, the president of the Congress, wrote, "All the way through the country as I passed, I found the people engaged in matters of interest, and in pursuit of pleasure."[20]

Greene's plan to retake South Carolina was based on obtaining the support of the partisan commanders, including Pickens, Marion and Sumter. The British still had some 8000 men in the state at outposts from Augusta, Georgia, on the Savannah River, to Georgetown on the coast. Andrew Pickens had left Greene's army by his own request to return to South Carolina before Guilford Court House, and received instructions from Greene to place

himself under Sumter's command. Pickens was back in South Carolina by the end of March, having joined up with Georgian Elijah Clarke. Together they hoped to carry out operations against Ninety Six and Augusta. When Pickens ran into Clarke, Clarke had just returned from a victory over loyalists at Beattie's Mill on the Little River. There, Clarke had attacked Major James Dunlap with 180 mounted men, driving off their dragoons, surrounding their infantry, and killing some 34 men. Dunlap had been captured in the engagement, much to the glee of Pickens. Dunlap had burned Pickens' home during 1780, causing Pickens to renounce his parole to the British and rejoin the patriot cause.

Pickens and Clarke agreed that Dunlap should be moved to Gilbert Town where he could be sent on as prisoner to Virginia. On the way Dunlap was murdered. Pickens reported the event to Greene saying, "A set of men chiefly unknown except one Cobb, an over Mountain Man forced the Guard and shot him." Pickens also provided the information to Colonel Cruger, the loyalist commander at Ninety Six, indicating that Americans regarded the murder with "horror and detestation" while noting that it might have been caused by "the many barbarous massacres committed by those calling themselves [loyalist] officers on our people after their capture."

The partisan war was becoming quite cruel. At Beattie's Mill, where the 34 loyalists were killed, not one American was a casualty. Pickens observed, "The country here is in great distress ... chiefly broken up for want of assistance by the Enemy's marauding parties, and unless something can shortly be done for them I am afraid they will in great measure altogether quit these parts...." Colonel Cruger sortied from his post at Ninety Six on March 31 with 500 regular and loyalist troops and attempted to set up a strong point on Fair Lawn River. The threat of Clarke and Pickens soon changed his mind, and they turned back home.[21]

Earlier Greene had sent colonels Lee and Oldham of the Maryland Continentals to feint towards Cross Creek, tracking Cornwallis' move to the coast. When Cornwallis was placed at Wilmington, Greene ordered Lee to break his pursuit and head to join Francis Marion. Marion had been working in the Pee Dee area for months with his usual success. Greene was sure Marion would cooperate with his operations. When Greene made comments that perhaps he had withheld captured horses, Marion sent in his resignation. Greene had to apologize to get Marion back into the fold. Another situation not to the liking of Marion was that he was now under the orders of Brigadier General Henry Harrington of Richmond County, North Carolina, but he did not actively resist.[22]

After eight days of travel, Lieutenant Colonel Lee joined with Marion on the Santee River. Lee wrote,

"These military friends very cordially rejoiced at being again united in the great attempt of wrestling South Carolina from the enemy."[23] They wasted no time. On April 1, Lee, with a number of mounted Continentals, and Marion, with some 80 men, attacked Fort Watson. This stockade fort was manned by about 130 loyalists under Colonel John Watson, and was located near Wright's Bluff on an eminence 30 to 40 feet high. Marion had fought with Watson several weeks earlier and Watson had retreated to Georgetown. While Lee and Marion outnumbered the garrison, they had no artillery to breach the stockade and abatis that surrounded it. The first move was to cut off the water supply coming from Scott's Lake. Watson countered by sinking his own well. The only way to cause the surrender was to starve them out. Such a move would not have lasted very long, since Watson might receive armed relief at any moment.

The answer to their problem came from Hezekiah Maham, a colonel in the South Carolina Militia, who suggested that a tower be built to give the riflemen a proper angle to shoot down into the fort. After five days of construction, on the night of April 22 a prefabricated tower was raised opposite the fort. The top of the tower had a platform with a log parapet to protect the riflemen as they fired down. The deadly fire came from the tower as two patriot assault parties attacked the walls. Since the loyalists could not man the walls due to the tower fire, the fort was quickly taken. The Americans lost two killed and six wounded. The first of the British strongholds was now broken.[24] Lee wrote of the victory, "The commandant, finding every resource cut off, hung out the white flag."[25]

Since leaving his camp, Greene's army had traveled for 13 days covering 130 miles. On April 19, exactly six years after the American Revolution began at Lexington and Concord, Greene reached Logtown, a cluster of huts one-half mile north of Rawdon's fort at Camden, South Carolina. After surveying Rawdon's defenses, Greene decided to fall back to camp at a place called Hobkirk's Hill on the road from Camden to Waxhaw, just one and one-half miles north of Camden, South Carolina. Hobkirk's Hill was a sandy ridge that ran east to west, with its eastern end falling to a swamp bordering Pine Tree Creek. The western end was a heavy forest area with much underbrush. The road ran through Hobkirk's Hill with open areas on either side. Greene ordered his units to form in camp as a defensive line, and sent out constant patrols to guard against surprise attacks.

Both Rawdon and Greene were expecting reinforcements. Greene had first expected Marion and Lee to come to his aid, but he understood the support they were providing as a flanking unit. Greene's real disappointment, and indeed his frustration, was with the ever-independent partisan, Thomas Sumter. Made a brigadier general by Governor Rutledge, Sumter was never a cooperative commander for any Continental commander or force. Greene remarked, "Sumter refuses to obey my orders, and carries off with him all active force of this unhappy State on rambling, predatory excursions, unconnected with the operations of the army." Without a larger force Greene could not carry out a siege action against Rawdon's force at Camden. Greene now expected Rawdon to meet him in open action.

Greene's force at Hobkirk's Hill consisted of four regiments of Continentals, two from Virginia and two from Maryland, for a total of 1200 men. In addition, he had 250 men from the North Carolina Militia, 100 cavalry under William Washington, Kirkwood's Delaware light infantry, and some 40 artillerymen. The total force of the American army at Camden was therefore a little over 1500 men.

The day after Greene encamped at Hobkirk's Hill, Thomas Kirkwood and his small unit of Delaware light infantry were directed to advance to Logtown to probe the British. Under cover of darkness Kirkwood had gotten "full possession of the place [Logtown], a scattering firing was kept all night, and at sunrise next morning had a smart schirmaze, Beat in the Enemy, about two hours afterwards had a Very agreeable Sight of the Advance [works] of the Army." The next day Kirkwood and William Washington's mounted men attacked Camden with a raid west of the town. The patriots "Burnt a House in one of the Enemy's Redoubts … took 40 hourses & 50 Head of cattle & returned to Camp."

Colonel Francis Lord Rawdon, the Irish 26-year-old, tall, dark, ugly and well-respected commander of the British forces in South Carolina, was well positioned in Camden. He directed some 900 troops, including the 63rd Regiment, three loyalist regiments from New York and Ireland, and some local supporters. Rawdon had 840 infantry and some 60 dragoons. He had continued to command the South Carolina posts with relative success since Cornwallis had moved to action in North Carolina. With the trust of his men and the respect of his earl, Lord Rawdon was ready to take on the Southern Army of Greene.[26]

Lord Rawdon's view of his situation was recounted in his letter to Cornwallis dated April 26:

> On the 19th General Greene appeared before us. I was so weak in troops, considering the extent I had to defend, that I would not risk men to harass him as he advanced. Three days after[ward] the South Carolina Regiment, which I had summoned from Ninety Six, arrived; and, although I had been obliged to abandon the ferry, I fortunately secured the passage of that corps into Camden. At the same time I received a letter from Lieutenant Colonel Balfour, giving me notice of Your Lordship's situation and signifying to me Your Lordship's wish that

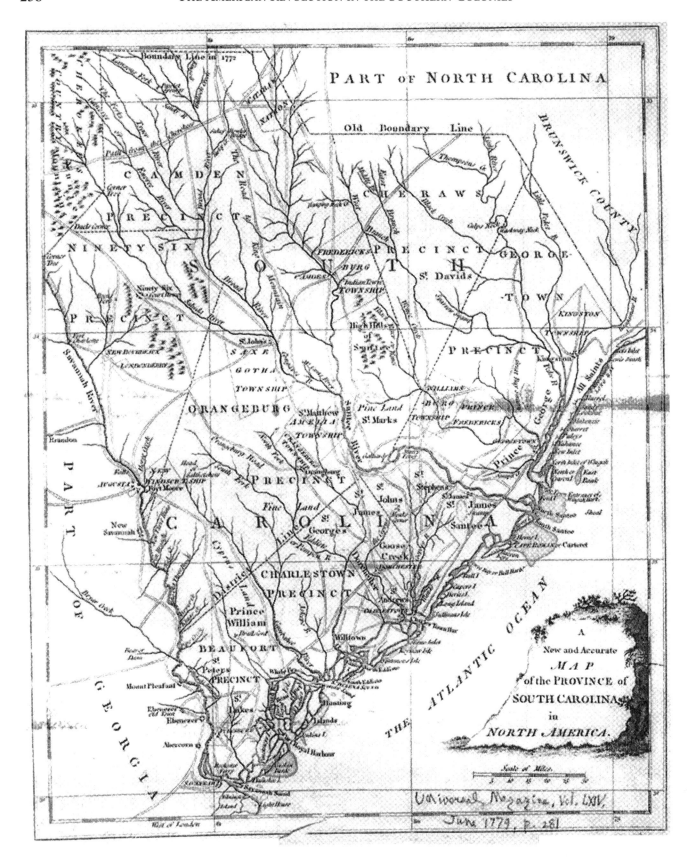

South Carolina. (Hargrett Rare Book and Manuscript Library, University of Georgia Libraries.)

I should retire within the Santee. The necessity of the measure was obvious, but it was no longer in my power.

The efforts of the enemy to examine our works, and in particular an attempt to destroy our mill, had in the meantime occasioned some skirmishing. From the prisoners whom we made in these excursions I gathered that General Greene's army was by no means so numerous as I had apprehended, but that reinforcement was daily expected by them. The position which Marion had taken near the high hills of Santee precluded the hope of Lieutenant Colonel Watson's joining me; I therefore conceived some immediate effort necessary. And, indeed, I did not think that the disparity of numbers was such as should justify a bare defense.[27]

Two events served to aid Rawdon in deciding what move he should make against Greene. The first circumstance was created while Greene was moving south. He was unable to transport the baggage and artillery through a swampy area at Sandhill Creek and decided to leave them behind with Lieutenant Colonel Edward Carrington, his quartermaster general, with a small detachment of infantry. Carrington moved to a point just north of Lynch's Creek to await instructions to move to meet Greene. The second event occurred on April 24 when dispatch riders reported to Greene that Lee and Marion had taken Fort Watson. Later that same day, prisoners and deserters from the British engagement entered the camp of Greene's army at Hobkirk's Hill.[28]

The intelligence that gave Rawdon confidence to take action against Greene was obtained from a deserter. Unfortunately for the Americans, a young drummer boy, one who had been recently returned to the patriot side, switched and went back to the British. The deserter told Rawdon of the American force composition and placement, as well as the situation with Carrington and the delayed artillery. Rawdon wrote of the event, "I had procured information that the enemy, with a view of hazarding an assault, had sent their cannon and baggage a day's march in their rear, but that, abandoning the resolution, they had detached all their militia to bring up against their artillery. Although my intelligence was somewhat tardy, I hoped I should still be in time to avail myself of this conjuncture. By arming our musicians, our drummers, and in short everything that could carry a firelock, I mustered above nine hundred for the field, sixty of whom were dragoons."[29]

Though Greene had given orders that "Every part of the army must be in readiness to stand at arms at a moment's notice," he was taken by surprise on the morning of April 25.[30] Rawdon's men moved rapidly through the thickets, brush and swamp, along the right side of the Waxhaw road, and off the road in the woods for much of the advance. At the head of the British in their rather narrow front were three regiments, the 63rd Regiment on the

right, in the center the New York Volunteers, and the King's American Regiment (Fanning's Regiment) on their left. In support on the right were the Volunteers of Ireland, and on the left many "walking wounded." In reserve were the South Carolina Provincial Regiment and the New York Dragoons.[31]

At around 10 in the morning on the 25th, while Greene was sipping his tea after the morning meal, with many of his men washing their clothes and cleaning their arms, the pickets were alerted to Rawdon's force as they came out of the woods. The pickets retreated in reasonable order as Captain Robert Kirkwood formed up his Delaware company and established a defensive line on the left flank as they fired at the British. Due to Kirkwood's quick thinking, Greene was able to have time to form up his order of battle. General Isaac Huger's two regiments of Virginia Continentals, the Fourth under Lieutenant Colonel Richard Campbell and the Fifth under Lieutenant Colonel Samuel Hawes, were formed on the right side of the road. On the left of the road were Colonel Otto Williams' Maryland Brigade, with the First Maryland under Colonel John Eager Howard and the Second Maryland under Lieutenant Colonel Benjamin Ford. In the center Greene placed the just arrived Colonel Carrington with his three six-pounders and the detachment of 40 artillerymen under Colonel Charles Harrison. The reserve consisted of Colonel Reade's North Carolina Militia and the 87th Cavalry commanded by Lieutenant Colonel Walham Washington.

Greene first ordered the two center regiments, the Fifth Virginia and the First Maryland, to close across the road to hide the artillery. As Rawdon moved out of the woods, the artillery fired canister into the ranks of the British. Rawdon engaged the American Army as Greene watched with intense focus. Greene directed Campbell's Fourth Virginia and Ford's Second Maryland to advance and turn toward the enemy's flanks to avoid the narrow front of Rawdon's force. At the same time Greene sent the two center regiments of Virginia and Maryland Continentals down the hill to attack the British with a bayonet charge. Huger's Virginia Brigade was pushing down the slope and moving the British left. William Washington's dragoons were ordered to swing in a wide arc around and attack Rawdon's force from the rear.[32]

Rawdon's force adjusted to Greene's maneuvers but the canister shot was having its effect. Just as the British were about to "begin to give way on all sides, and their left absolutely to retreat," one of Greene's premier regiments, the First Maryland, fell into confusion as Gunby tried to halt part of the line to allow the remaining troops to line up. During this delay Captain William Beatty was shot and the advance companies faltered. In the confusion the regiment began to retreat. Colonel Ford of the Second

4 Miles to Saunders Ferry

Salisbury Retreat 4½ two Miles

Light Infantry

Militia
Gen¹ Greene Reserve
Colonel Williams
Brig Gen Huger Maryland
Lt Col Campbell
Lt Col Howard
Virginia Brigade

Col of Ireland

Dragoons

King Somerville
Benj Capt Kirkwood Morgan N Y Dragoons
Lord Rawdon

Charlestown

American Pickel

Col Washington

Thickets with few trees.

Dragoons

Mill Branch

Open Ground

One and three Bub¹ Miles Dout (Charleston)

Log Town

Open and cleared of trees in the vicinity of Camden

To Cheraw

Original Plan of Gen¹ Greene.

Redoubt

Hobkirk Hill

Camden
Head Qrs

British.
American.
British Dragoons.

Compiled and Drawn by Col. Carrington.

Maryland was shot as his regiment hesitated and then fell back. Campbell's force also broke. Only Hawes' men remained steady in the face of the disorder of the moment.

With his units in almost total disorder, Greene had no choice but to order a retirement. As the men retreated, Harrison's artillery was in a desperate move to set up the cannons to help with the rear guard action. Greene even dismounted to help the men drag the cannons into place. Some 50 Americans were killed at the cannons, mostly by Captain John Coffin's New York dragoons. Eventually Washington arrived to drive the British off the cannon for a few moments. Greene retreated in reasonable order. While Washington was too late to make an impact on the battle, he did aid the retreat. Lee credited Washington with stopping the pursuit with a fierce saber charge against the British.[33]

Washington returned to patrol when Greene had reached Saunders' Creek, some four miles away. Washington was able to ambush 60 New York Provincial dragoons and defeated them soundly. Greene's army moved to the old Camden battleground after collecting the stragglers and wounded. The next day, April 26, Greene moved to Rugeley's Mill and camped. The American losses were 132 killed and 136 wounded, captured or missing. Rawdon's losses were 258, of whom 38 were killed. The British lost one officer killed and 13 wounded.[34]

The news of the American defeat at Camden was received with joy by the British garrison at Charles Town. An expression of the British sentiment appeared in print in the Charles Town *Royal Gazette* in a verse:

> To Camden, so fatal to Rebels, we're told
> That Greene with his army, and forces so bold,
> Of success so secure, advanc'd that the Tanner
> [Greene, from his younger days in that vocation]
> Promised laurels to each who fought under his banner.
> On the 25th ult., fatal day! What a hardship!
> Without the least warning, out sailed his Lordship
> Killed, wounded, and took, alas! My poor Tanner,
> How many of those who fought under your banner?

Greene was not entirely distressed by the results at Camden. In a letter to the French envoy, Chevalier de La Luzerne, Greene wrote, "We fight, get beat, rise and fight again." His letter revealed that he must indeed pull down the British outposts in South Carolina in order to free the lower South. Greene also gave more testimony of his disdain for the militia as he wrote, "North Carolina has got no men in the field and few militia and those the worst in the world." Unfortunately Greene was not sympathetic to those men from North Carolina who did support him. At Hobkirk's Hill, some 20 percent of the force engaged were from that state. Greene was most upset with five prisoners that had previously deserted the American cause. These men were immediately taken out and hanged. This event set in motion many reprisals throughout South Carolina in the coming weeks.[35]

Rumors came to Greene's camp that Cornwallis would be coming back into the fray in Carolina, rather than moving up to Virginia. But on May 6 Greene wrote to Sumter, "I am rather inclined to think that he will leave everything here, and move northward. I am led to entertaining this opinion from its being the original plan, and from the earl's being too proud to relinquish his object."[36] Greene must consider his next moves to further his goals of driving the British from South Carolina.

On May 7 John Watson with 1200 men managed to evade Marion and Lee and returned to Camden. Lord Rawdon now had an army nearly equal to Greene's, but with Sumter, Marion and Pickens operating around the area it was difficult to find comfort. Since Fort Watson had fallen, and the other posts were now threatened, Rawdon decided to abandon Camden and all the territory north of the Congaree River. He also sent orders to Lieutenant Colonel Harris Cruger to leave Ninety Six and join Thomas Brown at Augusta. The British commander at Fort Granby was ordered to abandon the post and go to Orangeburgh. Unfortunately for Rawdon, Greene's patrols intercepted each of these messages, and none got through.[37]

On May 10, Rawdon left his fortifications at Camden and burned the jail, the mills and several private homes owned by local patriots before heading off to Nelson's Ferry on the Santee River. In company with the British were "Militia who had been with us in Camden ... also the well affected Neighbours on our Route, together with the Wives, Children, Negroes and Baggage of almost all of them." Rawdon had left behind 31 wounded American prisoners, and 61 British wounded with three officers, who were too sick to travel by wagon or carriage.

At Nelson's Ferry, Rawdon joined with Colonel Balfour from Charles Town. In reflecting on the situation in the countryside, both Rawdon and Balfour agreed that "the whole interior Country had revolted."[38] Thus the British commanders made the decision to march on to Monck's Corner, just 32 miles from Charles Town. By his actions in abandoning Camden, Rawdon had lost the strategic initiative, even as Greene lost the battle at Hobkirk's Hill. This was another strong message to the local loyalists that the British could not be depended on to maintain control of the countryside.[39]

For those loyalist families that departed with Lord

Opposite page: Battle of Hobkirk Hill. (*Battles of the American Revolution.*)

Rawdon, the future would turn out to be a rather bleak one. When they arrived in Charles Town, no houses were provided for their convenience. They were forced to construct huts outside the works, which came to be known as Rawdontown. As fate would have it, many of these loyalist supporters were to perish in these huts under the eyes of the British authorities.[40]

Meanwhile, Greene was intent on continuing the offensive against the British in South Carolina. The day after the battle at Hobkirk's Hill, Greene sent word to Marion asking him to move up. Out of respect for Marion, Greene wrote, "I have detached a field piece to your assistance with an escort of a few Continental troops under the command of Major Eaton." Colonel Pinketham Eaton of the Third North Carolina Regiment unfortunately became lost in the swamps on the way to Marion. A guide finally led Eaton to Marion's concealed camp on the Pee Dee. Marion then departed and crossed the Santee, as Eaton was ordered to send his detachment to aid Lee and Pickens at Augusta.[41]

General Sumter, who was pursuing his independent operations, had moved to Fort Granby (near present-day Columbia) on the Congaree River. Finding the fort too strong to take, Sumter moved to Orangeburgh some 50 miles south. With a display of his troops and artillery, Sumter was able to force the garrison of 85 loyalists and regulars to surrender the post on May 11. Meanwhile Marion and Lee moved to Fort Motte. The "fort" was located at the confluence of the Congaree and Wateree rivers, and was actually the large residence of a patriot widow, Mrs. Rebecca Motte. A ditch with a reinforced abatis surrounded the house, which protected some 150 infantry.

In the act of digging parallel ditches, after two days the patriots received word that Rawdon was on his way to relieve the garrison. Knowing they might not have time to continue their offensive in the current manner, Lee and Marion decided to burn Mrs. Motte's house. After getting the approval of the patriot lady, the house was lit by fire arrows. Lee wrote of the circumstance, "The ... house was a large, pleasant edifice intended for the summer residence of the respectable owner.... Nevertheless the obligations of duty were imperative."[42] Soon the garrison was showing a white flag. In an act of chivalry, that night the patriots treated the British officers to a "sumptuous dinner" as the hostess, Mrs. Motte, conducted herself "with ease, vivacity, and good sense ... the engaging amiability of her manners, left it doubtful which set of officers constituted these defenders." Soon, General Greene himself joined the Americans at Fort Motte, where he met Francis Marion for the first time face-to-face. Greene remarked to Marion that he was "at a loss which to admire most, your bravery and fortitude, or your ad-

dress and management."

With this latest post taken, Greene directed Marion to move to position to take Georgetown on the coast, while Lee was sent up the Congaree River to take Fort Granby. Lee arrived at Fort Granby on May 15, and immediately called for the surrender of loyalist Major Andrew Maxwell and his garrison. Lee promptly began to construct a battery for his six-pounder at the edge of the woods to the west of Granby. The morning was rather foggy while the battery was built. When the fog lifted, Captain Finley ordered a single round to be fired over the fort's parapet, which sent the enemy in disarray. Lee's infantry then advanced with bayonets showing.

Lee sent Captain Joseph Eggleston in to conduct negotiations with Maxwell. Maxwell, a well-known plunderer, complied with Lee's direction and was allowed to leave with looted goods and some slaves. The Hessian troops were allowed to keep their horses. The surrender document was signed by Maxwell and Lee. The terms of the surrender allowed the British and loyalists to return to Charles Town and be exchanged for patriot prisoners. Lee also agreed to escort them to Charles Town under his protection. On May 15 the enemy garrison of 340 men, of whom 60 were regulars and 280 were loyalist militia, marched out of Fort Granby with two field pieces, all personal possessions and two covered wagons.[43] The decisions to grant these terms would later cause some conflict. Serious conflict came from the militia when they learned that Maxwell was allowed to take away his loot. They were even more concerned when they noticed that Lee's men appeared shortly afterward in new clothes.[44]

Sumter came to charge Lee with taking over his territory, since he had left a small detachment to watch Fort Granby while he moved south. Actually Sumter was most upset over not being able to engage "Sumter's Law," in having the opportunity to split up the loot as reward for taking Fort Granby. This greed factor was common among partisan units on both sides and made the pure military arrangements more difficult.[45]

Francis Marion marched to Georgetown, arriving outside the town to begin the siege operations. With no hope of reinforcements, the British garrison evacuated the town by sea on May 23, and sailed to Charles Town. Marion leveled the defensive works and occupied the town in another bloodless victory.[46]

At this point the British maintained only two major defensive outposts in the lower South — Augusta and Ninety Six — other than Charles Town and Savannah. After Camden, Greene decided to head for Ninety Six while he ordered operations against Augusta, Georgia, where loyalist Colonel Thomas Browne commanded his Florida Rangers in their strong entrenchment. Greene sent Lieutenant Colonel Henry Lee with his Legion, and the newly promoted Brigadier General Andrew Pickens commanding his South Carolina Militia, to take Augusta. Browne had constructed three forts around Augusta for defense — Galphin, Cornwallis and Grierson.

On his way to the Augusta area, covering some 75 miles in three days from Fort Granby, Lee had sent out strong patrols under Captain Ferdinand O'Neale. O'Neale discovered that the annual British gift to the Indians had just arrived at Fort Galphin only 12 miles away. The gift consisted of powder, balls, small arms, liquor, salt and blankets. Seeing this opportunity before him, Lee brought his forces around Fort Galphin. On the morning of May 18, Lee sent a detachment of mounted militia at the front gate in open defiance. Lee had sent a unit of his Legion infantry through cover of the woods to allow them to approach from the opposite direction if the enemy militia came out to pursue the mounted men. The loyalists took the bait, as most of the garrison came out to pursue the horsemen. The concealed infantry charged the open gate from the other side and took the fort with only a single casualty — a sunstroke victim. The British lost four killed, and a few were wounded out of the 126 prisoners taken. Now the gift supplies were in the hands of the patriots.

On the evening of May 21, Lee crossed the river and moved toward Augusta. At Augusta he joined with Pickens and Elijah Clarke commanding his Georgians to take on the two remaining Augusta British forts. Fort Cornwallis was located in the middle of the town and Fort Grierson was a mere one-half mile away up the river across a narrow creek swamp. Pickens ordered his artillery to construct batteries midway between the two forts. At Fort Grierson was Colonel Grierson, a hated loyalist, with a garrison of 80 loyalist Georgia Militia. From their encampment on the west of town, Lee, Pickens and Clarke decided to attack the weaker enemy garrison at Grierson first. At Fort Cornwallis on the riverbank Colonel Browne commanded 320 Provincial regulars with two artillery pieces. Supporting this facility were some 200 black slave laborers who maintained the fortifications. The plan was to attack Grierson and prevent his militia from joining with those at Fort Cornwallis.

The attack on Fort Grierson began on May 23. Pickens and Clarke attacked from the north and west as Major Eaton with the North Carolina Continentals engaged from the south along a swamp. Lee's Legion of infantry and artillery moved up from the swamp with Eaton. Captain Eggleston with the Legion Cavalry was positioned in the woods to the south of Lee with orders to support by attacking Browne's rear if he advanced toward Lee. When Colonel Browne noticed Lee's movements on the margin of the swamp, he came out of his fort with infantry and artillery. After a long-range and ineffective bombardment between Lee and Browne, Browne retreated back inside the fortification. The garrison fell quickly at Fort Grierson with the coordinated attack. The loyalists lost 30 killed, and many of the remaining wounded. American casualties were light, but among them was the promising young officer Major Eaton.

To the south of the swamp was a creek which flowed into the river. Located there was a large brick mansion belonging to a prominent loyalist. Here Lee took up his Legion while Pickens and Clarke positioned the militia in the woods on the left of Fort Cornwallis. Since the fort was near the Savannah River, its banks allowed the Americans to operate rather freely. The siege works began around the left and rear, as Browne continued strengthening his defensive works. To attempt to dislodge the Americans, Browne sent out a British assault unit just before midnight on May 28 to attack the trenches next to the river. The unit was able to drive the surprised Americans out, but a fierce battle led by Captain Handy fought off the British. That same night, Browne sent out another detachment. Likewise, this force was driven back by Captain Michael Rudolph of the Legion and troops who used bayonets and hand-to-hand combat to win.

Since the area around the fort was a flat river plain, Pickens, Lee and Clarke decided that a Maham Tower (named for Hezekiah Maham), such as the one used by Marion and Lee at Fort Watson, should be built. The timbers for the tower arrived on May 30 as construction began hidden by an old house. The frame for the tower was raised, steadied by a foundation of earth, stone and brick rubble. Anticipating that Browne would try to destroy the tower, Lee and Pickens placed a company of infantry around the tower to guard it. The night the tower was raised, Browne did come out for a third time and attacked Pickens' militia in the rear of Fort Cornwallis. Captain Rudolph's men fought off the river attackers as Captain Handy's troops swung around and came to the aid of Pickens' militia under bayonet attack from Browne. With losses on both sides, Browne finally retreated into the fort.[47] On May 31, a summons to surrender was sent to Browne, but he refused.[48]

Realizing the danger of the Maham Tower, Browne erected a tower opposite the American tower. On his tower he mounted two of his heaviest artillery pieces. The British fired at the American tower even as it was nearing completion. The American tower was completed on June 1, and a single six-pounder cannon was mounted on the top. At dawn on June 2 cannon-fire commenced immediately by the Americans with good effect. By noon of that day the Americans had dismounted the two British cannons on the tower, and were sending cannon and musket shot into the fort in all locations, except at the British tower, which was out of range.

Browne was getting desperate, but he would not

surrender. He sent a Scottish sergeant into Lee's camp pretending to be a deserter. The deserter told Lee that he knew where the British powder magazine was located. If red-hot cannon shot was fired at it, the whole place would go up in smoke. Apparently the mission of the Scottish sergeant was to set fire to the house before the tower, in the hopes that it would reach the tower itself. Lee became suspicious and removed the sergeant off the tower platform and placed him under guard. In frustration at the lack of success of the sergeant, Browne came out and burned two empty log cabins on the outside of the fort. The American commanders could not understand why Browne had spared two other houses. Pickens ordered a party of militia to prepare to occupy the tallest house on the early morning of June 4 to cover a planned attack. At about 3 A.M. that selected house was destroyed by a violent explosion. Apparently Browne had positioned a mine at the house and blew it up. It was fortunate for the designated party that they had not moved to occupy the house yet that morning.

At 9 A.M. Lee and Pickens were positioned to attack the fort. First they sent out a letter to Browne asking him to surrender the fort. Initially he refused, but later a white flag was seen from the fort and negotiations began. Since June 4 was the king's birthday, Browne would not surrender on that day. So, on the next day at 8 A.M. Browne's more than 300 troops marched out of their fort and laid down their arms. Captain Rudolph then marched in and raised the American flag. Augusta was now in American hands.[49]

Knowing of the hatred toward Browne and some of his officers, Browne was sent directly to Lee's headquarters for protection. Lee recorded, "This precaution suggested by the knowledge of the inveteracy with which the operations in this quarter have been conducted on both sides turned out to be extremely fortunate; as otherwise, in all probability, the laurels acquired by the arms of America would have been stained by the murder of a gallant soldier...." Pickens sent a heavy escort of the North Carolina Militia with the prisoners to Savannah to be paroled. This mission was successfully accomplished.

While Lee, Pickens and Clarke were engaging the enemy at Augusta, Greene had moved to the most notorious British stronghold at Ninety Six. Ninety Six, the place named because it was 96 miles from the chief Cherokee Indian town of Keowee, had been a continuous loyalist post since the British had occupied South Carolina. Since the summer of 1780 Ninety Six had been commanded by Colonel John Harris Cruger. Cruger, an officer from a prominent family of politicians and merchants in New York, commanded a force consisting of 150 men of the Second Battalion of DeLancey's New York Volunteers, 200 New Jersey Volunteers and some 200 South Carolina Loyalist Militia.

Cruger and his Ninety Six fortifications had served to make this area the most loyalist environment in South Carolina. It was felt that loyalists outnumbered patriots by a ratio of 5-to-1 in this country. The village at Ninety Six was enclosed by a stockade which was protected by a deep ditch and abatis. On one corner outside the main stockade, some 80 yards to the east of the village, was a unique star-shaped redoubt that had been built by a most skilled British engineer, Lieutenant Henry Haldane. The classic star redoubt, used by many European military engineers, contained eight points and 16 angles and provided a powerful defensive structure intended to prevent attack on these two sides of the fort. On the opposite and west side of the fort from the star redoubt was a similar four-sided structure positioned to defend the water supply, a rivulet fed by a spring. This defensive structure was joined to the stockade by a covered way. Cruger also had three three-pounders, and numerous black slaves as a labor battalion.[50] These fortifications were most impressive and fearsome for Greene and his American attackers.

Greene reached Ninety Six on May 22 with his force of 427 Continentals from Maryland and Delaware, 421 Virginia Continentals, 66 North Carolina Militia and 60 Delaware mounted scouts detachment directed by Captain Robert Kirkwood. The mission of these 974 Americans under Greene's command was to capture this fort and drive out Cruger and his loyalists. Even though Greene had nearly twice as many men as Cruger, he was not in a position to storm the fort due to the strength of Cruger's defensive works. Following the expert advice of his chief engineer, the Polish general and colonel in the American Army, Thaddeus Kosciuszko, Greene decided to lay siege to the fort and began preparations immediately.

Colonel Kosciuszko's force established a series of parallel trenches at only 70 yards from the star redoubt and a three-gun battery just 130 yards in front of the star redoubt. Seeing that the Americans were trenching at 70 yards away, contrary to the usual European principles of siege warfare, Cruger immediately built a gun battery at the nearest point to the besiegers and mounted all three cannons there. On May 23 the loyalists opened heavy fire at the Americans, as Lieutenant John Roney of DeLancey's New York Volunteers came out with 30 handpicked men to engage the Americans. The sally group bayoneted all those who did not quickly retreat, as a working party of loyalists and black slaves destroyed the American works and carried off their tools. The American losses were heavy, but the only loyalist casualty was Roney. The loyalists were back in the fort before Greene's reinforcements arrived. Greene had learned a hard lesson.

Greene now began his new trenches at a more respectable distance. He set two cannon batteries at 300 yards from the star redoubt, while Kosciuszko and his engineer assistant, Captain Dalzien, managed construction working parties day and night. The first parallel, located at 220 yards from the star, was completed on May 27, and was a 20-foot-high battery at just 140 yards back. This trench was four feet wide, three feet deep and some 60 yards long, with facines (wooden stakes bound together) at the lip and gabions (wicker baskets of earth).

On May 30 the patriot sappers completed a *flèche* located at 100 yards from the fort itself. This *flèche* consisted of two trenches that met at a point, which represented the second parallel. This work was intended to provide communications, flanking fire against British sallies and artillery position. Greene's men also started work on a third parallel trench only 60 yards from the star. As the British noted the Americans closing in on the redoubt, they started an intense fire at the laborers. The laborers were forced to use a wooden shield or mantelet in front of them for protection as they worked.

Greene decided to construct a Maham Tower near the third parallel at 30 yards from the star, and rising 40 feet in the air. From the tower on June 3 one American shot down a loyalist when he raised his head above the parapet in the star redoubt. To counter this move, Cruger raised the parapet three feet higher by stacking sandbags. Cruger attempted to burn the Maham Tower at the third parallel with red-hot cannon shot, but the logs were too green and he had no adequate furnaces. Not giving up, Cruger directed the construction of a 16-foot high transverse that provided protection as men moved from section to section within the works.

With the American trenches in place and the Maham tower established, Greene sent Colonel Otto Williams under a flag of truce to seek permission to deliver a written surrender demand to Cruger. Lieutenant Stelle, who was the British officer of the day, refused to allow Williams to advance, but he did take the message to Cruger. This communication revealed that Lord Rawdon had retreated to Charles Town and that all the British posts between the Wateree, Congaree and Santee rivers were captured. Greene's message demanded immediate surrender. Cruger rejected the demand, having considered his situation serious but not hopeless. He had lost only one officer killed and eight men wounded, and thought the demand an insult.

Now Greene tried to burn the fort by sending flaming arrows at the wooden fort's buildings. To counter, Cruger's men tore off the roofs of each building. From the American works musket fire and cannon fire rained down on the enemy. On June 8 Lee arrived from Augusta and promptly upset the enemy by inadvertently parading his prisoners from Augusta in front of the fort in plain sight of their British and loyalist brethren. The next day Pickens came in with his militia. Now Greene was in a better staffing situation. He directed Lee's Legion to counter the nightly sallies from the enemy garrison, as well as beginning to dig a trench toward the spring. Loyalist water was now getting short, but some came in with the black slaves who were sent out at night to retrieve the water. The summer heat was taking its toll on the British and loyalists.

By now Greene's third parallel was within six feet of the star redoubt. It was decided that a tunnel must be built into Cruger's star, under the wall. Greene was planning to blow up the British star works with barrels of gunpowder being acquired by Pickens. Greene was only a few feet away from having the tunnel complete on June 11 when he received intelligence from Sumter that British reinforcements had landed at Charles Town, and Rawdon had marched out of the city on June 7th. Three fresh regiments of infantry and grenadiers from Ireland — the Third, the 19th and the 30th Foot — had arrived at Charles Town on June 3rd. Greene immediately sent William Washington and his cavalry with a message to Sumter and Marion to gather as many militia as they could and do everything they could to intercept Rawdon before he reached Ninety Six.[51] Believing that Rawdon would move to retake Fort Granby, Sumter headed to the Congaree River. Unfortunately for the Americans, Rawdon moved through Orangeburgh. By the time Sumter learned of the movement, it was too late to intercept the British.[52]

On the night of June 12 a farmer, Hugh Aikens, came up riding along the American lines south of the town. Moving in a casual manner, he stopped to talk with the troops and met with little attention since he was a local resident and wanted to see what was happening. As Aikens came to the road that headed directly into Ninety Six, he put his horse in a gallop at full speed and raced toward the British gate waving a letter over his head. The garrison saw the rider and opened the gate quickly. From his letter Cruger learned that Rawdon had arrived at Orangeburgh, which was about 100 miles away, and was marching to Ninety Six with newly arrived reinforcements, a force totaling around 2000 men.

The news brought general cheering among the enemy garrison as Greene looked on. But the situation was still becoming rather difficult for the British. Lee had moved his lines, reinforced with artillery, to within a few yards of the outlying works on the hornwork at the stream. Cruger was so concerned that he evacuated the garrison from that redoubt on June 17. Now the water supply was in more peril. Without water, Cruger would eventually have to surrender.

Realizing that he could not use regular siege tactics with Rawdon on his way, Greene made the decision to undertake a frontal assault on the fort. On the morning of June 18, 1781, Greene directed all the cannons to bear on the star redoubt. Greene divided the attack into two groups. At noon one assault group of Virginia and Delaware Continentals to the east moved forward under the direction of Lieutenant Colonel Richard Campbell, assisted by Lieutenant Isaac Duvall of Maryland and Lieutenant Samuel Selden of Virginia. The other group commanded by Lieutenant Colonel Lee to the west, with Captain Michael Rudolph, crossed the abatis and ditch in two places, and advanced with much success.

The storming party, armed with hooks on long handles, had pulled down the sandbags on the parapets as the riflemen from the Maham Tower fired at the retreating enemy. For a moment it looked like the attack would succeed, but the flow of the engagement changed. Captain Thomas French of the New York Volunteers led some 30 men out on a flank on one side, as Captain Peter Campbell of New Jersey struck from the other flank at the Americans. A bloody struggle ensued with bayonets and muskets used as clubs on both sides. When two commanders of the attackers, Lieutenant Duvall and Lieutenant Seldon, were hit, the Americans soon retreated back to their trenches.[53]

With the loss of 127 American Continentals killed and wounded, and 20 missing, and with Rawdon nearing Ninety Six only 30 miles away, Greene called off operations and moved to retreat. The militia losses were not recorded. Lee reported, "Gloom and silence pervaded the American camp; every one mortified. Three days more and Ninety Six must have fallen; but this short space was unattainable.... Greene alone preserved his equanimity; and highly pleased by the unshaken courage displayed in the assault, announced his grateful sense of the conduct of the troops...." To avoid Rawdon, Greene moved his army northeastward toward Charlotte.[54]

At Ninety Six the loyalists had lost 27 killed and 58 wounded. Rawdon arrived at Ninety Six with 1800 infantry and 150 horsemen after traveling hard for 14 days in the heat of the South Carolina summer sun. When he arrived the day after the battle he was greeted with cheers. Rawdon sent out 800 infantry and 60 horsemen to chase Greene, as he rested the remainder of his forces. Rawdon gave the loyalist population two choices: either stay in the fortified fort with a small garrison and support it as best they could from Charles Town, or they could come with him to Charles Town. The locals elected to leave with the British. Rawdon ordered Cruger to destroy the remaining fortifications, and escort the refugees to safety. Rawdon would abandon this infamous fort and leave the Upcountry to the patriots.[55]

By the time Greene's forces reached Enoree, Rawdons' troops had approached the rear guard of Lee's Legion and Kirkwood's 60 light infantrymen. Thankfully, the British were exhausted in their heavy woolen uniforms in the 100-degree temperatures and high humidity. More than 50 British had died from heat exhaustion on the march. Rawdon and his British chasing force stopped and then moved back to Ninety Six. The British and loyalists left Ninety Six on June 29, and Greene's tactical failure was turned into strategic victory.

The real hero of the battle was Cruger, who had held off Greene for 27 days until Rawdon arrived. Greene had run out of time as his blocking forces under Sumter and Marion had failed. Greene revealed his disappointment as he wrote Marion, "It was my wish to have fought Lord Rawdon before he got to Ninety Six and could I have collected your force and that of General Sumter and Pickens, I could have done it, and am persuaded we should have defeated him.... I am surprised the people should be so averse to joining in some general plan of operations."

When Greene learned that Rawdon had evacuated Ninety Six, he turned his army to the southeast. Greene ordered Lee and Kirkwood to attempt to reach the front of Rawdon's forces. He also requested Marion and Sumter to join their forces at the lower Congaree River. Lee and Kirkwood were able to get into position, but Marion and Sumter did not move fast enough. Rawdon, with Lieutenant Colonel Alexander Stewart of the Third Regiment, known as the Buffs, halted at Orangeburgh. There they took up positions in a number of buildings in the village. Soon Greene arrived at Orangeburgh with Washington's dragoons and Lee's Legion. Surprisingly, Sumter managed to reach Orangeburg to meet Greene. Greene now considered his next move.

Even though Cruger's force had not yet joined up with Rawdon's, Greene made a decision not to attack Rawdon. His men were entirely fatigued. The Legion and Kirkwood's men were nearly staggering around. The Continentals had traveled 323 miles in the 23 days since Ninety Six. Greene wrote:

> Never did we suffer so severely as during the few days' halt here (Orangeburg). Rice furnished our substitute for bread, which, although tolerably relished by those familiarized with it ... was very disagreeable to the Marylanders and Virginians, who had grown up in the use of corn or wheat bread ... the few meagre cattle brought to camp as beef would not afford more than two ounces per man. Frogs abounded ... and on them chiefly did the light troops subsist.... Even alligator was used by a few; and very probably, had the army been much longer detained upon that ground, might have rivalled the frog in the estimation of our epicures.

Greene broke off the campaign and retired to the High Hills of the Santee. This area consisted of 20 miles of sand and clay hills rising some 200 feet above the north bank of the Santee River. This area was rich in grain and was free from most swamp diseases as the gentle breezes blew to provide some relief.[56]

As Greene retired to the Santee, Sumter requested to continue to harass the enemy. Greene therefore assigned Marion's force and Lee's Legion to his command. As intelligence arrived, Sumter moved to the area of Monck's Corner, just 30 miles from Charles Town, to attack the British. At Biggin Church, a strong brick building northwest of Monck's Corner, Colonel Peter Horry of Marion's force engaged Lieutenant Colonel James Coates with the 19th Regiment. Horry, with men from Marion's Brigade and some of Sumter's riflemen, had moved to within three miles of the church. There at 5 P.M. on July 16, Major Thomas Fraser with his mounted South Carolina Loyalist Rangers suddenly attacked them. After falling back and then regrouping, Horry's men fought off Fraser's men with support of Colonel Edward Lacey's riflemen. Fraser moved back to Biggin Church and Coates.

Believing that Horry's dragoons were the lead elements of Greene's entire army, on July 16 Coates set fire to the church, which was loaded with supplies and baggage, and crossed Fair Swamp and the Wadboo Bridge without problem. Coates was on his way back towards Charles Town. Sumter did not discover that the British had left until his scouts saw the fire at the church. At 3 A.M. on July 17 Sumter woke his troops and ordered them to pursue. Lee and Wade Hampton had arrived earlier, with much frustration over the inability of the Americans to block the retreat of Coates. Coates had now decided to send his mounted Rangers to Charles Town via the Bonneau Ferry road, while the 19th Regiment swung to the left and took the route toward Quinby Bridge.

Hampton rode off after the South Carolina Loyalist Rangers while Lee's Legion and Marion's cavalry went after the 19th Regiment. Hampton was unsuccessful and did not reach the Rangers until they have moved by boat to the other side at Bonneau Ferry, securing all the boats there. The only hope was with Lee. At a mile away from Quinby Bridge, Lee's force engaged 100 men of the 19th Regiment rear guard under Captain Colin Campbell, who was escorting the baggage. After a brief resistance, the entire rear guard surrendered. Unaware of the rear action, Coates crossed Quinby's Bridge and prepared to wait for Campbell with the baggage.

As Coates' men removed the planks from the bridge and placed a cannon at the southern end to protect the rear guard, the cavalries of Lee and Marion approached. In the lead was Captain James Armstrong with the lead elements of Lee's cavalry. When Armstrong came to the northern end of the bridge, he halted and sent a rider back to alert Lee. Lee replied to pursue immediately and Armstrong did. As he galloped over the bridge, the loos-

ened planks fell into the creek under the hooves of the horses. The British scrambled off to a plantation house nearby. The second section of cavalry under Lieutenant George Carrington had to jump the gap of missing planks in the center of the bridge left by Armstrong.

Coates had become separated from most of his men as he defended himself with his sword against Captain Armstrong's saber slashes. The third section of the Legion under Captain O'Neale hesitated in crossing the growing gap in the bridge, but Hezekiah Maham, leading Marion's cavalry, passed O'Neale's men and stormed the bridge. Maham went down as a musketball hit his mount. Soon Captain James McCauley, commanding the first infantry under Marion, crossed the bridge and joined with Armstrong and Carrington. The 19th Regiment was now rallying on the causeway as they began to put up a stiff resistance. Lee and Marion came up and directed that the bridge be repaired. After some hand-to-hand combat, Coates' men moved back with him to the large two-story house and outbuilding at Shubrick's Plantation a short distance off.

Frustrated over the lack of quick progress at repairing the bridge, Lee and Marion marched up Quinby Creek and forded it upstream. They then moved through some woods and came out in the open fields around the plantation. Seeing that they could not attack Coates' force without support, Marion and Lee decided to wait for Sumter to come up before engaging further. Sumter arrived late in the afternoon and immediately called for a general attack. Since the British had artillery, and the American six-pounder had not been brought up yet, Lee and Marion protested the decision. Sumter ignored them and began the attack anyway. With the cavalry covering any British retreat, Sumter's brigade advanced on the right by the rice fields along the creek and took up position at the slave quarters. From that location, Sumter kept up fire at a rather long distance from Coates' forces at the mansion and buildings. Colonel Thomas Taylor was ordered to attack with 45 men at the fences on the British left. As Taylor advanced under heavy fire from the British, Captain Scerett led a bayonet charge at Taylor, forcing him to retreat across the open field.

Marion, with his troops and Lee's infantry on the left, moved up to the fence and ordered the men to lie down and fire under the rails. The men remained there until their ammunition was gone. Under cover of darkness, Marion withdrew the men. The engagement had lasted three hours. Sumter retired from the action at sundown, moved across the repaired bridge and camped three miles away. With all the commanders back with Sumter, the anger came out with a passion. Sumter desired to engage the next morning, but most resisted. Taylor was the most irate at Sumter's actions that day.

Marion was so disgusted that he moved off with his men during the night. Lee followed Marion the next morning, heading back to join Greene on the Santee Hills without informing Sumter. Sumter, now too weak to engage, moved away from the area and moved back across the Santee River.

Coates had won the Battle of Quinby Bridge, as the Americans were humiliated and angered over Sumter's action. The Americans had lost 60 killed and wounded around the house, while the British lost six killed, 38 wounded and 100 captured.[57]

Meanwhile, Greene was still resting and building his army in the High Hills of the Santee. The heat of the midsummer in South Carolina was unbearable for all. To Greene's delight General Sumner with his commanders, Ashe, Armstrong, and Blount, marched from Salisbury, North Carolina, to join Greene. In all Sumner had around 500 men, including many who had experienced Guilford Court House. Also joining Greene were 75 mounted North Carolinians under Marquis Malmedy, a French officer who had taken part in the defense of Charles Town under General Lincoln.[58] Now Greene had a force of some 1500 men, made up of 1250 Continentals, 300 dragoons, some South Carolina Militia and another 150 North Carolinians. With the forces soon to join him, Greene had the most formidable force since Guilford Court House.

After Lord Rawdon had rescued the forces at Ninety Six, he retired back to Charles Town in ill health. In July, at the young age of 26, the sick Lord Rawdon departed for England and turned over his command to a Scottish officer, Lieutenant Colonel Alexander Stuart. Stuart had a force of around 2300 troops, including the survivors of the New York and New Jersey Loyalist Regiments under Lieutenant Colonel John Harris Cruger, and the experienced British regulars of the Third, 63rd and 64th regiments. In August Stuart moved out from Charles Town and moved his force to a point near the junction of the Congaree and the Wateree rivers, only 16 miles from Greene's camp. Even though these opposing forces were only 16 miles apart, they were divided by mostly flooded swampland.

With renewed confidence, Greene marched from the High Hills on August 22, towards Charles Town, with the primary intention of driving the British and loyalists out of South Carolina. Greene moved down the Wateree along the northern bank, crossed the river near Camden, and moved south and west to Friday's Ferry on the Congaree. There he was joined by General Andrew Pickens with the South Carolina Militia from Ninety Six and a small force of recently organized troops under Lieutenant Colonel William Henderson of the South Carolina Continentals.

On receiving intelligence that Greene had marched to the southwest, Stuart quickly marched his forces 40 miles to Eutaw Springs on the road to Charles Town to protect his lines of communications and meet a convoy coming up from the city. Greene had crossed the Congaree slowly in order to allow Francis Marion (now brigadier general by act of Congress in August) with his 250 partisans to join him from the Georgetown area. At Henry Laurens' Farm only a few miles from Eutaw Springs, Marion's force joined with Greene's army. Now Greene had a force of 2400 men ready to a take on Stuart.

At 4 A.M. on the morning of September 8, Greene broke camp at Burdell's Plantation and marched to meet the British, who were seven miles away. Stuart was camped near a stately two-story brick mansion with several outbuildings and gardens. At 6 A.M. two American deserters came into Stuart's camp with word that Greene was not far away and on the move to attack. Fortunately for Greene the deserters were ignored and arrested. American intelligence was good and Greene knew the exact location of Stuart. Stuart showed little immediate concern over the possibility of Greene's presence when he sent out an unarmed foraging party of 300 men to dig sweet potatoes under the protection of a small escort commanded by Major Coffin, a Boston loyalist. These foragers were to work in fields along the road that Greene was approaching on.

The American force was moving in two columns of cavalry with Lieutenant Colonel Lee at the head, and William Washington's cavalry in the rear with the Virginia Light Horse. At around 8 A.M., and at four miles from the British camp, Captain James Armstrong of Lee's Legion, who was leading a scouting unit, reported the approach of Stuart's army. Lee halted and drew up his Legion infantry across the road with the cavalry in the open woods on the right. On the left in the thick woods was placed William Henderson's South Carolina troops. As soon as the British foraging party appeared on the road, Lee's infantry attacked the head of the foragers while the Legion cavalry swung around and attacked the British from the rear. The unarmed foragers escaped into the woods while Major Coffin's British cavalry escort ran off at full gallop. Several of the infantry escort troops were killed and the remaining 40 were captured.

Alerted by Coffin's escort cavalry in retreat, Stuart hastily beat to quarters and started to organize his defense. Having little time to prepare, Stuart formed his troops in one line a few hundred yards in front of his tents. On the right flank resting at the Charles Town Road he placed his own Third Regiment of Foot, the Buffs. In the center were the three loyalist battalions — Lancey's New York Brigade, the New York Volunteers and the New Jersey Volunteers. On the left were placed the two veteran British infantry regiments, the 63rd and 64th, backed up

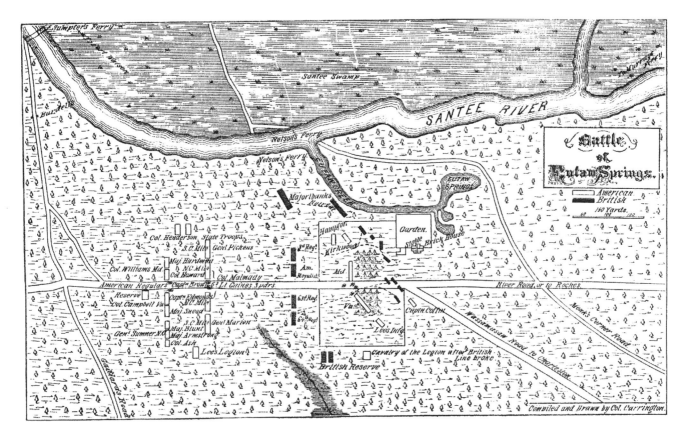

Battle of Eutaw Springs. (***Battles of the American Revolution.***)

with Coffin's loyalist cavalry. On the right, placed behind a thick "blackjack" hedge at an obtuse angle to Greene's force and with the Eutaw Creek behind, was Major John Marjoribanks' three light infantry companies and three companies of grenadiers. Two British artillery pieces were placed on the Charles Town Road between Marjoribanks and the Third Regiment, and two other pieces were located on the road that ran by Patrick Roche's Plantation toward St. John's and St. Stephen's parishes.

While Stuart was preparing, Lee requested Greene's support. Colonel Otto Williams soon brought up Captain William Gaines at full gallop with two three-pounder field guns. Under the umbrella of artillery fire from both sides, the forces of Greene and Stuart formed up for battle. Greene formed up the first line with the North and South Carolina Militia troops. In the center were the North Carolinians under Colonel Francis Malmedy, with equal numbers of South Carolinians on the left and right. Brigadier General Marion commanded the right, and Pickens led the left. Colonel William Henderson led his South Carolina State troops on the left flank, while Lee commanded the Legion cavalry and infantry on the right flank.

The second line was made up of Continental troops. General Jethro Sumner commanded on the right the three battalions under Colonel Ashe, Major Armstrong and Major Blount. The center, made up of Major Sneed's and Captain Edmunds' battalions of Virginia Continentals, was commanded by Lieutenant Colonel Richard Campbell. The veteran Maryland Continentals under Colonel Otto Williams commanded the left, with the two battalions commanded by Colonel John Eager Howard and Major Henry Hardman. Lieutenant Colonel William Washington commanded Baylor's Regiment of Horse. Captain Robert Kirkwood's Delaware Continental infantry made up the reserve placed under cover of woods. Captain William Gaines led the artillery unit in the center of the first line. Captain Browne commanded two six-pounders at the same place in the second line. In all, Greene had some 2400 American attackers.[59]

At 9 A.M. the Americans advanced the first line to engage the enemy's main front without faltering. To the surprise of Greene, the militia forces took losses but continued to move forward. "The militia advancing with alacrity, the battle became warm.... The fire ran from flank to flank; our line still advancing, and the enemy adhering to his position...."[60] Eventually the center forces under Colonel Malmedy broke after a counterattack bayonet charge by Cruger's loyalists. This forced the other militia on both sides of the American line to move back. Fighting savagely, they backed off with good order. Greene ordered Sumner's North Carolina Continentals to fill the gap caused by the militia's retreat. The movement worked as Sumner moved in line with Henderson's troops on the left and Lee's Legion on the right. Henderson's force was engaged with heavy fire from the Third Regiment and on the flank by Marjoribanks' light infantry and grenadiers. Finally Henderson was hit and the men briefly faltered until Lieutenant Colonel Wade Hampton took over to steady the line. The Americans advanced again and pushed the British back.

The fighting was extremely intense at this point on the entire front. The remaining militia retired with empty powder pouches. Sumner's Continentals who were sustaining severe British volleys fell back as Stuart's left swung forward with bayonets drawn. The critical point in the engagement had arrived. Greene now moved his Virginia and Maryland Continentals up with bayonets. These troops moved to within 40 yards of the British in perfect order, halted, and then fired a single fierce volley. They then moved in for hand-to-hand combat. The battle was deadly. Lee's infantry swung around and exposed the British left flank. The British left and center began to give way, finally retreating back into the open field around the brick mansion.

Major Coffin moved his cavalry back into the woods on the left of the field, while Marjoribanks held the right wing and covered the British retirement. The New York Volunteers under Major Sheridan occupied the mansion, while Lieutenant Lawrence Manning of Lee's Legion attempted to force his way into the house without success. As Marjoribanks held his position on the right, Stuart attempted to form a new line before the house in the field. Seeing that Marjoribanks was providing too much support to the British retirement, William Washington was ordered to attack Marjoribanks' force. The Virginia cavalry leader led his mounted force with his red banner flying. Washington carried out an impressive frontal attack, but was not able to dislodge Marjoribanks' force behind the hedges. The fire at Washington's flank was so deadly that all but two of Washington's officers went down. Washington, who was now wounded, was captured. Soon Kirkwood's Delaware Continentals arrived, and with Hampton's State troops and the remaining troops of Washington's force in support, they were able to drive Marjoribanks back. The British major moved his line back with his rear at Eutaw Creek. Marjoribanks, the solid rock of a force in the battle on the right, continued to resist all the American attempts to break his force.

As Stuart's British and loyalists pivoted around the house, through their own tents, the pursuing Americans came upon the camp tents. Except for a few units, most of the American forces began to break ranks and loot the British supplies. Apparently the Americans sensed that the battle was essentially over. The troops concentrated on consuming the goods, especially the rum. The British continued to keep up a fierce fire from the house. The Americans were in near total confusion. Lee's Legion infantry was an exception, as they found protection behind the outbuildings on the right of the American line. Kirkwood's force and Hampton's command on the left remained under control.

Seeing the American situation unfold before them, Marjoribanks on the British right and Coffin on the left immediately launched attacks on the American flanks. The Americans were driven back. Greene, now realizing the situation and determined not to lose his entire army, ordered a retreat from the field. As the American officers tried to gain some control over their troops, Major Coffin attacked through the tent area. Only the quick action of Wade Hampton to cover the retreat spared the Americans, as Coffin was driven back in brutal action. Hampton's men advanced near the house, but received so much fire that they had to move off. Marjoribanks charged out of his position and drove off the remaining Americans from the field of battle. In this action he was mortally wounded, and was carried, dying, into the garden for protection.[61]

What should have been an American victory turned into a defeat. Greene collected his wounded, and made an arrangement with Stuart for those who were too wounded to leave. The Americans moved toward Burdell's Plantation, seven miles away, with Wade Hampton serving as rear guard. Stuart maintained his position at Eutaw for the night, but the next day withdrew toward Charles Town. His plans to hold the area were abandoned. The Americans had lost nearly one-third of their force — 692 men — with 251 killed, 367 wounded and 74 missing. The British lost 85 killed, 350 wounded, and 257 missing. This loss represented one-quarter of the British force.

This bloody Battle of Eutaw Springs was the last major engagement in the American Revolution in the lower South. Again Greene had lost the battle but had gained his objective in opening up the South Carolina countryside.

17

THE VIRGINIA CAMPAIGN

While Nathanael Greene was fighting to regain South Carolina from the British, Lord Cornwallis was resting and rebuilding his damaged army at Wilmington from his residence at Judge Wright's white house at Third and Market streets. Though fresh from a technical victory at Guilford Court House, Cornwallis knew that his plan to take North Carolina had failed. Soon after he had arrived in Wilmington on April 7, news came in that Greene had marched south toward Camden. The time had come for this British leader to consider the present alternatives and make his next move. Each alternative was fraught with much danger.

Cornwallis had several possible moves at this point. He could attempt to intercept Greene and reenter South Carolina. He rejected this option because he could field only 1435 men and by the time he arrived to support Lord Rawdon's operations in South Carolina, it was quite likely the major action would have been already determined.

He could return to Charles Town via land down the coastal road, but the journey was full of problems marching through the swampy wild country with patriot partisans like Francis Marion hanging in his path. Going to the city by sail was available, but the trip would provide a visual indication of just how afraid the British commander was of American land forces. To Germain he wrote that a sea movement to Charles Town was "ruinous and disgraceful to Britain."[1] In addition a sea voyage always created the possibility of loss of the cavalry and artillery horses from broken legs in heavy weather.

The alternative of staying in Wilmington was inappropriate since it provided no opportunity for offensive action. Remaining in a port like Wilmington or Charles Town served little purpose if the British intended to defeat the rebels and return the colonies to their rightful condition. Also, dealing with the summer heat and humidity was an ever-present health danger for his troops. Malarial mosquitoes would decimate his remaining army. Less than a year earlier Cornwallis himself was laid up for weeks with a fever.

Cornwallis carefully considered his remaining option to move north to Virginia and join with Major General Phillips' forces. In a message to the general dated April 10, 1781, he outlined his strategy:

> Now my dear friend, what is our plan? Without one we cannot succeed, and I assure you that I am quite tired of marching about the country in quest of adventures. If we mean an offensive war in America, we must abandon New York and bring our whole force into Virginia; we then have a stake to fight for, and a successful battle may give us America. If our plan is defensive, mixed with desultory expeditions, let us quit the Carolinas (which cannot be held defensively while Virginia can be so easily armed against us) and stick to our salt pork at New York, sending now and then a detachment to steal tobacco, &c.

Convinced of this move to Virginia, Cornwallis wrote Clinton of this letter likewise on April 10.

> I am very anxious to receive your Excellency's commands, being as yet totally in the dark as to the intended operations of the summer. I cannot help expressing my wishes that the Chesapeak may become the seat of war, even (if necessary) at the expense of abandoning New York. Until Virginia is in a manner subdued, our hold of the Carolinas must be difficult, if not precarious. The rivers in Virginia are advantageous to an invading army; but North Carolina is of all the provinces in America the most difficult to attack (unless material assistance could be got

from the inhabitants, the country of which I have sufficiently experienced), on account of its great extent, of the numberless rivers and creeks, and the total want of interior navigation.[2]

After writing to Phillips and Clinton, Cornwallis sent a like appeal for a campaign in Virginia to the American secretary, Lord George Germain. To Phillips his lordship had declared, "By a war of conquest, I mean, to possess the country sufficiently to overturn the rebel government, and to establish a militia and some kind of mixed authority of our own."[3] Cornwallis now was clearly determined to go to Virginia and "take advantage of General Greene's having left the back of Virginia open and march immediately into that province to attempt a junction with General Phillips."[4] And, thus, with this fateful decision made, the final phase of the American Revolution and Southern operations was to begin.

Even though he had made his decision to go north, Cornwallis still did not want to close the door on Lord Rawdon's force under siege by Greene in South Carolina. As an insurance policy, on April 24 he ordered Balfour to send transports in case he needed them to return to Charles Town. After having made his decision, the British commander went about preparing his army for future operations.

While in Wilmington Cornwallis reflected on the sacrifices that had been made by his men during the North Carolina campaign. To Clinton he wrote that he felt "distress at having no power to gratify those whose zealous services, courage, & abilities have often relieved me in my most anxious moments." Cornwallis tried to promote several worthy officers but was only able to move Tarleton to the rank of lieutenant colonel. Aside from actions to tend to the sick and wounded, while rebuilding his offensive force, Cornwallis finally reached agreement with Greene on the details of a prisoner exchange that had been negotiated since the previous December. The exchange process involved the transfer of American prisoners from Charles Town, sailing on or before the 15th of June to Jamestown, Virginia, with the first British prisoners embarked there on or before the first week in July to sail to the nearest British port. Only a few exchanges were carried out after Greene stopped the process due to complaints over the actions of Balfour in Charles Town, including the hanging of a prisoner.[5]

During the period and after Lord Cornwallis was being hosted in Wilmington, Major Sir James Henry Craig carried out numerous actions against the patriots. One of his first activities was to build a stockade on the north side of Market Street between Second and Third streets to hold prisoners captured during various roaming cavalry patrols. One of the most well-known patriot prisoners was Colonel John Ashe who had been captured

trying to escape from his home on the Cape Fear. A servant who revealed that he was hiding in a swamp at Burgaw had betrayed him. While Ashe was paroled, unfortunately he died at Colonel John Sampson's house in Sampson County while moving to a new location.

Another popular patriot leader fell victim to Craig's roundups. After leaving his home at "Hilton" Cornelius Harnett was captured by the British at Colonel Spicer's house in Onslow County, some 30 miles from Wilmington. On his capture he was forced to walk back to Wilmington. After he was about spent, he was thrown over a horse and carried to the town. He soon died in Craig's prison at age 58. William Hooper, one of the signers of the Declaration of Independence, managed to escape from his home on Masonboro Sound with no more than the clothes on his back. He made it to Halifax and wrote to Judge James Iredell that "In the agony of my soul, I inform you that I am severed from my family, perhaps forever." With he and lawyer Archibald Maclaine they moved to Edenton where hospitable friends kept them.[6]

On April 25, Cornwallis left Wilmington with 1435 men and headed due north. Major James H. Craig was left to continue holding the port town. The editor of the *Annual Register* in 1781 wrote the following regarding Lord Cornwallis' departure from Wilmington:

> [He left with] the bold and vigorous resolution of marching to Virginia, and endeavouring a junction with General Phillips. This measure, in a situation which afforded only a choice of difficulties and dangers, was undoubtedly the best that could have been adopted; but yet it was a resolution of such a nature as could have been only conceived or entertained by an enterprizing and determined mind. It was indeed a perilous adventure. The distance was great, the means of substance uncertain, and the difficulties and hazards were sufficient to appall the boldest.[7]

Out of Wilmington the British Army moved up the curving road to Duplin Court House, which ran parallel with the northeast river of the Cape Fear. From here they crossed the Burgaw and Rock Fish creeks to the Neuse River. From there the force moved to Nahunta Swamp on May 5 and across Contentnea Creek to Tarboro, where a short opposition occurred. On Sunday, May 6, on the shore of Contentnea Creek some 400 militiamen under Colonel David Gorham tried to handle Tarleton's dragoons at Peacock's Bridge. They held for a bit, but were forced to scatter into the woods.

Six miles further at Fishing Creek there was another brief skirmish between militia forces from Edgecombe, Pitt and Northampton counties, before the British moved on to Halifax. At Halifax, the place renowned for the passage of the Halifax Resolves of April 12, 1776, the American Militia put up another spirited engagement against the British, but Tarleton scattered the troops. The Legion had come to attack the militia not from the expected direction in the south but from the opposite direction. Tarleton did suffer three dragoons dead and a number of horses killed. The militia gathered and built a breastwork on the other side of the Roanoke River to fire at the British. Cornwallis sent a small detachment across the river to drive the militia away. Unfortunately the British soldiers took it out on the local town citizens by looting and raping. As a result of these events, his lordship court-martialed and executed two British offenders.[8]

As Cornwallis moved north he was still concerned with the situation with Greene in South Carolina. Back on May 4 he wrote Major Craig in Wilmington: "I wrote to you yesterday to say, that when transports & provisions arrive in Cape Fear I will return to embark. Give me early notice and communicate this to Balfour immediately." But Cornwallis changed his mind at Halifax on May 12 when he received news that Lord Rawdon had defeated Greene at Hobkirk's Hill. With Rawdon in reasonable shape, he and his army moved out of Halifax on May 13 and crossed the Roanoke River.[9] The British Army headed northeasterly for 17 miles across Northampton County to the Meherrin River and into Virginia.

From the time Cornwallis had been engaged in his campaign to take North Carolina, events were taking place that would eventually culminate in Virginia with Cornwallis. Events in Virginia had not really improved from the time back on January 20, 1781, when the traitor, now the British Brigadier General Benedict Arnold, marched into Portsmouth to settle down for the winter after having raided Richmond and various patriot villages downstream along the James River. At General Washington's headquarters at Peekskill, New York, rather distressing intelligence continued to come in from General Friedrich Von Steuben regarding the poor support being given him by Jefferson and the Virginia leaders. Added to that information was the news of Arnold's invasion. Even though he could well afford to reduce his troop strength, General George Washington made a critical decision to send more troops to Virginia to handle this perilous situation in his own home state. On February 20, Washington directed the 24-year-old major general, the Marquis de Lafayette, to take command of 1200 Continental troops from New England and New Jersey and proceed to Virginia to confront, and even better, to capture Arnold.[10]

Meanwhile, at the request of Virginia leaders to "protect the American commerce in the Chesapeake Bay and attempt to destroy the fleet of Mr. Arnold which was laying waste the shores of that State," the French sent a small naval force under the command of Captain Le Gardeur de Tilly to Virginia. On February 8, a French

force consisting of one ship-of-the-line, two frigates and a cutter entered Hampton Roads to confront the British fleet. The British fleet immediately withdrew back up the Elizabeth River. Unfortunately for the French, the river was too shallow to enter with the French vessels. With the British fleet protected by the narrow river, shallow waters and the Portsmouth shore batteries ever-threatening, Tilly's naval squadron departed back to the French fleet headquarters at Newport, Rhode Island, after only 10 days in Hampton Roads.

With the French naval activity increasingly focused on the Chesapeake, Clinton was concerned. He wrote to Arnold, "Appearances at Rhode Island give some reason to suppose that the Ships seen last Wednesday were the *Avant Garde* from that place. Should they pay you a visit from Rhode Island, you may rest assured every attention will be paid to your Situation, and that our Movements will be regulated by theirs." As the Virginia Militia began to show increased activity, Arnold wrote Clinton the following on March 8:

> I have every reason to believe that [the enemy] have collected their Force to co-operate with the French ships and Troop which they hourly expect from Rhode Island. I have had several Conversations with Commodore Symonds upon the subject of the defence of this place, and His Majesty's Ships. He seems undetermined how to act. At one time he proposes opposing the Enemy at Crany Island Bar — at another of bringing his Ships up to Town. At present he is between both, and has lain there near four weeks, permitting the Enemy's Ships to go out & come in as they please. He informs me, that his orders from the Admiral are to get all the Ships in Shoal Water, out of the reach of the Enemy, and I believe he is sincerely inclined to follow his Instructions…. I am clearly of opinion that if the Commodore gives up Craney Island Bar, that every King's Ship and Transport here will fall a Sacrifice in Forty Eight hours after the Arrival of a superior fleet and Army to ours.[11]

On March 6 General Washington arrived at Newport, Rhode Island, to confer with Jean Baptiste Donatien de Vimeur, Comte, Lieutenant General de Rochambeau, the commander of the French Army in America. This Frenchman with thinning, gray hair and a paunch was a 56-year-old professional soldier who had gained a reputation as a soldier's soldier. As a veteran of numerous battles with the English and Prussians during a 40-year period, he had risen through the ranks by his deeds. "Papa Rochambeau," as he was known by his men, was no "court soldier" and preferred to spend his time in the field with the troops.[12]

Since July of 1780 the French had kept a force of 5000 troops under Rochambeau and a naval squadron under Admiral Ternay at Newport. As a result Clinton had always been concerned with the presence of the French only a few days' sailing distance from his headquarters at New York. After deliberations with Washington, Rochambeau agreed to cooperate with Washington to provide 1200 French troops and a fleet detachment to support Lafayette's operations in Virginia. Washington's hope was that a French fleet would be able to blockade Arnold as Lafayette handled the British army in the Tidewater. The French general quickly prepared the force, which sailed on March 8 with Admiral Chevalier Destouches' fleet of eight ships-of-the-line and three frigates to join with Lafayette at the Head of Elk, Maryland. The command had gone to Destouches as a result of the recent death of Admiral Ternay. Meanwhile, moving with due speed, Lafayette and his force of 1200 Continentals arrived at Head of Elk on March 3.[13] The command consisted of three light infantry battalions under Colonel Vose of Massachusetts, Lieutenant Colonel Barber of New Jersey, and a French officer and former aide to Lafayette, Lieutenant Colonel Gimat.

After reaching Head of Elk, Lafayette decided to leave the majority of his army behind to wait to sail down the Chesapeake with Destouches' fleet when it arrived. Ahead of his army, Lafayette proceeded with his advance party of his officers to Annapolis via open boat. They arrived at Yorktown on March 14, made their way to Williamsburg, then across the James to Suffolk on the 19th. There, General Muhlenberg, who was guarding the roads leading out of Portsmouth, met him. As Lafayette was making a reconnaissance of the Portsmouth area and Arnold's position, bad news arrived.[14] On March 10 a large British fleet had sailed southward from Gardiner's Bay, at the tip of Long Island, New York, commanded by Admiral Arbuthnot aboard the *Royal Oak*. On March 16, the day after the battle at Guilford Court House, Arbuthnot's fleet caught up with Destouches' French fleet off the Chesapeake Capes and a general sea engagement ensued.

Arbuthnot's *Royal Oak* led the British line of battle, as did Destouches. Both fleets were of equal size, so the maneuvering to get position was intense. The French attempted to get to the leeward of the British line. When the British *Robust* engaged the French line, a general battle raged with fierce cannonades from both forces. The French line soon was broken, but the wind now "settled down to the northeast … fair for entering the bay." Finally Destouches led his ships past the disabled British ships, firing as they passed and headed out to sea. Arbuthnot in *Royal Oak* attempted to follow the French, but soon lost sight of Destouches. British ships *Robust*, *Prudent* and *Europe* were disabled, having taken most of the French cannon fire. With these ships and the damaged *London*, Arbuthnot gave up the chase and moved back into the Chesapeake Bay. Within 24 hours, Arbuthnot's fleet was resting in Lynnhaven Bay.[15]

While the British had taken the brunt of the damage in the sea battle, Arbuthnot had succeeded in keeping the French from supporting Lafayette and blockading Arnold at Portsmouth. Destouches returned to Newport with his fleet and the 1200 troops intended for Lafayette. Having now realized the significance of the effort of Admiral Destouches to support the Virginia patriots, Clinton sent a force of 2000 men under the command of Major General William Phillips to reinforce General Arnold. Phillips and his force arrived aboard Admiral Arbuthnot's fleet of some 20 British warships in the Chesapeake Bay on March 26 with orders to defend Portsmouth, as well as follow any instructions from Lord Cornwallis. If orders from his lordship were unavailable, Phillips was to carry out operations to disrupt supply lines and destroy American magazines and warehouses. He was to select a permanent base in cooperation with the Royal Navy that could easily be defended and that was able to anchor large ships-of-the-line. If possible, Clinton desired that Phillips hold the Chesapeake while moving north to take Maryland and lower Pennsylvania.[16]

After learning of Destouches' naval engagement with the British, Lafayette immediately returned to Annapolis and then to the Head of Elk to rejoin his army. At Head of Elk Lafayette received a letter from Washington, dated April 6, directing him to continue southward and placing him under the command of General Greene. He also learned that British General Phillips was heading for the Chesapeake Bay and was expected to reinforce Arnold's forces. Without delay Lafayette marched his army to Baltimore, where he borrowed £2000 to acquire linen, shoes, and winter clothing for his troops. While at Baltimore, the ladies of the town held a ball in Lafayette's honor. These fair ladies offered to make shirts and blouses for the Continentals.

Unfortunately for Lafayette the thought of moving to the distant South did not sit well with many of the New England troops, and several desertions occurred. After hanging one deserter and dismissing another, Lafayette announced that any who did not desire to continue on this dangerous Southern campaign would be allowed to obtain a pass to rejoin the Northern Army. From that instance forward "all desertions ended" and not one man would leave the marquis. Realizing that Phillips and Arnold would probably move back up the James River and secure Richmond, Lafayette departed Baltimore on April 19 with his baggage, tents and artillery left behind to follow later. He hoped to be in place in Richmond before the British arrived.[17]

The day before, April 18, Phillips began his campaign to disrupt the Americans in Virginia. He ordered Arnold to depart Portsmouth and begin to head up the James River to attack. The lead force under Colonel John Simcoe landed at Burwell's Landing on April 20. As a result, the Virginia Militia under James Innes was compelled to move with his militia to Williamsburg. Two days later Arnold sailed upriver again and citizens in Richmond were in a panic. Phillips appeared on April 23 on the James River. Steuben ordered Innes to move his militia to the north bank of the James across from Hood's Landing, having not realized that Innes had already veered off and crossed the Pamunkey River. Twenty wagons of supplies and some 100 sick burdened Innes' travel from the military hospital at Williamsburg.

On the 24th the British were located at Westover and continued to threaten the Richmond citizens. With the British apparently coming toward Richmond, Jefferson ordered the public records moved. Meanwhile the British leaders were discussing their next move. Colonel Simcoe wanted an attack on Richmond, but Arnold was more interested in the patriot stockpile of supplies at Petersburg. On April 24 the British showed their hand by appearing at City Point, located at the confluence of the Appomattox and James rivers. This was a clear indication of the British desire to move away from Richmond.

On the afternoon of April 25 the Virginia Militia finally engaged the British a mile east of Petersburg at Blandford. Arnold, with some 2500 troops, met Steuben and Muhlenburg with 100 militiamen. The conflict lasted several hours with the British finally driving off the Americans across the Appomattox River with their artillery. Destroying the Pocahontas Bridge behind them, the militia forces fell back to the Chesterfield County Courthouse. With so many negative events in recent months, this militia engagement tended to raise the spirits of the Virginia citizens as well as the militiamen. Even though they had not claimed victory, they had made a good fight.

Meanwhile, Jefferson and Steuben were attempting to move the state supplies away from Petersburg and the British to Point of Fork, which was further inland. Even though they ran into much difficulty, "not the least article fell into the Enemy's hands" at Petersburg, according to Steuben. With Petersburg now under British control, Phillips announced that if the locals moved their tobacco outside the buildings, he would spare their storage buildings. Under these conditions the British successfully burned 4000 hogsheads of tobacco but only one warehouse.

On April 27 Phillips moved to Chesterfield County Courthouse, Steuben's headquarters, and burned the barracks, 300 barrels of flour and other supplies. Meanwhile, Arnold moved back to Osborne's on the James River where the Americans had gathered a number of merchant vessels under the protection of nine Virginia naval ships. As the little fleet lay "clustered at Osborne's," the British

moved in and attacked on that day. A battle continued until a cannonball severed a mooring cable and the largest ship, the *Tempest*, drifted into an exposed position. The crew of the *Tempest* panicked and abandoned the ship. The other crews followed suit, and the small Virginia Navy was lost. Arnold also captured 12 other vessels with 2000 hogsheads of tobacco as cargoes.[18]

Phillips and Arnold rejoined their forces and moved upriver toward Richmond, arriving at Manchester, Virginia, on April 30. Meanwhile, Lafayette's Continentals had moved south through Alexandria, Fredericksburg, and Bowling Green, and finally arrived in Richmond on the evening of April 29, only a few hours ahead of the British.[19] Even though Lafayette now had only 900 men with him, and no artillery, the Americans held strong positions. Expecting that Steuben was moving his militia toward their position, Phillips decided to fall back to Osborne's on the James after destroying some 1200 hogsheads of tobacco. Reports came into Lafayette that Phillips "flew into a violent passion and swore vengence" at being thwarted. In stark contrast, Lafayette and Steuben celebrated their hold action with a parade in a field just outside Richmond. Phillips moved to Bermuda Hundred where they gathered fresh provisions and then embarked to sail downriver on May 2. Along the way the British hurt the local planters by killing horses and cattle, and taking slaves. One dairyman wrote that the slaves "flocked to the Enemy from all quarters even from very remote parts."[20]

On May 7, as he was moving pass Burwell's Landing towards Portsmouth, Phillips received a letter from Cornwallis, dated April 24, indicating that both British armies should join at Petersburg. Phillips immediately turned around and headed to meet Cornwallis. Phillips landed his troops at Brandon that same day and marched to Petersburg. Meanwhile, Lafayette moved his force to Bottom's Bridge located on the Chickahominy River. This position was centered to react to any British actions at Fredericksburg, Williamsburg or Richmond. As Phillips changed direction toward Petersburg, Lafayette moved back to Richmond. The strength of the British under Phillips caused Lafayette to move no closer than Osborne's.

The Petersburg citizens were just in the process of returning back home when news that the British were returning arrived. The locals dreaded another attack with its resulting destruction. In the first occupation the state had lost a ton of lead and a wagon containing 6000 yards of cloth. Many citizens had lost their slaves and other property. Phillips "marched into that town [Petersburg] on the evening of the 9th of May."[21] He was in very poor health. Sadly for the British, Phillips died on May 15 of typhoid fever, and, thus, was not present when his lordship

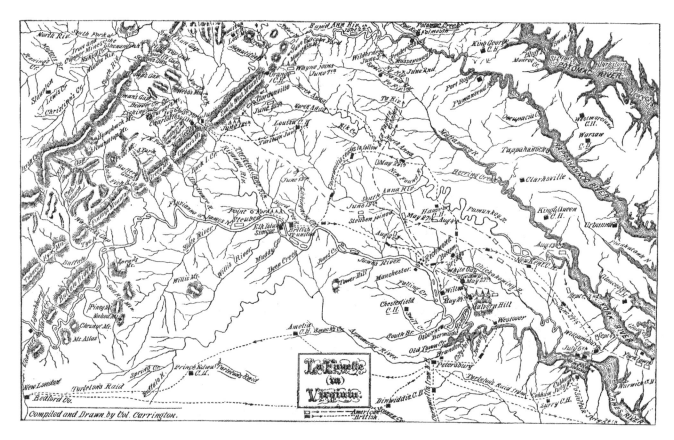

Lafayette in Virginia. (*Battles of the American Revolution.*) *Opposite:* Arnold at Petersburg and Richmond. (*Battles of the American Revolution.*)

arrived on May 20 at Petersburg. Cornwallis' troops were quite tired and especially hungry, as Tarleton had been unable to forage enough food. The streams had been so parched from drought that the meal the British could find could not be ground because the mill wheels would not turn.[22]

As Cornwallis sat at Petersburg he considered his situation. With Arnold's force of nearly 4000, his units of over 1400 effectives and with the welcomed reinforcements of the 17th and 43rd regiments, along with two German Anspach battalions of around 1500, Cornwallis now had at his disposal a combined army of 7200 men. Opposing him was Lafayette with a force of 1200 Continentals from regiments of Vose, de Gimat and Barber, some 2000 Virginia Militia and 40 dragoons from Armand's Legion, making the total at 3240 men. With his numerical superiority of professional troops, Cornwallis was confident of his condition.[23]

Cornwallis read Phillips' orders from Clinton and was somewhat distressed at the nature of the proposed activities from his commander. Carrying out raids from a naval base in the Chesapeake was not the grand offensive that Cornwallis had in mind for Virginia. For the first time in a great while Cornwallis felt the hand of Clinton's command over him. Since he had not received any letters from Clin-

ton, Cornwallis decided to essentially carry out Phillips' orders and proceed to establish a proper defensive port in the Chesapeake after engaging in raids to destroy Lafayette and the supply depots in the Virginia. Later on May 26 Cornwallis wrote Clinton confirming his decision:

> I shall now proceed to dislodge Lafayette from Richmond, and with my light troops to destroy any magazines or stores in the neighborhood which may have been collected either for his use or for General Greene's army. From thence I propose to move to the Neck at Williamsburg, which is represented as healthy, and where some subsistence may be procured, and keep myself unengaged from operations which might interfere with your plan for the campaign, until I have the satisfaction of hearing from you.

Cornwallis wasted no time in getting underway. On May 23, Tarleton struck at Chesterfield County Courthouse in a heavy rain. The rain prevented the Virginia Militia on guard there from firing their weapons. Tarleton captured them all. The next day Cornwallis left Petersburg, crossed the James River from Mead, and moved to Westover just 25 miles below Richmond. With words from Tarleton expressing that the movement was "an easy entrance into a fertile quarter of Virginia," Cornwallis camped near White Oak Swamp on May 27. The next day

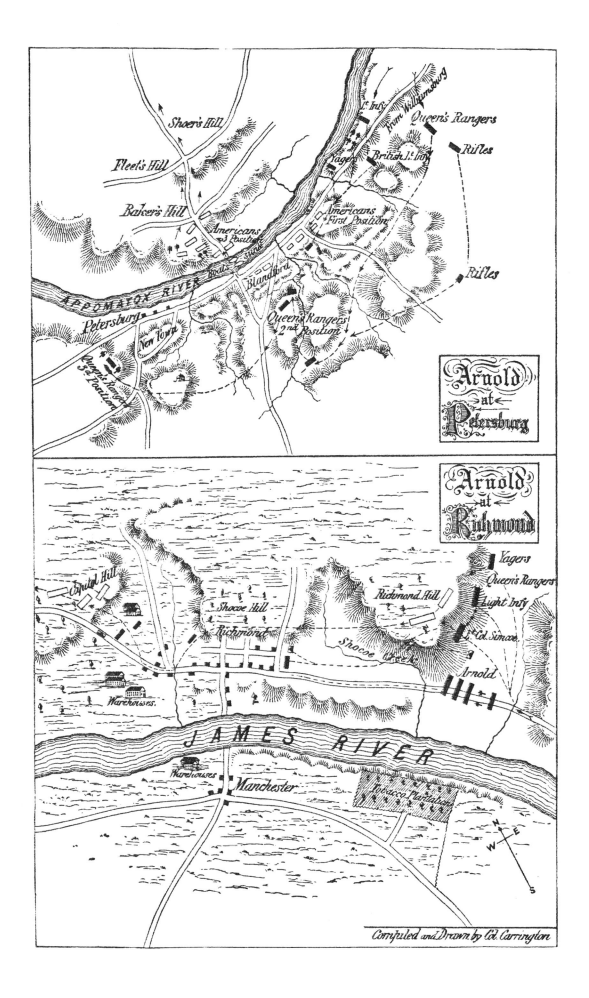

Shoer's Hill

Fleet's Hill

Baker's Hill

Lt. Infy

from Williamsburg

Queen's Rangers

Rifles

Yagers

British Lt. Infy

Americans
First Position

Rifles

Americans
3 Position

Blandford

Petersburg

Boat

Queen's Rangers
2nd Position

New Town

Queen's Rangers
3d Position

APPOMATOX RIVER

Arnold at Petersburg

Arnold at Richmond

Capitol Hill

Shocoe Hill

Richmond

Shocoe Creek

Richmond Hill

Yagers

Queen's Rangers

Light Infy

Lt. Col. Simcoe

Arnold

Warehouses

Warehouses

Manchester

Tobacco Plantation

JAMES RIVER

Compiled and Drawn by Col. Carrington

the British reached Bottom's Bridge on the Chickahominy River.

As Cornwallis moved north, Lafayette abandoned Richmond and moved to the northwest. As Cornwallis crossed the Chickahominy on May 27, Lafayette camped between Allen's Creek and Gold Mine Creek on the South Anna River. The marquis sent word to General Weedon to leave Hunter's Forge and move his militia to defend Fredericksburg. Cornwallis continued forward, looking to intercept Lafayette, and reached Newcastle on the Pamunkey River on May 29. The next day the British reached Hanover Court House to discover some spiked French 24-pounders that had been thrown into the river. At present day Hanovertown the British burned the tobacco warehouses of Page and Aylett, destroying large amounts of tobacco. Cornwallis then moved on to the North Anna River camping at Hanover Junction on June 1.[24]

Lafayette had retreated swiftly to avoid the British. Leaving Winston's Bridge on the 28th, he had proceeded to Dandridge's, located at a point where Goldmine Creek enters the South Anna River. Lafayette was then 25 miles west of the British. Lafayette was on the lookout for Brigadier General "Mad Anthony" Wayne and his Pennsylvania Continentals. Ever since February when Wayne's force had been ordered to move south, the Southern Department had awaited the arrival of these quality troops. But a number of difficulties in recruiting and obtaining stores had delayed the movement. In early May, Wayne's troops had even mutinied over the issue of pay. Word had it that General Wayne did not want to serve under Lafayette and that "Virginia was too grand — let her be humbled by the Enemy..." When Cornwallis entered the picture Lafayette had written to Wayne urging him to hurry south. Wayne replied that he could not be in Virginia until well into June.[25]

While still camped at Goldmine Creek on May 29, Lafayette wrote General Steuben the following:

> Lord Cornwallis has sent people to examine the fords of the James River — he did since intend to turn our left flank — these schemes he seems to have abandoned, and is on his way to Fredericksburg. I am apprehensive an expedition will go by water up Powtomack, as General Leslie is said to have gone down to Portsmouth. We march on a parallel line with the enemy, keeping the upper part of the country, and disposed to turn back in case this movement is only a feint. I wish all our stores may be collected at the Court House [Albemarle]. The enemy's cavalry increase every day. The gentlemen do not please to take our horses out of the way, and the impressing warrants are so contracted that we cannot get, while the enemy sweep everything that is in their way and many miles around. I request you will urge the Assembly to have us furnished with horses; if they do not, it is impossible we can defend this country.

Lafayette moved north on the 30th, crossing the North Anna River at Anderson's Bridge. The next day he moved to Mattaponi Church in Spottsylvania County only a few miles northeast of Mount Pleasant. Now Weedon was reporting from Fredericksburg that the stores had been moved out to a safe location. On June 3 Lafayette was at Corbin's Bridge on the Po River. There he wrote a letter to Morgan asking him to see that Burgoyne's prisoners be moved from the Shenandoah Valley to Maryland as Cornwallis might attempt to rescue them. On June 4 Lafayette headed across Spottsylvania and crossed the Rapidan River at Ely's Ford, some 20 miles above Fredericksburg. Here the marquis learned that Wayne's Continentals were marching from Frederick, Maryland, to the Potomac River. The Americans felt more secure now that the heavy rains had made the fords impassable.

At the North Anna River, Cornwallis halted and gave up the chase to outflank Lafayette. Unable to engage the main force with Lafayette, he then decided to send out two raiding parties. On June 1 Cornwallis sent out the first raid with Tarleton to "disturb the Assembly, then sitting at Charlottesville, and to destroy the stores there...." Taking 180 dragoons and 70 mounted infantry with him, he "proceeded west to Louisa Court House...."[26] On Saturday, June 2, 1781, the Virginia Assembly postponed the election of the successor to the present state governor, Thomas Jefferson, until Monday, June 4. No one seemed concerned that the legal term of the governor had technically ended. The weekend was partly taken up dealing with official correspondence for Jefferson, even without much authority to sign the papers.

Tarleton had taken the back roads to escape detection and by late Sunday night he had passed the Cuckoo Tavern near Louisa. Sitting in the tavern as Tarleton's dragoons rumbled past was the tall, strong rider, Jack Jouett, who at once ran to the window to see the British cavalry in the faint moonlight. Realizing the British were heading toward Charlottesville, Jouett set out to warn the Assembly. He rode to the Louisa Inn, alerted the innkeeper, and eventually wakened the leading patriot official in the area, Dr. Thomas Walker. On his way he woke up Thomas Jefferson at Monticello. A coach hurried off Mrs. Jefferson with her three children to a hideaway in the mountains. Jouett then continued on to Charlottesville to find the legislators having breakfast. Hearing that Tarleton was near, the Assembly quickly convened and then officially recessed to Staunton before leaving in a great hurry.

Meanwhile, Tarleton stopped at Walker Plantation for breakfast, where Mrs. Walker did her best to slow the British for the legislators' sake. When they finally reached Charlottesville on Monday, Tarleton rounded up seven tardy legislators, and stores consisting of 1000 flintlocks, 400 barrels of gunpowder, along with tobacco and clothing intended for Greene's forces in South Carolina.[27] Jefferson had stayed behind after sending off his family, but as the British riders with British Captain McLeod of the Legion approached Monticello, Lieutenant Hudson warned Jefferson this second time and he fled with the state papers to the woods on Carter Mountain. Captain McLeod entered Monticello only ten minutes after Jefferson had departed. Jefferson caught up with his family and took them on to a friend's home in Amherst County.

The Virginia Assembly quickly reconvened at Staunton and, after a number of complications and deliberations, on June 12 a new governor, Thomas Nelson, was elected to succeed Jefferson. Meanwhile in the Tidewater, Richard Henry Lee was drafting letters to Philadelphia urging Congress to send Washington as a dictator over Virginia. While Tarleton was "disturbing" Charlottesville, Cornwallis dispatched Colonel Simcoe with his loyalist legion, the Queen's Rangers, to attack Baron Von Steuben who was guarding the military stores at Point of Fork on the James River. With Simcoe were 200 men of the 71st Highlanders and some 300 of his Rangers, of which "nearly fifty [were] absolutely barefooted." On the night of June 3 Steuben received news that Simcoe was heading his way, but he discounted the intelligence and continued the task of removing the stores. At this point Steuben's force had shrunk to only 420 men, of which 250 were militia under General Robert Lawson.

The morning light of the next day came with an alert from a Continental officer, Major Richard Call, giving positive intelligence of the enemy moving in two columns through Goochland and Louisa counties toward them. Alarmed that one of Simcoe's columns might cross the Rivanna River and outflank him, Steuben moved over the James River to the south. By noon on June 4, Simcoe was on the northern bank of the James, and Steuben was 30 miles away. At Point of Fork on June 5, Simcoe captured 2500 arms, "a large quantity" of gunpowder and shot, 60 casks of saltpeter, sulfur, rum, brandy, "a great variety of small stores, necessary for the equipment of cavalry and infantry," a 13-inch mortar, five brass howitzers and four brass nine-pounders. In addition, Simcoe burned 150 barrels of gunpowder and a considerable amount of tobacco from warehouses on the James.

The affair at Point of Fork left the supply situation in Virginia in disarray. Steuben had mistaken Simcoe's force as the lead component of Cornwallis' main army. Simcoe had led his Highlander infantry in red coats up to the riverbank while keeping the cavalry who wore green out of sight in the rear. General Lawson, who was at Point of Fork, and later Lafayette, both agreed that Steuben should have been able to hold out at least 24 hours, which would have allowed the military supplies to be removed. Colonel Davie reported that the "business was illy executed by the State Officers." The stores that Steuben had been able to remove were scattered at Prince Edward, Charlotte and Halifax county courthouses "in such a manner that only part could fall into the Enemies Hands in any Rout they could take."[28]

On June 7 at Elk Hill, only a few miles from Point of Fork, both Tarleton and Simcoe rejoined with Cornwallis. During these days of enemy raids, Lafayette had moved from Ely's Ford along the northern bank of the Rapidan River to Raccoon Ford. While Lafayette was distressed at hearing the news of the two raiding parties' events, he was most focused on joining up with Wayne's Pennsylvania Line. Lafayette wrote of these times when he made "all his calculations so as to be able to effect a junction with that corps, without being prevented from covering the military magazines of the Southern States, which were at the foot of the mountains on the heights of the Fluvanna."

At Frederick, Maryland, Wayne wrote Lafayette of his continued delay:

> I well know the necessity of an immediate junction, and beg leave to assure you that our anxiety for that event is equal to your wishes; may it be speedy and propitious. I wish our numbers were something more; however, we must endeavor to stem this torrent; and if we have it not in our power to command success, I trust, my dear Marquis, that we shall produce a conviction to the world that we deserve it.

Wayne's forces crossed the Potomac River on May 31 at Noland's Ferry, passed Leesburg on June 4 and that night camped at Cook's Mills on Goose Creek. The next day their march continued, leaving their baggage and sick behind, advancing some 18 miles to Red House near Thoroughfare Gap. Wayne moved ahead of his forces and arrived to greet Lafayette on June 7. His troops moved slowly through the rain-soaked terrain until they reached Raccoon Ford at the Rapidan River on the 9th by way of Norman's Ford on the Rappahannock River. On June 10, Wayne's entire force finally joined with Lafayette's troops 12 miles south of the crossing.

Now Lafayette commanded a rather formidable army. Wayne's Brigade of Pennsylvania Continentals consisted of three regiments of approximately 1000 men under Colonels Richard Butler, Walter Stewart and Richard Humpton, and Proctor's Fourth Continental Artillery, made up of nine officers and 90 men.[29] On June 13 another 600 riflemen commanded by Brigadier General William Campbell of the Virginia Militia joined with Lafayette. Another 425 Virginia Continentals under veteran Colonel Christian Febiger arrived. With Lafayette were 2100 men of the three brigades of the Virginia Militia under generals Campbell, Edward Stevens and Robert Lawson. With the Second Artillery and 120 dragoons, Lafayette's army totaled over 4500 men.[30]

Cornwallis left Elk Hill on June 15th and marched back to Richmond on his way to Williamsburg. With his reconstituted army, Lafayette departed from the Rapidan in controlled pursuit of the British. The same day that Wayne's troops arrived, June 10th, they moved away with Lafayette to the North Anna River. They crossed the river at Brock's Bridge, located 12 miles east of present day Gordonsville. Moving through Louisa County south, they camped on June 11 at Boswell's Tavern at the South Anna. With caution, Lafayette marched down Three Notches Road to encamp the night of June 12th behind Mechunck Creek at "Allegree's," located 13 miles east of Charlottesville. Here the next morning Lafayette wrote Steuben the following:

> Our junction with the Pennsylvanians is formed, and we have again got between the enemy and our stores. Nothing has been lost but what was left on the Point, and the few articles that, notwithstanding your and my directions, it had been thought proper to send to Charlottesville. I have ordered the stores to be removed higher up, and am now in a better situation to defend them. I request, my dear sir, you will immediately return this way, and, with the Continentals and militia under your command cross the James River, what I do not believe, and none of them has yet attempted, it must be with a view to reconquer Carolina.

As Lafayette followed Cornwallis down southeastward, General Washington and Congress was being overwhelmed with appeals for the commander-in-chief to come to Virginia and take charge. Richard Henry Lee continued his writing campaign for such action, as did others. Lee's appeal read, "Let Washington be immediately sent to Virginia with two or three thousand good troops." Jefferson also sent support for Washington's saving his home state. John Cadwalader of Maryland wrote from Annapolis on June 5 saying, "That the enemy intend to make the Southern States the scene of action, the ensuing campaign, is past a doubt; and the consequences are easily foreseen, unless considerable reenforcements very soon arrive either from France or the Northern army." He closed with the common appeal that the wish of every person he had conversed with was that Washington should take command in Virginia.

But Washington could not bring himself to leave the northern operations he was planning as he wrote back to Jefferson on June 27, "I feel for the suffering of Virginia, and, if I had been supported here in time, I should have been there before this with a great part of our cavalry.... I have the highest opinion of the marquis's abilities and

zeal, and flatter myself that nothing will be left unattempted to give all the protection to the State that his force will admit." Lafayette would continue to carry out his orders to evade Cornwallis, yet attempt to contain the British while saving the military stores.

While Cornwallis had not been as successful at catching Lafayette or destroying all the stores above Richmond, he had created much fear in the upcountry as he carried out his inherited orders to raid, not conquer with a major campaign. Leaving Elk Hill on June 15, Cornwallis marched to reach Richmond on June 16. Meanwhile Lafayette departed Mechunk on June 14th and traveled along the line of the South Anna River staying about 20 miles away from Cornwallis. The heat and lack of supplies was having its effect on the men. Lieutenant Feltman wrote in his journal on June 15th, "A great scarcity of water, and a very fatiguing march.... Refreshed ourselves in an orchard with Colonel Robinson." Another letter to a home in Connecticut stated, "It found me very destitute of summer clothes and almost every other necessary requisite to render life tolerable in this uninhabited world. We frequently march whole days without seeing anything like a house except a log hut or two."

The South was a new experience for the men of the Northern Army. As they moved to Richmond, Lieutenant Feltman had his first encounter with Southern slavery. He wrote of the servants of the white women from the plantations: "They will have a number of blacks about them, all naked, nothing to hide their nakedness. I am surprised this does not hurt the feelings of the fair sex to see these young boys of about Fourteen and Fifteen years Old to Attend them...." Naked slaves also waited tables in the plantation houses along the river where Feldman and his fellow officers dined. A cruel circumstance was also recorded as the British left blacks with the disease smallpox along the road to Richmond to hopefully give the disease to the Americans. These blacks lay "starving and helpless, begging of us as we passed them for God's sake to kill them as they were in great pain and misery."

Lafayette had also developed his opinions of the South and of Southerners. In his dealing with the Virginia state officials with whom he had negotiated, he found them practicing polite evasiveness. In a letter to Washington he wrote, "There is a great slowness and great carelessness in this part of the world.... But the intentions are good, and the people want to be awakened." While Lafayette had the support of many including General Washington, there were detractors. A militia officer wrote, "I fear the Marquis may lose his credit about HDQuarters. The people do not love Frenchmen, every person they can't understand they take for a Frenchmen."

While Cornwallis rested at Richmond on June 17, Lafayette camped at Dandridge's on the South Anna in

Hanover County, to the northwest of Richmond. The marquis sent out patrols to ensure the location of the enemy was known. One of these patrols, made up of 400 riders and commanded by Muhlenberg, attempted to bring Tarleton out for some type of action. Tarleton was at Meadow Bridge on the Chickahominy River when he heard of the patrol. He engaged a forced march on June 18 to surprise it. Lafayette learned of the events and sent Wayne with some of his Continentals and light infantry to intercept Tarleton. Tarleton missed finding Muhlenberg, and after a night march of 13 miles, Wayne missed Tarleton, who had already turned back.

On June 19, General Steuben, accompanied by 450 Virginia 18-month militiamen, joined Lafayette.[31] This brought the total American force to over 5000 men. The marquis gave Steuben a rather cold reception as he came into camp riding his familiar horse and smoking his long pipe. Steuben's reputation was severely damaged by the Point of Fork affair. Lafayette wrote Washington, "The militia left him. His new levies deserted. All Virginia was in an uproar against him. The enemy laughed at him, and I cannot describe to you what my surprise has been." In a few days Steuben was overcome with fatigue and dejection, and he retired to the vicinity of Charlottesville to recover.

On June 20 Cornwallis left Richmond and continued his march toward the coast. His lordship crossed the Chickahominy River at Bottom's Bridge heading to Williamsburg at a leisurely pace. Lafayette entered the town 20 hours later to find that the British had burned 2000 hogsheads of tobacco and destroyed harnesses, uniforms, food, 600 bushels of flour and 5000 muskets.[32] On the 23rd Cornwallis stopped and seemed to be about to strike back at Lafayette. The alarm came into Wayne's camp and he eagerly formed up his troops for action. After waiting some two hours, no British came to engage them. The Americans continued their advance on word Cornwallis was moving again. They moved past Bottom's Bridge and on the 25th were at New Kent Court House. That same day Cornwallis reached Williamsburg.

Working to harass the British rear guard, Colonel John Simcoe's Queen's Rangers, Lafayette approved Wayne's request to intercept the Rangers as they returned from collecting cattle and burning stores above Williamsburg. Wayne sent out the advance party under a distinguished veteran officer, Colonel Richard Butler. Butler, with McPherson, Call and Willis, left the night of June 25 but failed to meet up with Simcoe's Rangers until the next day at Spencer's Ordinary, some six miles above Williamsburg. Simcoe was attacked with cavalry as the loyalists engaged in hand-to-hand combat. Simcoe feared a major attack might be started and he sent a rider to alert Cornwallis. The engagement ended when Simcoe's Rangers re-

treated. Lafayette reported that the loyalists lost 150 casualties, but British records show that 31 Americans were captured, while they lost 10 killed and 33 wounded. Regardless, it was a psychological victory for the Americans and a lift in spirit for all Virginia patriots.

The day Cornwallis arrived at Williamsburg, he received new and disappointing orders from Clinton. Clinton recalled his directions to Cornwallis as follows:

> I requested that His Lordship would in that case send to New York all the troops he could spare from the ample defense of whatever post he had chosen, and [from] such occasional desultory movements by water as might present themselves for breaking in upon the enemy's communications and destroying their magazines, etc.... We had likewise ... some letters from General Washington and several principal officers belonging to the French armament at Rhode Island, that were found in one of their mails just fallen into our hands, gave me to understand that the enemy had in a grand conference come to a resolution of attacking New York with all they could collect.[33]

Somewhere on the road between New Windsor and Morristown, New Jersey, on June 5, a young British officer, Ensign John Moody, had held up a public courier. Along with other letters, the robber had found dispatches from Washington intended for Lafayette revealing that a conference had been held between Washington with Rochambeau and the new French naval commander, Commodore de Barras, at Wethersfield, Connecticut, on May 21 concerning the upcoming campaign. At Wethersfield, Washington urged the French to launch a combined attack on Clinton at New York, but both Rochambeau and de Barras favored going to the assistance of Lafayette in Virginia. Washington finally convinced the French leaders of the merits of his plan.

Moody delivered all the dispatches to Clinton in New York, receiving 200 guineas for his effort. Clinton was delighted and called in former governor James Robertson and General Knyphausen to review the papers with him. British Lieutenant Mackenzie wrote of the event, "The capture of this Mail is extremely consequential, and gives the Commander in Chief the most perfect knowledge of the design of the Enemy."[34] Armed with this newfound intelligence, it was not surprising that Clinton called upon Cornwallis to send troops to defend his beloved New York.

This would turn out to be a turning point for Cornwallis and the American Revolution. With Clinton's orders, Cornwallis was now sure that any hope of an offensive campaign in Virginia and the Chesapeake was doomed. In his letter to his lordship, Clinton had even named the units he wanted transported to New York: six regiments of infantry, all the Rangers, as many cavalry he could get from the 17th Dragoons, all the light cavalry and all the artillery the earl could spare. On July 4 Cornwallis left Williamsburg and moved to Jamestown, where his forces encamped at the ford in front of the village. Colonel Simcoe's Rangers crossed over the James River to secure the other side. Cornwallis planned to move his entire force across the James and on to Portsmouth to embark troops for Clinton. While Cornwallis moved to Jamestown, Lafayette and his army celebrated Independence Day with parades and firing salutes at Tyree's Plantation located 20 miles from Williamsburg.

On July 5, while Cornwallis moved his baggage and supplies across the James, Lafayette moved his advance parties to Chickahominy Church, just eight miles from Jamestown. Lafayette's main army was camped back at Bird's Tavern. On the morning of July 6 Tarleton dispatched a dragoon with a black to be captured by the Americans with false intelligence. Acting as a deserter, the black told Wayne that the main British army had already crossed over to the other side of the James River, leaving only the Legion and a detachment of infantry on Lafayette's side. Brigadier General Wayne unfortunately believed the black deserter and set out with due haste and 500 men at 3 P.M. toward the British.

Wayne had managed to pick up the nickname "Mad Anthony" for his spirited military bravery. As a youth he spent time at the local tavern listening more to soldiers' talk than studying his Latin. At age 19 he had acquired many of the vices of a soldier — rum, wine, billiards and horse racing. He was skilled in mathematics, surveying and astronomy, which were useful in his chosen career as a military man. Wayne served in the Pennsylvania legislature in 1774-75. He started his military career in January 1776 as a colonel with command of the Fourth Battalion of the Continental Army of Pennsylvania. He served in Canada, and was promoted to brigadier general in February 1777. He served with distinction at Brandywine, Germantown, and Monmouth, and accomplished one of his greatest battlefield successes by retaking Stony Point, New York, in a brilliant night raid.

Cornwallis camped his forces northwest of Jamestown in a favorable position for an attack. On his right were several ponds, while on his left was a large morass that carried out to the James River. In front of the earl to the northwest was a narrow causeway to his position with access to Green Spring Farm. With swampy land on either side of the causeway, Cornwallis hoped to lure the Americans to move into the trap where he could outflank them and destroy the rebel army. On the morning of July 6, Cornwallis located Lieutenant Colonel Yorke's light infantry, Guard's Brigade and Hessians on the right, with the 76th, 80th and part of the 43rd regiments' light infantry companies under the command of Lieutenant

Colonel Thomas Dundas and the Legion on his left. All these forces were just out of sight in the woods, with only pickets posted out front to meet the Americans.[35]

Wayne advanced with Major MacPherson's cavalry, riflemen, volunteer dragoons and three artillery pieces toward Jamestown and Cornwallis. The earl had briefed the pickets to fall back slowly in mild resistance as the rebels approached. To entice the rebels, Cornwallis had left an artillery piece out in the open. For almost two hours the pickets skirmished with the advancing American force. Major William Galvin, a French officer, dashed out with some 60 light infantrymen in the open to seize the artillery piece. Wayne moved up with pleasure at the find just as a bullet clipped the plume in his hat. At this moment Cornwallis opened the attack on Wayne's force. The British fired artillery loaded with grape and canister shot, as the British right moved to outflank the American left with significant ease. Suddenly Wayne's force, which assumed it was working against rear guard units, was confronted with a major British attack.

About this time Lafayette rode up to a point where he could view the engagement. He saw in horror the British troops hiding along the riverbank as Wayne's forces had moved toward the causeway in harm's way. The marquis had tried to warn Wayne, but he was too late. A major part of Wayne's force had already moved beyond the swamp before the British attacked and the British were moving up in greater numbers than the American force. Out in front, Galvin's men fired a volley at the oncoming British and fell back in reasonable order. Wayne saw Galvin's predicament and had to make an instant decision. Retreating meant retracing the narrow corridor where his troops would no doubt receive deadly fire and be cut to pieces. Wayne made the fateful decision to charge the British.

Yelling at the top of his lungs, Wayne bravely ordered his men to fix bayonets and advance. The Americans moved forward toward the British through a cloud of heavy musket fire and grapeshot fire "making a devil of a noise of firing and huzzaing." Wayne's men advanced to within 50 yards of the shocked British. The British had stopped in their tracks, looking in pure surprise at the oncoming Americans. Why did the outnumbered rebels charge them? While the bewildered British hesitated in confusion, and as the darkness of the early evening arrived, Wayne quickly moved his forces back away from the British. Lafayette had rode up in a courageous attempt to help Wayne's retreat. He had one horse killed from under him and another wounded in the action.[36]

Wayne had somehow been able to avoid a disaster at the hands of Cornwallis. Only his personal bravery had changed the outcome. There were losses. Lafayette and Wayne had lost 28 killed, 99 wounded and 12 missing, including ten officers. Cornwallis had suffered 75 killed or wounded, including five officers. Cornwallis had attempted to follow the retreating Americans but the darkness had come too quickly and the cavalry could not pursue through woods and swamp in that condition. The earl wrote to Balfour that "the darkness of the evening prevented me from making use of the cavalry, or it is probable the Pennsylvania line would have been demolished."[37]

Tarleton wrote of the action: "His Lordship might certainly have derived more advantage from his victory." Tarleton felt that if Cornwallis had pushed harder to pursue the Americans, Lafayette's army "must have been annihilated ... such as exploit would have been easy, fortunate, and glorious...." British Colonel John Francis Mercer gave his view that Lafayette had been rather lucky and concluded, "Thus terminated one of the silly & misjudged affairs that took place during the war ... it required all the bravery of Wayne & his corps & above all, the misconduct of the enemy to save the whole from capture."[38]

While the affair was certainly not impressive, being a near defeat, Lafayette put a positive spin on events in his following general orders, emphasizing the bravery he saw:

> The General is happy in acknowledging the spirit of the detachment commanded by General Wayne, in their engagement with the total of the British army, of which he happened to be an eye-witness. He requests General Wayne, the officers and men under his command, to receive his best thanks.
> The bravery and destructive fire of the riflemen engaged rendered essential service.
> The brilliant conduct of Major Galvin and the Continental detachment under his command entitle them to applause.
> The conduct of the Pennsylvania field and other officers are new instances of their gallantry and talents.
> The fire of the light infantry under Major Willis checked the enemy's progress round our right flank.
> The General was much pleased with the conduct of Major Savage, of the artillery; and it is with pleasure, also, he observes that nothing but the loss of horses could have produced that of the field-pieces.
> The zeal of Colonel Mercer's little corps is handsomely expressed in the number of horses he had killed.

General Greene's reaction of the events caused him to write to Wayne, "It gives me great pleasure to hear of the success of my friends; but be a little careful and tread softly, for, depend upon it, you have a modern Hannibal to deal with in the person of Lord Cornwallis."[39]

The next day Tarleton took a patrol of 200 dragoons and 80 mounted infantry across the swamp and back toward Lafayette's army. He found the marquis camped six miles away at Chickahominy Church, but decided not to engage even though they "would have been an easy prey to a powerful detachment of the British...." With Lafayette's army humbled and the Battle of Green Spring Farm over, Cornwallis moved his forces over the James River.

On July 8 at Cobham, across from Jamestown, Cornwallis received the first in a series of rather confusing and contradictory letters from Sir Henry. Clinton requested in the first letter dated June 28 that his lordship send a new force to Philadelphia, if he had not already dispatched troops to New York as covered in his letters of June 11 and 15. Having earlier written to Clinton protesting his plans to attack Philadelphia, Cornwallis now adjusted to his fresh orders. Immediately he forwarded a dispatch to Leslie in Portsmouth to prepare the transports for the arrival of his troops.

As Cornwallis moved toward Portsmouth, a black servant named James, who was really a spy for Lafayette, was monitoring him. As the earl headed southeast, James reported all progress to Lafayette. Unfortunately, James was unable to gather detailed intelligence about British plans since "his Lordship is so shy of his papers that my honest friend says he cannot get at them." (After the war this black spy was given his freedom as "James Lafayette" by the Virginia legislature.) As Cornwallis moved toward Suffolk, he sent out Tarleton and the Legion to raid Prince Edward Court House to destroy stores. Unfortunately for Tarleton, the stores had already been shipped south to Greene's army in South Carolina.

On July 12, Cornwallis arrived at Suffolk to receive Clinton's letter of June 8 and the 19th, as well for May 29. These letters were distressing to Cornwallis, and they showed how Clinton was confused at the purpose that should be made with his army in Virginia. Clinton's letter of May 29 told of his disfavor at having Cornwallis move into Virginia. The letters of June 8 and 19 informed the earl of the need to send all the troops and supplies he could spare to New York. Clinton wrote that "the Enemy will certainly attack this Post," and "I am much in want of Howitzers &c I think your Lordship can spare some." Cornwallis wrote Clinton on July 12, "I have only now to inform your Excellency that every exertion shall be made to fit out the Expedition [for Philadelphia] in the completest manner without loss of time."

During the next days Cornwallis endeavored to carry out Clinton's orders with dispatch. He sent units to Leslie and gave orders to empower his officers to equip and prepare the expedition to Philadelphia. He would only keep six boats for his infantry and four for his horses. While focused on this work, Cornwallis sent out Tarleton again in more raiding parties to find and destroy stores in the area. By July 20 the preparations were made to embark troops. The Queen's Rangers had already embarked their transport when around 1 P.M. Cornwallis received new orders from Clinton:

> I have received your lordship's letter of the 30th June and the admiral has dispatched a frigate with his and my opinions in answer to it. I cannot be more explicit by this opportunity than to desire that, if you have not already passed the James River you will continue on the Williamsburg Neck until he arrives with my dispatches by Capt. Stapleton. If you have passed it and find it expedient to recover that station, you will please to do it and keep possession until you hear further from me. Whatever troops may have been embarked by you for this place [New York] are likewise to remain until further orders. And if they should have been sailed and within your call you will be pleased to stop them. It is the admiral's and my wish at all events to hold Old Point Comfort which secures Hampton Road.

Cornwallis was in a fury over these new orders that contradicted the former ones. Clinton was continuing to modify his plan entirely from letter to letter, with little strategic regard and certainly no consistency. Driven by new orders, Cornwallis instructed Leslie to halt embarkation, and sent out an engineer to survey Old Point Comfort. While awaiting the results of the survey, Cornwallis received yet another letter from Clinton dated July 11. This letter urged for a naval station in the Chesapeake Bay area and indicated that Admiral Graves, who had replaced Arbuthnot, had agreed with him that such a naval station was necessary. Cornwallis was told he could fortify Yorktown if he felt he needed added security to Old Point Comfort. Clinton indicated that the earl was "at full liberty to detain all the Troops now in Chesapeak ... which very liberal concession will I am persuaded convince your lordship of the high estimation in which I hold a Naval station in Chesapeak."

In a few days the engineer sent to survey Old Point Comfort, Lieutenant Sutherland, returned to report to Cornwallis that he found the ground totally unsuited for building fortifications designed to protect naval vessels. Aside from the ground, there was no bay to allow the ships to anchor under the protection of a fort's guns. To verify the report, Cornwallis personally visited the area with the captains of the British warships lying in Hampton Roads. All agreed that Old Point Comfort was not a viable location for a naval station. Cornwallis wrote Clinton of the findings and indicated that Yorktown, and Gloucester opposite, were feasible locations that were "easily accessible to the whole force of this province." On August 1, Cornwallis and his army sailed for Yorktown and Gloucester in Leslie's transports then available at Portsmouth. In the heat of the summer, work began immediately on the defenses.[40]

Before Cornwallis had departed Portsmouth, James the spy had reported that he knew the British were about to leave but he did not know where they were sailing. Lafayette wrote to Washington that he was forced to "guess at every possible whim of an enemy that flies with the wind and is not within reach of spies or reconnoiters." Lafayette also wrote of his respect for his adversary Cornwallis, and declared that "To speak plain English I am devilish afraid of him." As the British were about to evacuate Portsmouth, Lafayette received a letter from Washington indicating that "I shall shortly have occasion to communicate matters of very importance to you." Lafayette concluded that his commander-in-chief must be heading to Virginia. He replied to General Washington, "Should a French fleet now come in Hampton Road, the British army would, I think, be ours."

When Lafayette heard Cornwallis had landed at Yorktown and Gloucester, he sent word to Washington, "You must not wonder my dear General that there has been a fluctuation in my intelligence. I am positive the British Councils have been fluctuating." He continued, "His Lordship plays so well that no blunder can be hoped from him to recover a bad step of ours." Lafayette moved his forces to Malvern Hill to keep a close watch on Cornwallis. He sent Wayne's detachment to guard the road to Richmond. Now the British were settling in to defend Yorktown and the events to take place there would seal the fate of the British in the American Revolution.[41]

18

VIRGINIA GATHERINGS AND THE CHESAPEAKE CAPES

On May 1, 1781, before General Washington's meeting with Rochambeau and de Barras at Wethersfield, Connecticut, on May 21 on French naval matters, he had recorded his first entry in his war diary:

> Instead of having Magazines filled with provisions, we have a scanty pittance.... Instead of having our Arsenals well supplied with Military Stores, they are poorly, and the Workmen all leaving.... Instead of money and credit for quartermaster needs, having to resort to Military Impress ... oppressing the people — souring their tempers — and alienating the affections.... Instead of adequate troops, scarce any State in the Union has, at this hour, an eight part of its quota in the field.... In a word ... instead of having the prospect of a glorious campaign before us, we have a bewildered and gloomy defensive one — unless we should receive a powerful aid of Ships — Land Troops — and Money from our generous allies...."

This depressing entry served to reflect the state of Washington's spirit in this later point in the long struggle to evict the British. But only three months later the opportunity was developing in Virginia to accomplish what had been to this point a futile effort. Certainly Washington was not the only commander at his last wits about the war. Cornwallis had been reduced by Clinton's frustrating orders from carrying out a campaign to defeat Lafayette and take control of Virginia, to fortifying a naval station at Yorktown. All his efforts in making the Carolinas a loyalist controlled haven had been reduced to maintaining occupation of Charles Town. All his other South Carolina posts were now abandoned to Greene's Southern Army.

Washington's letter to Colonel John Laurens in Paris, written back on April 9, expressed his desire that France's war plans favor her "to keep a superior Fleet always in these Seas and France would put us in condition to be active by advancing us money, the ruin of the enemy's schemes would then be certain ... for they would be forced to concentrate thus giving up all gains in the Southern States, or be vulnerable every where ... if France delays, a timely and powerful aid ... it will avail us nothing should she attempt it hereafter ... we are at the end of our tether ... now or never our deliverance must come."[1]

Just four days before Washington wrote Laurens in Paris, Rear Admiral Francois Joseph Paul, the Count de Grasse, had detached the 50-gun warship *Sagittaire*, together with 30 other ships from his fleet then heading toward the West Indies to Newport, Rhode Island. The *Sagittaire* was carrying 650 troop replacements for Rochambeau's First Division and an important letter from the admiral to Rochambeau declaring his intentions:

> His Majesty has intrusted me with the command of the naval force destined for the protection of his possessions in southern America, and those of his allies in North America. The force which I command is sufficient to fulfill the offensive plans, which it is in the interest of the Allied powers to execute, that they may secure an honorable peace. If the men-of-war are necessary for fulfilling the projects which you have in view ... It will not be until the 15th of July at soonest, that I shall be on the coast of North America.[2]

Having left Brest on March 22, 1781, de Grasse's fleet had made a rapid and important voyage with the slower merchantmen in tow to arrive at Martinique on April 28. On learning that the French fleet had sailed, London was unsure as to the destination—West Indies or North America? News of the sailing took three weeks to reach the West Indies, which was too late to stop de Grasse. He had expected to encounter British fleets of Rodney and Hood. At the time Admiral George Rodney and his fleet were at the Dutch island of St. Eustatius nursing his gout and collecting loot. Back on February 3 Rodney, with 12 warships, had captured the Dutch island after war had been declared with Holland on December 20. Rodney had taken possession of 150 merchantmen vessels, 2000 Americans, and "naval stores of every kind … wharves … thronged with merchandise … cases of sugar and tobacco." The value of the booty was estimated at £3 million.[3]

Rodney had positioned Rear Admiral Samuel Hood with his main fleet of 17 ships-of-the line and five frigates off Martinique, blockading a small French squadron of four ships commanded by the Chevalier de Monteil in Fort Royal harbor. While Hood's fleet was fewer in number than de Grasse's fleet of 20 warships, all his ships had copper bottoms and were, therefore, faster. To alert Rodney of the news of de Grasse's presence, Hood detached a slow cutter, the *Swallow*. The ship did not arrive with the news until May 17. Hood's goal was to keep de Grasse from reaching his port destination at Martinique, but his position to the leeward caused him problems. Hood had not been premitted by Rodney to sail to the windward of the island to be able to intercept any approaching fleet and thus complained that "Never was a squadron so unmeaningly stationed…. Never was more powder and shot thrown away in one day before." The fleets of de Grasse and Hood engaged and soon Hood's fleet had six warships with heavy damage. Prevailing, de Grasse entered the harbor with his convoy.

He continued his operations against the British possessions. After taking the indigo-rich island of Tobago, he returned to Martinique on June 18. To gather available ships for the upcoming operations in North America, de Grasse had also sent frigates. Soon the French admiral had 150 vessels, which were escorted to Cape Francois, Haiti, on July 16. Eight days before, the frigate *Concorde* had arrived at Cape Francois from Boston with 25 American pilots aboard for de Grasse's fleet. Also waiting for de Grasse were three letters from Rochambeau for the admiral. The first letter, dated May 28, told of Cornwallis' Virginia campaign and Washington's desire to attack New York, and revealed that Rear Admiral Graves' fleet of seven ships-of-the-line were in New York. The text summarized the situation:

> That is the state of affairs and the very grave crisis in which America, and especially the states of the South,

finds herself at this particular time. The arrival of M. le Comte de Grasse would save this situation, all the means in our hands are not enough without his joint action and the sea superiority which he is able to command.

The letter went on to give de Grasse the choice of coming to New York, as Washington requested, or going to the Chesapeake. He continued with appeals for more troops, saying, "five or six thousand more new men would give us the means of making certain the operations." Rochambeau's second letter was an appeal for money to pay the French army beyond August 2, pointing out that "it would be to the greatest advantage for the interest of the King … up to the amount of one million two hundred thousand livres in specie…."

The third letter revealed that Washington had sent him four letters seeking support for the New York attack. Rochambeau wrote the following regarding the full measure of American force condition:

> …I must not conceal from you, Monsieur, that the Americans are at the end of their resources, that Washington will not have half of the troops he reckoned to have, and that I believe, though he is silent on that, that at present he does not have six thousand men; that M. de Lafayette does not have a thousand regulars with militia to defend Virginia, and nearly as many on the march to join him; that General Greene has pushed a small force far in advance of Camden, where he was repulsed, and that I do not know how and when he will rejoin M. de Lafayette; that it is therefore of the greatest consequence that you take on board as many troops as possible; that four or five thousand men will not be too many, whether you aid us to destroy the works at Portsmouth, Virginia, near Hampton Roads, where up to now they have always kept fifteen hundred men while the others operate in the country, and all their flotillas with which they have tormented the poor Marquis de Lafayette on the rivers in a very evil manner; whether then to force the Hook in seizing Sandy-Hook for your land troops, which ought to facilitate the entrance of your squadron over that bar … finally to aid us afterwards to lay siege to Brooklyn…. There, Monsieur, are the different objects that you may have in view, and the actual and sad picture of the affairs of this country. I am quite persuaded that you will bring us naval superiority, but I cannot too often repeat to you to bring also the troops and the money….[4]

Ever since the Wethersfield Plan had been formulated at the conference with the French that ended May 22, 1781, Washington had been preparing for the attack on New York. Washington wrote of the plan to Greene on June 1, "I have lately had an interview with Count de Rochambeau, at Wethersfield. Our affairs were very attentively considered in every point of view, and it was finally determined to make an attempt upon New York, with its present garrison, in preference to a southern operation, as we had not the decided command of the water."

Washington started to execute the plan immediately after the conference, staying an extra day, the 24th, at Wethersfield to write urgent letters to the New England governors asking them to fill their quotas of Continental troops for the campaign, and to provide necessary supplies. His letters read, "The enemy, counting upon our want of ability, or upon our want of energy, have, by repeated detachments to the southward, reduced themselves in New York to a situation which invites us to take advantage of it.... Our allies in this country expect and depend upon being supported by us in the attempt which we are about to make, and those in Europe will be astonished should we neglect the favorable opportunity which is now offered."

Washington had also written the French Minister in Philadelphia, Chevalier de la Luzerne, with his request to have de Grasse come up the coast to New York to aid in the joint attack. Luzerne replied to Washington, "Be persuaded that I shall use the most pressing motives to determine him, and I shall do it with so much the more zeal as I feel the necessity of it." Washington left Wethersfield at forenoon on the 24th and arrived at his headquarters at New Windsor on the Hudson at sunset the following day. Washington now devoted the majority of his time to preparations. He directed Knox and Duportial, the chiefs of artillery and engineers, to get their men as fully trained as possible. He pushed the troops to be drilled, and in all ways prepared for the attack. King Louis XVI of France had given Congress some six million livres, which were applied to purchase arms and clothing for the troops. Washington was given budgetary control of the surplus remaining of 1,500,000 livres.

As Washington prepared his forces, time seemed to move too slowly. It was not until June 13 that letters arrived from Rochambeau with welcomed intelligence that de Grasse had been heard from and was expected off American waters in midsummer. Washington wrote back that the news was important and that it was also quite clear from news coming from the South that Cornwallis had abandoned the Carolinas and was intent on campaigning in Virginia. Not until July 6 did Count de Rochambeau's French troops that had marched from Newport join with Washington's at Dobbs Ferry. The French Army marched southward from Newport on June 9, through Providence on June 18 through 21, passing through the towns of Plainfield, Canterbury, Windham, Bolton, Hartford, Farmington, Southington, Newtown, Ridgebury, Bedford, Northcastle, and White Plains. Every town and village they passed found the citizens cheering their allies with welcomed respect.[5] The combined American-French army had strength of some 9000 men.

Meanwhile, de Grasse found himself now pressed to bring three things with him to the American coast: a significant fleet to hold off the British; money to pay the troops; and troops to fill the gaps in the French and American forces to wage the upcoming campaign. Admiral de Grasse now made this most critical strategic decision to sail to the Chesapeake rather than to New York. His letter, dated July 28, was carried aboard the returning *Concorde*, arriving at Newport on August 12. It revealed that Chesapeake was "the point which appears to me to be indicated by you, Monsieur Comte de Rochambeau, and by Messieurs Washington, de la Luzerne, and De Barras, as the one from which the advantage you propose may be most certainly attained." Admiral de Grasse began to take actions to satisfy the three requests. To obtain additional troops, he approached the acting governor of Spanish San Domingo, Count de Lillancourt, for the loan of three French regiments — the Agenais, Gatinais and the Touraine — totaling 3200 troops that were then in the service of the Spanish in the West Indies. These forces, to be commanded by Spanish Claude Henri de St. Simon, were granted to de Grasse with an agreement to have them returned "by the month of November."

Next the admiral set off on the quest to raise 1,200,000 livres in specie, no small task. A young Swedish lieutenant, Carl Gustav Tornquist, who was serving with the French Navy, recorded the actions to raise the sum. He recorded how de Grasse tried to raise 300,000 piastres in San Domingo by pledging de Grasse's own plantation on the island, as well as his chateau of Tilly in France as collateral. That deal did not materialize, but he did manage to persuade the Spanish customs collector to go to Havana with his request to the governor and "to do his best to assist the public treasury by the purses of individuals." As recorded by an anonymous writer, "It must be said to the honor of the colonists, that all were eager to do so, ladies, even, offering their diamonds." The collector was sent aboard the French frigate *Avigrette* and once they arrived, the total required was raised in only six hours.

The greatest decision now facing de Grasse was how many ships could he gather to move northward to the Chesapeake. Although it was true that de Grasse's first obligation was to his country's territory and forces in the West Indies, along with those of their Spanish allies, he desired to come to the aid of the Americans. He wrote in his letter to Rochambeau, "I have read with great sadness of the distress in which the Americans find themselves and the necessity of prompt aid." As it occurred, "There happened to be at San Domingo a Spanish commissary from the island of Cuba; it was agreed with him that a Spanish squadron should protect the coasts and commerce...." The Spanish would not go north to aid the

American Revolution, but they would protect the Antilles and release de Grasse from his immediate responsibilities. Later Lafayette would write of these circumstances to Luzerne, "The Spanish have behaved like little angels."

The troops of the three infantry regiments, 100 dragoons and 350 artillerymen with their equipment were loaded aboard 15 chartered merchant vessels on August 3. On August 5, 1781, led by the admiral's mammoth flagship, the 110-gun *Ville de Paris*, de Grasse's fleet of 28 ships-of-the-line, seven frigates, two cutters and 15 merchant ships set sail toward Cuba. The ships were divided up into three squadrons commanded by de Monteil, de Grasse and de Bougainville. As recorded, "The fleet followed the old [Bahama] channel, the dreaded channel, where no French fleet had ever passed." The passage was known to be tedious and often difficult. While passing between Cuba and the Bahamas, the winds were violent. On August 17, at Matanza, the *Avigrette* rejoined the admiral with the cargo of money. The money was divided among the ships of the fleet and that night, "We were in the channel between Florida and the Bahama Islands, whose greatest width is ten German miles. The constant current which always flows northward with great speed brings it about that, although the wind may be contrary, one does not consider it remarkable to find oneself in twenty-four hours from twenty to thirty German miles more northerly than the most careful calculations would indicate."

Lieutenant Tornquist wrote, "On August 24, being off Charleston, the cutter *La Mouche* was sent off to Europe with dispatches." On the voyage several British ships were captured, including the 34-gun *Sandwich* which contained Lord Rawdon on his way to England. As a result, Rawdon was forced to witness Cornwallis' operations at Yorktown. Late in the evening of August 29 in calm waters, "The fleet anchored on the banks outside of Chesapeake Bay five leagues from land. Early the following morning the whole fleet weighed and steered into the bay and anchored again in the roadstead of Lynnhaven within the Horseshoe bank in three columns, the van farthest out in eight to ten fathoms, the bottom being sand mixed with shells. The British frigate *Loyalist*, 26 guns, was captured by the *Glorieux*, 74 guns, which pursued it into the bay. The other enemy frigate *Guadaloupe*, 28 guns, escaped to Yorktown under the protection of its batteries."[6]

On September 2 at 5 A.M. French officer Colonel Louis Duportail was the first from American headquarters to see that the French fleet had come to trap Cornwallis at Yorktown. He recalled that the sight of the mighty fleet "makes me forget all the hardships I experienced." For the British there was much apprehension at Yorktown over the news of the French fleet. Captain Thomas Symonds, the senior British naval officer on the York River, sent his lieutenant to reconnoiter the situation from a land position. Symonds reported the following:

> Between thirty & forty sail lay between the Horse shoe & middle, sixteen or seventeen if not more he took to be ships of the Line, besides these, one Line of Battle ship & two Frigates with the loyalists are laying off Toes marsh in full sight of us, so that this River is effectually blocked except a chance of a small schooner or row boat escaping the Enemy's vigilance. I am landing cannon from the *Charon* & shall cooperate with Ld. Cornwallis in everything he wishes for His Majesty's service.

Hessian soldier Ewald recorded:

> Now head banged against head in York and Gloucester. Now they hastily began to unload all the magazines and guns which had been brought from Portsmouth, but which—through negligence and laziness—were still on board the ships lying at anchor in the York River between the two towns. Now, if the French had been in better readiness, or perhaps had had better intelligence, the ships could be shot to pieces.[7]

Since the British had the 44-gun *Charon*, two smaller frigates and six sloops in the York, de Grasse immediately sent the *Vaillant* and *Triton* to join the *Glorieux* to block the river. Then the French admiral sent the 50-gun *Experiment* with the frigates 32-gun *Andromaque* and 26-gun *Diligente* up the James River with the majority of the promised troops. On August 31 some 40 boatloads of Marquis St. Simon's infantrymen rowed onto Jamestown Island to reinforce and join with Lafayette's army outside Williamsburg. Lieutenant Tornquist wrote of the landing and of a recent atrocity:

> On a beautiful estate two miles from Hampton, a pregnant woman was found murdered in her bed through several bayonet stabs: the barbarians had opened both her breasts and written above the bed canopy: "Thou shalt never give birth to a rebel!" In another room was just as horrible a sight, five cut-off heads, arranged on a cupboard in place of plaster-cast figures, which lay broken to pieces on the floor.... The pastures were in many places covered with dead horses, oxen and cows. A storehouse of tobacco, which had been collected from Virginia, Maryland, and the Carolinas during many years, containing ten thousand hogsheads of tobacco, was laid in ashes. Such was our first sight on landing in this unfortunate country. We did not find a single trace of inhabitants, for those who had been unable to flee lay on the ground, as a token of the godless behavior of their enemies.[8]

With the arrival of the French cutter *Serpent* under the command of Captain Amie de la Laune in Baltimore, which had been sent north by de Grasse just after his arrival, General Mordecai Gist of the Maryland Militia viewed the dispatches from de Grasse and Duportail with intense interest. With the news of the arrival of the French fleet now reaching Baltimore, the taverns were filled with locals drinking and militiamen firing muskets in the air with joy as the town was illuminated. An express rider headed north to find General Washington.[9] Cornwallis was trapped at Yorktown unless the British fleet could free him. Where was the British fleet?

The events related to the operations of the British Royal Navy were rather confused and mistimed at this point in 1781 to the advantage of the American cause. Realizing that de Grasse was a true threat to North America, the 61-year-old Admiral Sir George Brydges Rodney sent the sloop *Swallow* to New York from his headquarters at St. Eustatius in the West Indies on July 7 to warn Admiral Graves of the French admiral's presence in the West Indies. Rodney's letter to Graves told of the situation:

> As the enemy has at this time a fleet of twenty-eight sail of the line at Martinique, a part of which is reported to be destined for North America, I have dispatched His Majesty's sloop *Swallow*.... The enemy's squadron destined for America will sail I am informed in a short time...."

The *Swallow* arrived at Sandy Hook off New York on July 27, but by that time Graves was cruising off New England with his entire squadron of six ships-of-the-line. Admiral Graves at New York had been alerted by the British Admiralty back on July 19 that valuable convoy of "money, clothing, and military stores" obtained by John Laurens was sailing to Boston from France. The admiralty had indicated in the secret letter that the capture of the material would be "decisive of the state of America and the war." The *Swallow* left New York to find Graves and deliver the message of de Grasse's movement north. Unfortunately for Admiral Graves, while Captain Wells departed New York and sailed the *Swallow* through Long Island Sound, he sighted a Yankee privateer and set off to capture it. Captain Wells did capture their prize, but was soon attacked by three other privateers and the *Swallow* was "pushed on shore upon Long Island, eleven leagues to the eastward" of New York. Captain Wells managed to burn his prize, but the "privateers pillaged [the *Swallow* and] ... the dispatches were destroyed." Admiral Graves did not find out about de Grasse until he returned to New York in mid–August.

Later other attempts to warn Graves would be unsuccessful. Admiral Hood sent the brig *Active* northward to find Graves when he sailed, but the ship and crew were captured and brought to Philadelphia. The imprisoned captain was able to smuggle word out to New York, but

the news did not arrive until Hood had already arrived there. Rodney also sent the *Pegasus* on a 26-day trip to New York to warn Graves, but she arrived three days after the British and French fleets had already fought off Chesapeake Capes.

Meanwhile, having delayed his often discussed departure to England, the "sharp-tongued tyrant" and 50-year veteran of the British naval service, Admiral Rodney, sat at St. Eustatius in the West Indies auctioning off his seized treasures from the capture of this tiny Dutch island. While complaints continued from the Dutch officials that the British "acted like robbers, searching, digging, confiscating," Rodney, whose health was failing from gout and prostate trouble, could not make up his mind about when to leave. Admiral Hood, who had been defeated at Martinique, continued to lose his patience with his superior who, "one hour he says his complaints are of such a nature that he cannot possibly remain in this country, and is determined to leave the command with me; the next he says he has no thought of going home.... If he stays much longer, his laurels may be subject to wither." It had been hard for Rodney to leave St. Eustatius for it was the "richest island in the world," according to the admiral.

Finally on August 1, Rodney departed for England to consult with British surgeons and visit the healthy waters at Bath, leaving orders to Hood to sail to America. Rodney had hoped that the initial voyage would invigorate him, but by the time he reached the "point of no return" near Bermuda on August 13, he felt no better than he had at St. Eustatius. He sent the *Pegasus* off with warning dispatches to New York of de Grasse. Rodney also sent word that he had sent Admiral Hood "to the Capes of Virginia, where I am persuaded the French intend making their grand effort." With Rodney sailing to England was a fleet made up of the 80-gun *Gibraltar*, the 74-gun *Triumph*, and the 60-gun *Panther*.

Admiral Hood sailed north from Antigua with his reduced squadron of 14 ships on August 10. While he did not know it at the time, he was to reach the Chesapeake Capes ahead of de Grasse, who had departed Cape Francois on August 5. With his faster ships with their copper bottoms, and his choice to use a more favorable sea-lane, Hood arrived off the Virginia Capes on August 25 ahead of the French admiral. With no signs of a French fleet, Hood sailed north to New York.

On August 26 Hood's fleet encountered a brig from Jamaica with news that "on the 28th of July the Count de Grasse with his whole fleet, consisting of thirty sail of the line, was at the Cape, and that the Jamaica convoy only waited his departure to pursue their voyage to England." This news hurried Admiral Sir Samuel Hood to Sandy Hook on the morning of August 28 with his urgent message to rear Admiral Graves. Hood learned that Graves had returned from sea and his fruitless voyage on August 16 and was that day off with Clinton at Denis' on Long Island in discussions. Hood wrote that he immediately "got into my boat and met Mr. Graves and Sir Henry Clinton on Long Island, who were deliberating upon a plan of destroying the ships at Rhode Island." Hood remarked to them both, "You have no time to lose; every moment is precious."

Strangely, Rear Admiral Graves was not as interested in moving to the Chesapeake Capes with the speed that Hood expected. On August 29 the frigate *Richmond* arrived in New York from the Chesapeake Capes and reported that "Everything is quiet ... whether the French intend a junction or whether they have left the coast is only to be guessed at." Graves felt that perhaps it was a false alarm, and he sent Hood a message at Sandy Hook on August 30 that "No intelligence yet of de Grasse.... For my part I believe the mountain in labor."[10]

When Rochambeau marched to Washington's headquarters at Joseph Appleby's house on the Dobbs Ferry–White Plains Road near the Hudson River on July 6, he was able to see the deplorable state of the main American Army. Under orders to serve Washington as his commander-in-chief, Rochambeau was now able to see the results of six years of war on the Americans. Most of Washington's men still had no uniforms. Only the officers had uniforms of blue with buff facings. Baron Ludwig von Closen, a young Bavarian from the Royal Deux-Ponts Regiment and now on Rochambeau's staff, wrote of the American force, "It is really painful to see these brave men, almost naked, with only some trousers and linen jackets, most of them without stockings, but, would you believe it? Very cheerful and healthy in appearance." The only American regiment von Closen was impressed with was the Rhode Island Regiment, which was two-thirds Negro. He characterized this group as "the most neatly dressed, the best under arms, and the most precise in its maneuvers."

After the armies joined, Washington held a formal review of the French troops, while Rochambeau reviewed the Americans. Washington was treated to the color of the French uniforms that included white coats and long waistcoats. The coat lapels and color bands were of differing colors — crimson, pink, blue, green, yellow — depending on the regiment or unit. The artillery units wore long gray coats with red velvet lapels. In short, the French were dazzling in "parade-ground brilliance." The French forces looked like they actually were the finest French regiments in the French Army.

The contrast in living conditions was also extreme. Abbe Claude Robin, the French chaplain, was astonished to discover that the Americans slept three or four men per tent, with only 40 pounds of baggage, and few mattresses available. The French had traveled from Newport without their heavy equipment, which included some 14 baggage wagons allocated per regiment. French soldiers were nearly bent over "under the weight" of the material they carried with them. While in camp with the French, the Americans were quite embarrassed with the contrast between themselves and their ally.

While the American Army lived at best on starvation rations, the French lived well. One French general sent Washington an entire keg of claret. The French were always hosting dinners for the American officers and Washington that could not be reciprocated. While seeing the poor state of living for the Americans, they gained a high degree of respect for them. The French especially loved Washington. He was described by Count Axel Fersen as "handsome and majestic but at the same time kind and gentle, corresponding completely with his moral qualities. He looks like a hero; he is very bold and says little but is frank and polite." Major General Francois Jean de Chastellux viewed Washington as "Brave without temerity, laborious without ambition, generous without prodigality, noble without pride, virtuous without severity."[11]

As the days of July 1781 continued, Washington and Rochambeau set about reconnoitering and, to some extent, probing Clinton's defenses around New York. On one such scouting event on July 18 the 49-year-old Washington was escorted by 150 handpicked troops from the New Jersey Continentals as he joined up with Rochambeau and moved down the New Jersey bank of the Hudson. At a spot far enough down to allow the two generals to view Manhattan Island all the way to the sea, Washington looked with dismay through his spyglass to see the tents of the two Hessian camps near the ravine at Jumel's Mansion in Harlem. At Cox's Hill, a decaying old fort, sat 100 tents of the German riflemen. At McGowan's Heights his staff officer told Washington of the two battalions of British grenadiers camped there. There seemed no place around Manhattan that Washington could exploit to his advantage with an attack. Perhaps Rochambeau was right and they would be better served to support an attack on Cornwallis in Virginia than risk a direct assault on Clinton's defenses at New York.[12]

By July 21 it was becoming clear that Washington was beginning to think that he must abandon any hope of a frontal attack at New York. On August 1 Washington wrote, "Everything would have been in perfect readiness to commence the operations against New York if the States had furnished their quotas of Men ... of 6,200 ... pointedly and continually called for to be with the army by the 15th of last month, only 176 had arrived from Connecticut and two companies of York levies — about 80 men." Finally on August 12 Washington received discouraging news from his spies at Manhattan that a fleet of 20 British ships had arrived in New York harbor carrying what was believed to be some 2880 German reinforcements for Clinton.[13]

The final blow to the New York plan came on August 14, when Rochambeau and Washington learned in a letter from Admiral de Barras at Newport that Admiral de Grasse was sailing for the Chesapeake to support joint land-sea operations there. Quartermaster General Timothy Pickering and the Philadelphia financier Robert Morris saw Washington react to the news as the general was "striding to and fro in such a state of uncontrolled excitement...." Pickering wrote that Washington's "hopes were blasted, and he felt that the cause was lost and his country ruined." Both men excused themselves, but they returned a half hour later as the general spoke, "I must apologize for my extraordinary appearance when you came." Washington then exclaimed, "I wish to the Lord the French would not raise our expectations of a cooperation [not to] fulfill them." That night Washington wrote in his journal:

> Matters having now come to a crisis and a decisive plan to be determined on, I was obliged, from the shortness of Count de Grasse promised stay on this Coast, the apparent disinclination in their Naval Offices to force the harbor of New York and the feeble compliance of the States to my requisitions for Men ... to give up all idea of attacking New York; and instead therefore to remove the French Troops and a detachment from the American Army ... to Virginia.[14]

Now that the decision had been made, Washington set about preparing for the movement of a combined American-French army southward to Virginia. Realizing that Clinton no doubt had spies in his camp just as he had spies in New York, Washington chose to depart with as much secrecy as could be achieved. Numerous actions were taken to give the impression that the attack on New York was still the American objective. Washington ordered to have a new and large camp erected at Chatham in New Jersey, some four miles above Staten Island. French cooks began constructing four huge bread ovens as evidence that the new site was more permanent. The Canadian Regiment moved over the dunes at Sandy Hook under the guise of building artillery batteries.

Washington also met with a known spy and "old inhabitant of New York" and directly asked him if he knew anything about the water supply and landing sites on Long Island, and the terrain around Sandy Hook. He remarked that he had no special reason for asking other than he was "fond of knowing the Situation of different parts of the Country, as in the Course of the war he might unexpectedly be called into that part of the Country."[15]

Washington selected General William Heath to stay behind in New York with a force less than 4000 men including ten Massachusetts regiments, five Connecticut, two New Hampshire, Crane's Third Artillery, and Sheldon's Dragoons and militia units. Above New York to guard against threatened incursions from Canada, General Lord Stirling took up command of the fort at Saratoga, while at the Mohawk was placed the New York Continentals under Lieutenant Colonel Willett. The American forces directed to march south were some 2000 men including Colonel Alexander Scammell's Light Infantry, Colonel John Lamb's Regiment of Artillery, the New York regiments, two New Jersey, the Rhode Island and Hazen's Canadian regiments, a small corps of Engineers and the Sappers and Miners. Rochambeau's entire force of 4000 troops was to move out for Virginia.[16]

On August 17 Washington received the good news in a dispatch from Lafayette that Cornwallis had moved to Yorktown and was in the process of fortifying the area. Washington immediately sent out letters to General Henry Knox in Philadelphia with orders to prepare to move the American cannon stored there. Letters were also sent to the state governors urging more militia recruits to fill in the vacating forces around the Hudson. A rather curious general order from the commander-in-chief sternly instructed that "No women will be suffered to ride in waggons or walk in the ranks this campaign unless there are very particular reasons for it of which the general officer or the officer commanding the division or brigade is to be the judge. A written permission only will avail." The American Army was on the move with a truly serious mission.[17]

On August 19, the allied American and French armies broke camp at 2 A.M. and marched from Dobbs Ferry, crossing the Hudson River at King's Ferry. Washington had left his new headquarters at the Smith House at Haverstraw and moved to direct the American and French forces with their baggage and artillery. It took until the 25th to get all the forces over the river and camped. The French army moved farther to the west by way of Northcastle, Pine's Bridge and Compound. From the ferry crossing, the forces moved in three different routes toward Princeton, New Jersey, where they merged. The First New York under General Lincoln was to the left marching from Kakeat by way of Paramus and Second River, camping at Springfield on the 27th. The other column moved with the baggage, stores and artillery and the remaining forces through Pompton to Chatham. The French passed through Suffrens and Pompton to Whippany. On the 28th the entire allied force was encamped at Chatham.

The march was resumed with assembly ordered for 3:30 A.M. on the 29th and marching off by 4 A.M. General Lincoln relayed Washington's daily marching orders as follows: "General Hazen's regiment in front and the Sappers and Miners will cover your rear. You will march through the Scotch plains, Quibble Town, and Bound Brook. On the 30th to Princeton — 31st to Trenton, where you will meet me and further orders. You will keep these orders a perfect secret." The center of the forces moved to Boundbrook while the French moved through Morristown to Bullion's Tavern. As planned, the allies marched through Princeton on the 30th and at Trenton on the 31st. As the men headed toward the Delaware River, it was anticipated that boats would be there to take the troops down to Wilmington, Delaware.

Unfortunately the letters from Washington to Quartermaster Miles at Philadelphia and the efforts of Robert Morris yielded an insufficient number of vessels to transport the entire army. The land march was continued, therefore, for all except the Second New York Regiment and Hazen's men, who traveled by water. The allies crossed the Delaware River on September 1 and moved 17 miles to Lower Duplin. September 2 saw the Americans make 12 miles reaching and passing through Philadelphia and camping near the Schuylkill River. The French came into Philadelphia on the 3rd, having stayed behind the American forces by a full day since Princeton.[18]

Washington and Rochambeau hurried ahead to Philadelphia before the troops arrived. Under the escort of a troop of light horse, Washington arrived in the city at one o'clock on August 30 with the "universal acclamations of the citizens." Robert Morris, the superintendent of finance, received the commander-in-chief at the City Tavern as the local gentlemen called for toasts. After a short while, Washington retired to Robert Morris' home. Rochambeau and party traveled to the residence of Chevalier de la Luzerne. Morris held a dinner in Washington's honor with his party including Rochambeau, the Chevalier Chastellux, General Knox, General Moultrie and others. The assembled party raised toasts to the king of France, Spain, the United Provinces, the allied armies and to the swift arrival of de Grasse, as ships in the harbor fired salutes. The night was filled with great illumination in honor of Washington as the leader walked among the population on the principal avenues as crowds assembled.

On September 1 at 8 A.M. a dispatch rider from General Forman brought news from the north that the combined fleets of Graves and Hood had departed New York with 20 warships. Washington was concerned that this force might intercept de Barras, who was moving south from Rhode Island toward the Chesapeake. Would de Grasse be able to block Cornwallis without the support of de Barras?

When the troops marched in later on Sunday afternoon, led by Scammell's Light Infantry, citizens gathered

for continued salutes and cheering in the hot August sun. The marching column of troops, covering some two miles in length, raised much dust which was "like a smothering snow-storm as the ladies were viewing us from the open windows of every house as we passed through this splendid city." The officers were dressed in their military best "mounted on noble steeds elegantly caparisoned ... followed by their servants and baggage. The soldiers marched in slow and solemn step, regulated by the drum and fife...." The army was ordered to march straight through the city without stopping. It was believed that the sight of the rather prosperous citizens of Philadelphia would enrage the troops, who had suffered without even being paid for many months. "Great symptoms of discontent ... appeared on their passage through the city."[19]

Even a more delightful sensation came when the French Army arrived on the following days of September 3 and 4. The French formed in white with colored trimming and dressed "as elegantly as ever the soldiers of a garrison were on a day of review." Rochambeau, who had ridden out to meet his men, led his first division into America's capital as they passed in review before the Congress, the French minister, commanding generals and dignitaries. As a special salute to their ally, the president and delegates of Congress removed their hats as the troops passed. The streets were full of crowds and bands as the city was enveloped in spirited pride as Washington and the dignitaries looked on from the balcony of the State House. Count Dumas wrote of the spectacle as Washington moved through the crowds: "The Americans, that cool and sedate people ... are roused, animated, and inflamed at the very mention of his name, and the first songs that sentiment or gratitude has dictated, have been to celebrate General Washington." The stark contrast between the French and American troops was noticed, as the citizens saw just how poorly dressed and scraggly their own army was.

The lead units of the Continentals departed their encampment on the Schuylkill on the morning of September 3 and marched some ten miles to relocate within three miles of Chester, Pennsylvania. On the 4th Lieutenant Sanderson of the Light Infantry recorded that the army traveled 20 miles that day "through Chester, through Brandywine, through Wilmington [Delaware]," coming to camp one mile outside the town. The following day these troops moved through Christiana, where the artillery and many troops had landed from Trenton. On September 5 a courier arrived at Chester to deliver a message to Washington that de Grasse had arrived in the Chesapeake with his fleet. Washington was so delighted that he mounted his white horse and trotted off for the wharf to tell Rochambeau the great news. As the General saw Rochambeau's boat coming into sight, he was "standing on the shore and waving his hat and white handkerchief joyfully." As the boat came close enough, Washington shouted the message. When the French general came on shore, Washington showed himself to be out of character as he threw his arms around the portly Frenchman. When Washington reached Christiana Bridge on the Delaware for breakfast on September 6 he wrote the following order to his army:

> It is with the highest pleasure and satisfaction that the Commander-in-chief announces to the Army the arrival of Count de Grasse in the Chesapeak.... He felicitates the army on the auspicious occasion, he anticipates the glorious events which may be expected.... The general calls upon the gentlemen officers, the brave and faithful soldiers ... to exert their utmost abilities in the cause of their country, to share with him ... the difficulties, dangers, and glory of the enterprise.

There was celebration in all directions including Philadelphia as the news of de Grasse's fleet reached the patriot Americans. For the army, the real celebration came when finally they were mustered for payday, and paid from borrowed funds from barrels of silver half-crowns. Robert Morris had convinced the French that they must let the American troops receive some of their pay to help morale. Major William Popham of New York wrote of this event, "This day will be famous in the annals of History for being the first in which the Troops of the United States received one month's Pay in specie." The 130,000 livres were not sufficient to pay all that were worthy and Morris did all he could to make up the difference. Morris wrote in despair, "The late movements of the army have so entirely drained me of money that I have been obliged to pledge my personal credit very deeply ... besides borrowing money from my friends and advancing ... every shilling of my own."[20]

On September 6 the lead forces marched ten miles to the Head of Elk, Maryland, near the Chesapeake. It had been some 15 days and 200 miles since these units of the American Army had left the Hudson and Clinton behind. By the 8th the French Army joined these troops. In good spirits at Head of Elk, Pickering wrote his wife the following:

> Here I am, my dearest, in perfect health. Presently I set out for Williamsburg by land. It will be a seven or eight days' journey, and give me an opportunity of seeing Maryland and Virginia. I hope, in a little time, to congratulate you on the capture of Cornwallis and his army. Should we succeed at all, the work, I think, will be short; and the only chance of ill-success will arise from this — that Cornwallis may possibly attempt to save himself by flight, by marching his army up the country, and then pushing to South Carolina. But a few days' delay will render this impossible, as our troops will soon surround them.[21]

Back in New York Clinton had resisted the ever-increasing intelligence that the allied armies had left the area. Clinton seemed to hold on to the belief that Washington indeed planned to attack New York as revealed in the captured courier messages of British Ensign John Moody on June 5 between New Windsor and Morristown, New Jersey. But evidence was everywhere. On August 18, the day before Washington moved south, a spy reported to Clinton that Rochambeau's son, the viscount, had moved his mistress to Trenton, New Jersey. August 25 was the day Clinton called in Lieutenant Mackenzie to his office to discuss his scheme to attack the French fleet at Rhode Island. The next days passed as Sir Henry was active ordering troops, equipment and shipping to be made ready for the engagement at Newport.[22]

On August 27 Sir Henry wrote Cornwallis indicating that "I cannot well ascertain Mr. Washington's real intentions by this move of his army," as he continued to explain that he assumed that Washington was moving to his old winter headquarters at Morristown, New Jersey. Still Clinton was not moved on the issue. On the 29th from a spy known only as "Squib" came a scrap of paper hidden in a button with the message, "The Chesapeake is the Object — All in motion." On the next day Clinton sent another letter to Cornwallis: "Mr. Washington's force still remains in the neighborhood of Chatham and I do not hear that he has yet detached to move southward." That day Washington was entering Philadelphia.

It was not until September 2 when Clinton finally admitted that Washington's army was heading south. That day he wrote a dispatch in cipher to Cornwallis:

> Mr. Washington is moving an army to the southward with an appearance of haste; and gives out that he expects the cooperation of a considerable French armament. Your Lordship, however, may be assured that if this should be the case, I shall endeavor to reinforce your command by all means within the compass of my power; or, make every possible diversion in your favor....

Now Clinton warned Germain in London that "Things appear to be coming fast to a crisis ... with what I have, inadequate as it is, I will exert myself to the utmost to save Lord Cornwallis."[23]

While Washington was moving to Head of Elk, Maryland, the British fleets of Hood and Graves reached the entrance of Chesapeake Bay. The British scouting frigate *Solebay* signaled at around 9:30 A.M. that she had sighted the French ships in Lynnhaven Bay under Cape Henry at ten miles distance. The report indicated that "About an hour-and-a-half after the frigate had left Admiral Graves, the man at the masthead gave notice of a fleet at anchor in Lynnhaven Bay. The commanding officer, thinking the man might have mistaken the tall

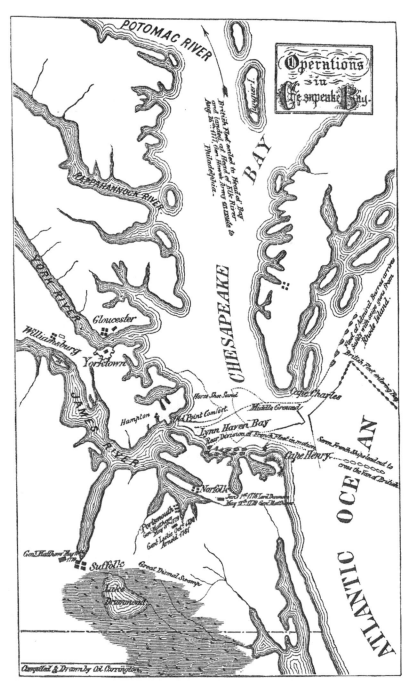

Operations in Chesapeake Bay. (*Battles of the American Revolution.*)

frigate *Avigrette*, which had been cruising off the entrance of the Chesapeake, discovered the presence of the British fleet. Before discovering the truth, the French crews rejoiced in the belief that these ships were those of the ten ships of de Barras' squadron. Thus, both the British and French had mistakenly believed that they had discovered de Barras, who was not present.

By 10 A.M. the British had seen some 16 French sails from the *Bedford*, and by 2 P.M. the count had risen to 24 "very large ships." At this point Graves believed that the dreaded event had already happened — the French fleets of de Barras and de Grasse had merged. It was not the case. The count of the British vessels discovered by the French had moved from ten at first to 25. They were mistaken, since there were only 19 warships with over 60 guns. The British combined fleet was five ships inferior to the French 25 warships, and was some 500 cannon short. The advantage the British fleet had was that all their ships had copper bottoms for greater speed, while the French fleet had only half the ships so equipped.

Admiral Graves gave the order to clear for action at 10:05 A.M., and called in his scouting frigates a short while later. Admiral de Grasse alerted his fleet to action at 11:30 A.M. as the ships' carpenters chopped their mooring cables with axes, but were still prevented from immediately coming out to meet the British due to the incoming tide into Lynnhaven Bay. By noon the tide had slowly reversed direction and de Grasse ordered his fastest ships to take the lead in leaving the channel. They moved on the south part of the ten-mile-wide channel just off the menacing sand bar known as Middle Ground Shoal. Commodore Louis Antoine de Bougainville commanding the 80-gun *Auguste* moved into the lead position. Captain de Monteil was ordered to take out the rear ships as de Grasse managed the center of the line aboard his flagship, the 110-gun *Ville de Paris*.

At 1:45 P.M. the 12th French warship in sequence, the flagship *Ville de Paris,* and the middle of the line cleared the capes and were at sea. If Graves had engaged the French fleet at this point as it moved out of the channel, the British might have won the sea battle quickly. But Graves followed the British fighting instructions to the letter. These instructions required the ships to be positioned

stumps of trees for masts, since it is customary there to burn the trees as they stand for tar, and many of the bare stumps remain standing twenty-feet high, went himself to the masthead, and saw the French fleet at anchor, and not even in any posture of defense." They first believed that they had spotted de Barras' fleet of eight warships.

Admiral de Grasse had placed his fleet in three irregular lines at anchor. He had sent ships to block the entrances to the York and James rivers. Three frigates were in the process of sailing up the bay when the advance in line-ahead order to be assured of supporting fire from adjacent ships during an engagement. Ordering a "general chase" command would have been an unorthodox method for a British admiral to deal with, even with this golden opportunity before Graves' fleet. As the British Admiral wrote in his account of events nine days later:

> My aim was to get close, to form parallel, and attack all together.... I therefore came to the same tack as the enemy, and lay with the topsail to the mast dressing the line and pressing toward the enemy, until I thought the enemy's van were so much advanced as to offer the moment for successful action; and I then gave the signal for close action.[24]

At about time when de Grasse had cleared the Cape, Graves had ordered the British line to form one cable length apart. Time passed as the British sailed inland while the French fleet struggled to get into a proper spread as they headed outbound to sea. At 2:05 P.M. Graves noticed that his lead ship, *Alfred*, was in danger of striking the Middle Ground Shoal. He immediately ordered the fleet to reverse course 180 degrees, which put them heading eastward in the same direction as the French line of ships. The closest point of the British line was still over four miles away from the French ships.

The British reversal of direction also created the second tactical problem for Graves. Now the British rear commanded by Drake's squadron of ships was in the lead and the former lead ships of Hood's squadron were at the rear. The three-deckers of the flagships of Hood and Graves were now in the rear and center of the British line, and Drake's squadron was opposite the strength of the French line. Two of Drake's ships, *Terrible* and *Ajax*, had just come from the West Indies in poor condition and were leaking so much the crews had to keep four pumps working at all times. Drake's ships were to take the brunt of the damage and death in the coming battle as a result of this poor placement by Graves of his warship assets.

The lead five ships of Bougainville's van were far in front of the main body of the French line as de Grasse's center lagged behind. As a British account recorded, "To the astonishment of the whole fleet, the French center were permitted without molestation to bear down to support their van." From the deck of the *Barfleur* Admiral Hood looked on with disbelief as Graves allowed one hour and a half to pass as the French closed the gaps in their line. A London paper wrote, "Brought to in order to let ye Center of the Enemy's Ships come a Brest of us."

At 2:52 and 3:09 P.M. British orders were signaled to "lead more to starboard, or toward the enemy." This was yet another tactical error dictating that the British vessels coming into the French would be in a piecemeal and disadvantageous angled line than optimum. The British warships would not be parallel with the French and, thus, the British ships would not be able have concentration of gunfire for maximum effect. As the two opposing fleets came toward each other, the lead and center ships were almost parallel while the rear divisions were many miles apart.

At 4:03 P.M. some six miles from shore, and some six and one-half hours after the opposing fleets sighted each other, Graves felt his ships were "pretty well formed" as the French ships were "very particularly extended ... as many of their rear were not clear of Cape Henry ... advancing very slow." Graves now raised the blue and white checked flag with a white pendant over it, which was the British signal "ye Ships to bear down and engage close." In error his order was confused by the fact that he still flew the "line ahead" signal, which was not taken down for another eight minutes. The two signals were contradictory and some ships, as those in Hood's rear squadron, continued to obey the "line ahead" signal. Graves in the *London* turned toward the French line to engage and others followed. Hood was upset with the spacing that had bunched the vessels too close together. Men on several British ships were bewildered to discover the flagship *London* between them and the enemy ship.[25]

At 4:15 P.M., as the lead ships of the fleets approached within musket range of 120 yards, both fleets opened fire with massive broadside cannonades with as many as 40 guns firing simultaneously. By convention, the French fired at the masts and rigging, trying to disable the enemy vessel for boarding, while the British fired at the hulls of the enemy in the hopes of sinking them. The first victim was the British 74-gun *Shrewsbury* in Drake's squadron, which fought "in a very gallant and spirited manner," but the fire from the French *Pluton* raked her, taking Captain Mark Robinson's leg, and killing his first lieutenant and 13 seamen. Before it was concluded, the *Shrewsbury* lost another 12 men dead and 48 others wounded. Her topmast was shot in three places, her mizzenmast riddled, and she had taken five cannonballs in her hull below the waterline. The ship dropped out of the battle line and signaled distress.

The British *Intrepid* moved up to come to the aid of *Shrewsbury*, only to be met with fierce fire from the 74-gun *Marseillais*. The *Intrepid* took some 64 shots in her starboard side and had to retire out of line. These two ships of Drake's squadron suffered half the British loss in dead and one-third of the wounded primarily because the British were only able to fire their bow guns. Drake's flagship *Princessa* was "shot through in three places; one shot went through the middle of the foremast ... several shot in the side and under the water." The *Alcide* suffered with

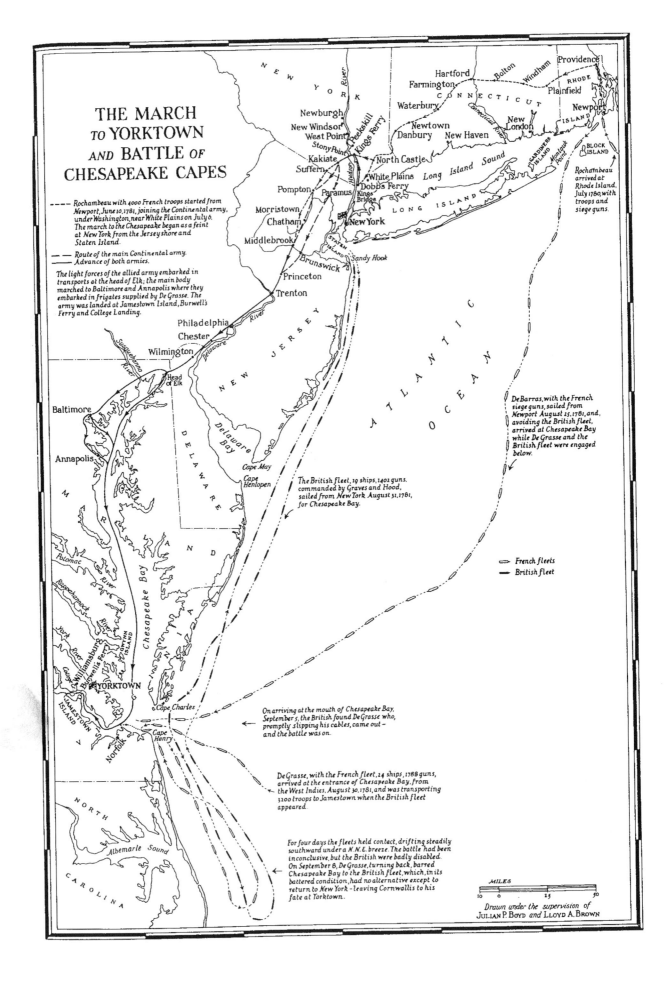

THE MARCH TO YORKTOWN AND BATTLE OF CHESAPEAKE CAPES

- - - - Rochambeau with 4000 French troops started from Newport, June 10, 1781, joining the Continental army, under Washington, near White Plains on July 6. The march to the Chesapeake began as a feint at New York from the Jersey shore and Staten Island.

- - - - Route of the main Continental army.
──── Advance of both armies.

The light forces of the allied army embarked in transports at the head of Elk; the main body marched to Baltimore and Annapolis where they embarked in frigates supplied by De Grasse. The army was landed at Jamestown Island, Burwell's Ferry and College Landing.

Rochambeau arrived at Rhode Island, July 1780, with troops and siege guns.

De Barras, with the French siege guns, sailed from Newport August 25, 1781, and, avoiding the British fleet, arrived at Chesapeake Bay while De Grasse and the British fleet were engaged below.

The British fleet, 19 ships, 1401 guns, commanded by Graves and Hood, sailed from New York August 31, 1781, for Chesapeake Bay.

⇨ French fleets
──── British fleet

On arriving at the mouth of Chesapeake Bay, September 5, the British found De Grasse who, promptly slipping his cables, came out — and the battle was on.

De Grasse, with the French fleet, 24 ships, 1788 guns, arrived at the entrance of Chesapeake Bay, from the West Indies, August 30, 1781, and was transporting 3100 troops to Jamestown when the British fleet appeared.

For four days the fleets held contact, drifting steadily southward under a N.N.E. breeze. The battle had been inconclusive, but the British were badly disabled. On September 8, De Grasse, turning back, barred Chesapeake Bay to the British fleet, which, in its battered condition, had no alternative except to return to New York — leaving Cornwallis to his fate at Yorktown.

MILES
10   0   25   50

Drawn under the supervision of
JULIAN P. BOYD and LLOYD A. BROWN

her "mizzen topmast shot through; one shot through the head of the mainmast; boats wounded by shot; running rigging and sails very much cut; two guns wounded and one dismounted."

The British fleet did not sustain the only damages. The *Princessa* managed to fire her first full broadside into the French *Reflechi*, killing her captain, M. de Boades, and later another officer who died of his wounds. One French onlooker wrote:

> That vessel soon bore away, as well as the *Caton*, on which the English kept up a brisk fire. The four ships of the French van found themselves, consequently, entirely cut off from the rest of the fleet, and constantly engaged with seven or eight vessels at close quarters. The *Diademe* was near Rear Admiral Drake, who set on fire to her at every shot, the wadding entering her side. This vessel was constantly engaged with two and sometimes three ships. The English could not cut off our van, which they might perhaps have taken, and they would, at all events, have rendered past repair. They contented themselves simply with cutting up that part of our fleet which kept up a distant fight.
>
> The *Diademe* was utterly unable to keep up the battle, having only four thirty-six-pounders and nine eighteen-pounders fit for use, and all on board killed, wounded, or burnt. At this juncture M. de Chabert, commanding the *Saint-Esprit*, which had for a long time been engaged with the British admiral, and who was himself wounded, seeing the imminent danger of the *Diademe*, hoisted sail and was soon in her wake; then he opened a terrible fire, that the gentlemen of Albion could not stand, and had to haul their wind.

The battle continued as Commodore de Bougainville with the *Auguste* came in close and almost boarded her, as Drake moved away. Then turning for the leaky *Terrible*, de Bougainville was able to send two French cannonballs through her foremast. The commodore noted in his journal that his flagship had shot 684 cannonballs during the battle and received 54 British shots in her own hull and 70 in the sails. The French ship had also lost 10 killed and 58 wounded. Captain D'Albert de Rions reported that his ship, the *Pluton*, had its masts and rigging damaged "prodigiously." The *Diademe* "had lost one hundred and twenty men and had no sails or rigging, having received one hundred and twenty-five balls in her hull and twelve under the waterline." Several other French ships, including the *Caton*, reported distress but were able to repair the damage after the battle.

Up to this point in the afternoon, all the fighting had occurred between the lead units of the fleets. Finally at 5 P.M. the center divisions came into contact, and general

firing commenced. The first two ships in the British center, *Europe* and *Montagu*, suffered severely. The *Europe*, now leaking, lost her rigging, masts and many gun carriages and had her hull shot full of holes. She also lost 27 casualties. The *Montagu* had sustained 30 casualties and dropped out of the line "in great danger of losing her masts, which might fall at any moment."

The remaining ships in the British line suffered less, being further from the van. The next ship in the line, the *Royal Oak*, had no casualties and was struck only 17 times. The flagship *London* had "one large shot through the mainmast and two in the foremast; a number of shot in the side … sails and rigging much cut; four men killed and eighteen wounded." The next four ships of the line, the *Bedford*, *Resolution*, *Centaur* and *Monarch*, had little damage. As it turned out, only 12 of the 19 British ships were in the battle engagement and only eight were in significant action. The French engaged 15 ships in the battle.

At 5:25 P.M. the ships of the rear were nearly in range of each other. Several French shots came over the British *Barfleur*. At 5:55 P.M. Hood opened up from the *Barfleur* and *Monarch*, but he was too far away to cause damage. Hood tried for 35 minutes to damage the French ships, but at 6:30 P.M. Graves pulled down the engagement signal flag and the battle was over. Now sailing at sunset, the two fleets were cruising in parallel tracks seaward some ten miles southeast of Cape Henry.[26]

The British fleet was battered. It had lost 90 killed and 246 wounded. Graves had sent two frigates, the *Fortunee* and *Solebay*, to survey the damage to his fleet and communicate the sailing orders for the British fleet. The news came back at 10 P.M. when the *Fortunee* returned to reveal that the *Shrewsbury*, *Intrepid* and *Montagu* could no longer sail in a line. The *Terrible* was barely afloat, the *Ajax* was leaking, and the *Princessa* was ready to lose her main topmast. Graves wrote, "the French had not the appearance of near so much damage as we sustained." The French had 209 casualties but much less physical ship damage. The French account revealed the condition that night:

> The fleet passed the night in the presence of the enemy in line of battle, the fires in all the vessels lighted. These signs of victory were not belied in the morning, for we perceived by the sailing of the English that they had suffered greatly.

The early morning of September 6 came with the fleets sailing southeast in "moderate and clear" weather. The numerical shortage of five ships at the beginning now

Opposite: **The March to Yorktown and the Battle of the Chesapeake Capes.** (*Atlas of American History.*)

had essentially been doubled because of the battle. Under these conditions Graves was uninterested in engaging the French on this day. The British fleet was busy repairing the damaged vessels and "in changing their topmasts, and one seemed to have a damaged mainmast." Captain Everett approached Rear Admiral Hood with a message from Rear Admiral Graves asking Hood of his opinion of whether the battle should be renewed. Hood answered coldly, "I dare say Mr. Graves will do what is right. I can send no opinion, but whenever he, Mr. Graves wishes to see me, I will wait upon him with great pleasure."

That evening Graves called a meeting aboard the *London* with Hood and Drake to discuss the situation. The *London Political and Military Journal* published in 1782 revealed the conversation that occurred that night. Graves asked why Hood did not bear and engage, which was answered by Hood, "You had up the signal for the line." Graves turned to Drake, who indicated that he had come to bear because of the signal for action. Graves responded, "What say you to this, Admiral Hood?" Hood exclaimed: "The signal for the line was enough for me." The day soon ended with de Grasse's fleet seven to eight miles away from the British fleet, continuing to bear away from Chesapeake Bay.

On September 7 the two fleets continued to sail in parallel lines. Admiral de Grasse sent several messages to de Bougainville, the second of which said:

> If the wind continues and the English do not escape us tonight, we shall meet them at closer range tomorrow morning, and I hope the day will be a happier one, which will permit us to go back and take those Johnnies in the Chesapeake. What a joy it will be to have the ships of De Barras united with ours! What a body blow that will be, and decisive, too, instead of this uncertain state of affairs where the forces are only equal and poorly manned. I have great hopes based upon the damages to the enemy which I can see. I judged by them that they are not as well-outfitted as we are, and by the slowness of their movements that they are not as ready for battle.

The wind "came onto blow pretty fresh" with some thunderstorms and lightning, according to Graves on the dawn of the 8th. Hood visited Graves at 7 A.M. for a short discussion. By 11:00 A.M. the sea was quite rough and soon the *Terrible* flew a distress signal, as the *Orpheus* and *Fortunee* came to her aid. By now the French had the windward advantage and were tacking to maintain this advantage. That evening Graves wrote, "At night about an hour after the fleet had been wore together, the *Intrepid* made a signal to speak with the admiral, upon which the fleet was brought to, and I was soon informed that her main topmast was gone over the side and they expected the fore-yard would go at every minute. These repeated misfortunes in sight of a superior enemy who kept us all

extended and in motion, filled the mind with anxiety and put us in a condition not to be envied."[27]

By the morning of September 9, the wind favored the British, but now the two fleets were slowly drifting apart. By now both the French and British were beginning to be concerned about the anchorage in Chesapeake Bay. Commodore de Bougainville wrote in his journal:

> I was very much afraid that the British might try to get to the Chesapeake … ahead of us. It is what we ought to have been doing since the battle: that is, our very best to get back into that bay, recover our ships, barges and boats…. Perhaps we would also find the squadron of M. de Barras."

As nightfall came de Grasse reached the same conclusion as de Bougainville and others. He ordered his fleet to turn and set sail for Chesapeake Bay. Rear Admiral Hood became alarmed as he watched the sails of the French ships bellow and soon disappear over the horizon. Hood grumbled, "I was distressed that Mr. Graves did not carry all the sail he could also, and endeavour to get to Chesapeake before him; it appeared to me to be a measure of the utmost importance to keep the French out, and if they did get in they should first beat us."

As morning came Hood wrote Graves:

> I flatter myself you will forgive the liberty I take in asking whether you have any knowledge where the French fleet is, as we can see nothing of it from the *Barfleur*…. I am inclined to think his aim is the Chesapeake…. If he should enter the Bay … will he not succeed in giving most effectual succour to the rebels?[28]

Graves responded by calling another conference aboard the *London*. When Hood arrived he was astonished to find Graves "as ignorant as myself where the French fleet was." The problem Graves had now was the slowly sinking *Terrible*. By September 10 the *Terrible* was taking on water at the rate of eight feet per hour. By then the crew had thrown overboard five lower-deck cannons. At this point the captain declared, "We make too much to give us any great hopes of being able to carry her into port." An eight-man survey party led by First Lieutenant Richard Nash concluded that it was "absolutely impracticable to carry her into port" and confirmed this opinion.

The issue was settled on the 11th when Graves called another council with Hood and Drake, when Graves revealed that "We are of the opinion to take out People and sink her." Accordingly, after the officers signed a statement that she was in a hopeless condition, the *Terrible* was stripped of her cannon, powder and crew. In the early darkness the last man to leave the *Terrible* opened her two-inch sea cock in the hull and set flame to her old oak.

The ship burned, then exploded, as it drifted away from the British fleet. At 9 P.M. Graves finally set sail toward the Chesapeake and sent Captain Duncan's *Medea* ahead to reconnoiter the bay.

At 11 A.M. on September 10 the lead ships in de Grasse's fleet came into sight of Cape Henry. According to de Loture:

> Behind the point of land there appeared the high masts of ships. They were at anchor, close to the entrance of the bay, twenty vessels of good size, approximately the number in Graves' fleet. Immediately orders were given to clear for action, and the Commodores of De Grasse's squadrons waited for the word to form a line of battle. But if it were only De Barras!
>
> Already a frigate had been sent ahead, with the recognition signal flying from its mainmast. Bravo! There, on one of the ships in the distance, the signal agreed-upon is unfurled. It is indeed De Barras, who, finding the way open, had entered in the nick of time with his eight warships and the ten vessels of his convoy carrying the siege train.

As it had turned out, de Barras had avoided the British by heading far out to sea, coming south of Albemarle Sound, and then circling back toward the Chesapeake. Aware of the battle of September 5, de Barras had been unable to distinguish the nationalities of the ships engaged, however. He had considered his highest objective to head for the bay, which he had accomplished and thereby had been able to "gain the anchorage before nightfall." As the French had arrived earlier than expected, they were able to surprise and capture the British frigates *Iris* and *Richmond* as they were engaged in "cutting the cables attaching the anchors to the [French] buoys...."

On the morning of September 13, Captain Duncan of the *Medea* returned to Rear Admiral Graves that the French fleet was back in their anchorage in the bay, and curiously making no reference to the number of French warships there. That morning Graves wrote Hood for his advice, asking, "Admiral Graves presents his compliments to Sir Samuel Hood, and begs leave to acquaint him that the *Medea* had just made the signal to inform him that the French fleet are at anchor above the Horse Shoe in the Chesapeake, and desires his opinion what to do with the fleet?" Hood replied, "Sir Samuel Hood presents his com-

pliments to Rear Admiral Graves, though it is more than what he expected, as the press of sail the fleet carried on the 9th and in the night of the 8th made it very clear to him what de Grasse's intentions were. Sir Samuel would be very glad to send an opinion, but he really knows not what to say in the truly lamentable state we have brought ourself."

Graves then called the final council of war to discuss the situation the British fleet now found itself in. The result of the session was the following resolution, which was signed by the three admirals, Graves, Hood and Drake:

> At a Council of War held on board His Majesty's ship *London* the 13th September, 1781, upon a report from Captain Duncan of his majesty's ship *Medea*, that they had seen the evening before, the French fleet at anchor off the Horseshoe Shoal in the Chesapeake ... Upon this state of the position of the Enemy, the present condition of the British Fleet, the season of the year so near the Equinox, and the impracticability of giving any effectual succour to General Earl Cornwallis in the Chesapeake, It was resolved that the British Squadron under the command of Thomas Graves, Esqr. Rear Admiral of the Red ... should proceed with all dispatch to New York, and there use every possible means for putting the Squadron into the very best state for service.[29]

On September 14 the *Medea* was ordered to sail to England. Captain Duncan landed at Weymouth, England, on October 5, and reached London the same evening with the first news of the infamous sea battle off the Chesapeake Capes. When King George III heard the news he wrote the Earl of Sandwich, "I nearly think the empire ruined ... this cruel event is too recent for me to be as yet able to say more." On September 17 Graves' dispatches to Clinton arrived on a small, fast-sailing packet boat ahead of the British fleet to a waiting crowd of 3000 anxious Tory citizens of New York. The locals saw the dejected looks of the officers as they disembarked. When Graves' fleet arrived on September 19, with ten ships in need of repair and four ships requiring a major refitting, one loyalist, Frederick Mackenzie, wrote, "I fear the fate of the Army in Virginia will be determined before our fleet can get out of the harbour again...." Many loyalist families now began to pack their most cherished possessions.[30]

The fate of Cornwallis at Yorktown was now sealed.

19

YORKTOWN

On September 6, 1781, after Washington reached the Head of Elk, Maryland, a tributary of the upper Chesapeake, he spent two days writing numerous letters to prominent leaders on the Eastern Shore urging them to send boats to carry the troops down the bay. After a conference Washington and Rochambeau decided to send 1200 French and some 800 Americans ahead on the available boats. The force included Lamb's artillery and siege equipment, Lauzan's infantry and "shock" troops of the French regiments. The rest of the army was to march with the generals to Baltimore.

Good news arrived from General Mordecai Gist of Maryland who came to announce that 1800 men had been recruited in the state and were ready to support him at Yorktown. Gist remarked, "They are young, terribly young, but they are lions' whelps and now they are under way. Some are riding, some are sailing, some are walking; they will be there, General, before you are." The morning of September 8 Washington, Rochambeau and Chastellux departed with troops toward Baltimore. Billy Lee, his mulatto servant, and Colonel David Humphreys, his aide, escorted Washington. Washington rode so hard that the French soon fell behind.

In the late afternoon the commander-in-chief approached Baltimore, where he was joined by a company of militia cavalry under Captain Nicholas Moore, a veteran of many earlier campaigns of the war. Cannons fired salutes as crowds on both sides of the streets watched in awe.

Washington rode to the Fountain Inn where he spent the night. The local officials read the general a formal address. Washington responded with a worthy speech. The city was illuminated with candles and torches in his honor.

Before Rochambeau or Chastellux reached Baltimore the next day, Sunday the 9th, Washington was already gone, having left the fair city before daybreak. After riding hard for 60 miles, Washington, with Lee and Humphreys, reached his home on the hill, Mount Vernon, at 6:30 P.M. It had been six years and four months since he had seen it last, when he had ridden off to Philadelphia as a Virginia congressman in the uniform of a retired militia colonel.

Martha and a growing family of four grandchildren by her son, Jacky Custis, greeted the commander-in-chief. Though Washington had ridden hard all day, he dictated a letter to a county militia lieutenant for support in repairing the ruts in the local roads he had encountered on his trip. Before he retired he reviewed the text of the letter with Humphreys and wrote in his journal, "I reached my own Seat at Mount Vernon (distant 120 Miles from the Hd. Of Elk)...." The next day was spent directing the servants, cooks and farm manager in preparing for his visitors. His staff arrived at mealtime, and Rochambeau arrived with his aides several hours later. General Chastellux saw Washington's home as "simple" and his wife as "somewhat fat, but fresh and with a pleasant face."[1]

On September 11 the Washingtons hosted a feast for the French, his own staff and a number of his neighbors. One of Washington's aides, the Connecticut-born Jonathan Trumbull, Jr., found the Mount Vernon plantation splendid: "A numerous family now present. All accommodated. An elegant seat and situation, great appearance of opulence and real exhibitions of hospitality and princely entertainment." Chastellux wrote of the dinner, "tea succeeded dinner, and lasted until supper. The war was frequently the subject...." The French general asked Washington which writings did he find the most instructive about military affairs. Washington replied, "the King of Prussia's Instructions to the Generals, and the Tactics of M. de Guilbert: from whence…." Chastellux responded, "I concluded that he knew as well how to select his authors as to profit by them."[2]

The next morning Washington and all his military guests were on the road from Mount Vernon to Williamsburg. Between the villages of Colchester and Dumfries the general's party was met by a courier from Lafayette with news that de Grasse had departed the Chesapeake blockade as a British fleet had arrived over the horizon. Sounds of gunfire were heard but both fleets had not been seen since September 5. Now ahead of him, Washington's letter to Lafayette was moving over the Virginia lowlands:

> We are thus far, my Dear Marquis, on our way to you. The Count de Rochambeau has just arrived … & we propose (after resting tomorrow) to be at Fredericksburg on the night of the 12th.–the 13th. We shall reach New Castle & the next day we expect the pleasure of seeing you at your encampment.
>
> Should there be any danger as we approach you, I shall be obliged if you will send a party of Horse towards New Kent Court House to meet us….
>
> P.S. I hope you will keep Lord Cornwallis safe, without Provisions or Forage until we arrive. Adieu.[3]

The night of September 12, after a hard day's riding, Washington and Rochambeau bedded down at a tavern in Fredericksburg, Maryland. At dawn Washington pushed ahead, soon leaving many in his party behind in his dust, unable to keep up. Thursday, September 13th came and went as Washington and party headed toward Williamsburg with due haste.

While Washington and his French and American armies marched south, Cornwallis was still sitting at Yorktown preparing his defense. His small fleet had arrived in the blue waters of the York River at Yorktown and Gloucester Point on August 1. The York River ran 20 miles inland, and was affected by the tides of the Chesapeake Bay, which ran at nine miles an hour. As the Queen's Rangers under Colonel John along with the 43rd Infantry Regiment and the German regiments went ashore at Yorktown, they were joyous to be off the transports. One German soldier, Johann Doehla, who kept a diary, wrote of "such astonishing heat that it could scarcely be endured on the ships." That first day, and for three days after, all spent the day on the beach sand without tents.

The quaint village of Yorktown, resting on the south bank of the York, was founded on land owned by the earliest known ancestor of George Washington, Nicholas Martiau, in 1691. In 1736, when the town was flourishing in the tobacco trade as the primary port on the Chesapeake Bay, an English visitor wrote, "You perceive a great air of opulence among the Inhabitants, who have some … Houses equal in Magnificence to many of our superb ones at St. James." Nicholas Creswell, an English visitor to America in the early days of the Revolution, wrote of Yorktown as "a pleasant town situated upon the York River which is navigable for the largest ships. Close to the town there are several very Gentlemen's houses built of brick and some of their gardens laid out with the greatest taste of any I have seen in America."[4] Yorktown was also described in a letter home from a German soldier:

> This Yorktown, or Little-York, is a small city of approximately 300 houses; it has, moreover, considerable circumference. It is located on the bank of the York River, somewhat high on a sandy but level ground. It has 3 churches, 2 reformed English and 1 German Lutheran, but without steeples, and 2 Quaker meeting houses, and a beautiful court or meeting house, which building, like the majority of the houses, is built of bricks. Here stood many houses which were destroyed and abandoned by their occupants. There was a garrison of 300 militia men here, but upon our arrival they marched away without firing a shot back to Williamsburg, which is 16 English miles from here. We found few inhabitants here, as they had mostly gone with bag and baggage into the country beyond.

The next 20 years had seen the economy of Yorktown decay, and most of the tobacco trade had moved to the other ports of Virginia. By 1781 most of the local merchants had moved inland for safety, as the area was an attractive place for British raids. The population was not over some 3000 inhabitants. Across the York River, one-half mile away, was the smaller village of Gloucester. It contained some dozen or so houses located on level ground. Cornwallis occupied Gloucester too in order to prevent the Americans from mounting cannonades across the river at Yorktown.

When Cornwallis disembarked at Yorktown on August 2 in the early humid morning, he moved up the steep hill to establish his headquarters in the finest home in view on the southeastern side of the town, the Thomas Nelson home. Nelson, the former Virginia secretary of the legislature, was in his 70s and still living in the house as his lordship took possession. The house was described by a visitor as being a "handsome house from which neither European taste nor luxury was excluded. The chimney piece and some bas reliefs of very fine marble were particularly admired." Nelson, who had not taken sides in the war, was treated with much respect by Cornwallis and his staff.[5]

In the heat of late summer of August and September in 1781 at Yorktown and Gloucester, Cornwallis' troops and blacks sweated in building the defensive works and fortifications around both towns. The plan for York-town called for inner and outer fortifications, each running in a semi-circle from east of the town to the west. The outer defensive works were about a half-mile out from the inner one. To the west was a ravine that extended from the river to "nearly half way around the inner works." Behind this ran Yorktown Creek along marshy ground. Wormley Creek ran about half a mile to the west of the ravine and was "curved slightly northeasterly." These natural features of the area served to provide Cornwallis some protection on the flanks of his outer works.

Though Cornwallis was afforded some natural protection, defending the Yorktown area with the troops he had would be extremely difficult even with the outer defenses he was currently building. It was simply too much ground to cover. The allied army could reach his place from any of four roads. The road to Williamsburg came from along the river from the west. Nearer the town the road split with one road branching off to intersect with Hampton Road, which ran north into Yorktown between the ravine and Wormley Creek. Coming from the east was the fourth road that came past the home of a local merchant, Augustine Moore.

Cornwallis built several outer fortifications on his left near the head of Wormley Creek. The British constructed the largest outer redoubt on the right near the river and to the right of the Williamsburg Road. In this redoubt he placed the fusiliers manned by the 23rd Regiment. He also anchored several small vessels in the river opposite the fusiliers' redoubt to aid them. Cornwallis' main defensive works were in the center between the ravine and Wormley Creek.

Around Yorktown's inner defensive works, Cornwallis constructed ten redoubts. Two were facing the river road from Williamsburg, three were in the back of the town, and three more were left along the river. The two most important redoubts, numbers 9 and 10, were positioned out from the other redoubts on the left. These were the two mostly likely locations on level ground for any allied attack. Cornwallis then placed 65 cannons in his 14 batteries along his earthen works. Most of the cannons were light field pieces. The heaviest artillery were 18-pounders that had come from the available ships.[6]

The British fortified Gloucester by constructing a log palisade from the point of a small triangular fort and a line of earthen works along the bluffs. The nearly 3000 blacks who had flocked to aid Cornwallis did most of the work at Gloucester and Yorktown. Regardless, Cornwallis suffered a number of desertions from his army and most especially from the Germans. On August 10, four men of the Bayreuth Regiment deserted and soon others followed. The British and Hessian troops suffered at Yorktown. Men were dying each day and one Hessian wrote,

"we get terrible provisions now, putrid ship's meat and wormy biscuits that have spoiled on the ships. Many of the men have taken sick here with dysentery or the bloody flux and with diarrhea. Also the foul fever is spreading, partly on account of the many hardships from which we have had little rest day or night, and partly on account of the wretched food; but mostly the nitre-bearing water is to blame for it."[7] A staff officer of Lafayette wrote of the British efforts with the work, "Lord Cornwallis neither pushes his works with rapidity on the land or water side. Like some of the heroes in romance, he appears to despise armour and to confide in his own natural strength." The heat was taking its toll.

It was not until August 10 that Cornwallis had received all the cavalry at Yorktown. Tarleton's dragoons arrived, having crossed Hampton Roads in flat boats, and then forcing their horses to swim in deep water to the peninsula shore. From there, Tarleton's cavalry rode across the peninsula, raiding as he went, toward Yorktown. Now Cornwallis had an opportunity to gather needed intelligence about his area situation with Lafayette's forces. With the arrival of all the troops from Portsmouth, Cornwallis' garrison consisted of over 7000 men.

Work on the Yorktown and Gloucester fortifications had continued when the news of the arrival of de Grasse's fleet came. The critical news arrived on August 29 when the British 28-gun *Guadeloupe* left Yorktown with dispatches from Cornwallis in the morning tide. Soon in the bay, the captain of the *Guadeloupe* saw a fleet of large ships to the southeast giving strange signals. He turned the ship around and fled back to Yorktown to warn his lordship. The news eliminated the rather leisurely trench digging, as Bayreuth Hessian Corporal Stephan Popp recorded, "We hardly have time for eating. Often we had to eat raw meat."

On August 31, Cornwallis sent the schooner *Mary* with dispatches to Clinton including the news of the French fleet. Clinton read the message from Cornwallis, coded in cipher on American Continental notes, five days later in New York. It read, "An enemy's fleet within the Capes, between thirty and forty ships of war, mostly large." Lord Cornwallis sent dispatches via small boats slipping past the French fleet almost every day after that with continuing news of the actions of the French and soon the arrival of the British fleet on September 5. The tempo picked up for the British and Hessians at Yorktown and Gloucester.

Cornwallis was concerned about the naval events, but he had every reason to believe that the blockade would soon be lifted and he would receive fresh troops. He reassured his men that the French troops of Saint-Simon who had reinforced Lafayette were "raw and sickly" and rather undisciplined from the West Indies, and "enervated

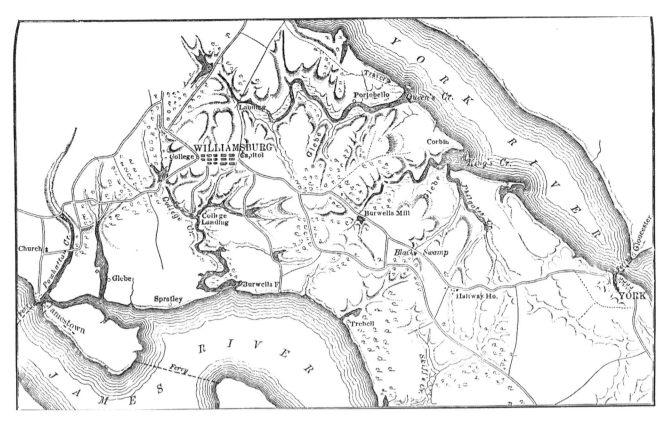

Section of the first United States survey of the Virginia Peninsula, 1818, showing topography and landings of 1781. (*Battles of the American Revolution*, map by Major James Kearney.)

by a hot climate" and would not be able to deal with the Virginia winter. On September 1 four French warships sailed up the York River and anchored two miles below the town, blocking the channel. The following day saw the sailors from the British fleet begin digging trenches that faced the river to guard against naval attack. His lordship tried to gain more intelligence about the naval situation by sending out the Legion to the shores of the James and York rivers to report all they could.

On September 2, Cornwallis received a dispatch from Clinton that revealed a fateful threat to the British at Yorktown and Gloucester: "it would seem that Mr. Washington is moving an army to the southward…. Your Lordship … may be assured that … I shall … reinforce the army under your Command." As preparation continued and Cornwallis contemplated his situation, the British heard the mysterious cannon fire from outside the capes on September 5. [8]

With de Barras' French fleet entering the bay on the night of September 5, soon to be joined by de Grasse on the 10th, the outcome of the naval situation was becoming clear to his lordship. Coupled with Clinton's warning that the allied army was on the way to Virginia, Cornwallis realized that he was in a most difficult situation as mid–September arrived. The earl considered the possibility of fighting Lafayette's army before the allied army

arrived. He ordered Tarleton's Legion to scout the Americans and to "use every expedient to obtain exact intelligence of their number." Tarleton, with three officers and six men from his Legion, scouted in the vicinity of Lafayette's headquarters on the grounds of the College of William and Mary in Williamsburg. He returned with the intelligence and urged a surprise attack along the main street in Williamsburg. He argued that the attack would scatter Lafayette's troops and allow the British to escape. That same night a female spy also revealed to Cornwallis of Lafayette's strength and disposition. Cornwallis was now convinced that the British should indeed break out of Yorktown.

Cornwallis and his staff had devised two schemes for the break out. The first plan called for the army to move down to Williamsburg before daybreak, and by using the natural terrain near the former capital, to advance with limited exposure to patriot discovery and gunfire. The second plan called for a two-prong attack on the Americans from the front and rear. One group of 2500 men in small vessels would move up the York River to Queen's Creek, a stream above Williamsburg, and advance up to the town. The main army would advance directly on the American front, converging with the first group in the rear of the enemy at the same time. Cornwallis weighed both plans and decided to execute the first plan. The second plan required too much coordination and good timing to be successful.

As Cornwallis worked with his staff to prepare for the breakout attack on Lafayette's post, a dispatch arrived from Clinton on September 14 with news of possible reinforcements from New York. Clinton's words served to change the earl's mind about his future plans and sealed his fate at Yorktown:

> As ... I can have no Doubt that Washington is moving with, at least, 6000 French and rebel Troops against you, I think the best way to relieve you, is to join you as soon as possible, with all the Force that can be spared from hence, which is about 4000 Men. They are already embarked, and will proceed the Instant I receive information from the Admiral that we may venture, and that from other intelligence the Commodore and I shall judge sufficient to move upon.... I beg your Lordship will let me know as soon as possible your ideas how the troops embarked for the Chesapeake may best be best employed for your relief, according to the state of circumstances when you receive this letter. I shall not however wait to receive your answer, should I hear, in the mean time, that the passage is open.[9]

On the same day Cornwallis received his reassurance of support and reinforcement from Sir Henry Clinton, September 14, Washington and Rochambeau rode into Lafayette's camp at Williamsburg. Colonel St. George Tucker described the event: "About four o'clock in the afternoon his approach was announced.... The French line had time to form. The Continentals had more leisure. He approached without any pomp or parade, attended by a few horsemen and his own servants."[10] Washington rode down the dusty streets of Williamsburg past the former Royal Governor's Palace, and came up to the camp of the French West Indian division. As the French officers formed the troops, Lafayette, Governor Thomas Nelson and General Marquis de Saint-Simon rode up between the tents. Lafayette jumped down from his horse and ran to Washington with his arms outstretched. Tucker recorded that Lafayette "caught the General round his body, hugged him as close as it was possible, and absolutely kissed him from ear to ear once or twice ... with as much ardor as ever an absent lover kissed his mistress on his return."

The French regiments poured out of their tents and formed on both sides of the road to see the great American general, who by this time was indeed a legend. After a quick review of the troops, Washington's party moved on to the American camps where he was met by a 21-gun salute. Lafayette's Light Infantry and the Pennsylvania Continentals stood in a line formation.[11] After another troop review, Washington inquired about the status of de Grasse, but sadly there was no news. Later on General

Saint-Simon hosted a dinner in his tent, followed by, according to Colonel Butler, "an elegant band of music played an introductive part of a contemporary French opera *Lucille*, signifying the happiness of the family when blessed with the presence of their father, and their great dependence upon him. About ten o'clock the company rose up, and after mutual congratulations and the greatest expressions of joy, they separated."[12]

Just past Bruton Parish Church, where the commander-in-chief had once joined in prayer with fellow Virginia patriots after the closing of the port of Boston in 1774, Washington made his Williamsburg headquarters at the home of his friend, George Wythe. In a past moment in history, Washington had traveled with Wythe to Congress to sign the Declaration of Independence. The General was to spend the next two weeks in his fine home planning the siege of Yorktown. On an adjacent green near the Wythes, at the handsome frame house of widowed Mrs. Peyton Randolph, Rochambeau made his headquarters.[13]

As midnight approached a courier came riding up with news that de Grasse was back in Chesapeake Bay and the British fleet had returned to New York. The next day Claude Blanchard, the French commissary, arrived in camp and brought additional insight into the naval engagement, which de Grasse had modestly called "only an encounter between two advance guards." Apparently Washington believed this was the case, as he wrote in his journal about the "partial engagement ... with Admiral Graves whom he [de Grasse] had driven back to Sandy Hook." It was apparent to all the generals that this was the golden opportunity the allied army had been looking for. It would be critical to take advantage of the circumstance now before Clinton could send another relief fleet to help Cornwallis. But there was one major problem. The men of the allied army were still far away up the Chesapeake.[14]

Washington moved quickly to action. On the 15th he sent Axel Fersen northward to order the boats on the upper Chesapeake to begin sailing to Virginia. General George Weedon and his militia were sent to keep a watchful eye on the British at Gloucester to prevent Cornwallis from escaping across the river. Picket boats were ordered to guard the upper York River by night so there would be no escape up the river. He sent word to General Lincoln in Baltimore that "every day we now lose is comparatively an age. As soon as it is in our power with safety, we ought to take our position near the enemy. Hurry on, then, my dear Sir, with your troops on the wings of speed...."

Washington wrote to de Grasse on September 15 asking to visit the admiral on his flagship. He wished to convince de Grasse of the necessity to remain in the Chesapeake until Cornwallis and his army had been taken.

Washington also issued general orders congratulating the troops regarding the current situation at hand and dined that night with Lafayette and his officers. The next day he rode toward Yorktown with aides to reconnoiter the British lines in person. He was to learn rather little about Cornwallis' actual condition. He also spent time reviewing General Nelson's Virginia Militia. After the review of the ragged troops, he sent word to Richmond urging them to acquire uniforms for the militia.

Washington felt it was important that the situation with Baron Von Steuben and his detractors be resolved. While the Prussian had tangled with Virginia State officials and Lafayette himself, he was the most experienced officer in siege warfare in the combined army. So Washington made a quick move and reinstated the baron as the inspector general of the army. Immediately Steuben ordered that the drilling of the troops should begin. Ensign Ebenezer Denny wrote of these days of renewed discipline: "The guards are told off; officers take their posts, wheel by platoons to the right; fine corps of music … strikes up; the whole march off, saluting the Baron and field officer of the day as they pass." In spite of some faults, the baron was a true patriot who had sacrificed for his men and America. The man was now a pauper, having spent all his money on the army. He asked Washington for a month's pay in coin but it was an impossible request. The baron was forced to sell some of his silver spoons in order to feed one of his aides who had become ill. His last dollars were spent entertaining the French and American officers with "a great dinner."[15]

De Grasse sent a boat to pick up Washington. On September 17, Washington, Rochambeau, Henry Knox and several aides including his secretary, Jonathan Trumbull, rowed out from Archer's Hope Landing to board the captured British cutter *Queen Charlotte* and sailed down the James River in a hearty wind. The next morning Trumbull wrote of reaching the French fleet:

> Come early in the Morng. In View of the Fleet — a grand Sight! 32 Ships of the Line in Lynn Haven Bay just under the point of Cape Henry, about 60 miles from where we had first embarked — get alongside the Admiral about 12 o'clock — go on board — received with great Ceremony & Military Naval Parade — & most cordially welcomed. The Admiral a remarkable Man for Size, Appearance & plainness of Address — with Compliments over, Business is proposed & soon dispatched to great Satisfaction; after which Dinner is served & then we view the ship & see her Batteries & accommodations — a noble prospect — the World in miniature. After receiving the Compliments of the Officers of the fleet, who are almost all come on Board the Admiral's ship, we take our Leave about Sunset to go on Board our little Ship — saluted by the Admiral's Guns, & the Manning of all the Ships of the fleet, who from the Yards Tops & etc. give us their several Feu de Joyes — or Vive Le Roy."[16]

The meeting aboard the *Ville de Paris* had been a grand affair. When Washington was greeted with a kiss on both cheeks by the shorter de Grasse, the admiral remarked, "My dear little General!" The American officers roared with laughter. The "business" part of the gathering had been directed by a list of written questions that Washington had brought with him. To the question of how long would he stay, de Grasse responded: "The Instructions of Count de Grasse fix his departure to the 15th of October…. But having already taken much upon himself, he will also engage to stay to the end of October." The issue of Saint-Simon's troops came up and de Grasse declared, "as my Vessels will not depart before the 1st of November, you may count upon those Troops to that period, for the Reduction of York." Washington then turned to various questions of supplies and logistics. He had asked if the admiral would consider blockading Charles Town and Wilmington, which de Grasse declined.

Meanwhile, at this time the main army that had marched down through Baltimore, was camped at Annapolis, Maryland. The advance force that had sailed from Head of Elk had encountered rough waters, and had also moved to Annapolis. Frigates from de Grasse's fleet met the army and on September 18, they sailed out of the port and headed southward down the Chesapeake toward Williamsburg via the James River. Scammell's Light Infantry was the first unit to arrive by ship and they disembarked at College Landing, only one mile from Williamsburg on Archer's Hope Creek. The trip was not without hazards, as Scammell's vessel ran aground and remained there until 8 A.M. on September 20, when they were boarded on a smaller boat and transported to the ultimate landing site in heavy headwinds. The French army landed in the vicinity at Jamestown Island, and at Burwell's Ferry, a mile below Archer's Hope Creek. The stores and equipment were unloaded at Trebell's Landing, some three miles below Burwell's Ferry. All the troops offloaded and were in Williamsburg by September 21. Some of the more unfortunate men had spent 14 days on board ships.[17]

As Washington's party had set out aboard the *Queen Charlotte* back on September 18 after seeing de Grasse, a cold wind came up blowing toward the sea, making it very difficult to make headway. The wind settled down eventually. Later the wind returned and served to help the cutter run aground. Washington spent the night of September 19 on a sandbar in the James River. The next morning Washington and Rochambeau were transferred to the frigate *Andromaque* and had breakfast before sailing upriver. Soon after getting underway they came upon the *Queen Charlotte* and they returned to her. Washington went to his cabin to write some letters but the severe rocking of the boat made the effort useless. Soon the cutter was forced to move nearer the shore to ride out the storm. On the morning of September 21 the wind was still raging as Washington insisted that the captain resume the trip. But it was impossible to move upriver and again Washington's party spent another day and night in the storm-tossed river. That day Washington was cheered to see the scores of flatboats and schooners at anchor at Hampton Roads with Lincoln's Chesapeake troops aboard.

Under gray skies on September 22 Washington left the *Queen Charlotte* and was transported by a smaller open boat, which was rowed the 30 miles toward Williamsburg. Finally at noon the general reached College Creek where he and his party landed and rode to Williamsburg. The fatigued Washington was delighted to hear that the British had not stirred while he had been gone. This trip to see de Grasse for six hours had cost him four and one-half days. The only pro–British news came in that same day to Washington's headquarters. The courier's message from the north indicated that British Admiral Robert Digby had arrived at the Chesapeake with three to ten warships. Washington was not concerned and he remarked that Digby's coming could not "have any influence on our operations while there are thirty-six French ships of the line in the Bay." The messenger was sent to warn de Grasse by Baron von Closen.[18]

When Baron von Closen arrived aboard the *Ville de Paris* he was surprised to find that the news had "alarmed and disquieted these excitable gentlemen of the navy, who think only of cruises and battles, and do not like to oblige or to cooperate with land troops." Admiral de Grasse's officers urged him to leave the bay before the British caught them at the mercy of the tide. Baron von Closen hurried back to Washington with the admiral's dispatch, which read:

> I will sail with my forces toward New York.... If the enemy do not come out, it is evident because they dare not. We shall then consider what course to pursue. In the meantime you will push Cornwallis vigorously, and we will act in concert, each on his own side. I shall set sail as soon as the wind permits.

Washington was shocked by de Grasse's dispatch. Why was it so difficult to impress upon de Grasse how important this blockade was? Frantically Washington called for a meeting with Rochambeau. Quickly the commander-in-chief called for John Laurens, who had just returned from France. To Laurens Washington dictated the following letter to de Grasse:

> "I cannot conceal from your Excellency the painful anxiety under which I have labored since the receipt of the letter with which you honored me on the 23rd inst.... Give me leave in the first place to repeat to your Excellency that the enterprise against York under the protec-

tion of your Ships is as certain as any military operation can be rendered by a decisive superiority of strength and means that it is in fact reducible to calculation —& that the surrender of the British Garrison will be so important itself and in its consequences; and that it must necessarily go a great way toward terminating the war, and securing the invaluable objects of it to the Allies.

> Your Excellency's departure from the Chesapeake by affording an opening for the Succor of York, which the Enemy would instantly avail himself of would frustrate these brilliant prospects, and the consequence would be not only the disgrace and loss of renouncing an enterprise upon which the fairest expectations of the allies have been founded after the most extensive preparations and uncommon exertions and fatigues, but the disbanding perhaps of the whole Army for want of provisions. The present theater of the war is totally deficient in means of land transportation, being intersected by large rivers and its whole dependence for interior communications being upon small vessels. The Country has been so exhausted besides the ravages of the enemy, and the subsistence of our army that our supplies can only be drawn from a distance and under cover of a fleet Mistress of the Chesapeake. I most earnestly entreat your Excellency rather to consider that if the present opportunity should be missed, that if you withdraw your maritime force from the position agreed upon, that no future day can restore to us a similar occasion for striking a decisive blow — that the British will be indefatigable in strengthening their most important maritime points; and that the epoch of an honorable peace will be more remote than ever....

Washington met with Rochambeau and the French general agreed with Washington fully. They both agreed that the best man to carry the appeal to de Grasse was Lafayette. Fortunately for all, the malaria that plagued Lafayette had left him now. So Washington gave the letter to his trusted Lafayette and with Baron von Closen they departed for the frigate *Richmond* at College Landing. By morning they were in the bay, being led by the frigate *Iris* out to the supposed anchorage of de Grasse. But the French fleet was not in sight. The captain reassured Lafayette that the admiral would not leave without word to them. The frigates sailed on another 12 hours and found the French fleet anchored at the mouth of the York River.

On board the *Ville de Paris* Lafayette and von Closen were to learn that the naval captains under de Grasse had totally vetoed the plan to leave the Chesapeake Bay. The only discomfort now was felt by Lafayette, who thought it was a mistake to have the French fleet only blockading the York River, leaving the James River open for a British troop landing or reinforcement. After some discussion de Grasse agreed with Lafayette and he moved his fleet back to Lynnhaven Bay at the mouth of the Chesapeake. With the French fleet secure in the bay, the land siege was the focus of attention. On receiving the news that de Grasse was staying in the Chesapeake, Washington exclaimed the "resolution that your Excellency has taken in our Circumstances proves that a great Mind knows how to make personal Sacrifices to secure an important general Good." Rochambeau wrote to the admiral, "You are the most amiable admiral I know. You meet all our wishes, and I believe we are going to turn this into a good business."

On September 27 Washington issued his orders indicating that the allied army would march the following day to Yorktown to engage Cornwallis. In the general orders the commander-in-chief gave his troops a full measure of the possibilities of the next day:

> The General particularly enjoins the troops to place their principal reliance on the Bayonet, that they may prove the Vanity of the boast which the British make of their particular prowess in deciding Battles with that Weapon.... generous Emulation will actuate the Allied Armies.... The Justice of the cause in which we are engaged and the Honor of the Two Nations must inspire every breast with sentiments that are the presage of Victory.

The veteran Sergeant Joseph Plumb Martin wrote of the events,

> We prepared to move down and pay our old acquaintance, the British, at Yorktown, a visit. I doubt not but their wish was not to have so many of us come at once as their accommodations were rather scanty. They thought, "the fewer the better cheer." We thought, "the more the merrier." We had come a long way to see them and were unwilling to be put off with excuses.[19]

At five o'clock on September 28 the allied armies started the 11-mile march under fair skies and warm temperatures. The American Continentals led the advance followed by the French formation. Only a force of 200 troops remained in Williamsburg under Claude Blanchard to guard the 300 sick and wounded in camp. Ahead of the French column was found the Marquis Saint-Simon, who was struggling with malaria and being carried in a litter. The American militia had moved farther to the right, going past Harwood's Mills, but joined the Continentals at Munford's Bridge.

The forces halted at noon for several hours as the meal fires were lit. After lunch the march was continued and near Half-way House on the "great road" from Williamsburg, the French moved off to the left directly to Yorktown as the Americans headed off toward the right. The French came within sight of Yorktown at around 3 P.M. The leading scouts ran into British pickets who fired some volleys and hastily moved back. The French took up their positions on the edge of a wood, along a creek bank. On their left the formation was on a high bank on the York, while the right ended at the American position at a marsh edge.

The Americans moved into positions on the south of town in front of a swamp. Tarleton's Legion cavalry came out and rode across the front of the Americans. They were turned back by some rounds of grapeshot, and retired to Moore House below the town. As the allies moved in, the British troops in the trenches were shocked by the display of the strength of the forces before them. One soldier wrote: "The whole camp was in alarm. Tents were hastily removed and all the baggage taken into the town." British Lieutenant James was likewise impressed, "At noon the enemy appeared in front of our works, in force about 26,000 extending from right to left of our lines; and a number of them advancing to reconnoiter a ravine in front of my battery. I opened a fire on them until they dispersed." In the late afternoon the allies were settled a mile in front of the British lines. Before he retired Washington was impatient to reconnoiter the British positions on his new white-legged horse, Nelson. After surveying the situation, Washington ordered up the heavy cannon. Everyone spent that night in the open. The headquarters tents did not arrive in time and Washington spent the night sleeping under a mulberry tree. The night was surprisingly calm and the troops were in good spirits. Dr. Thacher wrote in his diary, "unbounded confidence in our ... commanders...."[20]

The next morning at seven o'clock the American army changed positions by moving across the marsh in their front, and then moved to the right, to end up closer to the British redoubts. During the movement the British gunners opened fire at the exposed infantry and managed to wound one soldier severely in the leg with a cannonball. Now the siege army was in place to engage Cornwallis. French and American forces had formed a full semi-circle around the British and were ready. Washington's memorandum for the 29th read,

> Moved the American troops more to the right, and encamped on the east side of Beaverdam Creek, with a morass in front, about cannon-shot from the enemy's lines — spent this day in reconnoitering the enemy's position, and determining upon a plan of attack, and approach which must be done without the assistance of the shipping above the Town, as the admiral (notwithstanding my earnest solicitation) declined hazarding any vessels on that station.

The allied army opposite Cornwallis was divided into three components — the American Continentals, the American Militia and the French army. The French held the left portion of the semi-circle under Rochambeau and consisted of seven regiments of infantry totaling 900 men each, an artillery unit of 600 men, and a horse cavalry with around 600 men. The infantry units named Bourbonnois, Royal Deuxponts, Saintonge, Soissonois, Touraine, Agenais and Gatenois were commanded respectively by the

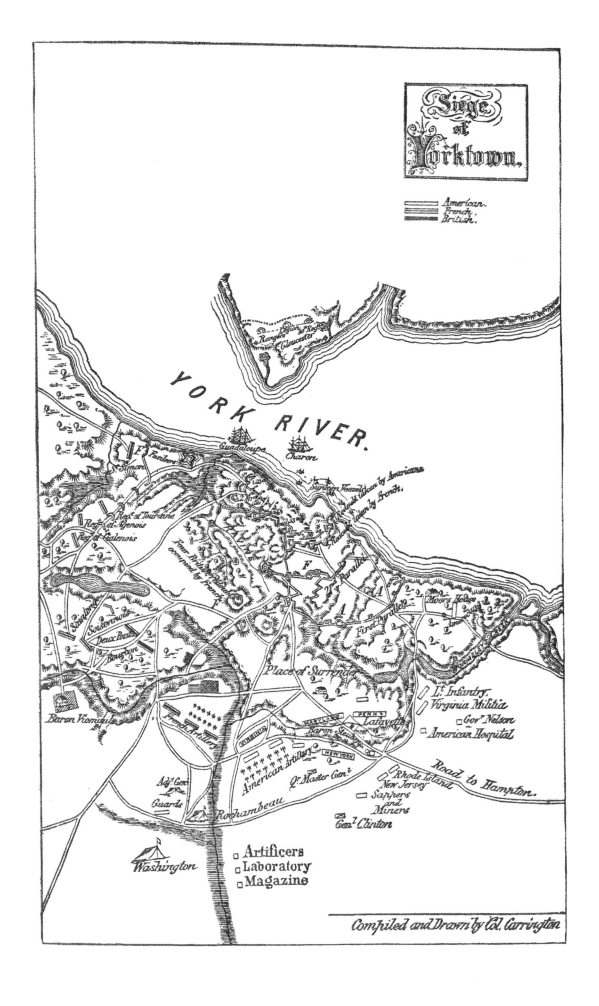

Siege
of
Yorktown.

American.
French.
British.

YORK RIVER.

Rangers
Gloucester

Guadaloupe   Charon

St Simon   F   Fusilers

Reg.t of Touraine
Reg.t of Agenois
Reg.t of Satenois   Ships Vessels taken by Americans
                                       taken by French.

                              F
Saintonge
Soissonois   First Parallel.
Deux Ponts   Moors House
Bourbon

Place of Surrender.   First Parallel.

Baron Viominds.   L.t Infantry.
                                             Virginia Militia
                                             Gor.r Nelson
                              PENN.s   American Hospital
                        MARYLAND   Lafayette
French Artillery   VIRGINIA Baron Steuben
                                   NEW YORK
                  American Artillery   Road to Hampton.
Adj.t Gen.l   Qr. Master Gen.l   Rhode Island
Guards   New Jersey
        Rochambeau   Sappers
                                                     and
                                             Gen.l Clinton   Miners

Washington   ☐ Artificers
                  ☐ Laboratory
                  ☐ Magazine

Compiled and Drawn by Col. Carrington

colonels Marquis de Laval, M. Guillaume de Deux-ponts, M. Custine, Viscount de Noailles, Viscount de Pondeux, Marquis d'Audechamp and Marquis de Rostaing. The French major generals included Baron de Viomenil, the Viscount de Viomenil, the Chevalier de Chastellux and the Marquis de Saint-Simon, with Brigadier M. de Choisy. The Baron de Viomenil, Antoine Charles du Houx, was Rochambeau's second in command.

The American Continentals were positioned in the center, with Beaverdam Creek separating them from the French positions on their left. They were organized at Williamsburg as three divisions under major generals Lincoln, Lafayette and Steuben with two brigades each. Lincoln's First Brigade of 675 troops under General James Clinton was made up of the First and Second New York regiments under colonels Van Schaick and Van Cortlandt. The 1050-man Second Brigade under Colonel Elias Dayton had Colonel Jeremiah Olney's Rhode Island Regiment, and the two New Jersey regiments under Colonel Mathias Ogden.

Lafayette's Light Infantry Division consisted of the First Brigade of 700 men under Brigadier General Peter Muhlenberg, supported by Colonel Joseph of Massachusetts, lieutenant colonel Gimat from Connecticut and Lieutenant Colonel Francis Barber from New Jersey. Lafayette's Second Brigade commanded by Brigadier General Moses Hazen included some 800 men in four battalions under lieutenant colonels Ebenezer Huntington, Alexander Hamilton, John Laurens and Edward Antill. Steuben commanded the brigades under generals Wayne and Gist. The First Brigade of 900 troops was made up of Colonel Walter Stewart's First Pennsylvania Battalion, Colonel Richard Butler's Second Pennsylvania Battalion and the Virginia Battalion under Lieutenant Colonel Thomas Gaskins. Gist's Second Brigade of 1000 troops was made up of the Third Maryland Regiment under Lieutenant Colonel Peter Adams and the Fourth Maryland Regiment of Major Alexander Roxburg.

General Thomas Nelson commanded the American Militia on the far right and east of Yorktown. This force consisted of three brigades totaling 3200 men under brigadier generals George Weedon, Robert Lawson and Edward Stevens. Also included was the State Regiment of 200 men under Lieutenant Colonel Dabney. Washington's Artillery Brigade was commanded by Brigadier General Henry Knox. In total the American Army at Yorktown totaled nearly 8900 and the French around 7800. The grand force of the allied army was nearly 17,000 strong.

Yorktown land forces under Cornwallis consisted of some 7500 troops. From his veteran Southern army were

the Brigade of Guards, the regiments of the 23rd, 33rd and 71st, the Light Infantry Company of the 82nd Regiment, Tarleton's Legion, the North Carolina Volunteers and the German Regiment under Colonel de Bose. The troops that had come with Arnold and Phillips included the two battalions of Light Infantry, the 17th, 43rd, 76th, 80th regiments, Simcoe's Rangers, the Anspachers of colonels de Voit and de Seybothen, the Hessians of Prince Hereditaire, and other small detachments of artillery, light dragoons, jagers, and light infantry. In addition to these forces were the 800 to 900 marines. While the allied army outnumbered them, the British forces were the elite of the king's army in North America.[21]

By the end of the day on September 29, Washington had retired to his tent where he slept on a hard cot. The worn gray headquarters tents had been set up and the commander-in-chief was resting under the alert eyes of the veteran Life Guard security troops which surrounded the immediate area.[22] After dark on this same day, a dispatch boat rowed into Yorktown harbor with a message from Clinton to Cornwallis. The message read:

> My Lord: At a meeting of the General and Flag officers held this day, it is determined that above five thousand men, rank and file, shall be embarked on board the King's ships, and the joint exertions of the navy made in a few days to relieve you, and afterwards co-operate with you.
>
> The fleet consists of twenty-three sail of the line, three of which are three deckers. There is every reason to hope we start from hence the 5th October.
>
> P.S. Admiral Digby is this moment arrived at the Hook with three sail of the line.

That night at his desk in the Nelson mansion Cornwallis wrote the following response to Sir Henry's message:

> Sir: I have ventured these last two days to look General Washington's whole force in the face in the position on the outside of my works, and I have the pleasure to assure your Excellency that there was but one wish throughout the whole army, which was, that the enemy would advance.
>
> I have this evening received your letter of the 24th, which has given me the greatest satisfaction. I shall retire this night within my works, and have no doubt, if relief arrives in any reasonable time, York and Gloucester will be both in possession of his Majesty's troops.

As Cornwallis' letter noted, at one o'clock the next morning the British regiments quietly abandoned their outer positions and moved across the meadows to the inner fortifications circling Yorktown. The event did not set well with the troops. Corporal Stephan Popp's diary recorded, "The regiments in the line moved back to the

Opposite: Siege at Yorktown. (*Battles of the American Revolution.*)

city because the enemy always came nearer and stronger…. In the night three of the men of our company deserted." Johann Doehla noted that he saw eight Germans slip away to desert to the enemy, including three from his own regiment. Doehla had also written that he had seen Private Zeilmann on picket duty mortally wounded, and had later helped others to bury him. His words rang with sadness as he recorded, "Today over thirty men were shot and wounded on the detached outposts."[23]

The first American to discover the incredible circumstance that the British had indeed moved back from their outer defenses was Colonel Alexander Scammell. Acting as the field officer of the day, Scammell rode out to examine one abandoned redoubt found by some pickets just after dawn. As he viewed the redoubt Tarleton's cavalry under Lieutenant Cameron came up and surrounded him. Scammell was prisoner for just a few minutes before he attempted to escape. A dragoon turned and shot the colonel in the back. Colonel Van Cortlandt soon came up and learned that Scammell had been shot and taken off by the British. The British took Scammell off to Yorktown, dressed his wounds and later that day paroled him back to the Americans. The officer retired to Williamsburg and died there on the evening of the 6th.[24] Washington was upset at the death of his fine officer, a loyal adjutant general for the last two years. He was one man who could get the commander-in-chief to laugh with his humorous stories. He replaced his friend with his Parisian emissary and true idealist, John Laurens, who was the commander of the First Light Infantry Regiment of the Second Brigade.[25]

By 8 A.M. it was clear that the British had abandoned the outer redoubts, and the allied troops moved to occupy them without opposition. When Washington heard of the news, he was joyous. He expressed his delight in a letter to President John McKean of Congress, "We are in possession of very advantageous grounds, which command their line of works." Rochambeau learned of the circumstance from his night duty officer, Baron d'Esebeck, and rode out with Count Deux-ponts and other officers to inspect the line. Deuxponts wrote of the reaction: "The enemy ought to have kept these redoubts until they were forced to abandon them … it would have compelled us to feel our way, and would have held us in doubt; it would have retarded our works … instead of leaving us masters of all the approaches to the place…."

The day was to see only a single engagement. It happened near the York on the far left of the French line. Troops from Saint-Simon's unit moved into the woods and drove off a number of enemy pickets who had been sniping at them. As the French approached they ran into a hail of gunfire and grapeshot from the British fortifications. The allies lost one French hussar and ten wounded men including an officer from the Agenais Regiment, M. de Bouillet. By early afternoon the French and American troops had taken possession of the trenches and the engineers were positioning the artillery. The allies were in rather high spirits as they settled into their new defenses.

Washington did some investigating with several of his generals along the line that day, heading first to an abandoned redoubt with large poplar trees. As Van Cortlandt sat and studied the British artillery position, the enemy fired a cannon shot that came over Washington's head and sent poplar twigs everywhere. The other officers waited for the second cannonball to land before they hurried away from the advanced position, but Washington stayed for a while perched on his horse, surveying the enemy with his spyglass with little regard for his safety. After he returned to his headquarters to conduct other business, he received a letter from Lafayette requesting that he be placed in charge of all American forces at Yorktown. The marquis suggested that General Lincoln should take command of the forces on the Gloucester side of the York. Lafayette wrote, "I am sure you will be so very kind to me as to adopt any plan consistent with propriety that may bring on an event so highly interesting to me…." But Washington rejected the suggestion and Lincoln remained as second in command.

The British saw 30 of their men killed or wounded in the line that day when the French attacked the fusilier's redoubt. Lieutenant James wrote of the battle, "After a smart action of two hours they were repulsed with some loss, retreating into the woods with the utmost precipitance and confusion, our batteries having much galled them." Stephan Popp watched from the trenches as the three French charges were repulsed and noted, "This month we had hard work and poor provisions." September 30 was soon ended.

The morning of October 1 was opened with a distressing sight as starving horses were being driven from Yorktown. They struggled to cover the distance through the sand and marshes, carrying their heads down and stumbling as they went. Later the American surgeon, James Thacher, discovered hundreds of bloated horse carcasses floating down the York River. He estimated that the British had killed approximately 600 of these animals rather than to feed them or let them escape to the allied army. Most of these horses had been gathered in the Southern operations and had served Cornwallis well.[26]

The first week of October was a time of preparation for the allied forces for the coming all-out battle for Yorktown. The allies made gabions, fascines and stakes to use in defensive protection. In addition the cannons were moved forward into the most advantageous positions. On the 1st Washington was again in the saddle reconnoitering and reviewing the preparations. Lieutenant Feltman, who was serving that day on picket duty at Moore's Mill at the head of Wormley Creek, noted, "This afternoon, three o'clock, his Excellency General Washington, General Duportail, and several other engineers crossed at the mill-dam to take a view of the enemy's works. His Excellency sent one of his *aides-de-camp* for Captain Smith and his guard of fifty men, to march in front of his Excellency as a covering party, which we did, and went under cover of a hill, where we posted our guard, when his Excellency General Washington and General Duportail with three men of our guard advanced within three hundred yards of the enemy's works, which is the town of York."

Most of the delay in opening the operations was due to the effort in moving the heavy siege guns from the James. Washington wrote, "Much diligence, was used in debarking and transporting the stores, cannon, etc., from Trebell's Landing (six miles away) on the James River to camp; which for want of teams went on heavily." The horse teams had been delayed from the Head of Elk. Washington sent his own baggage wagons to the loading area in the morning of October 2. The morning orders had instructed the other officers to follow in providing their wagons, for it was "of the utmost importance that the Heavy Artillery should be brought up without a moment's loss of time."

Nearly one-third of the allied men were detailed for work, including sandbagging, digging trenches, and gathering wicker material. Each regiment was required to furnish at least 6000 stakes, 2000 fascines, 600 gabions and another 600 saucissons. Drill and discipline were kept with care as the orders revealed on the 1st, "The health of the troops is an object of such infinite importance, that every possible attention ought to be paid to the preservation of it." Quartermasters were ordered to furnish straw for bedding, bread, and one gill of rum per man daily. The trench operations were to be done in the "greatest silence," with the covering guard always with musket in hand. Sentries were posted at proper intervals and instructed to call out when the enemy fired shells or for any approach of the enemy toward their fortifications. After a few men deserted to the British, an ominous order went out declaring that "every deserter from the American troops, after this public notice is given, who shall be found within the enemy's lines at York, if the place falls, will be instantly hanged." It was a serious time for the forces before Yorktown.[27]

Corporal Popp in the British trenches wrote of his observations on the first day in October, "October 1 the enemy began to fortify heavily to really block us up. They threw no shots against us, because they had no cannon yet. But we fired steadily upon them and destroyed much of their labor again. We … had no rest day or night…." The British fired at the allies during the day and continued into the night while the allies moved out into the no-man's land between the British and their former position. Captain James Duncan was surprised to see the light firing and wrote, "I am at the loss to account for it, for the moon shone bright, and by the help of their night glasses they must certainly have discovered us." A Pennsylvania officer lay awake and recorded that the British fired an average of 10 rounds of cannon per hour toward the allies.

On October 2 the British continued the cannonade with some increase, causing some American casualties. A drummer who shouted out at the British in defiance, "Damn my soul if I'll dodge for the buggers!" was soon hit and killed by a cannonball. A single ball killed four men from the Pennsylvania Regiment. At 10 o'clock that night the British ships in the York opened fire for a short while and then went silent. The mysterious event was conducted to cover the crossing of the cavalry to Gloucester to escort the infantry on a foraging party. This was soon to begin an interesting engagement.

Back in September Washington had sent General George Weedon with approximately 1500 Virginia Militia to guard Gloucester County and to prevent the British from escaping. On September 28 Washington sent Duke de Lauzun's Legion of 300 infantry and 300 cavalry over to the Gloucester side to join the inexperienced militia. The French officer and head of the hussar force was critical of Weedon's location of his force, some 15 miles from Gloucester at Dixon's Mill. The militia forces were moved forward, and as another 800 French marines arrived, Brigadier General M. de Choisy arrived to take command of all Gloucester-side forces.

On October 3 General Choisy with the militia and the Legion marched toward Gloucester on Severn Road, while another company of Legion dragoons under Dillon, accompanied by Lieutenant Colonel John Mercer's militia grenadiers, moved forward on the York River Road. At four miles from Gloucester the two roads merged as the American forces joined. On that same morning the British had decided to conduct "a grand forage" under Lieutenant Colonel Dundas along that same road as the allied army. The British had often conducted similar foraging operations using Simcoe's Rangers. That morning a section of the Rangers and Tarleton's Legion, which had crossed the York the evening before, had scoured the fields for Indian corn, and were returning with wagons loaded. At around 10 A.M. the two opposing forces met in the lane. Since the two armies were so close, they could not ignore each other and action was inevitable.

Tarleton immediately moved his force into the woods, formed up and advanced with part of his Legion into the battle. Duke de Lauzun raced into the lane with his dragoons. On passing a rather pretty woman in the doorway of her house next to the road, he inquired of the enemy. The woman replied, "Oh, Colonel Tarleton left this place only a few minutes ago; he said he was very eager to shake hands with the French Duke." Lauzun replied, "Ha, ha! I assure you, madam, I have come on purpose to gratify him." At full gallop the duke rode after Tarleton. He found Tarleton only 100 yards from the house and Lauzun recorded, "I saw the English cavalry in force three times my own. I charged it without halting; we met hand to hand. Tarleton saw me and rode towards me with pistol raised...."[28] When one of the horses of Tarleton's own men was struck by a lance from a French dragoon, his horse bounced against Tarleton's horse and threw Tarleton. The main body of the British cavalry came up at this exact instant, and Tarleton was able to find another mount and escape. Tarleton sounded the retreat under the cover of Captain Champagne's infantry company from the 23rd Royal Welsh Fusiliers.

The French chased Tarleton and the cavalry but were forced to disengage when the British infantry pressed them. Soon Tarleton attempted to return to attack the dragoons, but Lieutenant Colonel John Francis Mercer and Virginia militiamen who had just arrived met him. Lee wrote of the militia, "No regular corps could have maintained its ground more firmly than did this battalion of our infantry." Lauzun reinforced Mercer's force from the rear and prepared for another charge, but the British retired with the loss of 50 men and Lieutenant Moir of the infantry, who was killed. The engagement yielded the congratulations of General Washington the next day, delivered with the general orders. Washington called the engagement a "brilliant success" and felt the British were "decisively repulsed." Brigadier General Choisy set up camp on the field of the completed engagement, with advance posts now only a mile and a half from Gloucester. These forces would remain in this location throughout the remainder of the siege at Yorktown. The British had seen their last foraging operation on the north shore of the York River.[29]

Back on the Yorktown side, Washington was nearly ready to open up the parallels, which were trenches in advance of the line and nearer to the enemy. The excavation work must be completed under cover of darkness in a single night. The operation was started on the evening of October 5 in the rain, but after surveying the conditions, the engineers delayed the activities for the following night. On the British side some 500 yards from the allied trenches Johann Doehla lay on the ground for his two-hour guard duty. He did not dare sit up for fear the Americans would fire at him. The duty was lonely and quite dangerous. He wrote of the experience: "Everything must proceed quietly. One dares call out neither to sentry nor patrol except to give the agreed signal. Nor does one dare to smoke tobacco nor make a fire. The men call it the 'lost post' with all justice."

The final advance on Cornwallis and Yorktown was made with the construction of the new parallels. On October 6, Washington wrote President McKean of the Congress that "We shall this night open trenches." The allied commander had ordered 1500 men to be ready at dark to dig the first parallel, under the protection of another 2800 men standing guard over the workers. There was significant tension in the air, as the British would be expected to counter the trenching operation that night. Artilleryman John Lamb told another associate, "You may depend on its being a night of business."

After dark the troops moved out behind the engineers with their pickaxes, muskets and spades, and carrying fascines and gabions, with wagons loaded with sandbags to the rear. The engineers established the parallel at 800 yards from the enemy line. Washington had come out and according to Sergeant Martin had struck a few blows of a pickaxe so that "it might be said 'Gen. Washington with his own hands first broke ground at the siege of Yorktown.'" First the gabions were "placed in rows, and the soft, sandy soil from the ditch was thrown into them so that there was soon a four-foot trench behind a sturdy breastwork." The "diggers" worked for two hours and the enemy was still not alerted to the operation. Ahead of schedule, the planned French diversion of a false attack was started at 9 P.M. Washington learned that a French deserter had alerted the British, who immediately fired cannon and rockets at the French.

An American diversion consisting of large campfires set up near the marsh and away from the workers did draw British firing. But fortunately the British did not fire at the trench diggers. At dawn the British sentries looked out across the field to see a new allied trench just out of musket range manned with workers and guards under the cover of the breastwork. The new parallel was 2000 yards long and ran from the head of the Yorktown Creek near the center, across the Hampton Road, and in a long arc to the bluff above the York River to the right. The parallel was 600 yards from the British on the left and some 800 yards from them on the right. During the morning of the 7th Lieutenant Colonel Alexander Hamilton led his light infantry into the trench with drums beating and his flags flying. Captain James Duncan, who had moved out with Hamilton's color guard, was astonished:

> We were ordered to mount the bank, front the enemy, and there by word of command go through all the ceremony

Plan of the Siege of York Town, Virginia. (*A History of the Campaigns of 1780 and 1781.*)

of soldiery, ordering and grounding our arms; and although the enemy had been firing a little before, they did not now give us a single shot. I suppose their astonishment ... must have prevented them....[30]

That night the casualties had been light. The French lost one officer and 20 killed or wounded. Fifteen had been from Marquis Saint-Simon's corps. No American had been killed or wounded the entire evening. The work on completing the trench and mounting batteries of artillery continued during the 7th and 8th with little British disruption. Colonel Butler wrote of the time, "The enemy seem embarrassed, confused, and indeterminate; their fire seems feeble to what might be expected, their works, too, are not formed on any regular plan, but thrown up

in a hurry occasionally, and although we have not as yet fired one shot from a piece of artillery, they are as cautious as if the heaviest fire was kept up."

On the 8th Steuben's division relieved Lafayette's division in the trenches. On the 9th Lincoln relieved Steuben. On the French wing Chastellux, the Marquis de Saint-Simon, Viscount Viomenil and the Baron Viomenil succeeded each other at the trenches. On the morning of October 9 the sun came out as the French and American artillery batteries were nearing completion. The commander of the American Artillery Brigade, Brigadier General Henry Knox of Massachusetts, was delighted at the coming role of his forces. His artillery was already considered the most efficient arm in service to the Revolution. He maintained a strict and precise standard as the artillery batteries were positioned and ammunition brought up. The American batteries had installed three 24-pounders, three 18-pounders, two eight-inch howitzers and half a dozen mortars. A deserter had came into camp and told the story to the Pennsylvania troops that Cornwallis had told the men that they should not fear the Americans because they had no heavy cannon.

At 3 P.M. on October 9 the French battery on the extreme left was allowed to open fire at the British fusiliers' redoubt opposite them. The battery, constructed by the Touraine Regiment with four 12-pounders and six howitzers and mortars, had been completed first. The fire forced the British frigate *Guadaloupe* to move to the opposite Gloucester shore. At 5 P.M. on the extreme right on the river bank below, "His excellency Gen. Washington put the match to the first gun, and a furious discharge of cannon and mortars immediately followed," recorded Dr. Thacher. The battery contained six 18-pounders, six 24-pounders, four mortars, and two howitzers. Colonel Philip Van Cortlandt, who was closer to the front line, heard the first American shot into Yorktown. He noted, "I could hear the ball strike from the house to house, and I was afterwards informed that it went through the one where many officers were at dinner, and over the tables, discomposing the dishes and either killed or wounded the one at the head of the table...." Apparently the officers hit by the first shot were from the 76th Regiment.[31]

Washington ordered the guns to fire all night so that the enemy could not repair the defenses. Colonel Butler watched the bombardment for hours and noted, "The shot and shells flew incessantly through the night, dismounted the guns of the enemy, and destroyed many of their embrasures." Lieutenant Ebenezer Denny observed the mortar shells with spent glowing fuses, "A number of shells from the works of both parties passing high in the air and descending in a curve each with a long train of fire, exhibited a brilliant spectacle." British Lieutenant James recorded in his diary that special night, "It will be impossible to account for the number killed and wounded.... I must content myself with observing that the slaughter was great, and that among the killed on this day was the Commissary General, who with some other officers were killed at dinner." Cornwallis wrote, "The fire continued incessant[ly] from heavy cannon ... until all our guns on the left were silenced, our work much damaged and our loss of men considerable."

Corporal Popp and other companions were forced to pitch tents in the trenches as men "began to desert in large numbers, and left the commands, watches and posts. Why? Out of fear!" Johann Doehla wrote of the deadly action:

They threw bombs in here from 100, 150 pounds and also some of 200 pounds; and their howitzer and cannon balls.... One could therefore not avoid the horribly many cannon balls either inside or outside the city. Most of the inhabitants who were still to be found here fled with their best possessions eastward to the bank of the York river, and dug in among the sand cliffs, but ... many were badly injured and mortally wounded by the fragments of bombs which exploded partly in the air and partly on the ground, their arms and legs severed or themselves struck dead.

The next morning Washington rode out to admire the French gunners. These men had boasted that they could fire six shots into a narrow embrasure. Blanchard commented that the French guns were new and "the balls perfectly suited to their calibre." The French were surely the most expert in artillery, but Knox and his men were outstanding. Lafayette commented to Major Sam Shaw, the aide to Knox, that "You fire better than the French!" Major Shaw smiled and shook his head. Lafayette responded with renewed passion, "On my honor, it's the truth. Everyone knows the progress of your artillery is one of the wonders of the Revolution."[32]

By the 10th the Grand French Battery on the left of the parallel opened up with ten 18- and 24-pounders and six mortars. The Americans' battery, containing four 18-pounders and two mortars, and under the command of Captain Thomas Machin of the Second, was also opened. Lafayette, the general officer of the day, invited Virginia Governor Thomas Nelson to watch the events. The marquis asked Nelson, "To what particular spot would your excellency direct that we should point the cannon?" Nelson responded, "There, to that house. It is mine, and, now that the Secretary's is nearly knocked to pieces, is the best one in the town. There you will be almost certain to find Lord Cornwallis and the British head-quarters. Fire upon it, my dear marquis, and never spare a particle of my property so long as it affords a comfort or shelter to the enemies of my country." Nelson was a devoted patriot. The governor challenged the men, "I'll give five guineas to the first man to hit it." Soon the shots hit the house, plunging through the roof and shattering the walls. Lord Cornwallis had indeed vacated the home that same day.

That night the *Charon* was set on fire by a hot shot from the French battery on the left. An officer took in the sight, "The *Charon* was on fire from the water's edge to her truck at the same time. I never saw anything so magnificent." Two additional transports near her were also burned. Several other ships were scuttled by orders of the British. American John Laurens noted in his diary, "It was allowable to enjoy this magnificent nocturnal scene, as the vessels had previously been abandoned by their crews." Dr. Thacher saw the blaze of the 44-gun

Charon and two transports: "The ships were enwrapped in a torrent of fire, which spread with vivid brightness among the combustible rigging, and running with amazing rapidity to the tops of the several masts, while all around was the thunder and lightning from our numerous cannon and mortars.... Some of our shells, over-reaching the town, are seen to fall in the river, and bursting, throw up columns of water like the spouting of the monsters of the deep." From Yorktown British Lieutenant James watched the ship die and all the burned ships drifted down across the river to the Gloucester shore.

Johann Doehla sat on the beach and watched the volley, "It felt like the shocks of an earthquake." Some 3600 shells had fallen on the British in the first 24 hours. Doehla continued, "One saw men lying everywhere who were mortally wounded and whose heads, arms and legs had been shot off.... Enemy cannon balls of 24 and more pounds flew over our whole line and city into the river, where they struck through 1 and 2 ships." He even saw some shot skip across the water to the Gloucester side, where it wounded the troops on the beach. During the events of the evening of the 10th, a small open boat came slowly up the river and put out Major Charles Cochrane. He had a dispatch from Clinton, which read:

> I am doing every thing in my power to relieve you by a direct move, and I have reason to hope, from the assurances given me this day by Admiral Graves, that we may pass the bar by the 12th of October, if the winds permit, and no unforeseen accident happens; this, however, is subject to disappointment, wherefore, if I hear from you, your wishes will of course direct me and I shall persist in the idea of a direct move, even to the middle of November should it be your Lordship's opinion that you can hold out so long; but if, when I hear from you, you tell me that you cannot, and I am without hopes of arriving in time.... I will immediately make an attempt by Philadelphia....

By October 11 there were some 52 guns firing at Cornwallis and the troops about Yorktown. The British had almost silenced their return fire. By noon Cornwallis wrote to Clinton: "We have lost about seventy men, and many of our works are considerably damaged. With such works, on disadvantageous ground, against so powerful an attack we cannot hope to make a very long resistance." At 5 P.M. he added a postscript: "Since my last letter was written we have lost 30 men."

On the evening of the 11th the second parallel was constructed some 500 yards in advance and to the left of the first parallel. At dusk parties from Von Steuben's division moved out with the men carrying fascines, and each man with "a shovel, spade, or grubbing hoe." By the morning of the 12th the workers had opened up a trench 750 yards long, three and one-half feet deep and seven feet wide. Shells and alerts were everywhere. Steuben and Wayne were among the men in harm's way with their men. On one occasion when a shell landed nearby, Steuben jumped into a trench with Wayne stumbling over him. Steuben laughed, "Ah ha, Wayne, you cover your general's retreat in the best manner possible." Only two allied men were killed, having been caused by premature exploding of French shells in the crossfire.

After the new parallel was completed, it was more obvious that the redoubts nine and 10 on the right, near the riverbank, were a serious obstacle to the next activities of the siege operations. The redoubts must be stormed. The troops were in position on the 12th. Washington continued to be surprised with the lack of opposition: "Lord Cornwallis' conduct has hitherto been passive beyond conception; he either has not the means of defence, or he intends to reserve his strength until we approach very near him." Two days later Washington's guns began to soften up the redoubts in question, and by 2 P.M. the redoubts were ready to be stormed. The orders went out for a night attack. The American light infantry would attack on the right on the high bank on the York River. The French grenadiers and chasseurs of the Gatenois and Royal Deuxponts regiments were assigned. Both the American and French storming parties were approximately 400 strong.

With the designated signal, consisting of six shells fired off in rapid succession at 8 P.M. after dusk, the operations to take the redoubts was begun. The French advanced in platoon columns, with the 50 chasseurs carrying fascines to fill the ditch and eight men carrying ladders. As the French came to within 120 paces of redoubt nine, a Hessian sentinel discovered them and shouted, "Wer da?" meaning, "Who goes there?" The French did not respond and the Hessian units fired. For a few minutes the French were delayed under fire as the pioneers struggled to clear a path through a strong abatis. When the passage was cleared, the chasseurs moved quickly and mounted the parapet. Discovering the French at the edge of their redoubt, the Hessians charged at the French. But Deuxponts directed his men to fire and countercharge, and the Hessians immediately threw down their arms.

The Hessians lost 18 killed and 50 taken prisoner in redoubt nine. For his bravery in the engagement, Deuxponts received the title of chevalier in the Military Order of St. Louis. He wrote in his journal of his brave comrades, "With troops so good, so brave, and so disciplined as those I have the honor to lead against the enemy, one can undertake anything, and be sure of succeeding, if the impossibility of it has not been proved. I owe them the happiest day of my life, and certainly the recollection of it will never be effaced from my mind." The grenadiers of the Gatenois Regiment were awarded the honored name of "Auvergne sans tache," meaning "Good for Royal Auvergne!"

Meanwhile, the Americans met with like success in their attack on redoubt 10. Lafayette, the chief of the Light Division, selected Gimat's, Hamilton's, and half of Laurens' battalions for the operation. Lafayette had appointed the command to go to Gimat, but Alexander Hamilton protested since he had been assigned the field officer of the day. Lafayette wrote a note to Washington for direction, and the commander-in-chief yielded the honor to Hamilton. Though Hamilton was in command, Gimat's battalion retained the honored front position in the attack since they were the oldest forces in Virginia.

Redoubt 10 was square shaped and smaller than any the French had encountered. It was located some 20 feet from the riverbank and was commanded by British Major Campbell, with 70 men. When the six-shell signal was given, Hamilton's force advanced with unloaded muskets to take the redoubt by bayonets alone. Laurens' unit went around to the rear of the redoubt. The frontal unit rushed the enemy, not waiting to remove the abatis as the French did. The Americans moved over the obstacles, entered the ditch and scaled the parapet. The capture was completed in only 10 minutes. The column from the Fourth Connecticut under Lieutenant John Mansfield attacked with total focus and precision. Mansfield, who led the charge, received a bayonet wound and received Hamilton's favorable remark commending his "coolness, firmness, and punctuality." Sergeant Brown of the Fifth Connecticut was awarded the "badge of merit" for his gallant actions with Hamilton. This was the first decoration given in the American military without regard for rank, commonly known as the "Purple Heart."

Stephen Olney of the Rhode Island Regiment, the oldest captain in the military service at Yorktown, Captain Hunt of the Sappers and Gimat were also wounded in the engagement. Laurens, leading two companies, was successful at taking the British redoubt commander, Major Campbell, as prisoner as he cut off the enemy retreat. In all, the American losses were nine killed and 25 wounded. General Washington was overcome with joy at the brilliant action to storm the redoubts. His general orders of October 15, 1781, read:

> The Commander-in-Chief congratulates the army on the success of the enterprise against the two important works on the left of the enemy's line. He requests Baron Viomenil … and Marquis de La Lafayette … to accept his warmest acknowledgments, for the excellency of their dispositions, and for their own gallant conduct on the occasion; and he begs them to present his thanks to every individual officer, and the men of their respective commands, for the spirit and rapidity with which they advanced to the attacks assigned them, and for the admirable firmness with which they supported them, under fire of the enemy, without returning a shot.
>
> The General reflects with the highest degree of pleasure on the confidence which the troops of the two nations must hereafter have in each other. Assured of mutual support, he is convinced there is no danger which they will not cheerfully encounter — no difficulty which they will not bravely overcome.[33]

During the action, Washington, Lincoln and Knox had dismounted from their horses and were in the open viewing the fight. One of the staff aides, Colonel David Cobb, warned Washington that "Sir, you're too much exposed here. Hadn't you better step back a little?" Washington came back immediately with, "Colonel Cobb, if you are afraid, you have the liberty to step back." When the fighting had died down, Washington quietly told his fellow officers, "The work is done, and well done." He then turned to his personal servant, Billy Lee, and remarked, "Billy, hand me my horse." Washington trotted off to his headquarters to attend to his paper work. By morning the second parallel was extended to include the redoubts, and the deep trench now ran across the entire front to the riverbank. Guns had been moved into the redoubts and were facing the British. Washington's note to President McKean explained, "The works we have carried are of vast importance to us. From them we shall enfilade the enemy's whole line."

On the evening of the 15th Cornwallis wrote Clinton of his dire situation:

> Last night the enemy carried two advanced redoubts on the left by storm, and during the night have included them in their second parallel, which they are at present busy in perfecting. My situation now becomes very critical; we dare not show a gun to their batteries, and I expect that their new ones will open to-morrow morning. Experience has shown that our fresh earthen works do not resist their powerful artillery, so that we shall soon be exposed to an assault in ruining works, in a bad position, and with weakened numbers. The safety of the place is, therefore, so precarious that I cannot recommend that the fleet and army should run any risk in endeavoring to save us.

Cornwallis made one last attempt to counter the allied army's advance. At 3 A.M. on the 16th, after some British shelling of the nearest allied position on the second parallel, a party of some 400 men led by Lieutenant Colonel Robert Abercrombie attacked at the weakest point in the parallel, where the French and American lines met. Half of the force was a company of grenadiers from the Footguards and the other unit was Captain Murray's company from the 8th. The attacking party entered the second parallel undetected and fanned out toward the French to the west and the other moved in the trench toward the Savage battery of Colonel Henry Skip-with's Virginia Militia. Some 150 men of the French Agenais Regiment were attacked by the British western group as they slept. The British stabbed several French troops and ran the others off before spiking the cannons by breaking off their bayonets in the touchholes of the weapons.

Nearby, Viscount de Noailles shouted out for a countercharge from his troops, who were able to stab eight British as they advanced. The British attackers carried off the Agenais officer with two prisoners. The 100 of Skip-with's Americans were engaged by British and most fled away in the night. The assault had cost the British eight killed and six prisoners. The allied army had lost 17 killed or wounded. While the allied officers admired the "secrecy and spirit" of the British attack, Washington reported that the action was "small and ineffective and of little consequence to either party." Within six hours the six spiked guns were back in action firing at the British and Hessians.[34]

The day of the 16th saw increased and more accurate shelling on Yorktown and the defensive works of the British. The allied shells from over 100 guns shook the earth and caused the walls to come crashing in around the enemy. The only safety to be found in Yorktown was in the waterfront caves along the river. As the pandemonium of the roaring guns and explosions continued, Cornwallis planned his desperate move to escape from Yorktown. On the evening of the 16th Cornwallis sent his aide, Lord Chewton, across the river to Gloucester with orders for Tarleton to prepare to attack the allied army under Choisy the next night. At 11 P.M. Cornwallis sent over the first group of 1000 men from the 23rd Royal Welsh Fusiliers, the Footguards and the light infantry in 16 flatboats. The first group made it to the Gloucester side by midnight, and the flatboats returned to Yorktown for the second wave. But the weather turned against Cornwallis, as a violent squall blew in. At around 2 A.M. the weather began to moderate, but by then it was clear to Cornwallis that he could not move all his forces over to the Gloucester side in time to attack Choisy. His forces would be trapped on both sides of the river, which was an invitation for Washington to attack either weakened force. Frustrated, Cornwallis ordered his forces back across the river to Yorktown, which was accomplished by the morning of the 17th.

The roars of the guns were even more intense on the 17th as Dr. Thacher remarked, "The whole peninsula trembles under the incessant thundering of our infernal machines." At around 7 A.M. Cornwallis and General Charles O'Hara appeared in the hornwork and studied the scope of the allied firing. Cornwallis detailed his survey:

Our works were going to ruin, and not having been able to strengthen them by an abatis, nor in any other manner but by a slight fraizing, which the enemy's artillery were demolishing wherever they fired, my opinion entirely coincided with that of the engineer and principal officers of the army, that they were in many places assailable in the forenoon, and that by continuance of the same fire for a few hours longer, they would be in such a state as to render it desperate, with our numbers, to attempt to maintain them. We at that time could not fire a single gun; only one eight inch and little more than 100 Cohorn shells remained.

Cornwallis called a Council of War with his principal officers and discussed the situation. With the sick and wounded increasing every hour, and the ammunition almost expended, the earl asked his men whether they should surrender or fight to the last man. Brave officers responded mournfully that they voted for surrender. Slowly Cornwallis nodded in assent. He then turned to his aide and dictated the historic letter:

Sir, I propose a cessation of hostilities for twenty-four hours, and that two officers may be appointed by each side to meet at Mr. Moore's house to settle terms for the surrender of the posts at York and Gloucester.

I have the honour to be &c.
Cornwallis[35]

At 10 A.M. on the cold day of October 17, 1781, a drummer in red mounted the British parapet on the left and began to beat a "parley." The man could be easily seen and the cannonade soon stopped. Ebenezer Denny of Pennsylvania wrote of the event, "When the firing ceased, I thought I had never heard a drum equal to it—the most delightful music to us all." In company with the drummer was an officer waving a white handkerchief. Soon the officer was met and blindfolded by an American officer who escorted him to the rear of the lines with Cornwallis' letter. The letter was sent to Washington.

At noon Washington sent the British officer back into his lines. Allied cannon fired again briefly, but by 3 P.M. Washington sent out an officer with a reply to Cornwallis. The message read:

An Ardent Desire to spare the further Effusion of Blood, will readily incline me to listen to such Terms for the Surrender of your Posts.... I wish ... that your Lordship's proposals in writing, may be sent to the American Line: for which Purpose a Suspension of hostilities during two Hours from the Delivery of this Letter will be granted.

Cornwallis replied to the letter with:

The time limited for sending my answer will not admit of entering into detail ... but the basis of my proposals will be ... that the British shall be sent to Britain and the Germans to Germany ... not to serve against France,

America or their allies until released or regularly exchanged....

Washington noted the requests from Cornwallis and agreed to suspend firing until the next day for negotiations. Anticipating the ultimate signing of an agreement, the British began destroying as much equipment as possible. The navy scuttled the *Guadeloupe* and towed the *Fowey* to shallow water where carpenters bored holes in her for sinking. The British powder magazine exploded during the night killing some 13 men. The Virginia militiaman, St. George Tucker, wrote of the evening of the 17th: "A solemn sky decorated with ten thousand stars — numberless Meteors gleaming thro' the Atmosphere afforded a pleasing resemblance to the Bombs which had exhibited a noble Firework the night before, but happily divested of all their Horror."

In the mists of the rising sun Tucker noticed two French ships coming up the river under full sail. At noon the ships dropped anchor among the wrecks in the channel. That morning the British bagpipers played for the allies, and were answered by the French Deuxponts regiment musicians. Tucker noted the incredible sight:

> From the ... Rock Battery on our side our Lines completely mann'd and our Works crowded with soldiers ... opposite these at the Distance of two hundred yards ... The British Works; their parapets crowded with officers looking at those who were assembled at the top of our Works — the Secretary's house with one of the Corners broke off, and many large holes through the Roof and Walls part of which seem'd tottering with their weight.
>
> On the Beach of York ... hundreds of busy people might be seen moving to and fro — At a small distance from the Shore were seen ships sunk down to the Waters Edge — further out in the Channel the Masts, Yards and even the top gallant Masts of some might be seen....

On the morning of the 18th Jonathan Trumbull's draft of the allied proposal was delivered to Cornwallis:

Head Quarters before York, October 18, 1781

> MY LORD: To avoid unnecessary Discussions and Delays, I shall at Once ... declare the general Basis upon which a Definitive Treaty and Capitulation must take place. The Garrisons of York and Gloucester, including the Seamen ... will be received Prisoners of War. The Condition annexed, of sending the British and German troops ... to Europe ... is inadmissible. Instead of this, they will be marched to such parts of the Country as can most conveniently provide for their Subsistence ... the same Honors will be granted to the Surrendering Army as were granted to the Garrison of Charles Town....
>
> The Artillery, Arms, Accoutrements, Military Chests and Public Stores of every denomination, shall be delivered unimpaired....
>
> Your Lordship will be pleased to ... accept or reject ... In the Course of Two Hours from the Delivery of this Letter, that Commissioners may be appointed to digest the Articles of Capitulation or renewal of hostilities may take place.[36]

Soon the commissioners met. They included Lieutenant Colonel John Laurens representing the Americans, Viscount de Noailles representing the French, with Cornwallis' aide, Major Alexander Ross, and Lieutenant Colonel Thomas Dundas of the 80th representing the British. They met in the early afternoon at the handsome two-story frame house of Augustine Moore, located a half mile behind the American first parallel. Laurens, in his worn buff and blue uniform, and Noailles, in his immaculate white and gold one, arrived first in the garden to await the British representatives. Soon the two red-coated British officers came up out of the trenches toward them. The negotiations went on until nearly midnight before the drafts were ready for the review by Washington and Cornwallis. It was agreed that the truce would continue until nine o'clock the next morning. The peaceful night continued.

By the morning of October 19, 1781, the final minor points of the treaty were resolved and a copy was made. It was delivered to Cornwallis with a hand-written note from Washington indicating that he expected the articles to be signed by 11 A.M. and that the British garrison would march out and formally surrender by 2 P.M. Washington then had his breakfast, followed by a ride out to redoubt 10 to join Rochambeau and Admiral de Barras, with a crowd of other ranking officers. At about 11 A.M. Cornwallis put his signature to the bottom of the long document. Under his signature, Captain Thomas Symonds signed for the British Royal Navy. The signed surrender document was delivered to redoubt 10 where Washington signed, "G. Washington" and the French signatures included "Le Comte de Barras en mon nom & celui Comte de Grasse" and "Le Comte de Rochambeau." In silence Washington ordered an aide to place above the signatures the line: "Done in the trenches before Yorktown in Virginia, October 19, 1781."[37] All but the ceremony remained of this glorious victory.

At 1 P.M. the allied troops moved out of their camps on either side of the surrender field location in a meadow one-half mile down the Williamsburg Road. The French marched out in their best linen finery, with the officers adorned in their plumes and gold braid. The American troops polished their guns and boots and repaired their uniforms as best they could. In front were stationed the Continentals, with the militias in their rather tattered clothing in the rear. Baron von Closen wrote of the American troops' condition: "Most of these unfortunate persons were clad in small jackets of white cloth, dirty and ragged, and a number of them were almost barefoot…. What does it matter!… These people are much more praise-worthy to fight as they do, when they are so poorly supplied with everything." Washington and his officers were at the head of the American ranks on horses, with Rochambeau and his staff opposite them.

In silence except for occasional playing of the French band, the allied troops waited. At 2 P.M. in the distance was heard the roll of drums from the town. Soon the surrender column of the British and Hessian troops was seen with color guard carrying flags unfurled in the wind. Their bands were playing the unmilitary and rather melancholy tune of the day, "The World Turned Upside Down." At the head of the British was not Lord Cornwallis as expected, but General O'Hara in his jackboots. Count Dumas rode out to guide the column to the surrender field, as O'Hara called out, "Where is General Rochambeau?" Dumas nodded toward the French line, but guessing that he desired to surrender to Rochambeau, Dumas tried to block his way.

O'Hara came up to Rochambeau and held out his sword. Rochambeau shook his head, pointed to Washington and replied, "We are subordinate to the Americans. General Washington will give you orders." O'Hara swung his horse around and moved to Washington. Trying again to surrender his sword, Washington spoke out, "Never from such a good hand." O'Hara then apologized for the absence of Cornwallis indicating that he was sick.

Washington passed him off to Major General Lincoln, who pointed to the field beyond where the British were to lay down their arms.

Light Horse Harry Lee noted the near "universal silence" of the allied troops and civilians as the British column passed and gave up their arms. Most who wrote of the event felt the British soldiers were rather "disorderly and unsoldierly … their step was irregular and their ranks frequently broken." It was an emotional moment for the surrendering troops, and many wept as they marched. The Germans marched with more discipline and dignity. At 3 P.M. the ceremony was completed. The British and German troops marched back to Yorktown to await their plight. Some 3500 troops had come out for the surrender event, with the others of the sick and wounded remaining in their camps totaling 7247 plus 840 seamen. The ceremony on the Gloucester side had just begun as Tarleton and his cavalry rode out with their sabers drawn. The infantry under Lieutenant Colonel John Simcoe of the Queen's Rangers marched out with the colors cased, drums beating and trumpets blaring.[38]

The last major engagement of the American Revolution was now concluded. On this day of British surrender, October 19, 1781, exactly six years and six months had passed since the American Revolution began on Lexington Green — April 19, 1775. The day after the surrender Lafayette wrote to Count de Maurepas: "The play has ended … the fifth act has just been finished."[39]

20

AFTER SURRENDER

After the surrender ceremony was concluded, the officers of the defeated army congregated at Washington's headquarters. Like some cloud was lifted, the role of the Americans and French toward the British had turned from adversary to host. In the spirit of gentlemen General Washington invited General O'Hara to dinner that night as the French entertained other British officers.

Captain Samuel Graham wrote of the fine entertaining in Washington's tent: "The Americans behaved with great delicacy and forebearance while the French, by what motive actuated I will not pretend to say, were profuse in their protestations of sympathy. When I visited their lines immediately after our parade had been dismissed, I was overwhelmed with the civility of my late enemies."

The evening of October 20, Rochambeau hosted a dinner for General O'Hara and party. Again the air of the event was incredibly comfortable and easy. The French aide Cromot du Bourg noted that he "could not imagine that the day after such a catastrophe as had happened to them they could forget it." After borrowing 20 guineas from General Washington, the Baron Von Steuben held a "grand dinner" even though "I eat my soup with a wooden spoon forever after."[1]

From all the dining and general hosting going on, it was hard to believe the battle for Yorktown had really happened. Considering the bombardment that occurred, the losses for the British had been rather light. The official totals indicated the British and Hessians lost 153 killed, 326 wounded and 70 missing or deserted. The Americans lost 23 killed and 65 wounded, while the French gave 52 killed and 134 wounded. There were some 7247 prisoners who surrendered, plus additional 840 sailors. The military supplies and equipment lost by the British was impressive: 144 cannon and mortars, with 15,000 round shot, 500 shells, thousands of cartridges for the large guns, 600 hand grenades and 120 barrels of powder, 26 tomahawks, 11 blunderbusses, 800 muskets, 3400 flints, 266,000 musket cartridges, and 2000 swords.

The quartermasters took possession of 300 horses, 43 wagons, 400 saddles, three tons of hemp, three tons of iron, 1000 sandbags, four tons of coal, 500 bushels of corn, 836 sheets, 450 tents, 613 gross of buttons, over 1000 uniforms, 1300 pairs of shoes, 1100 pairs of hose, and thousands of yards of cloth and ribbon. Even though the enemy troops were hungry throughout the engagement, the stocks of food captured were plentiful: 73,000 pounds of flour, 60,000 pounds of bread, 20,000 pounds of pickled beef, 75,000 pounds of pork, 20,000 pounds of butter, 1200 pounds of oatmeal, 30,000 bushels of peas, 3000 pounds of sugar, 1500 pounds of rice, 3000 pounds of cocoa, 2500 pounds of coffee and some 1250 gallons of liquor.

After the dinner of the 19th Washington wrote his victory letter to the president of the Congress. Jonathan Trumbull, Jr., prepared it and it was sent via his loyal 36-year-old aide, Lieutenant Colonel Tech Tilghman, Jr., from Maryland. Having just recovered from malaria, Tilghman was still weak as he departed down the York River in a small sailboat. With favorable winds he sailed to the mouth of the river and turned north up the bay.

Anxious to get his message to Philadelphia as soon as possible, he was frustrated when the skipper ran the boat aground near Tangier Island. It took the entire night to free the sailboat and then, "The wind left us entirely on Sunday evening thirty miles below Annapolis." Concerned over the delay, Tilghman went ashore at Rock Hall on Maryland's Eastern Shore. He borrowed a horse and rode off. He changed horses numerous times as he rode on shouting to the farmers on the way, "Cornwallis is taken! A horse for the Congress!"

At midnight of October 23 Tilghman finally reached Philadelphia. He was sick with chills and a fever, but he still located President McKean at his home and gave him the glorious news and Washington's dispatch. The old German watchman who helped Tilghman find the president noted, "Past dree o'clock — und Corn-val-lis is ta-gen!" Tilghman went to bed as the Congress met in early session that next morning. The first order of business was to find some way to pay Tilghman for his expenses. The treasury was penniless, so a collection was taken up and each attendee gave one-dollar specie for the messenger.[2]

Celebrations opened everywhere in the city. Congress declared a day of national thanksgiving and voted Tilghman a horse, saddle, bridle and an "elegant sword" for his work. Citizen Elias Boudinot wrote her brother of "the glorious Success of the allied Arms, a Day famous in the annals of American History ... would to God, that a deep sense of Gratitude may follow this remarkable Smile of Heaven at the critical Era." At 2 P.M. on the 24th Congress went to the Lutheran Church "where divine service was performed" by one of the chaplains of Congress, Reverend Duffield. The Minister of France, the Supreme Executive Council and Assembly of Pennsylvania, and a large number of citizens also attended the service. That evening the city was illuminated by candles and fireworks. A large portrait of Washington, painted by Charles Willson Peale, was hung above Market Street.

Most of the Americans believed that the Yorktown victory would be the end of British struggle to subdue the colonies. James Madison wrote of the times: "If these severe doses of ill fortune do not cool the phrenzy and relax the pride of Britain, it would seem as if Heaven had in reality abandoned her to her folly and her fate.... With what hope or with what view can they try the fortune of another campaign?" Thomas McKean wrote this message to Washington: "Words fail me when I attempt to bestow my small tribute of thanks and praise to a Character so eminent for wisdom, courage and patriotism and one who appears to be no less the Favorite of Heaven than of his country; I shall only therefore beg you to be assured that you are held in the most grateful remembrance; and with a particular veneration, by all the wise and good in these United States." It is hard to imagine an event that could have solidified Washington's reputation in history any more than that of the Yorktown victory.

The loyalist reaction to Yorktown was predictable. Anne Rawle, a citizen of Philadelphia and a daughter of loyalist parents, wrote in her diary that the news of Cornwallis' surrender was "as surprizing as vexatious," while her family tried to console each other. Her uncle looked, "as though he had sat up all night ... as there is no letter from Washington, we flatter ourselves that it is not true...." After the celebrations Anne wrote, "I suppose, dear Mammy, thee would not have imagined this house to be illuminated last night, but it was. A mob surrounded it, broke the shutters and the glass of the windows, and were coming in, none but forlorn women here. We for a time listened for their attacks in fear and trembling till, finding them grown more loud and violent, not knowing what to do, we ran into the yard.... We had not been there many minutes before we were drove back by the sight of two men climbing the fence.... It was the most alarming scene I ever remember. For two hours we had the disagreeable noise of stones banging about, glass crashing, and the tumultuous voices of a large body of men, as they were a long time at the different houses in the neighborhood."[3]

The peace-loving Quakers of Philadelphia suffered a long night as the mobs attacked their homes. Elizabeth Drinker, who was the wife of a Quaker shipper, wrote from her bed in sickness at Front Street: "Scarcely one Friend's house escaped. We had nearly 70 panes of glass broken ... the door crashed and violently burst open; when they threw stones into the house for some time, but did not enter ... some houses, after breaking the door, they entered and destroyed the furniture. Many women and children were frightened into fits."[4] Anne Rawle wrote, "that Philadelphia will no longer be a happy asylum for Quakers that it once was. Those joyful days when all was prosperity and peace are gone, never to return; and perhaps it is as necessary for our society to ask for terms as it was for Cornwallis."[5]

Victory celebrations were held throughout America. At Harvard and Yale there were bonfires and orations. A "triumphal hymn" was sung by students at Yale, as their president, Dr. Stiles, was moved to write Washington, "We rejoice that the Sovereign of the Universe hath hitherto supported you as the deliverer of your country, the Defender of the Liberty and Rights of Humanity.... We share the public Joy, and congratulate our Country on the Glory of your arms, and that eminence to which you have ascended in the recent Victory over the Earl of Cornwallis and his army in Virginia." The *New York Journal* of November 12, 1781, read, "This very important and remarkable event, the capture of a whole British army, the second time, just four years after the first, both under commanders of the most approved characters and ability — an event in which the hand of heaven has been visibly displayed — has been celebrated, in various expressions of thankfulness and joy, by almost every town and society in the thirteen United States, at the different times when the news came to their knowledge."

On hearing of the victory, Louis XVI of France ordered

a "Te Deum" to be sung in the Metropolitan Church in Paris on November 27. The French Bureau de la Ville issued an ordinance requiring "all the bourgeois and inhabitants" of the city to illuminate the fronts of their houses "in order to celebrate with due respect a great victory in America, both by land and sea, over the English, by the armies of the King combined with those commanded by General Washington."[6]

On the very day of surrender at Yorktown, October 19, Admiral Graves, with his fleet and Sir Henry Clinton with 7000 troops aboard, sailed past Sandy Hook, south of New York, into the Atlantic. The mission was to save Cornwallis, but it was too late. Graves' fleet arrived off Chesapeake Bay on October 24 to the sight of de Grasses' 35 ships-of-the-line still blocking the way. The fleet was greeted by several small vessels carrying refugees from Yorktown, including the black pilot of the *Charon,* James Robinson, who had left the town on the 18th, before actual surrender. The news for Graves and Clinton was that Cornwallis was in the process of surrendering to Washington. A whaleboat was sent to rescue some loyalists off the beach on the 25th and they disclosed that the Yorktown garrison had indeed surrendered.

The information was confirmed when the fleet was joined by the 40-gun frigate *Nymphe* from New York with dispatches from Cornwallis dated October 15th, relaying that "The Safety of the Place is therefore so precarious that I cannot recommend that the Fleet and Army should run great Risque, in endeavouring to save us." Graves immediately sent the *Rattlesnake* to London, England, with the depressing news. He also dispatched *Nymphe* to New York for the same mission. Admiral Hood went to his cabin and wrote: "Mr. Graves has just sent me word he is about to send a ship to England. His messenger brings the most melancholy news Great Britain ever received ... my mind is too greatly depressed with the sense I have of my country's calamities to dwell longer upon the painful subject."[7]

Graves considered his next moves: "We stood close in to the back of the sands [shoals at the mouth of the bay] to offer them battle, for two successive days ... but the French showed no disposition to come out." Graves determined that "nothing was so proper as to return with the fleet to New York." The young Comte de Revel wrote in his diary, "Too late. The hen had been eaten." Graves' fleet departed northward from Chesapeake Bay on October 27.[8]

On the evening of Sunday, November 25, the official word of Cornwallis' surrender arrived at the house of Lord Germain in Pall Mall. Captain Melcome of His Majesty's sloop *Rattlesnake,* a captured American privateer, delivered it.[9] In his distress Germain hurried off to give the news to Lord Stormant, and then on to see Lord North at 10 Downing Street. North was said to have turned pale as Germain read the report. Germain noted that North took the depressing news "as he would have taken a ball in his chest." He talked wildly, waved his arms, while pacing back and forth in the room repeating "O God! It is all over!"

The question of the hour was whether the opening of Parliament, due in two days, should be postponed. Since the members were coming from distant boroughs it was impractical to delay. Most of them had already arrived in London for the event. After the meeting with Lord North, Germain returned home to have dinner with his three daughters, Lord Walsingham, Sir Nathaniel Wraxall, and several other members of his household. During the meal a message arrived from the king. After the women had left the room, Germain told the guests that the first minister of France, Comte Maurepas, was near death. Wraxall replied, "It would grieve me to finish my career, however far advanced in years, were I First Minister of France before I had witnessed the termination of this great contest between England and America." Germain exclaimed, "He has survived to witness that event." Wraxall looked puzzled and tried to explain again his meaning. Germain spoke, "He has survived to witness it completely.... The army has surrendered, and you may peruse the particulars of the capitulation in that paper." Germain took a letter from his pocket and handed it to Wraxall, "not without visible emotion."

Germain agreed to allow the king's response to be read aloud, "observing, at the same time, that it did the highest honour to his Majesty's fortitude, firmness and consistency of character." The account showed that the king was upset by the news "on account of the consequences connected with it and the difficulties which it may produce in carrying on the public business or in repairing such a misfortune. But I trust that neither Lord George Germain nor any member of the Cabinet will suppose that it makes the smallest alteration in those principles of my conduct which have directed me in past time and which will always continue to animate me under every event in the prosecution of the present contest." The king wanted to continue to fight the war against Americans.

The British Parliament convened on November 27 as Lord North attempted to handle open attacks from the opposition. The greatest fears of the North administration had come to pass, and the opposition pressed the issue with a passion. The king's address urged continued prosecution of the war: "I have no doubt but that by the concurrence and support of my Parliament, by the valour of my fleets and armies, and by a vigorous, animated and united exertion of the faculties and resources of my people, I shall be able to restore the blessings of a safe and honorable peace to all my dominions."

Angry questions began to fly. Sir James Lowther stood up and shouted that it was not appropriate to inquire whether the ministry was still resolved "to persevere in this war and feed it with more British blood." He said that the war "had been obstinately, fatally pursued. The country was drained, exhausted, dejected. Their hearts were against it. They consider it as a struggle against nature, in which everything was to be hazarded and nothing to be got." Lowther continued that they must put "an end to the war by a preemptory resolution." He read the proposed motion:

> That it is the opinion of this House that the war carried on in the colonies and plantations of North America has proven ineffectual either to the protection of his Majesty's loyal subjects in the said colonies, or for the defeating the dangerous designs of his enemies....

The motion was seconded as member Powys remarked, "We had persevered in this war against the voice of reason and wisdom, against experience that ought to teach, against calamity that ought to make us feel." Powys continued that the war had become "the idol of his Majesty's ministers, to which they have sacrificed the interests of the empire and almost half the territories; they bowed before it, they made the nation bow.... The illusion which had filled the minds of some gentlemen with the hope of seeing America reduced to her former obedience to this country was now no more." Powys declared: "Abandoned by all the world, we could not find a friend from pole to pole."

As the opposition continued to present arguments to stop the war, the ministry under North was embattled. The opposition was unsuccessful at resolving the matter to their satisfaction for several reasons. First, and foremost, the king continued to support the war as a matter of honor and prestige. The issue of separating the involvement of France from the issue of ending the American conflict was a difficult one to resolve. Another problem centered on the practical matter of formulating a plan to end the war that could be reasonably agreed upon by a majority in Parliament. With the North ministry still in place, it would continue to be difficult to win approval. On December 12 a vote on Sir James Lowther's to end "all further attempts to reduce the revolted colonies" was defeated by a government majority of 41 votes.

During this period North attempted to resign once more but the king refused to hear it. The king even went so far as to draft a statement of abdication, which contained a significant insight to his views. George III declared that he had "no object so much at heart as the maintenance of the British Constitution...." His frustration with rebelliousness of the House of Commons caused him to write that it "totally incapacitated Him from ei-

ther conducting the War with effect, or from obtaining any Peace but on conditions which would prove destructive of the Commerce as well as the essential Rights of the British Nation." His document continued with the statement that he felt he had no choice but to resign.

Word of this draft made the rounds throughout the government circles and Parliament, and did have a rather sobering effect on the opposition. The abdication of the king would create a serious constitutional crisis, which no one had any desire to foster. The stubborn king, filled with pride, was talked out of making this disasterous move by his ministers, and by both sides of the aisle. With the issue of what to do with the American colonial war unresolved, Parliament recessed for Christmas on December 20.[10]

Sir Henry Clinton had returned to New York and his headquarters with Admiral Graves' fleet on November 7. Lieutenant Mackenzie noted that there were no signs of despair in Clinton's mood at his headquarters, but certainly all was lost. Sir Henry began to take the predictable role of the embittered commander in his letters as he defended his actions and denounced all associated with the Yorktown loss. Judge Smith observed that Clinton took the path of defense, "a desultory justification of his own conduct and censure of everyone else — Lord Amherst, the Secretary of State, Sir George Rodney, Lord Cornwallis, General Robertson, General Knyphausen, General Tryon, Admiral Arbuthnot, Mr. Graves, the fleet, etc." Judge Smith wrote, "He is a distressed man, looking for friends and suspicious of all mankind, and complains of the number of his enemies.... The man is wild.... I pity him in his disgrace."

After the immediate surrender the allied armies had moved quickly to move Cornwallis' troops away from Yorktown. On Sunday, October 21, the prisoners were organized and marched down the road to Williamsburg. The French commissary, Claude Blanchard, noted that the British and Hessian troops were "very fine-looking men.... The remainder of the English were small; there were some Scotch troops, strong and good soldier." These troops, including the non-commissioned officers, were marched under guard of the Virginia Militia of General Lawson and divided between prison camps at Winchester, Virginia, and Frederick, Maryland. Some 1700 sick stayed at Gloucester for several additional weeks to recover before they were moved to join their fellow prisoners. Some 180 unfortunate officers were assigned to stay with the men. These officers had been placed on parole after having agreed not to fight again until exchanged. Unlike the rank and file troops who stayed behind in prison camps, these officers were free to leave for England or any British port in America.

The British, according to Blanchard, were disdainful

of their captors: "There was no call for this: they had not even made a handsome defense, and, at this very moment, were beaten and disarmed by peasants who were almost naked, whom they pretended to despise and who, nevertheless, were their conquerors." On the trip to the prison camps, a number were able to escape. Some took to the backwoods of America while others attempted to cross the country to New York. Several did make it there, but others like 20 British escapees were caught in New Jersey and put in prison in Morristown.

On the day the prisoners departed Yorktown, Washington sent General Choisy across the York to supervise the disarming of the Gloucester garrison. Meanwhile, Washington went out to see Admiral de Grasse and thank him for his part in the action. Only after the surrender did the commander-in-chief realize the significance of the sea battle won by the admiral. He wrote of such to General Heath: "The naval engagement appears to have been of much greater importance than was at first estimated." While Washington now acknowledged in writing de Grasse's contribution, America never did.[11] The other French leaders like Lafayette and Rochambeau were heroes in the legend of Revolutionary leadership. Admiral de Grasse was never to receive the historic respect he was indeed entitled to. While statues of Lafayette and Rochambeau stand opposite the White House today, the only monument to de Grasse in America was dedicated at Yorktown on October 29, 1881, exactly 100 years after it had been authorized.[12]

In an act of justice and compassion, Washington opened the stockades and freed all prisoners without regard to their sentences. Americans who had served the British throughout the war were freed, yet deserters discovered in Yorktown who had switched uniforms during the engagement were hanged. On October 23rd the British sloop *Bonetta* was allowed to depart Yorktown without American inspection as agreed to during the terms of surrender. It was believed that some 250 deserters and loyalists were aboard. It turned out to be "so extremely riotous" that the captain risked all during a storm to put the passengers ashore in New York.

Meanwhile, the dinners given by the American and French officers continued night after night at Yorktown. On November 2 Rochambeau held another grand dinner starting at four o'clock in the afternoon attended by the ranking allied officers and finally the elusive Cornwallis. The earl's "reflective, mild, and noble bearing" impressed the French. Cornwallis was rather open in dinner conversation and he revealed that even the Carolina campaign had contributed to his defeat. On November 3 the majority of the American troops left Yorktown in a fleet of small boats bound for Head of Elk, Maryland. Rochambeau and the French army now settled down to

their winter quarters at Yorktown, Hampton and Williamsburg.[13] The next day de Grasse and his fleet departed the Chesapeake for the West Indies. Washington had attempted to get the distinguished admiral to stay on the East Coast for coordinated actions against the British at Charles Town or Savannah, but he was compelled to return to honor his commitment with the Spanish.

On November 4, 1781, Cornwallis boarded the *Cochrane* and sailed down the York River toward a meeting with Clinton in New York. After a rough voyage, with selected officers including General O'Hara, they arrived off Sandy Hook on November 19. Not wanting to deal with Clinton, Cornwallis was determined to leave for England as soon as possible. He was able to leave New York on December 15, in a convoy. Some 12 days out of port the convoy began to disperse, with Cornwallis transferring to the *Greyhound* under the command of Thomas Tonken. Unfortunately for Cornwallis, on January 14, 1782, his ship was "taken off Scilly by a French privateer of St. Malo who took all our seamen & put French in their room...." Since the privateers crew were poor seamen, "Lord Cornwallis proposed to him as our lives were in danger of going to France in our present situation that in case he consented to go into an English port that the ship should be his, his Lordship having given his word to the Capt. Of the privateer that neither the officers or servants should in the least interrupt the prize master from navigating his ship. All my papers give you every information in my power when I have the honour of waiting on you."[14] Cornwallis finally did reach England.

Washington left down the Williamsburg Road with his staff on November 4 headed toward the west. He stopped at Williamsburg to visit the wounded in the local hospital. By evening he had reached Eltham at the head of the York River at the home of his brother-in-law, Burwell Bassett. Here he discovered Jacky Curtis in his last hours of life. Washington's stepson, who had traveled to support the American cause as an aide at Yorktown, died of camp fever during the night, leaving two children — Eleanor Parke Custis and George Washington Parke Custis. Washington adopted both children.

The commander-in-chief then moved on to Fredericksburg to visit his mother. From there he rode to Mount Vernon for a week's rest. While at home he wrote Lafayette, who was planning to sail to France, his "ardent Vows for a propitious voyage ... and a safe return in the spring." He also wrote to General Greene giving direction to keep a careful watch on the British at Charles Town. Washington wrote, "My greatest fear is that Congress, viewing this stroke in too important a point of light, may think our work too nearly closed, and will fall into a state of languor and relaxation."

The journey of General Washington from Mount

Vernon to the capital at Philadelphia was a triumphal one. In Annapolis the governor and all the citizens acclaimed him. The local newspaper reported that even loyalists joined "feebly in applauding the man, whose late successes had annihilated their hopes.... The evening was spent at the governor's elegant and hospitable board with festive joy, enlivened by good humour, wit and beauty. Every heart overflowed with gratitude and love, and every tongue grew wanton in his praise.... Unrival'd and unmatched shall be his fame, And his own laurels shade his envied name.'"

In Baltimore the commander-in-chief was again heralded. When he arrived in Philadelphia on November 26 the *Pennsylvania Journal* reported, "All panegyrick is vain and language too feeble to express our ideas of his greatness." The editor continued, "May the crown of glory he has placed on the brow of the genius of America, shine with untarnished radiance and lustre, and in the brightness of its rays be distinctly seen—WASHINGTON, THE SAVIOUR OF HIS COUNTRY!"

The citizens everywhere celebrated the grand victory. Charles Willson Peale painted a number of pictures as "expressions of ... respect and gratitude to the conquering Hero." One of the paintings had Washington and Rochambeau "with rays of glory and interlaced civic crowns over their heads, framed with palm and laurel branches, and the words of transparent letters, SHINE VALIANT CHIEFS...." The celebrations continued for over a week as Washington and his officers were wined and dined. The new nation had a real and grand hero.[15]

After the surrender at Yorktown, Virginia citizens tried to return to more normalcy. The militias guarding the prisoners at Winchester were constantly hearing complaints from the local farmers that the prisoners caused disturbances. The farmers had no interest in feeding the visitors, and with some impressment the public opinion was in an uproar. The Virginia administration informed Congress through its delegates that the state just could not maintain the number of prisoners under their supervision. Strangely, when Congress did decide to move all the prisoners to Maryland in December of 1781, the counties around Winchester protested the loss of business. The governor and administrator responded: "If they are loosers by it, it is their own doings."

After the American Army departed Virginia, the French set out destroying the fortifications at Yorktown and those built by Arnold in Portsmouth. Rochambeau set up winter quarters in Williamsburg, with detachments at Yorktown, Gloucester, Hampton and West Point. The winter of 1781-1782 turned out to be a mild one, and from letters and the journals of the French officers it was a rather enjoyable time. The local Virginia aristocracy was delighted to host the French to dinners, dances, cock-

fights, horse races, hunts and similar leisure events. On the evening of December 15 Rochambeau celebrated the Yorktown victory with a "Te Deum" mass sung at Williamsburg, followed by an evening dinner and ball for which Baron von Closen noted, "Everyone was very much pleased with it."

During the winter the French took over the main college building in Williamsburg as well as the hospital. The old governor's mansion was used for wounded Americans, but unfortunately it caught fire during the winter. Most Virginians liked having the disciplined and distinguished French in Virginia. When they left Williamsburg in the incredibly hot weather of early July 1782, the citizens were sorry to see them go. After a march of six months, the French reached Boston, where they embarked for their long voyage home and out of the Revolution in North America.

There was one issue that the Virginia officials and the French did not agree on and that caused conflict before they departed the fair state. The French had no interest in returning the slaves they had captured. The French officers were delighted to find the black slaves so cheap during the war, and as one French officer put it, they "garnered a veritable harvest of domesticks. Those among us who had no servant were happy to find one so cheap." Virginia officials complained to Rochambeau with no success. The difficulty for the Americans was producing proof of ownership, as the blacks cried they were already free. In a last ditch effort to stop the French, Benjamin Harrison proposed to Rochambeau that if the French would leave the slaves behind, he would "make it my Business" to sort out the blacks and return them to the rightful owners. Rochambeau refused to respond to this effort with his excuse that they had brought slaves with them: "You saw the French army when it came here."

Returning the Virginia legislature to active sessions was somewhat slow in coming during the fall of 1781. The schedule had been set for opening on October 1, but the session was delayed because of the pending battle at Yorktown. Governor Thomas Nelson had set the new date on the battlefield, but it took nine days to reach the council in Richmond, the capital, leaving only 11 days before the session was to begin. The session did not actually reach a quorum until November 19, and this was only achieved because the sergeant at arms borrowed horses and riders from the state quartermaster to bring in the delinquent delegates. Absenteeism was so bad that a quorum was reduced to only 55 members.

Governor Nelson became ill and returned to his plantation at Offley Hoo in Hanover County. He was never to return to Richmond as the governor. As soon as a quorum was reached, Nelson had his resignation submitted. Finally, on the last day of November the legislature filled the vacant positions, including electing the speaker of the House of Delegates, Benjamin Harrison, as Nelson's successor over the two other candidates, John Page and Richard Henry Lee.

The focus of the Virginia legislative agenda was the economic situation of the state, much as it had been during the war. Virginia was indeed broke. Harrison wrote, "We have not a Shilling in the Treasury." To cut back the "bleeding" the assembly took a number of dramatic actions. It reduced the number of western regiments, the three state regiments, the State Garrison Regiment, the artillery regiment and the hospital service, and reduced the navy to one single lookout vessel, the *Liberty*, and four new row galleys that were to be built to defend against privateers. The legislature also dismissed the paymasters general of the army and navy, reduced the size of the state quartermasters and commissioners of the state, and terminated the state agent in Europe, Philip Mazzei. When the request came for assistance to deal with the Indians from Colonel Arthur Campbell of Washington County, the governor sent back his recommendation that "the Executive therefore recommend to the Citizens on our Frontiers to use every means in their Power for preserving a good Understanding with the Savage Tribes."

Paying the militia was another difficult issue, as it was for all the state governments and for Congress too. At discharge the troops in Virginia were given back pay in certificates redeemable in gold in 1785. As the government of Virginia began to dismantle much of its military support, the possibility of letting down its guard too soon was a real concern. The former royal governor, Lord Dunmore, who sat the war out in New York in the winter of 1781-1782, advocated the establishment of a black army to invade the South from West Florida. Although the Richmond newspaper called the threat "a laughable circumstance," General Greene did issue a midwinter warning that the British might reinforce the Charles Town British garrison with 4000 men, as he called for 2000 Virginia Militia to defend Georgia and South Carolina. Other news from William Lee in Brussels indicated that Benedict Arnold might be outfitting an expedition for operations in the South. Richard Henry Lee was able to form an 11-man committee to consider a defensive plan, but the legislature took no action.

What was expected to be quite a spectacle that winter seemed to melt away in disinterest from the delegates. The impeachment of Thomas Jefferson was on the agenda ever since June 12, at the lowest point in the war as Cornwallis was roving the state, when George Nicholas moved "that on the next session of Assembly an inquiry be made into the conduct of the Executive of this State for the last twelve months." The accusations of poor handling of the

state had festered and Jefferson had become bitter over it. An election in Albemarle County had allowed the former governor, Jefferson, to have a seat in the House of Delegates some three weeks after the sessions started, but he gave only minimal attendance.

When the time came to present their case against Jefferson, even Nicholas was not interested in joining the investigative committee. Jefferson had been preparing for months to defend himself, and when the opposition folded he took the floor anyway and read his reply to the charges. On December 12 the House of Delegates thanked him for his dissent and for his "impartial, upright, and attentive administration." The Senate amended the charges to essentially eliminate any reference to the need for the inquiry, which was agreed upon by the lower chamber on December 19. Jefferson was so hurt by the past charges that he declined election to Congress, and received approval to be absent from further proceeding of the legislature. In the spring of 1782 the legislature tried to elect him to office but he declined because of his wife's illness, and the "wound" of his potential impeachment. Jefferson told his friends that he could "only be cured by the all-healing grave."

By this time the attention and anger of the delegates had turned to Thomas Nelson. He was attacked for his past aggressiveness in giving supplies to the allied army. The primary opposition came from a retired member of the legislature, George Mason. Mason had developed a petition on behalf of his fellow citizens of Prince William County, which accused Nelson of violating the constitution by authorizing impressments without consent of the council. He charged that Nelson placed no restrictions on the seizures "other than the arbitrary Will and Pleasure of the Persons" in charge. Mason compared the impressments to the oppressions of King Charles I, whom the English had beheaded, and to that of King James II, whose subjects drove him from the throne.

The majority of the delegates were more interested in Nelson's use of money. Nelson had persuaded the French to buy supplies from state agents who were forced to rely on impressment rather than having the French use gold specie to pay the merchants for their supplies. Nelson was also accused of giving away supplies to troops from other states. Mason claimed by example that at least one Pennsylvania cavalry unit that had not been equipped at home was sent directly to Virginia for outfitting. On December 22, Nelson asked to be heard, and was immediately sent to the Committee of the Whole House for a hearing. He pleaded his case and after some discussion, Nelson was successful in convincing his detractors "that what he did wrong was imputable to a mistake in his Judgement and not from a corrupt heart." The House resolved without dissent to forgive the former governor and passed an act of indemnity. But the legislature did act to revoke the impressment powers of the governor. Governor Harrison noted that the Virginia governor was "the poorest and the most impotent Executive perhaps in the world."

The next year the wartime positions withered away, and the economic issues ruled the agendas. Numerous offices were reduced or eliminated and more work fell to the governor and the council. The faces changed, as many that were mere assistants or clerks before the war were now in positions of much responsibility. The issue of economic recovery was dominant. After Yorktown the legislature abolished paper money as legal tender, effective December 1781, except for the payment of taxes to redeem it. The delegates adopted a scale of depreciation, ranging from one and one-half to one in January 1777 to 1000 to one in 1781 for all contracts. All currency had to be exchanged by October 1, 1782, for gold certificates redeemable in 1790 with annual interest guaranteed for use in paying land tax or in warrants on western land. Superior court cases and judgments, which had been suspended since the invasion, were to proceed after December 1783.

Another issue that the Virginia legislature had to confront was the relationship with Congress. There was much resentment among the Virginians that the Northern states had been slow in coming to the aid of Virginia during the Cornwallis invasion. Most locals felt that Virginia had done more than any other state to win the victory. This opinion had surfaced even though the Virginia support for the union had always been evident at the beginning and during the Revolution. A Virginia correspondent wrote James Madison that "Our people still retain their opinions of the importance of this State, its superiority in the Union, and the very great exertions and advances it has made." He continued, "Their views are generally local, not seeing the necessity or propriety of general measures now [that] the War is over." This Virginia opinion and view of their importance in the war, and the suspicion of the central authority, led Virginia to become one of the most anti-federal states in the activities to follow in ratifying the Constitution later in the decade.

Virginians believed with conviction that Congress owed a debt to them, and in financial terms as reported to Madison by Joseph Jones, "at least one million pounds." It was not until almost a decade later that negotiations forced Virginia to accept that it actually owed Congress $100,000, in large measure because the commissary general, John Brown, had not recorded deliveries to the Continental forces. When the superintendent of finance, Robert Morris, demanded payment of the Virginia funds, Virginians complained. Harrison called Morris' "Stile" as "illy suited to the character of the writer or to that of the

Supreme magistrate of any one of the United States, and savours much more of that passion and ignorance you so obligingly attribute to me, than that calmness and decency ever the Characteristic of the great Minister."

Quite another irritant of the postwar years for a number of Virginia delegates to Congress was the issue of claims to Western lands. Most of the members of the Virginia House of Delegates felt that Congress was wholly ungrateful and they saw much of their interests in the Western lands to go unsettled. Back in November 1781 when Congress had agreed to New York's cession and rejected Virginia's, there was much sentiment to withdrawing from acceptance of the 1781 Act of Cession. Even James Madison advised his colleagues that there was "ample justification for revoking or at least suspending their Act of Cession."

Another factor that clouded the issue was the suspicion of the involvement of many of the Congressmen who had personal claims to Western lands. In an attempt to deal with this situation, Arthur Lee proposed in 1782 that the members submit to "a purifying declaration from each member requiring that they declare upon his honour, whether he is ... interested ... in the claims of ... companies, which have petitioned against the territorial rights of any one of the state." The resolution was not carried. The deterioration of the federal government finances finally led to compromise in June of 1783. Congress agreed to Virginia's demands not to recognize claims prior to the date of cession provided that Virginia reenact the cession without legal conditions. On March 3, 1783, Congress passed Virginia's second condition for cession of the entire Northwest Territory.

Perhaps the most passionate legislation during the immediate postwar years in Virginia was associated with the issue of allowing masters to manumit slaves. For most of the previous century manumission required the consent of the governor and his council. It was rarely given unless the slave had performed "meritorious services," and, therefore, there were only a few thousand freed slaves out of some 200,000 who lived in Virginia at the time of the Revolution. An earlier attempt to change the law had failed. Now the issue was raised in a religious context rather than a constitutional one. The decision of the Quakers and Methodists in the 1770s to release their slaves ran into problems with the law. The lobbying activities of three Quakers, George Dillwyn, Warner Mufflin and John Parrish, was successful in allowing masters to free their slaves. Filing a deed with the county court was now adequate to make the change. As a result of this change to the law, some 10,000 slaves were freed during the following decade in Virginia. Unfortunately the next 20 years would see restrictions gradually narrow the flexibility of the statute until in 1806 the law was nullified, forcing all freed slaves to move out of the state or face the possibility of being resold into bondage.[16]

The situation in Maryland was, as expected, quite similar to that found in Virginia. But in South Carolina the aftermath of the Yorktown victory was even more complicated than in Virginia. The key difference was that the British still occupied Charles Town and the surrounding countryside. The scorched earth policy of the British and the roving bands of loyalists and patriots served to devastate the countryside. Evidence of this condition was everywhere. In the Georgetown District, which had been prosperous before the war, Wemyss disclosed in his final mission report that he had "burnt and laid waste about 50 houses and Plantations" in the area. Camden was in ruins, having been destroyed as the British evacuated. "They burnt the Court House, Gaol, & the greatest Part of the best Houses." Joseph Kershaw's mills and property were burned, and Sumter's property was also destroyed. Tarleton had obliterated General Richardson's holding too.

Farther up near the North Carolina border, Colonel William Hill's iron works were destroyed, and at Fishing Creek the citizens "were vastly plundered and distressed." The Reverend John Simpson's "property was destroyed, his house burned, not so much as a farthing's worth was left." William Drayton wrote, "from Camden to Charleston, we could trace ... [the British army's] last Retreat by the Stacks of Chimnies that appear'd along the road." General William Moultrie related his recollection that the area from Winyaw, on the Georgetown coast, to the Ashley River was as "the most dull, melancholy, dreary ride that any one could ... take." In the Lowcountry near the Georgia border in November 1783 Reverend Archibald Simpson wrote on returning home that "All was desolation.... Every field, every plantation, showed marks of ruin and devastation." In his mind the British had come to "conquer" or "conciliate" Carolinians.

Farther to the west, the work of loyalist William Cunningham devastated part of the Saluda River region. At Dutch Fork many plantations were destroyed. At Ninety Six James Dunlap had terrorized and plundered. When he destroyed Andrew Pickens' house in the area, Pickens felt compelled to free himself from the parole and he rejoined the fight. Before the British left Ninety Six, they burned the town.

While there was considerable destruction and loss throughout South Carolina at the hands of the British, the property damage in the Lowcountry was somehow less than elsewhere in the state. Strangely, the people in the Lowcountry around Charles Town were less affected than in the backcountry and other areas. From the time the British occupied the state in 1780, Lowcountry fighting was somehow less bloody and not as cruel. Most of the battles were not fought in the Lowcountry either. Of the 137 known engagements of the Revolution in South Carolina, 78 were fought in the backcountry. Of the important battles only four were fought in the coastal area, while some 14 took place in the interior.

David Ramsey wrote just after the war that even with the destruction, "the houses of the planters were seldom burnt." When it was reported that the British had burned the houses of William Somersall and his father, better information came in that "it was not the houses I have mentioned but the barns that were burnt...." The picture of the destruction was not black and white as it may have seemed. In November 1781, a good one and one-half years after the British had first occupied Charles Town, Colonel Henry Lee wrote as he moved his troops into the "country settled by the original emigrants into Carolina" that he saw "spacious edifices, rich and elegant gardens, with luxuriant and extensive rice plantations." In contrast to what they had expected, "Never before had we been solaced with the prospect of so much comfort."

For those in the Charles Town District, the war was not extremely harsh. The terror that took place in the backcountry and in parts of Georgetown never really touched these favored individuals. For one, the white population was small and rather united. Many lived the lives of prosperous people, not as hardened as those of the backcountry. The Lowcountry peoples did not fight among themselves for the most part. Even the British treated the aristocracy-dominated Lowcountry peoples better. Many were educated in England and were Anglican in religion. Many had friends in the army or among the British merchants. Even those who were exiled by the British to St. Augustine were fairly treated in most cases. Some were even allowed to take their servants, and were allowed to rent homes. The backcountry peoples were faced with the majority of the destructiveness and cruelty of the Revolution in South Carolina. The civil war in the backcountry, coupled with the battle engagements and the terror of the likes of Tarleton, served to make life in the backcountry significantly more distressing as the war ended.

What property the British did not destroy, they carried off with them. The incredible loss of furniture, silver, and goods of all types was hard to place a value on. The property taken from homes in the Beaufort area during Prevost's invasion was estimated by Edward Rutledge to be in the millions of pounds sterling. Even when the British finally departed Charles Town, the terms of the negotiated evacuation allowed Major Andrew Maxwell to carry off "private property of every sort, without investigation of title." Maxwell's own "take" took two wagons to hall away to the waiting transport. On departing in 1782 one British officer confiscated St. Michael's church bells for shipment in one of the 30 ships Edward Rutledge described as "inadequate to carry off" all the loot that he had.

Perhaps the most valuable war booty taken from Charles Town and the surrounding plantations were the slaves. The British had collected some 12,000 slaves in the city. In March 1782 when the British left South Carolina, they left with 5000 slaves. Although the greed factor was certainly the dominant reason for the significant loss of slaves, another reality was that the slaves had taken the opportunity to escape their masters. Of the estimated 20,000 to 25,000 slaves that were lost during the war, as many ran away as were stolen. As early as 1775 the flight of the blacks began. In that year there were so many slaves on Sullivan's Island that the Council of Safety ordered their camp destroyed. As a result William Moultrie took many prisoners and killed some 50 blacks that would not surrender. In numerous journals during the war were recorded statements like the following in March 1780: "Today came thirteen Negroes fleeing from Young's plantation on Wadmalaw Island." Most South Carolina plantation owners lost significant numbers of slaves. William Wigg lost 96, and Rawlins Lowndes lost some 75 blacks.

Everywhere the British moved, the black slaves gathered in large numbers. Unfortunately many of these people never saw the freedom they prayed for. For many sickness and death were more often their fate. The large numbers made it difficult for the British to care for them. As a result of their station and the condition that they were only used for labor, they were quite neglected in most cases. Crowded together under poor conditions, many died of smallpox, then known as "camp fever." The situation might have improved for the slaves if they had been able to fight with the British, and thereby be viewed as more tactically necessary. But this was impossible because the support of the slave-owning loyalists. When on that rare occasion blacks were used in battle, the resentment was severe and served to make the British situation often worse. In 1781 Thomas Sumter wrote that the black slave soldiers raised "the resentment and detestation of every American who possesses common feelings." The following year Charles Cotesworth Pinckney declared that armed blacks were "daily committing the most horrible depredations and murder in the defenceless parts of our Country."

During the summer of 1781 South Carolina Governor John Rutledge returned from North Carolina intent on re-establishing civil government. With the encouragement of General Greene, Rutledge tried to end the civil war by offering to most loyalists a full and free pardon if they would serve a six-month tour with the state militia. The only excluded persons were those who currently held military or civil commissions with the British

or those who had already refused pardons in the past proclamations of 1778 and 1779. Also not eligible were any that were well known as enemies of the American cause.

The attempt at allowing pardons was Greene's response to "the daily scenes of the most horrid plundering and murder." Greene knew that "vengeance would dictate one universal slaughter," while forgiving those who had stayed with the enemy could cut down on the level of post-war revenge at the hands of the victors. General Francis Marion agreed with Greene and Rutledge on the issue of leniency as a proper policy. Later in 1782 Marion worked with the loyalist leader in the Pee Dee River area of North Carolina, Major Micajah Gainey, to establish a truce that required the loyalists to restore plundered property and sign an oath of allegiance to South Carolina and the United States in return for a pardon. Some 500 loyalists took advantage of this opportunity. Gainey and his followers served six months and actually fought with the patriots against the British-backed black dragoons.

Thomas Sumter also worked to encourage this type of arrangement. In the Orangeburgh region he pardoned some 40 on December 13, 1782, and by December 22 some 300 loyalists had joined the program. There was even some cooperation among loyalists and patriots to maintain a truce while the crops were being cultivated. According to South Carolina Judge Aedanus Burke, the leniency policy indeed saved lives. In a report in May 1782 he recorded that the country had been "ravaged by small armed parties" who murdered "in Cold Blood." After the governor authorized a truce Burke wrote that the parties "are at last received on terms of pardon & reconciliation & now live at home."

Not everyone agreed with this policy of forgiveness. Many held revenge in their hearts. Sumter wrote that "nothing but the sword will reclaim" the loyalists. William Clay Snipes called for violence, and even many men in General Marion's group were determined to kill the Pee Dee region's infamous Jeff Butler saying that "To defend such a wretch is an insult to humanity...." Colonel Lemuel Benton, in command of the Cheraw Militia, protested that men who had plundered and killed should not be "restored to equal privileges with the men who have suffered every thing them that was in their power & savage disposition to inflict." The issue was controversial for many years.

In November 1781 Governor Rutledge called for new legislative elections in South Carolina. The election officials made provisions to find and elect representatives to speak for the parishes that were still in British hands. Even those newly confirmed loyalists were allowed to vote. With the circumstances of the British control over several of the parishes, the election was curious and Edward

Rutledge wrote, "I fear there will be damned strange works when once the Assembly get together." But a month later he had changed his mind, writing, "I like the Competent Appearance of the House very much…. We have the Flower of the Country." Judge and House member Aedanus Burke agreed, saying that the body was "composed of very respectable good men."

The legislators who finally gathered in January 1782 at Jacksonborough, a small village some 35 miles from Charles Town, were dominated by the military. Nineteen of the 28 elected senators appeared and ten of the 19 held the rank of captain or higher. The results of the election left the Lowcountry parishes around Charles Town without control of the legislature for the first time. With many voting by habit for absentee representatives, the Charles Town District was short 39 representatives, while the other regions were short only 26 members. This situation left the Charles Town District with only 57 representatives present, while the remaining regions of South Carolina had 80 representatives.

The new makeup of the controlling membership of the legislature gave Rutledge and others in the former controlling aristocracy considerable anxiety as the session opened. The character of the new majority was unknown, and their philosophy was untested. But eventually the uncertainty gave way to sound voting records. The vote that quieted the fears came when John Laurens appeared at Jacksonborough and proposed another plan to arm and free the slaves. The defeat of the plan by a vote of 15 to 100 was great satisfaction that all was well.

Rutledge opened the session of the legislature with remarks congratulating the recent American victories and noting that General Greene was entitled to "honourable and singular marks of … approbation and gratitude." Rutledge warned the British that the Americans would "never … return to a domination which, near six years ago, they unanimously and justly renounced." The governor continued in serious expressions that the legislators had been "prisoners of war … killed in cold blood, delivered up to savages … consumed in flames…." He reminded those present that as the British had destroyed the homes of the "widowed, the aged, the infirmed," the enemy was affected by "neither the tears of mother, nor the cries of infants…." The man who had pushed the idea of pardons for the loyalists was at that moment proclaiming the cruelty of the past sins of the foe.

The first act of the legislature was to elect Christopher Gadsden as governor. But Gadsden declined the office in what Burke called "the most illustrious action of his Life." In the end John Mathews became governor and Richard Hutson was elected lieutenant governor. After the other public officials were identified, including the delegates to Congress, the legislative session began. The acts passed were prolific. New regulations for the militia were passed, and Greene was rewarded for his leadership with an estate worth 10,000 guineas. The assembly rejected Laurens' plan to raise black troops, but it agreed to repeal the act making paper money legal tender. They approved the ad valorem tax of five percent on all imported goods to be in force when all the other states adhered to it through congressional action in progress.

Another act of the legislature in South Carolina was to open the Courts of Oyer and Terminer. According to Burke, the action was an absurd act since so many crimes had been committed that the civil courts "w[oul]d not be able to settle them in twenty years." Burke was convinced that enforcement would not allow "one thousand men … [to] escape the Gallows." Burke was not alone in his assessment. Judge John Faucheraud Grimke recommended mercy in 1783 or Carolina justice would force all to "wade" through a "field of blood." These judges could see that the courts could very well be used to gain legal revenge on the loyalists as opposed to gaining true justice. Burke was so outraged that he finally presented his resignation to the governor.

Certainly the most significant attack on loyalists was not in the courts but as a result of legislation to seize loyalist property. The legislature passed the Amercement Act, which placed a 12 percent annual tax on appraised value of any property owned by suspected British sympathizers. Since the Confiscation Act of 1776 state government could seize property owned by loyalists for sale and order the execution of the owner. This act had rarely been enforced but it was always looming over the heads of those who had much to lose.

While revenge was certainly a clear motive, another justification for the seizures of property was the poor financial condition the South Carolina government found itself in. The state was indeed destitute. Edward Rutledge was the first legislator in the Jacksonborough assembly to draft a bill confiscating estates to "raise a Tax." Francis Marion was supportive of this bill as he expected it to yield as least one million pounds sterling. Marion wrote, "Two regiments are to be raised as our Continental quota," and he proposed that they should be "giving each man a Negro per year … taken from the confiscated estates." Burke was not in agreement with the action, feeling that "a few Land Jobbers or Speculators … [would] engross them." To stop the act from being used to build large estates by those who were already wealthy, Gadsden pushed through the final bill with provisions that divided all confiscated estates into tracts from 200 to 500 acres. The new clause "met with general approbation," and was "oppos'd only by … the great land jobber in the State."

The Confiscation Act of 1782 was much discussed over the years after its passage. Edward Rutledge wrote,

"I hope they will be lenient, but as I said before, I fear." In a letter to Arthur Middleton, Rutledge noted that "the passions of some People run very high." The action of the crowd at Jacksonborough was so emotional that Burke observed in support of the confiscation that he would have had his "throat cut for saying this in publick." For men like Burke they saw the "miserable melancholy plight" of the British loyalists.

Gadsden also condemned the harsh actions of the Assembly and wrote that his colleagues must "be without passion" at their work of setting laws to correct "the rash impetuosity of the people." It was not until 1787 that a bill came up for vote to repeal the Jacksonborough Confiscation Act, but it was soundly defeated 121 to 37. Fortunately the results of the act were not as severe as had been expected. While not an insignificant number, only 377 estates were confiscated and 94 amerced with the 12 percent tax. Of the 700 names originally identified by a committee of the House of Representatives to be punished, only 119 were ultimately listed. The bill passed on February 13, 1782.

Full-scale fighting ended in South Carolina in 1781, and only minor skirmishes occurred after that. The British made no strategic moves back into the countryside, and only ventured out for provisions. On one such engagement, though, 27-year-old John Laurens was killed. Young Laurens was a rare humanitarian who was obsessed with ending slavery in his state. After his death John Adams wrote his father, Henry Laurens, expressing, "You have ... reason to say 'I would not exchange my dead son for any living son in the world.'"

As the war came to an end in South Carolina, the old ruling aristocracy attempted to exert its power and influence on the executive government. Actions like Governor John Mathews settling two agreements with the British, which protected the rights of the slave-owning planters, served to provide clear evidence that the influence of the upper class was still intact. The major interest of the old planter class was their English debt. The estimated pre-war debt was around £412,000 sterling. Many of the debtors were so hard hit by the war that they were not in any condition to pay what they owed. The ultimate Treaty of Paris did not sit well with the planters because it made no allowance for the hardships caused by the Southern debt to the English. That treaty indicated that there should be no "lawful Impediment" to repaying British creditors any debts owed.

Another distressed group was the Carolina merchants, especially those living in Charles Town. When the occupation of the city began in May 1780, the British refused to allow the local merchants to work and support their families. As a result, opportunist British merchants flocked to the fair port to conduct lucrative trade. When word came that all British were to be departing Charles Town in 1782 as a result of the act of Parliament, the English merchants lobbied Governor Mathews to allow them to stay an additional 18 months to sell their goods and collect debts. But as a result of the pressure placed on the governor by the desperate Carolina merchants, Mathews gave permission to allow the English to stay only an additional six months to settle their affairs. With the war winding down, the English and Carolina merchants knew that the planters would need to restock and resupply their plantations with goods.

The English merchant agreement was hotly contested and most especially because these merchants violated the spirit of the agreement by charging an "extravagant price" for their goods. When William Logan, a Charles Town merchant who had been exiled to St. Augustine, returned to his home city, he was outraged to find the English merchants charging more than they did when the British occupied the city. Logan and "a Number of Inhabitants" petitioned the legislature to solve the grievance. Unfortunately the local planters favored their access to the English goods more than supporting their merchant colleagues, and the Senate dropped any support for the grievance. In 1783 much of the £300,000 of merchandise shipped to South Carolina was by British merchants. In 1784 some 40 percent of the goods valued at over £1,000,000 were imported by alien merchants. Certainly, Charles Town was an expensive place to live for a number of years after the war.

After the Jacksonborough legislature adjourned in March 1783, the state was moving to at least some level of normalcy. While the war was over, the citizens of South Carolina faced troubles, like their fellow citizens throughout the South. Prices were high for everything, resentment against the loyalists and British remained, the grievances to the legislature often met inaction, and the pre-war sense of class conflict returned. It was a time for rebuilding the financial strength of the state and coming to terms with the day-to-day meaning of independence with a new central government on the rise.[17]

In Georgia in 1781 the actions of the state government were not unlike those of the other Southern states. After the patriot victory and retaking of Augusta in June 1781, General Greene sent Joseph Clay, his paymaster general, to the town in an attempt to re-establish the Georgia government, which had all but dissolved. The Georgia Assembly met on August 17 in Augusta with representatives from all the Georgia counties except Camden. The body elected Dr. Nathan Brownson as governor and chose other state officials, county officers and congressional representatives. The Assembly extended expiring laws and regulations, and set about dealing with the issues surrounding the loyalists' and citizens' rights.[18]

On January 1, 1782, the Assembly again met in Augusta. By this point, all of Georgia was clear of British control except Savannah. Like their fellow representatives in the neighboring states, the legislature passed an act allowing confiscation of property, both real and personal, belonging to those who had joined with the British. These loyalists were banished forever from the state by this act. The plan called for the property to be sold and all proceeds to be credited to the state treasury. Funds from the credit were issued in the form of certificates totaling some £22,100 sterling to meet government obligations. The certificates were redeemable in par value for gold or silver coin or Spanish milled dollars. The Assembly took other actions including appointing the executive and judicial officers, with their salaries fixed and paid in certificates. Certificates worth £15,000 were also allocated to pay in arrears the salaries due to the state militia.

After Yorktown, Brigadier General Anthony Wayne was ordered to Georgia as the Continental commander for the state. At that time the British had a total of some 1000 men in Georgia compared to the 500 or so patriot forces. Early in February 1782 Wayne was ordered to Ebenezer with 100 of Colonel Moylan's dragoons under Colonel Anthony Walton White to join with Colonel James Jackson's Georgia State Legion. Soon they were also combined with Colonel Posey's 300 Continental troops. Even with this strengthened force, General Wayne had to limit his activities to defending the countryside around Savannah from foraging and plundering parties from the British out of Savannah.

A most pressing problem for Wayne was feeding the army and assisting others west of Augusta who were in dire need. The need was so great that John Werreat used his own slaves and boats to ship rice upriver to help the citizens of the interior. When the British under Brigadier General Clarke were ordered in from other outposts to defend Savannah as a result of Wayne's move to Ebenezer, he directed that all food and goods they were unable to bring with them to the town were to be destroyed. The conflagration was so successful that for many miles from the coast to Sunbury and Savannah, the rice farms were in ruin. These British and loyalist actions forced Wayne to feed and supply his army from South Carolina.

The limited actions of the foraging parties of the British and loyalists were active even after most of the Savannah area was in patriot hands. On February 13 Colonel Jackson was attacked at his camp at Cuthbert's Sawmills at 11 A.M. by 50 loyalists and Indians from Savannah led by Colonel Hezekiah Williams. The patriots rallied after the attack, but not before three of Jackson's men were wounded. Unfortunately Williams' force was able to escape back toward Savannah.

Wayne turned his attention to the extensive amount of rice that was stored on Hutchinson's Island opposite Savannah. Rice fields had been ordered cultivated by Governor Wright. Unable to gain possession of the rice because of the number of cannons pointed in that direction, Wayne decided to have it destroyed. On the night of February 26 Wayne detached Major Barnwell of South Carolina with 50 men in boats down the north river to burn the rice on the island, as well as any available on the mainland. Meanwhile Colonel Jackson was ordered to take 30 dragoons to Royal Governor Wright's rice plantation. Jackson's mission was successful at burning all the rice without any casualties. Unfortunately Major Barnwell's detachment was not so successful. The enemy found out about the plan and ambushed his force on the island. Barnwell lost two men killed and four wounded. One of his boats ran aground and three of his men were taken prisoner.

Incidents continued around Savannah during the first six months of 1782. One action was prompted by the movement of a party of Indians passing through Savannah from the Creek Nation with horses stolen from patriots in Liberty County. Major Francis Moore with 15 men chased the Indians and overtook them at Reid's Bluff. Finding the Indians well settled in a log cabin, Moore attacked the superior numbers anyway with no success. Moore was killed and another man was wounded on the first trade of musketfire. The patriots were forced to retreat.

Realizing the value of using the local Indians to supplement his forces, General Clarke sent representatives to the Creek and Cherokee nations to enlist their support. A general gathering was planned for May 15 on the Southern frontier, but disagreements with the Indian councils delayed the movement to join. Though the grand council of the Cherokee and Creek nations did not sanction the British alliance, some 3000 Creek warriors under Guristersigo set out for Savannah in June. Using white guides, the Indians moved down the southern frontier of Georgia to the vicinity of Wayne's encampment at Joseph Gibbon's Plantation some seven miles from Savannah. The white guides alerted Guristersigo to the patriot camp position, as they changed their path to avoid Wayne's camp.

Fortunately for Wayne, he moved his camp on the afternoon of the 23rd to avoid being detected by foraging parties from Savannah, not realizing that an enemy force was coming from the opposite direction. The Indian force had some 15 miles to cover and did not reach Wayne's location until three o'clock the morning of June 24. Guristersigo sent out a party to kill the sentinels while he moved his force into the rear of Wayne's camp. The Indian warriors were able to reach the patriot camp undetected. Captain Parker realized the situation and ordered a retreat behind Gibbon's house. General Wayne sprang to his horse and ordered a bayonet defense, calling out "victory or death." Wayne's horse was shot out from under him. Wayne continued to advance with sword raised in hand toward the attacking Indians. Wayne's men were able to regain their field cannon, as the tide of the conflict turned in favor of the patriot forces. When it was all over, 17 warriors were dead plus Guristersigo. The remaining Indians fled and were pursued. Twelve warriors were captured while retreating. Wayne's force suffered four killed and eight wounded.[19]

With these and other small engagements, the area around Savannah was ever more in patriot control as the year of 1782 progressed. The Georgia government and executives spent most of their time securing food and supplies for themselves, the militia and for many of the citizens who had no hope for supplies until the next crop could be harvested. In May the Assembly moved to Ebenezer where Wayne had his encampment. In Georgia the focus now turned to determining when the British would finally leave the fair town of Savannah.

Meanwhile in North Carolina, the events in the second half of 1781 rather paralleled those of her neighboring states as the war wound down. With General Greene and all the British out of North Carolina except in Wilmington, the state was left to the mercy of loosely organized bands of armed men. For more than a year these groups, whether loyalist or patriot, carried out a continuing series of robberies, midnight raids, house burnings, murders, and other criminal acts.

The most notorious loyalist raider was David Fanning. Major James Craig, the British commander at Wilmington, made him colonel in the loyalist militia. Fanning became aligned with the British cause during the war and led numerous raids in both of the Carolinas. In July of 1781 he drove into Pittsboro to interrupt a court-martial of several loyalists and managed to capture 50 prisoners, including militiamen, Continental officers and three members of the General Assembly. Later on September 12 in a raid on Hillsborough he took another 200 prisoners, including Governor Thomas Burke. He took the prisoners to Wilmington.

Major Craig was not much better in terms of conducting cruel acts and creating continual instability in the region. He encouraged loyalist acts of violence and personally led numerous raids. Among his prisoners were the well-known North Carolina patriot leaders John Ashe and Cornelius Harnett, who were held in such unhealthy confinement that both became ill and died within days of being released from Craig's control.[20]

In August, the militia leader General Griffin Rutherford was released as a prisoner of war from Florida. On his return to North Carolina he organized a march on Wilmington. While it was not successful at forcing the British to leave, his force did eventually see Craig and his 400 British troops evacuate Wilmington on November 18, 1781, and move to Charles Town. This was the same day that General Greene left camp in the High Hills of the Santee and moved to resume actions in South Carolina. The British were out of North Carolina.

The results of the war had been devastating to the citizens of North Carolina. There were some 350,000 people in North Carolina after the war, but most were in poor economic shape. The state owed the Continental treasury $18,230,000 in August of 1781 and had great difficulty in recovering enough taxes to keep up with even the interest payments. When Robert Morris wrote Governor Martin of North Carolina in 1783, he indicated that only some $750,000 had been collected from the state since 1781. The state's paper money was worthless.[21]

The conditions in North Carolina were depressing. Commerce had all but stopped after the war. With so little money around, farmers saw no real opportunity to make a profit in agriculture. Intellectual, social and moral institutions were also in ruins in the state. No newspaper had been printed in the state since 1778. The postal service had discontinued. Most schools and academies had closed during the war. As the war turned against the British, the Church of England collapsed. The Protestant denominations fared little better. The loss in religious zeal was so bad that Francis Asbury, a Methodist leader, described the people of North Carolina as "gospel slighters." Even the social organization, the Grand Lodge of Masons, which had been established in Wilmington, ceased to exist after 1776.

The political landscape was also in chaos. The old conflicts and alignments that had dominated the colonial period before the war were again resurrected. Most decisions taken by the politically endowed were resolved by personal or sectional self-interest. The colonial distrust of lawyers and merchants remained alive after the war. Other factors that contributed to creating the unsatisfactory situation included issues of "national origin, economic status, religious preference, place of residence, and veterans' status." Those, including the wealthy planters, merchants and lawyers, who saw the pre-war North Carolina as favorable, cried out for the return to the colonial conditions. Those who wanted a change to low taxes, relief from pre-war debt to the British, and little governmental restrictions saw nothing good in the state's colonial past. The conflict between these two factions was to keep the legislature in continual turmoil for years to come. Conflict between these parties even made selecting an appropriate town for the new state capital a difficult decision. Between 1777 and 1794 the legislature met in seven different towns. The final site for the capital,

Raleigh in Wake County, was selected on April 2, 1792. The site cost £1,378 for 1000 acres on Joel Lane's Plantation. The capital was named for Sir Walter Raleigh.[22]

In April of 1782 the General Assembly took action to resolve the issue of back pay for the officers and men of the militia and state Continentals. The legislature allotted 640 acres of land across the mountains, in what is known today as Tennessee, to privates. Colonels received 7200 acres, 12,000 acres went to brigadier generals and other officers in proportion, and General Greene received 25,000 acres. That same month the Assembly elected the interim governor, Colonel Alexander Martin, to succeed Dr. Thomas Burke, who had broken his parole and escaped from his prison camp on James Island across from Charles Town in January of that year. As evidence of the continued fear among the troops that they would not be treated fairly, in November 1782 a riot took place at Bladen Court House when 30 men led by Captain Robert Raiford of the Continental Line charged that loyalists were being favored in land disputes.

In May of 1782 General Greene wrote General Marion that the North Carolina troops were to be "discharged" from duty in South Carolina. Greene also wrote Governor Martin that he had released all but one regiment of North Carolina troops. Greene had been concerned about reports that the British might attack Beaufort, North Carolina. The attack never occurred. The last North Carolina troops left South Carolina in April of 1783.[23]

Meanwhile back in England, the Parliament's Christmas recess lasted until January 21, 1782. The opposition forces led by Charles James Fox, Lord Rockingham and Lord Shelburne had been busy during the recess gathering support for ending the war. While the goal for the opposition was the downfall of the North ministry, the debate turned first to discredit the admiralty and perhaps more importantly, Lord Sandwich, who was serving as the first lord of the admiralty. Sandwich was labeled with accusations of neglect and incompetence. Fox was able to press the House of Commons "to inquire into the causes of the want of success of His Majesty's naval forces during this war, and more particularly in the year of 1781." The strategy shifted on February 22 to the wider question regarding the conduct of the war in general in the American colonies.

The pressure was so great that Lord North resigned to the king again on the 28th at 2 A.M., but, as before, the king refused to accept it. On March 8 Lord John Cavendish pushed forward several resolutions, the most significant of which included a vote of no confidence for the North ministry. The resolution lost by ten votes, but the end was near.[24] Finally on March 19 rumors reached Lord North that the opposition was about to present res-

olutions that he termed as just short of treasonous. He wrote the king, pressing, "in the most decided terms, resigning his employment." The letter reached the king just as he was ready to take off on a hunt. It was recorded that the king read the letter, put it in his pocket, mounted his horse and started off. A page ran after the king saying that Lord North requested a reply. The king responded, "Tell him that I shall be in town tomorrow morning, and will then give Lord North an answer." The king then turned to his companions and remarked "Lord North has sent me in his resignation; but I shall not accept it."

Lord North did meet with King George III for over an hour, as the word spread of the curious event. Uncharacteristically, some 400 members of Parliament were present at 5 P.M. when Lord North entered the hall in full dress, showing his ribbon of the Order of the Garter on his coat. The members scrambled to their seats as North attempted to address the chair. While Lord Surry still had the floor, the members were in pandemonium as North stood trying to talk in vain above the roar. Finally he was able to speak with the permission of the opposition. North declared, "His object was to save the time and trouble of the House by informing them that the administration was virtually at an end; that His Majesty had determined to change his confidential servants; and that he should propose an adjournment, in order to allow time for the new ministerial arrangements which must take place." The opposition responded with cries of triumph and frantic cheers. Wraxall wrote, "a more interesting scene had not been acted within the walls of the House of Commons since … Sir Robert Walpole retired from power." With incredible dignity, North continued to remain as the body soon recessed early for the night. From his waiting coach North spoke these words to his friends, "Good night, gentlemen, you see what it is to be in the secret." The 12 years of the North government had come to an end.[25]

Lord George Germain, who had been openly supportive of Clinton back in December of 1781, soon found it impossible to allow him to continue his command in light of disastrous American developments. The king also had assumed that Clinton wanted to resign and he suggested that Sir Guy Carleton take Clinton's place. Germain detested Carleton and indicated that he would not continue in office if Carleton were appointed. Germain appealed to North, but North responded, "Yet only by changing measures could the ministry maintain itself against the growing forces of the Opposition."

As the events unfolded, on January 2, 1782, Germain sent a dispatch to Clinton with directions that all existing British posts were to be retained on the Atlantic coast. He even proposed the possibility of combined land and naval operations. As the North ministry crumbled and the opposition pushed its points in Parliament, Germain's fate was sealed. On February 9, Lord George Germain resigned. This left the way clear for Carleton to assume the command in America. Germain's last letter to Clinton was written on February 7 indicating that the king had accepted Clinton's request to resign and that he was to sail home at the first opportunity after turning his command over to Major General James Robertson, the royal governor of New York. Clinton received the letter on April 27, less than a week before Carleton was to arrive in America.[26]

Carleton received his orders and sailed from Portsmouth, England, on April 8 for America. His primary orders were to evacuate all forces and equipment to Halifax from New York, Charles Town and Savannah, as well as to determine whether St. Augustine should also be abandoned. He was also ordered to provide for all loyalists who wanted to leave the colonies. On May 5 Carleton arrived at New York to be greeted by Clinton, Major General Robertson, and Admiral Robert Digby, who commanded all British naval activities in North America. Clinton wrote:

> Sir Guy Carleton being in consequence sent out to New York to relieve me, I had the happiness of resigning to him on the 8th of May the chief command of His Majesty's forces in North America — a command which I had neither solicited nor coveted but accepted with reluctance, and which I was afterward compelled to retain for four years, although I had each year prayed to be released from it from the thorough conviction of the impossibility of my doing anything very essential toward extinguishing the rebellion without more troops than I had the direction of, and a cooperating naval force constantly superior to that of the enemy.[27]

During some ten days of briefings from these and other officials, Carleton gained a clear view of the discouraging conditions before him. The garrison at New York, consisting of only 18,000 British, Hessian and loyalist troops, was barely enough to maintain the defenses of the city. Admiral Digby had only three ships-of-the-line and a few lesser vessels at Carleton's disposal. The majority of the British naval forces were in the West Indies and would be of little use in providing assistance if an attack was to be forced by the Americans on New York.

Reports from the Southern colonies were even more depressing for the British. Before Clinton departed from the Chesapeake Bay after discovering that Cornwallis had already surrendered, he had ordered Lieutenant General Alexander Leslie to move to Charles Town to assume command of the troops in the Carolinas, Georgia and East Florida. Soon after Leslie arrived at Charles Town on November 8, he realized that the British were in an extremely weakened condition. He immediately ordered Craig to abandon Wilmington, North Carolina, and bring the troops back to Charles Town. Leslie reported that the troops for duty in the South were down to 4576 at Charles Town, 691 at Savannah, and 476 at St. Augustine. Clinton could not spare any significant numbers of troops from New York as Leslie requested, but he did send 537 officers and men who belonged to units in the South.

Information from Savannah was also most distressing for Leslie. The former royal governor, Sir James Wright, and the British commander for the colony of Georgia, Brigadier General Alured Clarke, believed that the town could not be defended from an assault unless they received additional troops from New York. Clinton refused their request for troops and indicated that if Savannah were attacked, Leslie would provide assistance from Charles Town. To complicate matters in the South, Clinton had ordered 2000 troops to be sent to Jamaica to assist in the defense of that island. Leslie refused to send that number, but compromised by sending 1300 men in May of 1782.

While the British were indeed weakened, General Greene outside Charleston and his subordinate, General Anthony Wayne at Savannah, had insufficient troops to assault the two Southern towns. Their operations against the British were in intercepting foraging parties and supplies, and dealing with loyalist activities. The Americans were simply unable to mount a major operation against defenses at Charles Town and Savannah.

When Carleton left from Portsmouth, England, he had been issued orders that gave him authority to determine when to evacuate each of the British posts. On May 7, two days after he arrived in New York, Carleton directed a survey of the number of transport vessels in the colonies. The results revealed that the British had 32 transports and victuallers, and one hospital ship at New York, only seven transports at Charles Town, and five other vessels engaged in other operations in the South. It was a severe blow to realize that it would be impossible to remove all the British garrisons in America in 1782.

The years of the war had resulted in the loss of nearly 2000 transports and victuallers in North America. During most of the period from 1775 until 1781, the movement of British troops and supplies in amphibious operations had been hampered by the lack of transports, as the North administration had failed to secure adequate vessels for America. Although the new Rockingham government had desired that the colonies be evacuated as soon as possible, they likewise had no interest in providing additional seaborne transportation to accomplish the movements. Evacuating the British forces and other supporters from the American colonies would indeed be a complex and drawn-out task.

On May 23, Carleton issued directions to Leslie to abandon Savannah and St. Augustine. All troops, stores and supplies were to be sent to New York. No specific instructions were included telling him where to send the loyalists, except that he was not to bring them to New York. For some reason Carleton was of the opinion that not many loyalists would desire to leave the Southern colonies. Carleton also directed that plundering be strictly forbidden. After both the towns were evacuated, Leslie was instructed to leave Charles Town. After receiving these instructions from Carleton, Leslie immediately forwarded orders to Sir James Wright at Savannah and Patrick Tonyn, the royal governor of East Florida, at St. Augustine.

When Governor Wright was given the orders to evacuate Savannah, he was shocked. While it was true that the British influence around Georgia had only extended to the immediate fortifications around Savannah during the previous six months, Wright felt that he needed only some 500 reinforcements to shore up his force to maintain control in the colony. Governor Tonyn was also outraged, and with support of the Assembly of East Florida they protested to Leslie and Carleton. As it turned out, only four days after he had issued his evacuation orders to Leslie, Carleton had conferred with a naval officer, Captain Keith Elphinstone, who told him that there was an insufficient number of transports to evacuate both towns. Since it was believed that Savannah could be reinforced from Charles Town, Carleton decided to delay departing from St. Augustine. Carleton notified Wright that he could send loyalists to East Florida if it was necessary since he directed that no one would be allowed to land at Charles Town.

On June 20, 34 transports and victuallers sailed into Charles Town harbor. In early July these same vessels reached Tybee Island at the mouth of the Savannah River. Governor Wright had directed General Clarke to prepare the fortifications at Tybee for protection during the embarkation there. On July 11 the British troops along with 3200 loyalists and 3500 blacks departed Savannah and were camped at Tybee. Unfortunately the evacuation was a slow one, lasting over three weeks. Even after Lieutenant Governor John Graham hired on five private ships, there were not enough vessels to carry those fleeing Georgia. Some 5000 loyalist whites and blacks had to travel to St. Augustine overland or in small boats and canoes along the Georgia inland waterways. After getting approvals from Leslie, on July 20 six transports with ten white families and 1568 blacks onboard sailed to Jamaica. Two days later seven ships departed for St. Augustine with 580 loyalists and 748 blacks. The last 24 ships left for New York carrying 1996 British, German and provincial troops with all stores and equipment.

With the British out of Savannah, General Wayne immediately occupied the town. He chose not to interfere with the slow embarkation at Tybee. Before the British had departed, Wayne had promised protection to all loyalists who wished to stay in Savannah, as well as allowing the merchants to have six months to dispose of their goods. Additionally, Wayne permitted anyone who had supported the British to regain their citizenship by serving for two years in the Georgia Continental Army. As it turned out, Wayne did not stay at Savannah long. After a brief period, Wayne marched his army back to Charles Town where Greene was nervously waiting. Greene was concerned that the troops from Savannah would land at Charles Town and join the forces there to re-engage in offensive operations again. Thankfully, Carleton's plan did not include landing troops at the city.

Leslie disobeyed Carleton's orders and instructed 846 provincial troops, and significant food was brought ashore at Charles Town when the fleet arrived there on July 25. The 15 ships from Tybee arrived at New York in early August. Soon 28 victuallers from England joined these vessels. Even though it was the largest number of ships that Carleton had in New York harbor since his command had begun, it was still insufficient to evacuate Charles Town. Half the ships that were sent to Jamaica and St. Augustine had not returned yet. Carleton was concerned that he would not be able to evacuate from America until some time in 1783 at the current pace.

To his delight, news came that by the end of September some 20 transports and victuallers would arrive from the West Indies under the orders from Lord Shelburne to proceed to South Carolina. With the additional transports from Halifax, Jamaica and St. Augustine becoming available, Carleton announced that Charles Town would be evacuated beginning on August 7. He directed all who wanted to evacuate to register with the army specifying the desired destination and property to be transported. The Charles Town departure list within a week included some 4230 loyalists and 7163 blacks. Leslie ordered all private shipping be made available to support the evacuation, and authorized merchants disposing of their goods to negotiate with General Greene or Governor John Mathews of South Carolina.

By early August food supplies were so low in the city that Leslie reluctantly ordered armed troops to raid American plantations and farms. He regretted taking this action but General Greene had prevented Leslie from buying food from the Americans without getting authorization from Congress. Leslie was also disappointed that Greene would not approve the exchanging of prisoners either. Greene was not interested in trading American militia for regular British troops. Greene finally yielded, but the prisoner exchange did not occur until October.

On September 20 the first contingent of 27 transports and victuallers departed New York for Charles

Town. These ships arrived at the Southern port ten days later. On October 14 a large number of transports left for East Florida with 1383 loyalists and 1681 blacks and 1147 provincial troops. Several days later another nine ships left for Halifax with 166 soldiers, 534 loyalists and all of the heavy ordnance. On October 8 Carleton sent Leslie some 31 ships remaining at New York to the South under escort of eight warships under Admiral Digby. On October 21 the last transport vessels from New York arrived at Charles Town, joined in late November by vessels from East Florida. Finally there were enough ships in the harbor to evacuate Charles Town.

As the final plans were made for the British departure from Charles Town, Greene and Leslie carried out negotiations on the removal tactics for slaves, as well as the last day of troop evacuation from the city. Leslie was concerned that when his troops were in withdrawal out of the city, the American forces would enter and fire on his troops. On December 13 Leslie sent General Wayne a plan for the final evacuation. The plan called for the British troops to leave their posts at 9 A.M., with Wayne's troops following his rear guard by a distance of at least 200 yards. Leslie declared that if Wayne did not agree to these arrangements, he would destroy the city. Wayne quickly agreed to the plan. The last British troops departed from the city of Charles Town on December 14, 1782.

The departure of the transports was not as quick as had been planned. On December 18 five British fleets left Charles Town. Three of the fleets sailed south; one with eight ships carrying 134 loyalists, 142 blacks and a large quantity of provisions went to St. Augustine; five vessels went to St. Lucia with provincial soldiers, supplies and 50 cavalry horses; 29 ships with 1265 British troops, 597 loyalists and 1550 blacks sailed to Jamaica. The fourth fleet departed with 20 ships carrying 506 army officers, many loyalists and royal officials to England. The last fleet sailed toward New York aboard 48 transports and victuallers with 4071 British, German and provincial troops and stores. In total, 126 vessels — 35,794 tons of shipping — were used to evacuate Charles Town. While the British never made a final count of those evacuated from the city, the American estimate was 3794 whites and 5237 blacks.

During 1782 the records indicated that 5090 whites and 8285 blacks from Georgia and South Carolina traveled to East Florida, where the population swelled from 4000 to 17,375 souls. It was not until December of 1783 that the British were able to evacuate New York. Though the preliminary peace treaty ceding East Florida to Spain was signed on January 20, 1783, it was not until November 1785 that the British and loyalists from East Florida completed the evacuation. Those East Florida loyalists who did not wish to stay under Spanish rule were resettled in Nova Scotia, the Bahamas, Jamaica and England,

and some 421 whites and 2561 blacks came back to the United States. The final British evacuation from the South was accomplished.[28]

After the North ministry dissolved in England on March 20, 1782, Charles James Fox, the leader of the opposition, was presented as the successor of North. The king refused to accept him as his first minister and offered up Lord Shelburne, but he was unable to form a government. The Marquis Lord Rockingham was successful at forming a government with Shelburne as the secretary of state for the new Southern Department over home, Irish and colonial affairs, and with Fox as the secretary of state for the Northern Department heading foreign affairs.

From the outset confusion reigned over which British secretary was responsible for handling the treaty negotiations. Shelburne opened negotiations with the Americans, but both secretaries sent emissaries to the endless meetings held in Paris, Versailles and occasionally in London and Madrid. Spain, France and Holland were also parties to the treaty along with America. The British wanted a separate peace with America, to support the potential of breaking the French-American alliance. But Congress decided that it would not set aside the alliance, indicating that "Congress will not enter into the discussion of any overtures for pacification but in confidence and in concert with his Most Christian Majesty."

In the middle of the complex peace negotiations Lord Rockingham died and Shelburne became prime minister. While it was an initial setback for the Americans, as the secretary was an advocate for American independence, the American negotiators Benjamin Franklin, John Adams, Henry Laurens, and the New York lawyer, John Jay, were eventually able to obtain a satisfactory agreement. On November 30, 1782, in Paris the preliminary articles of peace between England and America were signed. The agreement stated that the treaty was not actually in effect until an agreement between England and France was completed. After the treaty was signed and sealed, American negotiators rode out to Passy to have dinner with Franklin. At dinner some Frenchmen joined them, one of whom expressed to the British of "the growing greatness of America" and exclaiming that "the Thirteen United States would form the greatest empire in the world." Caleb Whitefoord, who was the secretary to the British commissioners, responded, "Yes, sir, and they will all speak English; every one of 'em." The articles of peace between Britain, France and Spain were signed on January 20, 1783, while Holland's peace truce was delayed several months.[29]

The final signing of the peace treaty took place in Paris at the quarters of David Hartley, Fox's chief negotiator, in the Hotel d'York on September 3, 1783. The official text of the Treaty of Paris arrived in the United States with Joshua Barney of Baltimore on March 12, 1783, aboard the ship

Washington. The official announcement of the ratification of the treaty was published on April 19, 1783, exactly eight years after the war started at Lexington and Concord.[30] Article One of the Treaty of Paris reads as follows:

> His Brittanic Majesty acknowledges the said United States, viz., New Hampshire, Massachusetts Bay, Rhode Island and Providence Plantations, Connecticut, New York, New Jersey, Pennsylvania, Maryland, Virginia, North Carolina, South Carolina and Georgia, to be free

sovereign and independent states, that he treats with them as such, and for himself, his heirs, and successors, relinquishes all claims to the government, propriety, and territorial rights of the same and every part thereof.

The passion of King George III to retain the American colonies was dashed forever. The struggle in the Southern colonies was concluded, and the American Revolution was at an end.

Selected Post-Revolution Biographical Sketches

Though the American Revolution was now ended, the lives of the principal leaders were not concluded. The American, French and British who had taken key roles in the Southern engagements of the war now turned to new pursuits.

Marriot Arbuthnot sailed home on July 4, 1781, after he was replaced by Admiral Graves, never to return to sea duty. In 1793 he was promoted to Admiral of the Blue, and died the following year.

Benedict Arnold sailed to London in December 1782 where he attempted to continue a military life in the British Army. He was unable to receive a promotion, and disappointed, he went into business in Canada as a merchant-skipper at St. John, New Brunswick, and later the West Indies. His business failed and only his wife's commercial acumen saved them from total ruin. Arnold died a broken man in London in 1810.

Nisbet Balfour was rewarded for his war efforts and promoted to colonel and served as A.D.C. to the king. In 1790 he was elected to Parliament. Three years later he entered the war against the French as a major general. After serving in Flanders until December 1794, he ended his military career. By 1803 he was the sixth ranking general in the British Army. He died at age 80 after serving some 62 years in the military.

Archibald Campbell returned to England in 1779 and by 1782 was promoted to major general after becoming the governor of Jamaica. He distinguished himself by raising a black militia for defense of the island. He returned to England in September of 1785 and was knighted. He also served as Governor of Madras but in 1789 he went home to London in bad health, where he died two years later.

Sir Guy Carleton departed New York on November 25, 1783, and returned to England. In April 1786 he was appointed for the second time as governor of Quebec. Except for an absence of two years, he remained in Canada until July of 1796. He survived the shipwreck of the *Active* and reached Portsmouth on September 19. He retired until a sudden death on November 10, 1808.

Richard Caswell became the governor of North Carolina in 1785 for the second time. Afterwards he served as the speaker of the General Assembly until he died in 1789.

Elijah Clarke was granted an estate by county and state authorities of Georgia. He then took off in a series of dubious adventures. He negotiated with the Indians and later fought against them, defeating them at Jack's Creek in Walton County. In 1793 he entered the service of France as major general with a salary of $10,000 in planning actions against the Spanish. In 1794 he established the "TransOconee State" across the Oconee River in Creek territory with Georgia volunteers. President Hamilton ended the action, but later Clarke was suspected of continued involvement in designs against West Florida and the Yazoo Land Fraud deal. He died a popular hero in 1799.

Sir Henry Clinton returned home to a sympathetic welcome to begin his efforts at defending his actions in the Americas. He was consequently quarreling with Cornwallis and later the Duke of Newcastle, his cousin. Regardless of his detractors, he was promoted in 1793 to full general and the next year became the governor of Gibraltar, where he died on December 23, 1795.

George Collier sailed home mad in November 1779 when Arbuthnot took over the key naval command in North America. He served in command of Canada in the English Channel in 1780. The next spring he took part in Darby's Expedition to resupply Gibraltar under siege by the Spanish. On the way home he captured the Spanish frigate *Leocadia*. He then resigned and soon served in Parliament. In 1790 he returned to naval service, and was promoted in February 1793 to rear admiral. The next year he was promoted to vice admiral of the Blue. In January 1795 he took command of the Nore, an anchorage at the mouth of the Thames, but due to bad health he had to resign. He died on April 6 of that year.

Earl Cornwallis was appointed governor general and commander-in-chief of India in 1786, where he won a great reputation for the defeat of Sultan Tippoo and as an administrator. He returned to England in 1793 as a marquis. He continued to serve England with distinction as the lord lieutenant of Ireland and as the plenipotentiary to France in 1802, where he negotiated the Peace of Amiens. Cornwallis died in India on October 5, 1805.

James Henry Craig was promoted before he left America and served as lieutenant colonel of the 16th Regiment in Ireland. He was promoted to colonel in 1790, and served in the Netherlands against France, where he was moved up to major general in October 1794. Craig took part in the operations to capture the Dutch colony at the Cape of Good Hope against the Boer militia. After the capture he served as military governor until 1897 when he was knighted and returned to England. He served in Bengal and the Kingdom of Naples, but returned in bad health to England in 1805. In 1807 he was appointed the governor general of Canada and served until he resigned in October of 1811. He was promoted to full general in January of the next year and died 11 days later.

William Richardson Davie settled in Halifax in 1782 and continued his law practice on the circuit in North Carolina. He was a representative for Halifax in the legislature from 1786 until 1798. He played a prominent role in important state and national issues and was largely responsible for the establishment of the University of North Carolina. He was appointed as commander of the state troops in 1797 and became governor of North Carolina in 1798. The next year he was peace commissioner to France. Davie retired to his plantation, *Tivoli*, in Lancaster County, South Carolina, in 1805, where he enjoyed farming, horses, friends and books until he died in 1820.

Comte Charles Hector Theodat D'Estaing returned to France in 1780, and in 1783 at Cadiz he was involved in organizing fleet operations in the West Indies when the war ended. He was elected to the Assembly of Notables in 1787 when he returned to France. He was made commandant of the National Guard at Versailles when the French Revolution broke out in 1789. In 1792 he was promoted to admiral. Though he was in favor of reforms, he continued to support the king and defended Marie Antoinette. For his actions, he was tried and was guillotined in Paris during the Reign of Terror on April 28, 1794.

Horatio Gates had his name cleared by Congress after his defeat at Camden and joined the army at Newburgh in 1782. Gates retired to his farm after the war officially ended. He sold his farm, freed his slaves, and moved to New York City in 1790. He served in the state legislature in New York for 1801 and 1802. He died in New York in 1806.

George III had shown symptoms of insanity as far back as 1765 but it was concealed from the public. In October 1788 he became ill and by the next month it was obvious that he was truly mad. His son, the Prince of Wales, waited anxiously to take over the crown but the king lived and recovered somewhat from his insanity. In 1811 his mind did go with the death of his favorite child, Princess Amelia. His son became regent. George spent the next nine years "wandering through the rooms of his palace, addressing imaginary parliaments, reviewing fancied troops, holding ghostly courts...." Blindness and deafness closed in on him before he died on January 29, 1820.

George Germain became the Viscount Sackville after Lord North resigned. He lived in retirement and died at his country house, Stoneland Lodge, in Sussex in 1785.

Mordecai Gist retired in November 1783 with his third wife and bought a plantation near Charles Town. He died there in 1792.

Francois de Grasse returned to the West Indies after the successful Yorktown campaign. In February 1782 he captured St. Kitts, but in April he was defeated and taken prisoner by the British. After he was returned to London, he worked with Lord Shelburne to act as the intermediary between the French and English in the peace negotiations. In May 1784 he was exonerated for the losses in the West Indies. After he died in Paris at his town house on January 14, 1788, the French Revolution raged. As a result of the Revolution his beloved family country estate, Chateau de Tilly, located 50 miles outside Paris, was destroyed. His four daughters escaped to America and settled in Charles Town.

Thomas Graves sailed to Jamaica after the surrender of Yorktown, and then to England on the *Ramilies*, which became shipwrecked. He arrived in England aboard a merchant ship, where he was appointed commander-in-chief at Plymouth in 1787. When later the British again fought with France, he was in command of the Channel Fleet where he was severely wounded in his right arm. He was raised in Irish peerage to Baron Graves in 1794, and died in 1802.

Nathanael Greene returned to his home state of Rhode Island to a hero's welcome in 1783. He declined the secretary of war position after the war. Due to his poor financial condition, he was forced to sell his properties in the North and retired to the confiscated estate of loyalist Lt. Governor Graham that he was granted in Georgia. He died of sunstroke at age 44 at Mulberry Grove, Georgia, near Savannah, in 1786.

Patrick Henry, who had served as governor of Virginia during part of the war, was reappointed to that post in 1784. He left office in 1786 and though he was offered several positions with the federal government, he declined for health reasons. With the encouragement of Washington, he ran for a seat in the Virginia House of Delegates as a Federalist in January 1799. Though he defeated John Randolph for the seat, he died at Red Hill near Brookneal, Virginia, before he could take office.

Samuel Hood was made an Irish peerage for his part in the defeat of de Grasse off Saints Passage at St. Kitts. He entered Parliament in 1784 and was promoted to vice admiral in 1787. When war broke with France he became the commander-in-chief in the Mediterranean. He was promoted to full admiral in April of 1794 and returned to England. He never returned to sea and died in 1812 in his post as governor of Greenwich Hospital.

John Eager Howard was a delegate to the Congress in 1788 and governor of Maryland from 1788 until 1791. He also served as senator from 1796 until 1803. He died in 1827.

Robert Howe led forces against the disgruntled troops who drove Congress from Philadelphia in 1783. He returned to his rice plantation that same year but in 1785 was appointed by Congress to work to solve various boundary conflicts with the Indians. In 1786 he was elected to the North Carolina legislature, but he died before he could take office.

Thomas Jefferson succeeded Franklin as minister to France, and in 1789 was appointed as secretary of state by Washington. He became vice president of the United States in 1897 and in 1801 became the third president of the United States. He retired in 1809 to Monticello and died on July 4, 1826.

Robert Kirkwood moved to Ohio after the war and settled at a point opposite Wheeling. In the subsequent trouble with Indians he was commissioned as captain in the Second U.S. Infantry in 1791. He was killed in action that November. Harry Lee wrote, "It was the thirty-third time he had risked his life for his country and died as he lived, the brave, meritorious, unrewarded, Kirkwood."

Thaddeus Kosciuszko became a brigadier general in 1783 and returned to his home in Poland the next year. The rest of his life was devoted to the cause of Polish independence. In 1792 he led a futile campaign to invade Russia, and moved to Paris. The Russians captured him in 1794 after another attempt to defeat them. He was released and came to the United States, where he received a lump sum payment of $15,000 and 500 acres in Ohio for his service in the Revolution. He returned to Paris in 1798.

Marquis de Lafayette sailed to France on September 8, 1782, with a container of American soil which he would later be buried in. He was promoted to *marechal de camp* and in 1789 was appointed commander of the National Guard of Paris. In 1791 he resigned his position. With the fall of the French monarchy, he defected to Austria where he remained until 1802. He took up residence at his Lagrange estate during the First Empire. In 1824 he was elected a deputy for the Sarthe. In 1830 he was appointed commander of the National Guard again. The marquis

died in 1834. He had spent some $200,000 of his own money on the American war and never sought repayment. He was voted some $24,500 in 1794 by Congress and in 1803 was given 11,520 acres in Louisiana.

Henry Laurens was finally released from his miserable imprisonment in the Tower of London in 1782 in exchange for Lord Cornwallis. While he was in prison he was named by Congress as a peace commissioner, but by the time he was released the treaty was only days away from signing. From 1782 to 1783 he served as an unofficial ambassador to Great Britain. He returned to South Carolina after these events and retired to his plantation, Mepkin, on the Cooper River some 30 miles outside Charles Town, to focus his life on rebuilding his fortune. He died in 1792 after a long illness and was one of the first in America to be cremated.

Charles Lee (Continental officer) retired in 1779 to his estate in the Shenandoah Valley. He remained there as a recluse breeding horses and working his dogs. He died alone in a tavern in Philadelphia in 1782 at the age of 51. In his will he wrote, "I desire most earnestly that I may not be buried in any church, or churchyard, or within a mile of any Presbyterian or Anabaptist meeting-house; for since I have resided in this country, I have had so much bad company while living, that I do not chuse to continue it when dead."

Henry "Light Horse" Harry Lee became the governor of Virginia in 1791. Later he served in the House of Representatives from 1799 to 1801. He was imprisoned for debt associated with land speculation and later was badly hurt in a riot in Baltimore defending an unpopular newspaperman. In bad health in 1818, he died on his way back from the West Indies.

Benjamin Lincoln became the secretary of war in 1781 and in 1788 served as lieutenant governor of Massachusetts. He was the collector for the port of Boston from 1789 to 1809. On May 9, 1810, he died at Hingham.

Francis "Swamp Fox" Marion served in the South Carolina Senate from 1782 to 1790 and died at age 63 at his estate in Berkeley County in February of 1795.

Josiah Martin left for England in 1781. After being compensated for his losses of property in North Carolina, he died in London in 1786.

Daniel Morgan commanded federal troops sent to Pennsylvania in 1794 to put down the Whiskey Rebellion. He served in the House in Congress from 1787 to 1799. He died at his home in Winchester, Virginia, in 1802.

William Moultrie was appointed governor of Georgia in 1785 and served through 1787. He was re-elected and served another term from 1792 to 1794. He died in Charles Town in 1805.

John Murray, Lord Dunmore, returned to England in July 1776. He was appointed as the governor of the Bahama Islands in 1787 and returned home to England in 1796. He died in Kent in 1809.

Sir Frederick North dropped out from public life as his eyesight faded. By 1789 his sight was completely gone. He died in 1792.

Charles O'Hara was a prisoner of war in America until he was exchanged in 1782. He served in Gibraltar and later in Toulon, where he was captured by the French. He was exchanged for the Comte de Rochambeau. He was promoted to general in 1798 and appointed as the governor of Gibraltar. He died there as a wealthy man in 1802, leaving his fortune to his two mistresses and their children.

Sir Peter Parker was knighted in 1782 for his bravery in Charles Town. He became Admiral of the Fleet, and died in 1811.

Andrew Pickens served as a member of the House of Representatives from 1793 to 1795. He died in 1817.

Thomas Pinckney served as governor of South Carolina from 1787 to 1789. He was appointed as minister to Great Britain from 1792 to 1796. He negotiated the treaty with Spain in 1795. He died in 1828.

Augustine Prevost returned to England in 1779 from Georgia. He died in 1786.

Lord Francis Rawdon took the surname of Hastings and in 1793 succeeded his father as the second Earl of Moira. He was appointed as the governor general of India in 1813 and as Marquess of Hastings in 1817. He resigned his post in 1821 and later in 1824 became the governor of Malta. He died aboard the H.M.S. *Revenge* off Naples in 1826. His last request was that his right hand be cut off after his death and preserved until it could be placed in his widow's coffin.

Comte de Rochambeau sailed home to France in 1783. In 1791 he was appointed to command the Army of the North. He was later held in prison during the Reign of Terror in the French Revolution. In 1803 he was appointed to the position of marshal of France and died in Vendome in 1807.

John Simcoe was appointed the first lieutenant governor of Upper Canada in 1791. On his return to England he was appointed to command at Plymouth. In 1806 he was assigned as commander-in-chief in India, but died at Exeter before he could take his new post.

Baron Von Steuben settled in New York after the Revolution. Continuing his extravagant lifestyle, he fought severe indebtedness all his remaining days. In 1790 he was given an annual annuity of $2500 for life. He died near Ramsen, New York, in 1794.

Thomas Sumter served in the House of Representatives from 1789 to 1793 and later from 1801 to 1810. As the last surviving general officer of the Revolution, he died in South Carolina in 1832 at the age of 97.

Banastre Tarleton returned to England in 1782 after being paroled. He became a member of Parliament from Liverpool in 1790. He lived with a notorious actress, Mary Robinson, the former mistress of his friend the Prince of Wales. In 1787 he published his *History of the Campaigns of 1780 and 1781 in the Southern Provinces of North America.* In 1812 he was promoted to general, and died at Shropshire in 1833.

George Washington became the first president of the United States in 1789 and died at Mount Vernon in 1799.

William Washington settled in Charles Town and served in the legislature. He refused to run for governor "because he could not make a speech." He died in 1810.

Anthony Wayne was breveted as major general at the end of the war. After several years as an unprosperous farmer, he was elected to Congress in 1791 but denied his seat. The following year Wayne was appointed as major general to command the actions against the Indians in the Old Northwest. He was victorious in the Battle of Fallen Timbers in August 1794. He died in 1796.

William Woodford died in captivity at Charles Town on November 13, 1780. He was buried in Old Trinity Church Yard.[31]

NOTES

Chapter 1

1. Richard Brookhiser, *Founding Father; Rediscovering George Washington* (New York: The Free Press, 1996), pp. 187–188.

2. Captain Hugh McCall, *The History of Georgia, Vol. I* (Atlanta: A.B. Caldwell, Publisher, 1811/1909), p. 2.

3. Jedidiah Morse, *Annals of the American Revolution* (Hartford, Connecticut: Oliver D. Cooke & Sons, 1824), pp. 6–13.

4. Richard B. Morris, *The LIFE History of the United States Before 1775: Vol. 1, The New World* (New York: Time-Life Books, 1963), p. 49.

5. Jedidiah Morse, *Annals of the American Revolution* (Hartford, Connecticut: Oliver D. Cooke & Sons, 1824), p. 13.

6. *Ibid.*, p. 13.

7. Julia Cherry Spruill, *Women's Life and Work in the Southern Colonies* (New York: W.W. Norton & Company, Inc., 1972), pp. 4–8.

8. William B. Hesseltine, *The South in American History* (New York: Prentice Hall, Inc., 1936), pp. 14–19.

9. Jedidiah Morse, *Annals of the American Revolution* (Hartford, Connecticut: Oliver D. Cooke & Sons, 1824), p. 18.

10. Julia Cherry Spruill, *Women's Life and Work in the Southern Colonies* (New York: W.W. Norton & Company, Inc., 1972), p. 10. William B. Hesseltine, *The South in American History* (New York: Prentice Hall, Inc., 1936), p. 19.

11. William B. Hesseltine, *The South in American History* (New York: Prentice Hall, Inc., 1936), pp. 19–20. Julia Cherry Spruill, *Women's Life and Work in the Southern Colonies* (New York: W.W. Norton & Company, Inc., 1972), p. 11.

12. William B. Hesseltine, *The South in American History* (New York: Prentice Hall, Inc., 1936), pp. 20–22.

13. Hugh T. Lefler and William S. Powell, *Colonial North Carolina* (New York: Charles Scribner's Sons, 1973), p. 32.

14. Jedidiah Morse, *Annals of the American Revolution* (Hartford, Connecticut: Oliver D. Cooke & Sons, 1824), p. 19. Walter J. Fraser, Jr., *Charleston! Charleston!* (Columbia: University of South Carolina Press, 1989), p. 1. Julia Cherry Spruill, *Women's Life and Work in the Southern Colonies* (New York: W.W. Norton & Company, Inc., 1972), pp. 11–12.

15. Walter J. Fraser, Jr., *Charleston! Charleston!* (Columbia: University of South Carolina Press, 1989), pp. 2–8.

16. Jedidiah Morse, *Annals of the American Revolution* (Hartford, Connecticut: Oliver D. Cooke & Sons, 1824), p. 20.

17. William S. Powell, *North Carolina Through Four Centuries* (Chapel Hill: The University of North Carolina Press, 1989), pp. 86, 93–94

18. Jedidiah Morse, *Annals of the American Revolution* (Hartford, Connecticut: Oliver D. Cooke & Sons, 1824), p. 20.

19. Captain Hugh McCall, *The History of Georgia, Vol. I* (Atlanta: A.B. Caldwell, Publisher, 1811/1909), pp. 2, 21.

20. William B. Hesseltine, *The South in American History* (New York: Prentice Hall, Inc., 1936), pp. 71–73.

21. William S. Powell, *North Carolina Through Four Centuries* (Chapel Hill: The University of North Carolina Press, 1989), p. 5.

22. Dr. J.B.O. Landrum, *Colonial and Revolutionary History of Upper South Carolina* (Greenville: Shannon & Co., 1897), pp. 1–2.

23. Bernhard A. Uhlendorf, *The Siege of Charleston (Diary of Captain Hinrichs)* (Ann Arbor: University of Michigan Press, 1938), pp. 333–337.

24. Alden T. Vaughan, *America Before the Revolution* (Englewood Cliffs, New Jersey: Prentice Hall, Inc., 1967), p 1.

25. John Richard Alden, *The South in the Revolution, 1763–1789* (Baton Rouge: Louisiana State University, 1957), p 5.

26. Arthur M. Schlesinger, *The Birth of the Nation, 6th ed.* (New York: Alfred A. Knopf, Inc., 1976), pp. 8–9. John Richard Alden, *The South in the Revolution, 1763–1789* (Baton Rouge: Louisiana State University, 1957), p. 6.

27. Arthur M. Schlesinger, *The Birth of the Nation, 6th ed.* (New York: Alfred A. Knopf, Inc., 1976), pp. 8–9.

28. William B. Hesseltine, *The South in American History* (New York: Prentice Hall, Inc., 1936), p 56.

29. Robert Stanbury Lambert, *South Carolina Loyalists in*

the American Revolution (Columbia: University of South Carolina Press, 1987), p. 4.

30. John Richard Alden, The South in the Revolution, 1763–1789 (Baton Rouge: Louisiana State University Press, 1957), pp. 6–7.

31. Arthur M. Schlesinger, The Birth of the Nation, 6th ed. (New York, Alfred A. Knopf, Inc., 1976), pp. 5–6.

32. William S. Powell, North Carolina Through Four Centuries (Chapel Hill: The University of North Carolina Press, 1989), pp. 15–16.

33. Arthur M. Schlesinger, The Birth of the Nation, 6th ed. (New York, Alfred A. Knopf, Inc., 1976), p. 6.

34. Edwin J. Perkins, The Economy of Colonial America, 2nd ed. (New York: Columbia University Press, 1988), p. 8.

35. Hugh T. Lefler and William S. Powell, Colonial North Carolina (New York: Charles Scribner's Sons, 1973), p. 148.

36. Walter J. Fraser, Jr., Charleston! Charleston! (Columbia: University of South Carolina Press, 1989), p. 129.

37. Hugh T. Lefler and William S. Powell, Colonial North Carolina (New York: Charles Scribner's Sons, 1973), p. 149.

38. John Richard Alden, The South in the Revolution, 1763–1789 (Baton Rouge: Louisiana State University Press, 1957), pp. 12–15.

39. Edwin J. Perkins, The Economy of Colonial America, 2nd ed. (New York: Columbia University Press, 1988), pp. 91–102.

40. William B. Hesseltine, The South in American History (New York: Prentice Hall, Inc., 1936), pp. 38–39.

41. Robert M. Weir, Colonial South Carolina (New York: Kraus-Thomson Organization Press, 1983), p. 177.

42. Edwin J. Perkins, The Economy of Colonial America, 2nd ed. (New York: Columbia University Press, 1988), p. 219.

43. John Richard Alden, The South in the Revolution, 1763–1789 (Baton Rouge: Louisiana State University, 1957), p. 42.

44. Arthur M. Schlesinger, The Birth of the Nation, 6th ed. (New York, Alfred A. Knopf, Inc., 1976), p. 66.

45. Edwin J. Perkins, The Economy of Colonial America, 2nd ed. (New York: Columbia University Press, 1988), p. 99.

46. William B. Hesseltine, The South in American History (New York: Prentice Hall, Inc., 1936), pp. 65–66.

47. Robert M. Weir, Colonial South Carolina (New York: Kraus-Thomson Organization Press, 1983), p. 175.

48. Arthur M. Schlesinger, The Birth of the Nation, 6th ed. (New York, Alfred A. Knopf, Inc., 1976), pp. 64–65.

49. Robert M. Weir, Colonial South Carolina (New York: Kraus-Thomson Organization Press, 1983), p. 176.

50. Edwin J. Perkins, The Economy of Colonial America, 2nd ed. (New York: Columbia University Press, 1988), p. 101.

51. Arthur M. Schlesinger, The Birth of the Nation, 6th ed. (New York, Alfred A. Knopf, Inc., 1976), p. 67.

52. Edmund S. Morgan, American Slavery, American Freedom (New York: W.W. Norton & Company, 1975), p. 4.

53. Arthur M. Schlesinger, The Birth of the Nation, 6th ed. (New York, Alfred A. Knopf, Inc., 1976), p. 227.

54. Benson J. Lossing, Seventeen Hundred and Seventy-Six (New York: Edward Walker, 1849), p. 46.

55. Jedidiah Morse, Annals of the American Revolution (Hartford, Connecticut: Oliver D. Cooke & Sons, 1824), p. 89.

56. Edwin J. Perkins, The Economy of Colonial America, 2nd ed. (New York: Columbia University Press, 1988), p. 19.

57. Jedidiah Morse, Annals of the American Revolution (Hartford, Connecticut: Oliver D. Cooke & Sons, 1824), p. 92.

58. Edwin J. Perkins, The Economy of Colonial America, 2nd ed. (New York: Columbia University Press, 1988), p. 34.

59. Warren M. Billings, John E. Selby and Thad W. Tate, Colonial Virginia (New York: Kraus-Thompson Organization Press, 1986), pp. 265–266.

60. Theodore Draper, A Struggle for Power: The American Revolution (New York: Times Books, 1966), pp. 7–10.

61. Lawrence Henry Gipson, The Coming of the Revolution (New York: Harper & Brothers, 1954), pp. 137–138.

62. Aubrey C. Land, Colonial Maryland (New York: Kraus-Thomson Organization Press, 1981), p. xiii.

63. Esther Mohr Dole, Ph.D., Maryland During the American Revolution (Chestertown, Maryland: Esther Mohr Dole, 1941), p. 6.

64. Charles Albro Barker, The Background of the Revolution in Maryland (New Haven: Yale University Press, 1940), pp. 2–4, 70–72, 106.

65. Ibid., pp. 7–14.

66. Esther Mohr Dole, Ph.D., Maryland During the American Revolution (Chestertown, Maryland: Esther Mohr Dole, 1941), pp. 4–5.

67. Charles Albro Barker, The Background of the Revolution in Maryland (New Haven: Yale University Press, 1940), pp. 155, 171–172.

68. Esther Mohr Dole, Ph.D., Maryland During the American Revolution (Chestertown, Maryland: Esther Mohr Dole, 1941), p. 6.

69. Aubrey C. Land, Colonial Maryland (New York: Kraus-Thomson Organization Press, 1981), p. xiii–xiv.

70. John Richard Alden, The South in the Revolution, 1763–1789 (Baton Rouge: Louisiana State University Press, 1957), p. 145.

71. Esther Mohr Dole, Ph.D., Maryland During the American Revolution (Chestertown, Maryland: Esther Mohr Dole, 1941), pp. 8–9.

72. Lawrence Henry Gipson, The Coming of the Revolution (New York: Harper & Brothers, 1954), p. 138.

73. Edwin J. Perkins, The Economy of Colonial America, 2nd ed. (New York: Columbia University Press, 1988), p. 30.

74. Lawrence Henry Gipson, The Coming of the Revolution (New York: Harper & Brothers, 1954), pp. 139–140.

75. Edwin J. Perkins, The Economy of Colonial America (New York: Columbia University Press, 1988), pp. 29–30.

76. Richard L. Morton, Colonial Virginia, Vol. II (Chapel Hill: The University of North Carolina Press, 1960), p. 824.

77. Lawrence Henry Gipson, The Coming of the Revolution (New York: Harper & Brothers, 1954), pp. 139–140.

78. John Richard Alden, The South in the Revolution, 1763–1789 (Baton Rouge: Louisiana State University Press, 1957), p. 144–145, 64.

79. Lawrence Henry Gipson, The Coming of the Revolution (New York: Harper & Brothers, 1954), pp. 141–143.

80. Hugh T. Lefler and William S. Powell, Colonial North Carolina (New York: Charles Scribner's Sons, 1973), pp. xiii–xv.

81. William B. Hesseltine, The South in American History (New York: Prentice Hall, Inc., 1936), pp. 57–58.

82. Lawrence Henry Gipson, The Coming of the Revolution (New York: Harper & Brothers, 1954), p. 143.

83. William S. Powell, *North Carolina Through Four Centuries* (Chapel Hill: The University of North Carolina Press, 1989), pp. 143–154.

84. Benson J. Lossing, *Seventeen Hundred and Seventy-Six* (New York: Edward Walker, 1849), pp. 102–103.

85. Lawrence Henry Gipson, *The Coming of the Revolution* (New York: Harper & Brothers, 1954), pp. 144–146.

86. John Richard Alden, *The South in the Revolution, 1763–1789* (Baton Rouge: Louisiana State University Press, 1957), p. 6.

87. Robert M. Weir, *Colonial South Carolina* (New York: Kraus-Thomson Organization Press, 1983), p. xii.

88. Lawrence Henry Gipson, *The Coming of the Revolution* (New York: Harper & Brothers, 1954), pp. 149–150.

89. Robert M. Weir, *Colonial South Carolina* (New York: Kraus-Thomson Organization Press, 1983), pp. 146, 155–156.

90. Lawrence Henry Gipson, *The Coming of the Revolution* (New York: Harper & Brothers, 1954), pp. 147–148.

91. Robert M. Weir, *Colonial South Carolina* (New York: Kraus-Thomson Organization Press, 1983), pp. xvi–xv.

92. Robert Stanbury Lambert, *South Carolina Loyalists in the American Revolution* (Columbia: University of South Carolina Press, 1987), p.7.

93. John Richard Alden, *The South in the Revolution, 1763–1789* (Baton Rouge: Louisiana State University Press, 1957), pp. 146–152.

94. Kenneth Coleman, *Colonial Georgia* (New York: Charles Scribner's Sons, 1976), pp. xiii–xiv.

95. John Richard Alden, *The South in the Revolution, 1763–1789* (Baton Rouge: Louisiana State University Press, 1957), p. 147.

96. Lawrence Henry Gipson, *The Coming of the Revolution* (New York: Harper & Brothers, 1954), pp. 150–152.

Chapter 2

1. Henry Steele Commager and Richard B. Morris, *The Spirit of 'Seventy-Six* (New York: Harper & Row, Publishers, 1958), p. 1.

2. Edwin J. Perkins, *The Economy of Colonial America, 2nd ed.* (New York: Columbia University Press, 1988), pp. 20, 32.

3. John C. Miller, *Origins of the American Revolution* (London: Oxford University Press, 1943), pp. 82–83.

4. Ellen Chase, *The Beginnings of the American Revolution* (New York: The Baker and Taylor Company, 1910), p. 20.

5. Jedidiah Morse, *Annals of the American Revolution* (Hartford, Connecticut: Oliver D. Cooke & Sons, 1824), pp. 93–94.

6. John C. Miller, *Origins of the American Revolution* (London: Oxford University Press, 1943), pp. 87–88.

7. Edwin J. Perkins, *The Economy of Colonial America, 2nd ed.* (New York: Columbia University Press, 1988), pp. 195–197.

8. *The Regulations Lately Made Concerning the Colonies...Considered*, 92, Grenville Papers, II, *Public Advertiser*, January 13, 1766.

9. John C. Miller, *Origins of the American Revolution* (London: Oxford University Press, 1943), pp. 83–92.

10. Jedidiah Morse, *Annals of the American Revolution* (Hartford, Connecticut: Oliver D. Cooke & Sons, 1824), pp. 93–94.

11. Philip Vickers Fithian, *Journal and Letters*, edited by John Rogers Williams, Princeton, 1924, 193, 270, 286.

12. John C. Miller, *Origins of the American Revolution* (London: Oxford University Press, 1943), p. 90–93.

13. Benson J. Lossing, *Seventeen Hundred and Seventy-Six* (New York: Edward Walker, 1849), pp. 53–54.

14. Jedidiah Morse, *Annals of the American Revolution* (Hartford, Connecticut: Oliver D. Cooke & Sons, 1824), pp. 93–94.

15. John C. Miller, *Origins of the American Revolution* (London: Oxford University Press, 1943), p. 101.

16. Benson J. Lossing, *Seventeen Hundred and Seventy-Six* (New York: Edward Walker, 1849), pp. 53–54.

17. John C. Miller, *Origins of the American Revolution:* (London: Oxford University Press, 1943), pp. 84–86.

18. Lawrence Henry Gipson, *The Coming of the Revolution* (New York: Harper & Brothers, 1954), pp. 62, 65.

19. John C. Miller, *Origins of the American Revolution* (London: Oxford University Press, 1943), pp. 102–105.

20. Berhard Knollenberg, *Origin of the American Revolution: 1759–1766* (New York: The Macmillan Company, 1960), pp. 216–218.

21. Ellen Chase, *The Beginnings of the American Revolution* (New York: The Baker and Taylor Company, 1910), pp. 21–26, 52.

22. Lawrence Henry Gipson, *The Coming of the Revolution* (New York: Harper & Brothers, 1954), pp. 85–86.

23. Ellen Chase, *The Beginnings of the American Revolution* (New York: The Baker and Taylor Company, 1910), pp. 23–24.

24. Charles Campbell, *Introduction to the History of the Colony and Ancient Dominion of Virginia* (Richmond: B.B. Minor, 1847), pp. 135–136.

25. Ellen Chase, *The Beginnings of the American Revolution* (New York: The Baker and Taylor Company, 1910), pp. 28–29.

26. Charles Campbell, *Introduction to the History of the Colony and Ancient Dominion of Virginia* (Richmond: B.B. Minor, 1847), pp. 135–136.

27. Lawrence Henry Gipson, *The Coming of the Revolution* (New York: Harper & Brothers, 1954), pp. 86–87.

28. John Richard Alden, *The South in the Revolution, 1763–1789* (Baton Rouge: Louisiana State University Press, 1957), p. 75.

29. H.J. Eckenrode, *The Revolution in Virginia* (Hamden, Connecticut: Archon Books, 1916), pp. 25–26.

30. John C. Miller, *Origins of the American Revolution* (London: Oxford University Press, 1943), pp. 132–133.

31. Berhard Knollenberg, *Origin of the American Revolution: 1759–1766* (New York: The Macmillan Company, 1960), pp. 186–187.

32. Louis T. Moore, *Stories Old and New of the Cape Fear Region* (Wilmington: Wilmington Printing Company, 1956), p. 57.

33. Hugh T. Lefler and William S. Powell, *Colonial North Carolina* (New York: Charles Scribner's Sons, 1973), p. 245.

34. Ellen Chase, *The Beginnings of the American Revolution* (New York: The Baker and Taylor Company, 1910), p. 43.

35. John Richard Alden, *The South in the Revolution, 1763–1789* (Baton Rouge: Louisiana State University, 1957), pp. 86–87.

36. Louis T. Moore, *Stories Old and New of the Cape Fear*

Region (Wilmington: Wilmington Printing Company, 1956), pp. 57–58.

37. John Richard Alden, *The South in the Revolution, 1763–1789* (Baton Rouge: Louisiana State University Press, 1957), pp. 87–89.

38. Hugh T. Lefler and William S. Powell, *Colonial North Carolina* (New York: Charles Scribner's Sons, 1973), pp. 244–245.

39. Charles Albro Barker, *The Background of the Revolution in Maryland* (New Haven: Yale University Press, 1940), p. 299.

40. John C. Miller, *Origins of the American Revolution* (London: Oxford University Press, 1943), p. 132.

41. Charles Albro Barker, *The Background of the Revolution in Maryland* (New Haven: Yale University Press, 1940), pp. 300–301.

42. Esther Mohr Dole, Ph.D., *Maryland During the American Revolution* (Chestertown, Maryland: Esther Mohr Dole, 1941), p. 25.

43. John Richard Alden, *The South in the Revolution, 1763–1789* (Baton Rouge: Louisiana State University Press, 1957), p. 81.

44. John C. Miller, *Origins of the American Revolution* (London: Oxford University Press, 1943), p. 133.

45. Charles Albro Barker, *The Background of the Revolution in Maryland* (New Haven: Yale University Press, 1940), pp. 308–309.

46. Berhard Knollenberg, *Origin of the American Revolution: 1759–1766* (New York: The Macmillan Company, 1960), pp. 191–192.

47. John Richard Alden, *The South in the Revolution, 1763–1789* (Baton Rouge: Louisiana State University Press, 1957), pp. 89–90.

48. Berhard Knollenberg, *Origin of the American Revolution: 1759–1766* (New York: The Macmillan Company, 1960), p. 215, 237.

49. John Richard Alden, *The South in the Revolution, 1763–1789* (Baton Rouge: Louisiana State University Press, 1957), p. 92.

50. Walter J. Fraser, Jr., *Charleston! Charleston!* (Columbia: University of South Carolina Press, 1989), pp. 107–109.

51. John C. Miller, *Origins of the American Revolution* (London: Oxford University Press, 1943), p. 133.

52. Walter J. Fraser, Jr., *Charleston! Charleston!* (Columbia: University of South Carolina Press, 1989), p. 109.

53. Berhard Knollenberg, *Origin of the American Revolution: 1759–1766* (New York: The Macmillan Company, 1960), p. 235.

54. Robert M. Weir, *Colonial South Carolina* (New York: Kraus-Thomson Organization Press, 1983), pp. 298–299.

55. Walter J. Fraser, Jr., *Charleston! Charleston!* (Columbia: University of South Carolina Press, 1989), p. 110.

56. John C. Miller, *Origins of the American Revolution* (London: Oxford University Press, 1943), p. 320.

57. John Richard Alden, *The South in the Revolution, 1763–1789* (Baton Rouge: Louisiana State University Press, 1957), pp. 95–96.

58. Kenneth Coleman, *Colonial Georgia* (New York: Charles Scribner's Sons, 1976), pp. 246–252.

59. Ellen Chase, *The Beginnings of the American Revolution* (New York: The Baker and Taylor Company, 1910), pp. 51–52.

60. Kenneth Coleman, *Colonial Georgia* (New York: Charles Scribner's Sons, 1976), pp. 247–248.

61. Berhard Knollenberg, *Origin of the American Revolution: 1759–1766* (New York: The Macmillan Company, 1960), p. 235.

62. Kenneth Coleman, *Colonial Georgia* (New York: Charles Scribner's Sons, 1976), pp. 248–250.

63. Lawrence Henry Gipson, *The Coming of the Revolution* (New York: Harper & Brothers, 1954), p. 89.

64. Kenneth Coleman, *Colonial Georgia* (New York: Charles Scribner's Sons, 1976), p. 246.

65. Lawrence Henry Gipson, *The Coming of the Revolution* (New York: Harper & Brothers, 1954), p. 98.

66. John C. Miller, *Origins of the American Revolution* (London: Oxford University Press, 1943), pp. 139, 150–152.

67. Lawrence Henry Gipson, *The Coming of the Revolution* (New York: Harper & Brothers, 1954), pp. 106–114.

68. John C. Miller, *Origins of the American Revolution* (London: Oxford University Press, 1943), pp. 149–156.

69. Berhard Knollenberg, *Origin of the American Revolution: 1759–1766* (New York: The Macmillan Company, 1960), p. 237.

70. John Richard Alden, *The South in the Revolution, 1763–1789* (Baton Rouge: Louisiana State University Press, 1957), p. 100.

71. John C. Miller, *Origins of the American Revolution* (London: Oxford University Press, 1943), pp. 153–156.

72. Lawrence Henry Gipson, *The Coming of the Revolution* (New York: Harper & Brothers, 1954), pp. 106–114.

73. John C. Miller, *Origins of the American Revolution* (London: Oxford University Press, 1943), pp. 156–158.

74. Hugh T. Lefler and William S. Powell, *Colonial North Carolina* (New York: Charles Scribner's Sons, 1973), p. 250.

75. Charles Albro Barker, *The Background of the Revolution in Maryland* (New Haven: Yale University Press, 1940), pp. 311–312.

76. John C. Miller, *Origins of the American Revolution* (London: Oxford University Press, 1943), pp. 161–164.

77. William S. Powell, *North Carolina Through Four Centuries* (Chapel Hill: The University of North Carolina Press, 1989), p. 165.

78. Robert M. Weir, *Colonial South Carolina* (New York: Kraus-Thomson Organization Press, 1983), pp. 298–301

79. Charles C. Jones, Jr., LL.D., *History of Georgia* (Boston: Houghton Mifflin and Company, 1883), pp. 71–72.

80. John C. Miller, *Origins of the American Revolution* (London: Oxford University Press, 1943), pp. 161–164.

Chapter 3

1. Lawrence Henry Gipson, *The Coming of the Revolution* (New York: Harper & Brothers, 1954), pp. 169–170.

2. Samuel B. Griffith II, *In Defense of the Public Liberty* (New York: Doubleday & Company, Inc., 1976), p. 48.

3. John Richard Alden, *The South in the Revolution, 1763–1789* (Baton Rouge: Louisiana State University Press, 1957), p. 102.

4. Samuel B. Griffith II, *In Defense of the Public Liberty* (New York: Doubleday & Company, Inc., 1976), p. 48.

5. Lawrence Henry Gipson, *The Coming of the Revolution* (New York: Harper & Brothers, 1954), pp. 170–175.

6. Hugh T. Lefler and William S. Powell, *Colonial North Carolina* (New York: Charles Scribner's Sons, 1973), p. 251.

7. Aubrey C. Land, *Colonial Maryland* (New York: Kraus-Thomson Organization Press, 1981), pp. 259–263.

8. Matthew Page Andrews, *Virginia, The Old Dominion* (New York: Doubleday, Doran & Company, Inc., 1937), pp. 248–249.

9. Charles Campbell, *Introduction to the History of the Colony and Ancient Dominion of Virginia* (Richmond: B.B. Minor, 1847), pp. 139–140.

10. Mathew Page Andrews, *Virginia, The Old Dominion* (New York: Doubleday, Doran & Company, Inc., 1937), p. 251.

11. Hugh T. Lefler and William S. Powell, *Colonial North Carolina* (New York: Charles Scribner's Sons, 1973), pp. 252–254.

12. Robert M. Weir, *Colonial South Carolina* (New York: Kraus-Thomson Organization Press, 1983), pp. 302–304.

13. Walter J. Fraser, Jr., *Charleston! Charleston!* (Columbia: University of South Carolina Press, 1989), p. 125.

14. Kenneth Coleman, *Colonial Georgia* (New York: Charles Scribner's Sons, 1976), pp. 256–257.

15. Samuel B. Griffith II, *In Defense of the Public Liberty* (New York: Doubleday & Company, Inc., 1976, pp. 50–51, 67.

16. Robert M. Weir, *Colonial South Carolina* (New York: Kraus-Thomson Organization Press, 1983), pp. 304–305.

17. John Richard Alden, *The South in the Revolution, 1763–1789* (Baton Rouge: Louisiana State University Press, 1957), p. 116.

18. Aubrey C. Land, *Colonial Maryland* (New York: Kraus-Thomson Organization Press, 1981), pp. 267–269, 351–354.

19. William S. Powell, *North Carolina Through Four Centuries* (Chapel Hill: The University of North Carolina Press, 1989), pp. 167–168.

20. Walter J. Fraser, Jr., *Charleston! Charleston!* (Columbia: University of South Carolina Press, 1989), pp. 126–127.

21. Kenneth Coleman, *Colonial Georgia* (New York: Charles Scribner's Sons, 1976), pp. 258–262.

22. Walter J. Fraser, Jr., *Charleston! Charleston!* (Columbia: University of South Carolina Press, 1989), p. 136.

23. Ellen Chase, *The Beginnings of the American Revolution* (New York: The Baker and Taylor Company, 1910), pp. 333–334.

24. Samuel B. Griffith II, *In Defense of the Public Liberty* (New York: Doubleday & Company, Inc., 1976), pp. 85–86.

25. L. Edward Purcell and David F. Burg, *The World Almanac of the American Revolution* (New York: Scripps Howard Co., 1992), p. 21.

26. John C. Miller, *Origins of the American Revolution* (London: Oxford University Press, 1943), pp. 358–359.

27. Charles Campbell, *Introduction to the History of the Colony and Ancient Dominion of Virginia* (Richmond: B.B. Minor, 1847), pp. 140–141.

28. Samuel B. Griffith II, *In Defense of the Public Liberty* (New York: Doubleday & Company, Inc., 1976), p. 86.

29. L. Edward Purcell and David F. Burg, *The World Almanac of the American Revolution* (New York: Scripps Howard Company, 1992), p. 23.

30. John Richard Alden, *The South in the Revolution, 1763–1789* (Baton Rouge: Louisiana State University Press, 1957), p. 170.

31. John C. Miller, *Origins of the American Revolution* (London: Oxford University Press, 1943), pp. 355–357.

32. John Richard Alden, *The South in the Revolution, 1763–1789* (Baton Rouge: Louisiana State University Press, 1957), p. 170.

33. John C. Miller, *Origins of the American Revolution* (London: Oxford University Press, 1943), p. 358–259, 367.

34. Lawrence Henry Gipson, *The Coming of the Revolution* (New York: Harper & Brothers, 1954), p. 224–225, 228.

35. John C. Miller, *Origins of the American Revolution* (London: Oxford University Press, 1943), pp. 374–375.

36. Ellen Chase, *The Beginnings of the American Revolution* (New York: The Baker and Taylor Company, 1910), pp. 333–334.

37. John Richard Alden, *The South in the Revolution, 1763–1789* (Baton Rouge: Louisiana State University Press, 1957), p. 172.

38. Charles Campbell, *Introduction to the History of the Colony and Ancient Dominion of Virginia* (Richmond: B.B. Minor, 1847), p. 141.

39. Thomas J. Wertenbaker, *Norfolk, Historic Southern Port* (Durham: Duke University Press, 1931), pp. 54–55.

40. Walter J. Fraser, Jr., *Charleston! Charleston!* (Columbia: University of South Carolina Press, 1989), pp. 138–139.

41. Charles Albro Barker, *The Background of the Revolution in Maryland* (New Haven: Yale University Press, 1940), pp. 367–371.

42. Aubrey C. Land, *Colonial Maryland* (New York: Kraus-Thomson Organization Press, 1981), p. 300.

43. Robert M. Weir, *Colonial South Carolina* (New York: Kraus-Thomson Organization Press, 1983), p. 314.

44. Charles Campbell, *Introduction to the History of the Colony and Ancient Dominion of Virginia* (Richmond: B.B. Minor, 1847), p. 141.

45. H. J. Eckenrode, *The Revolution in Virginia* (Hamden, Connecticut: Archon Books, 1916), pp. 34–35.

46. William S. Powell, *North Carolina Through Four Centuries* (Chapel Hill: The University of North Carolina Press, 1989), p. 171.

47. Hugh T. Lefler and William S. Powell, *Colonial North Carolina* (New York: Charles Scribner's Sons, 1973), pp. 259–262.

48. William S. Powell, *North Carolina Through Four Centuries* (Chapel Hill: The University of North Carolina Press, 1989), pp. 171–172.

49. Kenneth Coleman, *Colonial Georgia* (New York: Charles Scribner's Sons, 1976), pp. 263–265.

50. John C. Miller, *Origins of the American Revolution* (London: Oxford University Press, 1943), pp. 379–381.

51. Robert M. Weir, *Colonial South Carolina* (New York: Kraus-Thomson Organization Press, 1983), p. 315.

52. John Richard Alden, *The South in the Revolution, 1763–1789* (Baton Rouge: Louisiana State University Press, 1957), pp. 174–175.

53. Charles Campbell, *Introduction to the History of the

Colony and Ancient Dominion of Virginia (Richmond: B.B. Minor, 1847), p. 142.

54. John C. Miller, *Origins of the American Revolution* (London: Oxford University Press, 1943), pp. 383–386.

55. John Richard Alden, *The South in the Revolution, 1763–1789* (Baton Rouge: Louisiana State University Press, 1957), p. 176.

56. John C. Miller, *Origins of the American Revolution* (London: Oxford University Press, 1943), pp. 381–384, 390–392.

57. Robert M. Weir, *Colonial South Carolina* (New York: Kraus-Thomson Organization Press, 1983), p. 315.

58. Hugh T. Lefler and William S. Powell, *Colonial North Carolina* (New York: Charles Scribner's Sons, 1973), p. 263.

59. Benson J. Lossing, *Seventeen Hundred and Seventy-Six* (New York: Edward Walker, 1849), p. 132.

60. John Richard Alden, *The South in the Revolution, 1763–1789* (Baton Rouge: Louisiana State University Press, 1957), p. 180.

61. Aubrey C. Land, *Colonial Maryland* (New York: Kraus-Thomson Organization Press, 1981), pp. 301–303.

62. Matthew Page Andrews, *Virginia, The Old Dominion* (New York: Doubleday, Doran & Company, Inc., 1937), p. 281.

63. John Richard Alden, *The South in the Revolution, 1763–1789* (Baton Rouge: Louisiana State University Press, 1957), p. 181.

64. L. Edward Purcell and David F. Burg, *The World Almanac of the American Revolution* (New York: Scripps Howard Co., 1992), p. 35.

65. John Richard Alden, *The South in the Revolution, 1763–1789* (Baton Rouge: Louisiana State University Press, 1957), pp. 181–182.

66. Charles Campbell, *Introduction to the History of the Colony and Ancient Dominion of Virginia* (Richmond: B.B. Minor, 1847), p. 146.

67. Thomas J. Wertenbaker, *Norfolk, Historic Southern Port* (Durham: Duke University Press, 1931), p. 55.

68. John Richard Alden, *The South in the Revolution, 1763–1789* (Baton Rouge: Louisiana State University Press, 1957), p. 182.

69. William S. Powell, *North Carolina Through Four Centuries* (Chapel Hill: The University of North Carolina Press, 1989), p. 173.

70. Hugh T. Lefler and William S. Powell, *Colonial North Carolina* (New York: Charles Scribner's Sons, 1973), pp. 263–264.

71. Robert M. Weir, *Colonial South Carolina* (New York: Kraus-Thomson Organization Press, 1983), pp. 316–317.

72. Kenneth Coleman, *Colonial Georgia* (New York: Charles Scribner's Sons, 1976), pp. 266–267.

73. John Richard Alden, *The South in the Revolution, 1763–1789* (Baton Rouge: Louisiana State University Press, 1957), p. 184.

74. Matthew Page Andrews, *Virginia, The Old Dominion* (New York: Doubleday, Doran & Company, Inc., 1937), p. 282.

Chapter 4

1. David Hackett Fischer, *Paul Revere's Ride* (New York: Oxford University Press, 1994), p. 85, 189–197, 325.

2. Aubrey C. Land, *Colonial Maryland* (New York: Kraus-Thomson Organization Press, 1981), pp. 304–306.

3. David Hackett Fischer, *Paul Revere's Ride* (New York: Oxford University Press, 1994), p. 325.

4. Matthew Page Andrews, *Virginia, The Old Dominion* (New York: Doubleday, Doran & Company, Inc., 1937), pp. 283–284.

5. Charles Campbell, *Introduction to the History of the Colony and Ancient Dominion of Virginia* (Richmond: B.B. Minor, 1847), p. 148.

6. Matthew Page Andrews, *Virginia, The Old Dominion* (New York: Doubleday, Doran & Company, Inc., 1937), p. 283–284.

7. Charles Campbell, *Introduction to the History of the Colony and Ancient Dominion of Virginia* (Richmond: B.B. Minor, 1847), pp. 148–150.

8. Ivor Noel Hume, *1775, Another Part of the Field* (New York: Alfred A. Knopf, Inc., 1966), pp. 222, 229.

9. John E. Selby, *The Revolution in Virginia, 1775–1783* (Williamsburg: The Colonial Williamsburg Foundation, 1988), p. 43.

10. Matthew Page Andrews, *Virginia, The Old Dominion* (New York: Doubleday, Doran & Company, Inc., 1937), pp. 284–286.

11. John E. Selby, *The Revolution in Virginia, 1775–1783* (Williamsburg: The Colonial Williamsburg Foundation, 1988), pp. 44–46.

12. Ivor Noel Hume, *1775, Another Part of the Field* (New York: Alfred A. Knopf, Inc., 1966), p. 235.

13. David Hackett Fischer, *Paul Revere's Ride* (New York: Oxford University Press, 1994), p. 325.

14. Hugh T. Lefler and William S. Powell, *Colonial North Carolina* (New York: Charles Scribner's Sons, 1973), p. 269.

15. William S. Powell, *North Carolina Through Four Centuries* (Chapel Hill: The University of North Carolina Press, 1989), p. 174.

16. John E. Selby, *The Revolution in Virginia, 1775–1783* (Willamsburg: The Colonial Williamsburg Foundation, 1988), p. 44.

17. William S. Powell, *North Carolina Through Four Centuries* (Chapel Hill: The University of North Carolina Press, 1989), pp. 176–177.

18. David Hackett Fischer, *Paul Revere's Ride* (New York: Oxford University Press, 1994), p. 325.

19. Walter J. Fraser, Jr., *Charleston! Charleston!* (Columbia: University of South Carolina Press, 1989), p. 141.

20. Robert M. Weir, *Colonial South Carolina* (New York: Kraus-Thomson Organization Press, 1983), p. 321.

21. Walter J. Fraser, Jr., *Charleston! Charleston!* (Columbia: University of South Carolina Press, 1989), pp. 141–143.

22. Robert M. Weir, *Colonial South Carolina* (New York: Kraus-Thomson Organization Press, 1983), p. 322.

23. Walter J. Fraser, Jr., *Charleston! Charleston!* (Columbia: University of South Carolina Press, 1989), pp. 141–146.

24. Charles C. Jones, Jr., LL.D., *History of Georgia* (Boston: Houghton, Mifflin and Company, 1883), pp. 175–176.

25. Kenneth Coleman, *Colonial Georgia* (New York: Charles Scribner's Sons, 1976), p. 268.

26. David Hackett Fischer, *Paul Revere's Ride* (New York: Oxford University Press, 1994), p. 275.

27. Benson J. Lossing, *Seventeen Hundred and Seventy-Six* (New York: Edward Walker, 1849), pg. 160–164.

28. L. Edward Purcell and David F. Burg, *The World Almanac of the American Revolution* (New York: Scripps Howard Co., 1992), pp. 46–50.

29. Charles Campbell, *Introduction to the History of the Colony and Ancient Dominion of Virginia* (Richmond: B.B. Minor, 1847), p. 151. H.J. Eckenrode, *The Revolution in Virginia* (Hamden, Connecticut: Archon Books, 1916), pp. 123–125.

30. Charles C. Jones, Jr., LL.D., *History of Georgia* (Boston: Houghton, Mifflin and Company, 1883), p.177.

31. Kenneth Coleman, *Colonial Georgia* (New York: Charles Scribner's Sons, 1976), pp. 273–275.

32. Charles C. Jones, Jr., LL.D., *History of Georgia* (Boston: Houghton, Mifflin and Company, 1863), pp. 180–181.

33. Aubrey C. Land, *Colonial Maryland* (New York: Kraus-Thomson Organization Press, 1981), pp. 306–307.

34. Hugh T. Lefler and William S. Powell, *Colonial North Carolina* (New York: Charles Scribner's Sons, 1973), pp. 269–271.

35. Ivor Noel Hume, *1775, Another Part of the Field* (New York: Alfred A. Knopf, Inc., 1966), p. 268.

36. Hugh T. Lefler and William S. Powell, *Colonial North Carolina* (New York: Charles Scribner's Sons, 1973), pp. 266–272.

37. William S. Powell, *North Carolina Through Four Centuries* (Chapel Hill: The University of North Carolina Press, 1989), pp. 177–180.

38. Robert M. Weir, *Colonial South Carolina* (New York: Kraus-Thomson Organization Press, 1983), pp. 323–324.

39. Walter J. Fraser, Jr., *Charleston! Charleston!* (Columbia: University of South Carolina Press, 1989), p. 147, Ivor Noel Hume, *1775, Another Part of the Field* (New York: Alfred A. Knopf, Inc., 1966), p. 342.

40. Walter J. Fraser, Jr., *Charleston! Charleston!* (Columbia, South Carolina: University of South Carolina Press, 1989), pp. 147–148.

41. Robert M. Weir, *Colonial South Carolina* (New York: Kraus-Thomson Organization Press, 1983), pp. 324–325.

42. Clifford Sheats Capps and Eugenia Burney, *Colonial Georgia* (New York: Thomas Nelson, Inc. 1972), p. 120.

43. Kenneth Coleman, *Colonial Georgia* (New York: Charles Scribner's Sons, 1976), p. 276.

Chapter 5

1. Ivor Noel Hume, *1775, Another Part of the Field* (New York: Alfred A. Knopf, Inc., 1966), pp. 222–226.

2. Ernest McNeill Eller, *Chesapeake Bay in the American Revolution* (Centreville, Maryland: Tidewater Publishers, 1981), pp. 56–57.

3. John E. Selby, *The Revolution in Virginia, 1775–1783* (Willamsburg: The Colonial Williamsburg Foundation, 1988), pp. 14–21.

4. Ivor Noel Hume, *1775, Another Part of the Field* (New York: Alfred A. Knopf, Inc., 1966), pp. 237–242.

5. John E. Selby, *The Revolution in Virginia, 1775–1783* (Willamsburg: The Colonial Williamsburg Foundation, 1988), pp. 46–47.

6. Ivor Noel Hume, *1775, Another Part of the Field* (New York: Alfred A. Knopf, Inc., 1966), pp. 265, 271–274.

7. Ernest McNeill Eller, *Chesapeake Bay in the American Revolution* (Centreville, Maryland: Tidewater Publishers, 1981), pp. 66–67.

8. Ivor Noel Hume, *1775, Another Part of the Field* (New York: Alfred A. Knopf, Inc., 1966), pp. 265, 271–274.

9. Thomas J. Wertenbaker, *Norfolk, Historic Southern Port* (Durham: Duke University Press, 1931), p. 4, 26–27, 56

10. Ernest McNeill Eller, *Chesapeake Bay in the American Revolution* (Centreville, Maryland: Tidewater Publishers, 1981), pp. 68–69.

11. H.J. Eckenrode, *The Revolution in Virginia* (Hamden, Connecticut: Archon Books, 1916), p. 63.

12. Ivor Noel Hume, *1775, Another Part of the Field* (New York: Alfred A. Knopf, Inc., 1966), pp. 281–284, 305.

13. Ernest McNeill Eller, *Chesapeake Bay in the American Revolution* (Centreville, Maryland: Tidewater Publishers, 1981), p. 71.

14. Ivor Noel Hume, *1775, Another Part of the Field* (New York: Alfred A. Knopf, Inc., 1966), pp. 282–285, 305–318.

15. Ernest McNeill Eller, *Chesapeake Bay in the American Revolution* (Centreville, Maryland: Tidewater Publishers, 1981), pp. 71–73.

16. Ivor Noel Hume, *1775, Another Part of the Field* (New York: Alfred A. Knopf, Inc., 1966), pp. 333–334. H.J. Eckenrode, *The Revolution in Virginia* (Hamden, Connecticut: Archon Books, 1916), p. 64.

17. Ernest McNeill Eller, *Chesapeake Bay in the American Revolution* (Centreville, Maryland: Tidewater Publishers, 1981), p. 74.

18. Ivor Noel Hume, *1775, Another Part of the Field* (New York: Alfred A. Knopf, Inc., 1966), pp. 346–348.

19. Ernest McNeill Eller, *Chesapeake Bay in the American Revolution* (Centreville, Maryland: Tidewater Publishers, 1981), p. 76.

20. Ivor Noel Hume, *1775, Another Part of the Field* (New York: Alfred A. Knopf, Inc., 1966), pp. 349–351.

21. Thomas J. Wertenbaker, *Norfolk, Historic Southern Port* (Durham: Duke University Press, 1931), p. 59.

22. Ivor Noel Hume, *1775, Another Part of the Field* (New York: Alfred A. Knopf, Inc., 1966), pp. 343–360.

23. Ernest McNeill Eller, *Chesapeake Bay in the American Revolution* (Centreville, Maryland: Tidewater Publishers, 1981), pp. 77–79.

24. Ivor Noel Hume, *1775, Another Part of the Field* (New York: Alfred A. Knopf, Inc., 1966), pp. 360–362.

25. Ernest McNeill Eller, *Chesapeake Bay in the American Revolution* (Centreville, Maryland: Tidewater Publishers, 1981), p. 80.

26. Ivor Noel Hume, *1775, Another Part of the Field* (New York: Alfred A. Knopf, Inc., 1966), pp. 367, 381–396.

27. H.J. Eckenrode, *The Revolution in Virginia* (Hamden, Connecticut: Archon Books, 1916), p. 54.

28 Ivor Noel Hume, *1775, Another Part of the Field* (New York: Alfred A. Knopf, Inc., 1966), pp. 396–430.

29. Ernest McNeill Eller, *Chesapeake Bay in the American Revolution* (Centreville, Maryland: Tidewater Publishers, 1981), pp. 83–84.

30. Ivor Noel Hume, *1775, Another Part of the Field* (New York: Alfred A. Knopf, Inc., 1966), pp. 431–441.

31. Thomas J. Wertenbaker, *Norfolk, Historic Southern Port* (Durham: Duke University Press, 1931), p. 64.

32. Ernest McNeill Eller, *Chesapeake Bay in the American Revolution* (Centreville, Maryland: Tidewater Publishers, 1981), pp. 85–86.

33. Ivor Noel Hume, *1775, Another Part of the Field* (New York: Alfred A. Knopf, Inc., 1966), pp. 445–447.

34. Ernest McNeill Eller, *Chesapeake Bay in the American Revolution* (Centreville, Maryland: Tidewater Publishers, 1981), p. 85.

35. Ivor Noel Hume, *1775, Another Part of the Field* (New York: Alfred A. Knopf, Inc., 1966), pp. 446–448.

36. H.J. Eckenrode, *The Revolution in Virginia* (Hamden, Connecticut: Archon Books, 1916), p. 85.

37. Ivor Noel Hume, *1775, Another Part of the Field* (New York: Alfred A. Knopf, Inc., 1966), pp. 449–456.

38. Thomas J. Wertenbaker, *Norfolk, Historic Southern Port* (Durham: Duke University Press, 1931), pp. 66–67.

39. Ivor Noel Hume, *1775, Another Part of the Field* (New York: Alfred A. Knopf, Inc., 1966), p. 457.

40. Thomas J. Wertenbaker, *Norfolk, Historic Southern Port* (Durham: Duke University Press, 1931), p. 68.

41. H.J. Eckenrode, *The Revolution in Virginia* (Hamden, Connecticut: Archon Books, 1916), p. 86–88.

42. Charles Campbell, *Introduction to the History of the Colony and Ancient Dominion of Virginia* (Richmond: B.B. Minor, 1847), p. 153.

43. L. Edward Purcell and David F. Burg, *The World Almanac of the American Revolution* (New York: Scripps Howard Co., 1992), p, 68.

44. Thomas J. Wertenbaker, *Norfolk, Historic Southern Port* (Durham: Duke University Press, 1931), p. 69.

45. Ernest McNeill Eller, *Chesapeake Bay in the American Revolution* (Centreville, Maryland: Tidewater Publishers, 1981), pp. 86, 89.

46. H.J. Eckenrode, *The Revolution in Virginia* (Hamden, Connecticut: Archon Books, 1916), p. 88.

47. Thomas J. Wertenbaker, *Norfolk, Historic Southern Port* (Durham: Duke University Press, 1931), p. 70.

48. H.J. Eckenrode, *The Revolution in Virginia* (Hamden, Connecticut: Archon Books, 1916), pp. 55–56, 89–90.

49. Thomas J. Wertenbaker, *Norfolk, Historic Southern Port* (Durham: Duke University Press, 1931), pp. 71–72.

50. Ernest McNeill Eller, *Chesapeake Bay in the American Revolution* (Centreville, Maryland: Tidewater Publishers, 1981), pp. 94–95.

51. Thomas J. Wertenbaker, *Norfolk, Historic Southern Port* (Durham: Duke University Press, 1931), p. 73.

52. Ernest McNeill Eller, *Chesapeake Bay in the American Revolution* (Centreville, Maryland: Tidewater Pub., 1981), p. 95.

53. H.J. Eckenrode, *The Revolution in Virginia* (Hamden, Connecticut: Archon Books, 1916), pp. 90–94.

54. Charles Campbell, *Introduction to the History of the Colony and Ancient Dominion of Virginia* (Richmond: B.B. Minor, 1847), p. 160.

55. Ernest McNeill Eller, *Chesapeake Bay in the American Revolution* (Centreville, Maryland: Tidewater Publishers, 1981), pp. 96–97.

56. Thomas J. Wertenbaker, *Norfolk, Historic Southern Port* (Durham: Duke University Press, 1931), pp. 74–79.

Chapter 6

1. Malcolm Ross, *The Cape Fear* (New York: Holt, Rinehart and Winston, Inc., 1965), pp. 109–112.

2. Blackwell P. Robinson, *A History of Moore County, North Carolina 1747–1847* (Southern Pines, North Carolina: Moore County Historical Association, 1956), p. 47.

3. Malcolm Ross, *The Cape Fear* (New York: Holt, Rinehart and Winston, Inc., 1965), pp. 109–112.

4. Blackwell P. Robinson, *A History of Moore County, North Carolina 1747–1847* (Southern Pines, North Carolina: Moore County Historical Association, 1956), p. 47.

5. Malcolm Ross, *The Cape Fear* (New York: Holt, Rinehart and Winston, Inc., 1965), pp. 114–116.

6. Donald Barr Chidsey, *The War in the South* (New York: Crown Publishers, Inc., 1969), p. 26.

7. Henry Lumpkin, *From Savannah to Yorktown* (New York: Paragon House Publishers, 1981), p. 4.

8. Malcolm Ross, *The Cape Fear* (New York: Holt, Rinehart and Winston, Inc., 1965), p. 116.

9. Blackwell P. Robinson, *A History of Moore County, North Carolina 1747–1847* (Southern Pines, North Carolina: Moore County Historical Association, 1956), pp. 51–52.

10. Hugh T. Lefler and William S. Powell, *Colonial North Carolina* (New York: Charles Scribner's Sons, 1973), p. 276.

11. Blackwell P. Robinson, *A History of Moore County, North Carolina 1747–1847* (Southern Pines, North Carolina: Moore County Historical Association, 1956), pp. 52–54.

12. Donald Barr Chidsey, *The War in the South* (New York: Crown Publishers, Inc., 1969), p. 29.

13. Blackwell P. Robinson, *A History of Moore County, North Carolina 1747–1847* (Southern Pines, North Carolina: Moore County Historical Association, 1956), pp. 54–59.

14. Malcolm Ross, *The Cape Fear* (New York: Holt, Rinehart and Winston, Inc., 1965), pp. 106–107, 117–118.

15. Donald Barr Chidsey, *The War in the South* (New York: Crown Publishers, Inc., 1969), p. 30.

16. Malcolm Ross, *The Cape Fear* (New York: Holt, Rinehart and Winston, Inc., 1965), pp. 118–124.

17. Dr. Dan L. Morrill, *Southern Campaigns of the American Revolution* (Baltimore: The Nautical & Aviation Publishing Company of America, 1993), pp. 8–9.

18. Malcolm Ross, *The Cape Fear* (New York: Holt, Rinehart and Winston, Inc., 1965), p. 124.

19. Dr. Dan L. Morrill, *Southern Campaigns of the American Revolution* (Baltimore: The Nautical & Aviation Publishing Company of America, 1993) pp. 9–10.

20. Dr. Dan L. Morrill, *Southern Campaigns of the American Revolution* (Baltimore: The Nautical & Aviation Publishing Company of America, 1993), pp. 10–11. Donald Barr Chidsey, *The War in the South* (New York: Crown Publishers, Inc., 1969), p. 32.

21. Malcolm Ross, *The Cape Fear* (New York: Holt, Rinehart and Winston, Inc., 1965), p. 126.

22. *Ibid.*, pp. 126–128. Blackwell P. Robinson, *A History of Moore County, North Carolina 1747–1847* (Southern Pines, North Carolina: Moore County Historical Association, 1956), p. 60.

23. Malcolm Ross, *The Cape Fear* (New York: Holt, Rinehart and Winston, Inc., 1965), p. 129.

24. Hugh T. Lefler and William S. Powell, *Colonial North Carolina* (New York: Charles Scribner's Sons, 1973), p. 278.

25. Malcolm Ross, *The Cape Fear* (New York: Holt, Rinehart and Winston, Inc., 1965), p. 129.

26. Dr. Dan L. Morrill, *Southern Campaigns of the American Revolution* (Baltimore: The Nautical & Aviation Publishing Company of America, 1993), p. 13.

27. Blackwell P. Robinson, *A History of Moore County, North Carolina 1747–1847* (Southern Pines, North Carolina: Moore County Historical Association, 1956), pp. 62–69.

28. Esmond Wright, *The Fire of Liberty* (New York: St. Martin's Press, 1983), p. 61.

29. Hugh T. Lefler and William S. Powell, *Colonial North Carolina* (New York: Charles Scribner's Sons, 1973), pp. 280–281.

30. Malcolm Ross, *The Cape Fear* (New York: Holt, Rinehart and Winston, Inc., 1965), pp. 131–132.

31. Hugh T. Lefler and William S. Powell, *Colonial North Carolina* (New York: Charles Scribner's Sons, 1973), p. 282.

32. Donald Barr Chidsey, *The War in the South* (New York: Crown Publishers, Inc., 1969), p. 37.

33. L. Edward Purcell and David F. Burg, *The World Almanac of the American Revolution* (New York: Scripps Howard Co., 1992), pp. 72, 73, 76.

34. Franklin and Mary Wickwire, *Cornwallis, The American Adventure* (Boston: Houghton, Mifflin and Company, 1970), pp. 81–82.

35. Edward McCrady, LL.D., *The History of South Carolina in The Revolution 1775–1780* (New York: Russell & Russell, 1901/1969), pp. 130–133.

36. Franklin and Mary Wickwire, *Cornwallis, The American Adventure* (Boston: Houghton Mifflin and Company, 1970), pp. 81–82.

37. Malcolm Ross, *The Cape Fear* (New York: Holt, Rinehart and Winston, Inc., 1965), pp. 132–133,

38. Hugh T. Lefler and William S. Powell, *Colonial North Carolina* (New York: Charles Scribner's Sons, 1973), p. 280. Franklin and Mary Wickwire, *Cornwallis, The American Adventure* (Boston: Houghton Mifflin and Company, 1970), pp. 83–84.

39. Henry Steele Commager and Richard B. Morris, *The Spirit of 'Seventy-Six* (New York: Harper and Row, Publishers, 1975), p. 115.

Chapter 7

1. Edward McCrady, LL.D., *The History of South Carolina in The Revolution 1775–1780* (New York: Russell & Russell, 1901/1969), pp. 136–137.

2. Paul H. Smith, *Loyalists and Redcoats* (Chapel Hill: The University of North Carolina Press, 1964), p. 28.

3. Henry Lumpkin, *From Savannah to Yorktown* (New York: Paragon House Publishers, 1981), p. 10.

4. Donald Barr Chidsey, *The War in the South* (New York: Crown Publishers, Inc., 1969), pp. 37–38.

5. A.J. Langguth, *Patriots* (New York: Simon & Schuster, Inc., 1988), p. 329.

6. Colonel R. Ernest Dupuy and Colonel Trevor N. Dupuy, *An Outline History of the American Revolution* (New York: Harper & Row Publishers, 1975), p. 40.

7. Donald Barr Chidsey, *The War in the South* (New York: Crown Publishers, Inc., 1969), p. 38.

8. A.J. Langguth, *Patriots* (New York: Simon & Schuster, Inc., 1988), pp. 330–331.

9. Henry Lumpkin, *From Savannah to Yorktown* (New York: Paragon House Publishers, 1981), p. 14.

10. Edward McCrady, LL.D., *The History of South Carolina in the Revolution 1775–1780* (New York: Russell & Russell, 1901/1969), pp. 137–142.

11. Dr. Dan L. Morrill, *Southern Campaigns of the American Revolution* (Baltimore: The Nautical & Aviation Publishing Company of America, 1993), pp. 20–21.

12. L. Edward Purcell and David F. Burg, *The World Almanac of the American Revolution* (New York: Scripps Howard Co., 1992), p. 361.

13. Henry Lumpkin, *From Savannah to Yorktown* (New York: Paragon House Publishers, 1981), p. 13.

14. Edward McCrady, LL.D., *The History of South Carolina in the Revolution 1775–1780* (New York: Russell & Russell, 1901/1969), p. 143.

15. Dr. Dan L. Morrill, *Southern Campaigns of the American Revolution* (Baltimore: The Nautical & Aviation Publishing Company of America, 1993), p. 22.

16. Edward McCrady, LL.D., *The History of South Carolina in the Revolution 1775–1780* (New York: Russell & Russell, 1901/1969), p. 144.

17. Colonel R. Ernest Dupuy and Colonel Trevor N. Dupuy, *An Outline History of the American Revolution* (New York: Harper & Row Publishers, 1975), p. 41.

18. Henry Lumpkin, *From Savannah to Yorktown* (New York: Paragon House Publishers, 1981), p. 12.

19. Edward McCrady, LL.D., *The History of South Carolina in the Revolution 1775–1780* (New York: Russell & Russell, 1901/1969), pp. 138–141.

20. Franklin and Mary Wickwire, *Cornwallis, The American Adventure* (Boston: Houghton Mifflin and Company, 1970), pp. 84–85.

21. Edward McCrady, LL.D., *The History of South Carolina in the Revolution 1775–1780* (New York: Russell & Russell, 1901/1969), pp. 144–152.

22. Henry Lumpkin, *From Savannah to Yorktown* (New York: Paragon House Publishers, 1981), p. 15.

23. Edward McCrady, LL.D., *The History of South Carolina in the Revolution 1775–1780* (New York: Russell & Russell, 1901/1969), pp. 152–153.

24. Esmond Wright, *The Fire of Liberty* (New York: St. Martin's Press, 1983), p. 62.

25. Henry Lumpkin, *From Savannah to Yorktown* (New York: Paragon House Publishers, 1981), p. 17.

26. Dr. Dan L. Morrill, *Southern Campaigns of the American Revolution* (Baltimore: The Nautical & Aviation Publishing Company of America, 1993), p. 23.

27. Edward McCrady, LL.D., *The History of South Carolina in the Revolution 1775–1780* (New York: Russell & Russell, 1901/1969), pp. 154–155.

28. Dr. Dan L. Morrill, *Southern Campaigns of the American Revolution* (Baltimore: The Nautical & Aviation Publishing Company of America, 1993), p. 23.

29. Henry Lumpkin, *From Savannah to Yorktown* (New York: Paragon House Publishers, 1981), p. 16.

30. Edward McCrady, LL.D., *The History of South Carolina in the Revolution 1775–1780* (New York: Russell & Russell, 1901/1969), pp. 157–158.

31. Henry Lumpkin, *From Savannah to Yorktown* (New York: Paragon House Publishers, 1981), p. 17.

32. Edward McCrady, LL.D., *The History of South Carolina in the Revolution 1775–1780* (New York: Russell & Russell, 1901/1969), pp. 155–159. Henry Lumpkin, *From Savannah to Yorktown* (New York: Paragon House Publishers, 1981), pp. 16–17.

33. Donald Barr Chidsey, *The War in the South* (New York: Crown Publishers, Inc., 1969), pp. 46–47.

34. Dr. Dan L. Morrill, *Southern Campaigns of the American Revolution* (Baltimore: The Nautical & Aviation Publishing Company of America, 1993), pp. 23–24.

35. Edward McCrady, LL.D., *The History of South Carolina in the Revolution 1775–1780* (New York: Russell & Russell, 1901/1969), pp. 159–160.

36. Donald Barr Chidsey, *The War in the South* (New York: Crown Publishers, Inc., 1969), p. 47.

37. Henry Lumpkin, *From Savannah to Yorktown* (New York: Paragon House Publishers, 1981), pp. 17–18.

38. Colonel R. Ernest Dupuy and Colonel Trevor N. Dupuy, *An Outline History of the American Revolution* (New York: Harper & Row Publishers, 1975), p. 42.

39. Donald Barr Chidsey, *The War in the South* (New York: Crown Publishers, Inc., 1969), pp. 47–48.

40. Henry Lumpkin, *From Savannah to Yorktown* (New York: Paragon House Publishers, 1981), p. 18.

Chapter 8

1. L. Edward Purcell and David F. Burg, *The World Almanac of the American Revolution* (New York: Scripps Howard Co., 1992), pp. 147–148.

2. John Richard Alden, *The South in the Revolution* (Baton Rouge, Louisiana State University Press, 1957) pp. 230–231.

3. Paul H. Smith, *Loyalists and Redcoats* (Chapel Hill: The University of North Carolina Press, 1964), pp. 79–85.

4. Samuel B. Griffith II, *In Defense of the Public Liberty* (New York: Doubleday & Company, Inc., 1976), p. 496.

5. *Ibid.*, p. 496. L. Edward Purcell and David F. Burg, *The World Almanac of the American Revolution* (New York: Scripps Howard Co., 1992), p. 329.

6. Paul H. Smith, *Loyalists and Redcoats* (Chapel Hill: The University of North Carolina Press, 1964), pp. 85–94.

7. Samuel B. Griffith II, *In Defense of the Public Liberty* (New York: Doubleday & Company, Inc., 1976), pp. 515–521.

8. John Richard Alden, *The South in the Revolution* (Baton Rouge, Louisiana State University Press, 1957). pp. 231–232.

9. Christopher Hibbert, *Redcoats and Rebels* (New York: W.W. Norton & Company, 1990), pp. 239–240.

10. Paul H. Smith, *Loyalists and Redcoats* (Chapel Hill: The University of North Carolina Press, 1964), p. 100.

11. Christopher Hibbert, *Redcoats and Rebels* (New York: W.W. Norton & Company, 1990), p. 239.

12. Dr. Dan L. Morrill, *Southern Campaigns of the American Revolution* (Baltimore: The Nautical & Aviation Publishing Company of America, 1993), p. 242.

13. Christopher Hibbert, *Redcoats and Rebels* (New York: W.W. Norton & Company, 1990), p. 240.

14. Dr. Dan L. Morrill, *Southern Campaigns of the American Revolution* (Baltimore: The Nautical & Aviation Publishing Company of America, 1993), pp. 42–44.

15. Christopher Hibbert, *Redcoats and Rebels* (New York: W.W. Norton & Company, 1990), p. 240.

16. Dr. Dan L. Morrill, *Southern Campaigns of the American Revolution* (Baltimore: The Nautical & Aviation Publishing Company of America, 1993), p. 45.

17. Christopher Hibbert, *Redcoats and Rebels* (New York: W.W. Norton & Company, 1990), pp. 240–241. Clifford Sheats Capps and Eugenia Burney, *Colonial Georgia* (New York: Thomas Nelson, Inc., 1972), p. 135.

18. Dr. Dan L. Morrill, *Southern Campaigns of the American Revolution* (Baltimore: The Nautical & Aviation Publishing Company of America, 1993), pp. 45–46.

19. Donald Barr Chidsey, *The War in the South* (New York: Crown Publishers, Inc., 1969), p. 60.

20. Dr. Dan L. Morrill, *Southern Campaigns of the American Revolution* (Baltimore: The Nautical & Aviation Publishing Company of America, 1993), pp. 44–46.

21. Paul H. Smith, *Loyalists and Redcoats* (Chapel Hill: The University of North Carolina Press, 1964), pp. 116–117.

22. Clifford Sheats Capps and Eugenia Burney, *Colonial Georgia* (New York: Thomas Nelson, Inc., 1972), pp. 136–139.

23. L. Edward Purcell and David F. Burg, *The World Almanac of the American Revolution* (New York: Scripps Howard Co., 1992), p. 196.

24. Henry Lumpkin, *From Savannah to Yorktown* (New York: Paragon House Publishers, 1981), p. 29.

25. L. Edward Purcell and David F. Burg, *The World Almanac of the American Revolution* (New York: Scripps Howard Co., 1992), p. 362.

26. Christopher Hibbert, *Redcoats and Rebels* (New York: W.W. Norton & Company, 1990), p. 242.

27. Dr. Dan L. Morrill, *Southern Campaigns of the American Revolution* (Baltimore: The Nautical & Aviation Publishing Company of America, 1993), p. 48.

28. Christopher Hibbert, *Redcoats and Rebels* (New York: W.W. Norton & Company, 1990), p. 242.

29. Robert Middlekauff, *The Glorious Cause* (New York: Oxford University Press, 1982), p. 443.

30. Henry Lumpkin, *From Savannah to Yorktown* (New York: Paragon House Publishers, 1981), p. 30.

31. Christopher Hibbert, *Redcoats and Rebels* (New York: W.W. Norton & Company, 1990), p. 242.

32. Henry Lumpkin, *From Savannah to Yorktown* (New York: Paragon House Publishers, 1981), p. 30.

33. L. Edward Purcell and David F. Burg, *The World Almanac of the American Revolution* (New York: Scripps Howard Co., 1992), pp. 199–200.

34. Dr. Dan L. Morrill, *Southern Campaigns of the American Revolution* (Baltimore: The Nautical & Aviation Publishing Company of America, 1993), pp. 48–49.

35. Clifford Sheats Capps and Eugenia Burney, *Colonial Georgia* (New York: Thomas Nelson, Inc., 1972), pp. 139–140.

36. Dr. Dan L. Morrill, *Southern Campaigns of the American Revolution* (Baltimore: The Nautical & Aviation Publishing Company of America, 1993), p. 50.

37. Clifford Sheats Capps and Eugenia Burney, *Colonial Georgia* (New York: Thomas Nelson, Inc., 1972), p. 144.

38. L. Edward Purcell and David F. Burg, *The World Almanac of the American Revolu*tion (New York: Scripps Howard Co., 1992), p. 202.

39. Clifford Sheats Capps and Eugenia Burney, *Colonial Georgia* (New York: Thomas Nelson, Inc., 1972), p. 144.

40. Edward McCrady, LL.D., *The History of South Carolina in the Revolution 1775–1780* (New York: Russell & Russell, 1901/1969), pp. 350–357, 362.

41. *Ibid.*, pp. 357–360.

42. L. Edward Purcell and David F. Burg, *The World Almanac of the American Revolution* (New York: Scripps Howard Co., 1992), pp. 362–363.

43. Edward McCrady, LL.D., *The History of South Carolina in the Revolution 1775–1780* (New York: Russell & Russell, 1901/1969), pp. 360–384.

44. Paul H. Smith, *Loyalists and Redcoats* (Chapel Hill: The University of North Carolina Press, 1964), p. 104.

Chapter 9

1. Edward McCrady, LL.D., *The History of South Carolina in the Revolution 1775–1780* (New York: Russell & Russell, 1901/1969), pp. 384–388.

2. *Ibid.*, pp. 390–391. Dr. Dan L. Morrill, *Southern Campaigns of the American Revolution* (Baltimore: The Nautical & Aviation Publishing Company of America, 1993), p. 54.

3. Edward McCrady, LL.D., *The History of South Carolina in the Revolution 1775–1780* (New York: Russell & Russell, 1901/1969), pp. 389–391.

4. Dr. Dan L. Morrill, *Southern Campaigns of the American Revolution* (Baltimore: The Nautical & Aviation Publishing Company of America, 1993), p. 54.

5. Edward McCrady, LL.D., *The History of South Carolina in the Revolution 1775–1780* (New York: Russell & Russell, 1901/1969), pp. 392–394.

6. Walter J. Fraser, Jr., *Charleston! Charleston!* (Columbia: University of South Carolina Press, 1989), p. 158.

7. Edward McCrady, LL.D., *The History of South Carolina in the Revolution 1775–1780* (New York: Russell & Russell, 1901/1969), pp. 392–396.

8. Clifford Sheats Capps and Eugenia Burney, *Colonial Georgia* (New York: Thomas Nelson, Inc., 1972), pp. 144–145.

9. Dr. Dan L. Morrill, *Southern Campaigns of the American Revolution* (Baltimore: The Nautical & Aviation Publishing Company of America, 1993), p. 55.

10. Charles C. Jones, Jr., LL.D., *The History of Georgia, Vol. II* (Cambridge: The Riverside Press, 1883), p. 373.

11. Paul H. Smith, *Loyalists and Redcoats* (Chapel Hill: The University of North Carolina Press, 1964), pp. 106–107.

12. Edward McCrady, LL.D., *The History of South Carolina in the Revolution 1775–1780* (New York: Russell & Russell, 1901/1969), p. 399.

13. Dr. Dan L. Morrill, *Southern Campaigns of the American Revolution* (Baltimore: The Nautical & Aviation Publishing Company of America, 1993), pp. 55–56.

14. Henry Lumpkin, *From Savannah to Yorktown* (New York: Paragon House Publishers, 1981), p. 32.

15. L. Edward Purcell and David F. Burg, *The World Almanac of the American Revolution* (New York: Scripps Howard Co., 1992), p. 332.

16. Captain Hugh McCall, *The History of Georgia, Vol. 1* (Atlanta: A.B. Caldwell Publisher, 1811/1909), p. 427.

17. Edward McCrady, LL.D., *The History of South Carolina in the Revolution 1775–1780* (New York: Russell & Russell, 1901/1969), p. 403.

18. Charles C. Jones, Jr., LL.D., *The History of Georgia, Vol. II* (Cambridge: The Riverside Press, 1883), p. 376.

19. Dr. Dan L. Morrill, *Southern Campaigns of the American Revolution* (Baltimore: The Nautical & Aviation Publishing Company of America, 1993), p. 56.

20. Captain Hugh McCall, *The History of Georgia, Vol. 1* (Atlanta: A.B. Caldwell Publisher, 1811/1909), pp. 428–429.

21. Charles C. Jones, Jr., LL.D., *The History of Georgia, Vol. II* (Cambridge: The Riverside Press, 1883), pp. 376–378.

22. Dr. Dan L. Morrill, *Southern Campaigns of the American Revolution* (Baltimore: The Nautical & Aviation Publishing Company of America, 1993), p. 56.

23. Charles C. Jones, Jr., LL.D., *The History of Georgia, Vol. II* (Cambridge: The Riverside Press, 1883), p. 377.

24. Clifford Sheats Capps and Eugenia Burney, *Colonial Georgia* (New York: Thomas Nelson, Inc., 1972), p. 147.

25. Charles C. Jones, Jr., LL.D., *The History of Georgia, Vol. II* (Cambridge: The Riverside Press, 1883), pp. 377–379.

26. Dr. Dan L. Morrill, *Southern Campaigns of the American Revolution* (Baltimore: The Nautical & Aviation Publishing Company of America, 1993), pp. 56–57.

27. Charles C. Jones, Jr., LL.D., *The History of Georgia, Vol. II* (Cambridge: The Riverside Press, 1883), p. 382.

28. Dr. Dan L. Morrill, *Southern Campaigns of the American Revolution* (Baltimore: The Nautical & Aviation Publishing Company of America, 1993), p. 57.

29. Charles C. Jones, Jr., LL.D., *The History of Georgia, Vol. II* (Cambridge: The Riverside Press, 1883), pp. 382–385.

30. Edward McCrady, LL.D., *The History of South Carolina in the Revolution 1775–1780* (New York: Russell & Russell, 1901/1969), p. 407.

31. Charles C. Jones, Jr., LL.D., *The History of Georgia, Vol. II* (Cambridge: The Riverside Press, 1883), pp. 379–381.

32. Edward McCrady, LL.D., *The History of South Carolina in the Revolution 1775–1780* (New York: Russell & Russell, 1901/1969), p. 407.

33. Captain Hugh McCall, *The History of Georgia, Vol. 1* (Atlanta: A.B. Caldwell Publisher, 1811/1909), pp. 435–436. Dr. Dan L. Morrill, *Southern Campaigns of the American Revolution* (Baltimore: The Nautical & Aviation Publishing Company of America, 1993), pp. 58–59.

34. Charles C. Jones, Jr., LL.D., *The History of Georgia, Vol. II* (Cambridge: The Riverside Press, 1883), p. 383.

35. Dr. Dan L. Morrill, *Southern Campaigns of the American Revolution* (Baltimore: The Nautical & Aviation Publishing Company of America, 1993), p. 59.

36. Captain Hugh McCall, *The History of Georgia, Vol. 1* (Atlanta: A.B. Caldwell Publisher, 1811/1909), pp. 436–437.

37. Edward McCrady, LL.D., *The History of South Carolina in the Revolution 1775–1780* (New York: Russell & Russell, 1901/1969), p. 410.

38. Charles C. Jones, Jr., LL.D., *The History of Georgia, Vol. II* (Cambridge: The Riverside Press, 1883), pp. 384–385, 404.

39. Edward McCrady, LL.D., *The History of South Carolina in the Revolution 1775–1780* (New York: Russell & Russell, 1901/1969), pp. 410– 411.

40. Charles C. Jones, Jr., LL.D., *The History of Georgia, Vol. II* (Cambridge: The Riverside Press, 1883), pp. 23, 388.

41. Edward McCrady, LL.D., *The History of South Carolina in the Revolution 1775–1780* (New York: Russell & Russell, 1901/1969), pp. 407–408.

42. Charles C. Jones, Jr., LL.D., *The History of Georgia, Vol. II* (Cambridge: The Riverside Press, 1883), p. 388.

43. Captain Hugh McCall, *The History of Georgia, Vol. 1* (Atlanta: A.B. Caldwell Publisher, 1811/1909), p. 438.

44. Charles C. Jones, Jr., LL.D., *The History of Georgia, Vol. II* (Cambridge: The Riverside Press, 1883), pp. 388–389.

45. Captain Hugh McCall, *The History of Georgia, Vol. 1* (Atlanta: A.B. Caldwell Publisher, 1811/1909), pp. 438–439.

46. Charles C. Jones, Jr., LL.D., *The History of Georgia, Vol. II* (Cambridge: The Riverside Press, 1883), p. 389.

47. Captain Hugh McCall, *The History of Georgia, Vol. 1* (Atlanta: A.B. Caldwell Publisher, 1811/1909), p. 439.

48. Charles C. Jones, Jr., LL.D., *The History of Georgia, Vol. II* (Cambridge: The Riverside Press, 1883), pp. 390–391.

49. Esmond Wright, *The Fire of Liberty* (New York: St. Martin's Press, 1983), pp. 175–176.

50. Charles C. Jones, Jr., LL.D., *The History of Georgia, Vol. II* (Cambridge: The Riverside Press, 1883), pp. 391–392.

51. Dr. Dan L. Morrill, *Southern Campaigns of the American Revolution* (Baltimore: The Nautical & Aviation Publishing Company of America, 1993), p. 60.

52. Charles C. Jones, Jr., LL.D., *The History of Georgia, Vol. II* (Cambridge: The Riverside Press, 1883), pp. 392–394.

53. Captain Hugh McCall, *The History of Georgia, Vol. 1* (Atlanta: A.B. Caldwell Publisher, 1811/1909), pp. 441–443.

54. Charles C. Jones, Jr., LL.D., *The History of Georgia, Vol. II* (Cambridge: The Riverside Press, 1883), pp. 394, 397.

55. Dr. Dan L. Morrill, *Southern Campaigns of the American Revolution* (Baltimore: The Nautical & Aviation Publishing Company of America, 1993), p. 62.

56. Charles C. Jones, Jr., LL.D., *The History of Georgia, Vol. II* (Cambridge: The Riverside Press, 1883), pp. 398–403.

57. Edward McCrady, LL.D., *The History of South Carolina in the Revolution 1775–1780* (New York: Russell & Russell, 1901/1969), pp. 415–416.

58. Charles C. Jones, Jr., LL.D., *The History of Georgia, Vol. II* (Cambridge: The Riverside Press, 1883), pp. 406–407.

59. Dr. Dan L. Morrill, *Southern Campaigns of the American Revolution* (Baltimore: The Nautical & Aviation Publishing Company of America, 1993), pp. 63–64.

60. Charles C. Jones, Jr., LL.D., *The History of Georgia, Vol. II* (Cambridge: The Riverside Press, 1883), pp. 402–403.

61. Captain Hugh McCall, *The History of Georgia, Vol. 1* (Atlanta: A.B. Caldwell Publisher, 1811/1909), p. 452.

62. Charles C. Jones, Jr., LL.D., *The History of Georgia, Vol. II* (Cambridge: The Riverside Press, 1883), pp. 411–412.

63. Captain Hugh McCall, *The History of Georgia, Vol. 1* (Atlanta: A.B. Caldwell Publisher, 1811/1909), p. 454–455.

64. Esmond Wright, *The Fire of Liberty* (New York: St. Martin's Press, 1983), p. 177.

65. Henry Lumpkin, *From Savannah to Yorktown* (New York: Paragon House Publishers, 1981), p. 39.

66. Edward McCrady, LL.D., *The History of South Carolina in the Revolution 1775–1780* (New York: Russell & Russell, 1901/1969), p. 419.

67. Charles C. Jones, Jr., LL.D., *The History of Georgia, Vol. II* (Cambridge: The Riverside Press, 1883), pp. 414–415.

68. Dr. Dan L. Morrill, *Southern Campaigns of the American Revolution* (Baltimore: The Nautical Aviation Publishing Company of America, 1993) pp. 64–65.

Chapter 10

1. Paul H. Smith, *Loyalists and Redcoats* (Chapel Hill: The University of North Carolina Press, 1964), pp. 107–108.

2. Ernest McNeill Eller, *Chesapeake Bay in the American Revolution* (Centreville, Maryland: Tidewater Publishers, 1981), pp. 434–445.

3. Samuel B. Griffith II, *In Defense of the Public Liberty* (New York: Doubleday & Company, Inc., 1976), pp. 549–550.

4. Ernest McNeill Eller, *Chesapeake Bay in the American Revolution* (Centreville, Maryland: Tidewater Publishers, 1981), pp. 445–446.

5. Charles Campbell, *Introduction to the History of the Colony and Ancient Dominion of Virginia* (Richmond: B.B. Minor, Publisher, 1847), p. 164.

6. Paul H. Smith, *Loyalists and Redcoats* (Chapel Hill: The University of North Carolina Press, 1964), pp. 109–111.

7. Ernest McNeill Eller, *Chesapeake Bay in the American Revolution* (Centreville, Maryland: Tidewater Publishers, 1981), pp. 443–452.

8. Samuel B. Griffith II, *In Defense of the Public Liberty* (New York: Doubleday & Company, Inc., 1976), pp. 549–550.

9. L. Edward Purcell and David F. Burg, *The World Almanac of the American Revolution* (New York: Scripps Howard Co., 1992), pp. 208–209.

10. Paul H. Smith, *Loyalists and Redcoats* (Chapel Hill: The University of North Carolina Press, 1964), pp. 117–120.

11. Franklin and Mary Wickwire, *Cornwallis, The American Adventure* (Boston: Houghton Mifflin Company, 1970), pp. 119–123.

12. Dr. Dan L. Morrill, *Southern Campaigns of the American Revolution* (Baltimore: The Nautical & Aviation Publishing Company of America, 1993), p. 56.

13. Paul H. Smith, *Loyalists and Redcoats* (Chapel Hill: The University of North Carolina Press, 1964), p. 124.

14. Dr. Dan L. Morrill, *Southern Campaigns of the American Revolution* (Baltimore: The Nautical & Aviation Publishing Company of America, 1993), p. 56.

15. Paul H. Smith, *Loyalists and Redcoats* (Chapel Hill: The University of North Carolina Press, 1964), p. 126.

16. Samuel B. Griffith II, *In Defense of the Public Liberty* (New York: Doubleday & Company, Inc., 1976), pp. 567–569.

17. Edward McCrady, LL.D., *The History of South Carolina in the Revolution 1775–1780* (New York: Russell & Russell, 1901/1969), p. 426.

18. Franklin and Mary Wickwire, *Cornwallis, The American Adventure* (Boston: Houghton Mifflin Company, 1970), pp. 125–126

19. Bernhard A. Uhlendorf, *The Seige of Charleston* (Ann Arbor: University of Michigan Press, 1938), pp. 105–111.

20. Franklin and Mary Wickwire, *Cornwallis, The Amer-*

ican Adventure (Boston: Houghton Mifflin Company, 1970), pp. 125–126. Christopher Hibbert, *Redcoats and Rebels* (New York: W.W. Norton & Company, 1990), p. 269. Bernhard A. Uhlendorf, *The Seige of Charleston* (Ann Arbor: University of Michigan Press, 1938), pp. 23, 111–141.

21. Bernhard A. Uhlendorf, *The Siege of Charleston (Diary of Captain Hinrichs)* (Ann Arbor: University of Michigan Press, 1938), pp. 173–177.

22. Robert Middlekauff, *The Glorious Cause* (New York: Oxford University Press, 1982), p. 440.

23. Bernhard A. Uhlendorf, *The Siege of Charleston (Diary of Captain Hinrichs)* (Ann Arbor: University of Michigan Press, 1938), pp. 177, 181.

24. Henry Lumpkin, *From Savannah to Yorktown* (New York: Paragon House Publishers, 1981), p. 42.

25. Bernhard A. Uhlendorf, *The Siege of Charleston (Diary of Captain Hinrichs)* (Ann Arbor: University of Michigan Press, 1938), pp. 181–201.

26. Henry Lumpkin, *From Savannah to Yorktown* (New York: Paragon House Publishers, 1981), pp. 42–43.

27. Walter J. Fraser, Jr., *Charleston! Charleston!* (Columbia: University of South Carolina Press, 1989), p. 159.

28. Edward McCrady, LL.D., *The History of South Carolina in the Revolution 1775–1780* (New York: Russell & Russell, 1901/1969), pp. 427–429.

29. Walter J. Fraser, Jr., *Charleston! Charleston!* (Columbia: University of South Carolina Press, 1989), p. 93.

30. Edward McCrady, LL.D., *The History of South Carolina in the Revolution 1775–1780* (New York: Russell & Russell, 1901/1969), pp. 429–430.

31. Walter J. Fraser, Jr., *Charleston! Charleston!* (Columbia: University of South Carolina Press, 1989), pp. 158–159.

32. Lieutenant Colonel Tarleton, *A History of the Campaigns of 1780 and 1781 in the Southern Provinces of North America* (London: T. Cadell, in the Strand, 1787), p. 6.

33. Edward McCrady, LL.D., *The History of South Carolina in the Revolution 1775–1780* (New York: Russell & Russell, 1901/1969), pp. 435–436.

34. Bernhard A. Uhlendorf, *The Siege of Charleston (Diary of General Von Huyn)* (Ann Arbor: University of Michigan Press, 1938), p. 375.

35. Bernhard A. Uhlendorf, *The Siege of Charleston (Diaries of General Von Huyn and Captain Hinrichs)* (Ann Arbor: University of Michigan Press, 1938), pp. 375, 197–199.

36. Bernhard A. Uhlendorf, *The Siege of Charleston (Diary of Captain Hinrichs)* (Ann Arbor: University of Michigan Press, 1938), pp. 325–327.

37. Edward McCrady, LL.D., *The History of South Carolina in the Revolution 1775–1780* (New York: Russell & Russell, 1901/1969), pp. 438–440. Henry Lumpkin, *From Savannah to Yorktown* (New York: Paragon House Publishers, 1981), pp. 43–44.

38. Edward McCrady, LL.D., *The History of South Carolina in the Revolution 1775–1780* (New York: Russell & Russell, 1901/1969), pp. 445–446.

39. Lieutenant Colonel Tarleton, *A History of the Campaigns of 1780 and 1781 in the Southern Provinces of North America* (London: T. Cadell, in the Strand, 1787), pp. 6–7.

40. Edward McCrady, LL.D., *The History of South Carolina in the Revolution 1775–1780* (New York: Russell & Russell, 1901/1969), pp. 446–447.

41. Lieutenant Colonel Tarleton, *A History of the Campaigns of 1780 and 1781 in the Southern Provinces of North America* (London: T. Cadell, in the Strand, 1787), p. 7.

42. Edward McCrady, LL.D., *The History of South Carolina in the Revolution 1775–1780* (New York: Russell & Russell, 1901/1969), p. 447.

43. Henry Steele Commager and Richard B. Morris, *The Spirit of 'Seventy-Six* (New York: Harper & Row, Publishers, 1958), pp. 1101–1102.

44. Franklin and Mary Wickwire, *Cornwallis, The American Adventure* (Boston: Houghton Mifflin Company, 1970), pp. 128–129.

45. Christopher Hibbert, *Redcoats and Rebels* (New York: W.W. Norton & Company, 1990), p. 268

46. Franklin and Mary Wickwire, *Cornwallis, The American Adventure* (Boston: Houghton Mifflin Company, 1970), pp. 128–129.

47. Edward McCrady, LL.D., *The History of South Carolina in the Revolution 1775–1780* (New York: Russell & Russell, 1901/1969), p. 440.

48. L. Edward Purcell and David F. Burg, *The World Almanac of the American Revolution* (New York: Scripps Howard Co., 1992), pp. 368–369.

49. A.J. Langguth, *Patriots* (New York: Simon & Schuster, Inc., 1988), p. 404.

50. Edward McCrady, LL.D., *The History of South Carolina in the Revolution 1775–1780* (New York: Russell & Russell, 1901/1969), pp. 450–451.

51. Lieutenant Colonel Tarleton, *A History of the Campaigns of 1780 and 1781 in the Southern Provinces of North America* (London: T. Cadell, in the Strand, 1787), p. 9.

52. Edward McCrady, LL.D., *The History of South Carolina in the Revolution 1775–1780* (New York: Russell & Russell, 1901/1969), pp. 451–453.

53. Bernhard A. Uhlendorf, *The Siege of Charleston (Diary of Captain Ewald)* (Ann Arbor: University of Michigan Press, 1938), pp. 31–33.

54. Robert Middlekauff, *The Glorious Cause* (New York: Oxford University Press, 1982), p. 443.

55. Bernhard A. Uhlendorf, *The Siege of Charleston (Diary of Captain Hinrichs)* (Ann Arbor: University of Michigan Press, 1938), pp. 31–35, 223–227.

56. Edward McCrady, LL.D., *The History of South Carolina in the Revolution 1775–1780* (New York: Russell & Russell, 1901/1969), pp. 454–455.

57. Bernhard A. Uhlendorf, *The Siege of Charleston (Diary of Captain Hinrichs)* (Ann Arbor: University of Michigan Press, 1938), pp. 231–233.

58. Edward McCrady, LL.D., *The History of South Carolina in the Revolution 1775–1780* (New York: Russell & Russell, 1901/1969), p. 455.

59. Bernhard A. Uhlendorf, *The Siege of Charleston (Diary of Captain Ewald)* (Ann Arbor: University of Michigan Press, 1938), pp. 41–43.

60. Samuel B. Griffith II, *In Defense of the Public Liberty* (New York: Doubleday & Company, Inc., 1976), p. 588.

61. Edward McCrady, LL.D., *The History of South Carolina in the Revolution 1775–1780* (New York: Russell & Russell, 1901/1969), pp. 457–458.

62. Bernhard A. Uhlendorf, *The Siege of Charleston (Diary*

of Captain Hinrichs) (Ann Arbor: University of Michigan Press, 1938), pp. 241–243.

63. Edward McCrady, LL.D., *The History of South Carolina in the Revolution 1775–1780* (New York: Russell & Russell, 1901/1969), pp. 459–461.

64. Lieutenant Colonel Tarleton, *A History of the Campaigns of 1780 and 1781 in the Southern Provinces of North America* (London: T. Cadell, in the Strand, 1787), p. 11.

65. Bernhard A. Uhlendorf, *The Siege of Charleston (Diary of Captain Ewald)* (Ann Arbor: University of Michigan Press, 1938), p. 53.

66. Edward McCrady, LL.D., *The History of South Carolina in the Revolution 1775–1780* (New York: Russell & Russell, 1901/1969), pp. 461–467.

67. Lieutenant Colonel Tarleton, *A History of the Campaigns of 1780 and 1781 in the Southern Provinces of North America* (London: T. Cadell, in the Strand, 1787), pp. 15–17.

68. Edward McCrady, LL.D., *The History of South Carolina in the Revolution 1775–1780* (New York: Russell & Russell, 1901/1969), pp. 470–471.

69. Bernhard A. Uhlendorf, *The Siege of Charleston (Diary of Captain Hinrichs)* (Ann Arbor: University of Michigan Press, 1938), pp. 249–255.

70. Edward McCrady, LL.D., *The History of South Carolina in the Revolution 1775–1780* (New York: Russell & Russell, 1901/1969), pp. 471–481.

71. Franklin and Mary Wickwire, *Cornwallis, The American Adventure* (Boston: Houghton Mifflin Company, 1970), pp. 129–130.

72. Edward McCrady, LL.D., *The History of South Carolina in the Revolution 1775–1780* (New York: Russell & Russell, 1901/1969), pp. 484–486.

73. Bernhard A. Uhlendorf, *The Siege of Charleston (Diary of Captain Hinrichs)* (Ann Arbor: University of Michigan Press, 1938), p. 271.

74. Edward McCrady, LL.D., *The History of South Carolina in the Revolution 1775–1780* (New York: Russell & Russell, 1901/1969), p. 491.

75. Bernhard A. Uhlendorf, *The Siege of Charleston (Diary of Captain Hinrichs)* (Ann Arbor: University of Michigan Press, 1938), pp. 279–285.

76. Edward McCrady, LL.D., *The History of South Carolina in the Revolution 1775–1780* (New York: Russell & Russell, 1901/1969), pp. 491–492.

77. Bernhard A. Uhlendorf, *The Siege of Charleston (Diary of Captain Hinrichs)* (Ann Arbor: University of Michigan Press, 1938), p. 285.

78. Edward McCrady, LL.D., *The History of South Carolina in the Revolution 1775–1780* (New York: Russell & Russell, 1901/1969), p. 493.

79. Henry Lee, *Memoirs of the War in the Southern Department of the United States* (New York: University Publishing Company, 1869), pp. 156–157.

80. Edward McCrady, LL.D., *The History of South Carolina in the Revolution 1775–1780* (New York: Russell & Russell, 1901/1969), pp. 495–500.

81. Bernhard A. Uhlendorf, *The Siege of Charleston (Diary of Captain Hinrichs)* (Ann Arbor: University of Michigan Press, 1938), p. 287.

82. Dr. Dan L. Morrill, *Southern Campaigns of the Amer-*

ican Revolution (Baltimore: The Nautical & Aviation Publishing Company of America, 1993), p. 72.

83. Edward McCrady, LL.D., *The History of South Carolina in the Revolution 1775–1780* (New York: Russell & Russell, 1901/1969), pp. 500–503.

84. Bernhard A. Uhlendorf, *The Siege of Charleston (Diary of Captain Hinrichs)* (Ann Arbor: University of Michigan Press, 1938), pp. 289–291.

85. Walter J. Fraser, Jr., *Charleston! Charleston!* (Columbia: University of South Carolina Press, 1989), p. 162.

86. Edward McCrady, LL.D., *The History of South Carolina in the Revolution 1775–1780* (New York: Russell & Russell, 1901/1969), p. 507.

87. Henry Steele Commager and Richard B. Morris, *The Spirit of 'Seventy-Six* (New York: Harper & Row, Publishers, 1958), p. 1110.

88. Edward McCrady, LL.D., *The History of South Carolina in the Revolution 1775–1780* (New York: Russell & Russell, 1901/1969), pp. 504–506.

89. Henry Lumpkin, *From Savannah to Yorktown* (New York: Paragon House Publishers, 1981), p. 49.

90. Bernhard A. Uhlendorf, *The Siege of Charleston (Diary of Captain Ewald)* (Ann Arbor: University of Michigan Press, 1938), p. 87.

91. Dr. Dan L. Morrill, *Southern Campaigns of the American Revolution* (Baltimore: The Nautical & Aviation Publishing Company of America, 1993), p. 73.

92. Bernhard A. Uhlendorf, *The Siege of Charleston (Diary of Captain Ewald)* (Ann Arbor: University of Michigan Press, 1938), p. 89, 95–97.

93. Edward McCrady, LL.D., *The History of South Carolina in the Revolution 1775–1780* (New York: Russell & Russell, 1901/1969), p. 514.

Chapter 11

1. Walter J. Fraser, Jr., *Charleston! Charleston!* (Columbia: University of South Carolina Press, 1989), pp. 162–163.

2. Bernhard A. Uhlendorf, *The Siege of Charleston (Diary of Captain Ewald)* (Ann Arbor: University of Michigan Press, 1938), pp. 97–99.

3. Paul H. Smith, *Loyalists and Redcoats* (Chapel Hill: The University of North Carolina Press, 1964), pp. 129–133.

4. Edward McCrady, LL.D., *The History of South Carolina in the Revolution 1775–1780* (New York: Russell & Russell, 1901/1969), pp. 516–518.

5. Lieutenant Colonel Tarleton, *A History of the Campaigns of 1780 and 1781 in the Southern Provinces of North America* (London: T. Cadell, in the Strand, 1787), p. 28.

6. Edward McCrady, LL.D., *The History of South Carolina in the Revolution 1775–1780* (New York: Russell & Russell, 1901/1969), p. 518.

7. Henry Steele Commager and Richard B. Morris, *The Spirit of 'Seventy-Six* (New York: Harper & Row, Publishers, 1958), p. 1111.

8. Edward McCrady, LL.D., *The History of South Carolina in the Revolution 1775–1780* (New York: Russell & Russell, 1901/1969), pp. 519–521. Lieutenant Colonel Tarleton, *A History*

of the Campaigns of 1780 and 1781 in the Southern Provinces of North America (London: T. Cadell, in the Strand, 1787), pp. 29–30.

9. Dr. Dan L. Morrill, *Southern Campaigns of the American Revolution* (Baltimore: The Nautical & Aviation Publishing Company of America, 1993), p. 78.

10. Edward McCrady, LL.D., *The History of South Carolina in the Revolution 1775–1780* (New York: Russell & Russell, 1901/1969), pp. 521–523.

11. Dr. Dan L. Morrill, *Southern Campaigns of the American Revolution* (Baltimore: The Nautical & Aviation Publishing Company of America, 1993), p. 79.

12. Edward McCrady, LL.D., *The History of South Carolina in the Revolution 1775–1780* (New York: Russell & Russell, 1901/1969), p. 523.

13. Lieutenant Colonel Tarleton, *A History of the Campaigns of 1780 and 1781 in the Southern Provinces of North America* (London: T. Cadell, in the Strand, 1787), p. 32.

14. Edward McCrady, LL.D., *The History of South Carolina in the Revolution 1775–1780* (New York: Russell & Russell, 1901/1969), pp. 524, 533–534.

15. Samuel B. Griffith II, *In Defense of the Public Liberty* (New York: Doubleday & Company, Inc., 1976), p. 590.

16. Edward McCrady, LL.D., *The History of South Carolina in the Revolution 1775–1780* (New York: Russell & Russell, 1901/1969), pp. 547–549.

17. Samuel B. Griffith II, *In Defense of the Public Liberty* (New York: Doubleday & Company, Inc., 1976), p. 590.

18. Christopher Hibbert, *Redcoats and Rebels* (New York: W.W. Norton & Company, 1990), p. 269.

19. Bernhard A. Uhlendorf, *The Siege of Charleston (Diary of Captains Ewald and Hinrichs)* (Ann Arbor: University of Michigan Press, 1938), pp. 101, 313.

20. Franklin and Mary Wickwire, *Cornwallis, The American Adventure* (Boston: Houghton Mifflin Company, 1970), pp. 133–134.

21. Edward McCrady, LL.D., *The History of South Carolina in the Revolution 1775–1780* (New York: Russell & Russell, 1901/1969), pp. 547–549. Lieutenant Colonel Tarleton, *A History of the Campaigns of 1780 and 1781 in the Southern Provinces of North America* (London: T. Cadell, in the Strand, 1787), p. 87.

22. Lieutenant Colonel Tarleton, *A History of the Campaigns of 1780 and 1781 in the Southern Provinces of North America* (London: T. Cadell, in the Strand, 1787), p. 87.

23. Franklin and Mary Wickwire, *Cornwallis, The American Adventure* (Boston: Houghton Mifflin Company, 1970), pp. 139–145.

24. Walter J. Fraser, Jr., *Charleston! Charleston!* (Columbia: University of South Carolina Press, 1989), pp. 164–165.

25. Franklin and Mary Wickwire, *Cornwallis, The American Adventure* (Boston: Houghton Mifflin Company, 1970), pp. 145–147.

26. Paul H. Smith, *Loyalists and Redcoats* (Chapel Hill: The University of North Carolina Press, 1964), pp. 137–138.

27. Lieutenant Colonel Tarleton, *A History of the Campaigns of 1780 and 1781 in the Southern Provinces of North America* (London: T. Cadell, in the Strand, 1787), p. 86.

28. Edward McCrady, LL.D., *The History of South Carolina in the Revolution 1775–1780* (New York: Russell & Russell, 1901/1969), p. 588.

29. Phillips Russell, *North Carolina in the Revolutionary War* (Charlotte: Heritage Printers, Inc., 1965), p. 153. Edward McCrady, LL.D., *The History of South Carolina in the Revolution 1775–1780* (New York: Russell & Russell, 1901/1969), pp. 579–580.

30. Edward McCrady, LL.D., *The History of South Carolina in the Revolution 1775–1780* (New York: Russell & Russell, 1901/1969), p. 580.

31. Phillips Russell, *North Carolina in the Revolutionary War* (Charlotte: Heritage Printers, Inc., 1965), p. 153.

32. Edward McCrady, LL.D., *The History of South Carolina in the Revolution 1775–1780* (New York: Russell & Russell, 1901/1969), pp. 580–581.

33. Phillips Russell, *North Carolina in the Revolutionary War* (Charlotte: Heritage Printers, Inc., 1965), p. 153.

34. Edward McCrady, LL.D., *The History of South Carolina in the Revolution 1775–1780* (New York: Russell & Russell, 1901/1969), pp. 584–585.

35. Dr. Dan L. Morrill, *Southern Campaigns of the American Revolution* (Baltimore: The Nautical & Aviation Publishing Company of America, 1993), p. 82.

36. John S. Pancake, *This Destructive War* (Tuscaloosa: University of Alabama Press, 1985), pp. 95–96.

37. Edward McCrady, LL.D., *The History of South Carolina in the Revolution 1775–1780* (New York: Russell & Russell, 1901/1969), pp. 620–621.

38. Henry Lee, *Memoirs of the War in the Southern Department of the United States* (New York: University Publishing Company, 1869), p. 169.

39. Edward McCrady, LL.D., *The History of South Carolina in the Revolution 1775–1780* (New York: Russell & Russell, 1901/1969), pp. 621–623.

40. *Ibid.*, pp. 572–575.

41. *Ibid.*, p. 589–598.

42. John S. Pancake, *This Destructive War* (Tuscaloosa: University of Alabama Press, 1985), p. 96.

43. Edward McCrady, LL.D., *The History of South Carolina in the Revolution 1775–1780* (New York: Russell & Russell, 1901/1969), pp. 598–635.

44. *Ibid.*, pp. 623–645.

45. *Ibid.*, pp. 645–647. Lieutenant Colonel Tarleton, *A History of the Campaigns of 1780 and 1781 in the Southern Provinces of North America* (London: T. Cadell, in the Strand, 1787), p. 98.

46. Edward McCrady, LL.D., *The History of South Carolina in the Revolution 1775–1780* (New York: Russell & Russell, 1901/1969), pp. 568–569, 620–652.

47. John S. Pancake, *This Destructive War* (Tuscaloosa: University of Alabama Press, 1985), p. 98.

Chapter 12

1. John S. Pancake, *This Destructive War* (Tuscaloosa: University of Alabama Press, 1985), pp. 98–99.

2. *Ibid.*, pp. 95–96. Robert Middlekauff, *The Glorious Cause* (New York: Oxford University Press, 1982), p. 453. L. Edward Purcell and David F. Burg, *The World Almanac of the American Revolution* (New York: Scripps Howard Co., 1992), pp. 330–331.

3. Samuel B. Griffith II, *In Defense of the Public Liberty* (New York: Doubleday & Company, Inc., 1976), pp. 589–590.

4. John S. Pancake, *This Destructive War* (Tuscaloosa: University of Alabama Press, 1985), p. 99.

5. Samuel B. Griffith II, *In Defense of the Public Liberty* (New York: Doubleday & Company, Inc., 1976), pp. 590–592.

6. Phillips Russell, *North Carolina in the Revolutionary War* (Charlotte: Heritage Printers, Inc., 1965), p. 154.

7. Henry Lee, *Memoirs of the War in the Southern Department of the United States* (New York: University Publishing Company, 1869), p. 171.

8. John S. Pancake, *This Destructive War* (Tuscaloosa: University of Alabama Press, 1985), p. 99.

9. Phillips Russell, *North Carolina in the Revolutionary War* (Charlotte: Heritage Printers, Inc., 1965), p. 157.

10. L. Edward Purcell and David F. Burg, *The World Almanac of the American Revolution* (New York: Scripps Howard Co., 1992), pp. 336–337.

11. M.F. Treacy, *Prelude to Yorktown, The Southern Campaign of Nathanael Greene 1780–1781* (Chapel Hill: The University of North Carolina Press, 1963), p. 25.

12. Franklin and Mary Wickwire, *Cornwallis, The American Adventure* (Boston: Houghton Mifflin Company, 1970), pp. 149–150.

13. Phillips Russell, *North Carolina in the Revolutionary War* (Charlotte: Heritage Printers, Inc., 1965), pp. 154–155.

14. M.F. Treacy, *Prelude to Yorktown, The Southern Campaign of Nathanael Greene 1780–1781* (Chapel Hill: The University of North Carolina Press, 1963), p. 24.

15. Phillips Russell, *North Carolina in the Revolutionary War* (Charlotte: Heritage Printers, Inc., 1965), pp. 157–158.

16. Edward McCrady, LL.D., *The History of South Carolina in the Revolution 1775–1780* (New York: Russell & Russell, 1901/1969), p. 658

17. Phillips Russell, *North Carolina in the Revolutionary War* (Charlotte: Heritage Printers, Inc., 1965), p. 155.

18. *Ibid.*, p. 158.

19. Paul H. Smith, *Loyalists and Redcoats* (Chapel Hill: The University of North Carolina Press, 1964), p. 144.

20. Clyde R. Ferguson, *Carolina and Georgia Patriot and Loyalist Militia in Action (The Southern Experience in the American Revolution*, Ed. by Jeffrey J. Crow and Larry E. Tise) (Chapel Hill: The University of North Carolina Press, 1978), p. 186.

21. Paul H. Smith, *Loyalists and Redcoats* (Chapel Hill: The University of North Carolina Press, 1964), p. 144.

22. Henry Steele Commager and Richard B. Morris, *The Spirit of 'Seventy-Six* (New York: Harper & Row, Publishers, 1958), p. 1126.

23. John S. Pancake, *This Destructive War* (Tuscaloosa: University of Alabama Press, 1985), p. 100.

24. Henry Steele Commager and Richard B. Morris, *The Spirit of 'Seventy-Six* (New York: Harper & Row, Publishers, 1958), p. 1126.

25. Henry Lumpkin, *From Savannah to Yorktown* (New York: Paragon House Publishers, 1981), p. 58.

26. John S. Pancake, *This Destructive War* (Tuscaloosa: University of Alabama Press, 1985), pp. 100–101.

27. Phillips Russell, *North Carolina in the Revolutionary War* (Charlotte: Heritage Printers, Inc., 1965), p. 159.

28. Samuel B. Griffith II, *In Defense of the Public Liberty* (New York: Doubleday & Company, Inc., 1976), p. 593.

29. Henry Lumpkin, *From Savannah to Yorktown* (New York: Paragon House Publishers, 1981), p. 59.

30. Henry Steele Commager and Richard B. Morris, *The Spirit of 'Seventy-Six* (New York: Harper & Row, Publishers, 1958), pp. 1127–1128.

31. John S. Pancake, *This Destructive War* (Tuscaloosa: University of Alabama Press, 1985), p. 101.

32. Samuel B. Griffith II, *In Defense of the Public Liberty* (New York: Doubleday & Company, Inc., 1976), p. 593.

33. Edward McCrady, LL.D., *The History of South Carolina in the Revolution 1775–1780* (New York: Russell & Russell, 1901/1969), p. 659.

34. Henry Lee, *Memoirs of the War in the Southern Department of the United States* (New York: University Publishing Company, 1869), p. 172.

35. Edward McCrady, LL.D., *The History of South Carolina in the Revolution 1775–1780* (New York: Russell & Russell, 1901/1969), pp. 660–661.

36. Henry Steele Commager and Richard B. Morris, *The Spirit of 'Seventy-Six* (New York: Harper & Row, Publishers, 1958), p. 1128.

37. Phillips Russell, *North Carolina in the Revolutionary War* (Charlotte: Heritage Printers, Inc., 1965), p. 160.

38. Edward McCrady, LL.D., *The History of South Carolina in the Revolution 1775–1780* (New York: Russell & Russell, 1901/1969), pp. 662–663.

39. Phillips Russell, *North Carolina in the Revolutionary War* (Charlotte: Heritage Printers, Inc., 1965), pp. 159–160.

40. Paul H. Smith, *Loyalists and Redcoats* (Chapel Hill: The University of North Carolina Press, 1964), pp. 144–145.

41. Edward McCrady, LL.D., *The History of South Carolina in the Revolution 1775–1780* (New York: Russell & Russell, 1901/1969), p. 663.

42. Phillips Russell, *North Carolina in the Revolutionary War* (Charlotte: Heritage Printers, Inc., 1965), p. 165.

43. Lieutenant Colonel Tarleton, *A History of the Campaigns of 1780 and 1781 in the Southern Provinces of North America* (London: T. Cadell, in the Strand, 1787), pp. 99–100.

44. Christopher Hibbert, *Redcoats and Rebels* (New York: W.W. Norton & Company, 1990), p. 276.

45. Franklin and Mary Wickwire, *Cornwallis, The American Adventure* (Boston: Houghton Mifflin Company, 1970), p. 151.

46. Edward McCrady, LL.D., *The History of South Carolina in the Revolution 1775–1780* (New York: Russell & Russell, 1901/1969), p. 666.

47. Franklin and Mary Wickwire, *Cornwallis, The American Adventure* (Boston: Houghton Mifflin Company, 1970), pp. 152–153.

48. Henry Lumpkin, *From Savannah to Yorktown* (New York: Paragon House Publishers, 1981), p. 60.

49. Franklin and Mary Wickwire, *Cornwallis, The American Adventure* (Boston: Houghton Mifflin Company, 1970), pp. 151–154.

50. Edward McCrady, LL.D., *The History of South Carolina in the Revolution 1775–1780* (New York: Russell & Russell, 1901/1969), pp. 667–671.

51. Henry Lumpkin, *From Savannah to Yorktown* (New York: Paragon House Publishers, 1981), pp. 60–61.

52. Lieutenant Colonel Tarleton, *A History of the Campaigns of 1780 and 1781 in the Southern Provinces of North America* (London: T. Cadell, in the Strand, 1787), pp. 103–104.

53. Phillips Russell, *North Carolina in the Revolutionary War* (Charlotte: Heritage Printers, Inc., 1965), p. 165. Henry Lumpkin, *From Savannah to Yorktown* (New York: Paragon House Publishers, 1981), p. 61.

54. Lieutenant Colonel Tarleton, *A History of the Campaigns of 1780 and 1781 in the Southern Provinces of North America* (London: T. Cadell, in the Strand, 1787), p. 104.

55. Henry Lumpkin, *From Savannah to Yorktown* (New York: Paragon House Publishers, 1981), p. 61.

56. Edward McCrady, LL.D., *The History of South Carolina in the Revolution 1775–1780* (New York: Russell & Russell, 1901/1969), pp. 673–674. Christopher Hibbert, *Redcoats and Rebels* (New York: W.W. Norton & Company, 1990), p. 276.

57. Phillips Russell, *North Carolina in the Revolutionary War* (Charlotte: Heritage Printers, Inc., 1965), p. 166.

58. Edward McCrady, LL.D., *The History of South Carolina in the Revolution 1775–1780* (New York: Russell & Russell, 1901/1969), p. 674.

59. Lieutenant Colonel Tarleton, *A History of the Campaigns of 1780 and 1781 in the Southern Provinces of North America* (London: T. Cadell, in the Strand, 1787), p. 105.

60. Henry Lumpkin, *From Savannah to Yorktown* (New York: Paragon House Publishers, 1981), pp. 63–64.

61. Franklin and Mary Wickwire, *Cornwallis, The American Adventure* (Boston: Houghton Mifflin Company, 1970), p. 160.

62. Edward McCrady, LL.D., *The History of South Carolina in the Revolution 1775–1780* (New York: Russell & Russell, 1901/1969), p. 676.

63. Lieutenant Colonel Tarleton, *A History of the Campaigns of 1780 and 1781 in the Southern Provinces of North America* (London: T. Cadell, in the Strand, 1787), p. 106.

64. Phillips Russell, *North Carolina in the Revolutionary War* (Charlotte: Heritage Printers, Inc., 1965), p. 166.

65. Franklin and Mary Wickwire, *Cornwallis, The American Adventure* (Boston: Houghton Mifflin Company, 1970), p. 160.

66. Phillips Russell, *North Carolina in the Revolutionary War* (Charlotte: Heritage Printers, Inc., 1965), p. 166.

67. Franklin and Mary Wickwire, *Cornwallis, The American Adventure* (Boston: Houghton Mifflin Company, 1970), p. 160.

68. Henry Lumpkin, *From Savannah to Yorktown* (New York: Paragon House Publishers, 1981), p. 64.

69. John S. Pancake, *This Destructive War* (Tuscaloosa: University of Alabama Press, 1985), p. 104.

70. Christopher Hibbert, *Redcoats and Rebels* (New York: W.W. Norton & Co., 1990), p. 277.

71. Franklin and Mary Wickwire, *Cornwallis, The American Adventure* (Boston: Houghton Mifflin Company, 1970), pp. 160–161.

72. Henry Steele Commager and Richard B. Morris, *The Spirit of 'Seventy-Six* (New York: Harper & Row, Publishers, 1958), p. 1131.

73. Phillips Russell, *North Carolina in the Revolutionary War* (Charlotte: Heritage Printers, Inc., 1965), p. 168.

74. Henry Lumpkin, *From Savannah to Yorktown* (New York: Paragon House Publishers, 1981), p. 64. M.F. Treacy, *Prelude to Yorktown, The Southern Campaign of Nathanael Greene 1780–1781* (Chapel Hill: The University of North Carolina Press, 1963), p. 26.

75. Henry Steele Commager and Richard B. Morris, *The Spirit of 'Seventy-Six* (New York: Harper & Row, Publishers, 1958), pp. 1131–1132.

76. Henry Lumpkin, *From Savannah to Yorktown* (New York: Paragon House Publishers, 1981), pp. 65–66.

77. Lieutenant Colonel Tarleton, *A History of the Campaigns of 1780 and 1781 in the Southern Provinces of North America* (London: T. Cadell, in the Strand, 1787), pp. 107–108.

78. Franklin and Mary Wickwire, *Cornwallis, The American Adventure* (Boston: Houghton Mifflin Company, 1970), p. 164.

79. John S. Pancake, *This Destructive War* (Tuscaloosa: University of Alabama Press, 1985), pp. 106–107.

80. Dr. Dan L. Morrill, *Southern Campaigns of the American Revolution* (Baltimore: The Nautical & Aviation Publishing Company of America, 1993), p. 94.

81. Edward McCrady, LL.D., *The History of South Carolina in the Revolution 1775–1780* (New York: Russell & Russell, 1901/1969), pp. 679–684.

82. John S. Pancake, *This Destructive War* (Tuscaloosa: University of Alabama Press, 1985), p. 106.

83. Phillips Russell, *North Carolina in the Revolutionary War* (Charlotte: Heritage Printers, Inc., 1965), pp. 168–170.

84. Samuel B. Griffith II, *In Defense of the Public Liberty* (New York: Doubleday & Company, Inc., 1976), p. 595.

85. Phillips Russell, *North Carolina in the Revolutionary War* (Charlotte: Heritage Printers, Inc., 1965), p. 170.

86. Dr. Dan L. Morrill, *Southern Campaigns of the American Revolution* (Baltimore: The Nautical & Aviation Publishing Company of America, 1993), p. 95.

87. Franklin and Mary Wickwire, *Cornwallis, The American Adventure* (Boston: Houghton Mifflin Company, 1970), pp. 164–165.

88. Phillips Russell, *North Carolina in the Revolutionary War* (Charlotte: Heritage Printers, Inc., 1965), p. 169.

Chapter 13

1. Edward McCrady, LL.D., *The History of South Carolina in the Revolution 1775–1780* (New York: Russell & Russell, 1901/1969), pp. 698–702.

2. Paul H. Smith, *Loyalists and Redcoats* (Chapel Hill: The University of North Carolina Press, 1964), p. 146.

3. John S. Pancake, *This Destructive War* (Tuscaloosa: University of Alabama Press, 1985), pp. 108–109.

4. Phillips Russell, *North Carolina in the Revolutionary War* (Charlotte: Heritage Printers, Inc., 1965), pp. 171–172.

5. *Ibid.*, pp. 172–173. John S. Pancake, *This Destructive War* (Tuscaloosa: University of Alabama Press, 1985), pp. 112–113.

6. John S. Pancake, *This Destructive War* (Tuscaloosa: University of Alabama Press, 1985), pp. 113–115.

7. Lieutenant Colonel Tarleton, *A History of the Campaigns of 1780 and 1781 in the Southern Provinces of North America* (London: T. Cadell, in the Strand, 1787), p. 158.

8. Rev. J.D. Bailey, *Commanders at Kings Mountain* (Gaffney: Ed. H. DeCamp Publisher, 1926), p. 97.

9. Edward McCrady, LL.D., *The History of South Carolina*

in the Revolution 1775–1780 (New York: Russell & Russell, 1901/1969), pp. 731–732.

10. Franklin and Mary Wickwire, *Cornwallis, The American Adventure* (Boston: Houghton Mifflin Company, 1970), pp. 206–208.

11. Edward McCrady, LL.D., *The History of South Carolina in the Revolution 1775–1780* (New York: Russell & Russell, 1901/1969), p. 732.

12. Rev. J.D. Bailey, *Commanders at Kings Mountain* (Gaffney: Ed. H. DeCamp Publisher, 1926), pp. 282–287.

13. Dr. J.B.O. Landrum, *Colonial and Revolutionary History of Upper South Carolina* (Greenville: Shannon & Co., 1897), pp. 173–174.

14. Edward McCrady, LL.D., *The History of South Carolina in the Revolution 1775–1780* (New York: Russell & Russell, 1901/1969), p. 732

15. Franklin and Mary Wickwire, *Cornwallis, The American Adventure* (Boston: Houghton Mifflin Company, 1970), p. 186.

16. Edward McCrady, LL.D., *The History of South Carolina in the Revolution 1775–1780* (New York: Russell & Russell, 1901/1969), pp. 733–740.

17. Lieutenant Colonel Tarleton, *A History of the Campaigns of 1780 and 1781 in the Southern Provinces of North America* (London: T. Cadell, in the Strand, 1787), p. 163.

18. Edward McCrady, LL.D., *The History of South Carolina in the Revolution 1775–1780* (New York: Russell & Russell, 1901/1969), pp. 737–739.

19. Franklin and Mary Wickwire, *Cornwallis, The American Adventure* (Boston: Houghton Mifflin Company, 1970), p. 195. John S. Pancake, *This Destructive War* (Tuscaloosa: University of Alabama Press, 1985), p. 108.

20. *Ibid.*, p. 112.

21. Edward McCrady, LL.D., *The History of South Carolina in the Revolution 1775–1780* (New York: Russell & Russell, 1901/1969), pp. 742–743.

22. Phillips Russell, *North Carolina in the Revolutionary War* (Charlotte: Heritage Printers, Inc., 1965), p. 175.

23. Edward McCrady, LL.D., *The History of South Carolina in the Revolution 1775–1780* (New York: Russell & Russell, 1901/1969), p. 744. Franklin and Mary Wickwire, *Cornwallis, The American Adventure* (Boston: Houghton Mifflin Company, 1970), p. 198.

24. Franklin and Mary Wickwire, *Cornwallis, The American Adventure* (Boston: Houghton Mifflin Company, 1970), pp. 197–198.

25. Edward McCrady, LL.D., *The History of South Carolina in the Revolution 1775–1780* (New York: Russell & Russell, 1901/1969), pp. 744–745.

26. Franklin and Mary Wickwire, *Cornwallis, The American Adventure* (Boston: Houghton Mifflin Company, 1970), p. 199.

27. Phillips Russell, *North Carolina in the Revolutionary War* (Charlotte: Heritage Printers, Inc., 1965), p. 174.

28. Lieutenant Colonel Tarleton, *A History of the Campaigns of 1780 and 1781 in the Southern Provinces of North America* (London: T. Cadell, in the Strand, 1787), pp. 159–160.

29. *Ibid.*, p. 160.

30. Phillips Russell, *North Carolina in the Revolutionary War* (Charlotte: Heritage Printers, Inc., 1965), pp. 175–176. John S. Pancake, *This Destructive War* (Tuscaloosa: University of Alabama Press, 1985), p. 115.

31. Phillips Russell, *North Carolina in the Revolutionary War* (Charlotte: Heritage Printers, Inc., 1965), p. 177.

32. Rev. J.D. Bailey, *Commanders at Kings Mountain* (Gaffney: Ed. H. DeCamp Publisher, 1926), p. 380.

33. Franklin and Mary Wickwire, *Cornwallis, The American Adventure* (Boston: Houghton Mifflin Company, 1970), pp. 201–205.

34. Dr. Dan L. Morrill, *Southern Campaigns of the American Revolution* (Baltimore: The Nautical & Aviation Publishing Company of America, 1993), pp. 101–102.

35. Franklin and Mary Wickwire, *Cornwallis, The American Adventure* (Boston: Houghton Mifflin Company, 1970), pp. 202–205.

36. Dr. J.B.O. Landrum, *Colonial and Revolutionary History of Upper South Carolina* (Greenville: Shannon & Co., 1897), p. 175.

37. Edward McCrady, LL.D., *The History of South Carolina in the Revolution 1775–1780* (New York: Russell & Russell, 1901/1969), p. 755.

38. Dr. Dan L. Morrill, *Southern Campaigns of the American Revolution* (Baltimore: The Nautical & Aviation Publishing Company of America, 1993), p. 103.

39. Edward McCrady, LL.D., *The History of South Carolina in the Revolution 1775–1780* (New York: Russell & Russell, 1901/1969), p. 756.

40. Dr. J.B.O. Landrum, *Colonial and Revolutionary History of Upper South Carolina* (Greenville: Shannon & Co., 1897), p. 183.

41. Edward McCrady, LL.D., *The History of South Carolina in the Revolution 1775–1780* (New York: Russell & Russell, 1901/1969), pp. 758–759.

42. Henry Lumpkin, *From Savannah to Yorktown* (New York: Paragon House Publishers, 1981), pp. 92–97.

43. Dr. J.B.O. Landrum, *Colonial and Revolutionary History of Upper South Carolina* (Greenville: Shannon & Co., 1897), p. 184.

44. Henry Lumpkin, *From Savannah to Yorktown* (New York: Paragon House Publishers, 1981), p. 97.

45. Franklin and Mary Wickwire, *Cornwallis, The American Adventure* (Boston: Houghton Mifflin Company, 1970), p. 207.

46. Rev. J.D. Bailey, *Commanders at Kings Mountain* (Gaffney: Ed. H. DeCamp Publisher, 1926), pp. 80–93.

47. *Ibid.*, pp. 15–28.

48. Henry Lumpkin, *From Savannah to Yorktown* (New York: Paragon House Publishers, 1981), p. 97.

49. Rev. J.D. Bailey, *Commanders at Kings Mountain* (Gaffney: Ed. H. DeCamp Publisher, 1926), pp. 324–326.

50. Dr. J.B.O. Landrum, *Colonial and Revolutionary History of Upper South Carolina* (Greenville: Shannon & Co., 1897), pp. 229–231.

51. Hank Messick, *King's Mountain* (Boston: Little, Brown and Company, 1976), pp. 99–103.

52. Edward McCrady, LL.D., *The History of South Carolina in the Revolution 1775–1780* (New York: Russell & Russell, 1901/1969), p. 778.

53. Dr. J.B.O. Landrum, *Colonial and Revolutionary History of Upper South Carolina* (Greenville: Shannon & Co., 1897), pp. 191–192.

54. Franklin and Mary Wickwire, *Cornwallis, The American Adventure* (Boston: Houghton Mifflin Company, 1970),

p. 209. Edward McCrady, LL.D., *The History of South Carolina in the Revolution 1775–1780* (New York: Russell & Russell, 1901/1969), p. 779.

55. Henry Lumpkin, *From Savannah to Yorktown* (New York: Paragon House Publishers, 1981), p. 97.

56. Dr. J.B.O. Landrum, *Colonial and Revolutionary History of Upper South Carolina* (Greenville: Shannon & Co., 1897), p. 186.

57. Rev. J.D. Bailey, *Commanders at Kings Mountain* (Gaffney: Ed. H. DeCamp Publisher, 1926), pp. 114–128.

58. *Ibid.*, pp. 370–372.

59 Hank Messick, *King's Mountain* (Boston: Little, Brown and Company, 1976), pp. 109–110.

60. Edward McCrady, LL.D., *The History of South Carolina in the Revolution 1775–1780* (New York: Russell & Russell, 1901/1969), pp. 762–763.

61. Hank Messick, *King's Mountain* (Boston: Little, Brown and Company, 1976), p. 112.

62. Edward McCrady, LL.D., *The History of South Carolina in the Revolution 1775–1780* (New York: Russell & Russell, 1901/1969), pp. 763–764.

63. John S. Pancake, *This Destructive War* (Tuscaloosa: University of Alabama Press, 1985), p. 118.

64. Dr. Dan L. Morrill, *Southern Campaigns of the American Revolution* (Baltimore: The Nautical & Aviation Publishing Company of America, 1993), p. 105.

65. Dr. J.B.O. Landrum, *Colonial and Revolutionary History of Upper South Carolina* (Greenville: Shannon & Co., 1897), p. 193.

66. Franklin and Mary Wickwire, *Cornwallis, The American Adventure* (Boston: Houghton Mifflin Company, 1970), pp. 206–208.

67. Dr. J.B.O. Landrum, *Colonial and Revolutionary History of Upper South Carolina* (Greenville: Shannon & Co., 1897), pp. 188–189. Edward McCrady, LL.D., *The History of South Carolina in the Revolution 1775–1780* (New York: Russell & Russell, 1901/1969), pp. 764–769.

68. Edward McCrady, LL.D., *The History of South Carolina in the Revolution 1775–1780* (New York: Russell & Russell, 1901/1969), pp. 770–772.

69. Dr. J.B.O. Landrum, *Colonial and Revolutionary History of Upper South Carolina* (Greenville: Shannon & Co., 1897), p. 194.

70. Edward McCrady, LL.D., *The History of South Carolina in the Revolution 1775–1780* (New York: Russell & Russell, 1901/1969), pp. 780–781.

71. Dr. J.B.O. Landrum, *Colonial and Revolutionary History of Upper South Carolina* (Greenville: Shannon & Co., 1897), p. 192.

72. Edward McCrady, LL.D., *The History of South Carolina in the Revolution 1775–1780* (New York: Russell & Russell, 1901/1969), pp. 779–780.

73. Dr. J.B.O. Landrum, *Colonial and Revolutionary History of Upper South Carolina* (Greenville: Shannon & Co., 1897), pp. 195–196.

74. Hank Messick, *King's Mountain* (Boston: Little, Brown and Company, 1976), pp. 125–126.

75. Edward McCrady, LL.D., *The History of South Carolina in the Revolution 1775–1780* (New York: Russell & Russell, 1901/1969), pp. 783–784.

76. Hank Messick, *King's Mountain* (Boston: Little, Brown and Company, 1976), pp. 127–130.

77. Dr. Dan L. Morrill, *Southern Campaigns of the American Revolution* (Baltimore: The Nautical & Aviation Publishing Company of America, 1993), pp. 107–108.

78. Edward McCrady, LL.D., *The History of South Carolina in the Revolution 1775–1780* (New York: Russell & Russell, 1901/1969), pp. 789–790.

79. Dr. J.B.O. Landrum, *Colonial and Revolutionary History of Upper South Carolina* (Greenville: Shannon & Co., 1897), pp. 204, 221. Edward McCrady, LL.D., *The History of South Carolina in the Revolution 1775–1780* (New York: Russell & Russell, 1901/1969), p. 788.

80. Dr. Dan L. Morrill, *Southern Campaigns of the American Revolution* (Baltimore: The Nautical & Aviation Publishing Company of America, 1993), pp. 106–107.

81. Hank Messick, *King's Mountain* (Boston: Little, Brown and Company, 1976), pp. 134–135.

82. Edward McCrady, LL.D., *The History of South Carolina in the Revolution 1775–1780* (New York: Russell & Russell, 1901/1969), pp. 791–799.

83. Dr. Dan L. Morrill, *Southern Campaigns of the American Revolution* (Baltimore: The Nautical & Aviation Publishing Company of America, 1993), pp. 109–110.

84. Edward McCrady, LL.D., *The History of South Carolina in the Revolution 1775–1780* (New York: Russell & Russell, 1901/1969), pp. 799–801.

85. *Ibid.*, pp. 802–803. Hank Messick, *King's Mountain* (Boston: Little, Brown and Company, 1976), pp. 147, 150.

86. Dr. Dan L. Morrill, *Southern Campaigns of the American Revolution* (Baltimore: The Nautical & Aviation Publishing Company of America, 1993), pp. 110–111.

87. Hank Messick, *King's Mountain* (Boston: Little, Brown and Company, 1976), pp. 151–160.

88. Edward McCrady, LL.D., *The History of South Carolina in the Revolution 1775–1780* (New York: Russell & Russell, 1901/1969), p. 804. Hank Messick, *King's Mountain* (Boston: Little, Brown and Company, 1976), p. 159.

89. Edward McCrady, LL.D., *The History of South Carolina in the Revolution 1775–1780* (New York: Russell & Russell, 1901/1969), p. 805.

90. Hank Messick, *King's Mountain* (Boston: Little, Brown and Company, 1976), p. 159. Franklin and Mary Wickwire, *Cornwallis, The American Adventure* (Boston: Houghton Mifflin Company, 1970), pp. 218–219.

91. Edward McCrady, LL.D., *The History of South Carolina in the Revolution 1775–1780* (New York: Russell & Russell, 1901/1969), pp. 804–805.

92. Hank Messick, *King's Mountain* (Boston: Little, Brown and Company, 1976), p. 167.

93. Dr. J.B.O. Landrum, *Colonial and Revolutionary History of Upper South Carolina* (Greenville: Shannon & Co., 1897), p. 220.

94. Dr. Dan L. Morrill, *Southern Campaigns of the American Revolution* (Baltimore: The Nautical & Aviation Publishing Company of America, 1993), p. 111.

Chapter 14

1. Blackwell P. Robinson, *William R. Davie* (Chapel Hill: The University of North Carolina Press, 1957), pp. 75–76.

2. John S. Pancake, *This Destructive War* (Tuscaloosa: University of Alabama Press, 1985), p. 120.

3. Edward McCrady, LL.D., *The History of South Carolina in the Revolution 1775–1780* (New York: Russell & Russell, 1901/1969), pp. 806–808.

4. Lieutenant Colonel Tarleton, *A History of the Campaigns of 1780 and 1781 in the Southern Provinces of North America* (London: T. Cadell, in the Strand, 1787), p. 166.

5. Blackwell P. Robinson, *William R. Davie* (Chapel Hill: The University of North Carolina Press, 1957), pp. 79–80.

6. Edward McCrady, LL.D., *The History of South Carolina in the Revolution 1775–1780* (New York: Russell & Russell, 1901/1969), pp. 809–810.

7. W.J. Wood, *Battles of the Revolutionary War, 1775–1781* (Chapel Hill: Algonquin Books of Chapel Hill, 1990), pp. 206–208.

8. M.F. Treacy, *Prelude To Yorktown, The Southern Campaign of Nathanael Greene 1780–1781* (Chapel Hill: The University of North Carolina Press, 1963), pp. 28–38.

9. Dr. Dan L. Morrill, *Southern Campaigns of the American Revolution* (Baltimore: The Nautical & Aviation Publishing Company of America, 1993), pp. 113–116.

10. M.F. Treacy, *Prelude To Yorktown, The Southern Campaign of Nathanael Greene 1780–1781* (Chapel Hill: The University of North Carolina Press, 1963), pp. 30–36.

11. Blackwell P. Robinson, *William R. Davie* (Chapel Hill: The University of North Carolina Press, 1957), pp. 80–84.

12. Dr. Dan L. Morrill, *Southern Campaigns of the American Revolution* (Baltimore: The Nautical & Aviation Publishing Company of America, 1993), pp. 116–117.

13. M.F. Treacy, *Prelude To Yorktown, The Southern Campaign of Nathanael Greene 1780–1781* (Chapel Hill: The University of North Carolina Press, 1963), pp. 56–59. Dr. Dan L. Morrill, *Southern Campaigns of the American Revolution* (Baltimore: The Nautical & Aviation Publishing Company of America, 1993), pp. 55–56, 117–118.

14. Robert Fallaw and Marion West Stoer, *Chesapeake Bay in the American Revolution (The Old Dominion Under Fire: The Chesapeake Invasions, 1779–1781)* (Centreville, Maryland: Tidewater Publishers, 1981), pp. 453–461.

15. *Ibid.*, pp. 455–458.

16. M.F. Treacy, *Prelude To Yorktown, The Southern Campaign of Nathanael Greene 1780–1781* (Chapel Hill: The University of North Carolina Press, 1963), pp. 59–60.

17. Dr. Dan L. Morrill, *Southern Campaigns of the American Revolution* (Baltimore: The Nautical & Aviation Publishing Company of America, 1993), p. 118.

18. Phillips Russell, *North Carolina in the Revolutionary War* (Charlotte: Heritage Printers, Inc., 1965), p. 182.

19. M.F. Treacy, *Prelude To Yorktown, The Southern Campaign of Nathanael Greene 1780–1781* (Chapel Hill: The University of North Carolina Press, 1963), pp. 60–63.

20. Blackwell P. Robinson, *William R. Davie* (Chapel Hill: The University of North Carolina Press, 1957), pp. 94–95.

21. Dr. Dan L. Morrill, *Southern Campaigns of the American Revolution* (Baltimore: The Nautical & Aviation Publishing Company of America, 1993), pp. 120–121.

22. Edward McCrady, LL.D., *The History of South Carolina in the Revolution 1775–1780* (New York: Russell & Russell, 1901/1969), pp. 748–751.

23. Henry Lumpkin, *From Savannah to Yorktown* (New York: Paragon House Publishers, 1981), p. 91.

24. Edward McCrady, LL.D., *The History of South Carolina in the Revolution 1775–1780* (New York: Russell & Russell, 1901/1969), pp. 749–752. Henry Lumpkin, *From Savannah to Yorktown* (New York: Paragon House Publishers, 1981), pp. 72–73.

25. Dr. Dan L. Morrill, *Southern Campaigns of the American Revolution* (Baltimore: The Nautical & Aviation Publishing Company of America, 1993), pp. 121–122.

26. Edward McCrady, LL.D., *The History of South Carolina in the Revolution 1775–1780* (New York: Russell & Russell, 1901/1969), pp. 819–834.

27. Dr. Dan L. Morrill, *Southern Campaigns of the American Revolution* (Baltimore: The Nautical & Aviation Publishing Company of America, 1993), pp. 121–123.

28. M.F. Treacy, *Prelude To Yorktown, The Southern Campaign of Nathanael Greene 1780–1781* (Chapel Hill: The University of North Carolina Press, 1963), pp. 63–64.

29. Dr. Dan L. Morrill, *Southern Campaigns of the American Revolution* (Baltimore: The Nautical & Aviation Publishing Company of America, 1993), pp. 123–124. Franklin and Mary Wickwire, *Cornwallis, The American Adventure* (Boston: Houghton Mifflin Company, 1970), pp. 250–251.

30. M.F. Treacy, *Prelude To Yorktown, The Southern Campaign of Nathanael Greene 1780–1781* (Chapel Hill: The University of North Carolina Press, 1963), p. 66. Franklin and Mary Wickwire, *Cornwallis, The American Adventure* (Boston: Houghton Mifflin Company, 1970), p. 251.

31. Dr. Dan L. Morrill, *Southern Campaigns of the American Revolution* (Baltimore: The Nautical & Aviation Publishing Company of America, 1993), p. 124.

32. Franklin and Mary Wickwire, *Cornwallis, The American Adventure* (Boston: Houghton Mifflin Company, 1970), pp. 251–252.

33. W.J. Wood, *Battles of the Revolutionary War, 1775–1781* (Chapel Hill: Algonquin Books of Chapel Hill, 1990), pp. 211–213.

34. Franklin and Mary Wickwire, *Cornwallis, The American Adventure* (Boston: Houghton Mifflin Company, 1970), pp. 255–256.

35. M.F. Treacy, *Prelude To Yorktown, The Southern Campaign of Nathanael Greene 1780–1781* (Chapel Hill: The University of North Carolina Press, 1963), pp. 70–75. L. Edward Purcell and David F. Burg, *The World Almanac of the American Revolution* (New York: Scripps Howard Co., 1992), p. 267.

36. M.F. Treacy, *Prelude To Yorktown, The Southern Campaign of Nathanael Greene 1780–1781* (Chapel Hill: The University of North Carolina Press, 1963), pp. 86. Franklin and Mary Wickwire, *Cornwallis, The American Adventure* (Boston: Houghton Mifflin Company, 1970), pp. 255–256.

37. W.J. Wood, *Battles of the Revolutionary War, 1775–1781* (Chapel Hill: Algonquin Books of Chapel Hill, 1990), pp. 213–214.

38. M.F. Treacy, *Prelude To Yorktown, The Southern*

Campaign of Nathanael Greene 1780–1781 (Chapel Hill: The University of North Carolina Press, 1963), pp. 83–85.

39. W.J. Wood, *Battles of the Revolutionary War, 1775–1781* (Chapel Hill: Algonquin Books of Chapel Hill, 1990), p. 215.

40. Franklin and Mary Wickwire, *Cornwallis, The American Adventure* (Boston: Houghton Mifflin Company, 1970), p. 259. M.F. Treacy, *Prelude To Yorktown, The Southern Campaign of Nathanael Greene 1780–1781* (Chapel Hill: The University of North Carolina Press, 1963), pp. 86–87.

41. Dr. J.B.O. Landrum, *Colonial and Revolutionary History of Upper South Carolina* (Greenville: Shannon & Co., 1897), p. 295–296.

42. W.J. Wood, *Battles of the Revolutionary War, 1775–1781* (Chapel Hill: Algonquin Books of Chapel Hill, 1990), pp. 216–220. M.F. Treacy, *Prelude To Yorktown, The Southern Campaign of Nathanael Greene 1780–1781* (Chapel Hill: The University of North Carolina Press, 1963), pp. 98–99.

43. W.J. Wood, *Battles of the Revolutionary War, 1775–1781* (Chapel Hill: Algonquin Books of Chapel Hill, 1990), p. 220.

44. Lieutenant Colonel Tarleton, *A History of the Campaigns of 1780 and 1781 in the Southern Provinces of North America* (London: T. Cadell, in the Strand, 1787), p. 215.

45. M.F. Treacy, *Prelude To Yorktown, The Southern Campaign of Nathanael Greene 1780–1781* (Chapel Hill: The University of North Carolina Press, 1963), pp. 100–101.

46. Dr. Dan L. Morrill, *Southern Campaigns of the American Revolution* (Baltimore: The Nautical & Aviation Publishing Company of America, 1993), pp. 129.

47. M.F. Treacy, *Prelude To Yorktown, The Southern Campaign of Nathanael Greene 1780–1781* (Chapel Hill: The University of North Carolina Press, 1963), p. 103.

48. W.J. Wood, *Battles of the Revolutionary War, 1775–1781* (Chapel Hill: Algonquin Books of Chapel Hill, 1990), pp. 221–224.

49. Franklin and Mary Wickwire, *Cornwallis, The American Adventure* (Boston: Houghton Mifflin Company, 1970), p. 264.

50. W.J. Wood, *Battles of the Revolutionary War, 1775–1781* (Chapel Hill: Algonquin Books of Chapel Hill, 1990), pp. 224–225.

51. M.F. Treacy, *Prelude To Yorktown, The Southern Campaign of Nathanael Greene 1780–1781* (Chapel Hill: The University of North Carolina Press, 1963), pp. 108–109.

52. W.J. Wood, *Battles of the Revolutionary War, 1775–1781* (Chapel Hill: Algonquin Books of Chapel Hill, 1990), p. 225.

53. Dr. Dan L. Morrill, *Southern Campaigns of the American Revolution* (Baltimore: The Nautical & Aviation Publishing Company of America, 1993), pp. 132.

54. M.F. Treacy, *Prelude To Yorktown, The Southern Campaign of Nathanael Greene 1780–1781* (Chapel Hill: The University of North Carolina Press, 1963), p. 109.

55. W.J. Wood, *Battles of the Revolutionary War, 1775–1781* (Chapel Hill: Algonquin Books of Chapel Hill, 1990), p. 226.

Chapter 15

1. M.F. Treacy, *Prelude To Yorktown, The Southern Campaign of Nathanael Greene 1780–1781* (Chapel Hill: The University of North Carolina Press, 1963), pp. 112–114.

2. John S. Pancake, *This Destructive War* (Tuscaloosa: University of Alabama Press, 1985), p. 159. Franklin and Mary Wickwire, *Cornwallis, The American Adventure* (Boston: Houghton Mifflin Company, 1970), pp. 270–271.

3. Dr. J.B.O. Landrum, *Colonial and Revolutionary History of Upper South Carolina* (Greenville: Shannon & Company, 1897), p. 299.

4. M.F. Treacy, *Prelude To Yorktown, The Southern Campaign of Nathanael Greene 1780–1781* (Chapel Hill: The University of North Carolina Press, 1963), pp. 115–116.

5. Franklin and Mary Wickwire, *Cornwallis, The American Adventure* (Boston: Houghton Mifflin Company, 1970), pp. 274–275.

6. M.F. Treacy, *Prelude To Yorktown, The Southern Campaign of Nathanael Greene 1780–1781* (Chapel Hill: The University of North Carolina Press, 1963), pp. 117–122.

7. Franklin and Mary Wickwire, *Cornwallis, The American Adventure* (Boston: Houghton Mifflin Company, 1970), pp. 276–277.

8. M.F. Treacy, *Prelude To Yorktown, The Southern Campaign of Nathanael Greene 1780–1781* (Chapel Hill: The University of North Carolina Press, 1963), p. 124.

9. Franklin and Mary Wickwire, *Cornwallis, The American Adventure* (Boston: Houghton Mifflin Company, 1970), pp. 277–278.

10. Phillips Russell, *North Carolina in the Revolutionary War* (Charlotte: Heritage Printers, Inc., 1965), pp. 192–195.

11. M.F. Treacy, *Prelude To Yorktown, The Southern Campaign of Nathanael Greene 1780–1781* (Chapel Hill: The University of North Carolina Press, 1963), pp. 129–130.

12. Robert Fallaw and Marion West Stoer, *Chesapeake Bay in the American Revolution (The Old Dominion Under Fire: The Chesapeake Invasions, 1779–1781)* (Centreville, Maryland: Tidewater Publishers, 1981), pp. 457–458.

13. John E. Selby, *The Revolution in Virginia, 1775–1783* (Williamsburg: The Colonial Williamsburg Foundation, 1988), pp. 222–224.

14. Samuel B. Griffith II, *In Defense of the Public Liberty* (New York: Doubleday & Company, Inc., 1876), p. 627.

15. John E. Selby, *The Revolution in Virginia, 1775–1783* (Williamsburg: The Colonial Williamsburg Foundation, 1988), pp. 223–224.

16. M.F. Treacy, *Prelude To Yorktown, The Southern Campaign of Nathanael Greene 1780–1781* (Chapel Hill: The University of North Carolina Press, 1963), pp. 132.

17. Samuel B. Griffith II, *In Defense of the Public Liberty* (New York: Doubleday & Company, Inc., 1976), p. 627.

18. John E. Selby, *The Revolution in Virginia, 1775–1783* (Williamsburg: The Colonial Williamsburg Foundation, 1988), pp. 224–225.

19. Samuel B. Griffith II, *In Defense of the Public Liberty* (New York: Doubleday & Company, Inc., 1976), pp. 627–629.

20. Phillips Russell, *North Carolina in the Revolutionary War* (Charlotte: Heritage Printers, Inc., 1965), pp. 193–194. M.F. Treacy, *Prelude To Yorktown, The Southern Campaign of Nathanael Greene 1780–1781* (Chapel Hill: The University of North Carolina Press, 1963), pp. 132–133.

21. Phillips Russell, *North Carolina in the Revolutionary War* (Charlotte: Heritage Printers, Inc., 1965), pp. 194–195.

22. M.F. Treacy, *Prelude To Yorktown, The Southern Cam-*

paign of Nathanael Greene 1780–1781 (Chapel Hill: The University of North Carolina Press, 1963), pp. 135–136. Dr. Dan L. Morrill, *Southern Campaigns of the American Revolution* (Baltimore: The Nautical & Aviation Publishing Company of America, 1993), p. 141.

23. John S. Pancake, *This Destructive War* (Tuscaloosa: University of Alabama Press, 1985), p. 163.

24. M.F. Treacy, *Prelude To Yorktown, The Southern Campaign of Nathanael Greene 1780–1781* (Chapel Hill: The University of North Carolina Press, 1963), p. 138.

25. Dr. Dan L. Morrill, *Southern Campaigns of the American Revolution* (Baltimore: The Nautical & Aviation Publishing Company of America, 1993), p. 142.

26. Franklin and Mary Wickwire, *Cornwallis, The American Adventure* (Boston: Houghton Mifflin Company, 1970), pp. 281–282.

27. W.J. Wood, *Battles of the Revolutionary War, 1775–1781* (Chapel Hill: Algonquin Books of Chapel Hill, 1990), pp. 231–232.

28. John S. Pancake, *This Destructive War* (Tuscaloosa: University of Alabama Press, 1985), p. 164.

29. Franklin and Mary Wickwire, *Cornwallis, The American Adventure* (Boston: Houghton Mifflin Company, 1970), pp. 282–283.

30. Phillips Russell, *North Carolina in the Revolutionary War* (Charlotte: Heritage Printers, Inc., 1965), pp. 197–198.

31. John S. Pancake, *This Destructive War* (Tuscaloosa: University of Alabama Press, 1985), p.165.

32. M.F. Treacy, *Prelude To Yorktown, The Southern Campaign of Nathanael Greene 1780–1781* (Chapel Hill: The University of North Carolina Press, 1963), pp. 141–143.

33. Phillips Russell, *North Carolina in the Revolutionary War* (Charlotte: Heritage Printers, Inc., 1965), pp. 200, 204.

34. M.F. Treacy, *Prelude To Yorktown, The Southern Campaign of Nathanael Greene 1780–1781* (Chapel Hill: The University of North Carolina Press, 1963), pp. 144.

35. Phillips Russell, *North Carolina in the Revolutionary War* (Charlotte: Heritage Printers, Inc., 1965), pp. 203–204.

36. John S. Pancake, *This Destructive War* (Tuscaloosa: University of Alabama Press, 1985), p. 167.

37. M.F. Treacy, *Prelude To Yorktown, The Southern Campaign of Nathaniel Greene 1780–1781* (Chapel Hill: The University of North Carolina Press, 1963), pp. 149.

38. Phillips Russell, *North Carolina in the Revolutionary War* (Charlotte: Heritage Printers, Inc., 1965), p. 205.

39. John S. Pancake, *This Destructive War* (Tuscaloosa: University of Alabama Press, 1985), p. 167.

40. M.F. Treacy, *Prelude To Yorktown, The Southern Campaign of Nathanael Greene 1780–1781* (Chapel Hill: The University of North Carolina Press, 1963), pp. 149.

41. W.J. Wood, *Battles of the Revolutionary War, 1775–1781* (Chapel Hill: Algonquin Books of Chapel Hill, 1990), p. 234.

42. John S. Pancake, *This Destructive War* (Tuscaloosa: University of Alabama Press, 1985), pp. 168–169.

43. M.F. Treacy, *Prelude To Yorktown, The Southern Campaign of Nathanael Greene 1780–1781* (Chapel Hill: The University of North Carolina Press, 1963), pp. 151.

44. John S. Pancake, *This Destructive War* (Tuscaloosa: University of Alabama Press, 1985), pp. 169–171.

45. W.J. Wood, *Battles of the Revolutionary War, 1775–1781* (Chapel Hill: Algonquin Books of Chapel Hill, 1990), pp. 237–238.

46. M.F. Treacy, *Prelude To Yorktown, The Southern Campaign of Nathanael Greene 1780–1781* (Chapel Hill: The University of North Carolina Press, 1963), pp. 152–153.

47. Sir Henry Clinton, *The American Rebellion* (New Haven: Yale University Press, 1954), p. 263.

48. Samuel B. Griffith II, *In Defense of the Public Liberty* (New York: Doubleday & Company, Inc., 1976), p. 626.

49. M.F. Treacy, *Prelude To Yorktown, The Southern Campaign of Nathanael Greene 1780–1781* (Chapel Hill: The University of North Carolina Press, 1963), pp. 155–156.

50. W.J. Wood, *Battles of the Revolutionary War, 1775–1781* (Chapel Hill: Algonquin Books of Chapel Hill, 1990), p. 239.

51. Franklin and Mary Wickwire, *Cornwallis, The American Adventure* (Boston: Houghton Mifflin Company, 1970), p. 285.

52. Phillips Russell, *North Carolina in the Revolutionary War* (Charlotte: Heritage Printers, Inc., 1965), p. 209.

53. John S. Pancake, *This Destructive War* (Tuscaloosa: University of Alabama Press, 1985), p. 175.

54. M.F. Treacy, *Prelude To Yorktown, The Southern Campaign of Nathanael Greene 1780–1781* (Chapel Hill: The University of North Carolina Press, 1963), p. 158.

55. Dr. Dan L. Morrill, *Southern Campaigns of the American Revolution* (Baltimore: The Nautical & Aviation Publishing Company of America, 1993), pp. 145–146.

56. John S. Pancake, *This Destructive War* (Tuscaloosa: University of Alabama Press, 1985), p. 174.

57. M.F. Treacy, *Prelude To Yorktown, The Southern Campaign of Nathanael Greene 1780–1781* (Chapel Hill: The University of North Carolina Press, 1963), pp. 156–157.

58. Phillips Russell, *North Carolina in the Revolutionary War* (Charlotte: Heritage Printers, Inc., 1965), p. 209.

59. M.F. Treacy, *Prelude To Yorktown, The Southern Campaign of Nathanael Greene 1780–1781* (Chapel Hill: The University of North Carolina Press, 1963), p. 159.

60. Phillips Russell, *North Carolina in the Revolutionary War* (Charlotte: Heritage Printers, Inc., 1965), pp. 211, 213.

61. M.F. Treacy, *Prelude To Yorktown, The Southern Campaign of Nathanael Greene 1780–1781* (Chapel Hill: The University of North Carolina Press, 1963), pp. 159–161.

62. Phillips Russell, *North Carolina in the Revolutionary War* (Charlotte: Heritage Printers, Inc., 1965), pp. 211–212.

63. M.F. Treacy, *Prelude To Yorktown, The Southern Campaign of Nathanael Greene 1780–1781* (Chapel Hill: The University of North Carolina Press, 1963), pp. 162.

64. John S. Pancake, *This Destructive War* (Tuscaloosa: University of Alabama Press, 1985), pp. 173–174.

65. Phillips Russell, *North Carolina in the Revolutionary War* (Charlotte: Heritage Printers, Inc., 1965), pp. 211–212.

66. Franklin and Mary Wickwire, *Cornwallis, The American Adventure* (Boston: Houghton Mifflin Company, 1970), p. 289.

67. W.J. Wood, *Battles of the Revolutionary War, 1775–1781* (Chapel Hill: Algonquin Books of Chapel Hill, 1990), pp. 241–242.

68. M.F. Treacy, *Prelude To Yorktown, The Southern Campaign of Nathanael Greene 1780–1781* (Chapel Hill: The University of North Carolina Press, 1963), pp. 164–165.

69. John S. Pancake, *This Destructive War* (Tuscaloosa: University of Alabama Press, 1985), p. 176–177.

70. Phillips Russell, *North Carolina in the Revolutionary War* (Charlotte: Heritage Printers, Inc., 1965), p. 213.

71. John S. Pancake, *This Destructive War* (Tuscaloosa: University of Alabama Press, 1985), p. 177.

72. Dr. Dan L. Morrill, *Southern Campaigns of the American Revolution* (Baltimore: The Nautical & Aviation Publishing Company of America, 1993), pp. 148–149.

73. John S. Pancake, *This Destructive War* (Tuscaloosa: University of Alabama Press, 1985), p. 177.

74. Phillips Russell, *North Carolina in the Revolutionary War* (Charlotte: Heritage Printers, Inc., 1965), pp. 216–217.

75. Franklin and Mary Wickwire, *Cornwallis, The American Adventure* (Boston: Houghton Mifflin Company, 1970), pp. 292–293.

76. John S. Pancake, *This Destructive War* (Tuscaloosa: University of Alabama Press, 1985), p. 178.

77. Dr. Dan L. Morrill, *Southern Campaigns of the American Revolution* (Baltimore: The Nautical & Aviation Publishing Company of America, 1993), p. 152.

78. John S. Pancake, *This Destructive War* (Tuscaloosa: University of Alabama Press, 1985), p. 178.

79. M.F. Treacy, *Prelude To Yorktown, The Southern Campaign of Nathanael Greene 1780–1781* (Chapel Hill: The University of North Carolina Press, 1963), pp. 175–176.

80. Dr. Dan L. Morrill, *Southern Campaigns of the American Revolution* (Baltimore: The Nautical & Aviation Publishing Company of America, 1993), p. 152.

81. W.J. Wood, *Battles of the Revolutionary War, 1775–1781* (Chapel Hill: Algonquin Books of Chapel Hill, 1990), p. 248.

82. Dr. Dan L. Morrill, *Southern Campaigns of the American Revolution* (Baltimore: The Nautical & Aviation Publishing Company of America, 1993), pp. 153–154.

83. M.F. Treacy, *Prelude To Yorktown, The Southern Campaign of Nathanael Greene 1780–1781* (Chapel Hill: The University of North Carolina Press, 1963), pp. 181–182.

84. W.J. Wood, *Battles of the Revolutionary War, 1775–1781* (Chapel Hill: Algonquin Books of Chapel Hill, 1990), pp. 251–252.

85. John S. Pancake, *This Destructive War* (Tuscaloosa: University of Alabama Press, 1985), pp. 182–185.

86. M.F. Treacy, *Prelude To Yorktown, The Southern Campaign of Nathanael Greene 1780–1781* (Chapel Hill: The University of North Carolina Press, 1963), pp. 186–188.

87. Franklin and Mary Wickwire, *Cornwallis, The American Adventure* (Boston: Houghton Mifflin Company, 1970), pp. 309–310.

Chapter 16

1. M.F. Treacy, *Prelude To Yorktown, The Southern Campaign of Nathanael Greene 1780–1781* (Chapel Hill: The University of North Carolina Press, 1963), p. 189.

2. Dr. J.B.O. Landrum, *Colonial and Revolutionary History of Upper South Carolina* (Greenville: Shannon & Co., 1897), p. 312.

3. Franklin and Mary Wickwire, *Cornwallis, The American Adventure* (Boston: Houghton Mifflin Company, 1970), p. 312.

4. Phillips Russell, *North Carolina in the Revolutionary War* (Charlotte: Heritage Printers, Inc., 1965), pp. 223–225.

5. Franklin and Mary Wickwire, *Cornwallis, The American Adventure* (Boston: Houghton Mifflin Company, 1970), pp. 311–312.

6. Samuel B. Griffith II, *In Defense of the Public Liberty* (New York: Doubleday & Company, Inc., 1976), p. 636.

7. Dr. Dan L. Morrill, *Southern Campaigns of the American Revolution* (Baltimore: The Nautical & Aviation Publishing Company of America, 1993), p. 157.

8. Sir Henry Clinton, *The American Rebellion* (New Haven: Yale University Press, 1954), p. 502.

9. Franklin and Mary Wickwire, *Cornwallis, The American Adventure* (Boston: Houghton Mifflin Company, 1970), pp. 314–315.

10. M.F. Treacy, *Prelude To Yorktown, The Southern Campaign of Nathanael Greene 1780–1781* (Chapel Hill: The University of North Carolina Press, 1963), pp. 191–193.

11. Henry Steele Commager and Richard B. Morris, *The Spirit of 'Seventy-Six* (New York: Harper & Row, Publishers, 1958), p. 1167.

12. Sir Henry Clinton, *The American Rebellion* (New Haven: Yale University Press, 1954), p. 268.

13. Franklin and Mary Wickwire, *Cornwallis, The American Adventure* (Boston: Houghton Mifflin Company, 1970), p. 316.

14. Sir Henry Clinton, *The American Rebellion* (New Haven: Yale University Press, 1954), p. 269.

15. John S. Pancake, *This Destructive War* (Tuscaloosa: University of Alabama Press, 1985), p. 189.

16. M.F. Treacy, *Prelude To Yorktown, The Southern Campaign of Nathanael Greene 1780–1781* (Chapel Hill: The University of North Carolina Press, 1963), p. 201.

17. Franklin and Mary Wickwire, *Cornwallis, The American Adventure* (Boston: Houghton Mifflin Company, 1970), pp. 316–317.

18. M.F. Treacy, *Prelude To Yorktown, The Southern Campaign of Nathanael Greene 1780–1781* (Chapel Hill: The University of North Carolina Press, 1963), p. 202.

19. Dr. J.B.O. Landrum, *Colonial and Revolutionary History of Upper South Carolina* (Greenville: Shannon & Co., 1897), p. 314.

20. Phillips Russell, *North Carolina in the Revolutionary War* (Charlotte: Heritage Printers, Inc., 1965), p. 225.

21. John S. Pancake, *This Destructive War* (Tuscaloosa: University of Alabama Press, 1985), pp. 189–191.

22. Phillips Russell, *North Carolina in the Revolutionary War* (Charlotte: Heritage Printers, Inc., 1965), p. 225.

23. Dr. Dan L. Morrill, *Southern Campaigns of the American Revolution* (Baltimore: The Nautical & Aviation Publishing Company of America, 1993), p. 160.

24. John S. Pancake, *This Destructive War* (Tuscaloosa: University of Alabama Press, 1985), pp. 191–192.

25. Dr. Dan L. Morrill, *Southern Campaigns of the American Revolution* (Baltimore: The Nautical & Aviation Publishing Company of America, 1993), p. 160.

26. John S. Pancake, *This Destructive War* (Tuscaloosa: University of Alabama Press, 1985), pp. 192–195.

27. Sir Henry Clinton, *The American Rebellion* (New Haven: Yale University Press, 1954), p. 513.

28. Henry Lumpkin, *From Savannah to Yorktown* (New York: Paragon House Publishers, 1981), pp. 178–179.

29. Sir Henry Clinton, *The American Rebellion* (New Haven: Yale University Press, 1954), p. 514.

30. Phillips Russell, *North Carolina in the Revolutionary War* (Charlotte: Heritage Printers, Inc., 1965), p. 258.

31. John S. Pancake, *This Destructive War* (Tuscaloosa: University of Alabama Press, 1985), pp. 195–196.

32. Henry Lumpkin, *From Savannah to Yorktown* (New York: Paragon House Publishers, 1981), pp. 181–182.

33. John S. Pancake, *This Destructive War* (Tuscaloosa: University of Alabama Press, 1985), p. 198.

34. Henry Lumpkin, *From Savannah to Yorktown* (New York: Paragon House Publishers, 1981), p. 183.

35. Phillips Russell, *North Carolina in the Revolutionary War* (Charlotte: Heritage Printers, Inc., 1965), pp. 260–261.

36. John S. Pancake, *This Destructive War* (Tuscaloosa: University of Alabama Press, 1985), p. 199.

37. Henry Lumpkin, *From Savannah to Yorktown* (New York: Paragon House Publishers, 1981), pp. 183–184.

38. John S. Pancake, *This Destructive War* (Tuscaloosa: University of Alabama Press, 1985), p. 200.

39. Henry Lumpkin, *From Savannah to Yorktown* (New York: Paragon House Publishers, 1981), p. 184.

40. Dr. J.B.O. Landrum, *Colonial and Revolutionary History of Upper South Carolina* (Greenville: Shannon & Co., 1897), pp. 317–318.

41. Phillips Russell, *North Carolina in the Revolutionary War* (Charlotte: Heritage Printers, Inc., 1965), p. 262.

42. Dr. Dan L. Morrill, *Southern Campaigns of the American Revolution* (Baltimore: The Nautical & Aviation Publishing Company of America, 1993), p. 162.

43. Henry Lumpkin, *From Savannah to Yorktown* (New York: Paragon House Publishers, 1981), pp. 184–185.

44. John S. Pancake, *This Destructive War* (Tuscaloosa: University of Alabama Press, 1985), pp. 200–201.

45. Henry Lumpkin, *From Savannah to Yorktown* (New York: Paragon House Publishers, 1981), p. 185.

46. John S. Pancake, *This Destructive War* (Tuscaloosa: University of Alabama Press, 1985), p. 201.

47. Henry Lumpkin, *From Savannah to Yorktown* (New York: Paragon House Publishers, 1981), pp. 187–190.

48. John S. Pancake, *This Destructive War* (Tuscaloosa: University of Alabama Press, 1985), p. 202.

49. Henry Lumpkin, *From Savannah to Yorktown* (New York: Paragon House Publishers, 1981), pp. 190–191.

50. John S. Pancake, *This Destructive War* (Tuscaloosa: University of Alabama Press, 1985), pp. 202–210.

51. Henry Lumpkin, *From Savannah to Yorktown* (New York: Paragon House Publishers, 1981), pp. 196–202

52. John S. Pancake, *This Destructive War* (Tuscaloosa: University of Alabama Press, 1985), p. 212.

53. Henry Lumpkin, *From Savannah to Yorktown* (New York: Paragon House Publishers, 1981), pp. 201–204.

54. John S. Pancake, *This Destructive War* (Tuscaloosa: University of Alabama Press, 1985), p. 214.

55. Henry Lumpkin, *From Savannah to Yorktown* (New York: Paragon House Publishers, 1981), p. 204.

56. John S. Pancake, *This Destructive War* (Tuscaloosa: University of Alabama Press, 1985), pp. 214–215.

57. Henry Lumpkin, *From Savannah to Yorktown* (New York: Paragon House Publishers, 1981), pp. 206–211.

58. Phillips Russell, *North Carolina in the Revolutionary War* (Charlotte: Heritage Printers, Inc., 1965), pp. 269–270.

59. Henry Lumpkin, *From Savannah to Yorktown* (New York: Paragon House Publishers, 1981), pp. 212–216.

60. John S. Pancake, *This Destructive War* (Tuscaloosa: University of Alabama Press, 1985), p. 219.

61. Henry Lumpkin, *From Savannah to Yorktown* (New York: Paragon House Publishers, 1981), pp. 214–220.

Chapter 17

1. Samuel B. Griffith II, *In Defense of the Public Liberty* (New York: Doubleday & Company, Inc., 1976), p. 649.

2. Franklin and Mary Wickwire, *Cornwallis, The American Adventure* (Boston: Houghton Mifflin Company, 1970), pp. 319–320.

3. Dr. Dan L. Morrill, *Southern Campaigns of the American Revolution* (Baltimore: The Nautical & Aviation Publishing Company of America, 1993), p. 172.

4. Samuel B. Griffith II, *In Defense of the Public Liberty* (New York: Doubleday & Company, Inc., 1976), p. 649.

5. Franklin and Mary Wickwire, *Cornwallis, The American Adventure* (Boston: Houghton Mifflin Company, 1970), pp. 317–318.

6. Phillips Russell, *North Carolina in the Revolutionary War* (Charlotte: Heritage Printers, Inc., 1965), pp. 250–251.

7. Samuel B. Griffith II, *In Defense of the Public Liberty* (New York: Doubleday & Company, Inc., 1976), p. 649.

8. Phillips Russell, *North Carolina in the Revolutionary War* (Charlotte: Heritage Printers, Inc., 1965), pp. 248–249. Sol Stember, *The Bicentennial Guide to the American Revolution* (New York: Saturday Review Press, 1974), pp. 148–150.

9. Franklin and Mary Wickwire, *Cornwallis, The American Adventure* (Boston: Houghton Mifflin Company, 1970), p. 321.

10. Harold A. Larrabee, *Decision at the Chesapeake* (New York: Clarkson N. Potter, Inc., 1964), p. 130.

11. John O. Sands, *Yorktown's Captive Fleet* (Charlottesville: University Press of Virginia, 1983), pp. 15–19.

12. Thomas J. Fleming, *Beat the Last Drum* (New York: St. Martin's Press, 1963), pp. 69–70.

13. W.J. Wood, *Battles of the Revolutionary War, 1775–1781* (Chapel Hill: Algonquin Books of Chapel Hill, 1990), p. 231.

14. Henry P. Johnston, *Yorktown Campaign and the Surrender of Cornwallis, 1781* (Arlington, Virginia: Honford House, 1975), pp. 33–34.

15. Robert Fallaw and Marion West Stoer, *Chesapeake Bay in the American Revolution (The Old Dominion Under Fire: The Chesapeake Invasions, 1779–1781)* (Centreville, Maryland: Tidewater Publishers, 1981), pp. 466–467.

16. John O. Sands, *Yorktown's Captive Fleet* (Charlottesville: University Press of Virginia, 1983), pp. 21–22.

17. Henry P. Johnston, *Yorktown Campaign and the Surrender of Cornwallis, 1781* (Arlington, Virginia: Honford House, 1975), pp. 33–34.

18. John E. Selby, *The Revolution in Virginia, 1775–1783* (Williamsburg: The Colonial Williamsburg Foundation, 1988), pp. 269–273.

19. Henry P. Johnston, *Yorktown Campaign and the Sur-

render of Cornwallis, 1781 (Arlington, Virginia: Honford House, 1975), pp. 33–34.

20. John E. Selby, *The Revolution in Virginia, 1775–1783* (Williamsburg: The Colonial Williamsburg Foundation, 1988), pp. 273–274.

21. Sir Henry Clinton, *The American Rebellion* (New Haven: Yale University Press, 1954), p. 281.

22. Franklin and Mary Wickwire, *Cornwallis, The American Adventure* (Boston: Houghton Mifflin Company, 1970), pp. 325–326.

23. W.J. Wood, *Battles of the Revolutionary War, 1775–1781* (Chapel Hill: Algonquin Books of Chapel Hill, 1990), p. 231.

24. Henry P. Johnston, *Yorktown Campaign and the Surrender of Cornwallis, 1781* (Arlington, Virginia: Honford House, 1975), pp. 37–39.

25. John E. Selby, *The Revolution in Virginia, 1775–1783* (Williamsburg: The Colonial Williamsburg Foundation, 1988), p. 276.

26. Henry P. Johnston, *Yorktown Campaign and the Surrender of Cornwallis, 1781* (Arlington, Virginia: Honford House, 1975), pp. 39–43.

27. Page Smith, *A New Age Now Begins, Vol. Two* (New York: McGraw-Hill Book Company, 1976), pp. 1631–1632.

28. John E. Selby, *The Revolution in Virginia, 1775–1783* (Williamsburg: The Colonial Williamsburg Foundation, 1988), pp. 279–282.

29. Henry P. Johnston, *Yorktown Campaign and the Surrender of Cornwallis, 1781* (Arlington, Virginia: Honford House, 1975), pp. 43–45.

30. W.J. Wood, *Battles of the Revolutionary War, 1775–1781* (Chapel Hill: Algonquin Books of Chapel Hill, 1990), p. 260.

31. Henry P. Johnston, *Yorktown Campaign and the Surrender of Cornwallis, 1781* (Arlington, Virginia: Honford House, 1975), pp. 46–53.

32. Page Smith, *A New Age Now Begins, Vol. Two* (New York: McGraw-Hill Book Company, 1976), pp. 1627–1635.

33. Sir Henry Clinton, *The American Rebellion* (New Haven: Yale University Press, 1954), p. 304.

34. Page Smith, *A New Age Now Begins, Vol. Two* (New York: McGraw-Hill Book Company, 1976), p. 1648.

35. Franklin and Mary Wickwire, *Cornwallis, The American Adventure* (Boston: Houghton Mifflin Company, 1970), pp. 339–344.

36. Page Smith, *A New Age Now Begins, Vol. Two* (New York: McGraw-Hill Book Company, 1976), pp. 1650–1651.

37. Franklin and Mary Wickwire, *Cornwallis, The American Adventure* (Boston: Houghton Mifflin Company, 1970), p. 345.

38. Page Smith, *A New Age Now Begins, Vol. Two* (New York: McGraw-Hill Book Company, 1976), p. 1652.

39. Henry P. Johnston, *Yorktown Campaign and the Surrender of Cornwallis, 1781* (Arlington, Virginia: Honford House, 1975), pp. 67–68.

40. Franklin and Mary Wickwire, *Cornwallis, The American Adventure* (Boston: Houghton Mifflin Company, 1970), pp. 345–353.

41. Page Smith, *A New Age Now Begins, Vol. Two* (New York: McGraw-Hill Book Company, 1976), pp. 1653–1655.

Chapter 18

1. Ernest McNeill Eller, *Chesapeake Bay in the American Revolution* (Centreville, Maryland: Tidewater Publishers, 1981), p. 488.

2. Harold A. Larrabee, *Decision at the Chesapeake* (New York: Clarkson N. Potter, Inc., 1964), pp. 148–149.

3. Ernest McNeill Eller, *Chesapeake Bay in the American Revolution* (Centreville, Maryland: Tidewater Publishers, 1981), p. 488.

4. Harold A. Larrabee, *Decision at the Chesapeake* (New York: Clarkson N. Potter, Inc., 1964), pp. 149–153.

5. Henry P. Johnston, *Yorktown Campaign and the Surrender of Cornwallis, 1781* (Arlington, Virginia: Honford House, 1975), pp. 76–83.

6. Harold A. Larrabee, *Decision at the Chesapeake* (New York: Clarkson N. Potter, Inc., 1964), pp. 154–159.

7. John O. Sands, *Yorktown's Captive Fleet* (Charlottesville: University Press of Virginia, 1983), pp. 46–47.

8. Harold A. Larrabee, *Decision at the Chesapeake* (New York: Clarkson N. Potter, Inc., 1964), pp. 159–160.

9. Burke Davis, *The Campaign that Won America* (New York: The Dial Press, 1970), pp. 66–67.

10. Harold A. Larrabee, *Decision at the Chesapeake* (New York: Clarkson N. Potter, Inc., 1964), pp. 173–183.

11. Thomas J. Fleming, *Beat the Last Drum* (New York: St. Martin's Press, 1963), pp. 73–77.

12. Burke Davis, *The Campaign that Won America* (New York: The Dial Press, 1970), pp. 10–16.

13. Thomas J. Fleming, *Beat the Last Drum* (New York: St. Martin's Press, 1963), pp. 86–88.

14. Page Smith, *A New Age Now Begins, Vol. Two* (New York: McGraw-Hill Book Company, 1976), pp. 1657–1658.

15. Thomas J. Fleming, *Beat the Last Drum* (New York: St. Martin's Press, 1963), p. 97.

16. Henry P. Johnston, *Yorktown Campaign and the Surrender of Cornwallis, 1781* (Arlington, Virginia: Honford House, 1975), pp. 87–88.

17. Thomas J. Fleming, *Beat the Last Drum* (New York: St. Martin's Press, 1963), p. 93.

18. Henry P. Johnston, *Yorktown Campaign and the Surrender of Cornwallis, 1781* (Arlington, Virginia: Honford House, 1975), pp. 88–91.

19. Burke Davis, *The Campaign that Won America* (New York: The Dial Press, 1970), pp. 73–74.

20. Page Smith, *A New Age Now Begins, Vol. Two* (New York: McGraw-Hill Book Company, 1976), pp. 1667–1669.

21. Henry P. Johnston, *Yorktown Campaign and the Surrender of Cornwallis, 1781* (Arlington, Virginia: Honford House, 1975), pp. 91–94.

22. Page Smith, *A New Age Now Begins, Vol. Two* (New York: McGraw-Hill Book Company, 1976), p. 1662.

23. Burke Davis, *The Campaign that Won America* (New York: The Dial Press, 1970), pp. 49–51.

24. Harold A. Larrabee, *Decision at the Chesapeake* (New York: Clarkson N. Potter, Inc., 1964), pp. 185–194.

25. Burke Davis, *The Campaign that Won America* (New York: The Dial Press, 1970), pp. 152–154. Harold A. Larrabee, *Decision at the Chesapeake* (New York: Clarkson N. Potter, Inc., 1964), pp. 194–198.

26. Burke Davis, *The Campaign that Won America* (New York: The Dial Press, 1970), pp. 155–158.

27. Harold A. Larrabee, *Decision at the Chesapeake* (New York: Clarkson N. Potter, Inc., 1964), pp. 211–216.

28. Burke Davis, *The Campaign that Won America* (New York: The Dial Press, 1970), pp. 163–164.

29. Harold A. Larrabee, *Decision at the Chesapeake* (New York: Clarkson N. Potter, Inc., 1964), pp. 217–223.

30. Page Smith, *A New Age Now Begins, Vol. Two* (New York: McGraw-Hill Book Company, 1976), p. 1687.

Chapter 19

1. Burke Davis, *The Campaign that Won America* (New York: The Dial Press, 1970), pp. 83–85.

2. Page Smith, *A New Age Now Begins, Vol. Two* (New York: McGraw-Hill Book Company, 1976), p. 1670.

3. Burke Davis, *The Campaign that Won America* (New York: The Dial Press, 1970), pp. 86–87.

4. Franklin and Mary Wickwire, *Cornwallis, The American Adventure* (Boston: Houghton Mifflin Company, 1970), pp. 364–365.

5. Thomas J. Fleming, *Beat the Last Drum* (New York: St. Martin's Press, 1963), pp. 62–64.

6. Franklin and Mary Wickwire, *Cornwallis, The American Adventure* (Boston: Houghton Mifflin Company, 1970), pp. 365–366.

7. Page Smith, *A New Age Now Begins, Vol. Two* (New York: McGraw-Hill Book Company, 1976), p. 1674.

8. Burke Davis, *The Campaign that Won America* (New York: The Dial Press, 1970), pp. 133–137.

9. Franklin and Mary Wickwire, *Cornwallis, The American Adventure* (Boston: Houghton Mifflin Company, 1970), pp. 360–362.

10. Dr. Dan L. Morrill, *Southern Campaigns of the American Revolution* (Baltimore: The Nautical & Aviation Publishing Company of America, 1993), pp. 181–182.

11. Thomas J. Fleming, *Beat the Last Drum* (New York: St. Martin's Press, 1963), pp. 137–138.

12. Henry P. Johnston, *Yorktown Campaign and the Surrender of Cornwallis, 1781* (Arlington, Virginia: Honford House, 1975), p. 102.

13. Burke Davis, *The Campaign that Won America* (New York: The Dial Press, 1970), pp. 175–178.

14. Thomas J. Fleming, *Beat the Last Drum* (New York: St. Martin's Press, 1963), pp. 138–139.

15. Burke Davis, *The Campaign that Won America* (New York: The Dial Press, 1970), pp. 177–179.

16. John O. Sands, *Yorktown's Captive Fleet* (Charlottesville: University Press of Virginia, 1983), p. 49.

17. Henry P. Johnston, *Yorktown Campaign and the Surrender of Cornwallis, 1781* (Arlington, Virginia: Honford House, 1975), pp. 101–102.

18. Burke Davis, *The Campaign that Won America* (New York: The Dial Press, 1970), pp. 181–182.

19. Thomas J. Fleming, *Beat the Last Drum* (New York: St. Martin's Press, 1963), pp. 152–160.

20. Burke Davis, *The Campaign that Won America* (New York: The Dial Press, 1970), pp. 189–194.

21. Henry P. Johnston, *Yorktown Campaign and the Surrender of Cornwallis, 1781* (Arlington, Virginia: Honford House, 1975), pp. 108–120.

22. Burke Davis, *The Campaign that Won America* (New York: The Dial Press, 1970), p. 196.

23. Thomas J. Fleming, *Beat the Last Drum* (New York: St. Martin's Press, 1963), pp. 189–191.

24. Henry P. Johnston, *Yorktown Campaign and the Surrender of Cornwallis, 1781* (Arlington, Virginia: Honford House, 1975), p. 123.

25. Thomas J. Fleming, *Beat the Last Drum* (New York: St. Martin's Press, 1963), p. 199.

26. Burke Davis, *The Campaign that Won America* (New York: The Dial Press, 1970), pp. 198–202.

27. Henry P. Johnston, *Yorktown Campaign and the Surrender of Cornwallis, 1781* (Arlington, Virginia: Honford House, 1975), pp. 124–127.

28. Burke Davis, *The Campaign that Won America* (New York: The Dial Press, 1970), pp. 206–207.

29. Henry P. Johnston, *Yorktown Campaign and the Surrender of Cornwallis, 1781* (Arlington, Virginia: Honford House, 1975), pp. 128–129.

30. Burke Davis, *The Campaign that Won America* (New York: The Dial Press, 1970), pp. 214–216.

31. Henry P. Johnston, *Yorktown Campaign and the Surrender of Cornwallis, 1781* (Arlington, Virginia: Honford House, 1975), pp. 132–138.

32. Burke Davis, *The Campaign that Won America* (New York: The Dial Press, 1970), pp. 217–220.

33. Henry P. Johnston, *Yorktown Campaign and the Surrender of Cornwallis, 1781* (Arlington, Virginia: Honford House, 1975), pp. 139–147. Burke Davis, *The Campaign that Won America* (New York: The Dial Press, 1970), pp. 220–224.

34. Burke Davis, *The Campaign that Won America* (New York: The Dial Press, 1970), pp. 234–235.

35. Franklin and Mary Wickwire, *Cornwallis, The American Adventure* (Boston: Houghton Mifflin Company, 1970), pp. 383–385.

36. Burke Davis, *The Campaign that Won America* (New York: The Dial Press, 1970), pp. 258–259.

37. Thomas J. Fleming, *Beat the Last Drum* (New York: St. Martin's Press, 1963), pp. 319–325.

38. Burke Davis, *The Campaign that Won America* (New York: The Dial Press, 1970), pp. 264–268. Thomas J. Fleming, *Beat the Last Drum* (New York: St. Martin's Press, 1963), pp. 332.

39. Harold A. Larrabee, *Decision at the Chesapeake* (New York: Clarkson N. Potter, Inc., 1964), p. 282.

Chapter 20

1. Thomas J. Fleming, *Beat the Last Drum* (New York: St. Martin's Press, 1963), pp. 333–335.

2. Burke Davis, *The Campaign that Won America* (New York: The Dial Press, 1970), pp. 274–278.

3. Page Smith, *A New Age Now Begins, Vol. Two* (New York: McGraw-Hill Book Company, 1976), pp. 1711–1713.

4. Burke Davis, *The Campaign that Won America* (New York: The Dial Press, 1970), p. 279.

5. Page Smith, *A New Age Now Begins, Vol. Two* (New York: McGraw-Hill Book Company, 1976), p. 1715.

6. Henry P. Johnston, *Yorktown Campaign and the Surrender of Cornwallis, 1781* (Arlington, Virginia: Honford House, 1975), pp. 159–160.

7. Burke Davis, *The Campaign that Won America* (New York: The Dial Press, 1970), p. 284.

8. John O. Sands, *Yorktown's Captive Fleet* (Charlottesville: University Press of Virginia, 1983), p. 88. W.J. Wood, *Battles of the Revolutionary War, 1775–1781* (Chapel Hill: Algonquin Books, 1990), p. 292.

9. Thomas J. Fleming, *Beat the Last Drum* (New York: St. Martin's Press, 1963), p. 342.

10. Page Smith, *A New Age Now Begins, Vol. Two* (New York: McGraw-Hill Book Company, 1976), pp. 1717–1722.

11. Burke Davis, *The Campaign that Won America* (New York: The Dial Press, 1970), pp. 279–280, 287–288.

12. Harold A. Larrabee, *Decision at the Chesapeake* (New York: Clarkson N. Potter, Inc., 1964), pp. 277–288.

13. Burke Davis, *The Campaign that Won America* (New York: The Dial Press, 1970), pp. 279–280, 285–286.

14. John O. Sands, *Yorktown's Captive Fleet* (Charlottesville: University Press of Virginia, 1983), p. 108.

15. Page Smith, *A New Age Now Begins, Vol. Two* (New York: McGraw-Hill Book Company, 1976), pp. 1746–1747.

16. John E. Selby, *The Revolution in Virginia, 1775–1783* (Williamsburg: The Colonial Williamsburg Foundation, 1988), pp. 311–322.

17. Jerome J. Nadelhaft, *The Disorders of War, The Revolution in South Carolina* (Orono: University of Maine at Orono Press, 1981), pp. 61–104.

18. Kenneth Coleman, *Colonial Georgia* (New York: Charles Scribner's Sons, 1976), p. 300–301.

19. Capt. Hugh McCall, *The History of Georgia, Vol. I* (Atlanta: A.B. Caldwell, 1811/1909), pp. 537–545.

20. William S. Powell, *North Carolina Through Four Centuries* (Chapel Hill: The University of North Carolina Press, 1989), 207–208.

21. Phillips Russell, *North Carolina in the Revolutionary War* (Charlotte: Heritage Printers, Inc., 1965), pp. 284–286.

22. William S. Powell, *North Carolina Through Four Centuries* (Chapel Hill: The University of North Carolina Press, 1989), pp. 208–212.

23. Phillips Russell, *North Carolina in the Revolutionary War* (Charlotte: Heritage Printers, Inc., 1965), pp. 286–288.

24. William Seymour, *The Price of Folly* (London: Brassey's Ltd., 1995), pp. 233–238.

25. Page Smith, *A New Age Now Begins, Vol. Two* (New York: McGraw-Hill Book Company, 1976), pp. 1721–1737.

26. William Seymour, *The Price of Folly* (London: Brassey's Ltd., 1995), pp. 231–236.

27. Sir Henry Clinton, *The American Rebellion* (New Haven: Yale University Press, 1954), pp. 361–362.

28. W. Robert Higgins, *The Revolutionary War in the South: Power, Conflict, and Leadership (The British Withdrawal from the South, 1781–85, Eldon Jones)* (Durham: Duke University Press, 1979), pp. 260–285.

29. Page Smith, *A New Age Now Begins, Vol. Two* (New York: McGraw-Hill Book Company, 1976), pp. 1721–1737.

30. Donald Barr Chidsey, *Victory at Yorktown* (New York: Crown Publishers, Inc., 1962), p. 158.

31. Mark Mayo Boatner III, *Encyclopedia of the American Revolution* (New York: David McKay Company, 1974), pp. 1–1287.

BIBLIOGRAPHY

Alden, John Richard, *The South in the Revolution, 1763–1789*, Baton Rouge: Louisiana State University Press, 1957.

Andrews, Matthew Page, *Virginia, The Old Dominion*, New York: Doubleday, Doran & Company, Inc., 1937.

Bailey, Rev. J.D., *Commanders at Kings Mountain*, Gaffney: Ed. H. DeCamp Publisher, 1926.

Barker, Charles Albro, *The Background of the Revolution in Maryland*, New Haven: Yale University Press, 1940.

Billings, Warren M., John E. Selby and Thad W. Tate, *Colonial Virginia*, New York: Kraus-Thompson Organization Press, 1986.

Boatner, Mark Mayo, III, *Encyclopedia of the American Revolution*, New York: David McKay Company, 1974.

Brookhiser, Richard, *Founding Father; Rediscovering George Washington*, New York: The Free Press, 1996.

Campbell, Charles, *Introduction to the History of the Colony and Ancient Dominion of Virginia*, Richmond: B.B. Minor, 1847.

Capps, Clifford Sheats, and Eugenia Burney, *Colonial Georgia*, New York: Thomas Nelson, Inc., 1972.

Chase, Ellen, *The Beginnings of the American Revolution*, New York: The Baker and Taylor Company, 1910.

Chidsey, Donald Barr, *The War in the South*, New York: Crown Publishers, Inc., 1969.

Ibid., *Victory at Yorktown*, New York: Crown Publishers, Inc., 1962.

Clinton, Sir Henry, *The American Rebellion*, New Haven: Yale University Press, 1954.

Coleman, Kenneth, *Colonial Georgia*, New York: Charles Scribner's Sons, 1976.

Commager, Henry Steele, and Richard B. Morris, *The Spirit of 'Seventy-Six*, New York: Harper & Row, Publishers, 1958.

Davis, Burke, *The Campaign that Won America*, New York: The Dial Press, 1970.

Dole, Esther Mohr, Ph.D., *Maryland During the American Revolution*, Chestertown, Maryland: Esther Mohr Dole, 1941.

Draper, Theodore, *A Struggle for Power: The American Revolution*, New York: Times Books, 1966.

Dupuy, Colonel R. Ernest, and Colonel Trevor N. Dupuy, *An Outline History of the American Revolution*, New York: Harper & Row Publishers, 1975.

Eckenrode, H.J., *The Revolution in Virginia*, Hamden, Connecticut: Archon Books, 1916.

Eller, Ernest McNeill, *Chesapeake Bay in the American Revolution*, Centreville, Maryland: Tidewater Publishers, 1981.

Fallaw, Robert, and Marion West Stoer, *Chesapeake Bay in the American Revolution (The Old Dominion Under Fire: The Chesapeake Invasions, 1779–1781)*, Centreville, Maryland: Tidewater Publishers, 1981.

Ferguson, Clyde R., *Carolina and Georgia Patriot and Loyalist Militia in Action (The Southern Experience in the American Revolution)*, Edited by Jeffrey J. Crow and Larry E. Tise, Chapel Hill: The University of North Carolina Press, 1978.

Fischer, David Hackett, *Paul Revere's Ride*, New York: Oxford University Press, 1994.

Fithian, Philip Vickers, *Journal and Letters*, edited by John Rogers Williams, Princeton, 1924.

Fleming, Thomas J., *Beat the Last Drum*, New York: St. Martin's Press, 1963.

Fraser, Walter J., Jr., *Charleston! Charleston!*, Columbia: University of South Carolina Press, 1989.

Gipson, Lawrence Henry, *The Coming of the Revolution*, New York: Harper & Brothers, 1954.

Griffith, Samuel B., II, *In Defense of the Public Liberty*, New York: Doubleday & Company, Inc., 1976.

Hesseltine, William B., *The South in American History*, New York: Prentice Hall, Inc., 1936.

Hibbert, Christopher, *Redcoats and Rebels*, New York: W.W. Norton & Company, 1990.

Higgins, W. Robert, *The Revolutionary War in the South: Power, Conflict, and Leadership (The British Withdrawal from the South, 1781–85, Eldon Jones)*, Durham: Duke University Press, 1979.

Hume, Ivor Noel, *1775, Another Part of the Field*, New York: Alfred A. Knopf, Inc., 1966.

Johnston, Henry P., *Yorktown Campaign and the Surrender of*

Cornwallis, 1781, Arlington, Virginia: Honford House, 1975.

Jones, Charles C., Jr., LL.D., *History of Georgia,* Boston: Houghton, Mifflin and Company, 1883.

Ibid., The History of Georgia, Vol. II, Cambridge: The Riverside Press, 1883.

Knollenberg, Berhard, *Origin of the American Revolution: 1759–1766,* New York: The Macmillan Company, 1960.

Lambert, Robert Stanbury, *South Carolina Loyalists in the American Revolution,* Columbia: University of South Carolina Press, 1987.

Land, Aubrey C., *Colonial Maryland,* New York: Kraus-Thomson Organization Press, 1981.

Landrum, Dr. J.B.O., *Colonial and Revolutionary History of Upper South Carolina,* Greenville: Shannon & Co., 1897.

Langguth, A.J., *Patriots,* New York: Simon & Schuster, Inc., 1988.

Larrabee, Harold A., *Decision at the Chesapeake,* New York: Clarkson N. Potter, Inc., 1964.

Lee, Henry, *Memoirs of the War in the Southern Department of the United States,* New York: University Publishing Company, 1869.

Lefler, Hugh T., and William S. Powell, *Colonial North Carolina,* New York: Charles Scribner's Sons, 1973.

Lossing, Benson J., *Seventeen Hundred and Seventy-Six,* New York: Edward Walker, 1849.

Lumpkin, Henry, *From Savannah to Yorktown,* New York: Paragon House Publishers, 1981.

Malcolm, M.F., *The Cape Fear,* New York: Holt, Rinehart and Winston, Inc., 1965.

McCall, Captain Hugh, *The History of Georgia, Vol. I,* Atlanta: A.B. Caldwell, Publisher, 1811/1909.

McCrady, Edward, LL.D., *The History of South Carolina in the Revolution 1775–1780,* New York: Russell & Russell, 1901/1969.

Messick, Hank, *King's Mountain,* Boston: Little, Brown and Company, 1976.

Middlekauff, Robert, *The Glorious Cause,* New York: Oxford University Press, 1982.

Miller, John C., *Origins of the American Revolution,* London: Oxford University Press, 1943.

Moore, Louis T., *Stories Old and New of the Cape Fear Region,* Wilmington: Wilmington Printing Company, 1956.

Morgan, Edmund S., *American Slavery, American Freedom,* New York: W.W. Norton & Company, 1975.

Morrill, Dr. Dan L., *Southern Campaigns of the American Revolution,* Baltimore: The Nautical & Aviation Publishing Company of America, 1993.

Morris, Richard B., *The LIFE History of the United States Before 1775: Vol. 1, The New World,* New York: Time-Life Books, 1963.

Morse, Jedidiah, *Annals of the American Revolution,* Hartford, Connecticut: Oliver D. Cooke & Sons, 1824.

Morton, Richard L., *Colonial Virginia, Vol. II,* Chapel Hill: The University of North Carolina Press, 1960.

Nadelhaft, Jerome J., *The Disorders of War, The Revolution in South Carolina,* Orono: University of Maine at Orono Press, 1981.

Pancake, John S., *This Destructive War,* Tuscaloosa: University of Alabama Press, 1985.

Perkins, Edwin J., *The Economy of Colonial America, 2nd ed.* New York: Columbia University Press, 1988.

Powell, William S., *North Carolina Through Four Centuries,* Chapel Hill: The University of North Carolina Press, 1989.

Purcell, L. Edward, and David F. Burg, *The World Almanac of the American Revolution,* New York: Scripps Howard Co., 1992.

The Regulations Lately Made Concerning the Colonies … Considered, 92, Grenville Papers, II, *Public Advertiser,* January 13, 1776.

Robinson, Blackwell P., *A History of Moore County, North Carolina 1747–1847,* Southern Pines, North Carolina: Moore County Historical Association, 1956.

Ibid., William R. Davie, Chapel Hill: The University of North Carolina Press, 1957.

Ross, Malcolm, *The Cape Fear,* New York: Holt, Rinehart and Winston, Inc., 1965.

Russell, Phillips, *North Carolina in the Revolutionary War,* Charlotte: Heritage Printers, Inc., 1965.

Sands, John O., *Yorktown's Captive Fleet,* Charlottesville: University Press of Virginia, 1983.

Schlesinger, Arthur M., *The Birth of the Nation, 6th ed.* New York: Alfred A. Knopf, Inc., 1976.

Selby, John E., *The Revolution in Virginia, 1775–1783,* Williamsburg: The Colonial Williamsburg Foundation, 1988.

Seymour, William, *The Price of Folly,* London: Brassey's Ltd., 1995.

Smith, Page, *A New Age Now Begins, Vol. Two,* New York: McGraw-Hill Book Company, 1976.

Smith, Paul H., *Loyalists and Redcoats,* Chapel Hill: The University of North Carolina Press, 1964.

Spruill, Julia Cherry, *Women's Life and Work in the Southern Colonies,* New York: W.W. Norton & Company, Inc., 1972.

Stember, Sol, *The Bicentennial Guide to the American Revolution,* New York: Saturday Review Press, 1974.

Tarleton, Lieutenant Colonel, *A History of the Campaigns of 1780 and 1781 in the Southern Provinces of North America,* London: T. Cadell, in the Strand, 1787.

Treacy, M.F., *Prelude to Yorktown, The Southern Campaign of Nathanael Greene 1780-1781,* Chapel Hill: The University of North Carolina Press, 1963.

Uhlendorf, Bernhard A., *The Seige of Charleston (Diaries of Captain Hinrichs General Von Huyn, and Captain Ewald),* Ann Arbor: University of Michigan Press, 1938.

Vaughan, Alden T., *America Before the Revolution,* Englewood Cliffs, New Jersey: Prentice Hall, Inc., 1967.

Weir, Robert M., *Colonial South Carolina,* New York: Kraus-Thomson Organization Press, 1983.

Wertenbaker, Thomas J., *Norfolk, Historic Southern Port,* Durham: Duke University Press, 1931.

Wickwire, Franklin and Mary, *Cornwallis, The American Adventure,* Boston: Houghton Mifflin Company, 1970.

Wood, W.J., *Battles of the Revolutionary War, 1775–1781,* Chapel Hill: Algonquin Books of Chapel Hill, 1990.

Wright, Esmond, *The Fire of Liberty,* New York: St. Martin's Press, 1983.

INDEX

gmented>

ML

12/06